The Kingfisher Children's Illustrated
Dictionary
&Thesaurus

KINGFISHER
NEW YORK

423

KINGFISHER
LONDON & NEW YORK

First published in 2003
This revised edition published in 2011

Material in this edition previously published by Kingfisher as
The Kingfisher Illustrated Junior Dictionary and *The Kingfisher Illustrated Thesaurus*

Distributed in the U.S. by Macmillan, 175 Fifth Ave., New York, NY 10010
Distributed in Canada by H.B. Fenn and Company Ltd., 34 Nixon Road, Bolton, Ontario L7E 1W2

Library of Congress Cataloging-in-Publication data has been applied for.

ISBN: 978-0-7534-6469-4

Kingfisher books are available for special promotions and premiums. For details contact:
Special Markets Department, Macmillan, 175 Fifth Avenue, New York, NY 10010.

For more information, please visit www.kingfisherbooks.com

Printed in China
2 4 6 8 10 9 7 5 3 1
1TR/0411/WKT/UNTD/140MA

Contents

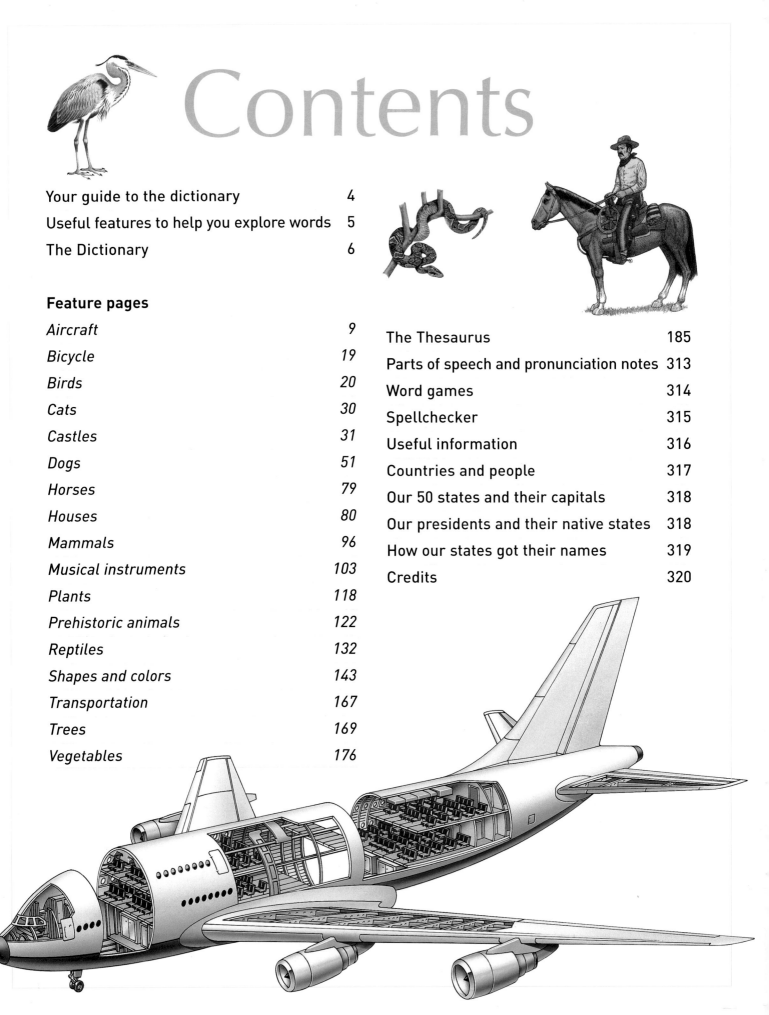

Your guide to the dictionary

How to find a word

All headwords (entries) in this dictionary are listed in the order of the alphabet.

Words that begin with **A** are followed by those which begin with **B**, and so on until you reach **Z**. All the words under each letter of the alphabet are themselves in alphabetical order, so **admit** follows **admire** and **form** follows **fork**.

guide words

show first headword on left-hand page and last headword on the right-hand page.

bold headwords

begin all entries and show how the word is spelled.

entries

include headword and all its information, including any different definitions and related words.

alpha rules

help you to find the right letter section. The highlighted **b** shows that you are in the **b** section.

definition

is what the word means.

different senses

refers to the fact that some words have more than one meaning. Each different sense or definition is numbered.

example sentences

show how a word is used to make the meaning clearer.

parts of speech

show whether the word is a noun, verb, adjective, adverb, conjunction, or preposition (see page 313) and tell what it does in a sentence.

changed forms

refer to the changes in spelling when words are used in different ways. All plurals of nouns, verb inflections, and the comparatives and superlatives of adjectives are shown.

verb tenses

show how each verb is written in the present, continuous present, and past tenses.

related words

belong to the same word family.

new letter section

is shown by a big, colored letter at the start of each section of the alphabet.

feature pages and panels

group words and pictures together by topic—birds, castles, or houses, for example. With their word boxes, these pages extend vocabulary and knowledge about the topic.

Useful features to help you explore words

thesaurus boxes
These show how you can vary and enrich your vocabulary by choosing a different word with a similar meaning to express yourself. The dictionary section of this book has thesaurus boxes for the following words: bad, big, eat, fast, good, happy, like, nice, piece, small.

happy

Some words that you can use instead of happy:

I'm happy that I've finished my homework.
contented, pleased, glad

They are happy with their wedding presents.
delighted, pleased, thrilled

small

Some words that you can use instead of small:

All small animals look cute.
baby, young

The writing is so small that you need a magnifying glass to read it.
minute, tiny

homophones
Words that sound the same but have different meanings are marked with this sign ●

pronunciation and rhyming words
Words that are difficult or awkward to say are marked with this sign ▲

opposites
The opposite meanings for some words are shown by this sign ▪

fair fairs noun
an outdoor place outside where rides and competitions are set up for people to have fun. ● A word that sounds like **fair** is **fare**.

fracture fractures noun
a break or crack in something, especially a bone. *Her arm is in a cast because she has a fracture.* ▲ Say frak-*sher*. **fracture** verb.*er*.

fill fills filling filled verb
If you fill something, you put as much into it as it can hold. *Frances filled the bottles with water.* ▪ The opposite is **empty**.

How our states got their names

On page 319, you will find a list of all 50 states, together with information about how they got their names. For example, did you know that Montana means "mountainous" in Spanish? You can learn a lot about words from their sounds.

spelling tips
If you cannot find a word under one letter, it may be under another letter. For instance, the correct spelling for "cangaroo" is "kangaroo."

SPELLING TIP
Some words that begin with a "co" sound are spelled with a "ko." For example, koala.

vocabulary boxes
Many topic pages have a list of special words connected to the topic.

VOCABULARY

chain
a series of metal rings called links.

hub
the center of a wheel.

gears
a set of toothed wheels (sprockets) over which the chain fits and which change the power and speed of the bicycle.

reflector
a red object that makes the bicycle visible in the dark by reflecting lights from vehicles behind it and in front of it.

First writing

At first, people would just draw a picture of the thing that they wanted to record—a woman, a horse, or a bird, for instance. The people of ancient Egypt could write very complicated messages using these types of pictures. The people of ancient China also drew pictures of things that they wanted us to know about. In time, these pictures became much simpler—just a few brush strokes known as "characters." Chinese is still written in characters to this day.

Around 3,000 years ago, a way of writing was developed that used signs for each sound in a word. A letter stood for a sound. We call letters that stand for sounds an alphabet. These are the "bricks" that we use to build our language.

5

abandon abandons abandoning abandoned verb
If you abandon somebody or something, you leave them behind.

abbreviation abbreviations noun
a short way of writing something. *"Rd." is an abbreviation of "Road."*

ability abilities noun
If you have the ability to do something, you can do it.

aboard adverb, preposition
If you are aboard a train, bus, ship, or plane, you are on it or in it.

abolish abolishes abolishing abolished verb
to put an end to something. *President Lincoln abolished slavery.*

above adverb, preposition
higher than something. *My bedroom is above the kitchen.* ■ The opposite is **below** or **beneath**.

abroad adverb, preposition
in another country.

absent adjective
If you are absent, you are not here. *Katie was absent from school yesterday.* ■ The opposite is **present**.

absorb absorbs absorbing absorbed verb
When a cloth or sponge absorbs water, it soaks it up.

abuse noun
words or acts that hurt or injure someone.

accelerator accelerators noun
the pedal that makes a car go faster.

accent accents noun
1 the way that a person from a certain place speaks. *He spoke with a Southern accent.*
2 a mark that shows how to pronounce a word. *"Café" has an accent on the "e."*

accept accepts accepting accepted verb
1 to take something that somebody gives you. *She accepted the gift.*
2 to say that you will come to a party. ■ The opposite is **refuse**.

accident accidents noun
something bad that happens without being planned. *Ella dropped the nail polish. It was an accident.*
accidentally adverb.

accompany accompanies accompanying accompanied verb
If you accompany others, you go with them. *The teacher accompanied the children on the field trip.*

account accounts noun
1 If you give an account of something, you describe what happened. *He wrote an account of the bank robbery in the local newspaper.*
2 money that you keep in the bank.

accurate adjective
exactly right. Is your watch accurate?
▲ Say **ak**-*yoo-rit*.

accuse accuses accusing accused verb
If you accuse somebody, you say that person has done something wrong. *The man was accused of stealing.*

ace aces noun
Somebody who does something very well.

ache aches noun
a pain in your body that keeps hurting, such as an earache.
▲ Rhymes with **take**.

achieve achieves achieving achieved verb
If you achieve something, you get it after trying very hard.

acid acids noun
a liquid that tastes sour, such as lemon juice or vinegar. Some strong acids can burn your skin.

acid rain noun
rain that has chemicals in it from factories and cars. Acid rain damages trees, rivers, and buildings.

acorn acorns noun
the nut that grows on an oak tree.

acrobat acrobats noun
a person who can do difficult and exciting balancing tricks. You can see acrobats in a circus.

across adverb, preposition
If you walk across something such as a field, you walk from one side to the other.

act acts noun
1 one part of a play. *This play has three acts.*
2 something that you do. *an act of kindness.*

act acts acting acted verb
1 When you act, you do something. *She acted quickly to save the boy from drowning.*
2 If you act in a play or movie, you play a part in it.

action actions noun
something that you do. *Frankie's fast actions saved the man's life.*

active adjective
If you are active, you are always busy and able to do lots of things.

activity activities noun
1 something that you do. *Playing football is Tom's favorite activity.*
2 a lot of things happening and people doing things. *During the summer, there is a lot of activity on the beach.*

actor actors
noun
a person who acts in a play or movie.

add adds adding added verb
1 When you add numbers, you put them together to find an answer. *If you add 2 and 3, you get 5.*
 ■ The opposite is **subtract**.
2 If you add something to something else, you put the two things together. *She put coffee in a mug and added sugar.*
addition noun.

address addresses noun
Your address is the number and name of the street where you live, and the city or town where it is. *Your zip code is also part of your address.*

adjective adjectives noun
a word that tells you what somebody or something is like. In the sentence "Tom has a new, red bike," "new" and "red" are adjectives.

admire admires admiring admired verb
If you admire somebody or something, you think that they are very good. *Everyone admired Katie's painting.*

admit admits admitting admitted verb
If you admit something, you agree that you have done something wrong. *Matthew admitted that he had broken the glass.*

adopt adopts adopting adopted verb
When people adopt a child, they take the child to live with them as part of their family.

adult adults noun
a person or an animal that is fully grown. *an adult bear.*

advance advances advancing advanced verb
When something advances, it moves forward. *The army advanced toward the enemy.*

advantage advantages noun
something that can help you do better than other people. *In the game of basketball, it is an advantage to be tall.* ■ The opposite is **disadvantage**.

adventure adventures noun
something exciting that happens to you. *We got lost in the snow. It was a real adventure!*

adverb adverbs noun
a word that tells you more about a verb, adjective, or another adverb. In the sentence "Mike quickly opened the package," "quickly" is an adverb.

advertise advertises advertising advertised verb
If you advertise, you tell people about things that you are selling. *These toys were advertised on television.*

advertisement advertisements noun
information on a poster, in a newspaper, or on the TV or Internet that tells you about something to buy or something to do.
▲ Say *ad-ver-**tize**-ment.*

advice noun
If somebody gives you advice, they tell you what they think you should do.

advise advises advising advised verb
If you advise somebody, you tell them what you think they should do.

aerial adjective
in the air or from the air. *an aerial photograph.* ▲ Say **air**-ee-ul.

aerobics noun
exercises like dancing and stretching that you do regularly. ▲ Say *air-**oh**-bix.*

aerosol aerosols noun
a can with liquid inside. You press a button to send out the liquid in a spray. ▲ Say *air-**oh**-sol.*

affect affects affecting affected verb
If something affects you, it makes you different in some way. *Smoking affects your health.*

affection noun
the feeling of loving or liking somebody. *Samantha shows great affection for her little sister Joan.*
affectionate adjective.

afford affords affording afforded verb
If you can afford something, you have enough money to buy it. *I've spent my allowance and I can't afford any more candy this week.*

afraid adjective
If you are afraid, you think that something bad will happen to you.

African-American noun
An American who has ancestors from Africa.

afternoon afternoons noun
the part of the day between noon and the evening.

again adverb
If you do something again, you do it once more. *Tell me that story again.*

against preposition
1 If you play against somebody in a game, you are on the other side.
2 next to, or touching something. *The ladder was against the wall.*
3 If you are against something, you do not agree with it. *I'm against violence in movies.*

age ages noun
1 Your age is how old you are.
2 a certain time in history.

agree agrees agreeing agreed verb
If you agree with somebody, you think the same about something. The opposite is **disagree**.
agreement noun.

agriculture noun
Agriculture is keeping animals and growing plants for food.
agricultural adjective.

ahead adverb
in front of somebody or something. *We walked slowly, but the dog ran ahead.*

aim aims aiming aimed verb
1 If you aim at something, you point something such as a bow and arrow at the thing that you want to hit.
2 If you aim to do something, you try to do it.

air noun
the mixture of gases that we breathe.

aircraft aircraft noun
any machine that can fly. Look at page 9.

airplane noun
a flying machine with wings and an engine.

airport airports noun
a place where airplanes take off and land.

aisle aisles noun
a place where you can walk between rows of seats, such as in a theater or a church. *The bride and groom walked down the aisle.* Say **eye-l**.

alarm alarms noun
1 something such as a bell or a flashing light that warns you of something. *a burglar alarm.*
2 a sudden feeling of fear.

album albums noun
1 a book that you keep things such as photographs or stamps in.
2 a CD, tape, or record with several different pieces of music on it.

alcohol noun
Drinks such as wine, beer, and whiskey have alcohol in them.
alcoholic adjective
Wine and beer are alcoholic drinks.

alien aliens noun
a creature from another planet. Say **ay-lee-un**.

alike adjective
If two things or people are alike, they are the same in some way. *The twins are not identical, but they are alike.*

alive adjective
A person, animal, or plant that is alive is living now. *Plants need water to stay alive.* The opposite is **dead**.

allergy allergies noun
an illness caused by something that does not normally make people sick. *Some people have an allergy to dust.*
allergic adjective.

alley alleys noun
a narrow path between buildings.

alligator alligators noun
a large reptile similar to a crocodile but with shorter, wider jaws. Alligators live in rivers in the southern United States and in China.

allow allows allowing allowed verb
If you are allowed to do something, somebody lets you do it. *I'm allowed to stay up later on weekends.*

allowance noun
money that is given each week to a child to spend.

Aircraft

single-engined trainer

short-haul jet

twin-engined executive jet

airborne early warning turboprop

"Stealth" bomber

fighter

VOCABULARY

aileron
a flap on the back of a wing that makes the plane roll sideways.

cabin
the part of a plane where the passengers sit.

elevator
a panel on the tailplane that makes the plane climb or descend.

flight deck
the area where the pilot and crew sit.

fuselage
the main part of a plane carrying passengers and crew.

galley
the kitchen.

rudder
a vertical piece on the tailplane that turns the plane left or right.

tail
a small horizontal wing at the back of the plane.

wing
one of the long, flat parts that keep the plane in the air.

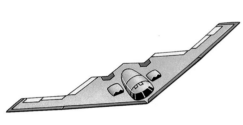
seven-seat utility helicopter

special-purpose transport plane

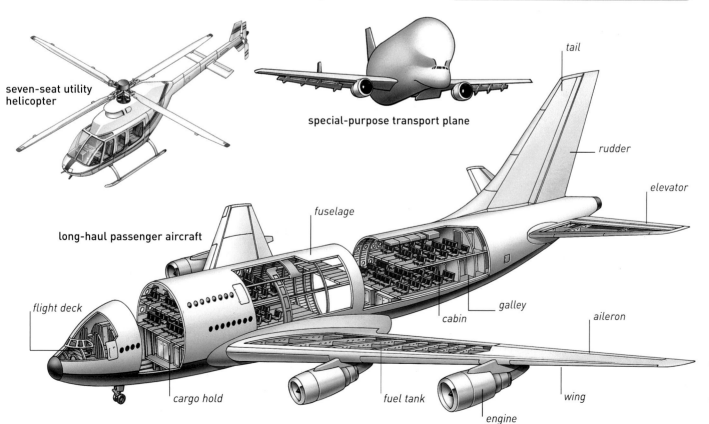
long-haul passenger aircraft

flight deck · cargo hold · fuselage · cabin · galley · fuel tank · engine · wing · aileron · elevator · rudder · tail

9

alone adjective, adverb
by yourself, with nobody else.
Sophie walked home alone.

aloud adverb
If you read or speak aloud, you
do it so that other people can
hear you. ● A word that sounds
like **aloud** is **allowed**.

alphabet alphabets noun
all the letters from A to Z that we use
to write words. The English alphabet
has 26 letters.

A a	A α	ꙣ ꙣ	A a		
B b	B β	ꙗ ꙗ	Б б		
C c	Γ γ	ꙗ ꙣ	В в		
D d	Δ δ	ꙙ ꙙ	Г г		
E e	E ε	ꙑ ꙑ	Д д		
F f	Z ζ	ꙅ ꙅ	E e		
G g	H η	ꙗ ꙗ	Ж ж		
H h	Θ θ	ꙩ ꙩ	З з		
I i	I ι	ꙩ ꙩ	И и		
J j	K κ	ꙣ ꙣ	Й й		
K k	Λ λ	ꙙ ꙙ	К к		
L l	M μ	ꙣ ꙣ	Л л		
M m	N ν	ꙗ ꙗ	М м		
N n	Ξ ξ	ꙗ ꙗ	Н н		

different types of alphabets

already adverb
before this time. *We ran to the bus
stop, but the bus was already gone.*

alter alters altering altered verb
If you alter something, you change it
in some way. *My father has altered his
working hours so that he can pick me up
from school.*
alteration noun.

altogether adverb
counting everybody or everything.
*My uncle gave me $5 and my aunt gave
me $10, so I've got $15 altogether.*

aluminum noun
a light, silver-colored metal.
Aluminum is used to make cans
and tinfoil. ▲ Say *uh-**loo**-muh-num*.

amateur amateurs noun, adjective
a person who does something such as
a sport because he or she enjoys it but
does not get paid for it. *Sarah is an
amateur at figure skating.*
▲ Say *am-at-ur*.

amaze amazes amazing amazed
verb
If something amazes you, it surprises
you very much.
amazement noun
We watched the acrobat in amazement.
amazing adjective
She told us an amazing story.

ambulance ambulances noun
a special motor vehicle that takes
people who are hurt or sick to the
hospital.

amigo amigos noun
Spanish-speaking people say "amigo"
to mean "friend."

among preposition
1 in the middle of. *The house stood
among the trees.*
2 shared between more than two
people. *She divided the candy bars
among the children.*

amount amounts noun
An amount of something is how
much there is. *I get the same amount
of allowance as my friend.*

amphibian amphibians noun
an animal that lives on land as well as
in water. Newts, toads, and axolotls
are amphibians. ▲ Say *am-fib-ee-un*.

amplifier amplifiers noun
a machine that makes sounds louder.
CD players and mp3 players have
amplifiers.

warty newt

common toad

axolotl

amuse amuses amusing amused
verb
If you amuse somebody, you make
someone laugh or you keep them
happy and busy. *The joke amused my
sister* or *We played games to amuse
ourselves on the long trip.*

ancestor ancestors noun
Your ancestors are members of your
family who lived a long time ago.

anchor anchors noun
a heavy, metal hook on a long chain
that you drop into the water from a
ship or boat to stop it from floating
away. ▲ Say *an-ker*.

ancient adjective
very old. *an ancient castle.*

anger noun
Anger is the strong feeling you have
when you think something is unfair.
angrily adverb.

angle angles noun
the corner where two lines meet.

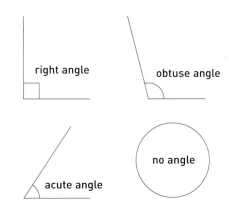

right angle

obtuse angle

acute angle

no angle

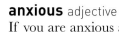

angry angrier angriest adjective
If you are angry, you feel anger.

animal animals noun
a living thing that is not a plant.
Birds, fish, insects, frogs, snakes,
rabbits, and elephants are all animals.

ankle ankles noun
Your ankle is the part of your leg that
connects to your foot.

anniversary anniversaries noun
a day when you remember something
special that happened on the same
date in another year. *Today is my
parents' eleventh wedding anniversary.*

announce announces announcing
announced verb
If you announce something, you
say it in front of a lot of people.
*She announced to the class that
the play would start tomorrow.*

annoy annoys annoying annoyed
verb
If you annoy somebody, you make
the person angry.
annoyance noun

annual adjective
If something is annual, it happens
once every year. *The fair is an
annual event.*

answer answers answering
answered verb
When you answer, you say something
to somebody who has asked you a
question or said something to you.
*"What's the capital of France?" "Paris,"
she answered.* ▲ Say **an**-*sur*. ■ The
opposite is **question**.
answer noun.

ant ants noun
a tiny insect. Ants live in groups
called colonies in a "hill."

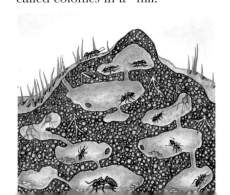

antelope antelope noun
an animal like a deer with
horns and long legs that
can run fast. Antelopes live
in Africa and parts of Asia.

a nilgar (front) and an eland (back)

antenna antennae noun
1 a long, thin part on the head of an
  insect that it uses for touching.
2 an aerial.

antifreeze noun
a substance that you add to a liquid
to keep it from freezing. *Dad put
antifreeze into the car's radiator.*

antique antiques noun
a thing that is very old and can be
worth a lot of money. ▲ Say *an*-**teek**.

antiseptic antiseptics noun
a cream, liquid, or spray that you put
on a wound in order to keep it clean
and germfree.

antler antlers noun
one of two large horns that grow
on the head of a male deer. The
male deer, called a "buck" or a
"stag," loses its antlers every year
and grows new ones.

anxious adjective
If you are anxious about something,
you worry about it. *Mom was anxious
because we were late coming home.*
▲ Say ang-*shuss*.

ape apes noun
an animal that is like a big monkey
with no tail. Gorillas, chimpanzees,
and gibbons are all apes.

apologize apologizes apologizing
apologized verb
If you apologize, you say you are
sorry. *Billy apologized for being late.*
apology noun.

apostrophe apostrophes noun
1 a mark that you use in writing
  to show that something belongs
  to somebody. *Lucy's book.*
2 a mark that you use in writing to
  show that a letter has been left out.
  In the word "I'm," which is short
  for "I am," the apostrophe shows
  that the letter "a" has been left out.
  ▲ Say a-**poss**-*trof-ee*.

gibbon

orangutan

gorilla

chimpanzee

apparatus noun
1 the pieces of equipment that you need to do a scientific experiment.
2 things such as bars and ropes that you use in gymnastics.

appear appears appearing appeared verb
1 to come into view. *He suddenly appeared from behind a tree* or *A black cloud appeared.* ▪ The opposite is **disappear**.
2 If something appears to be a certain way, it seems to be that way. *A magnifying glass makes things appear bigger than they really are.*

appearance appearances noun
1 If you make an appearance, you come to a place where people can see you. *She made a television appearance.*
2 Your appearance is what you look like. *Having her hair cut really changed her appearance.*

appendix appendixes or appendices noun
Your appendix is a small, closed tube inside your body. It is part of the intestines.

appetite appetites noun
If you have an appetite, you are ready to eat something. *I hope you have a good appetite, because I've made a really big dinner.*

applause noun
Applause is when people clap their hands together to show that they liked something.

apple apples noun
a hard, round, green, red, or yellow fruit that grows on a tree. *Apples are good for your health.*

apply applies applying applied verb
1 If something such as a rule applies to you, you must do what it says. *School rules apply to everyone in the school.*
2 If you apply for something such as a job, you write to somebody to ask for it.
application noun.

appointment appointments noun
a time that you have arranged to see somebody. *I have a doctor's appointment at 4 o'clock.*

appreciate appreciates appreciating appreciated verb
If you appreciate something, you are grateful for it. *I appreciate all your help.*
appreciation noun.

approach approaches approaching approached verb
If something approaches, it comes closer. *The train is approaching* or *The dog approached the cat.*

approve approves approving approved verb
If you approve of something, you think that it is good and right. *Mom doesn't approve of my new haircut.*

apricot apricots noun
a soft, round, orange-yellow fruit with a large pit in the middle.

apron aprons noun
a piece of clothing that you wear over your clothes to keep them clean while you are cooking.

aquarium aquariums or aquaria noun
1 a glass tank where fish and other water animals are kept.
2 a building with lots of glass tanks where people can look at fish.

arch arches noun
a part of a bridge, building, or wall that has a curved shape. Arches support buildings and let people, trains, boats, cars, and other vehicles pass underneath.

archery noun
the sport of shooting with a bow and arrow. You shoot at a circular target.

area areas noun
1 a part of a country, a city, or the world. *My uncle comes from this area.*
2 the size of a flat place. *If a room is 20 feet wide and 40 feet long, it has an area of 800 square feet.*
3 a place that you use for something special. *a picnic area.*

area code noun
three numbers that show the telephone region where you live.

arena arenas noun
a place with rows of seats in it where you can watch sports or concerts.

argue argues arguing argued verb
If you argue with somebody, you speak in an angry way because you do not agree with that person.
argument noun.

arithmetic noun
working with numbers to find answers to problems.

arm arms noun
Your arm is the part of your body between your shoulder and your hand.

armed adjective
If somebody is armed, the person has a weapon and is ready to fight.

armor noun
a suit of strong metal that soldiers used to wear to protect their bodies during battles.

arms noun
Arms are guns, swords, bombs, and other weapons used in fighting.

army armies noun
a large group of soldiers who are trained to fight on land in a war.

arrange arranges arranging arranged verb
1 If you arrange something such as a party, you plan it. *We are arranging a birthday party for my sister.*
2 If you arrange things such as flowers or your belongings, you set them out in a certain way or put them in order. *We arranged the books on the shelf in alphabetical order.*
arrangement noun.

arrest arrests arresting arrested verb
When the police arrest somebody, they catch the person and accuse him or her of breaking the law.

arrive arrives arriving arrived verb
If you arrive somewhere, you get there. *She arrived at 3 o'clock.* ■ The opposite is **depart** or **leave**.
arrival noun.

arrow arrows noun
1 a thin stick with a sharp point at one end that you shoot from a bow.
2 a sign that points to tell you the way to somewhere.

art noun
Art is something beautiful or interesting that somebody has made, such as a painting or a statue.

artery arteries noun
An artery is one of the large tubes that carry blood from your heart to all parts of your body.

artificial adjective
If something is artificial, it is made by people. ■ The opposite is **natural**.

artist artists noun
a person who draws or paints pictures or makes other beautiful things.

ash ashes noun
1 the gray powder that is left after something has been burned.
2 a tree that has gray bark and loses its leaves in the winter.

ashamed adjective
If you are ashamed of something you have done, you are sorry and unhappy about it. *William was ashamed that he had told a lie.*

ask asks asking asked verb
1 If you ask a question, you say that you want to know something. *"What time is it?" she asked.*
2 If you ask for something, you say that you want it. *Tom asked for a bike for his birthday.*

asleep adjective
sleeping. *The cat was asleep by the fire.* ■ The opposite is **awake**.

assembly assemblies noun
a meeting of a big group of people for something special. *We have a school assembly every Monday.*

assist assists assisting assisted verb
If you assist, you help somebody.
assistance noun, **assistant** noun.

assorted adjective
If things such as candy or cookies are assorted, all different kinds are mixed together.

asthma noun
an illness that makes it difficult for a person to breathe. ▲ Say **azz**-ma.

astonish astonishes astonishing astonished verb
If something astonishes you, it surprises you very much. *She was astonished to see the big rainbow.*

astronaut astronauts noun
a person who travels in space.

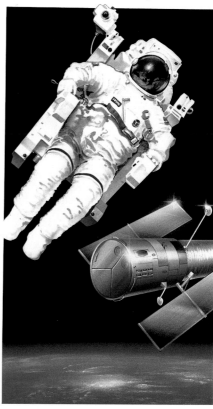

astronomy noun
the study of the Sun, Moon, planets, and stars.

ate past of **eat**.

athlete athletes noun
a person who is good at sports and
games like football or track and field.

athletics noun
sports such as football, baseball,
ice-skating, and track and field.

atlas atlases noun
a book of maps.

atmosphere noun
1 the layer of gases that surrounds
Earth.
2 the feeling that a room or a place
has. *The hotel has a warm, cozy
atmosphere.*

atom atoms noun
a very tiny part of something.
Everything is made of atoms.
Water is made of two kinds of atoms.

attach attaches attaching attached
verb
If you attach something to something
else, you join or fasten them together.
We attached the rope to a tree.

attack attacks attacking attacked
verb
to try to hurt someone by using
violence.
attack noun.

attempt attempts noun
a try. *After two attempts, I managed
to ski down the hill.*
attempt verb.

attention noun
listening to somebody or watching
that person carefully. *Pay attention!*

attic attics noun
a room or space under the roof of a
house. *We keep our old toys in the attic.*

attract attracts attracting
attracted verb
1 to like or to find somebody
or something interesting.
*Lisa was attracted to
the red car.*
2 To attract also
means to make
something come
closer. *Magnets
attract iron.*
attraction noun.

attractive adjective
very nice to look at.

audience audiences noun
a group of people who are watching
a play, movie, or concert.

audio adjective
1 relating to hearing a sound.
2 used to broadcast sounds.

aunt aunts noun
Your aunt is the sister of your
mother or your father, or the wife
of your uncle.

author authors noun
a person who writes stories or books.

autograph autographs noun
the signature of somebody famous.

automatic adjective
If a machine is automatic, it works
by itself instead of a person doing
the work.

autumn autumns noun
the season between summer and
winter, also known as fall. *Leaves
fall off trees in the autumn.*

avenue avenues noun
a street. Avenues are often wide
with trees along both sides.

average adjective
1 usual. *She is above average height
for her age.*
2 In math, to find the average of

three numbers, such as 5, 9, and 10,
add them up and divide by 3: $5 + 9 + 10 = 24$, and $24 \div 3 = 8$.

aviary aviaries noun
a place for keeping large numbers
of birds. *I love to visit the aviary at
the zoo.*

avoid avoids avoiding avoided verb
If you avoid something, you stay away
from it. *The driver swerved to avoid the dog.*

awake adjective
If you are awake, you are not asleep.

award awards noun
a prize for something you have done
well. *I won an award for swimming.*
award verb.

awful adjective
very bad. *This cake is stale. It tastes awful.*

awkward adjective
1 If you move in an awkward way,
you are clumsy.
2 difficult or not convenient. *Our cabin
is awkward to get to if you don't have a car.*

ax axes noun
a tool with a long handle and a sharp
blade for cutting down trees and
chopping wood.

Bb

baboon baboons noun
a large African monkey with a nose
and mouth the same shape as a dog's.

A family of baboons

baby babies noun
a very young child.

babysitter babysitters noun
a person who takes care of children
when their parents are out.
baby-sit verb.

back backs noun
1 Your back is the part of your body
behind you, between your neck
and your bottom.
2 The back of something is the
opposite part from the front.
■ The opposite is **front**.

background backgrounds noun
The background is everything behind
the main thing that you are looking
at. *This picture shows some camels with
pyramids in the background.*

bacon noun
meat from the back or sides of a hog
that has been prepared over smoke or
been treated with salt.

bacteria noun
Bacteria are living things that are so
tiny, you cannot see them without
a microscope. Bacteria live in air,
soil, water, and inside people and
animals, and some kinds can
make you sick.

bad worse worst adjective
1 not good.
2 If you are bad at something, you
cannot do it very well.
3 If food is bad, it starts to smell or
get moldy, so that you cannot eat it.

bad

*Some words that you can use
instead of bad:*

The weather was very bad last week.
unpleasant, nasty

You've been a bad girl.
naughty, disobedient

Candy is bad for your teeth.
harmful, damaging

Is the pain bad?
severe

Her car is in bad condition.
poor

The food has gone bad.
rotten

badge badges noun
a piece of metal or plastic with
a picture or words on it. A badge
is usually pinned or sewn onto
your clothes.

badger badgers noun
a wild animal with gray fur and black
and white stripes on its head. Badgers
live underground in holes called setts
and come out to eat at night.

badminton noun
a game in which players use rackets to
hit a light object called a shuttlecock,
or a birdie, over a high net.

bag bags noun
a thing that you use for carrying other
things in.

bait noun
a piece of food that you put on a
hook or put in a trap to catch fish
or animals.

bake bakes baking baked verb
When you bake food, you cook it
in an oven.

balance balances
balancing
balanced verb
If you balance,
you remain steady and
do not fall over.
*Connie balances
on the box.*

balcony
balconies
noun
a platform on
the outside wall
of a building
upstairs, with a wall or railing
around it.

bald balder baldest adjective
A man who is bald has no hair
on his head.

bald eagle noun
an eagle, the symbol of the U.S.A.
It is brown with a white head.

ball balls noun
1 a round thing that you use
to play games.
2 something made into a
round shape. *a ball of yarn.*
3 a fancy party where
people dance.

ballet noun
a kind of dance
set to music
that tells
a story. ▲ Say
bal-**lay**.

balloon
balloons noun
a round bag made of rubber and
filled with air or gas so that it floats.

bamboo noun
a tropical plant with a hollow stem.

ban bans banning banned verb
If somebody bans something, it is not allowed. *My parents have banned us from watching TV in the morning.*

banana bananas noun
a long, curved fruit with yellow skin.

band bands noun
1 a group of people who play music.
2 a group of people who do something together. *a band of soldiers.*
3 a narrow piece of material that goes around something. *Tennis players often wear wristbands.*

bandage bandages noun
a long strip of material that can be wrapped around a part of your body that is injured in order to protect it.

bandit bandits noun
an armed robber.

bang bangs noun
a sudden and very loud noise.
bangs noun.
hair across the forehead that is cut to just above the eyebrows.

bank banks noun
1 a building where people keep money.
2 the ground at the side of a river.

banner banners noun
a long piece of cloth with writing on it that people carry in a crowd or during a march.

bar bars noun
1 a long, straight piece of metal.
2 a flat solid piece. *a bar of soap.*
3 a place where you can buy a drink or food. *a salad bar.*
4 one of the short groups of notes that a piece of music can be divided into. When music is written down, the bars are shown by lines between the groups of notes.

barbecue barbecues noun
an outdoor grill on which you can cook things like hot dogs over hot charcoal. ▲ Say **bar-bi-*kew.***

bare bare barest adjective
1 without any clothes on. *bare feet.*
2 A bare closet or shelf is empty.
⬤ A word that sounds like **bare** is **bear**.

bargain bargains noun
a thing being sold that is much cheaper than you expected it to be.

barge barges noun
a long boat with a flat bottom, used on rivers and canals.

bark barks barking barked verb
When a dog barks, it makes a sudden loud noise.

bark noun
the rough outside covering of a tree's trunk and branches.

barley noun
a plant whose grain is used as food. *beef and barley soup.*

barn barns noun
a large farm building for storing crops such as hay or for keeping animals inside.

barrel barrels noun
a large container with curved sides that is used for storing liquids.

barrier barriers noun
a thing like a wall or fence that stops people or things from getting past.

base bases noun
the bottom part of something.

barrio barrios noun
a Spanish neighborhood.

baseball noun
a game played with a bat and ball by two teams of nine players each. Each player has to hit the ball and run around four bases on the field before the ball is caught.

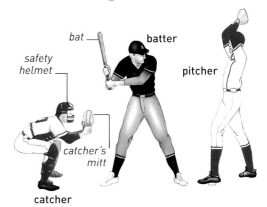

bat — batter
safety helmet
pitcher
catcher's mitt
catcher

basement basements noun
a room or rooms below the ground floor of a building.

basic adjective
Basic things are the important things that you cannot do without. *The one basic piece of equipment that you need for soccer is a ball.*

basket baskets noun
a kind of stiff bag made from cane or wire, used for carrying things.

basketball noun
a game played by two teams of five players each. The teams have to get a large ball through a high net attached to a ring at each end of the court.

bat bats noun
1 a small animal like a mouse with wings. Bats hunt for food at night.
2 a piece of wood or metal that you use for hitting the ball in sports such as baseball. **batter** noun.

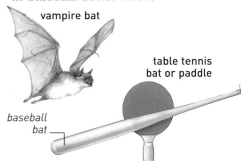

vampire bat
table tennis bat or paddle
baseball bat

bat bats batting batted verb
When you bat, you have a turn at hitting the ball in baseball.

bath baths noun

1 a very large container for water that you get into to wash your entire body.
2 When you have a bath, you get into a bath and wash yourself.
▲ Rhymes with **path**.

battery batteries noun

a metal object that makes and stores electricity. You put batteries in cameras, toys, and flashlights.

battle battles noun

a fight between armies or navies.

bay bays noun

a part of the sea that has land curving around it on three sides.

beach beaches noun

the land beside the sea that is covered with sand or pebbles.

bead beads noun

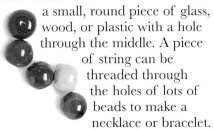 a small, round piece of glass, wood, or plastic with a hole through the middle. A piece of string can be threaded through the holes of lots of beads to make a necklace or bracelet.

beak beaks noun

the hard, pointed part of a bird's mouth.

beam beams noun

1 one of the thick, strong pieces of wood or metal that holds up a roof.
2 a line of bright light.

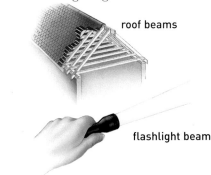

roof beams

flashlight beam

beam beams beaming beamed verb

If you are beaming, you have a big, happy smile on your face.

bean beans noun

a large seed that grows inside a pod. Sometimes you eat the whole pod, and sometimes you eat the seed. *green beans* or *baked beans.*

bear bears noun

a big, wild animal with thick fur. Bears are brown, black, or white.
● A word that sounds like **bear** is **bare**.

bear bears bearing bore borne verb

1 If you cannot bear something, you cannot put up with it. *She couldn't bear the pain any longer.*
2 If you bear something, you carry or support it. *He bore a heavy load.*
● A word that sounds like **bear** is **bare**.

beard beards noun

the hair on a man's chin and face.

beast beasts noun

a wild animal.

beat beats beating beat beaten verb

1 If you beat somebody in a competition or game, you win.
2 To beat somebody or something means to hit them, or it, very hard again and again, especially with your hand or a stick.
3 If you beat eggs or cream, you stir it fast with a fork, electric mixer, or whisk.
4 When your heart is beating, it is pushing the blood around your body regularly and keeping you alive.

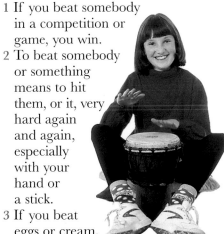

beat beats noun

the regular rhythm of your heart or of a piece of music. *the beat of a drum.*

beautiful adjective

very lovely to look at, listen to, or smell. *a beautiful painting.*
■ The opposite is **ugly**.

beaver beavers noun

a furry animal with strong teeth and a flat tail. Beavers live by rivers or streams, where they build homes called lodges.

become becomes becoming became verb

1 When one thing becomes another thing, it changes into it. *Caterpillars eventually become butterflies.*
2 When you become something, you change to be it. *She became worried about her son when he didn't come home at the usual time.*

bed beds noun

1 the piece of furniture that you sleep on. The room where your bed is and where you sleep is called a bedroom.
2 The seabed is the bottom of the sea.

bee bees noun

an insect with a yellow and black body that makes honey. ● A word that sounds like **bee** is **be**.

beef noun

meat from a cow.

beehive beehives noun

a box or place where bees live.

beetle beetles noun

an insect with hard, shiny wings.

beet beets noun

a round, red vegetable that grows in the ground.

beg begs begging begged verb

1 If somebody begs, he or she asks people for money in the street.
2 If you beg for something, you ask for it in a way that shows you want it very badly.

begin begins beginning began begun
verb
When something begins, it starts.
The opposite is **finish** or **end**.
beginning noun.

behave behaves behaving behaved
verb
The way you behave is the way that
you act. *The children behaved very badly.*
behavior noun.

believe believes believing believed
verb
1 If you believe something, you are
  sure that it is true or real even
  though you cannot prove it. *Do
  you believe in ghosts?*
2 If you believe somebody, you think
  that person tells the truth. *Mom
  believed my story.*
belief noun.

bell bells noun
a metal instrument like a large upside-
down cup that has a thin piece of
metal hanging inside called a clapper.
When the clapper hits the side of the
bell, it makes a ringing sound.

belong belongs belonging belonged
verb
1 If something belongs to you, it is
  yours.
2 If you belong to a club you are
  a member of it.

below adverb, preposition
underneath something else. *My room
is below the attic.*
The opposite is **above**.

belt belts noun
a strip of material or leather that you
wear around your waist.

bench benches noun
1 a long, hard seat made of wood or
  metal that more than one person
  can sit on. *a park bench.*

workbench   park bench

raspberry   huckleberry   cranberry

blackberry blueberry   strawberry   grape   gooseberry red currant black currant

2 a wooden table that people put
  things on when they work. *The
  carpenter was working at his bench,
  drilling a hole in a piece of wood.*

bend bends bending bent verb
1 If you bend, you move the top part
  of your body downward. *He bent
  down and stroked the dog.*
2 If you bend something, you make
  it curved instead of straight.

beneath preposition
If something is beneath something
else, it is below it. The opposite
is **above, over,** or **on top of**.

berry berries noun
a small, soft fruit with seeds in it.

beside preposition
next to something else.

best adjective, adverb
better than all others. *my best clothes*
or *I like math class best.*

bet bets betting bet verb
1 If you bet that something is
  going to happen, you are sure
  that it will.
2 If you bet someone is going to do
  something, you are very sure that he
  or she will do it. *I bet Jenny will win
  the race.*
bet noun.

betray betrays betraying betrayed
verb
If you betray somebody, you harm
that person on purpose even though
he or she trusted you. *She betrayed me
by telling lies.*
betrayal noun.

between preposition
in the middle.

beware verb
If somebody tells you to beware of
something, you are being warned to
be careful because it is dangerous.
The sign said "Beware of the dog."

bewildered adjective
If you are bewildered, you are
confused.

beyond preposition
If something is beyond something
else, it is on the far side of it. *The
parking lot is beyond the train station.*

bicycle bicycles noun
a vehicle with two wheels that you
ride by sitting on it and pushing
two pedals with your feet.
Say **by**-*si-kul*. Look at page 19.

bid bids bidding bid verb
If you bid for something, you offer an
amount of money for it. Other people
also offer an amount of money for it,
and the person who offers the most
gets it.

big bigger biggest adjective
large in size, or important.
The opposite is **small** or **little**.

bike bikes noun
a bicycle.

bill bills noun
1 a bird's beak.
2 a piece of paper money. *a $5 bill.*
3 a piece of paper showing how much
  money you owe for something. *After
  lunch, the waiter brought our bill.*

big

Some words that you can use instead of big:

There is a big crowd.
huge, large, great

This suitcase is too big for me to lift.
heavy, weighty

Canada is a big country.
massive

The wedding was a big occasion.
grand, impressive

As we sailed closer, we saw a big iceberg.
huge, great, gigantic

This was a big decision for her to make.
important, serious

bin bins noun
a container to store things in.

bind binds binding bound verb
If you bind something, you tie it up very firmly.

Bicycle

safety helmet

reflective jacket

handlebar

brake lever

elbow pads

front reflector

fork

tire

hub

spoke

saddle

rear reflector

pedal

knee pads

gears

chain

binoculars noun
An instrument with two lenses that you look through to make things that are far away look closer.

biodegradable adjective
Something that is biodegradable will decay naturally. Paper is biodegradable, but a lot of plastic is not. ▲ Say *by-oh-di-**gray**-di-bul.*

VOCABULARY

chain
a series of metal rings called links.

hub
the center of a wheel.

gears
a set of toothed wheels (sprockets) over which the chain fits and which change the power and speed of the bicycle.

reflector
an object that makes the bicycle visible in the dark by reflecting lights from vehicles behind it and in front of it.

spoke
one of the rods connecting the hub to the rim of a wheel.

tandem
a type of bicycle with seats and pedals for two riders.

biology noun
the scientific study of people, plants, and animals.
biological adjective.

bird birds noun
an animal that has wings, feathers, and a beak. Most birds can fly.
◆ Look at page 20.

birth births noun
The birth of a baby is when it comes out of its mother's body.

birthday birthdays noun
Your birthday is a day that you remember each year because it is the same day as the day you were born.

biscuit biscuits noun
a small bread raised with baking soda.
▲ Say **bis**-*kit.*

bit bits noun
1 a piece. *a bit of cheese.*
2 a little. *These shoes are a bit too small.*
3 the smallest unit of memory in a computer.

bite bites biting bit bitten verb
If you bite something, you close your teeth on it. ● A word that sounds like **bite** is **byte**.

bitter bitterest adjective
1 Food that is bitter has a sharp, bad taste. *bitter medicine.*
■ The opposite is **sweet**.
2 If you are bitter about something, you stay angry and upset about it for a long time after it happens.
3 If the weather is bitter, it is very cold.

blackbird blackbirds noun
a bird with black feathers that can often be seen in gardens.

blackboard blackboards noun
a large, dark-colored board that you write on with chalk.

Birds

condor

secondary feathers

feather

primary feathers

bill

talons

tail

tail feather

hummingbird

toco toucan

shaft

barn owl

starling

great blue heron

kiwi

black swan

pelican

great crested grebe

VOCABULARY

barb
a hairlike branch from the shaft of a feather.

barbule
a tiny hook of hair branching from the barb of a feather.

bird of prey
a bird that kills other birds and small animals for food.

down
the small, soft feathers beneath the outer feathers of water birds.

flipper
the armlike limb that birds such as penguins use for swimming.

primary feather, or **contour feather**
any one of the large feathers that covers a bird's wings, body, or tail.

talon
a sharp, hooked claw on the feet of a bird of prey.

webbed feet
water birds such as ducks and geese have a web of skin between their toes to help them swim.

blade blades noun
the sharp edge of a knife or sword.

blame blames blaming blamed verb
If you blame somebody for something, you say that it is that person's fault. *He blamed me for breaking his bike.*

blank blanker blankest adjective
If something is blank, it has nothing on it. *a blank sheet of paper.*

blanket blankets noun
a thick cover for a bed; a thick covering. *a blanket of fog.*

blast blasts noun
an explosion. *One person was injured in the blast when the bomb went off.*

blaze blazes blazing blazed verb
When a fire blazes, it burns very strongly. *The forest fire blazed for more than a week.*

bleed bleeds bleeding bled verb
When a part of your body bleeds, blood flows out. *He cut his arm, and it started bleeding.*

blew past of **blow**.
● A word that sounds like **blew** is **blue**.

blind adjective
A person who is blind cannot see.

blind blinds noun
a roll of material that you pull down to cover a window.

blindfold blindfolds noun
a piece of material tied over somebody's eyes so that he or she cannot see.

blink blinks blinking blinked verb
When you blink, you shut both your eyes and open them again very quickly.

blister blisters noun
a small bubble of liquid just under your skin that you get if something has rubbed your skin a lot or if you get burned.

blizzard blizzards noun
a snowstorm with very strong winds.

block blocks noun
1 a thick piece of something solid, with flat sides. *a block of wood.*
2 the area in a city or town within four streets is also a block.
3 an apartment block is a big building divided into apartments.

block blocks blocking blocked verb
If something blocks a place, it is in the way and nothing can get by.

blond blonde blonder blondest adjective
A person who is blond or blonde has light-colored hair. We use the spelling **blond** for men and boys and **blonde** for women and girls.

blood noun
the liquid that flows all around your body through your arteries and veins.

bloom blooms blooming bloomed verb
When a plant blooms, its flowers come out.

blossom noun
flowers on a tree. *cherry blossoms.*

blot blots noun
a drop of ink that has spilled onto something and left a mark.

blouse blouses noun
a piece of clothing like a shirt worn by a girl or woman.

blow blows blowing blew blown verb
1 If you blow, you breathe a lot of air out of your mouth at once. *He blew all nine candles out with one breath.*
2 When you blow your nose, you breathe out very hard through your nose and into a tissue.
3 If something blows somewhere, the wind is pushing it along. *Leaves were blowing around the street.*
blow up If something is blown up, it is destroyed by an explosion.

blow blows noun
a hard hit.

blunt blunter bluntest adjective
1 A blunt knife does not cut very well because it is not sharp anymore.
2 A blunt object has a rounded or flat end instead of a pointed one. *a blunt pencil.*
3 If you are blunt, you say exactly what you think, even if it is not polite or kind.

blur blurs blurring blurred verb
When something blurs, you cannot see it clearly. *My eyes were so tired that the TV was beginning to blur.*

B
C
D
E
K
N
T
U
X
Y
Z

B

blush blushes blushing
blushed verb
When you blush, your face gets red because you are embarrassed. *Mark blushed when Tina saw his baby picture.*

board boards noun
1 a long piece of sawn lumber.
2 a blackboard.
3 a surfboard.
● A word that sounds like **board** is **bored**.

board boarder boarding
boarded verb
to get into a big vehicle, such as an airplane.

boast boasts boasting boasted verb
If you boast, you talk in a way that shows you are too proud of something. *John boasted about his grades.*

boat boats noun
Boats carry people and things across water. Some boats have engines, some have sails, and some you row with oars or paddles.

body bodies noun
1 the parts of a person or of an animal that can be seen or touched.
2 a dead person.
3 a group of people. *our student body.*

boil boils boiling boiled verb
1 When liquid boils, it gets so hot that bubbles appear on the surface and it starts to change into steam.
2 When you boil food, you cook it in boiling water. *We boiled potatoes.*

boil boils noun
a big, painful spot on your skin.

bold bolder boldest adjective
not afraid to do dangerous things.
boldness noun.

bolt bolts noun
1 a metal bar that slides across to lock a door or window.
2 a metal pin that screws into a metal nut to fasten things together.

3 a big flash of lightning.
4 a large roll of cloth.

bolt bolts bolting bolted verb
1 When you bolt a door, you slide a bolt across it to hold it in place so that it cannot be opened.
2 When people or animals bolt, they suddenly run away. *The horse was frightened by the noise and bolted across the field.*

bomb bombs noun
a weapon containing chemicals that can be made to explode.

bone bones noun
A bone is one of the hard parts inside your body that make up your skeleton.

bonfire bonfires noun
a big fire that is made outdoors. *Campers sat around the bonfire.*

bonnet bonnets noun
1 a kind of hat that is tied with strings under the chin. Babies sometimes wear bonnets.
2 Pioneer women wore sun bonnets.

book
books
noun
sheets of paper fastened together inside a cover.

book books booking booked verb
When you book something, you ask somebody to keep it for you. *Mom booked seats on the plane.*

boomerang boomerangs
noun
a curved stick that comes back to the person who throws it. The first people who lived in Australia, called Aboriginal people, used the boomerang as a weapon for hunting.

boot boots noun
a shoe that covers your foot and ankle, and sometimes part of your leg. *Cowboys and cowgirls wear high-topped boots.*

border borders noun
1 the line that separates two countries.
2 a strip around the edge of something that is a different color or has a different pattern.

bore bores boring bored verb
1 If something bores you, you are not interested in it.
2 If you bore into something, you make a hole in it by using a drill. *The engineer bored a hole in the rock.*
boredom noun,
boring adjective.

bore past of **bear**.

born adjective
When a baby is born, it comes out of its mother's body.

borrow borrows borrowing
borrowed verb
If you borrow something, someone lets you have it for a time and then you give it back. *I borrowed books from the library.* ● The opposite is **lend**.

boss bosses noun
The boss is the person who is in charge.

both pronoun
When something is true about two people or things, you can say that it is true about both of them. *Both my sister and my aunt are named Mary.*

bother bothers bothering
bothered verb
1 If something bothers you, it makes you feel worried or uncomfortable.
2 If you bother about something you care about it and take trouble with it.

bottle bottles noun
a tall container of glass or plastic that you keep liquid in.

bottom bottoms noun
1 the lowest part of something. The opposite is **top**.
2 Your bottom is the part of your body that you sit on.

bought past of **buy**.
▲ Say **bawt**.

boulder boulders noun
a very large, smooth rock.

bounce bounces bouncing
bounced verb
When something bounces, it hits the ground or another hard surface and moves back up again. *Rachel sent the ball bouncing along the ground.*

bound bounds bounding
bounded verb
To bound is to move along by making big jumps. *The dog bounded up to the gate.*
bound to If something is bound to happen, it will definitely happen.

bound past of **bind**.

bouquet bouquets noun
a bunch of flowers. ▲ Say *bo-***kay**.

bow bows bowing bowed verb
If you bow, you bend your head or body forward. *Actors bow at the end of a play when people clap for them.*
▲ Rhymes with **cow**.

bow bows noun
1 a long piece of wood with a string fastened at each end that is used to shoot arrows.
2 a knot with two loops.
3 a long, straight piece of wood with horsehair stretched along it and fastened at each end. A bow is used to play a musical instrument such as a violin.
▲ Rhymes with **no**.

different types of bows

bowl bowls noun
a deep, round dish for food or liquids.

bowl bowls bowling bowled verb
When you bowl, you roll a heavy ball down a long alley to knock over pins. **bowling** noun, adjective.

box boxes noun
a container, usually with a lid, that is used for packing or storing things.

box boxes boxing boxed verb
When people box, they fight with their fists in a sport called boxing.

boy boys noun
a male child.

brace braces noun
a piece of wire that a dentist can put over your teeth to make them straighter.

bracelet bracelets noun
a piece of jewelry that you wear around your wrist.

Braille noun
a form of writing made up of patterns of raised dots that blind people can read by touching. *Paul is reading about frogs in his Braille textbook for science class.*

Braille writing

brain brains noun
the part inside your head that you use to think and that controls all parts of your body.

brake brakes noun
the part of a bicycle or car that you use to make it go slower or stop.
● A word that sounds like **brake** is **break**.

brake brakes braking braked verb
When you brake, you make a bicycle or car go slower or stop by using the brake. ● A word that sounds like **brake** is **break**.

branch branches noun
a part of a tree that grows out from the trunk. ▲ Rhymes with **ranch**.

brass noun
a yellow metal made from copper and another metal called zinc. *Trumpets and horns are made of brass.*

brave braver bravest adjective
If you are brave, you will do something frightening or dangerous without showing fear.

bread noun
a food that is made from flour and baked in an oven.

B

break breaks breaking broke broken verb
1 If you break something, you damage it so that it is in pieces or does not work anymore. *I think I've broken the CD player* or *He broke the dish*.
2 If you break a promise, you do not do what you promised that you would.
3 If you break the law, you do something that is against the law.
● A word that sounds like **break** is **brake**.

break breaks noun
a short rest from work. *She's having a coffee break.* ● A word that sounds like **break** is **brake**.

breakfast breakfasts noun
the first meal of the day. *We have cereal every morning for breakfast.*

breast breasts noun
part of a woman's body that makes milk to feed her baby.

breath breaths noun
the air that goes in and out of your lungs through your nose or mouth when you breathe.

breathe breathes breathing breathed verb
When you breathe, you take air into your lungs through your nose or mouth and then let it out again.

breed breeds noun
one kind of an animal. *Spaniels and Labradors are different breeds of dogs.*

breed breeds breeding bred verb
1 If you breed animals, you keep them in order to produce baby animals.
2 When animals breed, they produce baby animals.

breeze breezes noun
a gentle wind.

brick bricks noun
a block made out of baked clay that is used for building houses and walls.

bride brides noun
a woman on her wedding day.

bridegroom bridegrooms noun
a man on his wedding day; groom.

bridesmaid bridesmaids noun
a girl or woman who accompanies the bride on her wedding day.

bridge bridges noun
something built over a river, railroad line, or road so that people and vehicles can travel from one side to the other.

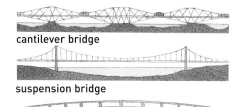

cantilever bridge

suspension bridge

arch bridge

cable-stayed bridge

brief briefer briefest adjective
Something that is brief only lasts for a short time. *We had a brief visit.*

bright brighter brightest adjective
1 A bright light shines very strongly. ■ The opposite is **dim**.
2 Bright colors are clear and strong. ■ The opposite is **dull** or **dark**.
3 A bright person is smart. ■ The opposite is **stupid**. ▲ Rhymes with **kite**.
brightness noun.

brilliant adjective
1 A brilliant person is very smart.
2 Brilliant light is very bright.

brim brims noun
1 If you fill a cup or glass to the brim, you fill it right up to the top.
2 the flat part that sticks out from the edge of a hat.

bristle bristles noun
1 a short, stiff hair on an animal.
2 Bristles are the stiff hairs fastened into the handle of a brush.

brittle adjective
If something is brittle, it is hard but easy to break. *Eggshells are brittle.*

broad broader broadest adjective
wide. *broad shoulders.* ■ The opposite is **narrow.**

broadcast broadcasts broadcasting broadcast verb
When a radio, TV, or online program is broadcast, it is sent out so that you can hear it online or on the radio or see it on TV.

broke, broken past of **break**.

bronze noun
a brown metal made from a mixture of copper and tin.

brooch brooches noun
a piece of jewelry with a pin that you can fasten onto your clothes. ▲ Rhymes with **coach**.

brook brooks noun
a small stream.

broom brooms noun
a brush with a long handle for sweeping the floor.

brother
A person's brother is a boy or man who has the same mother and father.

brought past of **bring**. ▲ Rhymes with **caught**.

brow brows noun
1 a person's forehead.
2 the top of a hill.
▲ Rhymes with **cow.**

bruise bruises noun
a dark mark on your skin where something has hit it or you have fallen over and bumped it. ▲ Say **brooz.**

brush brushes noun
a set of bristles fastened to a handle. You use different sizes and shapes of brushes for different jobs, such as painting, brushing your teeth, or sweeping the floor.

brush brushes brushing
brushed verb
If you brush something, you clean it with a brush. *Don't forget to brush your hair.*

bubble bubbles noun
a little ball of air or gas that you get in soft drinks or boiling water.

bucket buckets noun
a large container with a handle used for carrying liquid.

buckle buckles noun
a fastening on a belt or strap.
My belt has a silver buckle.

bud buds noun
a part of a plant that opens up to become a flower or a leaf.

Buddhist Buddhists noun
a person who follows a religion started by a religious teacher named Buddha. ▲ Say **buh**-*dist.*

buffalo buffalo or buffaloes noun
a wild member of the cattle family, with horns. The North American buffalo is called a bison.

bug bugs noun
1 an insect.
2 an illness such as a cold or flu.

build builds building built verb
When you build something, you make it by putting together different parts.

building buildings noun
a place that has walls and a roof like a house, department store, or school.

bulb bulbs noun
1 the thick, round root of a plant such as a daffodil or tulip that is under the ground, from which the plant grows.
2 the round glass part of a lamp or light.

bull bulls noun
the male of the cattle family. Male elephants and whales are also called bulls.

bulldozer bulldozers noun
a tractor with a wide blade in front of it that is used to move dirt or knock down buildings.

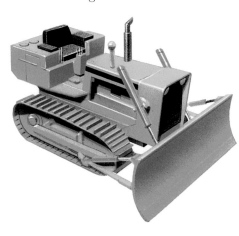

bullet bullets noun
a small piece of metal that is fired from a gun.

bully bullies noun, verb
a person who hurts or frightens other people.

bump bumps bumping bumped verb
If you bump into something, you hit it by accident. *I wasn't looking where I was going, and I bumped into the wall.*

bump bumps noun
1 the sound that something makes when it hits something else. *She fell off the chair and landed on the floor with a loud bump.*
2 a round lump or swelling on a surface. *Dad has a bump on his head where he banged it on the ceiling.*
bumpy adjective.

bunch bunches noun
a group of things. *a bunch of flowers.* or *a bunch of grapes.*

bundle bundles noun
a group of things tied together. *a bundle of sticks.*

bunk bunks noun
a small, narrow bed.

bunk beds noun
two beds, one above the other.

buoy buoys noun
a floating object fastened to the bottom of the sea or a river. A buoy shows a ship where it is dangerous to go. ▲ Say **boy** or **boo-**ee.

B

burglar burglars noun
a person who breaks into a house
or store to steal things.

burglary burglaries noun
breaking into a house or store to
steal things.

burn burns burning burned or
burnt verb
1 If something is burning, it is on fire.
2 If you burn something, you damage
it with fire or heat. *What's that
smell? Have you burned the steak?*

burn burns noun
when fire or heat causes a sore place
on your skin or a mark on something.

burrow burrows noun
a hole or tunnel under the ground
where an animal lives. Prairie dogs
live in burrows.

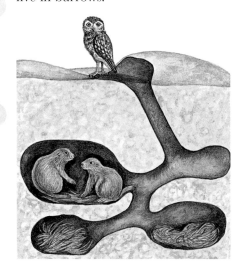

burst bursts bursting burst verb
When something bursts, it breaks
open suddenly, especially because
there is too much inside. *The little boy
was crying because his balloon had burst.*

bury buries burying buried verb
When you bury something, you
put it in a hole in the ground and
cover it up. *Squirrels bury their nuts
to store them for the winter.*
   Say **bair**-*ee.*

bus buses noun
a large vehicle that carries a lot of
passengers by road. *We ride the bus
to school.*

bush bushes noun
1 a large plant like a small tree with a
lot of branches.
2 The bush is a wild part of the
countryside in Australia or Africa.

business businesses noun
1 the work of making, buying, or
selling things. *The company does
a lot of business with England.*
2 a company or store that makes
or sells things. *a software business.*
   Say **biz**-*niss.*

busy busier busiest adjective
1 If you are busy, you have a lot
to do.
2 A place that is busy is full of people
doing things. *a busy supermarket.*
   Say **biz**-*ee.*

butcher butchers noun
a person whose job is to cut up meat.

butter noun
a yellow substance made from cream.
You spread it on bread and use it in
cooking.

butterfly butterflies noun
an insect with large white or colored
wings and a thin body.

button buttons noun
1 a small disk for fastening clothes.
2 a small part that you press to
make a machine work.

buy buys buying bought verb
to pay somebody money for
something.   A word that sounds like
buy is **bye**.   Rhymes with **pie**.

byte bytes noun
a unit of memory in a computer. One
letter or one number takes up one byte.
   A word that sounds like **byte** is **bite**.

peacock

red admiral

painted lady

small tortoiseshell

different types of butterfly

Cc

cab cabs noun
1 a taxi.
2 the part of a truck, train, or bus where the driver sits.

cabbage cabbages noun
a large, round vegetable with green, white, or dark red leaves.
◆ Look at page 176.

cabin cabins noun
1 a bedroom on a ship.
2 the part of a plane where the passengers sit.
3 a small house made of wood. *a log cabin in the woods.*

cable cables noun
1 a set of wires that carry electricity, television, or radio signals. *an underwater telephone cable.*
2 strong, thick wire or rope.

cable television cable televisions noun
a way of sending television programs using wires.

cactus cacti or cactuses noun
a plant with no leaves. Cacti are covered with sharp spikes. Cacti store water in their stems and grow in hot, dry places like deserts.

café cafés noun
a place where you can buy a drink and something to eat and sit down to eat it.
▲ Say ka-**fay**.

cage cages noun
a box or room with metal bars for keeping animals or birds. *a hamster cage.*

cake cakes noun
a sweet food that you make by mixing together flour, butter, eggs, and sugar and baking it in the oven.

calculator calculators noun
a small machine for doing math quickly. You work a calculator by pressing buttons with numbers on them.

calendar calendars noun
a list of all the days, weeks, and months in one year.

calf calves noun
1 a young cow. Young elephants, whales, and seals are also called calves.
2 the thick part at the back of your leg, between your knee and your ankle.

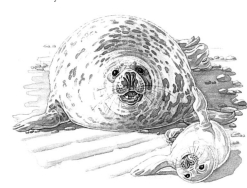

call calls calling called verb
1 If you call somebody, you shout. *"Dinner's ready!" he called.*
2 If you call somebody something, you give that person a nickname. *His name was Theodore, but she called him Ted.*
3 To telephone somebody. *Did anyone call while we were out?*
call noun.

calm calmer calmest adjective
1 quiet and not afraid. ■ The opposite is **nervous**.
2 If the sea is calm, there are no big waves on it.
▲ Say kahlm.

camcorder camcorders noun
a hand-held camera that can take movies and record sound.

camel camels noun
an animal with one or two humps on its back. Camels are used to carry people and things in the desert because they can travel for a long time without water.

camera cameras noun
a machine for taking photographs or making movies.

camouflage camouflages camouflaging camouflaged verb
If somebody or something is camouflaged, you cannot see it because it is the same color or shape as things around it. *Chameleons are lizards that change color and camouflage themselves for protection.*
▲ Say **kam**-uh-flahj.
camouflage noun.

a gecko has camouflaged itself

camp camps noun
a place where people live or stay in tents or cabins while on vacation.

SPELLING TIP

Some words that begin with a "ca" sound are spelled with "ka." For example kangaroo and karate.

camp camps camping camped verb
When you camp, you live in a tent or take a vacation in a tent. go camping *We're going camping this summer.*

can cans noun
a metal container for food, drink, or paint. *a can of cola.*

canal canals noun
a long, narrow strip of water made for boats to travel along.

cancel cancels canceling canceled verb
If you cancel something that you have planned, you stop it from happening. *We canceled our trip because Mom was sick.*

cancer noun
a serious illness that makes some cells inside the body grow too fast.

candle candles noun
a stick made of wax with a string called a wick inside. You light the wick, and the candle burns to give light.

candy candies noun
a sweet food that is made with sugar.

cane canes noun
1 the hard, hollow stem of some plants.
2 a long, thin stick.

cannon cannons noun
a big gun that fires heavy metal balls, or shells, that explode.

canoe canoes noun
a light, thin boat that you move with a paddle. ▲ Say *kun-oo*.

canopy canopies noun
1 a piece of material over a door or window that keeps out the sun.
2 a cover over something. *Tall trees form a canopy over the rainforest floor.*

canvas canvases noun
strong material that is used for making sails, tents, or shoes.

canyon canyons noun
a deep, rocky valley. *The Colorado River flows through the Grand Canyon in northwestern Arizona.*

cap caps noun
1 a flat hat with a peak at the front.
2 the top of a jar, bottle, or pen.

cape capes noun
1 a piece of land that sticks out into the sea. *Cape Cod.*
2 a loose coat with no sleeves that you wrap around your shoulders.

capital capitals noun
1 the most important city in a country or state, where the government is. *Washington, D.C. is the capital of the United States. Springfield is the capital of Illinois.*
2 an upper case letter in the alphabet.

captain captains noun
1 the person in charge of a ship or an aircraft.
2 an officer in the army, navy, or air force.
3 the leader of a sports team.

capture captures capturing captured verb
If you capture an animal, you catch it and make sure it cannot escape. *The hunters captured the bear.*

car cars noun
a machine with an engine and four wheels used for traveling on the road. The driver uses the steering wheel to turn the car and stops it by putting his or her foot on the brake.

caravan caravans noun
a group of people and animals, such as camels, that travel together. *Caravans in the desert use camels because they can travel long distances without needing water.*

carbohydrate carbohydrates noun
a substance in food that gives you energy.

card cards noun
1 a piece of stiff, thick paper with a picture and message on it. We send cards on birthdays and other special occasions. *My parents sent out more than 100 cards at Christmas.*
2 one of a pack of 52 cards that you play games with.

cardboard noun, adjective
very thick paper. *a cardboard box.*

cardigan cardigans noun
a sweater with buttons down the front.

care cares caring cared verb
1 If you care about somebody or something, you think that it is important. *I don't care who wins.*
2 If you care for somebody or something, you look after that person or thing.

care noun
If you do something with care, you try not to make a mistake or break something. *Wash the glasses with care—they are very delicate.*

career careers noun
a job that you learn to do and then do for a long time. *a career in teaching.*

careful adjective
If you are careful, you think about what you are doing so that you do it safely and well. *Be careful when you cross the street.* ■ The opposite is **careless**.
carefully adverb.

careless adjective
If you are careless, you make mistakes because you are not thinking about what you are doing. ■ The opposite is **careful**.

carnival carnivals noun
1 a special time when people dress up in colorful clothes and sing, dance, and play music as they move through the streets.
2 an outdoor entertainment where you can play games and go on rides. *At the carnival, we rode the Ferris wheel.*

carpenter carpenters noun
a person who makes or mends wooden things, such as chairs, tables, or doors.

carpool carpools noun
a group of people who take turns driving the rest of the group to and from a place.

carriage carriages noun
an old-fashioned vehicle with wheels that is pulled by horses.

carrot carrots noun
a long, orange-colored vegetable that grows under the ground.

carry carries carrying carried verb
When you carry something, you pick it up and take it to another place. *Tom carried the books upstairs.*

cart carts noun
a wooden vehicle with two or four wheels that is pulled by an animal, such as a horse or pony.

carton cartons noun
1 a cardboard or plastic container for holding food or drink. *a milk carton.*
2 a box containing something.

cartoon cartoons noun
1 a movie that uses drawings instead of real people or animals.
2 a drawing in a newspaper or magazine that makes a joke.

cartwheel cartwheels noun
If you do a cartwheel, you put your hands on the ground and swing your legs over sideways in a complete circle, ending up standing on your feet again.

carve carves carving carved verb
1 If you carve wood or stone, you cut it to make a shape out of it.
2 If you carve cooked meat, you cut it into slices.

case cases noun
1 a container such as a pencil case.
2 a crime that the police are trying to solve. *The detective was working on a murder case.*
3 a big box. *a case of sodas.*

cash noun
money in coins and paper bills.

cast casts noun
1 all the actors in a play or movie.
2 a hard plaster covering that holds a broken arm or leg in place while it is healing.

cast casts casting cast verb
1 If you cast something like a fishing line, you throw it.
2 If somebody in a story casts a spell, he or she uses magic to trick somebody. *The wicked witch cast a spell on the prince and changed him into a frog.*

castle castles noun
a large building with thick, high walls. Castles were built long ago to keep the people who lived inside them safe from their enemies.
◆ Look at page 31.

casual adjective
not fancy or formal. *We wore casual clothes to the picnic.*

casualty casualties noun
1 a person who is hurt or killed in an accident or a war. *There were three casualties in the traffic accident.*

cat cats noun
a furry mammal with sharp claws. Small cats are kept as pets. Big cats, such as lions and tigers, live in the wild.
◆ Look at page 30.

catalog catalogs noun
1 a book listing all the things that a company or store sells.
2 a list of all the books or other things in a library.

catapult catapults noun
a big weapon that soldiers used to shoot heavy rocks at an enemy.

catch catches catching caught verb
1 If you catch a ball, you take hold of it when it is moving.
2 If you catch a person or an animal, you stop it from running away.
3 If you catch a train or bus, you get on it.
4 If you catch an illness, you get it. *He caught a cold.*

Cats

Maine coon cat

red tabby

silver tabby

Japanese bobtails

black shorthair

Egyptian maus

red point Siamese

caterpillar caterpillars noun
a small animal like a hairy worm that
will turn into a moth or butterfly.

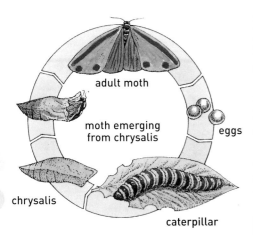

adult moth

moth emerging
from chrysalis

eggs

chrysalis

caterpillar

cathedral cathedrals noun
a large, important church. *St. Patrick's
Cathedral is in New York City.*

cattle noun
cows and bulls. *a herd of cattle.*

caught past of **catch.**

cauliflower cauliflowers noun
a large, round, white vegetable with
green leaves on the outside.

cause causes causing caused verb
If you cause something, you make
it happen. *Keep your dog on a leash,
or you'll cause an accident.*

cautious adjective
If you are cautious, you are very
careful because of danger.

cave caves noun
a big hole under the ground or in
the side of a mountain or cliff.

CD CDs noun
a flat, round piece of plastic that can
store music or information. CD is
short for **compact disk.**

CD-ROM CD-ROMs noun
a disk that you use with a computer to
show words and pictures. CD-ROM is
short for **compact disk read-only
memory.**

ceiling ceilings noun
the top part of a room over your
head. *The light is hanging from the
ceiling.*

celebrate celebrates celebrating
celebrated verb
When you celebrate something,
you do something that you enjoy
at a special time. *Let's have a party
to celebrate your birthday.*
celebration noun.

celery noun
a vegetable with a white or pale green
stem that you can eat raw or cooked.

Castle

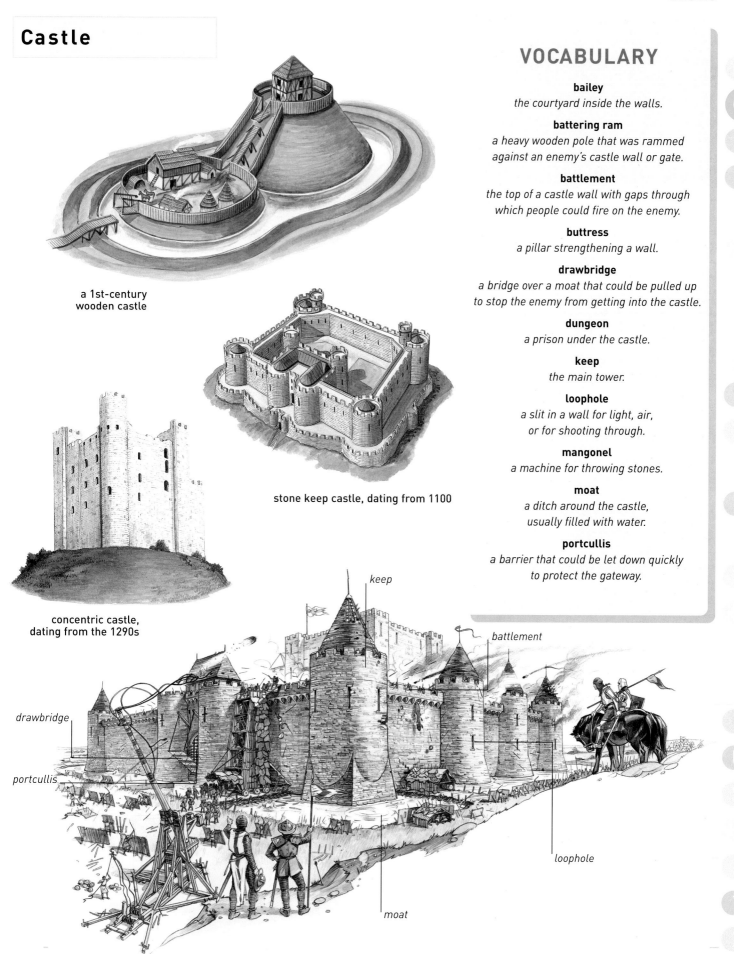

a 1st-century
wooden castle

stone keep castle, dating from 1100

concentric castle,
dating from the 1290s

keep

battlement

drawbridge

portcullis

loophole

moat

VOCABULARY

bailey
the courtyard inside the walls.

battering ram
*a heavy wooden pole that was rammed
against an enemy's castle wall or gate.*

battlement
*the top of a castle wall with gaps through
which people could fire on the enemy.*

buttress
a pillar strengthening a wall.

drawbridge
*a bridge over a moat that could be pulled up
to stop the enemy from getting into the castle.*

dungeon
a prison under the castle.

keep
the main tower.

loophole
*a slit in a wall for light, air,
or for shooting through.*

mangonel
a machine for throwing stones.

moat
*a ditch around the castle,
usually filled with water.*

portcullis
*a barrier that could be let down quickly
to protect the gateway.*

cell cells noun
1 one of the tiny parts that make up all animals and plants. The human body contains millions of red blood cells.
2 a small room in a prison or police station where people are locked up. ● A word that sounds like **cell** is **sell**.

cellar cellars noun
a room under a building where the furnace is.

cello cellos noun
a musical instrument like a big violin that you sit and hold between your knees. You play it by sliding a bow across the strings. ▲ Say **chel**-*lo*.

cement noun
a gray powder used in building that becomes hard when you mix it with water and leave it to dry.

cemetery cemeteries noun
a place where dead people are buried.

cent cents noun
a coin in the U.S.A. A dollar equals 100 cents. ● A word that sounds like **cent** is **scent** or **sent**.

center centers noun
1 the middle of something. *The table was in the center of the room.*
2 a place where people go to do something special, such as a daycare or a shopping center.

centipede centipedes noun
a tiny animal like a worm but with many sets of legs.

central adjective
in the middle. *central Dallas.*

century centuries noun
1 100 years.
2 The 20th century is the time between 1900 and the end of 1999.

cereal cereals noun
Cereals are plants such as rice and wheat that produce grain. We use the grain of cereal plants to make flour and bread. Breakfast cereals are made from grains such as rice and wheat.

● A word that sounds like **cereal** is **serial**.

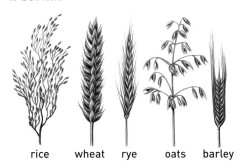

rice   wheat   rye   oats   barley

ceremony ceremonies noun
the actions and words that are used at a special and important event, such as a wedding.

certain adjective
1 If you are certain about something, you are sure that it is true. *I'm certain that I saw him yesterday.*
2 If something happens at a certain time, it happens then and not at other times. *The swimming pool is open only at certain times.*

certificate certificates noun
an important piece of paper that shows that something is true. *I got a certificate for swimming 100 yards.*

chain chains noun
A chain is made from rings of metal joined together. *a bicycle chain.*

chair chairs noun
a seat with four legs and a back, for one person to sit on. ▲ Rhymes with **hair**.

chalk chalks noun
1 soft, white rock.
2 a soft white or colored stick used for writing on a blackboard.
▲ Say **chawk**.

challenge challenges challenging challenged verb
If you challenge somebody, you ask that person to try to do something better than you.

challenge challenges noun
If something is a challenge, it is difficult to do. *This math problem is a real challenge!*

champion champions noun
a person who is the best at a sport or game. *She is the sports day champion.*

chance chances noun
1 a time when you can do something. *It was their last chance to escape.*
2 If there is a chance that something will happen, it might happen. *There's a chance that it will rain today.*
by chance If something happens by chance, it happens without being planned.

change changes changing changed verb
1 When something changes, it becomes different. *Tadpoles change into frogs.*
2 If you change your clothes, you put on different ones. *Sally changed into her jeans.*

change changes noun
1 If there is a change in something, it is different now.
2 the money that you get back if you have paid too much for something.
3 coins like 5¢, 10¢, and 25¢. *Do you have change for the phone?*

channel channels noun
1 a narrow part of a sea.
2 a television station. *Which channel is the show on?*

chapter chapters noun
a part of a book.

character characters noun
1 the way a person or thing is. *She has a kind and loving character.*
2 a person in a play, movie, or book.

charge charges charging charged verb

1 If somebody charges you a certain amount of money for something, he or she asks you to pay that amount. *He charged me 75¢ for the banana.*
2 When the police charge somebody, they say that person has done something wrong.
3 If you charge at people or things, you run toward them very fast. *The bull charged at the fence.*
4 If you charge a battery, you pass an electric current through it to make it work.

charge charges noun
the money that you have to pay for something. *There is a charge of $5 to get into the museum.*
in charge If you are in charge, you are the leader of a group of people. *The principal is in charge of the school.*

chariot chariots noun
a vehicle with two wheels that is pulled by a horse. Chariots were used in wars, races, and hunting a long time ago.

charity charities noun
an organization that collects money to help people who need it.

chart charts noun
1 a drawing that shows important dates or numbers. *The chart shows how long different animals live.*
2 a map of the sea or the stars.

Animal lifespans

Turtle

Elephant

Chimpanzee

Lion

Dog

10 20 30 40 50 60 70 80 90 100
Number of years

charter charters chartering chartered verb
to rent an airplane or bus for a trip.

chase chases chasing chased verb
to run after someone and try to catch him or her.

cheap cheaper cheapest adjective
Something that is cheap does not cost a lot of money. ■ The opposite is **expensive**.

cheat cheats cheating cheated verb
If somebody cheats, he or she does something that is not fair or that breaks the rules. *Play the game without cheating!*

check checks checking checked verb
When you check something, you look at it again to make sure that it is right. *Check your spelling in the dictionary.*

check noun
pattern of squares.

cheek cheeks noun
Your cheeks are the soft parts on each side of your face.

cheerful adjective
If you are cheerful, you feel happy. **cheerfully** adverb.

cheese cheeses noun
a white or yellow food made from milk.

cheetah cheetahs noun
a large, wild cat that can run very fast.

chef chefs noun
a person who cooks food in a restaurant. ▲ Say **sheff**.

chemical chemicals noun
a substance that is made by chemistry or used in chemistry.
chemical adjective

chemist chemists noun
a scientist who works with chemicals.

chemistry noun
the scientific study of what substances are made of and how they work together.

chemotherapy chemotherapies noun
Doctors treat people who have cancer with chemicals to kill the cancer cells. This is chemotherapy. We also call it "chemo."

cherry cherries noun
a small, round, red, yellow, or black fruit. Cherries have a small, smooth, hard seed in the middle.

chess noun
a game that two people play using 16 pieces each on a board with black and white squares. An expert in chess is called a "grand master."

chest chests noun
1 Your chest is the front part of your body between your neck and your waist.
2 a big, strong box with a lid. *The pirates stored gold in a wooden chest.*

chew chews chewing chewed verb
When you chew food, you use your teeth to make it soft and to break it into smaller pieces.

Chicano Chicanos noun
a Mexican-American who has ancestors from Mexico.

chicken chickens noun
a bird that people keep on farms for its eggs and meat.

chickenpox noun
an illness that gives you lots of itchy spots.

chief chiefs noun
the leader of a group of people.

child children noun
1 a young boy or girl.
2 a son or daughter. *They have two children.*

childish adjective
If you are childish, you are being silly and acting younger than your age.

chili chilies noun
a small, red or green vegetable. Chilies have a very hot taste.

chilly chillier chilliest adjective
If you are chilly, you feel cold. *The cold wind made me chilly.*

chime chimes chiming chimed verb
When a bell or a clock chimes, it makes a ringing sound. *The clock chimed midnight.*

chimney chimneys noun
a large pipe above a fire or fireplace that lets smoke and gas go outside into the air.

chimpanzee chimpanzees noun
a small African ape. Chimpanzees are very intelligent animals.

chin chins noun
Your chin is the part of your face below your mouth.

china noun
a kind of white clay that is made into things such as cups and plates. It breaks easily.

chip chips noun
1 a very thin piece of fried, dried potato: potato chip.
2 a tiny piece of a material called silicon that has an electronic circuit on it. Microchips are used in computers.
3 a small piece that has broken off something, or the gap that is left. *This plate has a small chip in it.*

chip chips chipping chipped verb
If you chip something, you accidentally break a small part off. *Mary chipped the plate.*

chipmunk chipmunks noun
a furry little animal with a stripe down its back. It looks a little like a squirrel.

chocolate chocolates noun
1 sweet, brown food made from cocoa.
2 a candy made of chocolate. *a box of chocolates.*

choice choices noun
1 all the things you can choose from. *There's a wide choice of books in the library.*
2 a person or thing that you choose. *Macaroni is my first choice for lunch.*

choir choirs noun
a group of singers, especially in a church. Say kwire.

choke chokes choking choked verb
If you choke, you cannot breathe because something is blocking your throat. *Tom choked on a fish bone.*

choose chooses choosing chose chosen verb
When you choose something, you take it because it is the thing that you want.

chop chops chopping chopped verb
If you chop something, you cut it with a knife or an ax. *Ricky is chopping carrots with his mother.*

chord chords noun
a group of notes that you play at the same time in a piece of music. Say kord. A word that sounds like **chord** is **cord**.

chorus choruses noun
1 the part of a song that you repeat at the end of each verse.
2 a group of singers. Say kor-*uss*.

chose, chosen past of choose.

Christian Christians noun
a person who believes in and follows the teachings of Jesus Christ. *a Christian festival.* **Christianity** noun.

chrysalis chrysalises noun
a moth or a butterfly at the stage between a caterpillar and an adult, when it has a hard case around it. Say kriss-*e-liss*.

chuckle chuckles chuckling chuckled verb
When you chuckle, you laugh quietly to yourself.

church churches noun
a building where Christians hold
religious services.

circle circles noun
1 a flat, round shape
   like a ring.
2 a group of
   people who are
   interested in
   the same things.
circle verb
*The plane circled the
airport.*

circumference
radius
diameter

circuit circuits noun
1 a complete path that an electric
   current can flow around.
2 a sports track, path, or route which
   starts and ends in the same place.

circular adjective
round like a circle. *a circular table.*

circulation noun
the movement of blood around the
body. Blood is pumped by the heart
and travels in arteries and veins.

circumference circumferences
noun
the distance around the edge of
a circle.

circus circuses noun
a traveling show with people such
as acrobats and clowns. A circus
can be held in a big, round tent.

city cities noun
a big and important town.

civilization civilizations noun
1 the way that people live in a
   certain place and at a certain time.

*We're learning about civilization in
ancient Greece.*
2 living in a group with lots of laws
   and certain ways of doing things.

claim claims claiming claimed verb
1 If you claim something, you say
   that it is yours. *Nobody has claimed
   the watch that I found.*
2 If you claim that something is true,
   you say it is true. *She claimed that the
   dog had eaten her homework.*

clap claps clapping clapped verb
When you clap, you hit your hands
together to make a noise. You clap
to show that you have enjoyed
something.

clash clashes clashing clashed verb
1 When metal objects clash, they hit
   together, making a loud, banging
   sound. *Cymbals clash.*
2 If colors clash, they do not look
   good together. *Do you think that red
   and orange clash?*

class classes noun
1 a group of people who learn
   together. *Sam and I are in the same
   class at school.*
2 a group of people, animals, or things
   that are the same in some way.

classical adjective
in a style that has been used for a
long time because people think that it
is good. *classical music of the 1800s.*

classroom classrooms noun
a room in a school where you
have classes.

claw claws noun
the long, sharp nails that an animal
or bird has on its feet.

clay noun
sticky red or gray
earth that
becomes hard
when it is dry.
Clay is used
to make
pots and
bricks.

clean cleaner cleanest adjective
having no dirt or marks on it. ■ The
opposite is **dirty** or **soiled.**

clean cleans cleaning cleaned verb
to make it clean. *You clean your teeth
by brushing them.* ■ The opposite
is **dirty.**

clear clearer clearest adjective
1 easy to see, hear, or understand.
   a clear photograph.
2 easy to see through.
3 free from things that are blocking
   the way or covering something.
   A clear sky does not have any clouds.

clear clears clearing cleared verb
When you clear something, you take
away things that you do not want
or need. *We cleared the snow from
the driveway.*

clever cleverer cleverest adjective
A person who is clever can learn and
understand things quickly.

cliff cliffs noun
the high, steep land, often by the sea
or along a river.

climate climates noun
the kind of weather that a place
usually has. *India has a hot climate.*

climb climbs climbing climbed verb
When you climb something, you move up by using your hands and feet. *Ella is climbing up Louis's back.*
climber noun.

cling clings clinging clung verb
If you cling to somebody or something, you hold on tightly. *He clung to the rope because he was afraid that he was going to fall.*

clinic clinics noun
a place where you can go to see a doctor.

clip clips noun
a small metal or plastic object used for holding things together. *a paper clip.*

clip clips clipping clipped verb
If you clip something, such as a bush or your fingernails, you cut off small pieces to make it neater.

cloak cloaks noun
a long, loose coat with no sleeves.

clock clocks noun
a machine that tells you the time.

clockwise adjective, adverb
If you turn clockwise, you move in the same direction as the hands of a clock.
The opposite is **counterclockwise**.

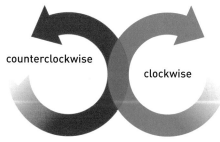

counterclockwise

clockwise

SPELLING TIP

Some words that begin with a "co" sound are spelled with a "ko." For example, koala.

close closes closing closed verb
When you close something, you shut it. *He closed the drawer quietly.*
Rhymes with **nose**. The opposite is **open**.

close closer closest adjective
1 near. *Our house is close to the train station.*
2 If you are close to someone, you know them very well. *Richard and Ray are close friends.*
Rhymes with **dose**.

cloth cloths noun
1 material made from something such as cotton or wool that we use to make clothes and other things.
2 a piece of material used for cleaning. *She wiped the table with a cloth.*

clothes noun
Clothes are things that you wear, such as jeans, skirts, shirts and blouses, and sweaters and coats.

cloud clouds noun
Clouds are made up of millions of droplets of water that sometimes fall as rain. On a cloudy day, the sky is full of white or gray clouds.

clown clowns noun
a person in a circus who wears funny clothes and makes people laugh.

club clubs noun
a group of people who meet to do something that they are all interested in. *a swimming club* or *a chess club.*

clue clues noun
something that helps you figure out the answer to a puzzle or a mystery. *I can't guess who it is. Give me a clue.*

clump clumps noun
a group of plants growing together. *a clump of grass.*

clumsy clumsier clumsiest adjective
If somebody is clumsy, they often fall over and drop things.
clumsily adverb.

clung past of **cling**.

clutch clutches clutching clutched verb
If you clutch something, you hold it tightly. *The child clutched her mother's hand.*

clutch clutches noun
the pedal in a car or other vehicle that you press when you switch gears.

coach coaches noun
1 a railroad car where passengers sit.
2 a large carriage that is pulled along by horses.
3 a person who teaches people a sport. *a tennis coach.*

coal noun
a hard, black substance that is dug out of the ground and burned to give heat. Coal is made from the remains of plants that died and were buried millions of years ago.

coast coasts noun
the part of the land that is next to the sea.

coat coats noun
1 You wear a coat on top of your other clothes to go outside when the weather is cold.
2 The fur that an animal has is called a coat. *A leopard has a spotted coat; a tiger has a striped one.*

cobweb cobwebs noun
a net of silky threads that a spider makes to catch insects. *The cobwebs were everywhere in the deserted house.*

cock cocks noun
1 a male bird.
2 a rooster.

cockpit cockpits noun
the front part of a plane, where the pilot sits. The part of a racecar where the driver sits is also called a cockpit.

cocoa noun
1 a brown powder made from the beans of the cacao tree and used to make chocolate.
2 a drink made from cocoa powder mixed with hot milk or water.

coconut coconuts noun
a large, round fruit with a hard, hairy brown shell. Inside there is a milky juice and sweet, white "meat" that you can eat. Coconuts grow on palm trees in hot countries.

coconut shell and "meat"

cocoon cocoons noun
a bundle of silky threads that some young insects make to cover themselves while they are developing into adults.

cod cod noun
a large sea fish that you can eat.

code codes noun
1 If you write something in code, you mix up the letters or change them into special signs. Only the people who know the code can read the message.
2 a group of letters or numbers that give information about something. *The zip code for this area of Virginia is 24523–1403.*

3 a collection of laws or rules. *the criminal code.*

coffee noun
1 a brown powder made from the roasted and ground beans of the coffee tree. You use coffee to make drinks.
2 a hot drink you make by mixing ground coffee beans with hot water.

coffin coffins noun
a box in which a dead person is buried.

cog cogs noun
1 a wheel with teeth around the edge. Cogs are used in machines to turn other things.
2 The teeth around the edge of the wheel are also called cogs.

coil coils noun
a thing that is twisted around into circles. *a coil of rope.*
coil verb. *The snake coiled around the branch.*

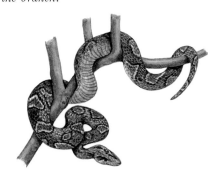

coin coins noun
a flat, usually round piece of metal that we use as money.

coincidence coincidences noun
A coincidence is when two things happen at the same time or in the same place by chance. ▲ Say *koh-in-si-denss.*

cold colder coldest adjective
1 not hot or warm. Ice and snow are cold.
2 unfriendly. *He gave me a cold look.*

cold colds noun
an illness that makes you sneeze and cough. *Lucy caught a cold.*

collage collages noun
a picture that you make by sticking lots of pieces of material or paper onto a surface.

collapse collapses collapsing collapsed verb
1 If something collapses, it falls down suddenly. *The tent collapsed.*
2 If somebody collapses, he or she falls over because of an illness. *She collapsed in the street.*
▲ Say **kul**-*lazh.*

collar collars noun
1 the part of a shirt or coat that goes around your neck.
2 a band that you put around the neck of a pet dog or cat.

collect collects collecting collected verb
1 When you collect things, you bring them together. *Please collect the bags and take them to the car.*
2 If you collect things such as stamps, you keep a lot of them because you like them. *I collect shells.*
collection noun
a stamp collection.

college colleges noun
a place where people go to study when they graduate from high school.

collide collides colliding collided verb
If something collides with another thing, it crashes into it. *The bus collided with a truck.*
collision noun.

colony colonies noun
a group of people who go to and settle in a land.

C
D
E
K
N
T
U
Y

color colors noun
Red, blue, yellow, and green
are colors.
colorful adjective. Look at
page 143.

column columns noun
1 a tall piece of stone
that holds up part of
a building or stands
on its own. *Columns
were often used in
Roman architecture.*
2 a long, thin strip
of writing in a book
or newspaper.

coma comas noun
If somebody is in a coma, he or she is
in a very deep sleep and cannot wake
up for a long time. People who have
had a serious accident sometimes go
into a coma.

comb combs noun
a flat piece of metal or plastic with
teeth along one edge. You use it to
make your hair neat. Rhymes with
home.
comb verb.

combine combines combining
combined verb
When you combine things, you join
or mix them together.
combination noun.

combine combines noun
a large machine that is used on a
farm. It cuts, separates, and cleans
grain.

comedy comedies noun
a funny play, movie, or TV show.

comet comets noun
a thing in space that looks like a star
with a tail and moves around the Sun.

comfortable adjective
If something is comfortable, it
is nice to wear, sit in, or lie on.
a comfortable bed.
comfortably adverb.

comic comics noun
1 a magazine that tells stories in
pictures.
2 comedian. A person who tells
jokes and makes people laugh.

comma commas noun
a mark (,) that you use in writing. You
put commas between words in a list.
Simon, Tom, Lee, and I went to the park.

command commands commanding
commanded verb
If somebody commands you to do
something, he or she tells you that you
have to do it. *The general commanded
the soldiers to march.*

comment comments noun
If you make a comment, you say
what you think about something.

common adjective
1 If a thing is common, it exists in
large numbers. *Robins and sparrows
are common birds.*
2 Something that happens often is
common. *These days, it is common
for people to have computers at home.*
 The opposite is **rare**.

communicate communicates
communicating communicated verb
If you communicate with somebody,
you talk or write to him or her. *Pilots
communicate with the airport by radio.*

communications noun
Communications are ways of sending
information to people, or ways of
moving from one place to another.
Roads, railroads, and telephones are
communications.

compact disk compact disks noun
a flat, round piece of plastic that can
store music or information. Also
known as a **CD**.

company companies noun
1 a group of people who work
together to make or sell something.
2 being with others so that you are
not alone. *My grandmother lives alone,
but she has a cat for company.*

compare compares comparing
compared verb
When you compare two things, you
look at them both together so that
you can see in what ways they are
the same or different. *When you have
finished the test, compare your answers
with the ones in the back of the book.*
comparison noun.

compartment compartments noun
1 a space with walls. *a luggage
compartment.*
2 a part of a container. *My bag
has a separate compartment for
my pencil case.*

compass compasses noun
1 a compass helps hikers and sailors
tell which direction they
are traveling. It has
a magnetic needle
that always
points north.
2 a tool that you
use for drawing
circles. One arm
has a sharp point, and
the other holds a pencil. You hold
the pointed arm still and move the
other around it to draw.

North

West ——————— Eas

South

competition competitions noun
a game or test that people try to win.
*Sophie won first prize in the skating
competition.*

complain complains complaining
complained verb
If you complain about something, you
say that you are not happy about it or
that it makes you angry. *He complained
about having to clean his room.*
complaint noun.

complete adjective
1 If something is complete, it has no
parts missing. *a complete pack
of cards.*
2 in every way. *a complete surprise.*
completely adverb,
complete verb.

complicated adjective
If something is complicated, it is difficult to do or understand. *The story had a very complicated plot.*

compliment compliments noun
If somebody pays you a compliment, he or she says something nice about you.

compose composes composing composed verb
To compose means to write music or poetry. *Beethoven composed nine symphonies.*
composer noun.

computer computers noun
a machine that can solve problems quickly, store information, or be used as a tool for games and music. *Mom uses her computer with a wireless mouse to design new buildings.*

compute computes computing verb.

conceal conceals concealing concealed verb
If you conceal something, you hide it. *She concealed the box under her bed.*

concerned adjective
If you are concerned about something, you worry about it.

concert concerts noun
a performance of music to a big group of people.

conclusion conclusions noun
1 the end of something. *The story had a sad conclusion.*
2 If you come to a conclusion about something, you decide what happened and why it happened. *We came to the conclusion that she went home because she was sick.*

concrete noun
a building material made from cement, sand, and small stones mixed with water that gets hard when it dries.

condition conditions noun
1 how somebody or something is. *The car is old, but it's still in good condition.*
2 how things are around you. *The animals in the zoo lived in good conditions.*
3 something that you must do before you are allowed to do something else. *You may go out on the condition that you clean your room first.*

condor condors noun
a big bird that lives in the Andes Mountains and in western North America. It is the biggest flying bird in the world.

conductor conductors noun
a person who stands in front of a group of musicians and directs how they play a piece of music.

cone cones noun
1 a solid shape that is pointed at the top and round at the bottom.
2 the hard fruit of a pine or fir tree.

confess confesses confessing confessed verb
If you confess something, you say that you have done something wrong. *Luke confessed that he had broken the fence.*
confession noun.

confidence noun
the feeling that you can do something well. *She climbed the tree with confidence.*
confident adjective,
confidently adverb.

confuse confuses confusing confused verb
1 If you confuse people, you mix up their ideas so that they cannot understand. *My sister tried to explain the rules of the game to me, but she spoke too quickly and I got confused.*
2 If you confuse two things, you mix them up so that you cannot tell the difference between them. *I always confuse the words "there" and "their" because they sound the same.*
confusing adjective, **confusion** noun.

congratulate congratulates congratulating congratulated verb
When you congratulate people, you tell them that you are pleased about something they have done. *I congratulated Anna on passing her math test.*
congratulations noun.

Congress noun
the two groups, the U.S. Senate and House of Representatives, that make laws in Washington, D.C.

conjunction conjunctions noun
a word that connects words or groups of words in a sentence. "And," "but," "if," and "yet" are conjunctions.

conjurer conjurers noun
a person who does magic tricks to entertain people at a show.

connect connects connecting connected verb
To connect things is to join them. *They are connecting parts of a toy.*
connection noun.

conquer conquers conquering conquered verb
If an army conquers its enemies, it wins the war and takes control of them.
conqueror noun.

39

conscience consciences noun
Your conscience is a feeling inside you that tells you about right and wrong. *Natalie didn't steal any candy; she has a clear conscience.* ▲ Say **kon**-*shunss*.

conscious adjective
If you are conscious, you are awake and you know what is happening around you. ▲ Say **kon**-*shuss*.
■ The opposite is **unconscious**.

consider considers considering considered verb
When you consider something, you think about it carefully. *We must consider what to do next.*

considerate adjective
If you are considerate, you think about other people's feelings and you are not selfish.

consist consists consisting consisted verb
If something consists of different things, it is made up of those things.

consonant consonants noun
any letter except *a, e, i, o,* or *u,* and sometimes *y,* which are vowels.

Constitution noun
a paper that lists the basic laws and rules of the U.S.A.

construct constructs constructing constructed verb
If you construct something, you build or put it together. *Tara is constructing a tractor.*

contact contacts contacting contacted verb
If you contact somebody, you write or telephone that person.

contact noun
If two things make contact, they touch each other. *The spaceship made contact with the Moon.*

contain contains containing contained verb
To contain something is to have something inside. *This jar contains coffee.*

container containers noun
A container is something that you put things in. Boxes, bottles, and cans are containers.

content adjective
If you are content, you feel happy. ▲ Say *kon*-**tent**.

contents noun
The contents of something are all the things inside. *Joanne dropped her bag, and all the contents fell out onto the floor.* ▲ Say **kon**-*tents*.

contest contests noun
a competition or game that people try to win. *a judo contest.*

continent continents noun
one of the seven big pieces of land in the world. The continents are: Africa, Asia, Europe, North America, South America, Australia, and Antarctica. See below.

continue continues continuing continued verb
When you continue doing something, you keep on doing it. *We continued playing outside until it got dark.*

contract contracts noun
a written agreement between two people or groups.

control noun
If you have control over somebody or something, you can make that person or thing do what you want. *You should have more control over your dog and not let it run into the road.*
control verb.

convenient adjective
If something is convenient, it is easy to do or use. *The theater is very convenient; it is just around the corner.*
■ The opposite is **inconvenient**.

conversation conversations noun
If you have a conversation with others, you talk to them. *Hank and Toby are having a conversation.*

convince convinces convincing convinced verb
to make somebody believe something.

cook cooks cooking cooked verb
When you cook food, you prepare and heat it, so that it is ready to eat.

cook cooks noun
a person who prepares and cooks food.

cookie cookies noun
a small, round, sweet cake. *I helped my mother bake four dozen chocolate-chip cookies.*

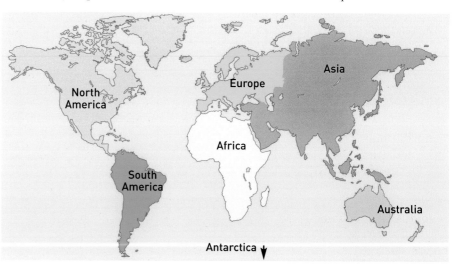

North America

Europe

Asia

Africa

South America

Australia

Antarctica ↓

cool cooler coolest adjective
If something like water or the weather is cool, it is cold, but not very cold. ■ The opposite is **warm**.

cool cools cooling cooled verb
When something cools, it becomes colder. *Take the cake out of the oven and leave it to cool.*

copper noun
a reddish-brown metal that is dug out of the ground. Copper wire is used to carry electricity.

copy copies copying copied verb
1 If you copy others, you try to do the same things or look the same as them. *Amanda copied her sister's way of talking.*
2 If you copy something, you write or draw something that is exactly the same as another thing. *The teacher asked us to copy the examples from the board.*

copy copies noun
a thing that is made to look exactly the same as another thing.

coral noun
Coral is found in shallow seawater, close to the shore. It is the skeletons of tiny creatures that are left when they have died. Most coral is pink, white, or red.

cord cords noun
strong, thick string. ● A word that sounds like **cord** is **chord**.

core cores noun
1 the middle part of some kinds of fruit that has seeds inside it. *an apple core.*

2 the center of Earth. *Earth's core is very hot.*

corn noun
a tall green plant that has ears, or corncobs. The yellow or white grains on the ears, called "kernels," are used for food. *I love corn on the cob with butter.*

corner corners noun
the place where two walls, roads, or edges meet.

corral corrals noun
an area with a fence around it that is used for horses, cattle, and sheep.
corral verb.

correct adjective
If something is correct, it is right and there are no mistakes. *Is your spelling correct?*
correction noun.

corridor corridors noun
a long, narrow space inside a building, such as a hotel, with rooms opening on each side of it.

cost costs noun
the amount of money that you must pay to buy something. *The cost of the tickets was $6 each.*

cost costs costing cost verb
If something costs $5, you have to pay $5 to buy it. *How much did it cost?*

costume costumes noun
the clothes that actors wear or that people wear at special times. *We all wore costumes to the party.*

cot cots noun
a small, narrow bed. *We slept on cots last summer while we were camping.*

cottage cottages noun
a small house in the country.

cotton noun
material that is made by weaving the soft white fibers of the cotton plant.

cough coughs coughing coughed verb
When you cough, you make a sudden loud noise in your throat. *The smoke made me cough.*
cough noun
I have a bad cough. ▲ Say **koff**.

council councils noun
a group of people who are chosen to plan and decide things for other people.

count counts counting counted verb
1 When you count, you say numbers one after another in the right order. *I can count from one to one hundred!*
2 to add things up to figure out how many there are. *Can you count the spoons and see if we have enough?*

counter counters noun
1 a long, high table in a store or bank where people are served.
2 a small, round piece of plastic that you use in some games.

counterclockwise adjective, adverb
if you turn counterclockwise, you move in the opposite direction as the hands on a clock. ■ The opposite is **clockwise**.

countertop noun
a counter used as a work surface in a kitchen or store.

country countries noun
1 an area of land in the world with its own people and government. *France, Spain, and Japan are countries.*
2 the rural land outside towns and cities.

41

county counties noun
one of the parts of a U.S. state that can make some rules for the people who live in it. *Broward County, Florida.*

couple couples noun
1 two people who are together.
2 two things. *a couple of oranges.*

courage noun
If you show courage, you are brave.
courageous adjective.

course courses noun
1 an area of ground used for some games and sports. *People play golf on a golf course.*
2 a set of lessons that you have when you learn something new. *I'm taking a course in Italian.*
3 one of the parts of a meal. *We had chicken for the main course.*

court courts noun
1 a place where a group of people, called a jury, and a judge decide if a person has done something wrong and what the punishment should be.
2 a piece of ground where you can play a certain sport. *a tennis court.*
3 a place where a king or queen lives.

courtyard courtyard noun
an area surrounded by walls.

cousin cousins noun
Your cousin is the child of your aunt or uncle.

cover covers noun
1 a thing that you put over another thing. *She got into bed and pulled the covers over her head.*
2 the outside of a book or magazine.

cover covers covering covered verb
1 to put something over something else to hide it or keep it warm.
2 When something covers another thing, it is all over it. *Snow covered the grass.*

cow cows noun
a large female farm animal that gives us milk. Female whales, seals, and elephants are also called cows.
Rhymes with **now** and **brow**.

coward cowards noun
a person who is easily frightened.

cowboy cowboys
cowgirl cowgirls noun
a person whose job is to look after cattle.

cozy cozier coziest adjective
If a place is cozy, it is warm and comfortable. *Birds build nests that are cozy for their eggs.*

crab crabs noun
a sea animal with a flat, hard shell and ten legs. The two front legs have big claws called pincers on the end.

crack cracks noun
1 a thin line on something where it has almost broken. *This cup has a tiny crack in it.*
2 a sudden loud noise. *a crack of thunder.*

crack cracks cracking cracked verb
If something cracks, it has a thin split in it, but it does not break into pieces. *Hot water will crack the glasses.*

cracker crackers noun
a thin, dry, crisp biscuit.

cradle cradles noun
a small wooden bed for a baby that usually rocks.

craft crafts noun
work or a hobby where you make things with your hands. Pottery and wood carving are crafts.

crane cranes noun
1 a tall machine that lifts and moves heavy things.
2 a large waterbird with a long neck and long legs.

crash
crashes noun
1 an accident when something that is moving hits another thing.
2 a loud noise like the sound of thunder. *There was a loud crash as he dropped the plates onto the floor.*

crash crashes crashing crashed verb
When something crashes, it hits another thing very hard and makes a loud noise.

crate crates noun
a wooden or plastic box for carrying things in. *a crate of bananas.*

crater craters noun
1 a huge hole in the ground that is made when something like a bomb or meteor lands on it.
2 the hole at the top of a volcano where fire and hot, liquid rock called lava comes out.

crawl crawls crawling crawled verb
When a baby crawls, it moves slowly along the ground on its hands and knees. When an insect crawls, it moves with its body close to the ground.

The baby is crawling across the floor.

42

crayon crayons noun
a colored pencil or wax stick that you draw with.

creak creaks creaking creaked verb
If something like a door creaks, it makes a strange squeaking sound. *The old floor creaked.*

cream noun
the thick, pale yellow liquid that is a part of milk. It contains a lot of fat.

crease creases creasing creased verb
If you crease something, you put lots of lines in it by crushing it or by not folding it carefully. *If you sit on your coat, you will crease it.*

create creates creating created verb
If you create something, you make something new.
creator noun, creation noun.

creature creatures noun
any animal. *Elephants are very big creatures.*

creep creeps creeping crept verb
If something creeps along, it moves slowly and quietly. *The cat crept toward the bird.*

crescent crescents noun
the curved shape of a new Moon.

crew crews noun
all the people who work on a ship or an airplane.

cricket noun
1 an insect like a grasshopper with wings and long legs that can jump high.
2 an outdoor game played by two teams of 11 players each with bats, wickets, and a ball.

cried past of **cry**.

crime crimes noun
something that is against the law. *Murder is a crime.*

criminal criminals noun
a person who does something that is against the law.

crisp crisper crispest adjective
If something like a cracker is crisp, it is hard, crunchy, and easy to break.

criticize criticizes criticizing criticized verb
If somebody criticizes you, that person says that you have done something badly or wrong. ■ The opposite is **praise**.

croak croaks croaking croaked verb
To croak is to make a deep, rough sound like the sound a frog makes. *"I have a sore throat," she croaked.*

crocodile crocodiles noun
a large reptile with a long body and sharp teeth. Crocodiles live in rivers in some hot countries.

crocus crocuses noun
a tiny plant with bright red, purple, yellow, or white flowers. It blooms in the spring or fall.

crooked adjective
not straight. *a crooked path through the trees.* ▲ Say **krook**-*id*.

crops noun
Crops are plants that farmers grow as food. Wheat, rice, and oats all are crops.

cross crosses noun
a mark like this **+** or this **x**.

cross crosses crossing crossed verb
When you cross something such as a road or a river, you go from one side to the other.

crouch crouches crouching crouched verb
When you crouch, you bend your knees so that your body is close to the ground. *Hank crouched to look at the plant.*

crow crows noun
a big, black bird that makes a loud noise.

crow crows crowing crowed verb
To crow means to make a noise like a rooster makes in the early morning.

crowd crowds noun
a lot of people together in one place. *There was a huge crowd at the football game.*

crowded adjective
If a place is crowded, it is full of people. *The swimming pool gets very crowded in hot weather.*

crown crowns noun
a ring of precious metal and jewels that kings and queens wear on their heads.

cruel crueler cruelest adjective
A person who is cruel hurts people or animals on purpose.

cruise cruises noun
If you go on a cruise, you have a vacation on a ship that stops at lots of different places.

a Nile crocodile

43

crumb crumbs noun
a tiny piece of bread, cake,
or a cookie.

crunch crunches crunching
crunched verb
If you crunch something hard and
firm like a cracker, you make a loud
noise when you eat it. *She crunched
a carrot.*
crunchy adjective.

crush crushes crushing
crushed verb
If you crush something, you press it
hard so that you break or squash it.

crust crusts noun
1 the hard layer on the outside of
something, like very cold snow.
2 Earth's crust is the thin outer layer.

crutches noun
two long sticks that fit under or
around your arms to help you walk
if you have hurt your foot or leg.

cry cries crying cried verb
1 When you cry, tears fall from your
eyes. *The baby is crying because he
is hungry.*
2 To cry also means to shout or make
a loud noise. *"Help!" she cried.*

crystal crystals noun
1 a hard kind of rock that looks
like glass.
2 a small, hard piece of something
such as salt or ice that has a regular
shape. ▲ Say **kriss**-*tal.*

cub cubs noun
a young bear, lion, tiger, fox, or wolf.

cube cubes noun
a solid shape with six square sides.
a cube of sugar.

cuckoo cuckoos noun
a bird that makes a sound like its
name. Cuckoos lay their eggs in the
nests of other birds.

cucumber cucumbers noun
a long vegetable that is dark green on
the outside and pale green inside. You
can eat it raw in salads.

cuddle cuddles cuddling
cuddled verb
When you cuddle somebody, you put
your arms around that person and
hold them. *The dad cuddled his baby.*

cup cups noun
1 a small container with a handle.
You drink liquids such as tea and
coffee from a cup.
2 a metal container with two handles
that you can win as a prize. *He won
a silver cup for winning the boat race.*

cupboard cupboards noun
a piece of furniture with shelves and
doors where you can keep things.
▲ Say **kub**-*erd.*

cupcake cupcakes noun
a small, round cake with icing.

cure cures curing cured verb
If something cures somebody, it
makes an illness go away.
cure noun.

curious adjective
If you are curious about something,
you want to know more about it.
*I was curious to know what the
noise was.*

curl curls noun
a piece of hair in a curved shape.
▲ Rhymes with **pearl.**
curly adjective.

curl curls curling curled verb
If something curls or curls up, it
bends into a curved shape. *The
porcupine curled up into a ball.*

currant currants noun
a small, dried grape. ● A word that
sounds like **currant** is **current.**

current currents noun
1 air or water that is moving. *It is too
dangerous to swim here because of the
strong currents.*
2 electricity that is passing through
a wire.
● A word that sounds like **current**
is **currant.**

curtain curtains noun
Curtains are pieces of cloth that you
pull across a window or the front of
the stage in a theater to cover it.

curve curves noun
a line that bends smoothly.

curved adjective
having the shape of a curve.

cushion cushions noun
a pad filled with soft material that you
put on a chair to make it comfortable.

custom customs noun
something that people usually do.
*It is the custom to give people presents
on their birthdays.*

customer customers noun
a person who buys something from
a store or company.

cut cuts cutting cut verb
1 You use scissors or a knife to cut
things into pieces.
2 If you cut yourself, you hurt yourself
by accident with something sharp.
cut noun.

cute cuter cutest adjective
If something like a kitten is cute,
you like it because it looks pretty
and sweet.

cycle cycles noun
Events that happen in a particular
order. *The life cycle of a butterfly.*

cycle cycles cycling cycled verb
When you cycle, you ride a bicycle.
cyclist noun.

cylinder cylinders noun
a long, round shape like a tube
or a can.

Dd

daffodil daffodils noun
a bright yellow, trumpet-shaped flower that blooms in the spring.

dagger daggers noun
a short sword with two sharp edges.

daily adjective, adverb
every day. *a daily newspaper.*

dainty daintier daintiest adjective
small and neat. *The doll's face is dainty.*

dairy dairies noun
a company that sells milk and other foods made from milk, such as butter and ice cream.

dairy adjective
Dairy foods are milk, butter, and cheese, as well as any other foods made from milk. A dairy farm produces milk.

daisy daisies noun
a small flower with narrow, white petals around a yellow center.

dam dams noun
a wall built across a river to hold back the water.

damage damages damaging damaged verb
If you damage something, you break or harm it. *A car hit the wall and damaged it.* ▲ Say **dam**-*ij*.
damage noun.

damp damper dampest adjective
a little wet.

dance dances dancing danced verb
When you dance, you move your body in time to music.
dance noun.

dandelion dandelions noun
a wildflower with a lot of bright yellow petals.

danger dangers noun
1 If you are in danger, you are in a situation in which something bad could happen to you. *The sign on the electric fence said: DANGER! Keep out!*
2 something that might harm you. *Smoking cigarettes is a danger to your health.*

dangerous adjective
Something that is dangerous might harm you. *It's dangerous to go near the edge of the cliff.* ■ The opposite is **safe**.

dare dares daring dared verb
1 If you dare to do something, you are brave enough to do it even though it is dangerous. *Sheila wouldn't dare to get near the angry bull.*
2 If you dare somebody, you ask that person if he or she is brave enough to do something. *I dare you to walk along the top of that wall.*

dark darker darkest adjective
1 without any light. *Open the curtains. It's dark in here.* ■ The opposite is **light** or **bright**.
2 Dark colors are closer to black than to white. *Ricky is wearing a dark blue T-shirt.* ■ The opposite is **light**, **pale**, or **fair**.
darkness noun.

dart darts noun
a short arrow that you throw at a round target called a dartboard in a game called darts.

dart darts darting darted verb
If you dart somewhere, you run there very quickly and suddenly. *Dad darted into the store and came out with ice cream cones for everybody.*

dash dashes dashing dashed verb
If you dash somewhere, you run there very quickly. *She put up her umbrella and dashed across the street.*

data noun
facts and information. Information stored on a computer is called data. ▲ Say **day**-*ta* or **dah**-*ta*.

date dates noun
1 the day, month, and sometimes year when something happens. *March 17th is Saint Patrick's Day.*

2 a brown, sticky fruit with a pit inside. Dates grow on a type of palm tree.

daughter daughters noun
A person's daughter is a girl or woman who is his or her child. ▲ Say **daw**-*ter*.

dawdle dawdles dawdling dawdled verb
If you dawdle, you walk very slowly.

dawn dawns noun
the beginning of the day when the Sun is just starting to come up.

day days noun
1 the time when it is light. ■ The opposite is **night**.
2 a measure of time. The 24 hours of a day start at midnight and end at the next midnight.

daze noun
If you are in a daze, you cannot think clearly and you are confused. *He hit his head and now he's in a daze.*

dazzle dazzles dazzling dazzled verb
If a light dazzles you, it shines straight in your eyes so that you cannot see.

dead adjective
no longer alive. The opposite is **alive**.

deaf adjective
A person who is deaf cannot hear very well or cannot hear at all.

dear dearer dearest adjective
If someone or something is dear to you, you love it and think that it is very special.
 A word that sounds like **dear** is **deer**.

death deaths noun
the end of a life, when a person or animal dies.

debt debts noun
money that you owe somebody and have to pay back. Say **det**.

decade decades noun
a measure of time. There are ten years in a decade.

decay decays decaying decayed verb
When something decays, it becomes bad or rotten.

deceive deceives deceiving deceived verb
If you deceive people, you trick them by making them believe something that is not true. *It is dishonest if you deceive your parents by sneaking out at night.*

decide decides deciding decided verb
If you decide something, you make up your mind about what you are going to do. *I'm trying to decide what to buy my brother for his birthday.*

deciduous adjective
A deciduous tree loses its leaves in the winter and gets new ones in the spring.
 Say *de-**sid**-yoo-uss*. The opposite is **evergreen**.

decimal decimals noun
a fraction that you write as a number, with amounts less than one written after the dot, called a decimal point. 2.5 is a decimal. It is the same amount as $2\frac{1}{2}$.

decision decisions noun
If you make a decision, you make up your mind about what you are going to do. *Have you made a decision yet?*

deck decks noun
1 a floor on a ship.
2 a platform with a railing that is part of a house. *We eat on the deck in the summer.*

declare declares declaring declared verb
If you declare something, you say something important to a lot of people. *I declare that the winner is Ben Watson.*

decorate decorates decorating decorated verb
1 If you decorate something, you add

things to it to make it look more beautiful. *Sam decorated the cake.*
2 If you decorate a room, you paint it or put wallpaper on the walls.
decoration noun.

decrease decreases decreasing decreased verb
If something decreases, it gets smaller or less. *The number of trees in the rainforests of South America has decreased in recent years.*
 The opposite is **increase**.

deep deeper deepest adjective
1 Something that is deep goes a long way down from the top. *The river is very deep.* The opposite is **shallow**.
2 A deep sleep is sleep that is hard to wake somebody up from.
3 A deep voice is very low. *Men's voices are usually deeper than women's.*

deer deer noun
a wild animal that eats grass and can run very fast. Male deer have big horns called antlers on their heads.
 A word that sounds like **deer** is **dear**.

defeat defeats defeating defeated verb
If you defeat people, you beat them in a game, competition, or battle.
defeat noun.

defend defends defending defended verb
When you defend somebody or something, you protect them when somebody else is attacking them. *Jack defended the goal.*
defense noun.

definite adjective
certain and not likely to change. *We haven't set a definite date for the trip.*
definitely adverb
I'm definitely going to do my homework early tonight.

defrost defrosts defrosting defrosted verb
To defrost is to thaw frozen food.

degree degrees noun
1 a measurement of temperature. Degree is sometimes written as °. *10°F is ten degrees Fahrenheit.*
2 a measurement of angles. *A right angle is 90°.*
3 a qualification that you get after studying at a college or university.

delay delays delaying delayed verb
1 If you delay doing something, you put it off until later. *We had to delay our vacation for a week because my sister was very sick.*
2 To delay somebody is to make him or her late.

delete deletes deleting deleted verb
If you delete something, you remove it from a piece of writing or from a computer's memory.

deliberate adjective
If something you do is deliberate, you do it on purpose.

delicate adjective
1 Something that is delicate is small and lovely, but it can be broken or damaged relatively easily. *A spider's web is very delicate.*
2 A person who is delicate gets sick quite easily. *He's a delicate child.*

delicious adjective
Food that is delicious tastes very good.
▲ Say *di-li-shuss.*

delight delights delighting delighted verb
If something delights you, it makes you feel very pleased.

deliver delivers delivering delivered verb
When you deliver something, you take it to the person that it is supposed to go to. *A post person delivers letters and packages to your home.*

delta deltas noun
muddy or sandy land shaped like a triangle that sits at the mouth of a river. *the Mississippi Delta.*

demand demands demanding demanded verb
If you demand something, you ask for it very strongly. *My father demanded to know why I was so late getting home from school.*
demand noun.

demolish demolishes demolishing demolished verb
To demolish something is to destroy it completely.
demolition noun.

den dens noun
the home of a wild animal, such as a lion.

dent dents denting dented verb
If you dent something that is made of metal, you damage it so that part of it is pushed in slightly instead of flat. *He dropped the can and dented it.*

dentist dentists noun
a person whose job is to take care of people's teeth.

deny denies denying denied verb
If you deny something, you say it is not true. *Tom denied taking the money.*

depart departs departing departed verb
If you depart, you leave. *The plane departs at 6:25.* ■ The opposite is **arrive**.
departure noun.

depend depends depending depended verb
1 If you depend on people or things, you need them. *The school depends on parents to raise money for school trips.*
2 If you depend on people, you trust them to do what they say they will do. *I'm depending on you to help me.*
3 To depend also means to be decided by something. *I don't know if we'll have a picnic tomorrow. It depends on the weather.*

depth depths noun
The depth of something is how deep it is. *What is the depth of the lake?*

deputy deputies noun
a person who does another person's job when that person is not there. *a deputy sheriff.*

descend descends descending descended verb
If something descends, it goes down. *We watched as the parachute slowly descended before landing.*
▲ Say *di-send.*

describe describes describing described verb
When you describe something, you say what it is like.
description noun
The woman gave the police a description of the man she had seen.

desert deserts noun
an area where it is very dry and hardly any plants can grow.
▲ Say **dez**-ert.

deserted adjective
If a place is deserted, there is nobody there. *The house was deserted.*

47

D

deserve deserves deserving
deserved verb
If you deserve something, it is fair that
it should happen to you. *He trained very
hard and deserved to win the medal.*

design designs designing designed
verb
If you design something, you decide
what it will be like and then you draw
it to show how it should be made.
△ Say *di-*zine

design designs noun
a pattern. *Each one of these sweaters has
a different design.*
△ Say *di-*zine.

desire desires noun
a very strong wish for something. *She
had a great desire to become an artist.*
desirable adjective
worth having. *a desirable house.*

desk desks noun
a table where you sit to write or read.
Desks often have drawers.

despair despairs despairing
despaired verb
If you despair, you feel no hope that
something good will happen.

desperate adjective
If you are desperate, you are in a very
bad situation and you will do almost
anything to change it.

destination destinations noun
the place where you are going.

destroy destroys destroying
destroyed verb
If you destroy something, you damage
it or break it so badly that it cannot
be fixed. *Fire destroyed the house.*
destruction noun
The storm caused a lot of destruction.

detail details noun
one of many small pieces of
information about something.

detective detectives noun
a person who tries to find out who
did a crime.

detention detentions noun
If the teacher keeps you after school
for bad behavior, that's detention.

detergent noun
a powder or liquid that you use to
clean clothes or dishes.

determined adjective
If you are determined to do
something, you are going to do it
and nothing can stop you. *Alex had
trained very hard; he was determined to
win the race.*

detest detests detesting detested
verb
to hate somebody or something
very much.

develop develops
developing
developed verb
When something
develops, it
changes as it
grows.
*A photograph
is developing.*
development noun
*The new housing
development.*

dew noun
Small drops of water that form in the
night on grass and plants. ● A word
that sounds like **dew** is **due**.

diagonal adjective
a line that slants from one corner of
something to the opposite corner.

diagram diagrams noun
a simple picture that explains
something.

dial dials noun
the part of something such as a clock
or speedometer that has numbers and
a pointer on it.

diameter diameters noun
a line drawn straight across a circle,
through the center.
◆ Look at page 35.

diamond diamonds noun
1 a very hard, clear jewel.
2 a shape like a square turned so that
   it is standing on one of its corners.

diary diaries noun
a book where you can write what has
happened during the day or what you
plan to do.

dice noun
small cubes with a different number
of dots on each side. You use dice
when you play some games. The
word for one of the dice is a **die**.

dictionary dictionaries noun
a book that gives the meanings of
words and how to spell them in
alphabetical order.

die dies dying died verb
When a person, animal, or plant dies,
it comes to the end of its life and
stops living. ■ The opposite is **live.**
● A word that sounds like **die** is **dye**.
death noun.

diesel noun
a kind of oil that is used as fuel in bus
and truck engines. Some cars use
diesel oil. △ Say **dee-***zil.*

diet diets noun
1 Your diet is the food that you normally eat. *A healthy diet includes plenty of fresh fruit and vegetables.*
2 If you go on a diet, you eat only certain foods either because you have an illness or because you are trying to lose weight.

different adjective
If something is different from another thing, it is not like it. ■ The opposite is **same**.
difference noun
Can you tell the difference between these two horses?

difficult adjective
hard to do. ■ The opposite is **easy** or **simple**.
difficulty noun.

dig digs digging dug verb
If you dig, you use something such as a spade or shovel to move dirt or make a hole in the ground. Animals dig using their claws.

digest digests digesting digested verb
When you digest food, it passes through your body and gets broken down so that your body can use it to make energy.
digestion noun.

digit digits noun
1 one of the numbers from 0 to 9.
2 a finger or a toe.

digital camera noun
A camera that uses a memory device, such as a memory card, instead of film, from which images can then be uploaded onto a computer.

dilute dilutes diluting diluted verb
When you dilute a liquid, you make it weaker by adding water.
dilution noun.

dim dimmer dimmest adjective
not very strong or bright. ■ The opposite is **bright.**

dinghy dinghies noun
a small, open boat that you row or sail.
▲ Say ding-*gi.*

dinner dinners noun
the main meal that you eat usually in the evening, or sometimes in the middle of the day.

dinosaur dinosaurs noun
a large reptile that lived millions of years ago and then became extinct.

dip dips dipping dipped verb
1 If you dip something into a liquid, you put it in for a moment. *He dipped his brush into the paint.*
2 If something dips, it slopes down. *The road dipped suddenly after the bridge.* ■ The opposite is **rise**.

direct adjective
The direct way to go somewhere is by the shortest way and without stopping.

direct directs directing directed verb
1 If you direct people to a place, you tell them the way to go.
2 A person who directs a movie or television show tells the actors what to do.

direction
directions noun
1 the way that something is pointing or moving. *Am I going in the right direction to get to the picnic area?*
2 Directions are instructions telling you how to do something.

dirt noun
mud, dust, or marks on something.

dirty dirtier dirtiest adjective
covered with dirt or marks. ■ The opposite is **clean**.

Word builder
Dis—is a little word called a prefix that you can add to the beginning of certain words, often to change their meaning.

1 Not, or the opposite of—disloyal.

2 To do the opposite of—disagree, dislike.

---

disabled adjective
A disabled person has a part of their body that does not work properly.
disability noun.

disagree disagrees disagreeing disagreed verb
When people disagree, they do not think the same way about something. *My brother and I often disagree about what to watch on TV.* ■ The opposite is **agree.**

disappear disappears disappearing disappeared verb
If something disappears, it goes out of sight. *We waved at the boat until it disappeared in the distance.* ■ The opposite is **appear**.
disappearance noun.

disappointed adjective
You feel disappointed when something you were looking forward to does not happen or when what happens is not as good as you had hoped it would be.
disappointment noun.

disaster disasters noun
a really terrible thing that happens. *An earthquake is a natural disaster.*

discover discovers discovering discovered verb
If you discover something, you find out about it or see it for the first time. *We discovered a secret hiding place.*
discovery noun.

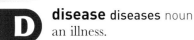

discuss discusses discussing
discussed verb
If you discuss something, you talk about it with other people.
discussion noun.

disease diseases noun
an illness.

disguise
disguises noun
something that you do to change the way you look so that other people do not know who you are.
▲ Say *dis*-**gize**.

disgust noun
a very strong feeling of not liking something that is really nasty or bad.
disgusting adjective

dish dishes noun
a plate or a bowl used for cooking or for putting food on.

dishonest adjective
If you steal, lie, or cheat, you are a dishonest person.

disk disks noun
1 a round, flat object.
2 a flat, plastic case with a magnetic metal part that stores information on a computer.

distance distances noun
Distance is how far apart two things are.
distant adjective.

distract distracts distracting
distracted verb
If something distracts you, it takes your attention away from what you are doing. *I can't do my homework with the radio on because I get distracted by it.*
distraction noun.

disturb disturbs disturbed
disturbing verb
If you disturb somebody, you stop them from doing something, such as working or sleeping. *Don't disturb her; she's asleep.*

ditch ditches noun
a long hole in the ground that has been dug along the side of a road so that water can drain away.

dive dives diving dived or **dove** verb
1 When you dive, you jump into water with your arms and head first.
2 to swim underwater with special breathing equipment.
3 To dive is to go underwater. *We watched the submarine dive.*
diver noun.

divide divides dividing divided verb
1 If you divide something, you separate it into smaller parts. *He is dividing the liquid into four equal amounts.*

2 You divide one number by another number to see how many times the smaller number goes into the larger one. When you write this, you use a division sign: ÷. *8 ÷ 2 = 4.* ■ The opposite is **multiply**.
division noun.

divorce divorces noun
the ending of a marriage.
divorce verb
She divorced her husband.

dizzy dizzier dizziest adjective
If you feel dizzy, you feel as if everything is spinning around and you are going to fall over.

dock docks noun
a place where ships stop to load or unload cargo or to be repaired.
dock verb.

doctor doctors noun
a person whose job is to help people who are sick to get better, by giving them medicine or advice. *M.D.* comes after a doctor's name.

document documents noun
a piece of paper with important information on it.

dog dogs noun
an animal that is often kept as a pet or for hunting or guarding things. A young dog is called a puppy.
◆ Look at page 51.

doll dolls noun
a toy in the shape of a person.

dollar dollars noun
an amount of money equal to 100 cents.

dolphin dolphins
noun
a mammal that lives in the sea but breathes air. Dolphins look like very large fish.
▲ Say **dol**-*fin*.

Dogs

Labrador retriever

dogue de Bordeaux

basenji

bull terrier

black and tan coonhound

beagle

domino dominoes noun
Dominoes are small, rectangular blocks of wood or plastic with different numbers of dots on them, used to play a game, also called dominoes.

donkey donkeys noun
an animal like a small horse but with longer ears.

door doors noun
a large piece of wood or glass that moves to open and close the way into a room, building, or closet.

dose doses noun
an amount of medicine that you have to take at one time.

dot dots noun
a small, round spot. *a blue shirt with white dots.*

double adjective
twice as large or twice as many. *Rebecca has double the number of blocks that Natasha has.* ▲ Say **dub**-*ul*.

doubt doubts noun
If you have a doubt about something, you are not sure about it. ▲ Say **dowt**.

dough noun
a mixture of flour, water, and other things that you cook to make bread, cake, or pastry. ▲ Say **doh**.

dove doves noun
a kind of pigeon.
▲ Say **duv**.

download verb
to transfer data from the Internet or another computer or device to your own computer.
download noun.

dozen dozen noun
twelve. *We made two dozen sandwiches for the party.*
▲ Say **duz**-*un*.

draft drafts noun
cold air coming into a room because there is a slight gap between a window or door and the wall.
drafty adjective.

51

D
E
K
N
T
U
Y

drag drags dragging
dragged verb
If you drag something, you pull it along the ground. *Freddy dragged his coat across the floor.*

dragon dragons noun
in stories, a very large animal with a long body covered in scales. Dragons sometimes have wings and can breathe out fire.

dragonfly dragonflies noun
an insect with a long, thin body and two sets of wings. Dragonflies live close to ponds and rivers.

drain drains
draining drained verb
1 When water drains, it flows slowly away.
2 When you drain food, you pour away the water that it cooked in. *Drain the spaghetti and serve with a spicy tomato sauce.*

drain drains noun
a pipe that carries water away. A sewer pipe is a large drain.

drama dramas noun
1 a serious play.
2 an interesting or exciting thing.

drank past of **drink**.

drastic adjective
severe or harsh.

draw draws drawing drew drawn verb
1 When you draw, you use a pencil, pen, or crayon to make a picture of something or someone.

2 If you draw the curtains, you move them together by pulling.
drawing noun.

drawbridge drawbridges noun
a bridge that opens to let ships pass underneath.

drawer drawers noun
a wooden box that slides in and out of a piece of furniture and holds things like clothes or paper and pens.

dream dreams dreaming dreamed
or **dreamt** verb
1 When you dream, you see pictures and hear sounds in your mind while you are sleeping. *Last night I dreamed that I could fly.*
2 When you dream of something, you think about how much you would love to be able to do it. *Madeleine dreams of becoming a world-famous ballet dancer.*
dream noun.

dress dresses dressing dressed
verb
When you dress, you put on clothes. ■ The opposite is **undress**.

dress dresses
noun
a piece of clothing that a woman or girl wears. A dress has a top part and a skirt connected together.

drew past of **draw**.

drift drifts drifting drifted verb
When something drifts, it is slowly carried along by the wind or by the movement of water. *She stopped the engine and let the boat drift.*

drill drills noun
a tool that is used for making holes.
drill verb.

drink drinks drinking drank drunk
verb
When you drink, you take liquid into your mouth and swallow it.
drink noun.

drip drips dripping dripped verb
When liquid drips, it falls in drops. *Rain dripped off the roof.*

drive drives driving drove driven
verb
to control something such as a car or bus and make it go where you want it to go.

drizzle noun
light rain in very small drops.

droop
droops
drooping
drooped
verb
When something droops, it hangs or bends down because it is weak or tired. *The flower drooped because it had no water.*

drop drops noun
a tiny amount of liquid.

drop drops dropping dropped verb
If you drop something, you let it fall. *I dropped the plate.*

drought droughts noun
a long period of time when there is no rain. ▲ Rhymes with **out**.

drove past of **drive**.

drown drowns drowning drowned
verb
to die because someone cannot breathe underwater.

drug drugs noun
1 medicine that a doctor gives you to treat an illness.
2 an illegal pill or chemical.

drugstore drugstores noun
a store where you can buy medicines and personal items.

drum drums noun
a musical instrument that you beat with a stick or your hands.

drunk adjective
When somebody is drunk, they have drunk too much alcohol.

drunk past of **drink**.

dry drier driest adjective
If something is dry, there is no water or liquid in it. ■ The opposite is **wet**.

dry dries drying dried verb
If you dry something, you make it dry. *Hal is drying himself with a towel.*

duck ducks noun
a water bird with webbed feet and a flat, broad beak. A male duck is called a drake, and a young duck is called a duckling.

due adjective
When something is due at a particular time, it should happen at that time. *They are due to arrive at 10 o'clock.*
● A word that sounds like **due** is **dew**.

duffle coat noun
a long, warm jacket made from thick wool. It usually has a hood and long wooden buttons called toggles.

dug past of **dig.**

dull duller dullest adjective
1 A dull color is not very bright. ■ The opposite is **bright**.
2 A dull day is cloudy and the Sun is not shining.
3 If something such as a movie or book is dull, it is not interesting.
4 not sharp. *a dull ache.*

dumb adjective
1 completely unable to speak.
2 stupid.

dump dumps dumping dumped verb
If you dump something, you put it down quickly and carelessly. *My parents get angry when my sister just dumps her clothes on the floor.*

dune dunes noun
a low hill of sand by the sea or in a desert.

models of sand dunes

dungarees noun
pants made out of a very strong cotton material, such as blue denim.

dungeon dungeons noun
an underground prison in a castle.
▲ Say **dun**-*jun*.

dusk noun
the time in the evening when it is almost dark but not quite.

dust noun
dirt that is like powder. *The furniture was covered with dust.*
dusty adjective.

duty duties noun
a job that you have to do. *The dog belongs to my brother, so it's his duty to take it for walks.*

DVD DVDs noun
a compact disk (CD) used for storing data, such as movies, music, or information.

dwell dwells dwelling dwelled or dwelt verb
When you dwell somewhere, you live there.
dwelling noun.

dye dyes noun
a liquid that you soak cloth or your hair in to change its color. ● A word that sounds like **dye** is **die**.
dye verb.

dyslexia noun
a learning difficulty that causes problems with reading and spelling.
dyslexic adjective.
▲ Say *dis*-**lex**-*ee-uh*.

Steller's eider

northern pintail

shelduck

garganey

mandarin

Ee

eager adjective
If you are eager to do something, you want to do it very much. *Ben was eager to help with the cooking.*

eagle eagles noun
a large bird with a curved beak and broad wings. Eagles are called birds of prey because they catch and eat small animals and other birds.

ear ears noun
Your ears are the part of your body that you hear with.

early earlier earliest adjective, adverb
1 near the beginning of a period of time. *Early cars had solid tires.*
2 before the usual time or the time that you are expected. *We went to the swimming pool early, before it got crowded.* ■ The opposite is **late**.

earn earns earning earned verb
If you earn money, you get money for work that you do. *Lauren sometimes earns extra allowance by washing her mother's car.*

earring earrings noun
a piece of jewelry that you wear on your ear.

earth noun
1 Earth is the planet that we live on. Earth moves around the Sun.
2 the ground that plants grow in.

earthquake earthquakes noun
An earthquake happens when part of the ground suddenly begins to shake. Earthquakes happen when rocks move deep beneath the surface of Earth.

easel easels noun
a stand for a blackboard or an artist's painting.

east noun
1 the direction from which the Sun rises.
2 the East is where countries such as China and Japan are located.
east adjective, **eastern** adjective.
■ The opposite is **west**, **western**.

easy easier easiest adjective
not difficult. ■ The opposite is **hard** or **difficult**.

eat eats eating ate eaten verb
When you eat something, you chew food in your mouth and swallow it.

eat

Some words that you can use instead of eat:

Rabbits eat carrots.
nibble

Apples make a crunchy sound when you eat them.
chew, munch, bite

We ate at the new Italian restaurant.
dined

echo echoes noun
An echo is the sound that comes back to you when you shout in a place such as a cave. ▲ Say **eck**-*oh*.

eclipse eclipses noun
1 An eclipse of the Sun happens when the Moon comes between Earth and the Sun so that you cannot see all the Sun's light (a).

Earth
a
Moon
Sun

2 An eclipse of the Moon happens when the Earth comes between the Sun and the Moon so that you cannot see all the Moon's light (b).

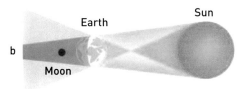

Earth
Sun
b
Moon

edge edges noun
An edge is the end or side of something. *Don't stand on the edge of the cliff.*

education noun
Education is teaching people to read, write, and learn about all kinds of things, usually in a school or college.

eel eels noun
a long, thin fish that lives in rivers or in the sea.

effect effects noun
An effect is a change that is caused by somebody or something. *The trash in the river had a bad effect on the fish.*

effort efforts noun
If you make an effort, you try hard to do something. *It takes a lot of effort to try to pull Kirsty off the floor.*

egg eggs noun
1 Birds, fish, some reptiles, and some other animals lay eggs. The young of these animals live inside the eggs until they are ready to hatch.
2 a hen, goose, or duck egg with a hard shell that you can cook and eat.

elastic adjective
A material that stretches when you pull it is elastic.

elbow elbows noun
Your elbow is the joint in the middle of your arm where it bends.

elderly adjective
rather old. *an elderly man.*

election elections noun
An election is when people vote to choose who they want to be their leader. *an election for a new president.*

electric adjective
A machine that is electric works by using electricity. *an electric fan.*

electricity noun
the form of energy that travels along wires. Rubbing a balloon on your hair creates a form of electricity called "static electricity." **electrical** adjective.

electronic adjective
An electronic machine, such as a computer, uses a piece of material called a silicon chip that has a tiny electric circuit in it.

elephant elephants noun
a very big, gray animal with a long trunk and two long teeth called tusks. Elephants live in Africa and Asia. They eat grass and parts of trees that they tear off with their trunks.

elevator elevators noun
a small moving room that can carry people from floor to floor in a building.

e-mail noun
electronic messages or mail that you send and receive from a computer.

embroider verb
to decorate cloth with tiny stitches. **embroidery** noun.

embryo embryos noun
a tiny person or animal that has only just begun to develop inside its mother and has not yet been born. ▲ Say **em**-*bree-oh.*

emerald emeralds noun
a bright green jewel.

emergency emergencies noun
An emergency is when somebody is in danger and needs help immediately. *In an emergency, you should call 911.*

emotion emotions noun
a strong feeling such as love, anger, or sadness. ▲ Say *em-oh-shun.*

emperor emperors noun
a man who rules over a group of countries, called an empire.

a Chinese emperor

employ employs employing employed verb
If you employ somebody, you pay them to work for you.

empress empresses noun
a woman who rules over a group of countries, called an empire.

empty adjective
If something is empty, there is nothing in it. *She drank all the milk and left the empty glass on the table.* ■ The opposite is **full**.

empty empties emptying emptied verb
If you empty something, you take out or throw away everything that is in it. *He emptied the entire pitcher.* ■ The opposite is **fill**.

enchanted adjective
A place that is enchanted has been put under a magic spell. *The story is about an enchanted forest where the trees come to life.*

encourage encourages encouraging encouraged verb
If you encourage people, you make them feel that what they are doing is good. *We encouraged the smaller kids to swim the length of the pool.* **encouragement** noun.

encyclopedia encyclopedias noun
a book that tells you about all kinds of facts and subjects in alphabetical order. ▲ Say *en-sy-clo-***pee***-dee-uh.*

end ends noun
1 the last part of something. *I'm almost at the end of my book.* ■ The opposite is **beginning** or **start**.
2 one of the short edges of something long. *They sat at opposite ends of the table.*

55

end ends ending ended verb
When something ends, it finishes. *What time does the movie end?* ■ The opposite is **begin** or **start**.

enemy enemies noun
An enemy is a person who hates someone else or a country that another country fights against in a war.

energy noun
1 Energy is the power that makes machines work and gives us heat and light. Electricity is one kind of energy.
2 Your energy is the strength that your body has to do things. *You need a lot of energy to run 1,000 yards.*
energetic adjective.

engaged adjective
1 If two people are engaged, they have agreed to get married.
2 If somebody is engaged in doing something like a job, he or she is busy doing it. *He is engaged in fixing the furnace.*

engine engines noun
1 a machine that makes things move. *a plane's engine.*
2 the front part of a train that pulls it along.

enjoy enjoys enjoying enjoyed verb
If you enjoy something, you like doing it. *I enjoy playing soccer.*
enjoyable adjective, **enjoyment** noun.

enormous adjective
very, very big. *China is an enormous country.* ■ The opposite is **tiny.**

enough adjective. adverb, noun
If you have enough of something, you have as much as you need. *Have you had enough to eat?*

enter enters entering entered verb
1 If you enter a place, you go into it. *She entered the room quietly.*
2 If you enter a race or competition, you take part in it. *Did you enter the bicycle race?*

entertain entertains entertaining entertained verb
If you entertain people, you do things that they find interesting or amusing. *The clown entertained the crowd while the acrobats changed their costumes.*
entertainment noun.

enthusiasm noun
a strong feeling of liking something or wanting to do something. *The children were full of enthusiasm for the party.*
enthusiastic adjective.

entrance entrances noun
the way into a place. *I'll meet you at the entrance to the store.* ■ The opposite is **exit**.

envelope envelopes noun
a folded paper holder for a letter or card. You write the address of the person that you are writing to on the front of the envelope.

environment noun
The environment is the air, water, land, and all the plants and animals around us. *We must all try to protect the environment.*
environmental adjective.

envy envies envying envied verb
to wish that you had the same things that other people have.
envious adjective.

episode episodes noun
An episode is one part of a long story on TV or radio that you watch or listen to in several parts. *The TV series had seven separate episodes.*

equal adjective
If things are equal, they are the same in size, amount, or number.

The children each had an equal number of candies.
equally adverb.

equator noun
The equator is an imaginary line on maps that goes around Earth at an equal distance between the North and South poles. Countries close to the equator are very hot.

equipment noun
all the things that you need to do something. *sports equipment* or *football equipment.*

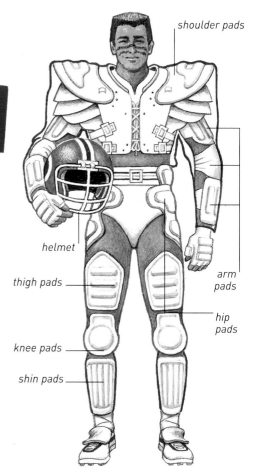

shoulder pads

helmet

arm pads

thigh pads

hip pads

knee pads

shin pads

error errors noun
a mistake.

erupt erupts erupting erupted verb
When a volcano erupts, it explodes
and very hot liquid rock called lava
shoots out of the top.
eruption noun.

escalator escalators noun
a staircase with moving steps.

escape escapes escaping escaped
verb
A person or an animal that escapes
gets away from somebody or
something. *The bird has escaped from
its cage.*

especially adverb
most of all. *I especially like cats.*

essential adjective
If something is essential, it is
absolutely necessary.

ethnic adjective
having to do with people who have
the same country, language, and way
of life.

evaporate evaporates evaporating
evaporated verb
When a liquid evaporates, it changes
into a gas or vapor and seems to
disappear. *Boiling water evaporates.*
evaporation noun.

even adjective
1 flat and smooth. *an even floor.* ■ The
opposite is **uneven**.
2 Even numbers can be divided
exactly by two. *2, 4, 6, and 8 are even
numbers.* ■ The opposite is **odd**.

evening evenings noun
the part of the day between afternoon
and night.

event events noun
something that happens, especially
something important or unusual.
The school field trip is a big event.

eventually adverb
after a very long time. *I waited for a
long time, then eventually the bus came.*

evergreen adjective
An evergreen tree does not lose
its leaves in the winter. Pine trees
are evergreen. ■ The opposite
is **deciduous**.

evidence noun
proof of something that happened.
*The paw prints were evidence that the cat
had jumped on the table.*

evil adjective
A person who is evil is very bad and
cruel. *an evil emperor.*

exact adjective
correct. *What is the exact time?*
exactly adverb.

exaggerate exaggerates
exaggerating exaggerated verb
If you exaggerate, you pretend that
something is bigger, better, or worse
than it really is. *Peter was exaggerating
when he said that he saw a spider as big
as a cat.* ▲ Say *eks-**zaj**-uh-rate.*

exam exams noun
a short word for examination. *a math
exam or a ballet exam.*

examination examinations noun
1 an important test that you are given
to see how much you have learned.
2 looking at somebody or something
closely and carefully. *a medical
examination.*

examine examines
examining
examined verb
If you examine
something, you
look at it closely
and carefully. *Freddie
examined the fossil with
a magnifying glass.*

example examples noun
a thing that shows what other things
of the same kind are like. *At the school
open house, we showed our parents examples
of our work.*

excellent adjective
Something that is excellent is very
good. *We had an excellent vacation.*

except preposition
but not. *Everyone except for Lee passed
the history test.*
exception noun.

exchange exchanges exchanging
exchanged verb
If you exchange something, you give
one thing and get something else in
return. *At the end of summer camp, we
exchanged addresses with our new friends.*

excited adjective
If you are excited,
you are so happy that
you cannot keep quiet
or calm. *Freddie is
so excited that he is
jumping for joy!*
excitement noun,
exciting
adjective.

exclaim
exclaims
exclaiming
exclaimed verb
To exclaim
means to say
something in
a loud voice
because you
are surprised
or angry. *"What
a mess!" she exclaimed.*
exclamation noun
*He gave an exclamation of surprise
when he saw the huge snake.*

exclamation point exclamation
points noun
a mark (!) that you use in writing. You
use an exclamation mark to show that
somebody is surprised or angry. *Oh no!*

excuse excuses noun
If you make an excuse, you try to
explain why you did something
wrong. *What's your excuse for being late
this time?* ▲ Say *ex-**kyoos**.*

excuse excuses excusing excused
verb
If you excuse people, you forgive
them for something that they did
wrong. *I'll excuse you for forgetting your
homework this time.* ▲ Say *ex-**kyooz**.*

exercise exercises noun
1 Exercise is something such as running or jumping that you do to keep your body strong and healthy. *The children are doing different kinds of exercise.*
2 An exercise is a piece of work that you do to help you learn something. *Our teacher asked us to finish exercise 2 for homework.*

exhausted adjective
very tired. *After running all the way up the hill, I was exhausted.*

exhibition exhibitions noun
a collection of things in a place such as a museum or gallery for people to come and look at. ▲ Say *ex-i-bish-un*.

exist exists existing existed verb
If something exists, you can find it in the real world now. *Do you think that ghosts really exist?*
existence noun.

exit exits noun
the way out of a building. *The exit is at the back of the theater.* ■ The opposite is **entrance**.

expand expands expanding expanded verb
If something expands, it gets bigger. *When you blow air into a balloon, it expands.*

expect expects expecting expected verb
If you expect something to happen, you think it will happen. *I expect that they will be here soon.*

expedition expeditions noun
a long journey to find or do something special. *Admiral Byrd led an expedition to the South Pole.*

expensive adjective
Something that is expensive costs a lot of money. ■ The opposite is **cheap**.

experience experiences noun
1 An experience is something that has happened to you. *What's the most frightening experience you've had?*
2 Experience is knowing about something because you have done it for a long time. *I can cycle to school once I've had more experience riding my bike on the road.*

experiment experiments noun
a test that you do to find out something. *We did an experiment to see which objects are magnetic.*

expert experts noun
a person who knows a lot about something. *a computer expert.*

explain explains explaining explained verb
1 If you explain how to do something, you tell somebody about it so that he or she can understand it. *My brother explained to me how to fix my bike.*
2 If you explain something that happened, you give reasons why it happened. *We explained that we were late because we had missed the bus.*
explanation noun.

explode explodes exploding exploded verb
If something such as a bomb explodes, it bursts suddenly with a very loud noise.
explosion noun.

explore explores exploring explored verb
When you explore, you look carefully around a place that you have never seen before.
exploration noun.

express expresses expressing expressed verb
If you express what you think or feel, you show it in words or actions.

expression expressions noun
Your expression is the look on your face that shows how you feel. *A smile is a happy expression.*

expressway expressways noun
a big road with many lanes.

extinct adjective
An animal or plant that is extinct no longer exists. *Dinosaurs became extinct millions of years ago.*
extinction noun.

extinguish extinguishes extinguishing extinguished verb
If you extinguish a fire, you put it out. *He extinguished the flames with a bucket of water.* ▲ Say *ex-ting-wish*.

extra adjective
more than you usually have. *I wore an extra sweater because I was cold.*

extraordinary adjective
very special or unusual. *I read an extraordinary story about a horse that could talk.*

extremely adverb
very. *Elephants are extremely large animals.*

eye eyes noun
Your eyes are the parts of your face that you use to see with. In the middle of the eye is a hole called a pupil that lets light onto the lens behind. ● A word that sounds like **eye** is **I**.

Ff

fable fables noun
a story, usually about animal characters, that teaches you something.

face faces noun
Your face is the front part of your head where your eyes, nose, and mouth are.

fact facts noun
something that is known to be true. *It's a fact that we live in San Jose.*

factory factories noun
a building where people use machines to make things. *a car factory.*

fade fades fading faded verb
1 If something fades, it becomes paler.
2 If a sound fades away, it slowly becomes quieter.

Fahrenheit adjective
having to do with a way of measuring temperature that shows the freezing point of water at 32 degrees and its boiling point at 212 degrees.

fail fails failing failed verb
If you fail at something, you do not succeed in doing it.
failure noun.

faint faints fainting fainted verb
If you faint, you become unconscious for a short time. *Alex fainted when he saw blood coming from the cut on his finger.*

faint fainter faintest adjective
Something that is faint is not very strong or clear. *There is a faint smell of smoke.*

fair fairer fairest adjective
1 A person who is fair has light-colored hair and skin.
■ The opposite is **dark**.
2 Something that is fair seems right or treats everybody the same. *It's not fair that I have to go to bed when Rachel is allowed to stay up.* ■ The opposite is **unfair**.
● A word that sounds like **fair** is **fare**.

fair fairs noun
an outdoor place outside where rides and competitions are set up for people to have fun. ● A word that sounds like **fair** is **fare**.

fairy fairies noun
in stories, a magical creature that looks like a very small person with wings.

faith noun
If you have faith in somebody, you trust that person to do what he or she says.

faithful adjective
If you are faithful to somebody who trusts you, you do not do anything to hurt that person; loyal. *She's very faithful to her friends.*

fake adjective
looking like the real thing. *It's a fake diamond.* ■ The opposite is **real**.

fall falls falling fell fallen verb
When something falls, it goes down or drops from a higher to a lower place.

Jason fell off the skateboard.
fall noun.

false adjective
1 not true. *The man gave a false name.* ■ The opposite is **true**.
2 not the real thing. *John is wearing false teeth.*

fame noun
being famous.

familiar adjective
If something is familiar to you, you know it well. *Her face was familiar, but I couldn't remember her name.* ■ The opposite is **unfamiliar** or **strange**.

family families noun
1 a group of people made up of parents, grandparents, and children. Aunts, uncles, and cousins are also part of your family.
2 a group of animals or plants that are like each other in certain ways. *Polar bears are members of the bear family.*

grizzly bear
black bear
sun bear   Asiatic black bear   polar bear

famine famines noun
a time when there is not enough food for the people in a country to eat.
▲ Say fam-*in*.

famous adjective
known by lots of people. *a famous movie star.* ▲ Say **fay-muss.**

fan fans noun
1 a machine with blades that spin quickly to keep a room cool in hot weather.
2 a flat object, often made of paper, that you wave in front of your face to keep you cool in hot weather.
3 a person who really admires somebody famous, such as a singer or an actor, or who likes a certain sport very much. *football fans.*

fancy fancier fanciest adjective
Something that is fancy has a lot of decoration on it. *My fanciest dress has a lace collar and a ruffled hem.*
■ The opposite is **plain.**
fancily adverb, **fanciness** noun.

fang fangs noun
a long, sharp, pointed tooth. Some snakes have fangs.

fantastic adjective
amazing or really good.

far adjective
a long distance from something or somebody. ■ The opposite is **near.**

fare fares noun
the money that you pay to go on a bus, train, or plane. ● A word that sounds like **fare** is **fair.**

farm farms noun
a place where people grow crops or raise animals to sell as food.
farmer noun.

fascinate fascinates fascinating fascinated verb
If something fascinates you, you are very interested in it. *Snakes fascinate me.* ▲ Say **fas-in-ate.**
fascination noun, **fascinating** adjective.

fashion fashions noun
a way of dressing or behaving that is very popular for a time.

fast faster fastest adjective
1 very quick. *She's a fast runner.*
2 If a watch or clock is fast, it shows a time that is later than the real time.
■ The opposite is **slow.**
fast adverb.

fast

Some words that you can use instead of fast:

We ate in a fast-food restaurant.

quick-service

She's a very fast talker.

quick, rapid

The news spread fast.

quickly, swiftly, speedily, rapidly

fasten fastens fastening fastened verb
If you fasten something, you close it firmly. *Fasten your seat belt.*
▲ Say **fa-sun.**

fat fatter fattest adjective
A person or animal with a large, heavy body. ■ The opposite is **thin.**

fat fats noun
oil, butter, or margarine that you can use to cook with.

father fathers noun
a male parent.

faucet faucets noun
a thing that you turn when you want water to come out of a pipe or when you want the water to stop.

fault faults noun
1 a mistake.
2 If something bad is your fault, it happened because of something you did.

favor favors noun
a kind and helpful thing that you do for somebody. *Could you do me a favor and carry this box for me?*

favorite adjective
Your favorite thing is the one that you like best.

fax faxes noun
1 a machine that sends a picture or message along a telephone wire to another machine that prints it out.
2 a message or picture sent on a fax machine.

an orignal document and a fax copy

fear noun
the feeling that you have when you are afraid. *He has a fear of heights.*

feast feasts noun
a large, special meal for a lot of people.

feather feathers noun
one of the light, soft parts that cover a bird's body.

federal adjective
If a government of a country is a group of states joined under single control, it is a federal government.

feed feeds feeding fed verb
1 If you feed others, you give them food. *We fed the ducks.*
2 When an animal feeds, it eats.

feel feels feeling felt verb
1 When you feel something, you touch it and know what it is like against your skin. *Feel my bear— it's so soft.*
2 If you feel sad, happy or angry, you are that way at the moment. *I feel really hungry.*

feeling feelings noun
A feeling is what you feel, like happiness.

feet plural of **foot**.

fell past of **fall**.

felt past of **feel**.

female adjective
A female person or animal belongs to the sex that can have babies or lay eggs. Girls and women are female. ▪ The opposite is **male**.

fence fences noun
a wall of wood or wire around land such as a garden or field. *a wooden fence.*

fern ferns noun
a plant that has leaves like feathers and no flowers.

Ferris wheel Ferris wheels noun
a big, high wheel with seats around the edge. People ride on Ferris wheels at carnivals and theme parks.

ferry ferries noun
a large boat that carries passengers and cars across a river or a narrow piece of sea.

fertile adjective
Fertile land is where plants grow well.

festival festivals noun
a special or religious holiday when people celebrate.

fetch fetches fetching fetched verb
When you fetch something, you go to get it and bring it back. *Our dog fetches the newspaper.*

fever fevers noun
an illness that makes the temperature of your body higher than usual.

few adjective
not many. ▪ The opposite is **many**.

fiber fibers noun
a thread of wool, cotton, nylon, or something similar that is used to make cloth.

fiction noun
stories that have been made up by somebody and are not about people who really exist or things that really happen.

field fields noun
an area of land where farmers grow crops or keep animals.

fierce fiercer fiercest adjective
An animal that is fierce is likely to attack you. *a fierce bull.*

fight fights fighting fought verb
When people or animals fight, they attack and try to hurt each other. *Lions sometimes fight over a kill.*
fight noun.

figure figures noun
1 one of the signs that we use to write numbers, such as 1, 2, and 3.
2 the shape of a person. *I could just make out the figure of a tall man in the fog.*

file files noun
1 a box, cardboard cover, or book where you can keep papers.
2 a set of information on a computer.
3 a tool with a rough surface that you use to make things smooth. *a nail file.*
single file a line of people or animals, one behind the other. *The children walked single file into the cafeteria.*

different types of file

fill fills filling filled verb
If you fill something, you put as much into it as it can hold. *Frances filled the bottles with water.*
▪ The opposite is **empty**.

film films noun
1 a movie. *Mom and Dad took me to see a foreign film.*
2 a long, thin strip of plastic that you put in some cameras for taking photographs. *I need new film for my camera.*

fin fins noun
A fin is one of the thin, flat parts on a fish's body that help it swim and balance.

final adjective
last. *the final episode of the TV series.*
finally adverb.

find finds finding found verb
When you find something, you see it again after it has been lost or you did not know where it was. *I've found my sneakers.* ▪ The opposite is **lose**.

fine finer finest adjective
1 healthy. *"How are you?" "I'm fine."*
2 bright and sunny. *The weather is fine for sailing.*
3 good enough. *There's nothing wrong with your work—it's fine.*
4 very thin. *Her hair is fine.*
5 very good. *She's a fine athlete.*

fine fines noun
Money that you have to pay as a punishment.

finger fingers noun
Your fingers are the long, thin parts at the end of your hands.

fingernail fingernails noun
the hard material over the tips of your fingers.

fingerprint
fingerprints noun
the mark made by the tip of your finger showing the lines on your skin. *The police couldn't find any fingerprints because the thief had worn gloves during the robbery.*

finish finishes finishing finished verb
When you finish something, you come to the end of it. ■ The opposite is **start** or **begin**.
finish noun.

fir firs noun
an evergreen tree with cones and leaves that are the shape of needles.
● A word that sounds like **fir** is **fur**.

fire fires noun
the hot, bright flames that come from something that is burning.

fire fires firing fired verb
1 to shoot bullets from a gun. *The thief fired at the police officer.*
2 to dismiss somebody from a job. *He was fired for stealing.*

fire engine fire engines noun
a large truck with hoses and ladders that firefighters ride in to get to a fire.

fire extinguisher fire extinguishers noun
a metal container full of special chemicals that you use to put out a fire.

firefighter firefighters noun
a person whose job is to put out dangerous fires and to rescue people who are in danger.

fireplace fireplaces noun
a hole in a wall in a room beneath a chimney where you can light a fire.

fireworks noun
small objects containing chemicals that explode noisily and make brightly colored sparks when you light them.

firm firmer firmest adjective
1 Something that is firm is quite hard and does not change its shape when you press it. *Bananas are firm when they are green but get soft when they are ripe.*
2 If you are firm about something, you are sure and you are not going to change your mind. *We haven't made a firm decision yet about where we are going on vacation.*

firm firms noun
a business company. *Dad works for a large law firm.*

first aid noun
medical help or treatment that is given to a sick or hurt person before he or she sees a doctor.

fish fish or fishes noun
an animal that lives in water and breathes through gills. A fish has fins and a tail for swimming, and its body is covered in scales.

fish fishes fishing fished verb
To try to catch fish. *My uncle taught us how to fish with a fishing rod.*

fishery fisheries noun
a place where fish are raised.

fist fists noun
You make a fist when you curl your fingers and thumb into your palm.

fit fits fitting fitted verb
1 If a thing fits, it is the right size or shape. *These jeans don't fit me anymore.*
2 If you fit things together, you join one thing to another. *I fitted the pieces of the puzzle together.*

fit fitter fittest adjective
If you are fit, your body is well and strong. *My parents exercise to keep themselves fit.*

fix fixes fixing fixed verb
1 When you fix something that was broken, you make it work again. *I've fixed your bike.*
2 When you fix something to another thing, you join the two things firmly. *She fixed the shelf to the wall.*

fizzy fizzier fizziest adjective
full of small bubbles.

flag flags noun
a piece of cloth with a pattern on it, on the end of a pole. Each country has its own flag.

flake flakes noun
a small, thin, light piece of something. *a snowflake.*

flame flames noun
the hot, bright, burning gas that comes from a fire.

flap flaps flapping flapped verb
When a bird flaps its wings, it moves them up and down quickly.

flap flaps noun
a flat piece that hangs down to cover an opening. *a tent flap.*

flare flares noun
a bright flame or light used as a signal.

flash flashes noun
a sudden, bright light that lasts a short time. *a flash of lightning.*

flashlight flashlights noun
a small tube with a lightbulb that gets power from batteries. When you press a switch, it lights up.

flat flatter flattest adjective
1 level and completely smooth and even, with no parts that are higher than the rest. *A table has to have a flat top so that things do not slide around.*
2 A flat tire does not have enough air in it. *My bike has a flat tire.*

flattery noun
too much praise. It can be insincere.

flavor flavors noun
The flavor of something is what it tastes like. *different flavors of ice cream.*

flea fleas noun
a tiny jumping insect with no wings. Fleas bite animals and people.

flesh noun
1 the soft part of your body that is under your skin, covering your bones.
2 the soft part of fruit or vegetables.

flew past of fly.
● A word that sounds like **flew** is **flu**.

flight flights noun
1 a journey in a plane. *It is a long flight from Chicago to Tokyo.*
2 flying through the air. *Have you ever seen geese in flight?*
3 a set of stairs. *We ran up six flights.*

float floats floating floated verb
1 When something floats in a liquid, it stays on the top and does not sink. *an experiment to see what floats.*
2 When something floats in air, it moves along gently in the air without falling to the ground. *We watched our balloon float through the backyard and over the fence.*

flock flocks noun
a group of animals of one kind. *a flock of sheep* or *a flock of geese.*

flood floods noun
A flood happens when a lot of water covers an area that is usually dry.

floodlight floodlights noun
very bright lights that light up a sports stadium or a building at night.

floor floors noun
1 the flat part that you walk on inside a building.
2 a level of a building; story.

floss flosses flossing flossed verb
to clean between your teeth with a special string.

flour noun
white or brown powder that is made by grinding grains, such as wheat. We use flour to make bread, cakes, and pastry. ● A word that sounds like **flour** is **flower**.

flow flows flowing flowed verb
When a liquid flows, it moves along smoothly. *Many rivers flow into seas* or *The water flowed down the drain.*

flower flowers noun
the part of a plant at the end of the stem that has colored or white petals. ● A word that sounds like **flower** is **flour**.

flown past of fly.

flu noun
an illness that gives you a high temperature and makes your body ache all over. Flu is short for **influenza**. ● A word that sounds like **flu** is **flew**.

fluffy fluffier fluffiest adjective
soft and light like wool or hair. *Baby chickens are fluffy.*

fluid fluids noun
a substance that flows. *Liquids are fluids.*

fluorescent adjective
A fluorescent object glows in the dark when you shine a light on it. *Cyclists wear fluorescent strips so that drivers can see them in the dark more easily.*
▲ Say *flor-es-ent.*

flush flushes flushing flushed verb
1 If you flush, your face gets red. *Thomas flushed with embarrassment.*
2 When you flush the toilet, you make a lot of water flow through it to clean it.

flute flutes noun
a musical instrument like a long, thin pipe. You hold it sideways and blow into the end, covering its holes with your fingers to play different notes.

flutter flutters fluttering fluttered verb
When something flutters, it makes quick, light, flapping movements. *A moth was fluttering against the window.*

fly flies noun
a small insect with two wings.

fly

fly flies flying flew flown verb
1 When something flies, it moves through the air. *A flock of geese was flying overhead.*
2 When you fly, you take a trip in a plane.

foal foals noun
a young horse.

foam noun
a mass of small air bubbles. *Laundry detergent makes a lot of foam.*

focus focuses focusing focused verb
When you focus a camera, a telescope, or binoculars, you move a part of it so that what you see through it is clear.

fog noun
a kind of thick cloud near the ground that makes it difficult to see things.
foggy adjective.

foil noun
a very thin sheet of metal used to wrap food.

fold folds folding folded verb
When you fold something, you bend one part so that it covers another. *Fred folded his sweater before putting it in his suitcase.* ■ The opposite is **unfold**.

follow follows following followed verb
1 If you follow others, you go along behind them. ■ The opposite is **lead**.
2 If one thing follows another, it comes after it. *Night always follows day.*

fond fonder fondest adjective
If you are fond of somebody, you like that person or thing very much and care about what happens to him, her, or it.

food noun
all the things that people and animals can eat.

foolish adjective
very silly. ■ The opposite is **sensible**.

foot feet noun
Your foot is the part of your body at the bottom of your leg that you stand on.

football footballs noun
1 a game played by two teams who try to get a ball into the other team's end zone. *high school football team.*
2 the ball that you use to play football.

footprint footprints noun
the mark that your foot or shoe leaves on a surface.

footstep footsteps noun
the sound that a person who is walking makes when each foot touches the ground. *I could hear footsteps coming down the stairs.*

forbid forbids forbidding forbade forbidden verb
If somebody forbids you to do something, he or she is telling you that you cannot do it. *Our teacher forbid us from bringing pets to school.* ■ The opposite is **permit** or **allow**.

force forces forcing forced verb
1 If somebody forces you to do something, he or she makes you do it. *He forced me to sit down.*
2 If you force something somewhere, you use your strength to make it go there. *She tried to force a package through the mail slot.*

force forces noun
power or strength. *A lot of trees were blown down by the force of the wind.*

forecast forecasts forecasting forecast or forecasted verb
If you forecast something, you say that it is going to happen in the future. *She forecasts that the weather will get warmer by the weekend.*
forecast noun
the weather forecast.

forehead foreheads noun
Your forehead is the part of your face above your eyes and below your hair.

foreign adjective
A person or thing that is foreign belongs to a country that is not your own. *Jane collects foreign stamps.*
▲ Say for-*en*.

forest forests noun
a very large group of trees.

forge forges forging forged verb
If somebody forges something, such as money, the person makes an exact copy of it to deceive people. *He was put in jail for forging another person's signature on checks.*
▲ Say forj.
forgery noun.

forget forgets forgetting forgot forgotten verb
When you forget something, you do not remember it. *Don't forget your keys.*

forgive forgives forgiving forgave forgiven verb
When you forgive somebody, you do not mind anymore about something bad that he or she did to you. *Lily finally forgave me for losing her pen.*

fork forks noun
1 a tool with long, pointed parts called prongs, or tines, at one end. You use a fork for putting food in your mouth.
2 the place where something divides into two parts. *a fork in the road.*

64

form forms noun
1 the shape of something. *a birthday cake in the form of a dog.*
2 a kind of something. *Gas and coal are forms of fuel.*
3 a printed paper that has questions and spaces for you to write the answers, usually for official purposes.

form forms forming formed verb
1 When things form a certain shape, they are arranged in that shape. *The chairs formed a semicircle.*
2 When something forms, it starts to appear. *A crowd was forming outside the theater.*

fort forts noun
an army base.

fortress fortresses noun
a big, strong building such as a castle that can be defended against enemies.

fortune fortunes noun
1 good or bad luck.
2 a lot of money. *They made a fortune on the movie.*

fossil
fossils noun
what remains of a plant or animal that died millions of years ago and that has become part of a piece of rock.
fossilized adjective.

foster adjective
taking care of someone else's child for a while. *foster parents of orphans* or *a foster family.*

fought past of fight.

found past of find.

fountain fountains noun
an object that sprays water up into the air.

fox foxes noun
a wild animal that looks like a small dog with reddish-brown fur and a long, thick tail.

fraction fractions noun
1 a part of a whole number. $\frac{1}{2}$ and $\frac{2}{5}$ are fractions.
2 a tiny part. *She only opened the cage a fraction, but the hamster escaped.*

fracture fractures noun
a break or crack in something, especially a bone. *Her arm is in a cast because she has a fracture.*
▲ Say frak-*sher*.
fracture verb.

fragile adjective
Something that is fragile can break easily. *Be careful not to drop that vase; it's very fragile.* ▲ Say fraj-*il.*

frame frames noun
1 an edge around something, such as a picture or window.
2 the shape of something such as a building or vehicle that is built first out of metal or wood, so that the rest can be built over it.
frame verb.

freckle freckles noun
a small brown spot on a person's skin.

free adjective
1 If you are free, you are able to do what you want or go where you want without anybody stopping you.
2 Something that is free does not cost any money.
3 not busy. *I'm busy now, but I'll be free after dinner.*
freedom noun.

freeway freeways noun
an expressway.

freeze freezes freezing froze frozen verb
1 When water freezes, it gets so cold that it turns into ice.
2 When you freeze food, you make it very cold by storing it at a very low temperature so that it will stay fresh for a long time.
3 If you are freezing, you are very cold.

freezer freezers noun
a large metal chest or part of a refrigerator that freezes food so that it stays fresh for a long time.

freight noun
things that a truck, train, ship, or plane is carrying. ▲ Rhymes with **late**.

french fries noun
long, thin pieces of potato fried until they are crisp.

frequent adjective
Something that is frequent happens or comes often. *There are frequent buses to the city from here.*

fresh fresher freshest adjective
1 Food that is fresh has been made or picked recently and is not old or spoiled. *fresh eggs.* or *fresh fruit.*
2 Fresh air is air that is clean and good to breathe. *We went outside to get some fresh air.*
3 Freshwater is water that is not salty.

freshman freshmen noun
a student who is in his or her first year of high school or college.

friend friends noun
a person that you like a lot. *Jane, Ali, and Rachel are friends.*
friendship noun.

friendly friendlier
friendliest adjective
A friendly person gets to know other people easily and acts like a friend toward them. *Erica is friendly to everybody.*

fright frights noun
a feeling of great fear. *The explosion caused fright among the people.*

frighten frightens frightening
frightened verb
If you frighten others, you make them feel afraid. *Don frightened me with his Halloween costume.*
frightened adjective,
frightening adjective.

frigid adjective
very cold. *Frigid weather conditions meant that the roads were icy.*

frog frogs noun
a small animal with long, powerful back legs that it uses to jump. Frogs lay their eggs in water, and these eggs develop into tadpoles.

front fronts noun
the part of something that faces forward or that you usually see first.
in front of not behind. *There is a flowerbed in front of our house.*
■ The opposite is **back** or **rear**.

frost noun
a layer of ice crystals that look like white powder and form at night when the weather is very cold.
frosty adjective.

froth noun
a mass of small bubbles on the surface of a liquid.
frothy adjective.

frown frowns frowning
frowned verb
When you frown, you lower your eyebrows and make your forehead wrinkle, often because you are angry or worried.

froze, frozen past of **freeze**.

fruit fruit noun
the part of a plant that contains seeds or a pit. You can eat many kinds of fruit.

fry fries frying fried verb
When you fry food, you cook it in hot fat or oil. You fry food in a frying pan.

fuel fuels noun
something such as coal, wood, or gasoline that we burn to make heat or power. *Cars and airplanes cannot run without fuel.*

full fuller fullest adjective
If something is full, there is so much inside it that there is no room for any more. *The bus was full of people.*
■ The opposite is **empty**.

fumes noun
smelly or poisonous smoke or gases that come from something that is burning or from chemicals. *gasoline fumes.*

fun noun
When you have fun, you enjoy yourself.

fund funds noun
an amount of money that is going to be used for a special purpose. *The school is raising funds to build a new gym.*

funeral funerals noun
a ceremony in which a dead body is buried or cremated.

fungus
fungi noun
a kind of plant that is not green and does not have leaves or flowers. Fungi grow in damp, dark places. Mushrooms and toadstools are common kinds of fungi.

funnel funnels noun
1 a tube that is wide at one end and narrow at the other. A funnel is used for pouring liquid into a narrow container, such as a bottle.
2 a chimney on a ship.

funny funnier funniest adjective
1 If something is funny, it makes you laugh or smile. *a funny story.*
2 strange. *There was a funny smell coming from the kitchen.*

fur noun
the soft, thick hair that covers the body of many animals, such as cats.
● A word that sounds like **fur** is **fir**.
furry adjective.

a furry hamster

furious adjective
very angry.

furniture noun
large things such as sofas, tables and chairs, beds, and desks that people have in their homes or offices.

fuss noun
If you make a fuss about something, you keep worrying and talking about it. *It would be better if you stopped making a fuss and actually did something.*

future noun
the time that has not happened yet. *Nobody can be sure what will happen in the future.* ■ The opposite is **past**.

Gg

gadget gadgets noun
a tool that you use to do a special job.

can openers are useful gadgets

gain gains gaining gained verb
1 To gain means to get or win something. *By the end of the game, our team had gained 10 points.*
2 To gain also means to get more of something. *The bicycle gained speed as it went down the hill.*

galaxy galaxies noun
a very large group of stars and planets in space. *Earth is part of one galaxy.*

gale gales noun
a very strong wind. *Gales can blow down trees and damage buildings.*

galleon
galleons noun
a big sailing ship that was used a long time ago.

a large galleon carrying treasure

gallery galleries noun
a place where you can go to look at paintings, sculptures, or photographs.

gallon gallons noun
four quarts of a liquid. You use about 10 gallons of water for every two minutes in the shower.

gallop gallops galloping galloped verb
When a horse gallops, it runs very fast.
gallop noun.

game games noun
A game is something that you play for fun. Games often have rules. *It rained, so we spent most of the day at home playing games.*

gang gangs noun
a group of people who do things together. *a gang of friends.*

gap gaps noun
a space between two things.

garage garages noun
1 a building where somebody can keep a car or store things.
2 a place that sells gasoline and where people repair cars.

garbage noun
pieces of food and trash that you put into cans and bags and throw away.

garden gardens noun
a piece of land near a house, where people grow flowers and vegetables.

garlic noun
a plant similar to a small onion with a very strong taste and smell. Garlic is used in cooking.

gas gases noun
A gas is something like air that is not liquid or solid and that you cannot see. Air is made up of several gases mixed together. We use another kind of gas for cooking and heating.

gasoline noun
a liquid fuel that comes from petroleum. Gasoline makes cars and trucks run. We also call it "gas."

gate gates noun
a gate is a kind of door in a wall or fence. *a garden gate.*

gather gathers gathering gathered verb
1 If you gather things, you collect them. *The Scouts gathered wood for the campfire.*
2 If people gather, they come together in a group. *The children gathered around the ice-cream truck.*

gaze gazes gazing gazed verb
If you gaze at something, you look at it for a long time. *He stood on the shore gazing out to sea.*

gear gears noun
1 a set of wheels that work together in a car, bicycle, or model to make it go faster or slower. *Gears on a bike move it forward or backward.*
2 the special clothes or things that you need for something.

geese plural of **goose**.

gem gems noun
a precious stone or jewel.

gene genes noun
Genes are the tiny parts of the cells of plants and animals that control what they look like. Genes are passed from parents to children. ▲ Say **jeen**.

general adjective
Something that is general has to do with most people or things. *The general feeling is that exercise is good for you.*
generally adverb.

generation generations noun
all the people who were born at about the same time. *This photo shows three different generations of my family: my grandparents, my parents, and me.*

generous adjective
If you are generous, you are kind and always ready to give money and other things to other people.
generosity noun.

genius geniuses noun
an unusually intelligent person.
▲ Say **jee**-*nee-uss*.

gentle gentler gentlest adjective
a gentle person is kind and careful. *Be very gentle when you pick up the baby.*
▬ The opposite is **rough**.

genuine adjective
real, not fake. *Is this a genuine dinosaur fossil?*
▲ Say **jen**-*yoo-in*.

geography noun
the study of the countries of the world and of its mountains and rivers.

gerbil gerbils noun
a small furry animal with long back legs. Some people keep gerbils in cages as pets.

germ germs noun
a very small living thing that can make you sick. *flu germs*.

ghost ghosts noun
the figure of a dead person that some people say they have seen. *Dad dressed up as a ghost.*

giant giants noun
a very big, strong person in stories.

gift gifts noun
1 a present. *birthday gifts*.
2 If you have a gift for something, you are very good at it. *Harry has a gift for music.*

gigantic adjective
very, very big. *a gigantic mountain.*
▲ Say *jy*-**gan**-*tik*.

giggle giggles giggling giggled verb
If you giggle, you laugh in a silly way. *We couldn't stop giggling at our teacher's funny shoes.*

gill gills noun
Gills are the parts of a fish that it breathes through. A fish has a pair of gills, one on each side of its head.

ginger noun
a plant that has a strong, hot taste. You can use the root or powder that is made from the root in cooking things. *gingersnaps* or *gingerbread*.

giraffe giraffes noun
a tall African animal with a very long neck. Giraffes feed on leaves and twigs from trees.

girl girls noun
a female child or a young woman.

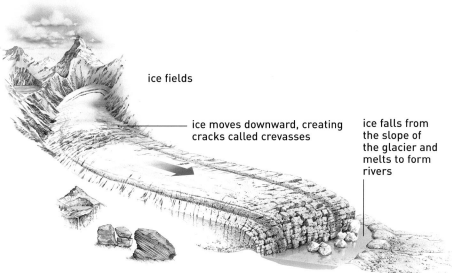

ice fields

ice moves downward, creating
cracks called crevasses

ice falls from
the slope of
the glacier and
melts to form
rivers

glacier glaciers noun
a huge mass of ice that moves
very slowly down a mountain valley.
▲ Say **glay**-*shur*.

glad adjective
happy. *I'm glad that you can come to my
birthday party.*

glance glances glancing glanced
verb
If you glance at something, you look
at it quickly. *She glanced at her watch.*

gland glands noun
one of the parts of your body that
make the chemicals that your body
needs. *Sweat glands produce sweat to
help your body cool down when you
are hot.*

glare glares glaring glared verb
If you glare at people, you look at
them in a very angry way.

glass glasses noun
1 Glass is a hard material that you
  can see through and that breaks
  easily. Windows and bottles are
  made of glass.
  *A greenhouse is
  made of glass.*
2 A glass is a
  container that you
  drink from, made
  of glass.

glasses noun
Glasses are two
pieces of special
glass, called

lenses, in a frame. Some people wear
glasses to help them see better.
She wears glasses to help her see more clearly.

gleam gleams gleaming gleamed
verb
To gleam means to shine with
a soft light. *The lake gleamed in
the moonlight.*

glide glides gliding glided verb
If something glides, it moves
smoothly along. *The dancers glided
gracefully across the floor.*

glider gliders noun
a very light aircraft that does not have
an engine. Gliders fly by floating on
currents of air.

glimpse glimpses glimpsing
glimpsed verb
If you glimpse people or things, you
see them only for a very short time.
*We just glimpsed the rabbit as it ran into
the woods.*

glitter glitters glittering glittered
verb
If something glitters, it shines
brightly with lots of flashes of
light. *The fresh snow glittered
like diamonds.*
glitter noun.

global warming noun
the scientific theory that Earth's
atmosphere is gradually warming.

globe globes noun
a ball with a map of the world on it.

gloomy gloomier gloomiest
adjective
1 If a room or a day is gloomy, it is
  dark and dull.
2 If you are gloomy, you feel sad.

glossy glossier glossiest adjective
shiny. *a dog with a glossy coat.*

glove gloves noun
a piece of clothing that you wear
on your hand. *woolen gloves.*

glow glows glowing glowed verb
If something glows, it shines with a
steady light. *The fire glowed in the dark.*

glue noun
a thick liquid that you use for sticking
things together. *Janice and Marina used
glue to fix the broken pottery.*
glue verb.

gnat gnats noun
a small, flying insect that bites people.
▲ Say **nat**.

gnaw gnaws gnawing gnawed verb
If you gnaw something hard, you keep biting it for a long time. *The dog was gnawing on a bone.*
▲ Say **naw**.

gnome gnomes noun
a little old man in fairy tales who lives underground. Gnomes usually have long beards and pointed hats.
▲ Say **nome**.

goal goals noun
1 A goal is the place where you have to make the ball go to score points in games such as soccer or hockey.
2 A goal is the point or points you score when the ball goes into the goal.
3 A goal can be something important that you want to do in your life. *My goal is to run the marathon in the Olympic Games.*

goat goats noun
an animal with horns and short, rough hair. A male goat is called a billy goat, a female is a nanny goat, and a young goat is a kid.

gobble gobbles gobbling gobbled verb
If you gobble food, you eat it very quickly and greedily. *She gobbled up all the cookies and cakes before anyone else could eat them.*

go-cart go-carts noun
a small, low, open racecar. *go-cart racing.*

god gods noun
a being that people believe controls them and nature. Some people pray to many different gods. *Brahma, Vishnu, and Shiva are the three main gods of the Hindu religion.*

goggles noun
special glasses that you wear to protect your eyes from water or dust. *He wears goggles when he's making models.*

gold noun
a shiny, yellow metal that is used to make rings and other jewelry.

goldfish goldfish or goldfishes noun
a small, orange fish that you keep as a pet.

golf noun
a game that you play by using long sticks called golf clubs to hit a ball into holes around a golf course.

gong gongs noun
a round piece of metal that you hit to make a loud noise.

good better best adjective
1 If something is good, people like it. *a good story.*
2 If you are good, you do as you are told.
3 If you are good at something, you can do it well. *Chris is good at spelling.*
4 If something is good for you, it makes you healthy. *Fruit is good for you.*

good

Some words that you can use instead of good:

We need a good plumber to fix the broken pipes.
skilled, experienced

He's a good pianist.
talented

The weather is good today.
marvelous

goods noun
things that can be bought and sold.

goose geese noun
a large bird with a long neck and webbed feet that lives near water. Some geese are wild, but others are kept on farms for their eggs, meat, and feathers. A male goose is called a gander, and a young goose is a gosling.

Canada goose

barnacle goose

Egyptian goose

gorge gorges noun
a deep, narrow valley. *The river runs through the gorge.*

gorgeous adjective
very beautiful. *a gorgeous day* or *a gorgeous view of the sea.* ▲ Say **gor**-*juss*.

gorilla gorillas noun
a very big African ape with dark fur.

gossip noun
stories about others that people repeat.

government governments noun
a group of people who are in charge of a country. ▲ Say **guv**-*er-ment*.

governor governors noun
the person that the people of a state elect as their leader.

gown gowns noun
1 a long dress that women wear at special times. *a ball gown.*
2 a long, loose piece of clothing that judges or graduates wear.

grab grabs grabbing grabbed verb
If you grab something, you take it quickly and roughly. *The robber grabbed the money and ran away.*

graceful adjective
beautiful or pleasing. *She is a graceful ice-skater.*

grade grades noun
a mark that a teacher gives you to show how good your work is. *My grades were great. My teacher gave me an A.*

gradual adjective
If something is gradual, it happens slowly and steadily. *I'm making gradual progress at learning to swim.*

graduate graduates graduating graduated verb
to pass tests and get a diploma from a school or college.

graffiti noun
writing and drawing on walls in public places. ▲ Say *gra*-**fee**-*tee*.

grain grains noun
1 Grain is the seeds of plants, such as wheat and rice, that we eat.
2 Grains are tiny, hard pieces of something such as salt, sugar, or sand.

grandchild grandchildren noun
A grandchild is the child of a person's son or daughter.

grandparent grandparents noun
The mother or father of your mother or father.

grape grapes noun
a small green, red, or black fruit that grows in bunches on a vine. Wine is made from grapes.

grapefruit grapefruit noun
a large, round yellow fruit that is similar to an orange but not as sweet.

graph graphs noun
a diagram that shows how numbers and amounts compare with each other. *We drew a graph to show how much rain there was in each month of the year.*

grasp grasps grasping grasped verb
If you grasp something, you hold it tightly. *She grasped the child's hand as they crossed the street.*

grass grasses noun
the thin, green leaves that cover fields and lawns. *Sheep, horses, and cows eat grass.*
grassy adjective.

grasshopper grasshoppers noun
a jumping insect with strong back legs and two pairs of wings. Grasshoppers feed on plants.

grate grates grating grated verb
If you grate food, you rub it over a metal tool called a grater to shred it into very small pieces. *grated cheese.*
● A word that sounds like **grate** is **great**.

grateful adjective
If you feel grateful to people, you want to thank them because they have done something for you. *I was very grateful to her for finding my purse.*
■ The opposite is **ungrateful.**
gratefully adverb.

grave graves noun
a hole in the ground where a dead person is buried.

grave graver gravest adjective
very serious and important. *a grave mistake* or *a grave illness.*

gravel noun
small stones that are used to cover roads and driveways.

gravity noun
the natural force that pulls everything down toward Earth.

gravy noun
a sauce made from the juices that come out of meat when you cook it.

graze grazes grazing grazed verb
1 When animals graze, they move around eating grass. *The sheep were grazing in the field.*
2 If you graze your skin, you cut it slightly by scraping it against something. *When she fell over, she grazed her knee badly.*

71

grease noun
thick oil or soft fat. *You will need very hot water to wash the grease off those dirty pots.*
greasy adjective.

great greater greatest adjective
1 very good. *a great movie.*
2 very important. *a great king.*
3 very big. *a great crowd of people.*
● A word that sounds like **great** is **grate**.

greedy greedier greediest adjective
People who are greedy want more of something than they really need. *Don't be so greedy—leave some cake for your brother and sister.*

greenhouse greenhouses noun
a building made of glass and used for growing plants.

greet greets greeting greeted verb
When you greet somebody, you do something friendly when you meet them, such as saying "hello", smiling, or shaking hands. *She greeted me by shaking hands.*

greeting greetings noun
words such as "hello," "good morning," or "Happy New Year" that you say when you meet somebody.

grew past of **grow**.

grief noun
great sadness. *She was filled with grief when her dog died.*

grill grills grilling grilled verb
If you grill food, you cook it on metal bars under or over strong heat. *We grilled hot dogs outside.*
grill noun.

grin grins grinning grinned verb
If you grin, you have a big smile. *She grinned at me when I said hello.*
grin noun.

grind grinds grinding ground verb
If you grind something, you crush it into tiny pieces or into a powder. *grinding peppercorns.*

grip grips gripping gripped verb
If you grip something, you hold it very firmly. *She gripped the branch and swung from it.*

groan groans groaning groaned verb
To groan is to make a long, deep sound because you are unhappy or in pain.

groom grooms noun
1 a person who takes care of horses.
2 a man on his wedding day.

groom grooms grooming groomed verb
If you groom an animal, you clean and brush it. *The children are grooming their horse before riding it.*

groundbreaking adjective
achieving something new. *a groundbreaking discovery.*

grouchy grouchier grouchiest adjective
If you are grouchy, you are in a bad mood and you feel like grumbling.

groove grooves noun
a long, thin line that is cut into a flat surface.

ground grounds noun
1 The ground is what you walk on when you are outside. *We sat on the ground to eat our picnic lunch.*
2 a piece of land that is used for something special. *a camping ground.*

ground past of **grind**.

group groups noun
1 a number of people or things that are together in one place. *A group of children stood near the corner.*
2 a group of musicians who play or sing together.

grow grows growing grew grown verb
1 When something grows, it gets bigger or more. *The puppy is growing very fast* or *The crowd grew.*
2 If you grow something, you plant it so that it will develop. *Flora grew this plant from a seed.*
3 To grow also means to become. *We are all growing older.*

growl growls growling growled verb
To growl is to make the low, rough noise that a dog or a bear makes when it is angry or frightened.
growl noun.

grownup grownups noun
an adult. *Parents are grownups.*
grown-up adjective

growth noun
the result of growing. *We measured the tree's growth every month.*

grumble grumbles grumbling **grumbled** verb
If you grumble, you complain about something in an angry way. *She grumbled about having to do her homework.*

grunt grunts grunting grunted verb
To grunt is to make the short, deep, rough sound that a pig makes.

guacamole noun
a dip made from mashed avocado and seasonings. ▲ Say **gwahk**-*uh*-**moh**-*lee.*

guarantee guarantees noun
1 a promise made by the makers of something that they will fix or replace it if it breaks.
2 a promise that something will happen.
▲ Say *ga-ran-***tee**.
guarantee verb.

guard guards noun
a person who keeps somebody or something safe, or who stops people from escaping. *a Swiss guard.*

guardian
guardians noun
a person who is told by a court to take care of someone else, usually a child.

guava noun
a sweet, tropical fruit with pink flesh.

guess guesses guessing guessed verb
When you guess, you try to give an answer to something when you do not really know if it is right. *Sometimes you can guess what is inside a box by looking at its shape.*
guess noun.
Guess how much the cake weighs.

guest guests noun
a person who is staying in your home because you have invited him or her. *We have guests staying with us this weekend.* ▲ Rhymes with **best**.

guide guides guiding guided verb
If you guide people, you show them where to go or what to do. *Her job is to guide people around the city.*
▲ Rhymes with **wide**.
guide noun.

guilty adjective
1 If you are guilty, you have done something wrong. ■ The opposite is **innocent**.
2 If you feel guilty, you feel sorry because you have done something wrong. *She felt guilty for being rude to her aunt.*

guinea pig guinea pigs noun
a small, furry animal with short ears and no tail. Some people keep guinea pigs as pets.
▲ Say **gih**-*nee pig.*

guitar guitars noun
a musical instrument with six strings that you play with your fingers.

gulf gulfs noun
a big part of the sea that has land partly around it.

gull gulls noun
a large, gray or white seabird.

gulp gulps gulping gulped verb
If you gulp, you swallow something very quickly. *Susan gulped down the orange juice because she was thirsty.*

gum gums noun
1 Your gums are the firm, pink flesh around your teeth.
2 chewing gum or bubble gum.

gun guns noun
a weapon that shoots bullets. *She aimed the gun and fired at the target.*

gutter gutters noun
an open pipe along the edge of a roof for carrying away rainwater. *We cleaned leaves out of the gutters.*

gym gyms noun
a large room where you can do exercises, often using special equipment. Gym is short for **gymnasium**.

gymnast gymnasts noun
a person who does difficult and carefully controlled movements with the body in competitions. *an Olympic gymnast.*

gymnastics noun
1 exercises for your body.
2 a sport in which people do difficult and carefully controlled movements with their bodies in competitions.

habit habits noun
something that you do often, usually
without thinking about it.

habitat habitats noun
The habitat of an animal or a plant
is the kind of place where it lives.

hacienda haciendas noun
a big farm in the southwest United
States.
▲ Say *hah-see-en-dah.*

hail noun
frozen rain falling as little balls of ice.

hair hairs noun
Hair is lots of thin threads that grow
on your head and other parts of your
body. ● A word that sounds like **hair**
is **hare**.

straight, curly, and wavy hair

hairdresser hairdressers noun
a person whose job is to cut and style
people's hair.

hairy hairier hairiest adjective
covered with hair. *The book is about
a big hairy monster.*

half halves noun
one of two equal parts of something.
You can write *half* as ½. *Half of ten
is five.* or *Two halves make a whole.*

hall halls noun
1 the part just inside the door of
a house or apartment building with
doors leading to rooms.
2 a large room or a building where
events such as concerts and
meetings take place. *our town hall.*

halt halts halting halted verb
When something halts, it stops.
The truck halted at the stoplight.

halve halves halving halved verb
If you halve something, you divide it
into two equal parts. *Halve the fruit
and remove the pit.*

ham noun
meat from a hog's leg that has been
treated with salt so that it can be kept
for a long time. *a ham sandwich.*

hamburger hamburgers
noun
chopped beef pressed into a flat,
round shape and eaten in a bun.

hammer hammers noun
a tool with a heavy part at one
end that you use for hitting nails
into things.

hammock hammocks noun
a bed made of canvas or
pieces of rope that is
hung at each end from
something such as a
tree or post.

hamster hamsters noun
a small animal that is often kept as a
pet. It is similar to a large mouse with
a very short tail. Hamsters can store
food in pouches inside their cheeks.

hand hands noun
Your hand is the part of your body at
the end of your arm.

hand hands handing handed verb
If you hand something to somebody,
you give it to him or her.

handicap noun
something that makes it more difficult
to do things. *Being tall can be a
handicap for getting into small cars.*

handkerchief handkerchiefs noun
a small square of cloth or paper tissue
that you use for blowing your nose.
▲ Say **hang-***kur-chief.*

handle handles noun
1 The handle of something such as a
cup or a bag is the part that you take
in your hand to carry it or pick it up.
2 The handle of a door is the lever or
knob that you move with your hand
to open and close it.

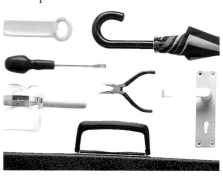

different types of handles

handlebar handlebars noun
the curved bar at the front of a bicycle
or motorcycle that you use for steering.

handsome adjective
A man who is handsome has an
attractive face.

handwriting noun
Your handwriting is the way that you
write with a pen or pencil.

hang hangs hanging hung verb
If you hang something somewhere, you
fasten it from the top to something
above it. *Hang your coat in the closet.*

hang glider hang gliders noun
a kind of large kite with a harness underneath, in which you fly through the air in the sport of hang-gliding.

happen happens happening happened verb
1 Something that happens or occurs takes place. *The accident happened because she was not paying attention.*
2 If you happen to do something, you do it by chance. *I happened to find your ball when I was in the garden.*

happy happier happiest adjective
If you are happy, you feel good because something nice has happened or because you are enjoying yourself. ■ The opposite is **unhappy** or **sad**.
happily adverb, happiness noun.

happy

Some words that you can use instead of happy:

I'm happy that I've finished my homework.
contented, pleased, glad

They are happy with their wedding presents.
delighted, pleased, thrilled

Christmas is a happy time of year.
merry, cheerful

harbor harbors noun
an area of sea by the coast where ships can tie up.

hard harder hardest adjective
1 If something is hard, you cannot break, cut, or bend it easily. *Stones, nuts, and bolts are hard.* ■ The opposite is **soft**.
2 hard to do. *a hard puzzle.* ■ The opposite is **easy**.

hard harder hardest adverb
a lot. *Stephanie has worked very hard this semester.*

hard disk hard disks noun
the part inside a computer where a large amount of information is stored.

harden hardens hardening hardened verb
When something hardens, it becomes hard. *Hold the pieces together until the glue has hardened.* ■ The opposite is **soften**.

hare hares noun
an animal that looks like a large rabbit with long ears and long legs. ● A word that sounds like **hare** is **hair**.

harm harms harming harmed verb
1 If you harm people, you hurt them. *The dog won't harm you.*
2 If you harm something, you damage it.

harmful adjective
If something is harmful, it could hurt you or make you sick. *Looking straight at the Sun is harmful to your eyes.* ■ The opposite is **harmless**.

harmless adjective
If something is harmless, it will not hurt you. *Our dog is harmless—it wouldn't bite anybody.* ■ The opposite is **harmful**.

harmony harmonies noun
a group of musical notes that sound nice when you hear them together.

harness harnesses noun
1 a set of straps and metal parts that go around a horse's head or body so that you can control it.
2 a set of straps for fastening something, such as a parachute, to a person's body.

harp harps noun
a musical instrument. It has a large frame with strings that you play (pluck) with your fingers.
harpist noun.

harsh harsher harshest adjective
1 If people behave in a harsh way, they are cruel or unkind. *That was a very harsh punishment.*
2 A harsh winter is very cold and difficult.
3 Harsh sounds are loud and unpleasant. *a harsh voice.*

harvest harvests noun
the time when farmers pick or cut their crops because they are ripe.

hat hats noun
a covering that you wear on your head.

hatch hatches hatching hatched verb
When a baby bird or other animal hatches, it breaks out of its egg.

hatchet hatchets noun
a small ax.

hate hates hating hated verb
If you hate somebody or something, you have a very strong feeling of not liking it. *I hate getting up early in the morning.* ■ The opposite is **love**.

haunted adjective
If a place is haunted, there is supposed to be a ghost there. *a haunted house.* ▲ Say **hawn**-*ted*.

hawk hawks noun
a large bird with a curved beak and strong claws that eats other birds and small animals.

hay noun
grass that has been cut and dried and is used to feed horses and cattle in the winter months.

hazard hazards noun
a danger or risk. *Patches of oil on the sea from leaking tankers are a hazard to seabirds and fish.*
hazardous adjective.

head heads noun
1 Your head is the top part of you.
2 the person who is in charge of a group. *the head of a large company.*
▲ Rhymes with **bed**.

headache headaches noun
a pain in your head.

headlight headlights noun
the lights on the front of a car.

headline headlines noun
words in larger print at the top of a story in a newspaper.

DAILY GLOBE
BOOKS STILL REIGN SUPREME!

headphones noun
small speakers for a stereo or radio that fit in your ears. Headphones let you hear music and other sounds without other people hearing them.

headquarters noun
the building where the people in charge of an organization work.

head start noun
an advantage that you get when you are allowed to start a race first.

heal heals healing healed verb
If something heals, it gets better after being sick or injured. ● A word that sounds like **heal** is **heel**.

health noun
Your health is how well you are. If your health is bad, you are sick. If your health is good, you are well.
▲ Say **helth**.

healthy healthier healthiest adjective
1 If you are healthy, you are fit and well.
2 Something that is healthy is good for you and helps you stay well. *Fresh fruit and vegetables are healthy foods.*
▲ Say **helth-y**. ■ The opposite is **unhealthy**.

heap heaps noun
a large, messy pile of things. *She left her clothes in a heap on the floor.*

hear hears hearing heard verb
When you hear a sound, you notice it through your ears. ● A word that sounds like **hear** is **here**.

heart hearts noun
Your heart is the part of you, inside your chest, that pumps the blood around your body.
▲ Say **hart**.

heat noun
warmth. *I can feel the heat from the Sun on my skin.*

heat heats heating heated verb
If you heat something, you make it hot. *He heated up his leftovers.*

heave heaves heaving heaved verb
If you heave something somewhere, you use a lot of energy to lift, push, or pull it. *Ben and Joe heaved the rope together in a tug-of-war.*

heavy heavier heaviest adjective
Something that is heavy weighs a lot. *The suitcase was too heavy for me to lift.*
■ The opposite is **light**.

hedge hedges noun
a line of bushes or small trees growing close together at the edge of a garden, yard, or road.

heed heeds heeding heeded verb
If you heed, you pay close attention. *Heed my advice.*

heel heels noun
1 Your heel is the back part of your foot.
2 the part of a shoe or boot that is under the back part of your foot.
● A word that sounds like **heel** is **heal**.

height heights noun
The height of something is how high it is from the bottom to the top.
▲ Rhymes with **kite**.

held past of hold.

helicopter helicopters noun
an aircraft without wings that is kept in the air by long blades that are attached to its roof and spin very fast.

hello interjection
People say hello when they answer the phone or meet and greet others.
■ The opposite is **goodbye**.

helmet helmets noun
a hard hat that protects your head.

help helps helping helped verb
If you help people, you make it easier for them to do something. *Amy helped me with my math homework.*
help noun.

helpful adjective
1 If you are helpful, you do what you can to help other people.
2 Something that is helpful is useful. *Thank you for your helpful advice.*

helpless adjective
If you are helpless, you cannot take care of yourself. *A baby is completely helpless when it is born.*

hem hems noun
the edge of a piece of material that is folded over and sewn flat in order to make it neat.

hen hens noun
1 a female chicken that lays eggs that we eat.
2 any female bird.

herb herbs noun
a plant that we use to give flavor to food or to make medicines. *Marjoram, yarrow, and mint are all herbs.*

yarrow

marjoram

herd herds noun
a large group of animals of one kind that live together. *Elephants live in herds.*

hero heroes noun
1 a person who is very brave or very good.
2 the main male character in a book, play, or movie.

heroine heroines noun
1 a woman who is very brave or very good.
2 the main female character in a book, play, or movie. ▲ Say **hair-oh-in**.

heron herons noun
a large, usually gray, bird with long legs and a long neck. Herons live near water and eat fish.

hesitate hesitates hesitating hesitated verb
If you hesitate, you stop for a short time before you do something, often because you are not sure what to do. *She hesitated before answering me.*
hesitation noun.

hexagon hexagons noun
a flat shape with six sides.
◆ Look at page 143.
hexagonal adjective.

hibernate hibernates hibernating hibernated verb
When an animal hibernates, it stays in a deep sleep all through the winter. *Bears hibernate.*
hibernation noun.

a dormouse hibernating

hiccup hiccups noun
a sudden, short breath in and a noise that sounds like "hic" that you cannot help making. You sometimes get hiccups when you eat or drink too quickly.
hiccup verb.

hickory hickories noun
a tall tree with hard wood and nuts that taste good.

hide hides hiding hid hidden verb
1 If you hide, you go where nobody can find you.
2 If you hide something, you put it where nobody can find it.

hieroglyphic adjective
a kind of writing that uses pictures instead of letters to make up words. Hieroglyphic writing was used in ancient Egypt. ▲ Say **hie-ro-glif-ik**.
hieroglyph noun.

high higher highest adjective
1 Something that is high goes up a long way from the bottom to the top.
2 High also means a long way above the ground. ■ The opposite is **low**.

high school high schools noun
a school for students from the ninth through the twelfth grades.

hijack hijacks hijacking hijacked verb
If people hijack a plane or ship, they take control of it by threatening the passengers and crew and then try to make it go where they want it to.
hijacker noun.

hill hills noun
an area of land that is higher than the land around it.

Hindu Hindus noun
a person who follows a religion called Hinduism. Hindus worship several different gods and believe that after you die, you are born again in a different body.

hinge hinges noun
a piece of metal that holds a door to its frame at one side, so that it can open and close.

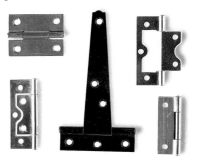

hint hints hinting hinted verb
When you hint, you let somebody know something without actually saying exactly what you mean.

hip hips noun
Your hips are at the sides of your body between your waist and the top of your legs.

hippopotamus hippopotamuses noun
a large animal with a thick, dark-gray skin and very short legs. Hippopotamuses live by lakes and rivers in Africa and are sometimes called **hippos** for short.
Hippopotomuses have only four toes on each foot.

hire hires hiring hired verb
If you hire someone, you pay him or her to work for you for a certain time. *Dad hired a person to paint our house.*

hispanic hispanics noun
an American who has ancestors from Spain, Mexico, or Latin America.

history noun
the study of things that happened in the past. *At school we are learning about the history of our state.*
historical adjective.

hit hits hitting hit verb
When you hit something, you touch it quickly and with force. *I hit the ball with the bat.*

hive hives noun
a special box for bees to live in where you can collect their honey.

hoarse hoarser hoarsest adjective
If you are hoarse, your voice sounds rough. *He yelled at the top of his voice all through the game until he was hoarse.* A word that sounds like **hoarse** is **horse.**

hobble hobbles hobbling hobbled verb
If you hobble, you walk with difficulty because your feet hurt. *He was hobbling because his feet were covered in blisters.*

hobby hobbies noun
something that you enjoy doing in your spare time. *My hobbies are swimming, reading, and collecting shells.*

hockey noun
a game played outdoors, or indoors on ice, by two teams of eleven players who try to get a puck or ball into a goal by hitting it with a long, curved stick.

hog hogs noun
a grown-up pig.

hold holds holding held verb
1 If you hold something, you have it in your hand or hands. *I held up the picture so that my sister could see it.*
2 If a container holds a certain amount, it can have that amount in it but no more. *A one-pint measuring cup holds up to 16 ounces.*

hole holes noun
a gap or space in something. *These jeans have a hole in the knee.* A word that sounds like **hole** is **whole**.

holiday holidays noun
a time when you do not have to go to school or work. *New Year's Day is a holiday in many countries.*

hollow adjective
Something that is hollow has an empty space inside it. The opposite is **solid**.

holly noun
a tree that has red berries and leaves with sharp points.

holy holier holiest adjective
Something that is holy is very special to a particular religion.

homage noun
an act that is performed to show respect to someone.

home homes noun
Your home is the place where you live.

homeless adjective
a homeless person has no place to live.

homeroom homerooms noun
a schoolroom where you often sit before classes start.

homework noun
work that a teacher gives to students to do at home.

honest adjective
If you are honest, you tell the truth. Say **on**-*est*. The opposite is **dishonest**.

honey noun
a sweet, sticky food that is made by bees. Rhymes with **funny**.

hood hoods noun
a part of a coat or jacket that you can pull over your head.

hoof hooves or hoofs noun
the hard covering on the foot of some animals, such as a horse or deer.

hoof   horseshoe

hoof prints

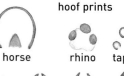

horse   rhino   tapir

water
deer   deer   wild boar   reindeer   elk

hook hooks noun
a curved piece of metal or plastic that is used for hanging things on or for holding or fastening things.

hoop hoops noun
a large ring made of wood, metal, or plastic.

hoot hoots hooting hooted verb
1 To hoot is to make the long "oo" sound that an owl makes.
2 When people hoot, they make a loud noise to show dislike for someone or something. *The crowd hooted loudly at the opposing team.*

hop hops hopping hopped verb
1 If you hop, you jump on one leg.
2 When an animal or insect hops, it moves along by jumping. *The frog hopped away.*

hope hopes hoping hoped verb
If you hope something will happen, you want it to happen and you think that it probably will. *I hope you will be able to come to my party.*
hope noun, **hopeless** adjective.

hopeful adjective
If you are hopeful, you think that what you want will probably happen. *The police are hopeful that they will soon be able to solve the crime.*

horizon horizons noun
the line in the far distance where the land or the sea seems to meet the sky.
▲ Say hor-**eye**-zin.

horizontal adjective
Something that is horizontal goes from side to side, parallel to the ground, not up and down. *The top of the table is horizontal.* ■ The opposite is **vertical**.
horizontally adverb.

horn horns noun
1 Horns are the hard, pointed, bony parts that grow out of the head of some animals, such as cows, goats, and some sheep.

2 A horn is a brass musical instrument that you blow into to make sounds.
3 A horn is also an instrument in a car or other vehicle that the driver uses to make a loud noise as a warning to other drivers or pedestrians.

horrible adjective
terrible or very unpleasant. *What a horrible thing to say!*
horribly adverb.

horror noun
1 a feeling that you get when you are very shocked and upset at something terrible. *We were filled with horror at the news of the famine in Africa.*
2 A horror story is a story that is meant to frighten you.

horse horses noun
a large animal with a long tail and a mane. People ride horses or use them to pull carts or carriages. A female horse is called a mare, a male horse is a stallion, and a young horse is a foal.
● A word that sounds like **horse** is **hoarse**.

horse chestnut noun
a large tree with white flowers that produces a large nut.

hose hoses noun
a long, plastic pipe that is used for spraying water. *You can use a hose to water the garden.*

hospital hospitals noun
a building where doctors and nurses take care of people who are sick or injured.

Horses

Przewalski's horse

wild donkey

Clydesdale horse

Arab stallion

Shetland pony

VOCABULARY

aids
the signals that a rider gives to tell the horse or pony what to do.

bit
the metal or rubber device attached to the bridle and placed in the horse or pony's mouth.

bridle
the part of saddle that is placed over a horse or pony's head and to which the bit and reins are attached.

colt
a male foal.

filly
a female foal.

gait
the pace of a horse or pony.

Houses

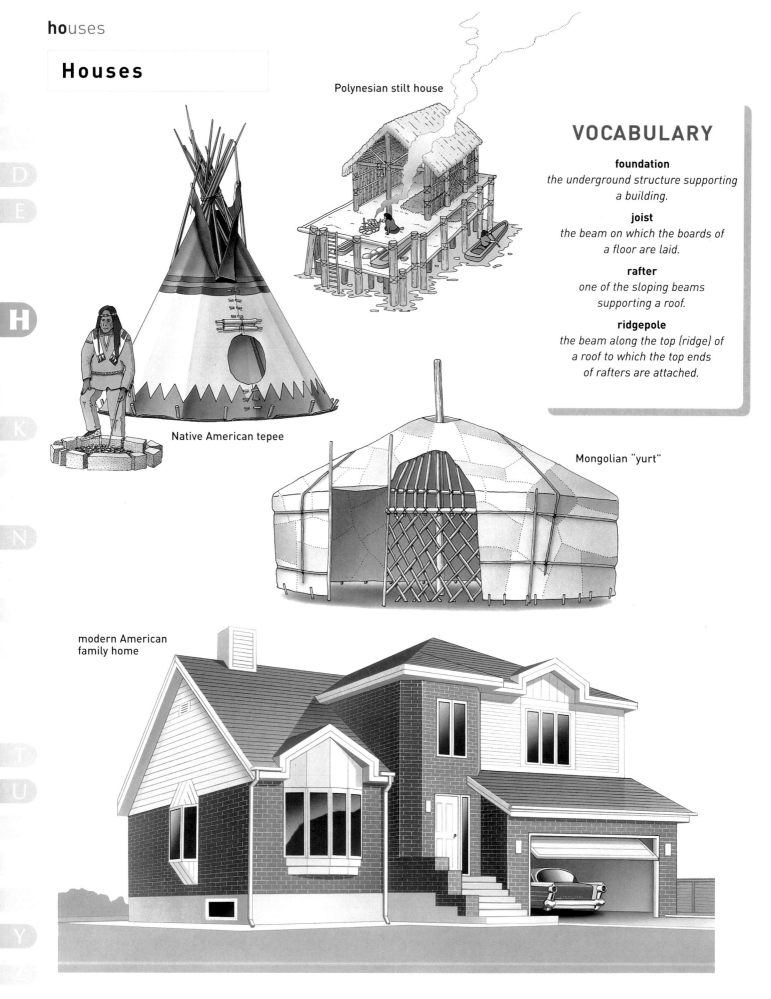

Polynesian stilt house

VOCABULARY

foundation
the underground structure supporting a building.

joist
the beam on which the boards of a floor are laid.

rafter
one of the sloping beams supporting a roof.

ridgepole
the beam along the top (ridge) of a roof to which the top ends of rafters are attached.

Native American tepee

Mongolian "yurt"

modern American family home

80

host hosts noun
a person who invites guests and takes care of them when they arrive.

hostage hostages noun
a person who is held prisoner by those who threaten to hurt or kill the prisoner if they do not get what they want.

hot hotter hottest adjective
1 Something that is hot has a high temperature. *Careful! That pan is very hot!*
2 Hot foods have a strong taste and make your mouth feel like it is burning when you eat them. *Some spices are hot.*

hotel hotels noun
a building with bedrooms where people pay to stay.

hour hours noun
a period of 60 minutes. There are 24 hours in a day. ▲ Rhymes with **tower**.
● A word that sounds like **hour** is **our.**

house houses noun
a building where people live.
◆ Look at page 80.

House of Representatives noun
One of the two branches of the U.S. Congress. Its members serve for two years.

hover hovers hovering hovered verb
If something hovers, it stays in one place in the air. *A rescue helicopter hovered over the boat.*

howl howls howling howled verb
When an animal howls, it makes a long, loud, crying sound.

hug hugs hugging hugged verb
When you hug people, you put your arms around them and hold them tight.
hug noun.

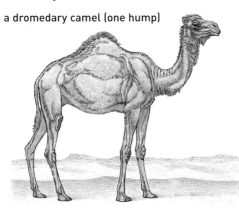

huge adjective
very, very big. ■ The opposite is **tiny**.

hum hums humming hummed verb
When you hum, you make a singing sound with your lips closed. *He was humming a tune while he worked.*

human humans noun
a person. *A lot of animals are afraid of humans.*

humid adjective
Humid weather is hot, sticky, and damp. ▲ Say **hyoo**-*mid*.

humor noun
the ability to make people laugh or to see when something is funny. *She has a good sense of humor.* ▲ Say **hyoo**-*mer*.
humorous adjective.

hump humps noun
1 a large, round lump on a camel's back, for example.
2 a bump in the road.

a dromedary camel (one hump)

a Bactrian camel (two humps)

hung past of **hang**.

hungry hungrier hungriest adjective
If you are hungry, you want to eat.
hunger noun.

hunt hunts hunting hunted verb
1 To hunt is to chase and catch wild animals to kill them, either to eat or as a sport.
2 If you hunt for something, you look everywhere for it. *I've been hunting for my watch all morning.*
hunt noun.

hurl hurls hurling hurled verb
If you hurl something, you throw it as

far and as hard as you can. *She hurled the stone into the lake.*

hurricane hurricanes noun
a powerful storm with winds that are strong enough to blow down trees or damage roofs.

hurry hurries hurrying hurried verb
If you hurry, you try to get somewhere or do something as quickly as possible. *You'd better hurry, or you'll miss the game.*
hurry noun.

hurt hurts hurting hurt verb
1 If you hurt yourself, you cause pain to a part of your body. *Did you hurt yourself when you fell over?*
2 If a part of your body hurts, it feels pain. *I have a bruised knee. It really hurts.*
3 To hurt people is also to upset them. *I think she was hurt when you didn't invite her to your party.*

husband husbands noun
A woman's husband is the man that she is married to.

hut huts noun
a small building, usually with one room.

hutch hutches noun
a wooden and wire cage for a rabbit.

hydrogen noun
a gas that is lighter than air. Oxygen and hydrogen together make up water.

hyphen hyphens noun
a mark in writing (-) to show that two parts of a word belong together. *self-esteem.*
▲ Say **hie**-*fen*.

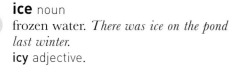

ice noun
frozen water. *There was ice on the pond last winter.*
icy adjective.

iceberg icebergs noun
a huge piece of ice floating in the sea. Icebergs are dangerous to ships because most of the ice is under the water where you cannot see it.

ice cream noun
a sweet, frozen food that is made from cream or milk.

ice-skating noun
sliding on ice in special boots called ice skates that have thin, metal blades on the bottom.

icicle icicles
noun
a hanging, pointed piece of ice made of dripping water that has frozen.

icing noun
a smooth, sweet covering for cakes that is made of sugar mixed with other things; frosting.

icy icier iciest adjective
very cold. *an icy wind.*

idea ideas noun
1 a new thought about something. *I have got an idea. Let's go to the beach!*
2 a picture in your mind. *The movie gives you a good idea of what India is like.*

ideal adjective
If something is ideal, it is perfect and just what you want. *The weather was ideal for a picnic.*
ideally adverb.

identical adjective
exactly the same. *Ben and Jason are identical twins.*

identify identifies identifying
identified verb
If you identify others, you know who or what they are and can name them. *Can you identify this wildflower and that bird?*
identification noun.

idle adjective
lazy, or not working.

igloo igloos noun
a round house built by Inuit people out of blocks of hard snow and ice.

ignorant adjective
not knowing about something.
ignorance noun.

ignore ignores ignoring ignored verb
If you ignore people, you take no notice of them. *She ignored me when I said hello.*

ill adjective
If you are ill, you are sick. *I didn't go to school today because I was ill.*

illegal adjective
If something is illegal, it is not allowed by law. ▪ The opposite is **legal**.

illness illnesses noun
something such as measles or a cold that makes you feel unwell.

illusion illusions noun
something that you think you can see, but that is not really there.

illustration illustrations noun
a picture in a book or magazine. *This dictionary has lots of illustrations.*

image images noun
1 a picture on paper, on a screen, or in a mirror. *A ghostly image appeared in the mirror.*
2 a picture in your mind. *I have an image of how I want to look when I'm a grownup.*

imaginary adjective
Something that is imaginary is not real and exists only in your mind. *I read a story about a boy who had an imaginary friend.* ▲ Say i-**maj**-in-ar-ee.

imagination noun
Your imagination is your ability to think of new ideas or create pictures in your mind. *Use your imagination and draw whatever you want.*
imaginative adjective.

imagine imagines imagining
imagined verb
When you imagine something, you create a picture of it in your mind. *Can you imagine living in a cave like people did in the Stone Age?*

imitate imitates imitating
imitated verb
If you imitate others, you copy the way that they talk or act. *Paul is imitating Nick taking a photograph of the magician.*
imitation noun
It is not a real Christmas tree, but a plastic imitation.

immediately adverb
now. *The ambulance arrived immediately after we called it.*

immigrant immigrants noun
a person who comes to live in one country from another country.

immune adjective
If you are immune to a disease, you cannot catch it.

impatient adjective
If you are impatient, you do not like waiting for things. ■ The opposite is **patient**.
impatience noun.

important adjective
1 If something is important, it matters a lot. *It is important to look both ways before you cross the street.*
2 One who is important has power. *Our president is an important man.*
importance noun.

impossible adjective
If something is impossible, you cannot do it or it cannot happen. ■ The opposite is **possible**.

impress impresses impressing impressed verb
If you impress people, they think that what you have done is very good. *Her drawings impressed us.*

impression impressions noun
1 thoughts and feelings that you have about somebody or something. *My first impressions of the new school were that it was very large and noisy.*

2 If you make an impression on people, they remember what you are like and what you have done. *The ballet dancer made a great impression on all of us.*

impressive adjective
If something is impressive, people admire it, especially because it is very good or very big. *an impressive fort.*

improve improves improving improved verb
If something improves, it gets better.
improvement noun.

include includes including included verb
To include is to have somebody or something as part of a group or as part of the whole thing. *Dan was pleased to be included on the football team.*

inconvenient adjective
If something is inconvenient, it is hard to do or use. ■ The opposite is **convenient**.

increase increases increasing increased verb
If something increases, it gets bigger in size or amount. ■ The opposite is **decrease**.
increase noun.

incredible adjective
If something is incredible, it is difficult to believe. *an incredible story.*

incubator incubators noun
1 a container where babies who are born early are kept until they grow bigger and stronger.
2 a container where eggs are kept warm until they hatch.

independent adjective
If you are independent, you do not want or need help from other people.
independence noun.

index indexes noun
a list of words from A to Z at the end of a book. The index lists things in the book and where they are.

Indian Indians noun
a person from India or South America.

indigestion noun
an uncomfortable feeling that you have in your stomach when you have eaten too much or eaten the wrong food.

individual adjective
to do with one person or thing, not an entire group. *individual voters.*

individual individuals noun
one person. *Every individual is different.*

indoors adverb
inside a building. *We went indoors when it started to rain.* ■ The opposite is **outdoors**.

industry industries noun
the work of making things in factories. *the car industry.*
industrial adjective.

infant infants noun
a baby or young child.

infection infections noun
sickness that is caused by germs. *a throat infection.*

infectious adjective
If an illness is infectious, it travels easily from one person to another. *Measles is a very infectious disease.*

inflate inflates inflating inflated verb
If you inflate something such as a balloon or a tire, you blow it up with air or gas.
inflatable adjective.

influence noun
If somebody or something has an influence over you, they have a certain effect on you so that you change the

way you think or act. *My parents don't like me to play with Louis because they say that he is a bad influence on me.* **influence** verb, **influential** adjective.

inform informs informing
informed verb
If you inform people about something, you tell them about it. *The teacher informed us that there would be a history test next week.*

information noun
the facts about something. *This dictionary gives you information about words and how to spell them.*

ingredient ingredients noun
Ingredients are all the things that you put in when you make something. *The ingredients for making a cake are butter, sugar, flour, and eggs.*

inhabitant inhabitants noun
The inhabitants of a place are the people or animals that live there. *The inhabitants of the island are mainly fishermen and their families.* **inhabit** verb.

initial initials noun
the first letters of each of your names. *Tom Jackson's initials are T.J.*

injection injections noun
If a doctor or nurse gives you an injection, he or she puts medicine into your body through a needle. **inject** verb.

injure injures injuring injured verb
If you injure yourself, you hurt a part of your body. *He injured his leg playing football.* **injury** noun.

ink noun
a colored liquid that is used for writing or printing. *The words on this page were printed with ink.*

inland adjective, adverb
toward the middle of a country, away from the sea. *an inland lake.*

inner adjective
1 in the middle of a place. *He lives in the inner city.*
2 inside something. *A bicycle tire has an inner tube.*
■ The opposite is **outer**.

innocent adjective
If you are innocent, you have not done anything wrong. *The police have accused him of stealing the money, but he says that he is innocent.*
■ The opposite is **guilty**.
innocence noun.

inquire inquires inquiring
inquired verb
If you inquire about something, you ask about it. *We inquired about the cost of flights to Dallas.*
inquiry noun
an official inquiry into the disaster.

insect insects noun
a small creature with six legs and a body that is divided into three sections. Many insects have wings. *Ants, grasshoppers, and butterflies are insects.*

insert inserts inserting inserted verb
If you insert a thing into something else, you put it inside it. *She inserted the key into the lock and opened the door.*

insist insists insisting
insisted verb
If you insist on doing something, you say very firmly that you want to do it so that no one can stop you. *Eleanor insisted on wearing her new sneakers.*
insistence noun.

inspect inspects inspecting
inspected verb
to look at something carefully.
inspection noun.

instant adjective
If something is instant, it happens very quickly or you can make it very quickly.

instead adverb
in the place of somebody or something else. *I don't like ice cream. May I have fruit instead?*

instinct instincts noun
something that makes people and animals do things without having to think or learn about them. *Birds build their nests by instinct.*

instructions noun
words that tell you how to do something. *She gave us instructions on how to look after the puppies.*

instrument instruments noun
1 a thing that is used for doing a special job. *A telescope is an instrument for looking at things, such as stars.*
2 A musical instrument is something that you play to make music. *Recorders and pianos are instruments.*

telescope

recorder

insult insults insulting
insulted verb
If somebody insults you, he or she upsets you by saying rude things to you.
insult noun.

integrate integrates integrating
integrated verb
to open something like a school to all people of all races.

intelligent adjective
A person who is intelligent is able to learn and understand things quickly. **intelligence** noun.

intend intends intending intended verb
If you intend to do something, you plan to do it. *What do you intend to do now?* **intention** noun.
My intention is to pass the class.

interest interests interesting interested verb
If something interests you, you like it and want to know more about it. *Football doesn't interest Mom at all.* **interesting** adjective.

interior noun
The interior of something is the part inside it. *The interior of the room was dark and gloomy.*

international adjective
If something is international, it has to do with more than one country. *an international flight.*

Internet noun
a system of networks that connects computers around the world.

interrupt interrupts interrupting interrupted verb
If you interrupt people, you stop them while they are saying or doing something. *Please don't interrupt me.* **interruption** noun.

intersection intersections noun
the place where streets cross.

interview interviews noun
a meeting when you answer questions about yourself. *The senator gave a television interview.*

intestine intestines noun
Your intestines are the long tubes inside your body that carry food to and from your stomach.

introduce introduces introducing introduced verb
If you introduce two people who have never met before, you tell each other's names so that they can get to know one another. *Tim introduced me to Bob.* **introduction** noun.

Inuit Inuits noun
a person or a people whose ancestors were the first people who lived in Alaska or the northern part of Canada.

invade invades invading invaded verb
When an army invades, it goes into another country to attack it. **invasion** noun.

invent invents inventing invented verb
If you invent something, you make something that has never been made or thought of before. **invention** noun.

inventor inventors noun
a person who invents something.

investigate investigates investigating investigated verb
When you investigate something, you try to find out all about it. *The police investigated the accident.* **investigation** noun.

invisible adjective
If something is invisible, you cannot see it.
■ The opposite is **visible**.

invitation invitations noun
If somebody gives you an invitation, the person writes or speaks to you to ask you to go somewhere.

invite invites inviting invited verb
If you invite people, you ask them to go somewhere with you.

involve involves involving involved verb
1 If you are involved in something, you take part in it. *Are you involved in the school play?*
2 If something is involved in an activity, it is part of it. *Tennis involves a lot of skill.*

iron noun
1 Iron is a strong, hard metal that is found in rocks. Iron is used for making tools, gates, and other things.
2 An iron is an electric tool that you use to get wrinkles out of clothes.
▲ Say eye-*urn*.

irritate irritates irritating irritated verb
If something irritates you, it annoys you. **irritation** noun.

Islam noun
the religion that Muslims follow.

island islands noun
a piece of land with water all around it.
▲ Say eye-*land*.

itch itches itching itched verb
When a part of your body itches, you have a feeling that you want to scratch that part of your skin. **itch** noun, **itchy** adjective.

ivy ivies noun
a plant with shiny pointed leaves that stay green in the winter. Ivy climbs up walls and trees.

Jj

jacket jackets noun
a short coat.

jack-o'-lantern jack-o'-lanterns noun
a pumpkin with a face cut into it. *Roy put a candle in the jack-o'-lantern.*

jackrabbit jackrabbits noun
a big rabbit with strong legs.

jaguar jaguars noun
a wildcat that has brown and yellow fur with black spots. Jaguars live in North and South America.

jail jails noun
a prison.

jam noun
1 a food made by cooking fruit with sugar. *Bill loves strawberry jam on toast.*
2 a traffic jam is a large number of vehicles that are unable to move.

jam jams jamming jammed verb
If something jams, it cannot move. *The paper has jammed in the printer.*

jar jars noun
a glass container for jam or other foods. *a jar of pickles.*

jaw jaws noun
Your jaws are the two large bones in your mouth that hold your teeth. Your jaws move up and down when you speak and eat.

jealous adjective
If you are jealous, you want what somebody else has, and it makes you angry and unhappy. *Joe was jealous of his little sister because she always seemed to get what she wanted.* ▲ Say **jel-***uss*. **jealousy** noun.

jeans noun
pants made from thick, strong cotton material called denim. ● A word that sounds like **jeans** is **genes**.

jelly jellies noun
a clear, spreadable food with a fruit flavor.

jellyfish jellyfish or jellyfishes noun
a sea animal that has a clear, round body and long tentacles that sting.

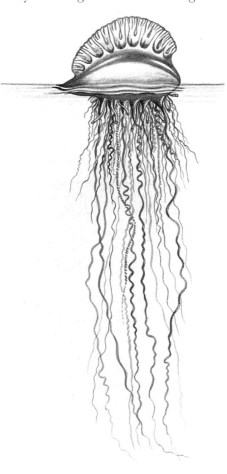

jerk jerks jerking jerked verb
To jerk is to make a sudden, sharp movement. *She jerked her hand away from the flame.*

jet jets noun
1 a fast plane with an engine that sucks air in and then forces it out at the back.
2 a fast, thin stream of liquid. *A jet of water was coming out of the burst pipe.*

Jew Jews noun
a person who belongs to the race of people who lived in Israel in ancient times or a person who follows the religion called Judaism.
Jewish adjective.

jewel jewels noun
a beautiful and valuable stone such as a diamond, ruby, or emerald.

jewelry noun
rings, bracelets, necklaces, brooches, and other things that people wear to decorate their bodies. Jewelry is often made of valuable metals, such as gold or silver, and jewels, such as diamonds or rubies.

jigsaw jigsaws noun
a puzzle made up of a lot of small pieces of wood or thick cardboard that fit together to make a picture.

job jobs noun
1 the work that a person does to earn money. *My mother is looking for a job at the moment.*
2 a piece of work that you have to do. *My sister and I were given the job of washing the car.*

jockey jockeys noun
a person who rides a horse in races.

jog jogs jogging jogged verb
If you jog, you run quite slowly, for exercise.

join joins joining joined verb
1 When you join things, you put them together. *I joined the pieces of the jigsaw puzzle.*
2 If you join a group, you become a member of it. *Maria has joined the school band.*

joint joints noun
a part of your body where two bones are joined together, such as your elbow, wrist, knee, or ankle.

joke jokes noun
something that somebody says or does to make people laugh.

journalist journalists noun
a person who writes news and stories for newspapers or television.
▲ Say jer-*na-list*.
journalism noun.

journey journeys noun
When you go on a journey, you travel from one place to another. *It's a three-hour journey by car from here to the beach.* ▲ Say jer-*nee*.

joy noun
a feeling of great happiness.
■ The opposite is **sorrow**.
joyful adjective.

Judaism noun
the religion that Jews follow.

judge judges noun
1 A judge is the person who controls what happens in a court of law and who decides what a guilty person's punishment should be.
2 a person who decides the winner in a competition.

judo noun
a sport from Japan in which two people try to throw each other to the ground using various special movements.

jug jugs noun
a large pitcher; a container with a handle and a shaped part at the top that is used for pouring liquids.

juggle juggles juggling juggled verb
If you juggle, you throw several things into the air and catch them, one after another, so that there is more than one thing in the air at once. *Chris is juggling.*
juggler noun.

juice juices noun
the liquid from fruit, vegetables, or meat. *orange juice* or *carrot juice.*
juicy adjective.

jump jumps jumping jumped verb
When you jump, you push your body quickly and suddenly up into the air.
jump noun.

jungle jungles noun
a thick forest in a tropical country.

junior adjective
younger. ■ The opposite is **senior**.

junior juniors noun
a student who is in his or her third year of high school or college.

jury juries noun
a group of 12 ordinary people in a court of law who have to hear all the evidence and decide whether the person on trial is guilty or innocent.

justice noun
a way of treating people that is both fair and right.

juvenile adjective
young.

Kk

kaleidoscope kaleidoscopes noun
a tube that you look through and see
lots of colored patterns as you turn it.
▲ Say *ku-lie-du-skope.*

kangaroo kangaroos noun
a wild animal that lives in
Australia. It has strong back
legs and moves by making
long jumps. A female
kangaroo has a kind
of pocket called a
pouch at the front
where she keeps
her baby.

a kangaroo and
its baby

karate noun
a sport from Japan in which two
people fight with their hands and feet
using special movements.
▲ Say **ku**-*rah-tee.*

kayak kayaks noun
a canoe that is covered on top. It has
a small opening where the paddler
sits. *The Inuit use kayaks.*

kennel kennels noun
a small house for a dog.

ketchup noun
a thick red sauce made with tomatoes.
*We put ketchup on our hamburgers and
french fries.*

kettle kettles noun
a container with a handle and a spout
that is used for heating water.

key keys noun
1 a piece of metal that is shaped so that
when you turn it, it locks or unlocks
something such as a door or padlock.
2 The keys of a piano are the parts
that you press when you play to
make different musical notes.
3 The keys of a computer are the
parts with letters and numbers that
you press to type.
4 The key to a map is a list that
tells you what the symbols on
the map mean.

keyboard keyboards noun
1 the part of a computer with
buttons, called keys, that have letters
and numbers on them.
2 the row of keys on a piano or other
musical instrument.
3 an electronic keyboard makes
musical sounds.

kick kicks kicking kicked verb
If you kick something, you hit it with
your foot. *Ben kicked the ball.*

kid kids noun
1 a young goat.
2 a child.

kidnap kidnaps kidnapping
kidnapped verb
When people kidnap someone, they
take them away and hide them so that
their family or friends will have to pay
money to free them.

kidney kidneys noun
Your kidneys are the two organs
inside your body that help clean
your blood.

kill kills killing killed verb
To kill somebody or something means
to make them die.

kind kinder kindest adjective
A person who is kind is friendly
and gentle and likes to help
other people.
■ The opposite is **unkind**.

kind kinds noun
a sort or type. *There are thousands of
different kinds of insects.*

kindergarten kindergartens noun
a class or a school for children who
are four to six years old.

king kings noun
A king is a man who leads his people
and who is a member of a royal family.

kiss kisses kissing kissed verb
When you kiss people, you
touch them with your lips in a
friendly way.
kiss noun.

kit kits noun
1 all the things that you need in order
to do something. *a tool kit.*
2 pieces that you put together to
make something. *a model airplane kit.*

kitchen kitchens noun
a room where food is kept and cooked.

kite kites noun
a toy that you fly in the wind. It is
made of a light frame covered with
paper or plastic, attached to a long
piece of string.

kitten kittens noun
a very young cat.

knee knees noun
Your knees are the parts in the middle of your legs where they bend. *He fell over and grazed his knee.*
▲ Say **nee**.

kneel kneels kneeling knelt or kneeled verb
to go down on your knees.
▲ Say **neel**.

knew past of **know**.
● A word that sounds like **knew** is **new**.

knife knives noun
A knife is a tool for cutting. It has a handle and a long, sharp piece of metal called a blade.
▲ Say **nife**.

knight knights noun
a soldier who wore armor and rode a horse hundreds of years ago. Knights fought in battles for their king or queen. ● A word that sounds like **knight** is **night**.

knit knits knitting knitted verb
When you knit, you use yarn and two long needles to make clothes. *My grandmother knitted this sweater for me.*
▲ Say **nit**.

knob knobs noun
1 a round handle that you use to open a door or a drawer.
2 A knob is also a button that you turn or press to make a machine work.
▲ Say **nob**.

knock knocks knocking knocked verb
1 If you knock on something such as a door, you hit it hard so that people will hear you.
2 If you knock something over, you hit it so that it falls. *I knocked over the vase and broke it.*
▲ Say **nock**.

knot knots noun
a place where a piece of string, thread, or rope is tied. *Can you undo this knot?* ● A word that sounds like **knot** is **not**.

know knows knowing knew known verb
1 If you know something, you have it in your mind and you are sure that it is true because you have learned it. *Do you know what the capital of Texas is?*
2 If you know people, you have met them before. *I know them because they are in my class.*
● A word that sounds like **know** is **no**.

knowledge noun
what you know and understand about something. *She has a good knowledge of computers.* ▲ Say **nol**-*edge*.

knuckle knuckles noun
Your knuckles are the bony parts in the middle of your fingers and where they bend. ▲ Say **nuk**-*ul*.

koala koalas noun
an animal that looks like a small bear with thick, gray fur. It lives in trees in Australia and feeds on their leaves and bark. A female koala has a kind of pocket called a pouch at the front where she keeps her baby.

Ll

label labels noun
a small piece of paper put onto something that gives you information about it. *The label on the dress gives its price and size.*

SALE

laboratory laboratories noun
a room where scientists work and do experiments using special equipment. ▲ Say **lab**-*ruh-tor-ee*.

lace noun
thin, delicate material with a pretty pattern of tiny holes in it. *a pair of lace gloves.*

laces noun
pieces of cord or string that you use to tie shoes or clothing.

lack noun
If there is a lack of something, it is missing or there is not enough of it. *The lack of rain meant that the crops did not grow well.*

ladder ladders noun
two long metal or wooden poles with bars, called rungs, between them that you can use to climb up or down. *The firefighter climbed up the ladder to rescue our cat from the tree.*

ladle ladles noun
a big, deep spoon with a long handle, used for serving soup.

ladybug ladybugs noun
a small, round beetle. Ladybugs are usually orange or red with black spots on their wings. They eat aphids, which are harmful to plants.

laid past of **lay**.

lake lakes noun
a large area of water with land all around it. *Lake Tahoe is a popular vacation spot.*

lamb lambs noun
1 a young sheep.
2 meat from a young sheep.

lame adjective
If a person or an animal is lame, it cannot walk well because its leg has been hurt. *The dog was lame in one leg.*

lamp lamps noun
an object that uses electricity, gas, or oil to give light.

land lands noun
1 the solid, dry part of the world that is not covered by sea. *The sailors were glad to be on land again after spending three months at sea.*
2 a country. *He told the children tales of the foreign lands he had visited.*

land lands landing landed verb
When a plane lands, it comes down to the ground and stops. ■ The opposite is **take off**.

lane lanes noun
1 a narrow road.
2 part of a main road or expressway that is wide enough for one car at a time. *Drivers should always signal before they change lanes.*
● A word that sounds like **lane** is **lain**.

language languages noun
the words that people use to talk and write to each other. *These books*

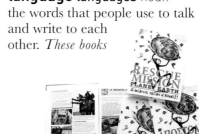

are written in different languages. ▲ Say **lang**-*wij*.

lantern lanterns noun
a light inside a glass and metal or paper case that you can carry.

lap laps noun
1 Your lap is the top half of your legs when you are sitting down.
2 one journey around a racetrack.

laptop laptops noun
a small computer that you can carry and use on your lap.

large larger largest adjective
big in size or amount. ■ The opposite is **small** or **little**.

larva larvae noun
an insect after it has come out of an egg but before it has become an adult.

laser lasers noun
a machine that produces a very powerful beam of light. People use laser beams for many different things, such as surgery.

lasso lassos or lassoes noun
a piece of rope with a large loop at one end that you can make bigger or smaller. Cowboys use lassos to catch cattle. ▲ Say **lass**-*oh*.

last adjective
coming after everybody or everything else.

late later latest adjective, adverb
If you are late, you arrive after the time that you were supposed to. ■ The opposite is **early**.

laugh laughs laughing laughed verb
When you laugh, you make sounds that show that you find something funny. *All the children laughed and laughed at the funny clowns in the circus.* ▲ Say **laff**.

laughter noun
the sound of somebody laughing.
▲ Say laff-ter.

launch launches launching
launched verb
1 When people launch a ship or boat, they make it go into the water.
2 When a rocket or missile is launched, it is sent up into the sky.

laundry laundries noun
1 dirty clothes.
2 dirty clothes that you have just washed.
3 a place where people's dirty laundry is washed. *We picked up the clean sheets and towels from the laundry.*

lava noun
hot, liquid rock that flows from a volcano when it erupts.

lavatory lavatories noun
a bathroom. ▲ Say lav-uh-tor-ee.

law laws noun
a rule or a set of rules made by a government that everybody in a country has to obey. *Stealing is against the law.*

lawn lawns noun
an area of short grass in front of a house.

lawyer lawyers noun
a person who advises people about the law and speaks for them in court. *Two lawyers defended the man who had been accused of robbery.*
▲ Say loy-yer.

lay lays laying laid verb
1 If you lay something down, you put it down carefully.
2 When you lay a table, you put knives, forks, spoons, and other things on it, ready for a meal.
3 When a hen lays an egg, it produces it.

lay past of lie.

layer layers noun
a flat piece of something that lies between two other pieces of it or that lies on the top. *A sandwich usually has three layers, two slices of bread and the filling in between—this one has five!*

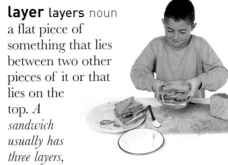

layoff layoffs noun
a time when people are dismissed from their jobs because there is not enough work for them to do.

lazy lazier laziest adjective
Somebody who is lazy does not want to work or do very much. *She gets a ride to school every morning because she's too lazy to walk.*

lead leads leading led verb
1 If you lead others, you go in front of them to show them the way. *Follow me and I'll lead you to the church.* ■ The opposite is **follow**.
2 If you lead a group of people, you are in charge of them. *The general led the troops into battle.*
3 If you are leading in a race or game, you are winning at the time. *John was leading for most of the race.* ▲ Say leed.
leader noun.

lead noun
a soft, heavy, gray metal. ▲ Rhymes with **bed**. ● A word that sounds like **lead** is **led**.

leaf leaves noun
Leaves are the thin, flat parts of a plant that grow

from the stem or from branches or twigs. Leaves are usually green.

league leagues noun
a group of sports teams. *a hockey league.*

leak leaks leaking leaked verb
If something leaks, liquid or gas escapes from it through a crack or hole. *The washing machine is leaking, and there's water all over the floor.*

lean leans leaning leaned verb
1 If you lean against something, you rest against it so that part of your weight is on it. *She leaned against the wall.*
2 If you lean somewhere, you bend your body in that direction. *Ray leaned across the table to talk to me.*

leap leaps leaping leaped or leapt verb
If you leap, you jump high or a long way. *The dog leaped over the fence.*
leap noun.

leap year leap years noun
a year that has an extra day, February 29, so that the year has 366 days instead of 365. Leap years happen once every four years.

learn learns learning learned or learnt verb
When you learn something, you find out about it or how to do it.

leash leashes noun
a long, thin piece of leather or a chain that you attach to a dog's collar to stop it from running away.

leather noun
a strong material made from an animal's skin. Leather is used to make shoes.

leave leaves leaving left verb
1 When you leave, you go away from somewhere. ■ The opposite is **arrive**.
2 When you leave something, you let it stay where it is.

led past of **lead**.
● A word that sounds like **led** is **lead**, the metal.

91

left noun, adjective
When you write the word "left," the "l" is to the left of the "e." *Carla writes with her left hand.* ■ The opposite is **right**.

leg legs noun
1 Your legs are the two long parts of your body that you use for walking.
2 The legs of a table or chair are the long, narrow parts that stand on the floor and support the top part.

legal adjective
If something is legal, the law says that you can do it. ▲ Say **lee**-*gul*. ■ The opposite is **illegal**.

legend legends noun
a story from long ago that may or may not be true. ▲ Say **lej**-*end*.

legislature legislatures noun
A legislature is elected by the people. It makes laws.

lemon lemons noun
a bright yellow fruit with sour juice.

lend lends lending lent verb
If you lend something to others, you let them have it for a while and then they give it back to you. *Can you lend me a pen?* ■ The opposite is **borrow**.

length noun
The length of something is how long it is. *My desk is three feet in length.*
lengthen verb
to make or become longer.

lens lenses noun
a curved piece of glass or transparent plastic used in a camera, a pair of glasses, a telescope, or something similar to help you see more clearly.

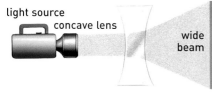
light source
concave lens
wide beam

light source
convex lens
focused beam

lent past of **lend**.

leopard leopards noun
a wild cat that has yellow fur with black spots. Leopards live in Africa and South Asia. ▲ Say **lep**-*erd*.

leotard leotards noun
a tight piece of clothing that covers you from your shoulders to your thighs, made of material that stretches. Dancers wear leotards. ▲ Say **lee**-*o-tard*.

lesson lessons noun
a period of time when you are taught something by a teacher.

let lets letting let verb
If you let somebody do something, you do not stop that person from doing it. *Will you let me try on your jewelry?*

letter letters noun
1 one of the signs that we use to write words, such as a, b, and c.
2 a written message that you send or receive by mail in an envelope.

lettuce lettuces noun
a plant with large green leaves that we eat raw in salads. ▲ Say **let**-*iss*.

level adjective
flat and not sloping.

lever levers noun
1 a long bar that you put under something heavy at one end so that you can lift the heavy object by pushing on the bar at the other end.
2 a long handle like a stick that you use to make a machine work. ▲ Say **leh**-*ver*.

liar liars noun
a person who does not tell the truth.

library libraries noun
a building or room that has books, CDs, and DVDs for people to borrow.

license licenses noun
an official piece of paper that gives you permission to do something. *a driver's license.* ▲ Say **lie**-*sense*.

lick licks licking licked verb
If you lick something, you move your tongue over it. *The dog licked my hand.*

lid lids noun
a cover for a box, pot, can, or jar.

lie lies lying lied verb
If you lie, you say something that you know is not true.
lie noun.

lie lies lying lay lain verb
When you lie down, you rest your body in a flat position—for example, on the floor or on a bed.

life lives noun
A person's or an animal's life is the time that they are alive, until death. *I'll remember today for the rest of my life.*

lifeboat lifeboats noun
a boat that is used for rescuing people who are in danger at sea.

lift lifts lifting lifted verb
If you lift something, you pick it up or raise it. *I can't lift this suitcase—it's too heavy.*

lift lifts noun
1 If somebody gives you a lift, he or she takes you somewhere in a car. *Can you give me a lift home from the party?*
2 a very happy feeling. *Your comments about my singing gave me a lift.*

light lights noun
1 Light is the bright rays that come from the Sun, the Moon, or from a lamp that lets you see things.
2 A light is a thing that produces light. *Can you turn on the light?*

light lighter lightest adjective
1 Something that is light does not weigh very much and you can pick it up easily. *A feather is light.* ■ The opposite is **heavy**.
2 not dark. *My room is very light because it has two big windows.*
3 pale in color. *light green.* ■ The opposite is **dark**.

light lights lighting lit verb
If you light something, you make it start burning. *Mom lit the candles on the birthday cake.*

lighthouse lighthouses noun
a tower with a very bright light on top that flashes to warn ships that they are near rocks or to show them the safe way to go.

lightning noun
a flash of very bright light that you see in the sky when there is a storm.

like likes liking liked verb
1 If you like others, you think that they are nice.
2 If you like doing something, you enjoy it. *I like swimming more than any other sport.*
■ The opposite is **dislike**.

like

Some words that you can use instead of like:

I like firefighters because they help people.
admire, respect

I would like an ice cream.
enjoy, want

He's a vet because he likes animals.
is fond of, loves

like preposition
very similar to somebody or something. *Jack looks just like his dad.* ■ The opposite is **unlike**.

likely likelier likeliest adjective
If something is likely, it is probably going to happen. ■ The opposite is **unlikely**.

limb limbs noun
an arm or a leg. ▲ Rhymes with **him**.

lime limes noun
a fruit that is similar to a lemon, with green skin and sour juice.

limit limits noun
the largest amount of something that is allowed. *The speed limit on this road is 55 miles per hour.*

limp limps limping limped verb
If a person or an animal limps, it walks in an uneven way because its leg or foot has been hurt.

line lines noun
1 a long, thin mark on something. *Draw a line under the title of the book.*
2 a number of people or things next to each other or one behind the other. *There was a long line of people waiting to get into the theater.*
3 a long piece of rope or string. *He's hanging the clean sheets on the line to dry.*

link links noun
1 a ring in a chain.
2 a connection between things or people. *The police believe that there is a link between the two crimes.*

lion lions noun
a large wildcat that has light brown fur and lives in parts of Africa and Asia. The male lion has a large mane. A female lion is called a lioness, and a young lion is a cub.

lip lips noun
Your lips are the two soft parts that form the edges of your mouth.

liquid liquids noun
water or anything else that flows like water. ■ The opposite is **solid**.
liquid adjective.

list lists noun
a line of things that are written down, one under the other. *a shopping list.*
list verb.

listen listens listening listened verb
When you listen, you pay attention to sounds so that you can hear them. *Listen carefully to the instructions.*

lit past of light.

litter noun
1 trash such as pieces of paper and cans that are thrown away in the street or in a public place instead of being put in a trash can.
2 a group of baby animals that are born at the same time to one mother. *Our cat had a litter of four kittens.*

little adjective
1 small in size. ■ The opposite is **big** or **large**.
2 A little child is a young child. *I loved drawing when I was little.*
3 small in amount.

live lives living lived verb
1 To live means to be alive. ■ The opposite is **die**.
2 If you live somewhere, that is where your home is. *I live with Grandma.* ▲ Rhymes with **give**.

live adjective
1 A live animal is alive. *Have you ever seen a real, live crocodile?* ■ The opposite is **dead**.
2 A live TV or radio show is being broadcast as it is happening. ▲ Rhymes with **five**.

lively livelier liveliest adjective
full of energy or excitement. *The old man is lively for his age.*

liver livers noun
Your liver is a large organ in your body that helps clean your blood.

living noun
When you do something for a living, you earn money by doing it. *She earned her living as a journalist.*

lizard lizards noun
a reptile with four very short legs, rough skin, and a long tail.

a thorny devil lizard

load loads noun
something that is being carried somewhere. *The truck carried a very heavy load of wood.*

load loads loading loaded verb
1 If you load a car or other vehicle, you put a lot of things into it to take somewhere. *The men loaded the furniture into the truck.* The opposite is **unload**.
2 If you load a gun, you put bullets in it.
3 If you load a camera, you put film in it.
4 If you load a computer, you put information or a program into it.

loaf loaves noun
bread that is cooked in one piece and then cut up into slices.

loan loans noun
money or something else that somebody lends you and that you have to pay or give back later.

lobster lobsters noun
a sea animal with a hard shell, eight legs, and two large claws in front. Lobsters can be eaten.

local adjective
close to where you live.
locally adverb.

lock locks noun
an object that fastens a door or lid so that you cannot open it without a key.

lock locks locking locked verb
If you lock something such as a door, you fasten it with a key. The opposite is **unlock**.

log logs noun
a piece of a thick branch cut from a tree. *We need some logs to put on the fire.*

lonely lonelier loneliest adjective
If you are lonely, you are sad because you are on your own or because you do not have any friends. *Emily feels lonely in her new school.*

long longer longest adjective
1 far between one end and the other. *a long bridge.*
2 for more time than usual. *The movie was very long, and we got bored.* The opposite is **short**.

long longs longing longed verb
If you long for something, you want it very much. *She longed to have a pony of her own.*

look looks looking looked verb
1 When you look at something, you use your eyes to see it.
2 If somebody looks a certain way, they seem that way to you. *You look tired and sleepy.*
3 If you look for something, you try to find it.
4 If you look after somebody or something, you take care of them. *Dad looked after us while Mom was in the hospital.*

loop loops noun
a circle made in a piece of string, rope, thread, or wire.

loose looser loosest adjective
1 not fixed firmly in place. *a loose tooth.*
2 too big to fit properly. *My pants are loose.* The opposite is **tight**.

lose loses losing lost verb
1 If you lose something, you do not know where to find it. The opposite is **find**.
2 If you lose a competition, game, or fight, you do not win it.
3 If you have lost weight, you now weigh less than you did before.

loss losses noun
The loss of something is not having it anymore. *Julie felt sad about the loss of her necklace.*

lot lots noun
1 a large number.

2 a piece of land. *Dad and Mom bought a big lot on the beach.*

loud louder loudest adjective
Something that is loud makes a lot of noise. *loud music.* The opposite is **quiet** or **soft**.
loudness noun.

love loves loving loved verb
to have a very strong feeling of liking for somebody or something. The opposite is **hate**.

lovely lovelier loveliest adjective
beautiful, or very pleasant. *The park looks lovely in the spring when all the flowers are in bloom.*

low lower lowest adjective
1 not very far from the ground. *There was a low wall between the houses.*
2 deep in sound. *He has a very low voice.* The opposite is **high**.

lower lowers lowering lowered verb
If you lower something, you bring it down slowly. *They lowered the flag.* The opposite is **raise**.

loyal adjective
If you are loyal to somebody, you always support him or her. *Janice has always been a very loyal friend.* The opposite is **disloyal**.
loyally adverb.

luck noun
1 Luck is when something happens by chance instead of when you plan it or make it happen. *There is no skill needed to play this game. It's just luck whether you win or not.*
2 good things that happen to you by chance. *Wish me luck on my exam!*

luggage noun
all the bags and suitcases that you take with you when you travel.
Say lug-*ij*.

lung lungs noun
Your lungs are the two parts like bags inside your chest that fill up when you breathe in and then empty again when you breathe out.

Mm

macaroni noun
hollow tubes of dough that we cook and eat. *a macaroni and cheese casserole.*

machine machines noun
a thing with parts that move to do work or to make something. We use machines in the home to help us sew, cook, and clean. A washing machine cleans our clothes, and a machine called a vacuum cleaner sucks up dirt from rugs.
machinery noun.

mad madder maddest adjective
A person who is mad at someone or about something is angry.

magazine magazines noun
a thin book with pictures, stories, and information about things in it. Most magazines come out every week or every month.

maggot maggots noun
a creature that looks like a worm and grows up to become a fly. Maggots are often found in dead flesh.

magic noun
1 a power that some people think makes strange and wonderful things happen. *The witch turned the frog into a prince by magic.*
2 the skill of doing clever tricks, such as making things disappear.
magic adjective.

magical adjective
1 produced by magic. *a magical hat that makes you disappear.*
2 strange or very exciting. *a magical fireworks display.*

magician magicians noun
a person who can do magic tricks.

magnet magnets noun
a piece of metal that makes iron or steel move toward it.
magnetic adjective.

magnificent adjective
very beautiful or grand. *a magnificent view.*

magnify magnifies magnifying magnified verb
When you magnify something, you make it look bigger. *We magnified the insect under the microscope.*

magnifying glass noun
a special piece of glass called a lens that can makes things look bigger.

mail noun
letters, postcards, and packages that you send by post. ● A word that sounds like **mail** is **male**.

main adjective
most important. *the main entrance.* ● A word that sounds like **main** is **mane**.

major adjective, noun
1 large, important, or serious. *Miami is a major city.* ■ The opposite is **minor**.
2 an officer in the army, air force, or marines.

make makes making made verb
1 If you make something, you put things together so that you have a new thing. *Sandy is making a cake.*
2 to cause something to happen. *The balloon made a loud bang when it burst.*
3 to do something. *I made a mistake.*
4 If you make somebody do something, you force him or her to do it. *Dad makes me go to bed early.*

makeup noun
special powders, paints, and creams that women and actors put on their faces. Eye shadow and lipstick are kinds of makeup.

male males adjective
a person or animal that belongs to the sex that cannot have babies or lay eggs. Boys and men are male. ■ The opposite is **female**. ● A word that sounds like **male** is **mail**.

mammal mammals noun
an animal that drinks milk from its mother's body when it is young. People, horses, and whales are all mammals. ◆ Look at page 96.

man men noun
a grown-up male person.

manage manages managing managed verb
1 If you manage to do something difficult, you do it well. *Those problems were hard, but I managed to do them.*
2 If you manage people at work, you are in charge of them.

manager managers noun
a person whose job is to run or control such things as a bank, store, or hotel.

mane manes noun
the long hair on the neck of a horse or male lion.

manner manners noun
1 the way that you do something. *She smiled in a friendly manner.*
2 Your manners are the way that you behave when you are eating or talking to other people. *It's bad manners to talk with your mouth full.*

many more most adjective
a large number of people or things.

map maps noun
a drawing that shows you what a place looks like from above. Maps show things such as roads, mountains, and rivers. *Will you draw me a map of how to get to your house?*

Mammals

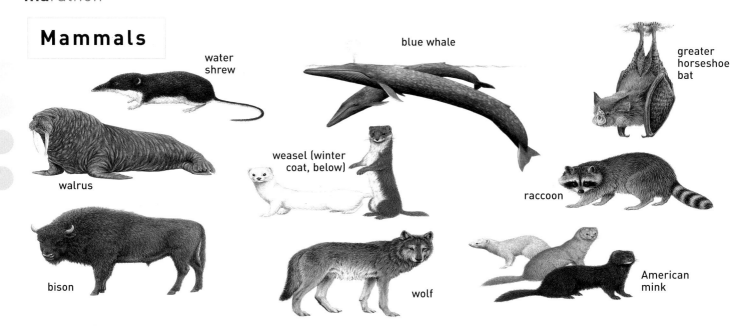

water shrew

blue whale

greater horseshoe bat

walrus

weasel (winter coat, below)

raccoon

bison

wolf

American mink

marathon marathons noun
a race when people have to run 26.2 miles. *He won the Boston Marathon.*

marble noun
a kind of very hard stone that can be polished until it is shiny. Marble is used to make statues and buildings.

marbles noun
small colored glass balls that you use in some games.

march marches marching marched verb
When you march, you walk like a soldier with regular, even steps. **march** noun.

margarine noun
a soft, yellow fat that looks like butter, but is not made from milk.

margin margins noun
a blank space around the writing or printing on a page.

mark marks noun
1 a spot, stain, or line on something that spoils it. *Your shoes have left a dirty mark on the rug.*
2 Marks are numbers or letters that your teacher gives you to show how good your work is. *Ben got the highest marks in the class.*
mark verb.

market markets noun
a place, usually in the open air, with lots of little stores or stalls where you can buy things such as fruit and vegetables.

marmalade noun
a jam made from oranges or lemons.

marriage marriages noun
1 the special ceremony or wedding when a man and a woman become husband and wife.
2 the time a man and woman live together as husband and wife. *Grandma and Grandpa have had a long and happy marriage; they have four children and seven grandchildren.*

marry marries marrying married verb
When a man and a woman marry, they become husband and wife.

marsh marshes noun
an area of land that is soft and wet.

marsupial marsupials noun
a mammal, the female of which has a pouch for carrying her babies. Opossum and koalas are marsupials.

marvelous adjective
very good, wonderful. *We had a marvelous day at the seaside* or *What a marvelous idea!*

mascot mascots noun
a person or thing that is supposed to bring good luck. *Our team's mascot is a donkey.*

mask masks noun
something you wear on your face to hide it or to protect it.

honey possum

brown bandicoot

potoroo

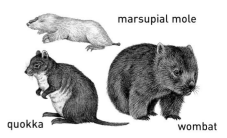

marsupial mole

quokka

wombat

mass masses noun
1 a large number of people or things.
2 a large amount of something solid. *a mass of rock.*
3 A Mass is a service in the Catholic Church.

massacre massacres noun
the violent killing of a lot of people. *Hundreds were massacred in the battle.*

massive adjective
very big, strong, and heavy. *massive castle walls.*

mast masts noun
a tall pole that holds a flag or the sails on a boat.

mat mats noun
1 a small carpet. *Please wipe your feet on the mat at the door.*
2 a piece of wood or material that you put on the table under a plate. *Put the dishes on the place mats.*

match matches matching matched verb
If two things match, they are the same color, shape, or pattern, or they look good together. *Stuart's hat and scarf match.*

match matches noun
1 a small, thin stick of wood or cardboard with a tip that makes fire when you rub it against something rough. *My father struck a match and lit the bonfire.*
2 a game that is played between two teams or two players. ◆ *a tennis match.*

mate mates noun
1 a merchant marine officer. *a third mate.*
2 one of two animals that have come together to have young ones. *Most birds choose a mate in the spring.*
mate verb.

material materials noun
1 things that you use to make other things with. Glass, wood, and stone are materials that we use to build houses.
2 a cloth that we use to make things such as clothes. *Jack bought material to make new curtains.*

maternal adjective
to do with being a mother. *Mothers have maternal feelings.*

math noun
adding, subtracting, multiplying, and dividing numbers. Math is short for *mathematics.*

matter noun
1 something that you must talk about or do. *Mom said that there were some important matters she had to discuss.*
2 a problem or difficulty. *What's the matter with your computer?*
3 a thing that you can see or touch. *The world is made of matter.*

matter matters mattering mattered verb
If something matters, it is important. *Ben has lost my ruler, but it doesn't matter because I have another one.*

mattress mattresses noun
the soft part of the bed that you lie on.

mature adjective
If you are mature, you have grown up or you behave in a grown-up way.

maximum noun
the most you can have of something. *We have a maximum of $5 to spend on Zack's present.*
maximum adjective
What's the maximum speed of this car?
■ The opposite is **minimum**.

mayonnaise noun
a thick sauce for sandwiches or salads. It is made of oil, eggs, lemon juice or vinegar, and mustard.

mayor mayors noun
a person who is in charge of the government of a city or town.

meadow meadows noun
a field of grass. Wildflowers often grow in meadows. ▲ Say med-*oh*.

meal meals noun
the food that you eat at certain times of the day. Breakfast, lunch, and dinner are all meals.

mean adjective
Somebody who is mean does not like other people and is not good or kind to others.

mean means meaning meant verb
1 If you ask what something means, you want somebody to explain it so that you can understand it. *What does this word mean?*
2 If you mean to do something, you plan and want to do it. *I meant to clean my room, but I forgot.*
meaning noun.

meanwhile adverb
If something happens meanwhile, it happens at the same time as something else, or before something else happens. *I'm getting a new bike next week; meanwhile, I'll have to borrow my sister's bike.*

measles noun
an illness that gives you little red spots all over your skin. *Jim wasn't at school today; he has the measles.*

measure measures measuring measured verb
When you measure something, you find out how big, tall, long, wide, or heavy it is. *Angela is being measured by Susan.*
measurement noun.

meat noun
the part of an animal that we eat.

97

mechanical adjective
If something is mechanical, it is done, made, or works by a machine. *a mechanical clock.*

medal medals noun
a kind of badge that somebody gives you when you win something or when you do something very brave or special. *She won a gold medal in the swim meet.*

sports day medals

meddle meddles meddling meddled verb
If you meddle with something, you touch or move it when you have been told not to. *The teacher told us not to meddle with the art supplies.*

media noun
newspapers, radio, Internet, and TV.

medicine medicines noun
the tablets, liquid, and drugs that a doctor gives you when you are sick to make you feel better.

medium adjective
not large or small but a size in between. *Do you want a small, medium, or large shirt?*

meet meets meeting met verb
When you meet people, you go to the same place at the same time as them. **meeting** noun.

meet meets noun
a sports contest. *the swim meet.*

melody melodies noun
a tune that you sing or play.

melon melons noun
a big, round, yellow or green fruit with lots of seeds inside.

melt melts melting melted verb
When something melts, it changes into a liquid. *Fran's ice cream is beginning to melt in the sun.*

member members noun
a person who belongs to something such as a club or a sports team. *Bill is a member of the school football team.*

memorize memorizes memorizing memorized verb
To memorize is to learn something so that you can remember it exactly. *Have you memorized the names of all the players on the team?*

memory memories noun
1 being able to remember things. *It is easy to learn spellings, if you have a good memory.*
2 Your memories are the things that happened to you a long time ago and that you can still remember. *My grandmother has lots of happy memories of her childhood.*
3 the part of a computer where it stores information.

men plural of **man.**

mend mends mending mended verb
When you mend something, you make it useful again. *Tracy is mending her sweater.*

mental adjective
If something is mental, it is in your mind or you do it in your mind. *mental arithmetic.*

mention mentions mentioning mentioned verb
If you mention something, you say a little bit about it. *Did Jay mention where they were going?*

menu menus noun
1 a list of things that you can eat in a restaurant.
2 a list on a computer that tells you what you can do.

mercury noun
a metal that has a silver color and is usually liquid. Mercury is used in thermometers.

mercy noun
If you show mercy to people, you do not hurt them or punish them.

mermaid mermaids noun
a sea creature in stories that has the head and body of a woman and the tail of a fish.

merry merrier merriest adjective
happy and full of fun. *Merry Christmas!*

merry-go-round merry-go-rounds noun
1 A fairground ride with wooden animals and seats that go around and around.
2 a playground ride.

mesa mesas noun
a high hill with a flat top.
▲ Say **may-***suh.*

mess noun
Things are a mess when they are dirty or not where they belong. *Your bedroom is in a mess—please clean it up!*
messy adjective.

message messages noun
words that you say or write when the person you want to speak to is not there. *Tom isn't in. Leave a message for him.*

messenger messengers noun
a person who brings a message.

met past of **meet**.

metal metals noun
a hard material that is used to make things such as cars and airplanes. Metal becomes soft or liquid when it is heated. Silver, iron, and copper are different kinds of metals.

meteor meteors noun
a piece of rock or metal that travels in space and burns when it gets close to Earth.

meteorite meteorites noun
a piece of rock or metal from space that has landed on Earth.

meter meters noun
an instrument that measures how much gas, electricity, or water has been used. *a gas meter* or *a parking meter.*

method methods noun
a way of doing something. *Baking, frying, and boiling are methods of cooking.*

mice plural of **mouse**.

microphone microphones noun
an instrument that is used to record sound or to makes sounds louder than they really are. *She sang with a microphone.*

microscope microscopes noun
an instrument that makes very small things look much bigger. *We looked at the insect under the microscope.*

microwave oven microwave ovens noun
a kind of oven that cooks food very

quickly using waves called electromagnetic waves.

midday noun
12 o'clock in the middle of the day; noon. ■ The opposite is **midnight**.

middle noun
the part of something that is not near the outside edges. *There is a vase of flowers in the middle of the table.*

midnight noun
12 o'clock in the middle of the night. ■ The opposite is **noon** or **midday**.

migrate migrates migrating migrated verb
When birds and animals migrate, they move to another part of the country or world for part of the year so that they can find food. *Some ducks and geese migrate to Florida from Maine in the winter.*
migration noun.

milk noun
the white liquid that human mothers and female mammals make in their bodies to feed their babies. People drink the milk that cows make.
milky adjective.

mill mills noun
1 a factory for making things such as steel, paper, or materials, such as wool or cotton.
2 a building where a machine grinds grain into flour.
3 a small tool that grinds or crushes things. *a pepper mill.*

millionaire millionaires noun
a rich person who has more than a million dollars.

mime mimes miming mimed verb
If you mime something, you use actions but you do not speak. *Ross mimed blowing up a balloon, and we had to guess what he was doing.*

mind minds noun
Your mind is the part of you that thinks, feels, learns, and remembers things.

mind minds minding minded verb
If you mind about something, you feel unhappy or angry about it. *Do you mind if I borrow your bike? No, I don't mind.*

mine mines noun
1 a place where people dig under the ground to get things such as coal, gold, or diamonds. *a coal mine.*
2 a bomb put in water or under the ground.

mineral minerals noun
Minerals are things such as coal, gold, salt, or oil that are found in rocks or under the ground.

miniature miniatures noun
a very small copy of something much bigger.
miniature adjective
miniature furniture. ▲ Say **min**-*at-cher*.

minimum noun
the smallest amount that you can have of something. *We need a minimum of four people to play this game.*
minimum adjective
Sixteen is the minimum age for driving in this state. ■ The opposite is **maximum**.

minister ministers noun
a person who directs services in church.

minnow minnows noun
a very tiny fish that lives in fresh water.

minor adjective
not very serious or important. *a minor injury.* ■ The opposite is **major**.

minor minors noun
If you are a minor, you are too young to decide and do things like an adult.

mint noun
1 a plant called an herb. It is used to add flavor to things such as meat, toothpaste, and candy.
2 a hard piece of candy with a strong mint flavor.
3 the place where coins are made by the government.

minus noun, preposition
1 You use the minus sign (–) to show that you have taken one number away from another. *Seven minus four is three (7 – 4 = 3).*
2 below zero. *The temperature was minus ten degrees.*

minute minutes noun
a measure of time. There are 60 seconds in a minute and 60 minutes in an hour. ▲ Say **min**-it.

minute adjective
very, very small. *a minute insect.*
▲ Say my-*newt*.

mirror mirrors noun
a piece of special glass that you can see yourself in. Mirrors reflect light.

Some mirrors can make you look funny.

mischief noun
bad or annoying behavior.
mischievous adjective
Mike played a mischievous trick on his uncle.

miserable adjective
If you are miserable, you feel very unhappy or sad. *Leah is miserable because she can't go on vacation.*

miss misses missing missed verb
1 If you miss a ball, you do not hit or catch it.
2 If you miss a bus or a train, you are not there in time to catch it.
3 If you miss somebody, you are sad because that person is not there. *I really missed my friend when he moved out of town.*

mist mists noun
a low cloud of tiny drops of water that is difficult to see through. *In the early morning, the fields were covered with mist.*

mistake mistakes noun
something that you do wrong. *I only made one spelling mistake.*

mix mixes mixing mixed verb
1 When you mix things, you stir them or put them together so that they make something new. *If you mix blue and red paint, you get purple* or *Oil and water do not mix.*
2 When people mix, they come together and talk to each other. *I mix with lots of different people at school.*

mixture mixtures noun
something that is made when two or more things are mixed together. *There are butter, flour, and sugar in this cake mixture.*

moan moans moaning moaned verb
1 When a person or an animal moans, they make a low, sad sound because of being in pain or unhappy. *The dog was moaning because it was locked in the pen.*

2 If you moan, you keep complaining about something that you do not like. *He was moaning about having to study for so long.*

mobile adjective
If something is mobile, it can move or you can move it easily. *a mobile home.*

mock mocks mocking mocked verb
If you mock others, you make fun of them.

model models noun
1 a small copy of something. *a model ship.*
2 a person who sits or stands so that an artist can draw him or her.
3 a person who wears new clothes so that people can see what the clothes look like before they buy them.

modern adjective
new or happening now. *We live in a modern house.*

modest adjective
If you are modest, you do not boast about how good or smart you are.

moist adjective
damp or a little wet. *The ground was moist after the rain.*
moisten verb.

moisture noun
small drops of water on something or in the air.

mole moles noun
a small animal with dark fur that lives under the ground and digs tunnels with its strong claws. Where moles have been digging, they leave piles of earth called molehills.

moment moments noun
a very short time. *I'll be back in a moment.*

money noun
the coins and bills that we use to buy things with.

mongrel mongrels noun
a dog whose mother and father are different types of dogs.

monk monks noun
Monks are a group of men who obey rules and live and pray together in a building called a monastery because of the religion that they believe in.

monkey monkeys noun
an animal with long arms and legs and a long tail that lives mainly in trees in hot countries.

monster monsters noun
a big, frightening creature that you can read about in stories.

month months noun
a measure of time. There are 12 months in a year. *January is the first month of the year.*
monthly adjective, adverb
a monthly magazine.

monument monuments noun
a large statue or building that people have made to remember an important person or event. *The Washington Monument is in Washington, D.C.*

mood moods noun
the way that you feel at different times. *Joe was in an angry mood today, but Sara was in a cheerful mood.*

moon moons noun
The Moon is a small satellite that travels around Earth once every four weeks. You can often see it in the sky at night.

moose mooses noun
a big animal that is related to deer but that is heavier and has much bigger antlers.

mop mops noun
a mop is a tool with a long handle for washing floors.

morning mornings noun
the early part of the day before noon. *What time do you get up in the morning?*

mosque mosques noun
a building where Muslims go to pray. ▲ Say **mosk**.

mosquito mosquitoes noun
a small flying insect that lives in hot, wet places. Female mosquitoes bite people and animals. People can get a serious illness called malaria from mosquito bites. ▲ Say *mos-kee-toe*.

moss mosses noun
a soft, green plant like a rug that grows on trees and damp ground.

moth moths noun
an insect that looks like a butterfly but that usually flies around at night.

mother mothers noun
a woman who has children.

motion noun
movement or the way of moving. *The motion of the boat on the rough sea made him feel sick.*

motor motors noun
the part inside a machine that makes it move or work. Washing machines have electric motors.

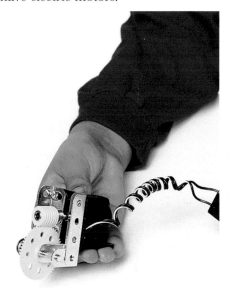
a small motor for a model

motorbike motorbikes noun
a kind of bicycle with an engine.

motorcycle motorcycles noun
a two-wheeled vehicle with a motor and handlebars that is heavier and faster than a motorbike.

mountain mountains noun
a very high piece of ground. The highest mountain in the world is Mount Everest.

mountain lion mountain lions noun
a big yellow wildcat. It is also called a *cougar* or a *puma*.

101

mouse mice noun
1 a small, furry animal with sharp teeth and a long tail. Mice are rodents.
2 a small instrument connected to your computer that you use to make the cursor on your computer screen move.

mouth mouths noun
1 the part of your face that you open and close to talk and eat.
2 The mouth of a cave is the way into it.
3 The mouth of a river is the place where it enters the sea.

move moves moving moved verb
1 When you move, you go from one place to another. *Don't move—I want to take your picture.*
2 If you move something, you put it in another place. *We moved the piano into the living room.*
movement noun.

movie movies noun
a story in moving pictures that you watch in a theater or on TV.

mow mows mowing mowed verb
When you mow grass, you cut it with a machine called a lawn mower.
▲ Rhymes with **low**.

MP3 noun
a means of sharing data, such as a song, so that it can be transmitted via the Internet and read by an MP3 player.
MP3 player noun.
a device that plays MP3s.

mud noun
soft wet dirt. *After playing football, Tom was covered with mud.*
muddy adjective.

mug mugs noun
a tall cup with a handle that you use without a saucer. *a mug of hot chocolate.*

mule mules noun
an animal whose parents are a female horse and a male donkey.

multiply multiplies multiplying multiplied verb
When you multiply a number, you add the number to itself several times. Four multiplied by three is twelve $(4 + 4 + 4 = 12$, or $4 \times 3 = 12)$.
■ The opposite is **divide**.
multiplication noun.

mumps noun
a sickness you can get from others that makes your neck and jaws swell and hurt.

munch munches munching munched verb
When you munch something hard, you bite and chew it in a noisy way. *Cal was munching an apple.*

murder murders murdering murdered verb
To murder somebody means to kill somebody on purpose.
murder noun, **murderer** noun.

murmur murmurs murmuring murmured verb
If you murmur, you say something softly and quietly.
murmur noun.

muscle muscles noun
Your muscles are the parts inside your body that stretch so that you can bend and move. Muscles are attached to your bones.
muscular noun.

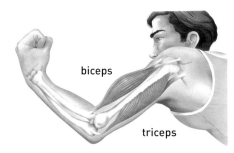
biceps
triceps

museum museums noun
a building where lots of interesting things are kept for people to look at. *We saw a model of a dinosaur at the museum.*

mushroom mushrooms noun
a small plant without leaves that looks like a tiny umbrella. People can eat some kinds of mushrooms; other kinds are poisonous. A mushroom is a fungus.

music noun
the sounds that come from somebody singing or playing a musical instrument, like a piano, flute, or guitar.
musical adjective.

musical instrument musical instruments noun
something that you play to make music. Violins are musical instruments. ◆ Look at page 103.

musician musicians noun
a person who plays a musical instrument well. *six musicians in the band.*

Muslim Muslims noun
a person who follows the religion of Islam. The religion is based on the teachings of the prophet Muhammad.

mustache mustaches noun
hair that grows above a man's top lip.
▲ Say mus-*tash*.

mutter mutters muttering muttered verb
If you mutter, you speak in a quiet and angry way. *"I don't want to go home," she muttered.*

muzzle muzzles noun
1 the nose and mouth of an animal such as a dog or a fox.
2 something that you can put over a dog's mouth to stop it from biting.

mystery mysteries noun
something strange that has happened and that you cannot explain.

myth myths noun
1 a very old story with a special meaning. Greek myths are about gods and goddesses.
2 a story that is not true.

Musical instruments

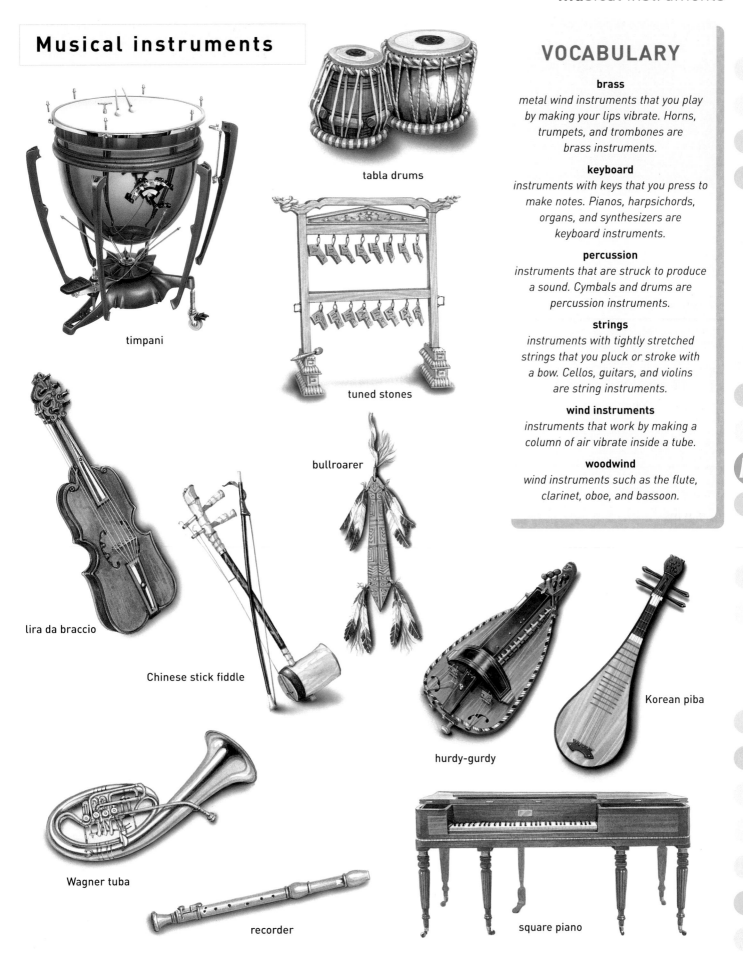

tabla drums

timpani

tuned stones

lira da braccio

Chinese stick fiddle

bullroarer

hurdy-gurdy

Korean piba

Wagner tuba

recorder

square piano

VOCABULARY

brass
metal wind instruments that you play by making your lips vibrate. Horns, trumpets, and trombones are brass instruments.

keyboard
instruments with keys that you press to make notes. Pianos, harpsichords, organs, and synthesizers are keyboard instruments.

percussion
instruments that are struck to produce a sound. Cymbals and drums are percussion instruments.

strings
instruments with tightly stretched strings that you pluck or stroke with a bow. Cellos, guitars, and violins are string instruments.

wind instruments
instruments that work by making a column of air vibrate inside a tube.

woodwind
wind instruments such as the flute, clarinet, oboe, and bassoon.

103

Nn

nail nails noun
1 a thin piece of metal with one pointed end and one flat end, like a very large pin. *She's hammering a nail into the wall to hang a picture.*
2 Your nails are the hard parts at the ends of your fingers and toes.

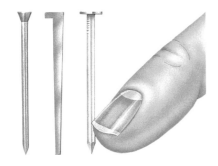

name names noun
the word we use to call somebody or something. *The dog's name is Spot* or *her last name is Jones.*

nap noun
a short sleep.

napkin napkins noun
a piece of paper or cloth that you use to wipe your fingers and mouth when you eat food.

narrator narrators noun
a person who tells a story out loud or explains to somebody how something happened. ▲ Say **nar-**ate-or.

narrow narrower narrowest adjective
If something is narrow, it is thin and does not measure very much from one side to the other. *The willow's leaves are narrow.* ■ The opposite is **broad** or **wide.**
narrowness noun.

nasty nastier nastiest adjective
1 horrible or not nice. *a nasty smell.*
2 unkind or cruel. *He was really nasty to me.*
nastily adverb, **nastiness** noun.

nation nations noun
a country with its own laws and government. The people of a nation share the same history and language.

national adjective
to do with an entire nation or the people in a nation. *the national news.*

Native American Native Americans noun
a person who is descended from the original peoples who lived in North America before the explorers and European settlers came.

natural adjective
If something is natural, it is made by nature and not by human beings.
■ The opposite is **artificial.**
naturally adverb.

nature noun
animals, plants, and all the things that are not made by human beings.
▲ Say **nay-**cher.

navigate navigates navigating navigated verb
If you navigate a ship or aircraft, you find out and say which way to go.
navigator noun.

navy navies noun
the ships and the sailors that are used to defend a country or fight an enemy.

near nearer nearest adjective, preposition
close by or a short distance from something or somebody. *Where's the nearest subway station?* or *In the picture, I'm standing near the statue.*
■ The opposite is **far.**

nearly adverb
almost but not quite. *She nearly won.*

neat neater neatest adjective
clean and tidy with everything in its correct place.

necessary adjective
If something is necessary, it is needed or has to happen. *It is necessary to have a passport when you travel to another country.*
necessarily adverb.

neck necks noun
The neck is the part of a person or animal that connects the head to the body. *The giraffe has a very long neck.*

necklace necklaces noun
a piece of jewelry such as a chain that you wear around your neck.

nectar noun
a sweet liquid in flowers that insects collect and that bees make into honey.

need needs needing needed verb
If you need something, you have to have it in order to live or to do a job. *People and animals need air and water or they die.* or *I need some more green thread to finish my sewing.*

needle needles noun
1 a thin, pointed piece of metal with a hole at one end for thread that is used for sewing.
2 a long, thin stick used for knitting.
3 a long, thin leaf on a pine tree.
4 a short tube with a thin, sharp point at one end that doctors use to give injections.

negative adjective, noun
1 meaning "no." *She gave a negative answer.*
2 A negative number is less than zero. −20.
3 film from a camera from which photographs are printed.
■ The opposite is **positive.**

neglect neglects neglecting neglected verb
1 If you neglect people or things, you do not take care of them and give them the time and attention they need. *He neglected the garden.*
2 to fail to do something. *He neglected to answer the letter.*

neighbor neighbors noun
a person who lives near or next to you. *We have very friendly neighbors.*
▲ Say **nay-***ber.*

neighborhood neighborhoods noun
the area where you live. *I've lived in this neighborhood all my life.*
▲ Say **nay-***ber-hood.*

nephew nephews noun
the son of your brother or sister.
▲ Say **nef-***you.*

nerve nerves noun
1 Your nerves are the long, thin parts inside your body that link your brain to other parts of your body. They carry the messages to and from your brain that make your body move and feel.
2 brave and calm when something is difficult or frightening.

nervous adjective
1 worried about something that is going to happen. *I'm nervous about the test.*
2 easily frightened. *a nervous horse.*
■ The opposite is **calm.**

nest nests noun
a home made by birds, squirrels, wasps, and other animals for their babies.

net nets noun
1 material made of thread, string, or rope joined with knots so as to leave small holes between.
2 the long barrier that you string between two poles so that you can play tennis, volleyball, or badminton. *Jill hit the ball over the net.*

nettle nettles noun
a wild plant with hairy leaves that sting you if you touch them. *Johnny got caught in the stinging nettle.*

network networks noun
1 a system of things that are connected at many different points. *a railroad network.*
2 a company or group of companies that broadcasts the same radio or television programs.

never adverb
at no time ever in the past or the future. *It is a beautiful horse, but it has never won a race.*

new newer newest adjective
1 If something is new, it has only just been made, or you have only just bought it. *I got some new games for my birthday.*
2 different from somebody or something you knew before. *We have a new teacher.*
■ The opposite is **old.**

news noun
information about what is going on or has just happened.

newspaper newspapers noun
sheets of folded paper that have news stories and pictures and other information printed on them.

newt newts noun
a small amphibian with short legs and a long tail that lays its eggs in water.

nib nibs noun
the pointed part of a pen that touches the paper when you write.

nibble nibbles nibbling nibbled verb
If you nibble, you slowly eat something, taking very small bites of it.

nice nicer nicest adjective
1 If you think something is nice, you like it or enjoy it.
2 kind and easy to like. *a nice person.*

nice
Some words that you can use instead of nice:

We had a nice dinner.
delicious, tasty

The woman next door is nice.
kind, friendly, likable

We had a nice time on vacation.
enjoyable, pleasant, wonderful

What nice weather we are having.
good, fine, beautiful, mild

nickname nicknames noun
a short or special name that people call you instead of your real name.

niece nieces noun
the daughter of your brother or sister.
▲ Say **neess.**

night nights noun
the time when it is dark and most people are asleep. ■ The opposite is **day.** ● A word that sounds like **night** is **knight.**

nightmare nightmares noun
a frightening dream.

nocturnal adjective
awake and active mostly at night rather than during the day. *The owl is a nocturnal animal.*

nod nods nodding nodded verb
When you nod, you move your head up and down to show that you agree with something.

noise noises noun
1 a sound. *I heard a strange noise.*
2 sounds that are too loud and unpleasant. *Please stop making so much noise!*
■ The opposite is **silence.**
noisily adverb, **noisy** adjective.

noodle noodles noun
a long, thin strip of pasta. *Do you want rice or noodles with your meal?*

noon noun
12 o'clock in the middle of the day; midday. ■ The opposite is **midnight**.

noose nooses noun
a loop made in rope with a special knot that gets smaller when you pull on the rope.

normal adjective
ordinary, the same as usual. *Cold weather is normal in the winter.* ■ The opposite is **unusual**.
normally adverb
I normally go to bed at 9 o'clock.

north noun
a direction that is to your left if you face the Sun as it is rising in the morning.
north adjective, **northern** adjective
a north wind or *a northern accent.*
■ The opposite is **south, southern**.

nose noses noun
Your nose is the part that sticks out in the middle of your face that you use for breathing and smelling. At the end of your nose there are two holes called nostrils.

Different types of animal noses

elephant

elephant seal

mandrill

note notes noun
1 a few words that you write down to remind yourself of something. *I've made a note of your phone number.*
2 a short letter. *I'll send a note to the school to explain that you have to go to the dentist.*
3 a single sound in music or a symbol written to show a sound. *Some opera singers can sing very high notes.*

notice notices noticing noticed verb
If you notice something, you start to see it or hear it or smell it. *I suddenly noticed that there were lots of people in the yard.*

SPELLING TIP

Some words that begin with an "n" sound are spelled with "gn" or "kn," such as gnat, gnome, knee, and knight.

notice notices noun
a written message that is put in a public place so that many people will be able to read it. *I saw the notice about the town council meeting.*

notify notifyer notifying notified verb
to tell someone about something.

noun nouns noun
a word that gives the name of a thing, state, feeling, idea, person, or place. *Table, talent, happiness, sadness, Ben, and Texas are all different nouns.*

nourishment noun
food that is good for you and makes you strong and healthy. ▲ Say nu-*rish*-ment.
nourishing adjective.

snow leopard

duck-billed platypus

giant anteater

spear-nosed bat

proboscis monkey

novel novels noun
a long written story that has been made up by someone about people and events that do not really exist.
novelist noun.

nudge nudges nudging nudged verb
If you nudge somebody, you push him or her with your elbow to make that person notice something. *Cindy stayed quiet but nudged Michael and pointed to the deer.*

nuisance nuisances noun
a person or thing that annoys you.
▲ Say new-*sense*.

numb adjective
unable to feel anything in a part of your body. *It was so cold that my feet were numb.* ▲ Say **num**.

number numbers noun
a word or sign that shows you how many of something there are.

numerous adjective
very many. *Numerous people were invited.* ■ The opposite is **few**.

nun nuns noun
Nuns are a group of women who obey rules and live and pray together in a building called a convent because of the religion that they believe in.

nurse nurses noun
a person whose job is to take care of people who are sick or injured.

nursery nurseries noun
1 a place where young children can go during the day when they are too young to go to school.
2 a place where plants and flowers are grown to be sold.

nut nuts noun
the fruit of a tree that has a seed inside of a hard shell.

Oo

oak oaks noun
1 a large tree that acorns grow on.
2 the wood from this tree.

oar oars noun
a long pole with one flat end that you use to row a boat. ▲ Say **or**.

oasis oases noun
a place in a desert with water, plants, and trees. ▲ Say *oh-**ay**-sis*.

oats noun
Oats are plants that farmers grow for their seeds called grain.

obey obeys obeying obeyed verb
If you obey a person, you do what he or she tells you to do. ■ The opposite is **disobey**.
obedient adjective.

object objects noun
1 a thing that you can see and touch. *The box was full of objects of all shapes and sizes.*
2 the purpose or thing that you are trying to achieve. *Her object was to win the contest.*
3 in the sentence, *"Jim hit the ball,"* the object of the sentence is *ball*.
▲ Say **ob**-*jekt*.

object objects objecting objected verb
If somebody objects to something, he or she does not like it or agree with it. *The teacher objects to fighting.*
▲ Say *ob*-**jekt**.

oblong oblongs noun
a shape with two long opposite sides and two short opposite sides.
oblong adjective
The pages of this dictionary are oblong.

observe observes observing observed verb
When you observe someone or something, you watch them carefully. *We observed a bird feeding its babies.*

obstacle obstacles noun
something that is in your way and stops you from doing something. *The fallen tree was an obstacle in the road.*

obstinate adjective
An obstinate person does not like to change what he or she thinks or do what other people want. *Rod is so obstinate that he will do only what he wants to do.*

obvious adjective
If something is obvious, it is easy to see or understand. *The answers to the quiz were obvious.*

occasion occasions noun
a time when something happens. *A wedding is an important occasion.*

occasionally adverb
If something happens occasionally, it does not happen very often. *I usually walk to school, but occasionally I go by bicycle.*

occupant occupants noun
somebody who lives or works in a place.

occupy occupies occupying occupied verb
1 If you occupy a house, you live in it.
2 If someone or something occupies a space, they are in it. *All of the parking spaces were occupied.*

3 If you are occupied, you are busy.
occupation noun.

occur occurs occurring occurred verb
1 When something occurs, it happens. *The storm occurred last night.*
2 If something occurs to you, you suddenly think about it. *It occurred to me that I had been very rude to my aunt.*

ocean oceans noun
any of the very large areas of sea. *the Atlantic Ocean.*

ocelot ocelots noun
a big wildcat with yellow and black fur that lives in Mexico and South America.

octagon octagons noun
a shape with eight straight sides.

octopus octopuses noun
an animal that lives in the ocean. It has eight long arms called tentacles.

odd odder oddest adjective
1 strange or unusual.
2 Odd things do not belong together in a pair or a set. *Todd is wearing odd socks; one is green and the other one is brown.*
3 An odd number is any number that ends in 1, 3, 5, 7, or 9. You cannot divide these numbers by two without carrying something over. ■ The opposite is **even**.

odds and ends noun
1 a number of things. *The eraser was among the odds and ends in the drawer.*
2 things you still have to do. *Debbie had some odds and ends to take care of.*

odor odors noun
a strong smell. *Dominic's socks have a strong odor!*

offend offends offending
offended verb
If you offend someone, you upset them and hurt their feelings. *Her mean remarks offended me.*
offense noun, **offensive** adjective
offensive behavior.

offer offers offering offered verb
1 If you offer people something, you ask them if they would like it. *She offered me a cookie.*
2 If you offer to do something, you say that you are willing to do it. *He offered to do the dishes.*

office offices noun
1 a place where people go to work. Offices have things such as desks, chairs, computers, and telephones.
2 a place where you can buy something or get information. *the post office.*

officer officers noun
1 a person in the army, navy, air force, marines, or coast guard who gives orders to other people.
2 a member of a police force. *police officer.*

official adjective
If something is official, it is important and people must believe it or do it. *an official report from the government.*
▲ Say oh-**fish**-al.

oil noun
1 a smooth, thick liquid that comes from the ground. You can burn oil to make heat or to make machines work.
2 a smooth liquid that comes from plants and animals. Some people use it for cooking.
oily adjective.

ointment noun
a cream that you put on a cut or on sore skin to heal it.

old older oldest adjective
1 Someone who is old has lived for a long time. *My great-grandfather is very old—he is 90!*
　■ The opposite is **young**.
2 Something that is old was made a long time ago. *This castle is very old—it was built 500 years ago.*
　■ The opposite is **new**.
3 having a certain age.
4 You also use "old" to talk about something that you had before. *Yesterday I saw an old friend while I was out shopping.*

olive olives noun
a small green or black fruit. Olives are used to make olive oil, which is used in cooking.

Olympic
adjective
of the Olympic Games or the Olympics, international sports contests that are held every four years in a different country.

onion onions noun
a round vegetable with a strong taste and smell that grows under the ground. *I like onions in a salad.*

only adjective, adverb, conjunction
1 with no others. *This is the only photo I have of her.*

2 no more than. *I have only one brother.* or *It will take only five minutes to prepare the food.*
3 but. *This is a good story, only it's too long.*

open adjective
1 not closed or covered. *The dog escaped through the open gate.*
2 ready for people to come in. *The store is open at nine o'clock.*

open opens opening opened verb
1 If you open a door, you let people or things go through.
2 To open means to move something so that it is not closed or covered. *Open your eyes!* or *He opened the box and found a present inside.*
　■ The opposite is **shut**.
3 If you open a store or office, you make it ready for people to come in.
opening noun.

open house open houses noun
a reception for visitors, as at a school.

opera operas noun
a play where actors sing most of the words. The Magic Flute *is an opera by Mozart.*

operate operates operating
operated verb
1 When surgeons operate, they take away or fix part of patients' bodies to make them well again.
2 If you operate a machine, you use it or make it work. *Can you operate this forklift?*

operation operations noun
When someone has an operation, a surgeon takes away or fixes a part of that person's body.

opportunity opportunities noun
a time or chance that is right for doing something. *On vacation, we had the opportunity to go sailing.*

opposite opposites noun
something that is different from another thing in every way. *Bad is the opposite of good.*

opposite adjective, adverb
1 different in every way. *North is in the opposite direction to south.*
2 across or on the other side. *The women stood opposite each other.*

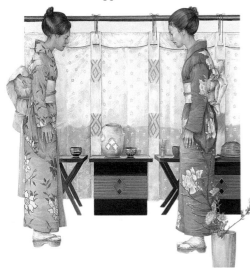

optician opticians noun
a person who tests your eyes to see if you need glasses or contact lenses.

orbit orbits noun
the invisible path that something such as a planet or a spaceship follows as it travels around Earth, another planet, or the Sun.
orbit verb.

orchard orchards noun
an area of land where fruit trees grow.

orchestra orchestras noun
a group of people who play different musical instruments together.
▲ Say **or-*kess-tra***.

order orders noun
1 Order means the way that things follow one another. *The letters of the alphabet always come in the same order.*
2 An order is something that you must do because someone tells you to do it. *The officer gave the soldiers an order to march.*

order orders ordering
ordered verb
1 If you order something, you say that you would like it. *We ordered bacon, toast, and eggs.*

2 If you order someone to do something, you say that the person must do it. *The doctor ordered Paul to stay in bed for a week.*

ordinary adjective
not exciting or special. *Yesterday was my birthday, but today is just an ordinary day.*

organ organs noun
1 An organ is a part of your body that does something special. Your heart, liver, and kidneys are all organs.
2 a big musical instrument like a piano with pipes that air goes through to make sounds. *a church organ.*

organization organizations noun
a group of people who work together.

organize organizes organizing
organized verb
If you organize something, you arrange or plan it. *The school has organized a trip to New York City.*

origin origins noun
1 the beginning of something and how and why it began. *We are learning about the origins of life on Earth.*
2 where someone or something came from. *a statue of African origin.*

original adjective
1 Something that is original is the first to be made. *This is an original painting. All of the others are copies.*
2 different and exciting. *What an original idea!*

ornament ornaments noun
an object that you like and use to make a place look pretty. *china ornaments.*

orphan orphans noun
a child whose mother and father are dead.

ostrich ostrich noun
a very large bird with long legs and a long neck that lives in Africa. Ostrich can run fast, but they cannot fly.

otter otters noun
a small animal with brown fur. Otters swim well and catch fish to eat.

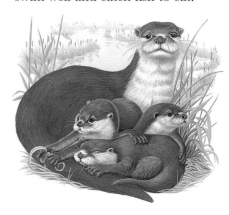

a gamelan orchestra from Indonesia

109

ought verb
If you ought to do something, you should do it because it is important. *You ought to brush your teeth before you go to bed.*

outdoors adverb
outside a building. *We went outdoors when the sun came out.*
■ The opposite is **indoors**.

outer adjective
1 not in the middle of a place. *I live in the outer suburbs of Houston.*
2 the outside of something. *His outer clothing was covered with mud.*
■ The opposite is **inner**.

outing outings noun
a short trip that you go on to enjoy yourself.

outline outlines noun
1 a line around the edge of something that shows its shape.
2 a drawing where you just draw a line to show the shape of something.
3 a list of topics that you want to write about. *Zeke made an outline before he wrote his essay.*

oval ovals noun
An oval is a shape like an egg.
oval adjective.

oven ovens noun
the boxlike part inside a stove where food is cooked. *Steve baked a chocolate cake in the oven.*

overalls noun
clothes that you wear to keep your other clothes clean when you do things such as painting.

overflow overflows overflowing overflowed verb
If something like a bathtub overflows, the water comes over the top of it. *I forgot to turn off the faucet, and the tub overflowed so much that water came out of the bathroom and ran down the stairs!*

overgrown adjective
If a garden is overgrown, it is covered with weeds and the plants look messy.

overhead adjective, adverb
above your head. *an overhead light* or *a plane flew overhead.*

overhear overhears overhearing overheard verb
When you overhear something, you hear what someone says when he or she is speaking to someone else. *I overheard Stacy say that she liked me.*

overlap overlaps overlapping overlapped verb
When two things overlap, part of one thing covers part of the other thing. *The shingles on the roof overlap.*

overseas adverb
across an ocean. *We flew overseas to London and Paris for our summer vacation.*

owe owes owing owed verb
If you owe money, you have to give the money back to the person who lent it to you. *I owe you 50¢ for the candy.*

owl owls noun
a bird with large eyes that sees well in the dark and hunts small animals, such as mice, at night.

own owns owning owned verb
If you own something, you have something that belongs to you. *Do you own that bike or did you borrow it?*

owner owners noun
a person who has or owns something. *Who is the owner of this pencil case?*

ox oxen noun
a bull that is used in some countries for pulling carts.

oxygen noun
a gas in the air that we breathe. People, animals, and plants need oxygen to live, and things cannot burn without it.

oyster oysters noun
a sea animal that lives inside a pair of shells. Some oysters produce pearls inside their shells.

ozone noun
a gas in the air. Ozone forms a layer called the ozone layer around Earth. It protects us from the harmful rays of the Sun.
ozone-friendly not harmful to the ozone layer. *We buy only ozone-friendly spray cans.*

Pp

pace noun
the speed at which something happens or moves. *They started off at a fast pace.*

pack packs packing packed verb
When you pack, you put clothes and other things you need into a suitcase or box to take away with you.

package packages noun
1 Something wrapped in paper so that you can mail it. *Mom wrapped up Grandma's birthday present and mailed the package to her.*
2 a box or bag of something. *a package of cheese.*

pad pads noun
1 a thick piece of soft material that can be used to protect something.
2 a lot of pieces of paper to write or draw on that are held together at one edge.
3 the soft part on the underneath of an animal's paw.

paddle paddles paddling paddled verb
1 If you paddle, you walk in the shallow water at the edge of the ocean or a lake.
2 When you paddle a canoe, you move it through the water.

paddle paddles noun
a short, flat oar for a boat or canoe.

padlock padlocks noun
a small metal block with a bar in the shape of a U at the top that you can use to lock things such as gates and bicycles and some doors.

page pages noun
one side of a piece of paper in a book or newspaper. *This dictionary has lots of pages.*

paid the past of pay.

pain noun
the feeling that you have in a part of your body when it hurts. *I have a bad pain in my lower back.* ● A word that sounds like **pain** is **pane**.

painful adjective
When something is painful, it hurts a lot. *I fell over, and my knee is now very painful.*
painfully adverb.

paint paints noun
a liquid that you can use to make colored pictures or to give a new color to the walls and ceilings in a house.
paint verb
I am going to paint a picture.

painter painters noun
1 a person whose job it is to put paint on walls, doors, and window frames.
2 an artist who paints pictures. *Monet was a French painter.*

painting paintings noun
a picture made using paint. *We hung our painting on the wall.*

pair pairs noun
1 two things that go together or that you use together. *a pair of gloves.*
2 We also talk about pairs of things such as pants, scissors, or binoculars that have two parts that are the same but are joined together.
● A word that sounds like **pair** is **pear**.

pajamas noun
pants and a top that you wear to sleep in.

palace palaces noun
a large building for a king or queen.

pale paler palest adjective
Something that is pale is almost white. *pale blue.* ■ The opposite is **dark**.

palm palms noun
1 a tree with no branches but that has long leaves that grow from the top of the trunk.
2 the flat part inside your hand between your wrist and your fingers.

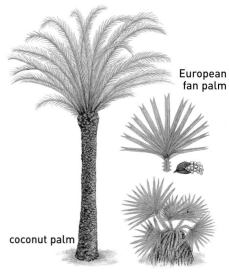

European fan palm

coconut palm

date palm

pan pans noun
a container with a handle that you use for cooking food. *a frying pan.*

pancake pancakes noun
a flat cake made from flour, baking powder, eggs, and milk and fried in a pan.

panda pandas noun
an animal that looks like a black and white bear, or a raccoon.

giant panda

red panda

pane panes noun
a flat piece of glass. *a windowpane.*
● A word that sounds like **pane** is **pain**.

panel panels noun
a long, flat piece of wood or glass that is part of a door or fence.

panic panics panicking panicked verb
If you panic, you feel so worried or afraid that you do not know what to do and you cannot act or think in a sensible or calm way.
panic noun.

pant pants panting panted verb
If people or animals pant, they breathe quickly with their mouth open. *Dogs pant when they get hot in order to cool themselves down.*

panther panthers noun
a black leopard.

pantomime pantomimes noun
a play with a story that is told by actors who do not speak but use arm and other body movements.

pants noun
a piece of clothing that you wear to cover all or part of your legs. Pants have two holes for your legs to go through.

paper noun
1 thin material that you use for writing on or wrapping things in and that books, newspapers, and magazines are printed on.
2 a newspaper.

parable parables noun
a story that teaches people something.

parachute parachutes noun
a large piece of cloth attached to a person with ropes that opens up like an umbrella so that the person can jump from a plane and float safely to the ground. ▲ Say **pair**-*a-shoot*.

parade parades noun
a lot of people marching along, often with decorated vehicles and music, to celebrate something special. *There was a big parade to celebrate the 4th of July.*

paragraph paragraphs noun
several sentences about the same idea that are written or printed together.

The first sentence of a paragraph starts on a new line. ▲ Say **pair**-*a-graf*.

parallel adjective
Parallel lines are straight and always the same distance from each other. *The rungs of a ladder are parallel.*

paralyzed adjective
If part of your body is paralyzed, you cannot move it or feel anything in it. *She is paralyzed from the waist down but is able to move around in a wheelchair.*

parcel parcels noun
a package. *At Christmas, we mailed many parcels.*

parchment noun
a material made from the skin of a sheep or goat that was used for writing on in ancient times.

pardon pardons pardoning pardoned verb
If you pardon people, you forgive them. *The governor pardoned the criminal.*

parent parents noun
a mother or a father.

park parks noun
an area of land, usually in a town, with grass and plants where people can go to walk and children can play.

park parks parking parked verb
to leave a car somewhere.

parliament parliaments noun
a group of people who meet to discuss or make new laws for a country. ▲ Say **parl**-*e-ment*.

parrot parrots noun
a tropical bird with brightly colored feathers and a curved beak. Some parrots can be taught to copy human speech.

part parts noun
1 one piece or a bit of something.
2 If you have a part in a play, you act as one of the characters in the play.

part parts parting parted verb
1 to divide. *hair parted in the middle.*
2 to separate. *We parted at the crossroad.*

particular adjective
A particular thing or person is the one that you mean and not anything or anyone else. *I don't want any old kitten; I want that particular one over there.*

partner partners noun
A partner is someone who does something with another person. *She's my favorite partner when we go square dancing.*

party parties noun
1 a group of people who get together to have fun. *a birthday party.*
2 a group of people who have the same ideas about politics. *the Democratic Party* or *the Republican Party.*

pass passes passing passed verb
1 If you pass something, you go by it without stopping.
2 If you pass a test, you do it well enough to succeed.
3 If you pass something to others, you give or hand it to them. *Pass us that pair of scissors, please.*
● A word that sounds like **passed** is **past**.

pass passes noun
a ticket or card that allows you to do something, such as travel free or enter a building.

passage passages noun
a narrow place with walls on each side like a corridor.

passenger passengers noun
a person who is traveling in a vehicle but not driving it.

passport passports noun
a small book or document that you take with you when you travel to another country that shows who you are and what country you come from.

password passwords noun
a secret word that you have to know to get into a place or to be able to work on a computer.

past noun
the time up until now. *In the past, there was no gas or electricity.* ▪ The opposite is **future**. ● A word that sounds like **past** is **passed**.

past preposition
farther on than something, or after it. *Go past the church and then turn left.* ● A word that sounds like **past** is **passed**.

pasta noun
a food made from flour that is formed into different shapes. Spaghetti and macaroni are types of pasta.

types of pasta

paste noun
1 a thick, soft glue.
2 a thick, soft mixture of food.

pastel pastels noun
a special colored crayon that looks like chalk that you can use for drawing.

pastime pastimes noun
a hobby or sport that you do when you are not working.

pastry noun
a mixture of flour, fat, and water that is rolled flat and used for making pies.

pasture pastures noun
a field with grass for animals such as cows and sheep to eat.

pat pats patting patted verb
If you pat something, you hit it gently with your hand. *He patted the dog.*

patch patches noun
1 a piece of material that you put over a hole to fix it. *Sid has a patch on his knee and over his eye.*
2 a small area that is different from the rest. *a patch of white fur.*

path paths noun
a narrow piece of ground where people can walk to get somewhere. *There's a path across the field.*

patience noun
If you have patience, you stay calm when something takes a long time or is very difficult. ▲ Say **pay-shenss**.

patient adjective
If you are patient, you stay calm and do not complain when something takes a long time. ▪ The opposite is **impatient**.
patiently adverb.

patient patients noun
a person who is being treated by a doctor or a dentist. *The doctor sees 30 patients a day.* ▲ Say **pay-shent**.

patrol patrols noun
a group of soldiers, guards, or police officers who regularly go around an area to protect it and make sure that there is no trouble or danger.

pattern patterns noun
a design or arrangement of colors and shapes on something. *It is fun to make patterns using different colors and shapes.*

pause pauses pausing paused verb
If you pause, you stop what you are doing for a short time before you continue with it.
pause noun
● A word that sounds like **pause** is **paws**.

pavement pavements noun
the hard surface of a road or sidewalk. *The pavement was covered with ice.*

paw paws noun
an animal's foot. ● A word that sounds like **paws** is **pause**.

pay pays paying paid verb
When you pay people, you give them money for something you have bought or for work they have done. *How much did you pay Don to wash your car?*

pea peas noun
a small, round green vegetable that grows in a pod.

peace noun
1 a time when people are not fighting. ▪ The opposite is **war**.
2 a time when there is no noise or no worry.
peaceful adjective.

peach peaches noun
a soft, round fruit with a pale, fuzzy orange skin and a large pit inside.

peacock peacocks noun
a large male bird with a tail made of blue and green feathers that it can spread out like a fan. The female is called a peahen.

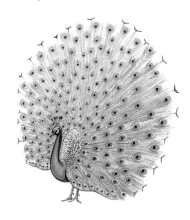

peak peaks noun
1 the pointed top of a mountain.
2 the front top part of a cap.

peanut peanuts noun
a light brown, oily seed that grows in a pod. The pod ripens underground.

pear pears noun
a sweet fruit that is round at the bottom but narrower at the top where the stalk is. ● A word that sounds like **pear** is **pair**.

pearl pearls noun
a small, hard, round white ball that is used as jewelry and that grows inside the shell of an oyster. *a pearl necklace.* ▲ Rhymes with **curl**.

pebble pebbles noun
a small, smooth stone.

pecan pecans noun
a flat nut that is good to eat. *salted pecans.*

peck pecks pecking pecked verb
When a bird pecks, it pushes its beak at something and picks it up. *The hens were pecking at the food scattered on the ground.*

pedal pedals noun
a part on a machine that you push with your foot. You push the pedals around on a bicycle to make it move. You push the pedals down in a car to make the car go faster or slower.

pedestrian pedestrians noun
a person who is walking across or along a street.

peel peels peeling peeled verb
If you peel a fruit or vegetable, you take off the skin. *She is peeling an apple.*

peel noun
the outside skin of a fruit or vegetable. *orange peel.*

peep peeps peeping peeped verb
If you peep, you look quickly at something. *The movie was so frightening that he just peeped at it.*

peer peers peering peered verb
You peer at something when it is difficult to see, so you have to look hard to see it. ● A word that sounds like **peer** is **pier**.

peg pegs noun
a piece of wood, plastic, or metal that is used to hold something down or to hang something up. *tent pegs* or *a peg to hang your coat on.*

pelican pelicans noun
a large water bird with a long, narrow beak with a pouch under it that it uses for holding fish.

pen pens noun
a long, narrow object with a point called a nib at one end that you use for writing with ink.

penalty penalties noun
a punishment given if you do not obey a rule or if you do something wrong.

pencil pencils noun
a long, thin stick made of wood with a substance called graphite in the middle that you use for writing or drawing.

pendulum pendulums noun
a weight on the end of a rod inside some clocks. It swings from side to side to make the clock work.

penguin penguins noun
a large black-and-white bird that swims but cannot fly. Penguins live mostly in the Antarctic, the very cold land and ocean in the far south of the world. Penguins feed on fish.

penitentiary penitentiary noun
a federal or state prison for people guilty of crimes.

penknife penknives noun
a knife with blades that fold back into the handle.

pennant pennants noun
a flag in the shape of a triangle.

penny pennies noun
In the United States and Canada, 100 pennies make one dollar.

pen pal pen pals noun
a person who lives far away whom you get to know by writing letters back and forth. *Lucy finally met her pen pal after writing for six years.*

pentagon pentagons noun
a shape with five sides.

people noun
men, women, and children. *A lot of people were waiting at the bus stop.*

pepper peppers noun
1 a spice with a hot taste that is ground into a powder and put on food. *black pepper.*

different types of peppers

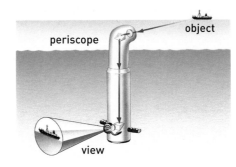

2 a green, red, or yellow vegetable that is hollow inside.

percent noun
the number of parts of something in every 100. *Eight percent of people or eight people in every 100 travel to work by bus.* The sign for percent is % *(8%).* ▲ Say *per*-sent.

perch perches noun
1 a place for a bird to stand.
2 a type of fish that lives in fresh water.
perch verb
The birds perched on the fence.

percussion noun
all of the different musical instruments, such as drums, that you play by hitting them.

perfect adjective
A perfect thing has no mistakes or faults.
perfection noun, **perfectly** adverb.

perform performs performing performed verb
1 If actors perform, they act, sing, dance, or tell jokes in front of an audience.
2 to do or carry out. *The surgeon performed an operation.*
performer noun.

perfume perfumes noun
a liquid with a pleasant smell that you put on your skin to make it smell nice. *a bottle of perfume.*

perimeter perimeters noun
the outside edge of something. *the perimeter of the circle.* ▲ Say *per*-imi-*ter*.

period periods noun
1 an amount of time.
2 a particular time in history.
3 a dot that you put at the end of a full sentence.

periscope periscopes noun
a tube with mirrors inside that are arranged so that when you look in one end of the tube, you can see things through the top that you would not normally be able to see.

Periscopes are used in submarines to see what is happening above the surface of the water.

permanent adjective
lasting forever or for a very long time. ■ The opposite is **temporary**.

permission noun
If people give you permission to do something, they say that you are allowed to do it. *My teacher gave me permission to go home early.*

permit permits permitting permitted verb
If people permit you to do something, they allow you to do it. *My parents permit me to stay up late on Friday and Saturday nights.* ■ The opposite is **forbid**.

person noun
a man, woman, or child.

personal adjective
belonging to one person.

persuade persuades persuading persuaded verb
If you persuade somebody to do something, you manage to make him or her do it.
▲ Say *per*-swade.

pest pests noun
1 an insect or animal that damages plants or is harmful to people.
2 a person who is annoying or causes trouble.

pet pets noun
a tame animal that you keep in the house and take care of.

petal petals noun
one of the white or colored parts that make the outside of a flower.

petroleum noun
a yellow-black oil under the ground that people use to make gasoline and other fuel.

phantom phantoms noun
a ghost. ▲ Say **fan**-*tom*.

pharmacist pharmacists noun
a person who prepares and sells medicine. ▲ Say **far**-*ma-cyst*.

pharmacy pharmacies noun
the part of a drugstore that sells medicines. ▲ Say **far**-*ma-see*.

phone phones noun
a telephone. ▲ Say **fone**.
phone verb

photo photos noun
a picture that you make by using a camera. ▲ Say **foh**-*toh*.

photocopy photocopies noun
a copy of a document made by a machine called a photocopier.

physical adjective
to do with people's bodies rather than their minds. ▲ Say **fiz**-*i-cul*.
physically adverb.

piano pianos noun
a large musical instrument with a row of black-and-white keys. When you press a key, a small hammer inside the piano hits a string to make a sound.
pianist noun.

pick picks picking picked verb
1 When you pick something, you choose it from a group of things because it is the one that you want. *Pick your favorite book, and we'll buy it.*
2 If you pick a fruit or a flower, you take it off the plant. *We're going to the farm tomorrow to pick strawberries.*
3 When you pick something up, you lift it from where it is lying. *Can you pick up those bags and bring them into the house?*
4 If you pick at something, you eat a little bit of it. *He wasn't very hungry and only picked at his food.*

pickle pickles noun
a vegetable that has been kept in vinegar. *I like cucumber pickles.*

picnic picnics noun
a meal that you take somewhere with you and eat outside.

picture pictures noun
a drawing, painting, or photograph.

pie pies noun
a piece of pastry with fruit, custard, meat, fish, or vegetables cooked inside it.

piece pieces noun
1 a part or bit that is cut off something bigger. *Cut the pie into four equal pieces.*
2 a single thing. *a piece of paper.*

piece

Some words that you can use instead of piece:

May I have a piece of cake?
slice, portion

She tore the paper into pieces.
bits, scraps

There were huge pieces of meat in the soup.
chunks, lumps

On this piece of land we grow roses.
part, section

pier piers noun
a long platform built out over the water where people can walk or where boats can be tied up. A word that sounds like **pier** is **peer**.

pierce pierces piercing pierced verb
When a sharp object pierces something, it makes a hole in it. *Have you had your ears pierced?*

pig pigs noun
a farm animal with a flat nose, short legs, and a short, curly tail. Male pigs are called boars, and female pigs are called sows. The meat of pigs is eaten as bacon, pork, and ham.

pigeon pigeons noun
a gray bird with a fat body. Some pigeons have been trained to carry messages, and some are used for racing.

pile piles noun
a lot of things that have been put on top of each other. *a pile of books.*

pill pills noun
A pill is a medicine that has been made into a small, round object that you swallow.

pillar pillars noun
a tall, round column made of stone or brick that holds up part of a building. *The Lincoln Memorial has tall white marble pillars.*

pillow pillows noun
a soft cushion that you put your head on when you are in bed.

pilot pilots noun
a person who flies an aircraft.

pin pins
noun
a small, thin metal stick with a sharp point at one end  that you use for holding two pieces of cloth or paper in place.
pin verb
She pinned the badge to her dress.

pinch pinches pinching pinched verb
1 If you pinch somebody, you squeeze a little bit of the person's skin with your thumb and finger.

pine pines noun
a tall evergreen tree that has narrow, pointed leaves called needles and its seeds held in cones.

pineapple pineapples noun
a large sweet fruit that is yellow inside and has a thick, prickly skin and leaves growing out of the top.

pint pints noun
sixteen ounces of a liquid. *Two cups equal one pint.*

pipe pipes noun
a tube, usually made of metal or plastic, that carries things like water and gas.

pirate pirates noun
a person who attacks and robs ships and private boats.

pistol pistols noun
a small gun that is held in the hand.

pit pits noun
1 a large hole in the ground.
2 the large seed of a fruit.

pitch pitches noun
1 a way of throwing a ball, as in softball or baseball.
2 The pitch of a sound is how low or high the sound is. *Her voice rose in pitch.*
pitch verb.

pity noun
If you feel pity for people, you feel sorry for them. *He feels pity for children who do not have enough to eat.*
pity verb.

pixie pixies noun
a small fairy.

pizza pizzas noun
a round piece of flat dough with things on top such as tomatoes and cheese that is baked in the oven.
▲ Say pee-*tsa*.

place places noun
1 an area or building. *Show me the place on your leg that hurts.*
2 a position in a race. *He was in third place.*

plague plagues noun
a serious disease that spreads quickly. *Plague can be spread by rats and fleas.*

plain plainer plainest adjective
1 Something that is plain has no pattern or marks on it. *Take a piece of plain paper and write the essay title at the top.* or *He wore a plain red tie.*
2 A plain person is ordinary and not beautiful. *She had a plain face, but she was very kind.*
3 If something is plain to you, it is clear and easy to understand. *She made it plain that she expected good behavior at all times.*
● A word that sounds like **plain** is **plane**.

plait plaits verb
to divide into strands and weave one over the other until a smooth line like a rope is formed. *She plaited her thick hair into two long braids.* ▲ Rhymes with **cat**.

plan plans
noun
a set of ideas that show how you are going to do something.

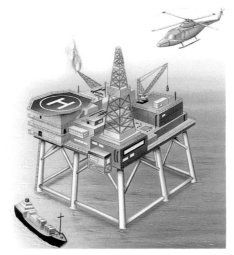

plan plans planning planned
verb
When you plan something, you figure out what you are going to do and how you are going to do it.

plane planes noun
an airplane that takes people to places by air.
● A word that sounds like **plane** is **plain**.

planet planets noun
a very large, round object in space, such as Venus, Mars, or Earth, that moves around a star such as the Sun.

plank planks noun
a long, flat piece of wood. *The floors are made of planks.*

plant plants noun
a tree, flower, bush, or other living thing that grows in one place and has roots, a stem, and leaves.
◆ Look at page 118.

plant plants planting planted verb
When you plant things such as flowers or trees, you put them into the ground where you want them to grow. *The garden club has planted trees on both sides of the street.*

plaster plasters noun
1 a wet material that a doctor puts around a broken arm or leg and that becomes hard. A cast made of plaster keeps the part from moving.
2 a soft, wet mixture that you use to cover walls and ceilings inside a house. It becomes hard and smooth, and you can paint or wallpaper over it.

plastic noun
a material that is made in a factory for a lot of different uses. It is light in weight and does not break easily.

plate plates noun
a flat dish that you put food on.

platform platforms noun
1 the part of a railroad station where you get on and off the trains.
2 a flat area that is built higher than the floor so that the people on it can be seen more easily.
3 a flat structure that is higher than the ground or built over water. *an offshore oil platform.*

play plays playing played verb
1 When you play, you do things that you enjoy doing, such as games.
2 If you play a musical instrument, you use it to make music. *She plays the clarinet.*

play plays noun
a story that is performed in the theater, on television, or on the radio. *Our school play starts Friday.*

playful adjective
liking to play and have fun.

playground playgrounds noun
an area of land where children can play. *Freddie plays in the school playground.*

plead pleads pleading pleaded or pled verb
If you plead with someone, you strongly ask that person to do something. *She pleaded to be allowed to go home.*

pleasant pleasanter pleasantest adjective
A pleasant thing is something that you enjoy or like. *We had a pleasant afternoon at the beach.*

please interjection
You say "please" to be polite when you are asking for something. *Would you pass me the magazine, please?*
please verb.

Plants

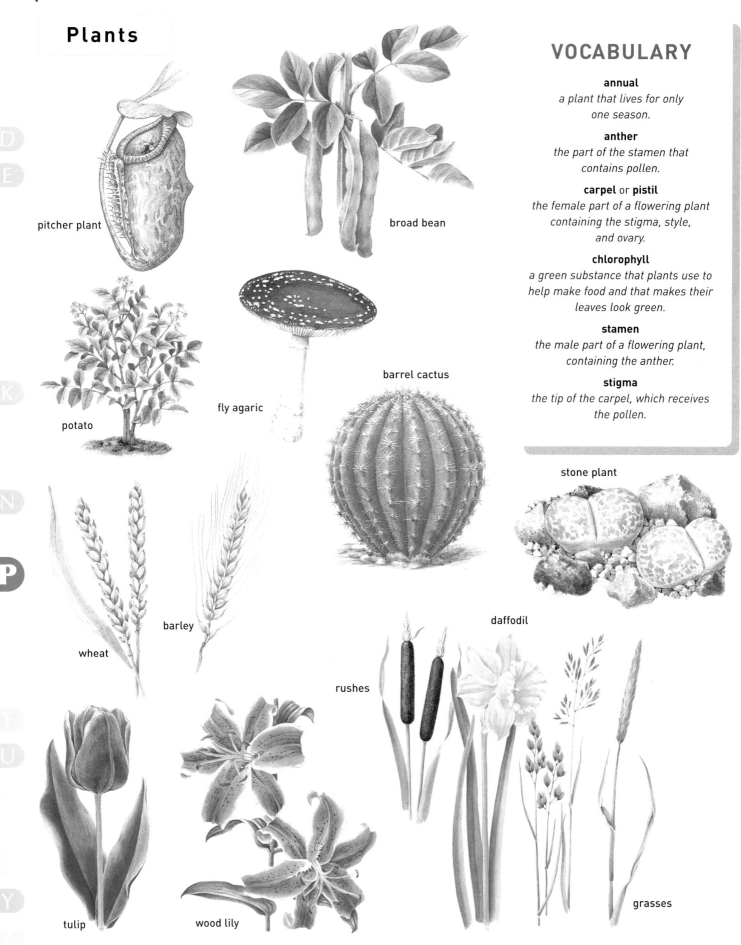

pitcher plant

broad bean

potato

fly agaric

barrel cactus

stone plant

wheat

barley

rushes

daffodil

grasses

tulip

wood lily

VOCABULARY

annual
a plant that lives for only one season.

anther
the part of the stamen that contains pollen.

carpel or **pistil**
the female part of a flowering plant containing the stigma, style, and ovary.

chlorophyll
a green substance that plants use to help make food and that makes their leaves look green.

stamen
the male part of a flowering plant, containing the anther.

stigma
the tip of the carpel, which receives the pollen.

pleasure noun
the feeling you get when you are happy and enjoying something. ▲ Say plej-*ur*.

plenty noun
a large amount of something and more than is needed. *There's plenty of cake, so you can all have a piece.*

plot plots noun
1 a secret plan by a group of people to do something, usually bad.
2 the story in a book, film, or TV show.
3 a small area of ground. *a vegetable plot.*

plow plows noun
a tool that is used for turning over the soil to prepare it for planting seeds. It is pulled along by a tractor or an animal. ▲ Rhymes with **cow**. **plow** verb.

pluck plucks plucking plucked verb
1 When you pluck a musical instrument such as a guitar, you pull on the strings in order to make the sounds of the notes.
2 When you pluck a flower or fruit, you pick it from the place where it was growing.

plug plugs noun
1 a round object that you put into the drain hole of a bathtub or sink to stop the water from running out.
2 a thing at the end of a wire on a machine that fits into a socket on the wall so that the machine can be connected to the power supply.

plum plums noun
a soft, purple or yellow fruit with a thin skin and a pit in the center.

plumber plumbers noun
a person whose job it is to put in water pipes in a house and to fix them when they break. *The plumber has come to fix the drain.* ▲ Say plum-*er*.

plump plumper plumpest noun
nicely fat. *The baby had plump cheeks.*
■ The opposite is **slim**.

plural plurals noun
the form of a word that you use when you are talking about two or more things instead of just one. The plural of "desk" is "desks" and the plural of "mouse" is "mice." ▲ Say pler-*rel*.
■ The opposite is **singular**.

plus preposition
You use the word "plus" to talk about adding numbers together. In arithmetic, you can use the sign + to mean plus. *Six plus five equals 11 is the same as 6 + 5 = 11.*

pocket pockets noun
a part like a flat bag in your clothes that you can put things in.

pod pods noun
a long, narrow part of some plants that seeds grow inside. Peas and beans grow in pods.

poem poems noun
a piece of writing arranged in short lines. The words in the lines make a rhythm, and sometimes the words at the ends of the lines rhyme.

some poetry books

poet poets noun
a person who writes poetry.

poetry noun
Poems are poetry.

point points noun
1 the end of something sharp like a needle or a pencil.
2 a particular place or time. *At this point, she suddenly saw that everybody had left the room.*
3 a score that somebody gets in a game or competition.
4 the purpose of doing something. *What's the point in taking off your coat if you're going right out again?*

point points pointing pointed verb
If you point, you show where something is by using your finger.

pointed adjective
A pointed thing has a point at one end.

poison noun
a substance that will make you sick or kill you if it gets inside your body. **poisonous** adjective.

poke pokes poking poked verb
To poke somebody is to push something into them. *She poked me in the back with her finger.*

polar bear polar bears noun
a large white bear that lives near the North Pole.

pole poles noun
1 a long, narrow, round piece of wood or metal. *a telephone pole.*
2 a point at each end of Earth that is farthest from the equator. *the North Pole and the South Pole.*

police noun
those whose job it is to protect people and make sure that everyone obeys the law.
policeman noun, **policewoman** noun, **police officer** noun.

polish polishes polishing polished verb
If you polish something, you rub it to make it shine. *David is polishing his shoes.* **polish** noun.

polite politer politest adjective
If you are polite, you behave well toward other people and think about how to make them feel comfortable. *It is polite to say "thank you" and "please."*
■ The opposite is **rude**.
politely adverb.

politics noun
all of the activities having to do with
the government of a country.
political adjective.

pollen noun
a fine powder inside flowers that the
wind or insects take to other flowers
of the same type so that they can
produce seeds.

pollution noun
poisonous chemicals and other forms
of dangerous dirt that cause damage
to the air, water, and environment.

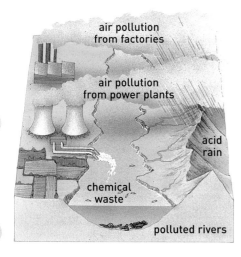

pond ponds noun
a small area of water.

pony ponies noun
a small type of horse.

pool pools noun
1 a small area of water.
2 a swimming pool.

poor poorer poorest adjective
1 A person who is poor has very little
money. ■ The opposite is **rich**.
2 not good enough. *My spelling is
very poor.*
3 unlucky or in a bad situation.
Poor John failed his driver's test.

pop pops noun
1 modern popular music.
2 a short, sharp sound.

popcorn noun
corn that you cook in hot oil to make
it pop open.

popular adjective
liked by a lot of people. *a popular song*
or *a popular girl.*
popularly adverb.

population populations noun
all of the people who live in a
particular area or country.

porch porches noun
a floor with a roof that is attached to
the front, back, or sides of a house. *I
love to sit on the porch and watch the sun set.*

porcupine porcupines noun
an animal that has stiff hairs on its
back called quills.

pork noun
the meat from a pig.

port ports noun
a place or town beside a large river or
the ocean where ships can stay and
load and unload.

portable adjective
Something that is portable is small
enough or light enough to be carried
around easily. *a portable computer* or
a portable television.

portion portions noun
an amount of food for one person.
a portion of peas.

portrait portraits noun
a picture of a person.

position positions noun
1 the place where something is. *I'm
not sure where we are, so can you check
our position on the map?*
2 the way in which you are sitting,
standing, or lying down. *Get into
a comfortable position.*

positive adjective
1 certain about something. *I'm positive
I saw him.*
2 A positive number is higher than
zero. ■ The opposite is **negative**.

possess possesses possessing
possessed verb
If you possess something, you
own it and it belongs to you.

Do you possess a TV and a stereo?
possession noun.

possible adjective
If something is possible, it can be done
or it can happen. *Come as soon as possible.*
■ The opposite is **impossible**.
possibility noun

post posts noun
a long, thick, strong pole or piece of
wood fixed in the ground. *a fence post.*

post posts posting posted verb
When you post a notice, you put it on
a wall in a public place.

postal service noun
the government department that sells
stamps and picks up and delivers the
mail.

postcard postcards noun
a small piece of cardboard, usually
with a picture on one side, that you can
use to send a short message to someone.

poster posters noun
a large picture, notice, or
advertisement that is put up on
a wall.

post office post offices noun
1 a place where you can send letters
and packages and buy stamps.
2 a local organization or group of
people who collect, sort, and deliver
people's letters and packages.

postpone postpones postponing
postponed verb
If you postpone something, you put it
off until later. *The race was postponed
because of bad weather.*

pot pots noun
1 a round container.
a pot of honey.
2 a container for plants to grow in
made of plastic or clay.

potato potatoes
noun
a white vegetable
with a thin brown
skin that grows under
the ground.

pottery noun
dishes and other objects made out of clay and then baked hard in a special oven called a kiln.

pouch pouches noun
1 a small bag.
2 a pocket of skin that female kangaroos and some other female animals have on their stomach that they use for carrying their babies.

pounce pounces pouncing pounced verb
To pounce is to suddenly jump forward and catch hold of something. *The kitten pounced on the ball of string.*

pound pounds noun
A pound of something weighs 16 ounces.

pour pours pouring poured verb
When you pour a liquid, you tilt a container such as a jug or bottle so that the liquid flows out.

poverty noun
People who live in poverty are very poor.

powder noun
tiny, dry grains that you get when you crush or grind something well.

power noun
1 the ability to do something. *Human beings have the power of speech.*
2 the force or strength of something. *The power of the wind knocked down the trees.*
3 A person who has power can control what happens to a lot of people.

powerful adjective
A powerful person or thing has a lot of power. *a powerful king* or *a powerful engine.* ■ The opposite is **weak**.

practical adjective
1 to do with actually working or doing something rather than knowing or having ideas about it. *Do you have practical training in Web design?*
2 sensible, useful, and likely to work. *a practical suggestion.*
practically adverb
almost. *I've practically finished eating.*

practice noun
doing something again and again until you can do it well. *guitar practice.*

practice practices practicing practiced verb
If you practice something, you keep doing it until you can do it well.

prairie prairies noun
flat land with lots of tall grass and few trees.

prairie dog prairie dogs noun
Prairie dogs live in burrows. They can stand on their hind legs. They have brown fur and can bark.

praise praises praising praised verb
When you praise someone, you say how well they have done something. *Everyone praised the brave firefighters.* ■ The opposite is **criticize**.

pray prays praying prayed verb
If you pray, you talk to God or Allah. ● A word that sounds like **pray** is **prey**.

prayer prayers noun
the words somebody says when they are talking to God or Allah.

precious adjective
very valuable or important to you. ▲ Say pre-*shus*.

predict predicts predicting predicted verb
If you predict something, you say that you think it is going to happen. *The weather forecast predicts rain for the weekend.*
prediction noun.

prefer prefers preferred verb
If you prefer one thing to another thing, you like it better. *Would you prefer an apple or a peach?*

prehistoric adjective
belonging to a very long time ago before history was remembered and written down. *Dinosaurs lived in prehistoric times.* ◆ Look at page 122.

prepare prepares preparing prepared verb
When you prepare something, you make it ready. *Leonard helped his dad prepare lunch.*
preparation noun.

preposition prepositions noun
a word that you use for such things as where and how. "Down," "on," and "in" are prepositions used in the following sentences: "He ran down the hill." "The phone was on the table." "The milk is in the bottle." A preposition shows how the words before and after it are related.

prescription prescriptions noun
the piece of paper that a doctor uses to write down the medicines or pills you need to get from a drugstore.

present adjective
1 being in a place or being there. *Many people were present at the concert.* ■ The opposite is **absent**.
2 happening now. *the present time.*

present presents noun
1 a thing that you give to someone. *What presents did you get?*
2 the time now. *We've had no trouble up to the present.*

121

prehistoric animals

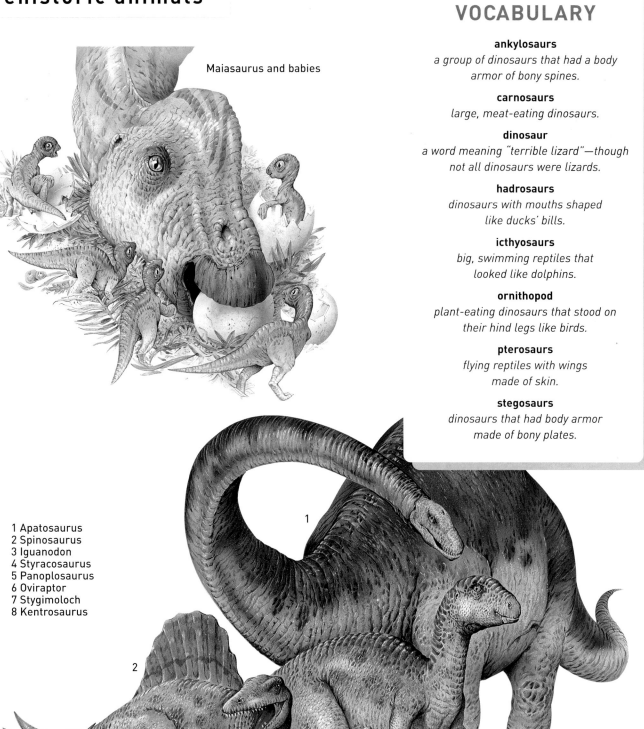

Maiasaurus and babies

VOCABULARY

ankylosaurs
a group of dinosaurs that had a body armor of bony spines.

carnosaurs
large, meat-eating dinosaurs.

dinosaur
a word meaning "terrible lizard"—though not all dinosaurs were lizards.

hadrosaurs
dinosaurs with mouths shaped like ducks' bills.

icthyosaurs
big, swimming reptiles that looked like dolphins.

ornithopod
plant-eating dinosaurs that stood on their hind legs like birds.

pterosaurs
flying reptiles with wings made of skin.

stegosaurs
dinosaurs that had body armor made of bony plates.

1 Apatosaurus
2 Spinosaurus
3 Iguanodon
4 Styracosaurus
5 Panoplosaurus
6 Oviraptor
7 Stygimoloch
8 Kentrosaurus

122

preserve preserves preserving **preserved** verb
1 If you preserve something, you keep it the way it is without changing it. *Most people want to preserve the old buildings, though the city council wants new ones.*
2 If you preserve food, you do something to it so that it will not spoil.

president presidents noun
A person who is chosen to lead a country that does not have a king or queen.

press presses pressing pressed verb
If you press something, you push hard on it. *You press a button and the door slides open.*

pressure noun
the force of one thing pressing or pushing on another. *If you apply pressure to that cut, it will stop bleeding.*
▲ Say **presh**-*ur*.

pretend pretends pretending pretended verb
If you pretend, you try to make other people believe something that is not true. *David's pretending to be a tree!*

pretty prettier prettiest adjective
attractive and nice to look at. *Flowers are pretty.*

prevent prevents preventing prevented verb
If you prevent something, you stop it from happening. *Shut the gate to prevent the horse from running away.*

previous adjective
The previous thing is the thing that came before or earlier. *I went over to Jane's house on Wednesday like we had arranged on the phone the previous day.*
▲ Say **pree**-*vee-us*.
previously adverb.

prey noun
any animal that is hunted for food. *Mice are an owl's natural prey.*
▲ Rhymes with **may**. ● A word that sounds like **prey** is **pray**.

price prices noun
the amount of money that you have to pay to buy something. *What's the price of that pair of sneakers?*

prick pricks pricking pricked verb
If you prick something, you make a small hole in it with something sharp. *Dominic said he'd prick the balloon with a pin.*

prickle prickles noun
a sharp point or thorn. *Be careful of this bush; it's covered with prickles.*
prickly adjective.

pride noun
the good feeling you get when you are proud and have done something well or someone you love or admire has done something well.

priest priests noun
a specially trained person in the Christian religion who leads people in religious services. ▲ Say **preest**.

primary adjective
1 first and most important. *Our primary concern is to make sure that everyone has enough to eat.*
2 to do with teaching children who are in kindergarten and grades one through four or five.

prime adjective
first and most important. *a matter of prime importance.*

prime number noun
a number that can be divided only exactly by itself or one. 7 and 17 are prime numbers.

prince princes noun
the son of a king or queen or a man or boy who is a member of a royal family.

princess princesses noun
the daughter of a king or queen or a woman or girl who is a member of a royal family.

principal principals noun
a person who is in charge of an elementary, middle, or high school.

principle principles noun
an important rule that you have about what is right and wrong. *It's against my principles to take drugs.*

print prints printing printed verb
1 When people print a book, magazine, or newspaper, they make copies of it on paper using a machine called a printer.
2 If you print something out from a computer, you use a machine called a printer to put information from the printer onto paper.
3 If you print words, you write using letters that are not joined up.
printer noun.

prison prisons noun
a building where people who have broken the law are kept locked up for a period of time.
prisoner noun.

private adjective
Something that is private is for only one person or one small group of people and not for everybody. *You can't see my letter; it's private.*
■ The opposite is **public**.
privately adverb.

prize prizes noun
a thing that you are given for winning a competition or for doing good work.

probably adverb
Something will be sure or likely to happen if you think that it is probably true or will probably happen.

problem problems noun
A problem is something that is difficult to figure out, understand, or do.

procession processions noun
a number of people walking or driving in a public place as part of a ceremony. *A brass band led the procession.*

prod prods prodding prodded verb
If you prod something, you push at it with something such as a stick or finger. *I prodded him in the ribs.*

produce produces producing produced verb
1 To produce something is to make it. *The factory produces hundreds of new cars each week.*
2 If you produce something, you take it out and show it. *She looked in her bag and produced a clean handkerchief.*
3 To produce a play, movie, or TV show is to organize the people making it and get it ready to show to the public.
▲ Say *pruh*-**dooss**.

product products noun
a thing that is made to be sold. *Maple syrup is a product of Canada.*

profession professions noun
a job that needs special knowledge and training, such as being a doctor or teacher.

professor professors noun
a person who is a teacher at a college or university. *My cousin is a professor at Iowa State University.*

profit profits noun
money that you get when you sell something for more than it cost to buy or make it.

program programs noun
1 a television or radio show.
2 a printed piece of paper that gives you information about such things as a play, concert, ballet, or game.

3 a list of instructions that make a computer work.

progress progresses noun
the way something or someone moves forward or gets better. *Jennifer is making good progress learning Spanish.*

project projects noun
a piece of work in which you find out as much as you can about a subject. *We're doing a project on World War II at school.*

prom proms noun
a fancy high-school dance.

promise promises promising promised verb
When you promise that you will do something, you say you will do it and you really mean it. *Pam promised not to make noise.*

prompt adjective
When you are prompt, you do something quickly or immediately, without delay.

pronoun pronouns noun
a word like "you," "her," or "one" that you use when you know the person or thing that is being talked about. "Me," "I," "it," "her," and "one" are pronouns in the following sentences. *Jane tossed me the ball, and I threw it back to her.* or *I don't want the red crayon; I want the green one.*

pronounce pronounces pronouncing pronounced verb
When you pronounce a word right, you say the sound of the word in the correct way. *Some English words are hard for French people to pronounce correctly.*
pronunciation noun.

proof noun
To have proof of something is to have all of the facts to show that it is true.

prop props propping propped verb
If you prop something, you put it or lay it against something. *She propped her bike up against the wall.*

propeller
propellers
noun
a set of blades that spin around to make a ship, plane, or helicopter move.

proper adjective
The proper way to do something is the right or correct way to do it.

property properties noun
1 things that you own. *Those books don't belong to the school; they're my property.*
2 a building and the land around it.

prosecute prosecutes prosecuting prosecuted verb
To prosecute people is to accuse them of crimes and make them go to court. *Trespassers will be prosecuted.*

prospector prospectors noun
a person who hunts for valuable minerals, such as gold.

protect protects protecting protected verb
If you protect others, you try to keep them from being hurt.

protest protests protesting protested verb
If you protest, you say that you think something is wrong and should be changed.

proud adjective
feeling good or pleased because you or someone else has done something very well. *I got better grades and I was really proud of myself.*
proudly adverb.

prove proves proving proved verb
When you prove something, you show that it is true. ▲ Rhymes with **move**.

provide provides providing provided verb
If you provide something, you get it and make sure that you give it when it is needed. *I'll provide the sandwiches.*

prune prunes pruning pruned verb
When you prune a tree or bush, you cut back its branches to keep it healthy or stop it from getting too big.

public adjective
for everybody to use or see. *a public phone booth* or *public transportation*.
The opposite is **private**.

public school public schools noun
a school in a city, town, or county that you attend for free.

publish publishes publishing published verb
To publish a book, magazine, or newspaper is to have it printed and ready for people to buy copies.

puck pucks noun
a hard rubber disk that ice hockey players push with long sticks.

puddle puddles noun
a pool or small area of water left on the ground after it has rained.

pueblo pueblos noun
a Native American village in the southwest United States that has stone and adobe buildings.

puff puffs noun
a small amount of moving air, smoke, or wind. *a puff of smoke.*

pull pulls pulling pulled verb
When you pull something, you hold it and move it toward you.

pulp noun
the soft part inside a fruit or vegetable.

pulse noun
the regular beat or throbbing that your blood makes as it goes through your body. You can feel your pulse by putting your fingers on your wrist.

pump pumps noun
a machine that is used to push air, liquid, or gas into or out of something.

pump pumps pumping pumped verb
to force air or liquid with a pump.

pumpkin pumpkins noun
a large, round orange vegetable that grows above the ground.

pun puns noun
a joke that works because a word has two meanings. "Two pears make one pair."

punch punches punching punched verb
1 If you punch someone, you hit him or her with your fist.
2 If you punch something, you make a hole in it. *The guard inspected everyone's tickets and punched them.*

punctual adjective
arriving on time.
punctually adverb.

punctuation noun
marks such as periods, commas, and quotation marks that you use when you are writing.

puncture punctures noun
a hole in a bicycle or car tire.
Say **punk**-*cher*.

punish punishes punishing punished verb
To punish someone is to make them hurt or suffer because he or she has done something wrong.
punishment noun.

pupa pupae noun
a stage in an insect's life cycle after it is a larva but before it is an adult insect with wings. Say **pew**-*pa*.

pupil pupils noun
1 a person who is studying at school.
2 the small, round black part at the center of the eye.

puppet puppets noun
a type of doll that you can make move by pulling strings that are attached to the different parts of the puppet, or by putting your hand inside the puppet and moving it with your fingers.

puppy puppies noun
a young dog.

purchase purchases purchasing purchased verb
If you purchase something, you buy it.

pure purer purest adjective
Something that is pure is not mixed with anything else. *pure apple juice.*
Say **pyuer**.

Puritan Puritans noun
a person in North America in the 1600s who wanted simple religious ceremonies.

purpose purposes noun
the reason that something is being done or what it is supposed to do. *The purpose of the trip is to see some famous places.*
on purpose If you do something on purpose, you intend to do it.

purr purrs purring purred verb
When a cat purrs, it makes a low sound to show that it is pleased.

push pushes pushing pushed verb
If you push something, you move it away from you. *When the car broke down, the entire family had to get out and push it off the road.*

Qq

quack quacks quacking
quacked verb
To quack is to make the sound that
a duck makes.
quack noun.

quaint quainter quaintest adjective
pretty and unusual. *a quaint old cottage.*

qualify qualifies qualifying
qualified verb
1 If you qualify, you pass a test that
allows you to do a job. *She qualified
as a teacher.*
2 You qualify if you win part of a
competition and are able to go on
to the next part. *Our team qualified
for the championship.*
qualification noun.

quality noun
1 how good or bad something is. *a dress
made from material of good quality.*
2 what makes something what it is.
*One quality of lemons is that they
are sour.*

quantity
quantities noun
an amount
of something.
*Birds need large
quantities of twigs
to make a nest.*

quarrel quarrels quarreling
quarreled verb
If you quarrel with others, you have
an angry argument with them.

quarry quarries noun
a place where things such as stone are
dug out of the ground.

quart quarts noun
A quart equals two pints. Four quarts
equal one gallon.

SPELLING TIP:

*Words that begin with "qu"
sound like they are spelled with
"cw" or "kw."*

quarter
quarters noun
1 one of four
equal parts
of something.
2 a coin worth
25 cents.

quay quays
a place in a harbor where boats are
tied up to be loaded or unloaded.

queen queens noun
a woman who rules a country or
who is the wife of a king and a
member of a royal family.

queer adjective
very strange. *queer sounds.*

query queries noun
a question. *Does anyone have any
queries?*

quest quests noun
a long and hard search for something
important. *a quest for a cure for cancer.*

question questions noun
You ask a question when you want to
find out about something. *I asked my
teacher a question about the computer.*
■ The opposite is **answer**.

question mark
question marks noun
a mark (?) that you use in writing.
You put a question mark at the end
of a sentence to show that some
body has asked a question. *What
did you say?*

quick quicker quickest adjective
1 fast. *If you're not quick, we'll miss
the bus.*
2 done in a short time. *We had
a quick breakfast before we went out.*
quickly adverb
Go as quickly as you can.

quiet quieter quietest adjective
making no noise or very little noise.
She played quiet music.
■ The opposite is **loud**.

quill quills noun
1 a large, stiff feather from a bird's
wing or tail.
2 the sharp spines of a porcupine.

quilt quilts noun
a soft, light
cover for a bed
made from
two layers of
cloth filled
with
padding.

quintuplet quintuplets noun
one of five babies that are born all at
the same time to one mother.

quit quits quitting quit verb
If you quit, you stop doing something.
I am going to quit studying German.

quite adverb
1 more than a little. *He's quite tall.*
2 completely. *You're quite right.*

quiver quivers noun
a case for carrying arrows.

quiz quizzes noun
a short test.

quotation quotations noun
words that you say or write that
someone else has said before. *"We
the people" is a quotation from the
U.S. Constitution.*

quotation mark
quotation marks noun
marks (" ") that you use in writing.
You put quotation marks before and
after the words that someone has said.
"What did you say?" he asked.

quote quotes quoting
quotes verb
1 to say or write something that
someone else has said before.
2 to name a price. *He quoted a price
of $100.*

Rr

rabbi rabbis noun
a teacher of the Jewish religion and the leader of a synagogue.

rabbit rabbits noun
a small wild animal with soft fur and long ears. Rabbits live in burrows.

rabies noun
Rabies is a disease that kills dogs and some other animals.

raccoon raccoons noun
a small animal that has masklike black markings on its face and black rings around its tail.

race races noun
1 a competition to see who is the fastest.
2 a large number of human beings whose ancestors all came from the same area and who look alike in some way—for example, in skin color.

race races racing raced verb
If you race, you go very fast. *She was racing along the bicycle path.*

rack racks noun
a frame or set of shelves that you can put things on or hang things on.

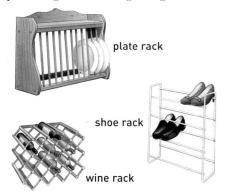

plate rack

shoe rack

wine rack

racket rackets noun
a sports bat with an oval frame for hitting a ball in tennis or badminton.

radar noun
a device that shows on a screen the exact position and speed of a plane or ship that cannot be seen.

radiator radiators noun
a flat metal object fixed against a wall that steam or hot water runs through to heat up a room.
▲ Say **ray**-*di-ay-ter*.

radio radios noun
a machine that receives sounds sent through the air so that you can hear them. You turn on a radio to listen to music, news, and other shows.

radius radiuses noun
a straight line from the center of a circle to the edge. ◆ Look at page 35.

raft rafts noun
a flat boat made of rubber or wood.

rag rags noun
an old piece of material that you can use to clean things.

rage noun
very great anger. *He was purple with rage.*

raid raids noun
a sudden attack on a place. *a raid by soldiers on a village.*

rail rails noun
1 a bar for people to hold onto or to stop them from falling. *She held onto the rail as she climbed the stairs.*
2 the long parallel metal bars (lines) that trains run on.
3 a railroad system. *We traveled all around Europe by rail.*
railings noun.

railroad railroads noun
the system of trains, stations, and tracks used when people travel by train.

rain noun
water that falls to the ground from clouds in small drops.
rain verb, **rainy** adjective.
rainy weather.

rainbow rainbows noun
an arc or curve of light of different colors that you can sometimes see in the sky when there are rain and sunshine at the same time.

rainforest rainforests noun
an area of thick, tropical forest where a lot of rain falls. Most are in Central and South America, Africa, and Southeast Asia.

raise raises raising raised verb
If you raise something, you lift it up or move it so that it is higher. *Raise your hand if you know the answer.*
■ The opposite is **lower**.

raisin raisins noun
a dried grape.

rake rakes noun
a garden tool with a long handle and a row of metal teeth like a comb that you use to make the dirt even or to gather leaves into a pile.
rake verb.

rally rallies noun
1 a large public meeting.
2 a car or motorcycle race that takes place over a long distance.

ram rams noun
a male sheep.

ran past of **run**.

ranch ranches noun
a very large farm for cattle, horses, or sheep. ▲ Rhymes with **branch**.

rang past of **ring**.

range ranges noun
1 a choice of things of the same type. *The store stocks a wide range of sneakers.*
2 a long line of mountains.
3 the area or distance over which something can be used.
4 a big area of land where animals feed.

ransom ransoms noun
money demanded in return for letting a kidnapped person go free.

rap raps noun
1 a short, sharp sound like a single knock on a door.
2 a type of music where the words are spoken in rhythm and not sung.

rapid adjective
very quick. *a rapid heartbeat.*
rapidly adverb.

rare rarer rarest adjective
not often seen or done.
■ The opposite is **common**.

rash rashes noun
a lot of small red spots that you get on your skin if you have an illness like the measles.

raspberry raspberries noun
a small, sweet red fruit that grows on a bush. ◆ Look at page 18.

rat rats noun
an animal that is like a very large mouse with a long tail.

a black rat

rate rates noun
1 the speed at which something happens. *Scientists are worried by the rate at which rainforests are being cut down.*
2 the amount of money that you pay for a service. *You pay a cheaper rate for phone calls in the evenings and on weekends.*

rattle rattles rattling rattled verb
When something rattles, it makes the noise of things knocking together.

rattlesnake rattlesnakes noun
a snake with a poisonous bite. It has hard rings on its tail that rattle.

raw adjective
Food that is raw has not been cooked. *raw cabbage* or *raw meat.*

ray rays noun
a line of light. *the Sun's rays.*

razor razors noun
a tool with a very sharp blade for shaving.

reach reaches reaching reached verb
1 When you reach a place, you get there. *When we reach Denver, we'll stop and have lunch.*
2 When you reach for something, you stretch out your arm toward it. *I'm not tall enough to reach the books on the top shelf.*

react reacts reacting reacted verb
When you react to something, you behave in a certain way because of that thing and as a kind of answer to it. *Rose is tapping Freddie's knee to see if his leg reacts.*
reaction noun.

read reads reading read verb
When you read something, you look at written words and understand what they mean. ● A word that sounds like **read** is **reed**.

ready adjective
When you are ready, you are prepared and can do something right away. *Are you ready to go yet?*
▲ Say **red-ee**.

real adjective
1 truly existing and not made up. *Do you think that unicorns were real?*
2 not a copy. *real leather.*
■ The opposite is **fake**.

realize realizes realizing realized verb
When you realize something, you start to know or understand it. *I realize that I can't have everything I want.*

reap reaps reaping reaped verb
When you reap crops such as wheat, you cut them and gather them.

rear noun
the back of something. *There's a large garden at the rear of the house.*
■ The opposite is **front**.

reason reasons noun
a fact that explains why something happens. *The reason I'm afraid of snakes is that I was once bitten by one.*

rebel rebels rebelling rebelled verb
When people rebel, they refuse to obey the people who are in charge.
▲ Say ri-**bell**.

receipt receipts noun
a piece of paper that shows how much money you paid for something.
▲ Say ree-**seet**.

receive receives receiving **received** verb
If you receive something, you get it when it has been given or sent to you. *Connie and Ted received a cup for winning the school spelling bee.*
▲ Say ree-**seev**.

recent adjective
from or happening a short time ago. *a recent photo of my brother.*
recently adverb.

reception receptions noun
a big party to honor or introduce somebody. *We attended the reception after my sister's wedding.*

recess recesses noun
a short period to relax. *We played soccer at noon recess.* or *The judge announced a short recess.*

recipe recipes noun
a list of things you need to cook something and the instructions on how to cook it. ▲ Say res-*i-pee*.

recognize recognizes recognizing **recognized** verb
If you recognize people, you know who they are because you have seen them before. *You look so different that I didn't recognize you at first.*

recommend recommends **recommending recommended** verb
If you recommend something, you say that you think it is good. *I recommend the apple pie and ice cream.*

record records recording **recorded** verb
1 If you record something, you write down what happened. *Every night, before he went to bed, Darren recorded the day's events in his diary.*
2 To record something is to store it on film, tape, DVD, or CD so that it can be played or shown again.
▲ Say re-**kord**.

record records noun
1 a written list of what has happened. *I kept a record of everything I spent while we were on vacation.*
2 a round black piece of plastic that has music or other sounds recorded on it in a special sound studio.
3 the best performance so far. *She holds the record for the high jump.*
▲ Say rek-*erd*.

recorder recorders noun
a machine that records sounds, such as music.

recover recovers recovering **recovered** verb
1 When you recover from an illness, you get better. *He's recovering from the flu.*
2 If you recover something, you get it back after it has been lost or stolen.

recreation noun
a way of exercising, relaxing, and having fun.

rectangle rectangles noun
a shape with four sides and four corners. Each side of a rectangle is the same length as the side opposite to it.
rectangular adjective.

recycle recycles recycling **recycled** verb
To recycle things is to make them into something new after they have already been used instead of throwing them away. *recycled paper.*

reduce reduces reducing **reduced** verb
To reduce is to make something smaller or less. *I'm trying to reduce the amount of chocolate that I eat.*

reed reeds noun
a plant with long, hollow stems that grows near water. ● A word that sounds like **reed** is **read**.

reef reefs noun
a long line of rocks, sand, or coral in the ocean. *In very bad weather, ships sometimes hit the reef and sink.*

reel reels noun
a round object that you wrap film, tape, or fishing line around.

referee referees noun
a person who makes sure that everyone playing in a game obeys the rules. *The referee's decision was final.*

reference book reference books noun
a book with facts and information in it.

reflect reflects reflecting reflected verb
1 If a surface reflects light, the light hits the surface and bounces back rather than passing through it.
2 A mirror reflects something in front of it and shows what it looks like.
reflection noun.

refrigerator refrigerators noun
a metal cabinet where you can place food to keep it cold and fresh.
▲ Say re-**frij**-*er-ay-ter*.

refugee refugees noun
If you are a refugee, you have been forced out of your country and must look for a new place to live.

refuse refuses refusing **refused** verb
If you refuse to do something, you will not do it. *Jill refused to wash the dishes and said that someone else would have to do it.*
■ The opposite is **accept**.

regard regards regarding **regarded** verb
If you regard something in a certain way, that is what you think about it. *She regarded the uniform as old-fashioned.*

region regions noun
an area of land or part of a country. *a mountain region.* ▲ Say **ree**-*jun*.

register registers noun
a book containing a list of names or important information. *The teacher checked her register at the beginning of the class.*

regret regrets regretting regretted verb
If you regret something, you are sorry about it and wish that you had not done it or that it had not happened.

regular adjective
Regular things have exactly the same amount of time between them. *When you exercise, your pulse gets faster, but it stays regular.*
regularly adverb.

rehearse rehearses rehearsing rehearsed verb
If you rehearse, you practice something before doing it for an audience. *We rehearsed the play every night for a week.* ▲ Say *re*-**hurse**.
rehearsal noun.

reign reigns reigning reigned verb
To reign is to be the king or queen of a country. ▲ Rhymes with **pain**. ● A word that sounds like **reign** is **rain**.

reindeer noun
a large deer with very big antlers that lives in northern countries where it is very cold. ▲ Say **rain**-*deer*.

rein reins noun
Reins are long leather straps that you use to guide a horse.
▲ Say **rain**.

reject rejects rejecting rejected verb
If you reject something, you will not accept it. *He rejected my advice.*

related adjective
If you are related to people, you are in the same family.

relation relations noun
a link between things. *the relation between smoking and cancer.*

relative relatives noun
a person who is in your family.

relax relaxes relaxing relaxed verb
When you relax, your body becomes less tense and you feel calm and less worried.

relay relays noun
a race between teams of runners. Each member of the team takes a turn to run a part of the race. A special stick called a baton is passed to the person whose turn it is to run.

release releases releasing released verb
When you release a person or an animal that has been held in some way, you set them free. *Robert released the bird after it was caught in a bush.*

reliable adjective
If someone is reliable, you can trust and depend on that person.
▲ Say *re*-**lie**-*uh-bul*.

relief noun
the good feeling that you get when you can stop worrying. *It was a great relief when I was told that I'd passed the test.* ▲ Say *re*-**leef**.

religion religions noun
believing in God or gods and a certain way of worshiping.
religious adjective.

rely relies relying relied verb
If you can rely on people, you know you can trust and depend on them.
▲ Say *re*-**lie**.

remain remains remaining remained verb
1 If people remain in a place, they stay there. *He did not go out to play but remained in the house all day.*
2 If something remains, it is still there. *The roof has gone, but most of the rest of the building remains.*

remark remarks noun
a thing that you say about someone or something. *She made a nice remark about my dress.*

remedy remedies noun
1 an answer to a problem.
2 a way of curing an illness.
remedy verb.

remember remembers remembering remembered verb
When you remember something, you have it in your mind or bring it into your mind again. *Can you remember what you did on vacation last year?*

remind reminds reminding reminded verb
1 If you remind someone, you tell the person something again in case he or she has forgotten. *Will you remind me to phone David?*

2 If something reminds you, it makes you remember something.

3 If someone reminds you of someone else, that person is like the other person in some way.

remote remoter remotest adjective
very far away.

remote control remote controls
noun
an electronic device used to turn a TV on and off and choose channels.

remove removes removing
removed verb
to take something away.

renew renews renewing renewed
verb
1 When you renew something, you arrange for it to go on longer. *You have to renew your subscription to the magazine.*
2 When you renew something, you start doing it again. *He renewed his efforts to spell better.*
3 If you renew a book you have borrowed from the library, you ask to keep it for longer.

rent rents noun
money that you pay to live in a place or to use something that you do not own yourself. *The rent for this apartment is $1,500 a month.*
rent verb.

repair repairs repairing repaired
verb
If you repair something that is broken or does not work, you fix it.

repeat repeats repeating
repeated verb
If you repeat something, you say it or do it again. *Will you repeat the question?*
repetition noun.

replace replaces replacing replaced
verb
1 If you replace something, you put it back where it came from. *She replaced the book on the shelf.*
2 When you replace something, you get a new one instead of the old one. *The school is replacing all of the old computers with newer ones.*

reply replies replying replied verb
When you reply, you give an answer. *"Must I reply to this letter?" "I don't know," he replied.*

report reports noun
Something that someone says or writes that tells you about something that has happened.

report card report cards noun
a written report that teachers give to parents to say how well a student has done in school.

represent represents representing
represented verb
If one thing represents another thing, it is a picture or symbol of it.

representative
representatives noun
a person who speaks for a group of people, as in a legislature.

reproduction reproductions noun
1 a copy of something old.
2 making new young animals or plants.

reptile reptiles noun
an animal with cold blood that has scales on its skin. Female reptiles lay eggs. Snakes, crocodiles, turtles, and lizards are reptiles.
◆ Look at page 132.

request requests requesting
requested verb
to ask politely for something.

require requires requiring
required verb
to need something or to ask for it.

rescue rescues rescuing
rescued verb
If you rescue people, you save them from danger. *This man is about to be rescued by a helicopter patrol squad.*

reserve reserves reserving
reserved verb
To reserve is to ask for something to be kept for you to use later. *William reserved a table for six at the restaurant.*
reservation noun.

reservoir reservoirs noun
a lake used to hold water that is sent through pipes to people's houses.
▲ Say rez-*er-vwar*.

resist resists resisting
resisted verb
If you resist something, you fight against it or try to stop it from happening.

resort resorts noun
a place where people go to have fun. *a beach resort.*

resources noun
things that are found naturally in a country, such as gas or oil, that can make the country richer.

respect noun
the feeling that you have for someone you like and admire because he or she is good, knows a lot, or is smart.

Reptiles

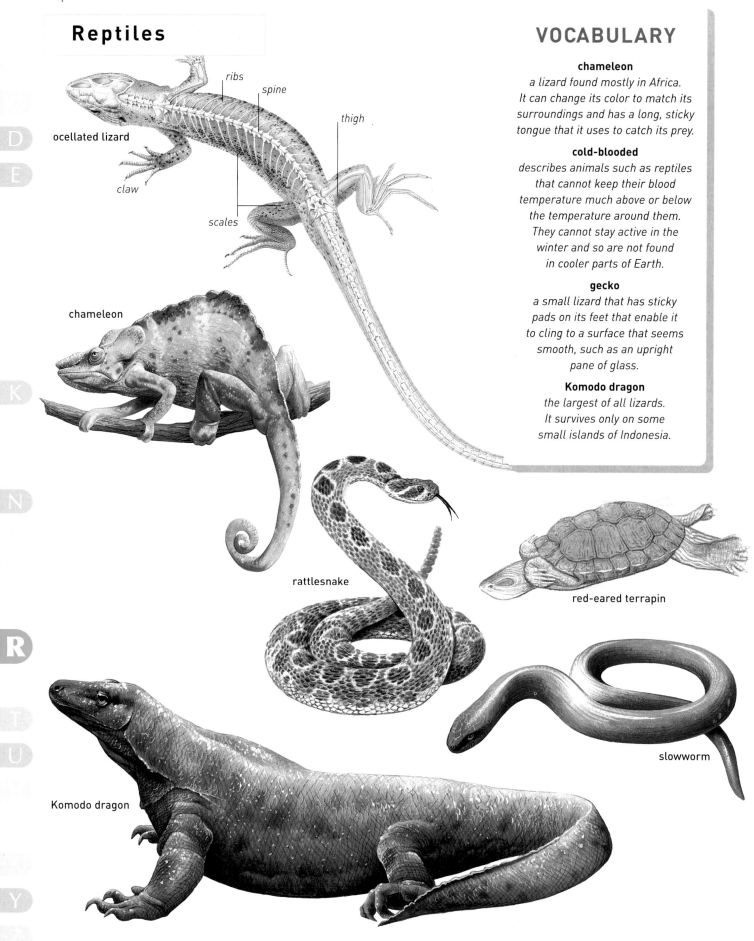

ocellated lizard

ribs

spine

thigh

claw

scales

chameleon

rattlesnake

red-eared terrapin

slowworm

Komodo dragon

VOCABULARY

chameleon
a lizard found mostly in Africa.
It can change its color to match its
surroundings and has a long, sticky
tongue that it uses to catch its prey.

cold-blooded
describes animals such as reptiles
that cannot keep their blood
temperature much above or below
the temperature around them.
They cannot stay active in the
winter and so are not found
in cooler parts of Earth.

gecko
a small lizard that has sticky
pads on its feet that enable it
to cling to a surface that seems
smooth, such as an upright
pane of glass.

Komodo dragon
the largest of all lizards.
It survives only on some
small islands of Indonesia.

respond responds responding responded verb
If you respond to someone, you answer that person.
response noun.

responsible adjective
1 A responsible person is sensible and can be trusted.
2 If you are responsible for someone or something, you are in charge.

rest noun
1 a time when you are quiet and do not work or do anything energetic. *Trent was having a rest reading a book.*
2 everything or everyone that is left over. *Jim and his friends went home, but the rest went swimming.* or *What shall we do for the rest of the afternoon?*

restaurant restaurants noun
a place where you can pay to eat a meal. ▲ Say **rest-er-ont**.

restrict restricts restricting restricted verb
If you restrict something, you keep it within a limit so that it is not too large. *The hall isn't very big, so we have to restrict the number of people coming to the concert.*

result results noun
1 a thing that happens because of something else. *The fence fell down as a result of the storm.*
2 the score at the end of a contest. *the election results.*

retire retires retiring retired verb
When someone retires, the person gives up a job, usually because of getting older.
retirement noun.

retreat retreats retreating retreated verb

If people retreat, they move back from something dangerous.

return returns returning returned verb
1 If you return to a place after going away, you come back or go back there.
2 If you return something, you give it back. *James returned his library books after he had read them.*

revenge noun
a thing that one person does to hurt someone else for being mean to him or her.

reverse reverses noun
the opposite of something else. *"Fast" is the reverse of "slow."*
reverse verb.

review reviews noun
something that someone says or writes in a newspaper or on radio, TV, or online telling people what a new movie, book, restaurant, or TV show is like and whether it is good or bad.

revolution revolutions noun
a fight to get a new type of government.
revolutionary noun.

revolver revolvers noun
a small gun that can be fired several times before it needs to be loaded again.

reward rewards noun
a nice thing that you are given because you have done something very well or been very helpful.
reward verb.

rewind rewinds rewinding rewound verb
To rewind a tape or video is to make it go backward so that it can be played again.

rhinoceros rhinoceros noun
a large, heavy wild animal with thick skin. It has one or two horns on its nose. Rhinoceros live in Africa and Asia. They are called **rhinos** for short. ▲ Say *reye-**noss**-er-us*. See below.

rhyme rhymes noun
a set of words that sound the same except for the first letters. ▲ Say **rime**.

rhythm rhythms noun
a pattern of repeated sounds that are regular. Music and poetry have rhythm. ▲ Say **rith**-um.

rib ribs noun
Your ribs are the bones that curve around your chest to protect your heart and lungs.

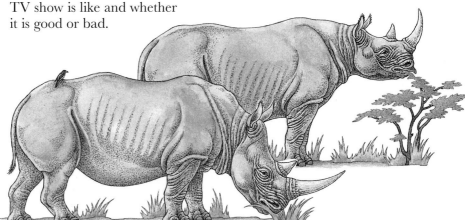

ribbon

ribbon ribbons noun
a strip of colored material that can be
used to tie hair or for decorating things.

rice noun
white or brown grains that you cook
and eat. Rice plants grow in wet
ground in hot regions. *China and
India produce the biggest rice crops in
the world.*

rich richer richest adjective
A person who is rich has a lot of
money. ■ The opposite is **poor**.

rid rids ridding rid verb
to free someone or something from
something harmful or annoying.
get rid of to throw something away.
Get rid of those old comic books.

riddle riddles noun
a question that is a puzzle and has
a smart or funny answer. *"What goes
up when the rain comes down?" Answer:
"An umbrella."*

ride rides noun
a trip in a car or on a horse, bicycle,
bus, boat, or train.

ride rides riding rode ridden verb
1 When you ride a horse or a bicycle
  or motorcycle, you sit on it and
  travel along.
2 When you ride in something such
  as a car or bus, you travel in it.

rifle rifles noun
a long gun.

right adjective
1 When you write the word "right,"
  the "i" is to the right of the "r."

I write with my right hand. ■ The
opposite is **left**.
2 If something is right, it is correct.
  Congratulations, that's the right answer!
  ■ The opposite is **wrong**.
  ● A word that sounds like **right**
  is **write**.

right adverb
correctly. *Did I guess right?* ■ The
opposite is **wrong**. ● A word that
sounds like **right** is **write**.

right angle right angles noun
an angle of 90 degrees, like the
corners of a square.

rigid adjective
If something is rigid,
you cannot bend
or stretch it.
*You can't bend a
rigid metal bar.*

rim rims
noun
the edge
around the top
of such things
as a glass, jar,
or cup. *The rim
had a chip.*

ring rings noun
1 a round piece of metal that you
  wear on your finger.
2 a circle with an empty center.
3 the noise of a bell.

ring rings ringing rang rung verb
When something rings, it makes the
sound of a bell. *The phone rang.* or
Has the phone rung this morning?

rinse rinses rinsing rinsed verb
to wash in clean water, not using soap.

rip rips ripping ripped verb
If you rip something, you tear it.
He ripped his shirt on a nail.

ripe riper ripest adjective
When a fruit is ripe, it is ready to eat.
The banana isn't ripe yet—it's still green.

ripple ripples noun
a very small wave or movement on
the surface of water.

rise rises rising rose risen verb
To rise is to move upward. *The smoke
was rising.* or *The bread dough has risen.*
■ The opposite is **fall**.

risk risks noun
a danger that something bad or
harmful will happen. *She took a risk
when she rushed into the burning house.*
risk verb, **risky** adjective.

rival rivals noun
someone who is trying to win the
same thing as you are.

river rivers noun
a large amount of water flowing
across the land toward the ocean
or a lake.

road roads noun
a long piece of hard ground that cars,
bicycles, and trucks can travel on.
● A word that sounds like **road**
is **rode**.

roam roams roaming roamed verb
To roam is to wander around without
trying to go anywhere in particular.
Cattle roamed the big fields.

roar roars roaring roared verb
To roar is to make a very loud noise.
The lion roared. or *The car engine
roared.*

roast roasts roasting roasted verb
When you roast food, you cook it
in an oven. *Dad roasted the chicken
for dinner.*

rob robs robbing robbed verb
To rob people is to steal from them.
robber noun, **robbery** noun.

robe robes noun
a long, loose piece of clothing.

robin robins noun
a small brown bird with red feathers on the front of its body.

European robin

American robin

robot robots noun
a machine controlled by a computer that can do jobs that people would otherwise do. *In factories, robots do a lot of work.*
▲ Say roh-*bot*.

rock rocks noun
1 stone; the material that mountains and hard ground are made of.
2 a large piece of stone.
3 pop music with a very strong rhythm.

rock rocks rocking rocked verb
When you rock, you move or move something gently from side to side or backward and forward. *He was rocking the baby in his arms.*

rocket rockets noun
1 an engine in a tall metal tube that is used to send spacecraft into space or to carry bombs.
2 a firework that is sent high up into the air and then explodes in different colors.

rod rods noun
a long, thin, round piece of wood or metal. *a fishing rod.*

rode past of **ride**.
● A word that sounds like **rode** is **road**.

rodent rodents noun
a small animal with sharp front teeth that gnaws things. Mice, rats, and squirrels are all rodents.

rodeo rodeos noun
a show in which cowboys and cowgirls ride horses and rope cattle.

roll rolls noun
1 a very small round loaf of bread.
2 a long, thin tube made by rolling around a piece of paper or material.

roll rolls rolling rolled verb
1 When something rolls, it moves along the ground, turning over and over.
2 To roll something is to wrap it around itself several times in the shape of a long, thin tube.

roller coaster roller coasters noun
a high railroad in a theme park that has steep bends and turns.

roof roofs noun
the top of a building or car.

room rooms noun
1 a part inside a building that is separated from the other parts inside the building by walls.
2 space. *There's not enough room in our car for ten people!*

rooster roosters noun
a grown male chicken.

root roots noun
1 a part of plant that grows underground and takes in water and food from the soil.
2 the part of a tooth or hair growing under the gum or skin that you cannot see.

rope ropes noun
very thick, strong string that is used for tying things.

rose roses noun
a garden flower that has lots of petals and sharp-pointed parts on its stem called thorns.

cultivated rose   wild prairie rose

rose past of **rise**.

rot rots rotting rotted verb
When something rots, it spoils or starts to get soft and weak. *The tomatoes were rotting on the ground.* or *Wood rots in water.*

rotate rotates rotating rotated verb
If something rotates, it turns around and around like a wheel. *Earth rotates as it goes around the Sun.*

rotten adjective
If something is rotten, it has gone bad and is so spoiled that it cannot be used. *That fruit is rotten.*

rough rougher roughest adjective
1 bumpy or uneven; not smooth. *A cat's tongue is very rough.*
2 not exact. *a rough guess.*
3 using a lot of force. *Soccer is a rough game.* ■ The opposite is **gentle**.
▲ Say **ruff**.
roughly adverb, **roughness** noun.

This sandpaper is rough.

135

round adjective
shaped like a circle or a ball. *Most coins are round.*

roundtrip roundtrips noun
a trip that you take from one place to another and back.

roundup roundups noun
When cowboys and cowgirls gather cattle to ship them to a market, it's called a roundup.

rout routs verb
To cause complete disorganization or defeat. *Our football team routed the opposing team.* ▲ Rhymes with **out**.

route routes noun
the way you go from one place to another place on a trip. *Please figure out the best route on the map before we leave.* ▲ Rhymes with **boot**.

row rows noun
things or people in a line. *a row of jars.*

row rows rowing rowed verb
When you row a boat, you make it move by pushing against the water using oars.
▲ Rhymes with **low**.

royal adjective
belonging to a king or queen. *a royal family* or *a royal palace.*

rub rubs rubbing rubbed verb
1 If you rub something, you move your hand up and down it. *She yawned and rubbed her eyes.*
2 To rub is to press one thing backward and forward against another. *People say that you can make*

a fire by rubbing two sticks together, but I've never been able to do it.

rubber noun
a strong, waterproof material that stretches and bounces. *Tires are made of black rubber.*

rubber band rubber bands noun
a piece of rubber in a circle that stretches.

ruby rubies noun
a valuable red jewel. *a necklace made of rubies.* ▲ Say **roo**-*by.*

rucksack rucksacks noun
a bag for carrying things in that you wear on your back. *We need rucksacks to take on our hike.*

rude ruder rudest adjective
If somebody is rude, that person behaves in a bad way and is not polite. ■ The opposite is **polite**.

rug rugs noun
a small piece of thick, heavy material that you put on the floor.

rugby noun
a game played mostly in England between two teams using an oval ball. Players score points by trying to carry the ball over a line or by kicking it over a bar.

ruin ruins ruining ruined verb
To ruin something is to completely spoil it. *The rain ruined our picnic.* ▲ Say **roo**-*in.*

ruins noun
the parts of a building left after the rest has fallen down or been destroyed. *the ruins of a castle.* ▲ Say **roo**-*ins.*

rule rules ruling ruled verb
To rule a country is to be in charge of it.

rule rules noun
something that says what you are allowed to do and what you are not allowed to do. *the rules of soccer.*

ruler rulers noun
1 a long, narrow piece of wood, metal, or plastic that is used for drawing straight lines and measuring.
2 a person who rules a country.

rumble rumbles rumbling rumbled verb
When something rumbles, it makes a long, low sound like thunder. *The trucks rumbled past.*

run runs running ran run verb
1 When a person or animal runs, it moves along on its feet much faster than when it walks.
2 If you run something, you are in charge of it and you make sure that it works properly.
3 When liquid runs, it flows. *Tears were running down his face.*

rung past of **ring**.

runway runways noun
the long, level strip of land at an airport on which airplanes take off and land.

rush rushes rushing rushed verb
If you rush, you are going somewhere or doing something very quickly. *He was rushing to get to the bus stop before the bus arrived.*

rust noun
a reddish-brown substance that covers iron or steel after it has gotten wet. *He left the tool outside in the rain, and it got covered in rust.*
rusty adjective.

rustle rustles rustling rustled verb
To rustle is to make the soft sound that leaves make as they move together in the wind. ▲ Say **russ**-*el.*

sauce

Ss

sabotage noun
When someone destroys enemy property during a war, it is sabotage.

sack sacks noun
a large, strong bag that you put things such as coal, potatoes, or trash in.

sad sadder saddest adjective
unhappy. ■ The opposite is **happy**.

saddle saddles noun
1 a seat for a rider on a horse.
2 a seat on a bicycle.

safe adjective
1 If you are safe, you are unharmed. *The lost kitten was found safe and sound hiding in the garage.*
2 not harmful or dangerous. ■ The opposite is **dangerous**.
safety noun.

safe safes noun
a strong box with a lock that you can keep money or valuables in.

said past of **say**.

sail sails noun
a big piece of cloth on a boat. When the wind blows against the sail, the boat moves along.

sail sails sailing sailed verb
To sail means to move along in a boat using its sails. *Sam went sailing on the river.*

sailor sailors noun
a person who works on a ship or boat.

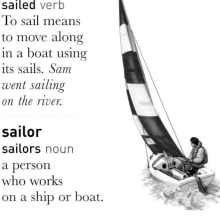

salad salads noun
a cold food made of raw vegetables, such as lettuce, tomato, and cucumber.

salary salaries noun
the money that people are paid for the work that they do. *Teachers' salaries are regularly paid every month.*

sale sales noun
a time when a store sells things at a cheaper price than usual. *Mom bought some shoes in the sale.*

saliva noun
the liquid in your mouth.

salmon salmon noun
a fish with silver skin and pink flesh that can be eaten. ▲ Say **sa-**mun.

salt noun
a white powder put on food to give it a stronger taste. Seawater has salt in it.
salty adjective
The soup that I made was too salty.

salute salutes saluting saluted verb
When soldiers salute, they make a sign by lifting their right hands to their foreheads as a greeting or to show respect to someone. *She saluted the general.*

same adjective
exactly alike. ■ The opposite is **different**.

sample samples noun
a small amount of something that shows what the rest of it is like.

sand noun
a white or yellow substance that is made from many tiny pieces of rock.

sandal sandals noun
a light shoe made of a sole with straps that go over your foot.

sandwich sandwiches noun
two slices of bread with food in between.

sang past of **sing**.

sank past of **sink**.

sap noun
the sticky liquid inside the stems of plants and the trunks of trees. Sap carries food to all parts of a plant.

sapphire sapphires noun
a bright blue jewel.

sari saris noun
a long piece of printed material that many Indian women and girls wrap around the body like a dress. ● A word that sounds like **sari** is **sorry**.

sat past of **sit**.

satellite satellites noun
1 a natural object in space, like a moon, that moves around a larger object, such as a planet.
2 A satellite is also a machine that is sent into space to pick up and send back signals and information. Satellite television comes to us by satellite. ▲ Say **sat-**il-ite.

satisfy satisfies satisfying satisfied verb
If you satisfy people, you please them and give them what they want or need. *Nothing I do ever satisfies you.*

sauce noun
a thick liquid that can be poured over food to add to its flavor. *Do you like sauce on your steak?*

137

saucepan saucepans noun
a metal pot with a handle and a lid
for cooking food.

saucer saucers noun
A saucer is a type of small plate for
placing a cup on.

sausage sausages noun
meat that is cut up into very small
pieces and made into long, thin
shapes like a tube.

savanna noun
a flat, grassy plain that has only a
few trees.

save saves saving saved verb
1 If you save someone, you take them
away from danger. *The man saved the
child from drowning.*
2 If you save money or something
else, you keep it somewhere to use
later. *I'm saving my allowance for a
new computer game.*

saw past of **see**.

saw saws noun
a tool for cutting wood. It has a metal
blade with sharp points called teeth
along one edge.
saw verb.

saxophone saxophones noun
a musical instrument made of brass
that is played by blowing into it.
saxophonist noun.

say says saying said verb
If you say something, you speak
words. *My uncle said that he didn't like
eating meat very often.*

scab scabs noun
a piece of dried blood that forms over
a cut in your skin when it is healing.

say

*Some words that you can
use instead of say:*

*I heard her say that she has
read the book.*
remark, comment, mention

How do you say "sari"?
pronounce

*She said that I would have
to work much harder.*
explained, announced

Other ways of saying things:
**chat, exclaim, have a conversation,
murmur, mutter, scream, shout,
shriek, talk, tell, whisper**

scald scalds scalding scalded verb
If you scald yourself, you burn
yourself with very hot liquid or steam.

scale scales noun
1 a row of marks on something such as
a ruler that is used to measure things.
2 a way of showing distances between
places on a map. *This map has a
scale of one inch to one mile.*
3 one of the small, hard pieces of
skin that cover the body of a fish
or reptile.

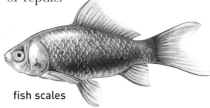

fish scales

4 a series of musical notes. *You play
or sing the notes of a scale one after
the other.*
5 You use a scale to find out how
heavy you are or to weigh things
such as fruit and vegetables.

scar scars noun
a mark on your skin left by a cut that
has healed.

scarce scarcer scarcest adjective
If things are scarce, they are difficult
to find because there are only a few of
them. *Flowers are scarce in the winter.*
scarcely adverb
I was so happy that I could scarcely speak.

scare scares scaring scared verb
If something scares you, it frightens
you. *That ghost story really scared me.*

scarecrow scarecrows noun
a thing that looks like a person
dressed in old clothes. Farmers put
scarecrows in their fields where crops
are growing to frighten away birds.

scarf scarves noun
a long piece of material or knitted
wool that is worn around the neck.

scatter scatters scattering
scattered verb
1 If animals or things scatter, they
move quickly in different directions.
*The loud noise frightened the squirrels,
and they scattered in many different
directions.*
2 If you scatter things, you throw
them around in different directions.
Ian scattered some bread for the ducks.

scene scenes noun
1 what you see in the area around
you. *a mountain scene.*
2 a place where something happens.
the scene of the murder.
3 a part of a play. *Does the hero get
killed in the last scene?*

scenery noun
1 what you see around you, such as
mountains, forests, rivers, and lakes.
2 the things on the stage of a theater
that make a play more real to the
audience.

scent scents noun
1 a nice smell. *a beautiful scent.*
2 a liquid that you can put on your skin to make you smell nice.
● Words that sound like **scent** are **sent** and **cent**.

school schools noun
a place where children go to learn.
▲ Say **skule**.

school schools noun
a group of fish that swim together. *a school of minnows.*

science sciences noun
finding out about things such as animals, plants, and natural materials. **scientific** adjective.

scientist scientists noun
a person who finds out about animals, plants, and other things in the world by looking closely at them, writing down information about them, and doing experiments.

scissors noun
a small tool for cutting paper and other things. A pair of scissors has two sharp blades that are connected.

scoop scoops scooping scooped verb
To scoop is to lift something up using your hands or with a type of spoon called a scoop. *Nick scooped some ice cream out of the container.*

scooter scooters noun
1 a motorcycle with a small engine.
2 a type of child's bicycle with a board that you stand on with one foot while pushing the ground with the other foot.

scorch scorches scorching scorched verb
If you scorch something like a piece of material, you burn it a little, leaving a brown mark.

score scores noun
In a game, the score is how many points each team has.

score scores scoring scored verb
To score means to get a point in a game.

scorpion scorpions noun
an animal related to a spider. It has a poisonous stinger on its tail.

scout scouts noun
a Boy or Girl Scout.

scowl scowls scowling scowled verb
If you scowl, you have an angry, bad-tempered look on your face.

scramble scrambles scrambling scrambled verb
If you scramble over rocks or rough ground, you use your hands and feet to help you move quickly.

scrap scraps noun
a small piece of something such as paper or material.

scrapbook scrapbooks noun
a book with blank pages that you can paste pictures, postcards, or clippings in.

scrape scrapes scraping scraped verb
1 If you scrape your knee, you hurt it by rubbing it against something hard or rough.
2 If you scrape mud off your shoes, you get it off with a thing such as a knife.

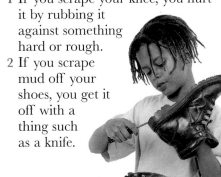

scratch scratches scratching scratched verb
1 If you scratch your skin, you make thin cuts on it by rubbing something sharp against it. *Sarah scratched her hand on the thorns.*
2 If you scratch yourself, you rub your nails across your skin because it itches.
scratch noun.

scream screams screaming screamed verb
If you scream, you shout in a very loud, high voice because you are excited or frightened. *Sophie screamed when she went on the big ride at the carnival.*

screen screens noun
1 the flat part of a TV or computer where you see the pictures or words.
2 the place on a wall where the movie is shown in a theater.

screw screws noun
a thin piece of metal like a nail with a sharp point at one end and a slot in the top. Screws are used to join things, such as pieces of wood, together. You use a screwdriver or drill to turn the screw into the piece of wood.

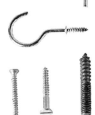

screw screws screwing screwed verb
1 to join things together using screws. *He screwed the shelf to the wall.*
2 If you screw things up, you make a mess out of them. *She screwed up on her test.*

scribble scribbles scribbling scribbled verb
to write quickly and without care.

script scripts noun
all of the words that have been written for the actors to say in a play or movie.

scrub scrubs scrubbing scrubbed verb
If you scrub something, you rub it hard to clean it. *Paul scrubbed the floor with a stiff brush.*

scruffy adjective
messy and dirty. *scruffy clothes.*

sculpture sculptures noun
1 a person, animal, or shape that has been made of stone, wood, or metal by an artist called a sculptor.
2 Sculpture is the art of carving or modeling things.

scurry scurries scurried verb
to move in a hurried, confused way. *We tried to catch my hamster, but each time we got near it, it scurried away.*

sea seas noun
a large area of salt water. *We went swimming in the sea.*

sea horse sea horses noun
a tiny fish with a head shaped like a horse's head and a long, curling tail.

seal seals noun
an animal with short gray fur that lives near the ocean. Seals spend a lot of time in the water and catch fish to eat.

seam seams noun
a line made where two pieces of material are sewn together. *These two pieces of fabric are joined with a seam.*

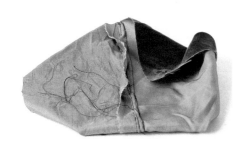

search searches searching searched verb
If you search for people or things, you look very carefully for them. *We searched everywhere for the lost kitten.*

season seasons noun
one of the four parts of the year. They are spring, summer, fall, and winter.
seasonal adjective
seasonal vegetables.

seat seats noun
a thing you sit on. Buses and cars have seats. *We sat in the front seats at the movie theater.*

seaweed noun
a red, green, or brown plant that grows in the ocean. *After the storm, the beach was covered with seaweed from the ocean.*

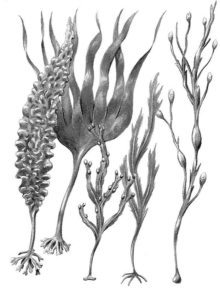

second seconds noun
a very short measure of time. There are 60 seconds in one minute.

second adjective
Second means next after the first. *Tom won the race, and Dan came second.*

secret secrets noun
something that only a few people know about. *I'm not telling you what you're getting for your birthday—it's a secret!*

secretary secretaries noun
a person who works in an office. Secretaries answer the phone, make appointments, and type letters.

section sections noun
one of the separate parts of something. *Rob was trying to fit the sections of the model airplane together.*

security noun
feeling safe or trying to keep things safe. *She locked the door for extra security.*

see sees seeing saw seen verb
1 When you see people or things, you look at them with your eyes.
2 To see also means to understand something. *Do you see what I mean?*

seed seeds noun
a tiny, hard part inside the flower or fruit of a plant. If you put seeds into the ground they will grow into new plants.

seek seeks seeking sought verb
To seek means to look for someone or something. *The police are seeking a woman who was seen near the bank at midnight.*

seem seems seeming seemed verb
To seem means to look or feel like something.

seen past of **see**.

seesaw seesaws noun
a ride in a playground. One person sits at each end of a long piece of wood, and they take turns going up and down.

segregate segregates segregating segregated verb
to not open something like a school to all people of all races.
segregation noun.

seize seizes seizing seized verb
If you seize something, you grab it. ▲ Rhymes with **freeze**. ● A word that sounds like **seize** is **sees**.

seldom adjective
not very often.

select selects selecting selected verb
When you select people or things, you choose them.
selection noun.

self-esteem noun
a good feeling about who you are and what goals you can reach. *Your compliment boosted my self-esteem.*

selfish adjective
A selfish person does not like to help or share things with other people.

sell sells selling sold verb
If people sell something to you, they give it to you and you pay them money for it.

semicircle semicircles noun
one half of a circle.

Senate noun
one of the two branches of U.S. Congress. Its members serve for six years.

send sends sending sent verb
To send is to make someone or something go to another place.

senior adjective
older in years or more important.
■ The opposite is **junior**.

senior seniors noun
a student in the fourth, or last, year of high school or college.

sense senses noun
1 the powers that most people have to see, hear, touch, taste, and smell.
2 knowing and being careful to do the right thing.

sensible adjective
A sensible person thinks carefully about what he or she is doing and does not do anything silly or foolish.
■ The opposite is **foolish**.

sensitive adjective
1 A sensitive person cares about other people's feelings.
2 If your skin is sensitive, it is sore or it gets sore very easily.

sent past of **send**.
● A word that sounds like **sent** is **scent**.

sentence sentences noun
a group of words that make sense together. A written sentence begins with a capital letter and ends with a period or other punctuation mark. *Joan is late today.* and *Where is the cat?* are sentences.

separate adjective
If two things are separate, they are not joined together. ▲ Say *sep*-ur-ut.

separate separates separating separated verb
to set or keep apart. *Hal separates the white from the yolk.* ▲ Say **sep**-ur-rate.

serial serials noun
a story that is told in parts on television or in a magazine. ● A word that sounds like **serial** is **cereal**.

series noun
1 a set of things of the same type that follow one another.
2 a number of shows on radio or television on the same subject that follow one another. *I am watching a series on dinosaurs.*

serious adjective
1 important or very bad. *a serious accident.*
2 A serious person is quiet and does not laugh or joke very often.

servant servants noun
A servant is a person who works in someone else's house, doing such things as cooking and cleaning.

serve serves serving served verb
1 If people serve you in a restaurant, they bring you food and drinks.
2 If people serve you in a store, they help you choose things to buy.

service services noun
1 something useful that a person or a company does for other people. *the train service* or *the postal service.*
2 A service is also a meeting in a church where people pray and sing.

session sessions noun
a time when people meet to do something. *a session of Congress.*

set sets noun
a group of things that belong together. *a china tea set* or *a chess set.*

set sets setting set verb
1 When something liquid like cement sets, it gets hard.
2 When the Sun sets, it goes down below the horizon and then the sky gets dark.
3 When you set a table, you put all of the things on it that you need for a meal such as glasses, plates, knives, and forks.
4 When you set a clock or a watch, you move the hands to a certain time. *I set my alarm clock for 7:30.*
5 To set also means to choose a date. *They set May 30th as their wedding date.*

settee settees noun
a long, comfortable seat for two or more people; also called a sofa.

settle settles settling settled verb
If you settle, you go to a place and stay there. *A ladybug settled on my hand.* or *Nita and Bill have settled in Georgia.*

several adjective
more than two but not very many.
Several people walked by.

severe adjective
very bad. *a severe headache* or *severe winter storms.*

sew sews sewing sewed sewn verb
When you sew, you join together pieces of material or join something to material using a needle and thread. *Can you sew this button back on my shirt, please?* ▲ Say **so**.

sewer sewers noun
a large pipe under the ground that takes waste away from houses and other buildings. ▲ Say **su**-*er*.

sex sexes noun
the two groups that people and animals belong to. These two groups are the *male sex* and the *female sex.*

shade noun
1 a place where the Sun cannot reach. *We sat in the shade of an oak tree.*
2 a cover for a lamp.
3 a variety of a color. *a dark shade of blue.*
shady adjective.

shadow shadows noun
a dark shape that you see close to someone or something that is under or in front of the light. *When you place your hands in front of a light, you can have fun by making hand shadows like these.*

shake shakes shaking shook shaken verb
1 When you shake something, you move it up and down or backward and forward. *I shook the bottle of salad dressing.*
2 If your body shakes because you are cold or frightened, it wobbles around.
shaky adjective, **shakily** adverb.

shallow adjective
not very deep. *This water is shallow; it only just covers my feet.* ■ The opposite is **deep**.

shame noun
the guilty feeling that you have if you have done something wrong.
shameful adjective.

shampoo shampoos noun
a liquid that is used to wash your hair.

shape shapes noun
what you see if you draw a line around the outside of something. Circles, squares, triangles, and rectangles are different shapes. ◆ Look at page 143.

share shares sharing shared verb
1 If you share something, you give some of it to someone else. *I shared my birthday cake with my friends.*
2 to use something together with another person. *I share a bedroom with my sister.*
share noun.

shark sharks noun
a big fish that has sharp teeth and a big mouth.

great white shark

sharp sharper sharpest adjective
1 Something that is sharp has an edge or a point that is good for cutting. *Knives and scissors are usually sharp.*
2 sudden and severe. *a sharp pain.*
sharply adverb.

shatter shatters shattering shattered verb
If something such as glass shatters, it breaks into many small pieces.

shave shaves shaving shaved verb
To shave is to cut hair off the skin with a razor.

shawl shawls noun
a wide scarf that is worn around the shoulders.

shed sheds noun
a small building made of wood. *a toolshed* or *a cowshed.*

shed sheds shedding shed verb
1 If an animal sheds hair, some of its hair falls out.
2 When trees shed their leaves, the leaves drop off because it is the fall.

sheep sheep noun
an animal that farmers raise for their wool and meat. A male sheep is called a ram, and a female sheep is called a ewe.

sheet sheets noun
1 a large piece of material for putting on a bed.
2 a thin, flat piece of paper, glass, or metal. *a sheet of writing paper.* or *The road was like a sheet of ice.*

shelf shelves noun
a long, flat piece of wood or glass attached to a wall or in a closet where you can put things.

Shapes

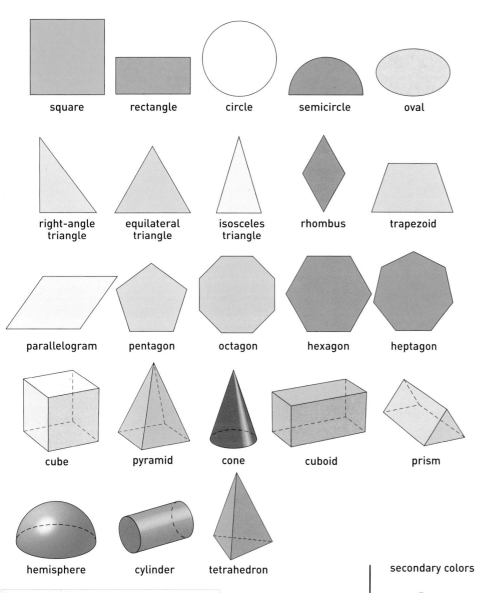

square · rectangle · circle · semicircle · oval

right-angle triangle · equilateral triangle · isosceles triangle · rhombus · trapezoid

parallelogram · pentagon · octagon · hexagon · heptagon

cube · pyramid · cone · cuboid · prism

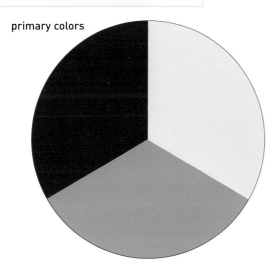

hemisphere · cylinder · tetrahedron

VOCABULARY

hemisphere
one half of a sphere or ball shape.

heptagon
a flat figure with seven sides.

parallelogram
a quadrilateral with two sides parallel (lying in the same direction but never meeting) in one direction and two sides parallel in the other direction.

polygon
any figure with many sides, such as a heptagon (7 sides), hexagon (6), octagon (8), and pentagon (5).

quadrilateral
a flat figure that has four sides.

rhombus
a diamond-shaped parallelogram.

spiral (not shown)
a line that coils around the same spot like a spring in smaller and smaller or bigger and bigger circles.

trapezium (not shown)
a quadrilateral with no parallel sides.

trapezoid
a quadrilateral with two parallel sides and two sides that are not parallel.

Colors

primary colors

secondary colors

green · orange · purple

143

shell shells noun
1 the hard outside part of some living things. Eggs, nuts, snails, and crabs have shells.
2 a very large type of bullet.

shelter shelters noun
a covered place where you are safe from bad weather or danger.

sheriff sheriffs noun
a county police officer.

shield shields noun
a large piece of wood or metal that soldiers carried in the past to protect their bodies from enemy weapons.

shin shins noun
Your shin is the front part of your leg between your knee and your ankle.

shine shines shining shone verb
When something shines, it gives out light or is bright like silver.
shiny adjective
a shiny new coin.

shingle shingles noun
a piece of material that covers a roof.

ship ships noun
a big boat for carrying people and things.

shipwreck shipwrecks noun
a bad accident when a ship is broken up by rocks or rough water.

shirt shirts noun
a piece of clothing that is worn on the top part of your body. Shirts have a collar, sleeves, and buttons down the front.

shiver shivers shivering shivered verb
When you shiver, you shake because you are cold or frightened. *The rabbit was shivering with fright.*

shoal noun
a large group or number; a crowd or school. *a shoal of fish.*

shock shocks noun
1 a sudden and bad thing that happens to you. *The news of the plane crash was a shock.*
2 An electric shock is a sharp pain that is felt if electricity goes through your body.

shod adjective
wearing shoes.

shoe shoes noun
things that are worn on your feet. Shoes are usually made of leather or canvas.

shone past of shine.
I polished my shoes until they shone.

shook past of shake.

shoot shoots shooting shot verb
1 to fire bullets from a gun or to use a bow and arrow.
2 to kick or throw a ball at a goal in sports like basketball or soccer.
3 to move somewhere very fast. *The kitten shot under the sofa.*

shop shops noun
a place where you go to buy things or to have things fixed; a store.

shop shops shopping shopped verb
When you shop, you go to stores to buy things. *We went shopping for food in the supermarket.*
shopper noun.

shore shores noun
the land along the edge of the ocean or a lake. *We walked along the sandy shore.*

short shorter shortest adjective
1 not having great height. ■ The opposite is **tall**.
2 not long. *Gerald has short hair.*
3 not lasting long. *The senator made a short speech.* ■ The opposite is **long**.
4 **short for** a short way of writing or saying something. *"Phone" is short for "telephone."*

shorts noun
short pants that usually do not cover your knees. *Freddie and Rose are wearing matching shorts.*

shot past of shoot.

shoulder shoulders noun
Your shoulder connects your arm to the rest of your body.

shout shouts shouting shouted verb
If you shout, you say something in a very loud voice. *Jill had to shout so that we could hear her.*

show shows showing showed shown verb
1 When you show someone something, you let them see it or you point it out to them. *Show me your photos.* or *Show me the girl who hit you.*
2 When you show someone how to do something, you explain how to do it. *Can you show me how to use the computer?*

show shows noun
1 something you can see at the theater or on television. *It's time for my favorite TV show.*
2 things arranged so that people can look at them. *a dog show.*

shower showers noun
1 a place where you can wash by standing under water that sprays down on you.
2 rain that falls for only a short time.

shrank past of shrink.

shred shreds noun
a small, thin piece that has been cut or torn from something larger.

shrimp shrimp or shrimps noun
a small sea animal that is related to a lobster and that people eat.

shrink shrinks shrinking shrank shrunk or shrunken verb
When something shrinks, it gets smaller. *Lou's T-shirt shrank in the wash.*
shrunken adjective.

shut shuts shutting shut verb
1 If you shut something, you move a door, window, lid, or book so that it is no longer open.
2 To shut something like a store means that people cannot go into it until it opens again. *What time did you shut the restaurant?*
■ The opposite is **open**.

shuttle shuttles noun
1 an airplane or bus that goes backward and forward between two places. *the New York—Washington shuttle.*
2 a type of spaceship. *the space shuttle.*

shy shier or shyer shiest or shyest adjective
If someone is shy, he or she does not feel happy or comfortable with unfamiliar people. *Sharon was shy and found it difficult to talk to strangers.*

sick sicker sickest adjective
1 If you are sick, you are not well.
2 related to being unwell. *a sick day.*

sickness sicknesses noun
something such as a cold that makes you feel unwell.

side sides noun
1 the left or right of something. *Mom sat on my right side, and Dad on my left.*
2 the flat surfaces of something.
3 the edges of something. *A square has four sides.*
4 one of the two teams that are playing against each other in a game.

sidewalk sidewalks noun
pavement next to a street to walk on.

sieve sieves noun
a frame or container with a mesh bottom or with many tiny holes in it. You use a sieve to separate small pieces from larger pieces or a liquid from something solid. ▲ Say **siv**.

sigh sighs sighing sighed verb
When you sigh, you breathe out loudly because you are tired, sad, or bored.

sight sights noun
1 the ability to see things with your eyes. *Owls have good sight in the dark.*
2 Things such as interesting old buildings that people go to see are also sights.

sign signs noun
1 a notice that tells you something or where to find something. *Can you see a sign to the airport?*
2 a movement that you make to tell someone something. *His sister made a sign to him to keep quiet.*
3 a mark that means something special. In math, a sign like this + means add.

sign signs signing signed verb
1 When you sign your name, you write it. *He signed the check.*
2 **sign up** to agree to do something. *Jack signed up for the club.*

signal signals noun
a sound, light, or movement that tells you something. *The referee blew a whistle as a signal to start the game.*

signature signatures noun
your name written in your own writing.

silence silences noun
1 no sound.
2 a very quiet state.
■ The opposite is **noise**.

silent adjective
not making any noise. *The house was silent and empty.*
silently adverb.

silk silks noun
a smooth, shiny material made from threads produced by an insect called a silkworm. *a silk scarf.*
silky adjective.

silly sillier silliest adjective
stupid and not sensible or smart. *You were very silly to run across the road.*

silver noun
a gray, shiny metal. Rings, bracelets, and necklaces are often made of silver.
silver adjective
the silver Moon.

similar adjective
If two things are similar, they are almost the same. *A horse, a zebra, and a donkey are similar.*

simple simpler simplest adjective
easy to do or understand. *These questions are simple!* ■ The opposite is **difficult**.
simply adverb.

sing sings singing sang sung verb
When you sing, you make music with your voice. *Sing that song again.* or *The birds start singing very early in the morning.*
singer noun
Who's your favorite singer?

single adjective
1 one. *I can't find a single sock anywhere!*
2 A person who is single is not married.

singular noun
one person or thing. *the singular of geese is goose.*
The opposite is **plural**.

sink sinks sinking sank or sunk verb
If something like a ship sinks, it goes underwater. *The ship sank in the storm.* or *The rock has sunk.*

sink sinks noun
a basin; a large bowl attached to water and drains.

sip sips sipping sipped verb
If you sip a drink, you slowly drink it, taking a little bit at a time. *She slowly sipped her cocoa because it was hot.*

sister sisters noun
A person's sister is a girl or woman who has the same mother and father.

sit sits sitting sat verb
1 When you sit somewhere, you rest your bottom there. *We sat on the sofa.*
2 When a bird sits on its nest, it stays there to cover its eggs.

sitcom sitcoms noun
a funny TV show that is on each week.

situation situations noun
something that is happening in a place at a particular time. *the political situation in China.*

size sizes noun
The size of something is how big it is. *What size shoe do you wear?*

skate skates noun
1 Roller skates are special boots with wheels on the bottom that you wear for moving around on smooth ground.
2 Ice skates are boots with sharp blades on the bottom that you wear for moving around on ice.
skate verb.

skateboard skateboards noun
a long piece of wood or plastic with wheels that you stand on to move along fast and to do jumps and turns.

skein skeins noun
a length of yarn or thread coiled loosely around a spool. ▲ Rhymes with **rain**.

skeleton skeletons noun
all of the bones that are joined together inside the body of a person or an animal.

sketch sketches noun
a picture that you draw quickly.

ski skis noun
a long, flat piece of plastic, wood, or metal that is attached to a boot for moving over snow. ▲ Say **skee**.
ski verb.

skill skills noun
If you have a skill, you have the ability to do something very well.
skillful adjective.

skin noun
1 the natural outside covering of the bodies of people and many animals.
2 the outside covering of many fruit and vegetables. *a banana skin.*

skin diving noun
swimming under the water while you wear flippers, a mask, and oxygen tanks.

skip skips skipping skipped verb
When you skip, you move with little jumps from one foot to the other.

skirmish skirmishes noun
1 a small fight in a larger battle.
2 a verbal conflict.

skirt skirts noun
a piece of clothing that women and girls wear. A skirt hangs down from the waist.

skull skulls noun
Your skull is the round, bony part of your head. Your brain is in your skull.

skunk skunks noun
an animal with black-and-white fur and a full tail. It can spray a bad-smelling liquid when it is scared.

sky skies noun
the space above Earth.

skyscraper skyscrapers noun
a very tall building.

slam slams slamming slammed verb
When a door slams, it closes with a bang. *She slammed the door.*

slang noun
words that you use in conversation, especially with people of your own age, but not when you are writing or being polite. *"Cool" is slang for "good."*

slanted adjective
Something that is slanted is not straight but leans in one direction.

slap slaps slapping slapped verb
If you slap someone, you hit him or her with the palm of your hand.

slave slaves noun
a person who is kept as a prisoner and forced to work very hard for someone else without being paid.
slavery noun.

sled sleds noun
a small, flat vehicle with runners that you ride down hills in the snow.

sleep sleeps sleeping slept verb
When you sleep, you close your eyes and rest your body as you do in bed at night.

sleepy sleepier sleepiest adjective
When you are sleepy, you feel tired.

sleeve sleeves noun
the part of a shirt, blouse, coat, or dress that covers your arm.

sleigh sleighs noun
a vehicle that you sit on to move over snow. Sleighs are usually pulled by animals such as horses or reindeer.

slept past of **sleep**.

slice slices
noun
a thin, flat piece that has been cut from something. *a slice of cake.*

slide slides sliding slid verb
When something slides, it moves smoothly over a surface. *The children were sliding on the ice.*

slight adjective
small or not very important. *I have a slight earache.*

slim slimmer slimmest adjective
If you are slim, you are thin, but not too thin. ■ The opposite is **plump**.

slingshot slingshots noun
a Y-shaped stick with a piece of elastic stretched over it. You pull back the elastic to shoot small stones.

slink slinks slinking slunk verb
to move secretly or by creeping. *Jaguars slink through the rainforests.*

slip slips slipping slipped verb
If you slip, you slide by mistake and fall down. *I slipped on the wet floor and sprained a muscle in my back.*

slipper slippers noun
a soft, comfortable shoe that is sometimes worn in the house.

slippery adjective
Something that is slippery is very smooth and difficult to hold or to stand on without sliding and falling over. *a slippery floor* or *a wet, slippery fish.*

slit slits noun
a long, thin cut in something. *They cut a slit in the material.*

slope slopes noun
ground that goes upward or downward. *We walked down the mountain slope.*

slot slots noun
a short, thin hole in something. *You put coins in the slot to use the machine.*

slow slower slowest adjective
Someone or something that is slow does not move quickly. *Snails and turtles are very slow animals.* ■ The opposite is **fast**.
slowly adverb
We walked home slowly.

slug slugs noun
a small, slimy animal like a snail without a shell. Gardeners do not like slugs because they eat plants.

sly slyer slyest adjective
If someone is sly, he or she is smart in a secretive and not very nice way. *The sly salesman sold us rotten corn.*

small smaller smallest adjective
not very big. *Ants are small insects.* or *My brother is smaller than me.* ■ The opposite is **big** or **large**.

smart smarter smartest adjective
A person who is smart can learn and quickly understand things.

smash smashes smashing smashed verb
If something smashes, it breaks into a lot of pieces. *I dropped the plate, and it smashed on the floor.*

small

Some words that you can use instead of small:

All small animals look cute.
baby, young

The writing is so small that you need a magnifying glass to read it.
minute, tiny

Don't worry. It's only a small mistake.
unimportant, slight, minor

Centipedes have many small legs.
short

smell smells smelling smelled or **smelt** verb
1 When you smell something, you use your nose to find out about it. *I can smell food cooking in the kitchen.*
2 When something smells, you notice it with your nose. *This rug smells.*
smelly adjective
smelly old socks.

smile smiles smiling smiled verb
When you smile, the corners of your mouth turn up to show that you are happy.

smog noun
fog mixed with smoke.

smoke smokes smoking smoked verb
When people smoke, they have cigarettes, cigars, or pipes in their mouths and breathe the smoke in and out.

smoke smokes noun
the white, gray, or black stuff that you see going up in the air when something is burning.

smooth smoother smoothest adjective
If something is smooth, you cannot feel lumps or any rough parts when you touch it. *These vases have smooth surfaces.*

smudge smudges noun
a dirty mark on something.

smuggle smuggles smuggling
smuggled verb
to take things such as alcohol, drugs, or cigarettes into or out of a country when it is illegal.
smuggler noun.

snack snacks noun
a small amount of food that you eat when you are in a hurry. *We had a quick snack of cheese and crackers.*

snail snails noun
a small creature with a hard shell on its back. Snails move along slowly.

snake snakes
noun
a long, thin type of animal called a reptile. Snakes have no legs and move by sliding along the ground. *Some snakes have a poisonous bite.* ◆ Look at page 132.

snap snaps snapping snapped verb
1 When something snaps, it breaks and makes a sudden sharp sound. *The pencil snapped when I stepped on it.*
2 When a dog snaps, it tries to bite someone or something. *The dog snapped at us when we walked by.*
3 When people snap, they speak in an angry way. *"Be quiet!" she snapped.*

snatch snatches snatching snatched
verb
If you snatch something, you take it quickly and roughly. *The thief snatched her purse.*

sneak sneaks sneaking sneaked
verb
If you sneak somewhere, you move in a quiet and secretive way. *No one saw him sneak out of the room.*

sneeze sneezes sneezing sneezed
verb
When you sneeze, you blow air out of your nose and mouth with a sudden loud noise. You sometimes sneeze when you have a cold.

sniff sniffs sniffing sniffed verb
When you sniff, you breathe air in through your nose in a quick and noisy way. You often sniff when you are crying or when you have a cold.

snore snores snoring snored verb
When people snore, they breathe noisily when they are asleep.

snorkel snorkels noun
a tube that you breathe through when you swim close to the surface of the water.

snow noun
small white pieces of frozen water that fall from the sky when it is very cold.

snowboarding noun
a sport where you move down snowy hills on a piece of wood or metal that looks like a skateboard without wheels.

snowflake snowflakes noun
a small piece of falling snow. Snowflakes are six-sided ice crystals.

soak soaks soaking soaked verb
1 When you soak something, you put it in water and leave it for a long time.
2 If you get soaked, you get very wet. *We got soaked in the rain.*

soap noun
a substance that can be solid, liquid, or powder that you use with water for washing. *This bar of soap smells nice.*

sob sobs sobbing sobbed verb
When you sob, you cry loudly.

soccer noun
a game played by two teams of 11 players each. The teams try to score goals by kicking a ball into a net at each end of a field.

society societies noun
1 all of the people who live in the same country or area and have the same laws and customs.
2 a type of club for people who are involved in the same things. *our local theater society.*

sock socks noun
a thing that you wear on your foot inside your shoe.

soda sodas noun
a drink that has bubbly water in it; pop.

sofa sofas noun
a long, comfortable seat for two or more people; also called a couch.

soft softer softest adjective
1 bending easily. ■ The opposite is **hard**.
2 not firm or stiff. *soft snow.*
3 not loud; quiet and gentle. ■ The opposite is **loud**.
softly adverb, soften verb

soften softens softening softened
verb
When something softens, it becomes soft. *The butter began to soften in the heat.* ■ The opposite is **harden**.

software noun
the part inside a computer or on a computer disk that has the instructions to make a computer program work.

soil noun
the brown stuff, which is also called dirt, that plants grow in.

solar adjective
to do with the Sun. *solar heating.*

sold past of **sell**.

soldier soldiers noun
a person in an army. ▲ Say **sole**-*jer*.

sole soles noun
the bottom of your foot or your shoe.

solid solids noun
an object that is hard and not a liquid or a gas. ■ The opposite is **liquid**.

solid adjective
1 hard. *solid rock*.
2 with no space inside. *a solid brick wall*.
■ The opposite is **hollow**.

solve solves solving solved verb
1 If you solve a problem, you find the answer to it.
2 If you solve a mystery, you find out why it happened.

sombrero sombreros noun
a tall hat with a wide brim.

some adjective
describing an amount that you don't give or know exactly. *I need some peas.* ● A word that sounds like **some** is **sum**.

somersault somersaults noun
rolling your body in a circle so that your feet go over your head.

son sons noun
Someone's son is a boy or man who is their child. ● A word that sounds like **son** is **sun**.

song songs noun
a short piece of music with words that are sung.

soot noun
black powder that comes from smoke after a fire.

sophomore sophomores noun
a student who is in their second year of high school or college.

sore adjective
If a part of your body is sore, it hurts. *I have a sore throat.*

sorrow noun
the feeling that you have when you are very sad. *He felt great sorrow when his mother died.* ■ The opposite is **joy**.

sort sorts sorting sorted verb
If you sort things, you put them into different groups. *Hal sorts the blocks into plain, colored, and patterned ones.*

sort sorts noun
a type. *What sort of animal is it? It's a lizard.*

sought past of **seek**.

sound sounds noun
something that you can hear. *I can hear the sound of someone playing a guitar.*

soup soups noun
a hot liquid food that you make by boiling vegetables or meat in water. *tomato soup* or *chicken soup*.

sour sourer sourest adjective
1 Something that tastes sour is not sweet. *Lemons are sour.*
2 When milk is sour, it is not fresh.

source sources noun
1 the place, person, or thing that something comes from. *The library is a good source of information.*
2 the place where a river starts. *The source of the river is in the mountains.*

south noun
the direction that is on your right if you face the Sun as it rises in the morning. ■ The opposite is **north, northern**.
south adjective, **southern** adjective
Peru is in South America. or *Miami is in southern Florida.*
south adverb
The Arctic tern flies south from the Arctic to Antarctica every winter.

souvenir souvenirs noun
something that you keep to remember a place or something that happened. *My friend bought me a Dutch doll as a souvenir of the Netherlands.*

sow sows sowing sowed sown verb
When you sow seeds, you put them in the soil so that they will grow into plants. ▲ Rhymes with **low**.

space spaces noun
1 an empty place with nothing in it. *There is space in this closet for your clothes.* or *Mom couldn't find a space to park the car.*
2 the place above Earth where the Sun, stars, and other planets are.

spacecraft noun
a vehicle that travels in space.

spade spades noun
a tool with a long handle and a wide, flat blade that is used for digging.

spaghetti noun
a type of pasta; long strings of dough made of flour and water that are cooked by boiling them.

span spans spanning spanned verb
When something like a bridge spans a river, it goes across it.

spare adjective
Something that is spare is not being used now, but you can use it when you need to. *When my friend stayed over, he slept in the spare room.*

spark sparks noun
a tiny piece of fire. Sparks can be made by electricity. *Sparks from the fire flew up the chimney.*

sparkle sparkles sparkling sparkled verb
When something sparkles, it shines with little flashes of light. *sparkling fabric.*

spat past of spit.

speak speaks speaking spoke spoken verb
When you speak, you say words. *Melissa was speaking to her friend on the telephone.* or *Can you speak Spanish?*

spear spears noun
a weapon made from a long stick with a sharp point at one end.

special adjective
1 If something is special, it is not ordinary but better or more important than other things. *Today is a special day because it's my birthday.*
2 describes a particular person or thing, or having to do with a particular job. *An ambulance is a special vehicle for taking people to the hospital.*
specially adverb
a specially designed classroom.

species noun
a group of animals or plants that are the same in some way. *different species of rodents.*

desert hedgehog

European hedgehog

Mindanao moonrat   moonrat

spectator spectators noun
a person who watches something. *There were thousands of spectators at the football game.*

speech speeches noun
1 the ability to talk. Speech is one of the main ways of communicating.
2 a special talk that you give in front of a group of people.

speed noun
how fast something goes or happens. *The car was traveling at a speed of 60 miles per hour.*

speedometer speedometers noun
an instrument that shows how fast a vehicle is traveling.

spell spells spelling spelled verb
When you spell a word, you say or write the letters in the right order. *"How do you spell tiger?" "T-i-g-e-r."*
spelling noun.

spend spends spending spent verb
1 When you spend money, you use it to buy something. *I must stop spending so much money on candy.*
2 When you spend time with someone, you stay with them. *I spent a week with my aunt and uncle.*

sphere spheres noun
a solid shape like a ball. *Earth is a sphere.*
spherical adjective.

spice spices noun
powder or seeds from a plant that you put in food to give it a stronger taste. *Cinnamon, ginger, and nutmeg are spices.*
spicy adjective.

spider spiders noun
a small creature with eight legs and no wings. *Many spiders spin webs to catch insects.*

spike spikes noun
a piece of metal or wood with a sharp point at one end. *The fence has spikes along the top.*

spill spills spilling spilled or spilt verb
If you spill a liquid, you let it flow out of a container by mistake. *I spilled my drink on the rug.*

spin spins spinning spun verb
1 When something spins, it turns around and around very fast. *The ball spun through the air.*
2 to pull cotton or wool into long, thin pieces and then twist them together to make thread or yarn.

spinach noun
a dark green leafy vegetable.

spine spines noun
1 the row of bones down your back.
2 one of the sharp points on some animals and plants. *Porcupines and cactuses have spines.*
3 The spine of a book is the part of the cover between the front and the back.

spirit spirits noun
1 the part of a person or animal that some people believe does not die when the body dies.
2 a ghost.

spit spits spitting spat verb
If you spit, you send food or liquid out of your mouth. *We spat out the cherry pits.*

splash splashes splashing splashed verb
If you splash someone or something, you make that person or thing wet with drops of water or some other liquid.

split splits splitting split verb
1 When something splits, it breaks open. *The bag split, and all of the groceries fell out.*
2 To split also means to share something. *We split the candy between us.*

spoil spoils spoiling spoiled or spoilt verb

1 If somebody spoils something, he or she makes it less good than it was before. *I spoiled my shirt when I spilled paint all over it.*
2 If people spoil a child, they give the child everything that the child wants.

spoke, spoken past of **speak**.

sponge sponges noun
1 a soft thing that is full of holes. You use a sponge to wash yourself or to clean things. *Wendy washed the car with a sponge.*

a natural sponge
2 also a sea creature with a soft part inside that is full of holes.

sponsor sponsors noun
a person or a company that gives money to someone or a group of people for doing something special, such as running for a charity. *A famous sportswear company is the sponsor of the city marathon.*

spooky spookier spookiest adjective
Something that is spooky is frightening.

spool spools noun
a round thing you wind thread or film on.

spoon spoons noun
a metal tool that you use for eating liquid things such as soup and cereals.
spoonful noun
six spoonfuls of sugar.

sport sports noun
something that you do to keep your body strong and healthy and to have fun. *Football, tennis, soccer, and swimming are all sports.*

spot spots noun
1 a small, round mark. *Leopards have yellow fur with dark spots.*
2 a small red mark on your skin; a pimple.
3 a place. *This is the spot where I fell off my horse.*
spotted adjective
a spotted horse.

spotty adjective
a spotty dress.

spout spouts noun
a part of a container such as a teapot or coffeepot where the liquid comes out.

sprain sprains spraining sprained verb
When you sprain something such as your ankle or your wrist, you hurt it by suddenly twisting it.

sprang past of **spring**.

spray sprays spraying sprayed verb
When you spray something, you make lots of small drops of liquid fall on it. *Jenny sprayed the fern with water.*

spread spreads spreading spread verb
1 If you spread something such as butter, you cover something else with it. *Freddie spread honey on the waffle.*
2 When something spreads, it moves all over a place. *The rain has spread to all parts of the country.*
3 When you spread your arms, you stretch them out. *The bird spread its wings.*

spring springs noun
1 the season of the year between winter and summer. *Plants start to grow in the spring.*
2 A spring is a piece of wire that is twisted around in circles. *A spring will jump back into the same shape if you press or pull it and then let it go.*

spring springs springing sprang sprung verb
to jump. *The cat sprang onto the wall.*

sprinkle sprinkles sprinkling sprinkled verb
If you sprinkle something, you throw small drops or pieces of something onto it. *She sprinkled the cake with some cinnamon.*

sprung past of **spring**.

spun past of **spin**.

spy spies noun
a person who tries to find out secret information about another person or country.

square squares noun
a flat shape with four straight sides that are the same length.
square adjective
a square table.

squash squashes squashing squashed verb
If you squash something, you press it hard and make it flat. *He sat on my hat and squashed it.*

squeak squeaks squeaking squeaked verb
To squeak is to make the small, high sound that a mouse makes. *The door squeaks when you open it.*

squeeze squeezes squeezing squeezed verb
If you squeeze something, you press it hard on its sides. *I squeezed the water out of the sponge.*

squirrel squirrels noun
a small gray or brown animal with a big, thick tail. Squirrels climb well and live in trees.

squirt squirts squirting squirted verb
When something squirts, liquid comes out very fast. *I opened the bottle, and soda squirted everywhere.*

stab stabs stabbing stabbed verb
To stab is to stick a knife or weapon into someone or something.

stable stables noun
a building where horses are kept.

stadium stadiums noun
a large area for sports such as football or track and field. There are usually seats around the edges so that people can watch. *an ancient stadium.*

stage stages noun
1 A stage is the part of a theater where the actors perform.
2 If you do something in stages, you do it in parts. *It will take a long time to build the tree house, so we'll have to do it in stages.*

stain stains noun
a dirty mark on something that is very difficult to get rid of. *Joe's football uniform was covered with grass stains.*

stair stairs noun
one of a set of steps for going up or down inside a building.

staircase staircases noun
a set of stairs inside a building.

stale staler stalest adjective
not fresh. *Sheri threw away the last piece of cake because it was stale.*

stalk stalks noun
the stem or long, thin part of a plant that flowers, leaves, and fruit grow on.

stall stalls noun
1 a place in a shed for one cow or in a stable for one horse.
2 a spot on an open table in a market where you can sell things.

stamp stamps noun
a small piece of paper with a picture and price on it. *You have to put a stamp on a letter before you drop it into the mailbox.*

stamp stamps stamping stamped verb
1 If you stamp your foot, you put it down hard on the floor. *My little sister stamps her foot when she is angry.*
2 To make a mark on paper or an object using a special tool. Stamping something often shows that you have paid for it or that you have returned it.

PAID
Date..............
Signed...............

RETURN TO LIBRARY

stampede stampedes noun
When cattle suddenly run fast together, they are in a stampede.

stand stands standing stood verb
to be on your feet.

standard standards noun
a measure of how good or bad something is. *a high standard.*

star stars noun
1 a small, bright light that you can see in the sky on a clear night.
2 a shape with five or six points. *We put a star on top of the Christmas tree.*
3 a famous person who sings, acts, or plays a sport. *a movie star.*

stare stares staring stared verb
If you stare at someone or something, you look at them for a long time. *Steve and James stared at each other.*

start starts starting started verb
1 When something starts, it begins. *What time does the movie start?* The opposite is **end** or **finish**.
2 When you start something like a car, you make it move or work.

start noun
the beginning. The opposite is **end**.

startle startles startling startled verb
If people or things startle you, they surprise you in a frightening way. *You startled me when you jumped out from behind the curtain.*

starve starves starving starved verb
If people or animals starve, they get sick and can die because they do not have enough to eat. *Many birds starve during the winter months.*
starvation noun.

state states noun
1 a country and its government. *The state runs the armed forces.*
2 a part of a country. *California is one of the western states of the United States of America.*
3 how someone or something looks or is. *Your clothes are in a terrible state!*

station stations noun
1 a place where trains and buses stop and pick up or drop off passengers.
2 a building that is used for something special. *a police station.*

station wagon station wagons noun
a rectangular car with back seats that fold down and a door in the back.

statue statues noun
a sculpture or model of a person or an animal that is made of stone or metal.

stay stays staying stayed verb
1 If you stay somewhere, you do not move from that place.
2 If you stay with someone, you live in their home for a short time.

steady steadier steadiest adjective
Someone or something that is steady

is not moving around or shaking. *The ladder must be steady when I climb it.* The opposite is **unsteady**.

steal steals stealing stole stolen verb
to take something that does not belong to you and keep it. *Someone stole my purse.*

steam noun
Steam is the gas that water turns into when it boils. *Steam was coming out of the kettle.*

steel noun
a strong metal that is used for making such things as knives, tools, and machines.

steep steeper steepest adjective
If something such as a hill is steep, it goes up or down sharply. *This mountain is too steep to climb.*

steer steers steering steered verb
When you steer a car, you turn the wheel so that it goes in the direction that you want it to.

stem stems noun
the long, thin part of a plant that grows above the ground.

step steps noun
1 what you do when you lift your foot and put it down in a different place. *Try to follow these dance steps.*
2 the flat part of stairs where you place your foot for going up or down.

step steps stepping stepped verb
to lift your foot and put it down in another place as you walk. *You stepped on my foot!*

stereo noun
music or sound that comes from two different loudspeakers at the same time. *a stereo CD player.*

stick sticks noun
a long, thin piece of wood. *We supported the young plants with sticks.*

stick sticks sticking stuck verb
1 When you stick two things together, you join them with glue. *Camille stuck a picture into her book.*
2 If something sticks, it cannot be moved. *The car is stuck in the mud.*
3 When you stick a pointed thing into something else, you push it in. *If you stick a pin into a balloon, it will burst.*
sticky adjective
Her fingers are sticky with glue!

sticker stickers noun
a small piece of paper with a picture or words on it that you can attach to something. *My suitcase is covered with stickers.*

stiff stiffer stiffest adjective
1 If something is stiff, it does not bend easily. *a stiff piece of cardboard.*
2 not moving easily. *a stiff neck.*

still adjective, adverb
1 not moving. *Please stand still while I take your picture.*
2 going on and on. *It's still raining.*

sting stings stinging stung verb
If an insect or a plant stings you, a small, sharp point goes into your skin and hurts you.
sting noun.

stingray stingrays noun
a sea animal that has a flat body and a long tail that looks like a whip. It also has a poisonous spine.

stir stirs stirring stirred verb
When you stir a liquid, you move a spoon around to mix it. *Rose stirred the soup.*

stitch stitches noun
a loop that is made when you put a needle and thread through a piece of material and bring it out again a little farther along.

stock stocks noun
all of the things that a store keeps ready to sell. *This store has a large stock of children's shoes.*

stocking stockings noun
a piece of clothing like a long, thin sock that women and girls wear over their legs and feet.

stole, stolen past of **steal**.

stomach stomachs noun
the place in the middle of your body where food goes after you have eaten it.

stone stones noun
1 a small piece of rock.
2 a large mass of rock that is used for building. *a stone wall.*

stood past of **stand**.

stool stools noun
a type of chair without a back or arms.

stop stops stopping stopped verb
1 If you stop what you are doing, you do not do it any more. *Stop talking and listen for a moment.*
2 When something that was moving stops, it stands still. *The bus stopped.*
3 If you stop someone from doing something, you do not allow them to do it. *I tried to stop the dog from sitting on the sofa.*
4 When a machine stops, it does not work any more. *My watch has stopped.*

stoplight stoplights noun
a set of red, yellow, and green lights on a street that tell you to stop, be careful, or go.

store stores noun
a shop that sells things.

store stores storing stored verb
If you store something somewhere, you put it there so that you can use it later. *The cans of food were stored in the pantry.*

stork storks noun
a big white bird with long legs and a large beak. *Storks live near water.*

153

storm storms noun
very bad weather with strong winds and a lot of rain or snow. *Many storms also have thunder and lightning.*
stormy adjective
stormy winter weather.

story stories noun
1 A story tells you about things that have happened. Some stories are about real things, and others are made up. *I read a story about a boy who made friends with a ghost.*
2 all of the rooms on one floor of a building. *This skyscraper has 50 stories.*

stout stouter stoutest adjective
1 bulky and thick. *a stout woman.*
2 sturdy and strong. *stout hiking boots.*

stove stoves noun
A stove has an oven inside for baking and broiling and parts on the top that heat up for boiling and frying.

straight straighter straightest adjective
not bending or curving.

strain strains straining strained verb
1 If you strain a part of your body, you hurt it by stretching a muscle too much.
2 If you strain food, you put it through a utensil called a strainer or sieve to separate the solid parts from the liquid. *James strained the can of tomatoes.*

strand strands noun
a long, thin piece of something. *strands of long, blond hair.*

strange stranger strangest adjective
1 odd or unusual. *I read a story about a strange animal that could talk.*
2 not known or seen before. *a strange house.* ■ The opposite is **familiar**.

stranger strangers noun
a person whom you do not know. *A complete stranger waved at me.*

strap straps noun
a long, thin piece of material that you use for fastening, carrying, or holding things. *How many types of straps can you see?*

straw straws noun
1 the dried stems of plants such as wheat. Straw is used for animals such as horses and pet rabbits to lie on. You can make hats out of straw.
2 a long, thin tube made of paper or plastic for drinking through.

strawberry strawberries noun
a small, soft red fruit that grows near the ground. ◆ Look at page 18.

streak streaks noun
a long, thin line of something. *There are streaks of paint on the floor.*

stream streams noun
1 a small, narrow river.
2 a long line of things going in one direction. *a stream of traffic.*

street streets noun
a road in a town or city with houses and other buildings along each side.

strength noun
how strong someone or something is. *Do you have the strength to move the table?*

stress noun
too much worry or work. *Stress has caused his headaches.*

stretch stretches stretching stretched verb
1 If you stretch something, you make it longer or wider by pulling on it. *My sweater has stretched.*
2 If you stretch your body, you push your arms and legs out and make yourself as tall as you can.

strict stricter strictest adjective
Strict people expect others to do what they say and to obey their rules.
strictly adverb.

stride strides striding strode stridden verb
to walk or run with long steps.

strike strikes striking struck verb
1 If you strike people or things, you hit them. *The ball struck me on the back of the head.*
2 When lightning strikes, it hits and goes through someone or something. *The tree was struck by lightning.*
3 When a clock strikes, it rings a bell to show the time. *The clock struck ten.*
4 When you strike a match, you rub it on something rough to make a flame.
5 When people strike, they stop working because they want more money or because they want to protest about something.

strike strikes noun
when people stop working because they want more money or because they want to protest about something.

string noun
1 very thin rope. You use string to tie up things such as packages.
2 Musical instruments such as guitars and violins have thin wires called strings that you touch to make sounds.

strip strips noun
a long, thin piece of something such as paper or material.

stripe stripes noun
a colored line on something. *My soccer*

jersey has red and white stripes.
striped adjective
a striped dress.

stroke strokes stroking stroked verb
When you stroke an animal such as a cat, you gently move your hand across its body.
stroke noun.

strong stronger strongest adjective
1 If you are strong, you have a lot of power in your muscles.
■ The opposite is **weak**.
2 not easy to break. *These toys are made of strong plastic.*
3 If a taste or smell is strong, you can easily notice it. *This cheese has a very strong smell.*

struck past of **strike**.

struggle struggles struggling
struggled verb
1 to fight to get away from someone or something. *The thief struggled to get away from the police.*
2 If you struggle to do something that is difficult, you try hard to do it. *Lauren and Joe struggled to get dressed.*

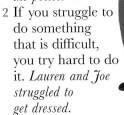

stubborn adjective
Stubborn people do not easily change their minds and do not like doing what other people tell them to do.

stuck past of **stick**.

student students noun
a person who is learning something at a school, university, or college.

studio studios noun
1 a room where an artist or a photographer works.
2 a place where movies, TV or radio shows, or albums are made.

study studies studying studied verb
1 If you study something, you spend time learning about it. *I am studying history at school.*
2 To study something is to look at it very carefully. *David was studying the stars through his telescope.*
studious adjective
Someone who is studious spends a lot of time studying. *a studious girl.*

stuff noun
something that we don't have a word for. *What's this stuff on the floor?* or *Please clean up all that stuff in your room.*

stumble stumbles stumbling
stumbled verb
If you stumble over something, you almost fall over it. *I stumbled over a pair of shoes on the floor.*

stung past of **sting**.

stupid stupider stupidest adjective
silly; not smart, bright, or sensible.
■ The opposite is **bright**.
stupidity noun.

style styles noun
the way in which something is done or made or how it looks. *a new style of shoe.*

subject subjects noun
1 something you learn about. *My best subjects at school are English and history.*
2 what something such as a story is all about. *Animals are the subject of this book.*
3 The subject of a sentence is the person or thing that does the action. In the sentence *Marie climbed a tree,* "Marie" is the subject.

submarine submarines noun
a boat that can travel underwater.

substance substances noun
something that you can see, touch, or use for making things. *This vegetable contains a very sticky substance.*

subtract subtracts subtracting
subtracted verb

To subtract is to take one number away from another number. *If you subtract 4 from 6, you get 2.*
■ The opposite is **add**.
subtraction noun

suburb suburbs noun
an area near a city.
suburban adjective.

subway subways noun
a railroad under city streets.

succeed succeeds succeeding
succeeded verb
If you succeed, you do or get the thing that you want.

success successes noun
doing something well or getting what you want. *We wish you success in the race.* or *The party was a great success.*
successful adjective,
successfully adverb.

suck sucks sucking sucked verb
to pull liquid into your mouth from something. *The baby is sucking milk from a bottle.*

sudden adjective
happening quickly when you are not expecting it. *We ran inside to get out of the sudden rain.*
suddenly adverb.

suffer suffers suffering suffered
verb
If you suffer, you feel pain because you have been hurt, are sick, or because you are unhappy. *Tom suffers a lot when he has a cold.*

suffocate suffocates suffocating
suffocated verb
If people or animals suffocate, they die because they have no air to breathe.

sugar noun
something that you put in food and drinks to make them sweet. Sugar comes from sugar cane or sugar beets.

sugar cane noun
a tall grass with thick stems. We get sugar from the stems, called "canes."

suggest suggests suggesting suggested verb
If you suggest something to others, you tell them about an idea that you have for doing something. *Sophie suggested that we go to the beach.*

suicide noun
killing yourself on purpose.

suit suits noun
a set of clothes made out of the same material that you wear together. A suit can be a jacket and pants or a jacket and a skirt.

suit suits suited verb
1 If clothes suit you, they look good on you. *Does this dress suit me?*
2 If something suits you, it is right for what you want or need. *This bedroom suits me.*

suitable adjective
right for someone or something. *This coat is suitable for rainy weather.*

suitcase suitcases noun
a large box or bag with a handle that you can carry your clothes in when you travel.

sulk sulks sulking sulked verb
If you sulk, you refuse to talk to anyone because you are angry about something. *Dominic is sulking because he's not allowed to watch anymore television.*

sum sums noun
a result of adding numbers. *The sum of 3 + 2 is 5.* ● A word that sounds like **sum** is **some**.

summer noun
the season of the year between the spring and the fall. *Summer is the hottest part of the year.*

summit summits noun
the top of a mountain.

summon summons summoning summoned verb
If you summon someone, you call that person to come. *We were summoned to the principal's office.*

Sun suns noun
the bright star that you can see in the sky during the day. The Sun gives us light and heat. ● A word that sounds like **Sun** is **son**.

sunbathe sunbathes sunbathing sunbathed verb
to sit in the Sun and let it make your skin get darker.

sung past of **sing**.

sunglasses noun
special dark glasses that are worn to protect your eyes from the bright light of the Sun.

sunk past of **sink**.

sunny sunnier sunniest adjective
with the Sun shining brightly. *It's a sunny day—let's have a picnic!*

sunrise noun
the time when the Sun comes up (rises) in the morning.

sunset noun
the time when the Sun goes down (sets) at night.

sunshine noun
the light and heat from the Sun.

super adjective, interjection
great; excellent.

superb adjective
wonderful. *We had a superb vacation in Europe last year.*

superior adjective
better than someone or something else. *Suzanne's drawing of the school building is superior to mine.*

supermarket supermarkets noun
a big store where you can buy food and lots of other things, which you pay for all at one time at a checkout counter.

supersonic adjective
If an aircraft, rocket, or bullet is supersonic, it goes faster than the speed of sound.

superstitious adjective
A superstitious person believes that bad luck will happen if he or she does or does not do certain things. *Superstitious people think that it is bad luck to walk under ladders.*

superstore superstores noun
a huge store that sells many things of one type, such as computers.

supervise supervises supervising supervised verb
If you supervise someone or something, you watch them to make sure that they are doing things the right way.

supper suppers noun
a light evening meal.

supply supplies noun
an amount of something that is needed. *We took a large supply of food on the camping trip.*

support supports supporting supported verb
1 to hold up someone or something. *Joe supported Connie when she twisted her ankle.*

2 If you support a club, team, or other group, you try to help and encourage it. *Which team do you support?*
support noun **supporter** noun.

suppose supposes supposing supposed verb
If you suppose that something is true, you think that it is probably true. *I suppose you are right.*

sure surer surest adjective
1 If you are sure about something, you know that it is true. *I'm sure I packed my raincoat.*
2 If you are sure that something will happen, you know that it will. *I'm sure it will snow tomorrow.*
surely adverb.
without a doubt.

surf noun
the foam or white part on top of the waves on the ocean.

surf surfs surfing surfed verb
to ride on top of the waves by standing on a long piece of wood or plastic called a surfboard.

surface surfaces noun
the outside part of something.

surgeon surgeons noun
a doctor whose job it is to operate on people in a hospital.

surgery noun
cutting someone's body to take out or fix a part inside. *heart surgery.*

surprise surprises surprising surprised verb
If you surprise someone, you do something that the other person does not expect. *You surprised me when you came home early.*
surprise noun
Don't tell Chris about the party—it's a surprise!
surprising adjective.

surrender surrenders surrendering surrendered verb
When an army surrenders, it stops fighting and gives in to the enemy.
surrender noun.

surround surrounds surrounding surrounded verb
to be or go all around something. *An island is surrounded by water.* or *The police surrounded the office building.*

survive survives surviving survived verb
to stay alive after something very bad or dangerous has happened. *Our cat was lucky to survive after being hit by a car.*

suspect suspects suspecting suspected verb
If you suspect someone of doing something wrong, you think that person did it. *The police suspected her of stealing the money and jewelry.*
suspect noun.

suspense noun
a feeling of fear or excitement that you have when you do not know what is going to happen. *We waited with suspense for the results of the election.*

suspicious adjective
If you are suspicious, you think that something is wrong or you do not believe someone. *I was suspicious when he said that he had lost my money.*

swallow swallows swallowing swallowed verb
When you swallow food or a drink, it goes down your throat.

swam past of **swim.**

swamp swamps noun
a marsh or an area of wet ground. There are some big swamps in the southeast of the United States.

swan swans noun
a big white or black bird with a long neck that lives on water. Young swans are gray and are called cygnets. *We saw swans swimming on the lake.*

swap swaps swapping swapped verb
to change something for something else. *May I swap my book for your camera?*
swap noun.

sway sways swaying swayed verb
When people or things sway, they move slowly from side to side for some time. *The daffodils were swaying on their long stems in the wind.*

swear swears swearing swore sworn verb
1 If people swear, they say bad or rude words.
2 If you swear, you promise something in a very serious way. *I swear that I will tell the truth.*

sweat sweats sweating sweated verb
When you sweat, you lose liquid from your body through your skin. *Everyone was sweating because it was so hot.*
sweat noun.

sweater sweaters noun
a piece of clothing that is knitted. You wear it to cover the top part of your body.

sweep sweeps sweeping swept verb
When you sweep something, you clean it with a brush. *Would you please sweep the porch?*

sweet sweeter sweetest adjective
1 Sweet foods and drinks have a taste like sugar. *Honey is sweet.*
2 A sweet person is gentle and kind. *It was very sweet of you to help me.*
sweetness noun.

swell swells swelling swelled swollen verb
When something swells, it gets bigger and thicker. *My ankle swelled up when I twisted it.* or *The insect bite made her hand swell up.*
swelling noun.

swept past of **sweep**.
Gerry swept the snow from the path.

swerve swerves swerving swerved verb
When something that is moving swerves, it goes quickly to one side. *The bicyclist swerved in order to avoid being hit by the car.*

swim swims swimming swam swum verb
When you swim, you use your arms and legs to move along in water. *We are going swimming in the sea.* or *We watched the fish swimming in the pond.* **swim** noun.

swimming pool swimming pools noun
a large indoor or outdoor water-filled tank for swimming and diving in.

swing swings swinging swung verb
When something swings, it moves backward and forward through the air. *The soldiers swung their arms as they marched.*

swing swings noun
a seat for swinging that hangs from two strong ropes or chains. *It is relaxing to sit in a swing and move gently backward and forward.*

switch switches noun
a thing that you press or turn to stop or to start something working. *Use the light switch to turn on the light.*

switch switches switching switched verb
1 to change one thing for another thing. *My friend and I switched places.*
2 When you switch on something, you use a switch to make it work. *Will you switch on the lights?*
3 When you switch off something, you use a switch to make it stop working. *Did you switch off the lights?*

swivel swivels swiveling swiveled verb
To swivel is to twist or turn around on the same spot.

swollen past of **swell**.

swoop swoops swooping swooped verb
to rush or fly downward suddenly. *The bird swooped down to catch the worm.*

sword swords noun
a weapon with a handle and a long metal blade with a sharp point at the end. Long ago soldiers used to fight with swords and shields.
⚠ Say **sord**.

SPELLING TIP
Some words that start with the sound "s," as in "simple," are spelled with a "c," such as "certain", "city," and "cycle."

swore, sworn past of **swear**.

swum past of **swim**.

swung past of **swing**.

syllable syllables noun
a word or part of a word that has one sound. The word "but" has one syllable, the word "butter" has two syllables, and the word "America" has four syllables.

symbol symbols noun
1 a sign or mark that means something. This symbol + means add in math.
2 a thing that stands for something else. *The dove is a symbol of peace.*

symmetrical adjective
If a shape is symmetrical, both sides are the same. If you draw a line through the middle of a circle, you will see that both sides are symmetrical. **symmetry** noun.

sympathy noun
If you feel or show sympathy for someone, you are very kind to that person because he or she is hurt or sad. **sympathetic** adjective, **sympathize** verb.

symphony symphonies noun
a long piece of music written for a large orchestra. **symphonic** adjective.

symptom symptoms noun
something that is wrong with you and shows that you are sick. *A sore throat and a temperature are symptoms of a bad cold.*

synagogue synagogues noun
a building where Jews go to pray.
⚠ Say **sin**-*a-gog*.

synonym synonyms noun
a word that means almost the same as another word. *Little* and *small* are synonyms. ■ A word that means opposite is **antonym**.

synthetic adjective
created artificially using chemicals. Nylon is a synthetic fabric.
⚠ Say *sin*-**thet**-*ik*.

syringe syringes noun
a special needle that doctors can push into your skin when they give you an injection of medicine or when they take blood out of your body.

syrup noun
a sweet, sticky food made from water boiled with sugar and often flavored.

system systems noun
1 an organized way of doing something. *We have changed the system for borrowing books from the library.*
2 a group of machines or other things that work together. *a computer system* or *a transportation system.*

Tt

table tables noun
1 a piece of furniture with a flat top that you can put things on.
2 a set of numbers or words arranged in columns.
3 a list of the multiplication of all the numbers between 1 and 12.

Telephone numbers:		
1	Janet	370 1037
2	Jill	265 0075
3	John	321 0076
4	Freddie	254 3084
5	Fran	828 1928
6	Sue	262 0208
7	Ray	976 4146
8	Carol	263 8043
9	Judy	883 0040
10	Kate	377 7767

Conversion table

Liters		Gallons
4.546	1	0.222
9.092	2	0.440
13.638	3	0.660
18.184	4	0.880
22.730	5	1.100
27.277	6	1.320
31.823	7	1.540
36.369	8	1.760
40.915	9	1.980
45.460	10	2.220

1 x 9 =	9
2 x 9 =	18
3 x 9 =	27
4 x 9 =	36
5 x 9 =	45
6 x 9 =	54
7 x 9 =	63
8 x 9 =	72
9 x 9 =	81
10 x 9 =	90
11 x 9 =	99
12 x 9 =	108

tablet tablets noun
a small, round piece of medicine that you swallow.

table tennis noun
a game for two or four people who stand at each end of a table with a net across the middle and hit a very small ball to each other, bouncing it off the table, using small bats. Also called Ping-Pong.

tackle tackles tackling tackled verb
1 If you tackle somebody when playing a game such as football, you try to get the ball away from him or her.
2 When you tackle something, you do whatever is needed, even if it is difficult.

tactful adjective
careful not to say anything that would hurt somebody else's feelings.
tactfully adverb.

tadpole tadpoles noun
a tiny animal that lives in water and that will grow into a frog or toad. Tadpoles have tails.

tail tails noun
the part at the back end of an animal, bird, or fish. *The dog wagged its tail.* or *Airplanes have tails.* ● A word that sounds like **tail** is **tale**.

tailor tailors noun
a person who makes suits, jackets, and coats.

take takes taking took taken verb
1 If you take something, you get hold of it or carry it. *Can you take these books back to the library?*
2 If someone takes you, they drive you or you go with them. *Dan took me to school on his way to work.*
3 If you take something, you remove it. *She took her purse out of her bag.* or *Have you taken my bag?*
take off When a plane takes off, it leaves the runway and moves into the air. ■ The opposite is **land**.

tale tales noun
a story. *a tale of love and adventure.* ● A word that sounds like **tale** is **tail**.

talent talents noun
If you have a talent for something, you have a natural ability for it and can do it well. *Clive's got a real talent for acting.*
talented adjective.

talk talks talking talked verb
When you talk, you say words. *We talked on the phone for hours.* ▲ Say **tawk**.

tall taller tallest adjective
1 higher than usual. *She's very tall.* or *a tall building.* ■ The opposite is **short**.
2 having a certain height. *He's just over five feet tall.*

tambourine tambourines noun
a small, round musical instrument that you shake or tap with your fingers.
▲ Say *tam-ber-een*.

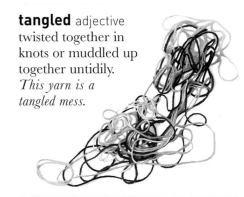

tame tamer tamest adjective
A tame animal or bird is used to living with people and is not afraid of them.
■ The opposite is **wild**.

tan noun
If you have a tan, your skin is a darker color than usual because you have been in the Sun.

tandem tandems noun
a special bicycle for two people.

tangled adjective
twisted together in knots or muddled up together untidily. *This yarn is a tangled mess.*

tank tanks noun
1 a big container that holds liquid or gas.
2 a big, heavy vehicle with a gun in it that is used in a war.

tanker tankers noun
1 a very big, long ship that carries oil.
2 a big truck that carries gasoline or some other liquid.

tap taps noun
a thing that you turn on to make water or gas flow out of a pipe and turn off to stop it from flowing.

tap taps tapping tapped verb
If you tap someone or something, you hit them gently. *He tapped a few keys, and data came up on the screen.*

tape tapes noun
1 a long, narrow piece of material. *a tape measure.*
2 a long strip of plastic that you can record sounds or pictures on and then play back on a tape machine.
tape verb.

tape recorder tape recorders noun
a machine that you use to play a tape or to record sounds onto a tape.

tapestry tapestries noun
a piece of material that has a picture on it made from colored threads.

tar noun
a thick, black, sticky substance that is mainly used for building roads.

tardy tardier tardiest adjective
arriving late. *tardy students.*

target targets noun
an object that people aim at or try to hit when they are shooting.

task tasks noun
a job that must be done.

taste tastes tasting tasted verb
1 When you taste something, you try a little of it to see if you like the flavor. *Please taste this fish and tell me if you like it.*
2 If something tastes good or bad, you think that the flavor is good or bad. *I like that ice cream; it tastes great.* or *This milk tastes funny.*

taste tastes noun
1 the ability to recognize the flavor of something by touching it with your tongue. *Sugar has a sweet taste.*
2 the way something tastes. *This bread has no taste at all.*

tattoo tattoos noun
a permanent or temporary pattern on a person's skin made by putting colored dyes under the skin using a needle or by using makeup.

taught past of teach.
▲ Say **tawt.**

tax taxes noun
money that people have to pay to the government for running the country. *income taxes.*

taxi taxis noun
a car that will take you where you want to go if you pay the driver.

tea noun
a drink that you make by pouring boiling water on to the dried leaves of the tea plant.

teach teaches teaching taught verb
1 When people teach you, they tell you about a subject and help you learn about it. *Mrs. Jones teaches history.*
2 to show somebody how to do something. *I'll teach you how to surf this summer.*
teacher noun.

team teams noun
a group of people who work together or play a sport together. *a football team.*

teapot teapots noun
a container for making tea in with a spout for pouring it out.

tear tears noun
one of the drops of liquid that comes from your eyes when you cry.
▲ Rhymes with **here.** ● A word that sounds like **tear** is **tier.**

tear tears tearing tore torn verb
When you tear something, you pull one part away from the rest. *If you tear paper in a special way, you can make different shapes and patterns.*
▲ Rhymes with **chair.**

tease teases teasing teased verb
When you tease people, you laugh at them or make jokes about them. *Tony's friends teased him because of his new haircut.* ▲ Say **teez.**

technology technologies noun
machines or ways of doing things that have been invented because of discoveries by scientists.
▲ Say *tek-**nol**-o-jee.*

teenage adjective
between 13 and 19 years of age.
teenager noun.

teeth plural of tooth.

telephone telephones noun
an instrument that you use to speak to another person who is not in the same place as you. ▲ Say *tel-u-fone.*

telescope telescopes noun
an instrument in the shape of a tube with a lens at each end that makes things, such as stars, that are far away look clearer and closer when you look through it.

160

television televisions noun
an instrument in the shape of a box or flat square that receives shows that are broadcast and shows them in sound and pictures.

tell tells telling told verb
1 If you tell somebody something, you give that person information in words about it. *I told him how to fix a tire.* or *She told me a very funny joke.*
2 If you tell somebody to do something, you say that the person must do it.

temper noun
1 If you have a bad temper, you get angry easily. *His temper gets bad when he loses.*
2 If you lose your temper, you get very angry.

temperature noun
1 how hot or cold something is. *Water freezes at a temperature of 32 degrees.*
2 If you have a temperature, your body is hotter than it should be.
▲ Say **temp-*re-cher.***

temple temples noun
a building where some people go to pray.

temporary adjective
lasting for a short time. *He has a temporary job.* ■ The opposite is **permanent**.
temporarily adverb.

tempt tempts tempting tempted verb
If something tempts you, you want it very strongly even if you know that you should not have it.
temptation noun.

tenant tenants noun
a person who pays another person in order to rent and live in an apartment or a house.

tend tends tending tended verb
If something tends to happen, it usually happens or happens often. *I tend to miss the bus if I leave after 8 o'clock.*

tender tenderer tenderest adjective
1 easy to chew. *This is very tender meat.* ■ The opposite is **tough**.
2 a little sore. *My ankle is still tender from when I fell over.*
3 gentle and loving.
tenderly adverb
She spoke tenderly to the little girl.
tenderness noun.

tennis noun
a game for two or four players. The players hit a soft ball with rackets backward and forward to each other over a net that is stretched across the middle of an area called a tennis court.

tense tenser tensest adjective
1 nervous and anxious about something.
2 If your muscles are tense, they are stiff and tight. *After running the marathon, my legs were very tense.*
tensely adverb.

tent tents noun
a shelter made of strong cloth that is held up by poles and ropes.

tepee tepees noun
The Native Americans made tepees out of animal skins or the bark of trees. These were their tents.

tepid adjective
slightly warm. *Babies have tepid baths so that they don't get burned.*

term terms noun
1 a length of time. *He served a four-year term as the President of the U.S.A.*
2 a word or phrase. *"Adagio" and "forte" are musical terms.*

terminal terminals noun
a building at an airport from which passengers leave and arrive.

terrible adjective
very bad or unpleasant. *What a terrible noise!*
terribly adverb.

terrific adjective
very good. *The movie is terrific—I've seen it five times.*

terrify terrifies terrifying terrified verb
If you terrify somebody, you make them very frightened. *The explosion terrified the horses.* or *Many dogs are terrified of thunder.*

territory territories noun
1 land that belongs to or is controlled by a country, army, or ruler.
2 an area where an animal lives that it will fight for if another animal tries to come and live there.

terror noun
very great fear. *He screamed with terror when he thought that he'd seen a ghost.*

test tests noun
1 a way of finding out what you know about something by asking you a set of questions or getting you to show what you can do. *a driver's test.* or *a spelling test.*
2 a check to see if part of your body is working correctly. *an eye test.*

an eye test

test tests testing tested verb
1 When you test something, you use or examine it to see if it works well. *I'm testing the brakes to make sure that they're working correctly.*
2 When you test somebody, you try to find out how much he or she knows by using a test.

text texts noun
written words. *Books for very young children have a lot of pictures and not a lot text.*

texture textures noun
the way that something feels. *This wool has a smooth texture, almost like silk.*

thank thanks thanking thanked verb
When you thank people, you tell them
how nice it was of them to do
something for you or to give you
something. *Thank you very much for
taking us all to the movie.*

thaw thaws thawing thawed verb
When something frozen thaws, it
becomes warm enough to melt.
*The Sun's out, and the snow has started
to thaw.*

theater theaters noun
a building where people go to see
plays. ▲ Say **thee**-*u-ter.*

theft thefts noun
the crime of stealing. *He was sent to
jail for the crime of theft.*

theme park theme parks noun
a place you go to have fun where
all the games and activities have to
do with the same subject—for
example, space.

thermometer thermometers noun
an instrument that shows what the
temperature of something is.

thick thicker thickest adjective
1 Something that is thick measures a
lot from one side to the other or
from top to bottom. *The castle wall
was three feet thick.* ■ The opposite
is **thin**.
2 A thick liquid does not flow easily.
Honey is thick. ■ The opposite
is **thin**.

3 Something that is thick is not easy
to get through or see through.
*The airport shut down because of
thick fog.*
thicken verb
The fog thickened.
thickly adverb.

thief thieves noun
a person who steals something.
*Thieves broke into the store and stole all
the silver and jewelry.* ▲ Say **theef.**

thigh thighs noun
Your thigh is the part of your leg
above your knee. *Your thighs are the
fattest part of your legs.*

thin thinner thinnest adjective
1 narrow from side to side or from
top to bottom. *a thin slice of cake.*
or *There was a thin layer of ice on
the pond.* ■ The opposite is **thick**.
2 A thin person does not have much
flesh covering their bones and
weighs less than most people.
■ The opposite is **fat**.
3 A thin liquid flows easily. *This soup
is too thin.* ■ The opposite is **thick**.
thinly adverb.

think thinks thinking thought verb
1 When you think, you have ideas or
words in your mind. *What are you
thinking about?*
2 When you think that something is
true, you believe it. *I think Mike's
plan for the party is great.*

thirsty thirstier thirstiest adjective
If you are thirsty, you need something
to drink. *Exercise can make you thirsty.*

thistle thistles noun
a wild plant with very prickly leaves
and purple or white flowers.

thorn thorns noun
a little sharp point on the stem of a
plant such as a rose.
thorny adjective.

thorough adjective
complete and careful. *a thorough
investigation.* ▲ Say **thu**-*ro.*
thoroughly adverb.

thought thoughts noun
an idea or something that you think.
*Any thoughts about what you'd like for
your birthday?* ▲ Say **thawt.**

thought past of **think**.
I thought I could solve the problem.

thoughtful adjective
1 quiet and serious while you are
thinking about something carefully.
2 If you are thoughtful, you think
about what other people want and
try to behave in a way that makes
them more
comfortable
or happy.
▲ Say
thot-*ful.*
**thoughtfully,
thoughtless**
adverbs
*thoughtless
behavior.*

Hal is looking
thoughtful.

thread threads noun
a long, thin piece of cotton, wool, or synthetic material that you use for sewing or weaving. ▲ Say **thred**. **thread** verb.

threat threats noun
a warning that something bad may happen. ▲ Say **thret**.

threaten threatens threatening threatened verb
If somebody threatens you, that person says that he or she will do something mean if you do not do what they want.

three-dimensional adjective
Something that is three-dimensional is like a real thing with height, width, and depth and not like a flat picture. A hologram is three-dimensional; 3-D.

threw past of throw.
● A word that sounds like **threw** is **through**.

thrill thrills noun
a sudden feeling of excitement or pleasure.
thrilling adjective.

throat throats noun
Your throat is the front part of your neck and the tube that goes down from inside your mouth, taking food and air into your body.

throne thrones noun
a special chair for a king or queen.

through preposition
from one side to the other. *The train went through a tunnel.* or *Water is coming through a hole in the ceiling.* ▲ Say **throo**. ● A word that sounds like **through** is **threw**.

throw throws throwing threw thrown verb
When you throw something, you send it through the air from your hand. *Throw the ball up into the air and then hit it with your racket.*

thumb thumbs noun
Your thumb is the short, thick finger at the side of your hand. ▲ Say **thum**.

thumbtack thumbtacks noun
a small object with a sharp point and a broad, flat head that you push into a wall or board to hold up notices and other paper.

thump thumps thumping thumped verb
If you thump somebody or something, you hit them with your fist.

thunder noun
the loud noise that you hear after a flash of lightning during some storms.

tick ticks noun
a tiny animal with eight legs that is related to the spider. It sucks blood from people and animals.

ticket tickets noun
a small piece of paper that shows you have paid for something. *Have you bought the movie tickets yet?* or *a train ticket.*

tickle tickles tickling tickled verb
When you tickle people, you touch them very softly in a place where it makes them laugh and wriggle away.

tide tides noun
the everyday movement of the sea coming toward land and then away from land. *The tide is coming in.* or *The tide is going out.*

tidy tidier tidiest adjective
neat; with everything in its correct place. *a tidy ship.*
tidy verb, **tidily** adverb.

tie ties tying tied verb
1 When you tie something, you fasten it using string or something similar. *The box was tied with red and white ribbons.* or *She tied the dog to a tree.*
2 When two people or teams tie in a race or competition, they finish in an equal position. *They tied for second place.*
tie up *Ships were tied up at the dock.*

tie ties noun
a long, thin piece of material that you wear around the neck of a shirt. It has a knot at the front.

tier tiers noun
one of a series of rows or layers that are placed one above the other. *There are several tiers of seats in the theater.* or *a wedding cake with three tiers.*
● A word that sounds like **tier** is **tear**, as in crying.

tiger tigers noun
a large wild animal in the cat family that has orange fur with dark stripes. Tigers live in Asia.

tight tighter tightest adjective
1 fitting very close to your body. *Connie's shoes are very tight—Joe is trying to pull them off.*
2 When something is tight, it is firmly fastened so that it will not move. *Make sure that the lid is on tight.* ▲ Say **tite**. ■ The opposite is **loose**.
tightly adverb.

tighten tightens tightening tightened verb
If you tighten something, you make it tighter. If something tightens it gets tighter. ▲ Say **teye**-ten.

tightrope tightropes noun
a rope high up in the air that acrobats walk along in the circus.
▲ Say **tite**-rope.

tights noun
a thin piece of clothing that tightly covers your body, sometimes from the neck down and sometimes from the waist. ▲ Say **tites**.

tile tiles noun
a thin piece of hard material that you use to cover a wall, floor, or a roof. *The bathroom tiles have pictures of fish and shells on them.*

till preposition
until. *We had to wait two weeks till we heard the test results.*

time noun
1 what we measure in units such as minutes, hours, days, weeks, and years.
2 a particular point in time. *What time is it?*
3 a period of time. *Did you enjoy your time in San Francisco?*

timetable timetables noun
a list that shows when things are going to happen. *Let's read the timetable to find out when to board the train.*

time zone time zones noun
a region where the same time is used.

timid adjective
shy and not very brave. *A mouse is a timid creature.*
timidly adverb.

tin noun
a type of silver-colored metal.

tiny tinier tiniest adjective
very small. *Bacteria are so tiny that you can only see them through a microscope.*
■ The opposite is **enormous** or **huge**.

tip tips noun
1 the end of something long and thin. *the tips of your fingers.*
2 an extra amount of money that you give to someone, such as a waiter, for helping you. *Dad gave the waiter a big tip.*

tiptoe tiptoes tiptoeing
tiptoed verb
to quietly walk on your toes.

tire tires noun
a circle of rubber around the rim of a car or bicycle wheel. ● Rhymes with **fire**.

tired adjective
If you are tired, you want to go to sleep.

tissue tissues noun
1 a thin piece of soft paper that you can use as a handkerchief.
2 a lot of tiny cells of the same type that make up part of the body. *muscle tissue.*

title titles noun
1 the name of something such as a book, movie, or picture.
2 a word such as *Professor, Dr., Mrs.,* or *Ms.* that a person can have in front of their name.

toad toads noun
an animal like a big frog. It lives on land but lays its eggs in water.

fire-bellied toad

giant toad

toadstool toadstools noun
a poisonous fungus that looks like a mushroom.

toast noun
a slice of bread that has been browned on both sides to make it crunchy.
toaster noun.

tobacco noun
the cut and dried leaves of the tobacco plant that are used in cigarettes, cigars, and pipes.

toboggan toboggans noun
a vehicle like a long seat attached to two long strips of wood or metal called runners that you use to slide downhill on snow.

toddler toddlers noun
a very young child who is just learning to walk.

toe toes noun
the five parts at the end of your foot. ● A word that sounds like **toe** is **tow**.

toilet toilets noun
a large bowl with a seat that you use to get rid of liquid and solid waste from your body.

token tokens noun
a metal disk that you can use instead of money to buy something. *a game token.*

told past of **tell**.

toll tolls noun
money that you pay to use a big road.

tomato tomatoes noun
a soft, round, red fruit that you eat in salads.

tomb tombs noun
a grave or place where somebody important is buried. ▲ Say **toom.**

tongue tongues noun
the long, pink part inside your mouth that you use to lick something and that helps you taste things and speak. ▲ Say **tung.**

tonsil tonsils noun
Your tonsils are the two small, soft lumps at the back of your throat. They sometimes swell and hurt in an illness called tonsillitis.

took past of **take**.

tool tools noun
anything that you use to help you do a particular job. Hammers and saws are tools.

tooth teeth noun
1 one of the hard, white parts inside your mouth that you use to bite and chew.
2 one of the thin parts that stick out in a row on such things as a comb, saw, or zipper.

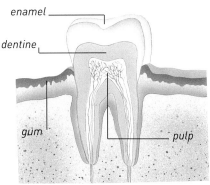

enamel
dentine
gum
pulp

toothbrush toothbrushes noun
a small brush with a handle that you use to brush your teeth.

toothpaste noun
a cleaning paste that you put on your toothbrush to brush your teeth.

top tops noun
1 the highest part of something. *We walked to the top of the hill.* ■ The opposite is **bottom**.
2 a lid or cover for something. *Screw the top tightly on the jar.*

topic topics noun
something that is being talked about or written about. *The topic of my essay is solar energy.*

topple topples toppling toppled verb
If something topples, it falls over because it is too heavy at the top. *The tree toppled over in the wind.*

tore, torn past of **tear**.

tornado tornadoes noun
a very strong wind that travels in circles and that can do a lot of damage to buildings.
▲ Say tor-**nay**-doh.

tortilla tortillas noun
a flat piece of bread made with water and cornmeal. ▲ Say tor-**tee**-yah.

tortoise tortoises noun
a turtle that lives on land and moves very slowly. Tortoises are reptiles.
▲ Say **tor**-tus.

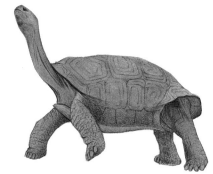
a giant Galapagos tortoise

torture tortures torturing tortured verb
To torture is to make somebody feel great pain as a punishment or to get information from him or her.
▲ Say **tor**-cher.

toss tosses tossing tossed verb
1 If you toss something, you throw it upward in a careless way. *She tossed me a pen.*
2 If something tosses, it moves around from side to side. *The ship tossed on the waves.*

total adjective
complete. *a total disaster.*

total totals noun
the amount that you get when you add everything together. *If you add 12, 17, and 8, you get a total of 37.*

touch touches touching touched verb
1 When you touch something, you feel it with your hand or another part of you.
2 If two things touch, there is no space between them.
▲ Say **tuch**.

touchdown touchdowns noun
a score of six points in football made by passing or running the ball into the opponent's end zone.

tough tougher toughest adjective
1 strong and hard to break or damage.

2 difficult. *a tough decision.*
3 difficult to chew. *This meat is tough.*
■ The opposite is **tender**.
▲ Say **tuff**.

tour tours noun
a trip to different interesting places. *a tour of Chicago.* ▲ Say **toor**.

tourist tourists noun
a person who is visiting interesting places on vacation. ▲ Say **tor**-ist.

tournament tournaments noun
a competition in which a lot of games are played until one person or team wins over all the others.
▲ Say **tor**-na-ment.

tow tows towing towed verb
To tow a vehicle is to pull it along behind another vehicle. *The car is towing a boat trailer.* ● A word that sounds like **tow** is **toe**.

towel towels noun
a large piece of soft, thick material that you use to dry yourself.

tower towers noun
a very tall, narrow building or part of a building. *the Eiffel Tower.* or *the Leaning Tower of Pisa.*

the Leaning Tower of Pisa

town towns noun
a place with streets, houses, stores, and other buildings where people live and work. *a small Midwestern town.*

toy toys noun
a thing for a child to play with.

trace traces tracing traced verb
1 When you trace a picture, you put a thin piece of paper over it and draw over the lines that show through.
2 If you trace others, you find them after looking for them. *He is trying to trace an uncle whom nobody in the family has heard from for many years.*

trace traces noun
a tiny amount. *There are traces of garlic in this soup.*

track tracks noun
1 footprints or other marks left by a person or animal that show where they have been.
2 an area of ground where races take place.
3 the rails that a train runs on.
4 one of the songs or pieces of music on a CD or MP3.

tractor tractors noun
a powerful vehicle with very large back wheels used on a farm for pulling heavy machinery and plowing.

trade noun
buying and selling things. *The U.S.A. does a lot of trade with Mexico.*

tradition traditions noun
a way of doing something that has been the same for a very long time.
traditional adjective
traditional songs.
traditionally adverb.

traffic noun
cars, trucks, buses, and other vehicles that are moving along the roads. *A lot of traffic goes through the city.*

tragedy tragedies noun
1 a very sad event. *Two of his brothers and a sister died in the tragedy.*
2 a serious play with a sad ending.
▲ Say **traj**-*e-dee*.
tragic adjective
a tragic accident.

trail trails noun
1 a track or path for people to follow or go along in the country. *the Appalachian Trail.*
2 marks or other signs left behind where a person or animal has been. *He left a trail of muddy footprints across the kitchen floor.*

trailer trailers noun
1 a vehicle that is towed behind a car or truck to carry very large or heavy things, such as a boat.
2 an advertisement that shows short scenes from a movie or TV show.

train trains noun
a set of railroad cars that move along rails pulled by an engine. Some trains carry passengers, and some trains carry freight.

train trains training trained verb
1 When you train, you practice a sport or do exercises to get fitter. *He's training for the Olympics.*
2 To train a person or animal is to teach them how to do something. *She's training the dog to roll over.*
3 If you train, you learn the skills that you need to do a job. *Sue's training to be a doctor.*
trainer noun.

traitor traitors noun
a person who helps the enemy of his or her country.

trample tramples trampling trampled verb
If you trample on something, you walk on it and crush it. *Please don't trample the flowers.*

trampoline trampolines noun
a piece of very strong material attached to a metal frame with springs that is used for jumping up and down in gymnastics.
▲ Say **tramp**-*o-leen*.

transfer transfers transferring transferred verb
To transfer something is to move it to a different place.

transform transforms transforming transformed verb
If you transform something, you change it completely. *With makeup, a wig, and good acting, he transformed himself into an old man.*

translate translates translating translated verb
If you translate something, you change the same thing into a different language. *Richard translated the story from Spanish into English.*

transparent adjective
If something is transparent, you can see through it. *This folder is transparent.*

transplant transplants noun
an operation in which a surgeon takes out a damaged part of the body and replaces it with one that is not damaged. *a heart transplant.*

transport transports transporting transported verb
To transport people or things is to take them from one place to another in a vehicle. *The boxes were transported by air.*

transportation noun
cars, buses, trains, and other vehicles that take people or goods from one place to another.

trap traps noun
a thing to catch an animal or bird. *a mousetrap.*
trap verb.

trapeze trapezes noun
a bar hanging from ropes high up in the air that acrobats in a circus swing from.

Transportation

B
C
D
E
K
N
T
U
V
X
Y
Z

VOCABULARY

bypass
a road built around a busy town so that traffic does not pass though it.

crosswalk
parallel white lines painted on a road to show where people may cross and where traffic must stop at lights.

freeway
a wide road with several lanes on which traffic can travel faster than on other roads.

intersection
a place where two or more roads cross one another.

lane
the part of a road used by vehicles going in the same direction.

on-ramp/off-ramp
a ramp by which one joins or leaves a freeway.

overpass
a highway or bridge crossing over another highway.

stoplights
lights of changing colors for controlling traffic at intersections and crosswalks.

dirt bike

road/racing motorcycle

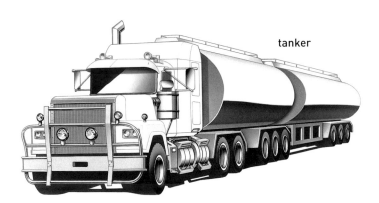

tanker

sports car

family car

Terex "Titan"

rickshaw

trash noun
things that you do not want that you throw away.

travel travels traveling traveled verb
When you travel, you go from one place to another. *We'll be traveling back to Fort Worth on Wednesday.*
travel noun, **traveler** noun.

trawler trawlers noun
a boat for catching fish that pulls a wide net behind it in the sea.

a trawler

tray trays noun
a flat piece of wood, metal, or plastic that you carry things, such as food, on.

tread treads treading trod trodden or **trod** verb
When you tread on something, you put your foot down on it. *Ouch! You trod on my toe!* ▲ Rhymes with **head**.

treasure treasures noun
a collection of very valuable objects such as gold, silver, or jewels. *The pirates hid the treasure in a cave.* ▲ Say **tre-**zure.

treat treats treating treated verb
1 When you treat somebody in a particular way, you behave toward that person like that. *He always treats me politely.*
2 To treat people is to give them medicine or to look after them in a way that will make them well. *The doctor treated her for an earache.*

treatment treatments noun
1 how a doctor treats somebody who is sick. *What's the right treatment?*
2 how somebody behaves toward a person, animal, or thing. *cruel treatment.*

tree trees noun
a big plant that has a thick, hard stem of wood called a trunk and branches and leaves. ◆ Look on opposite page.

tremble trembles trembling trembled verb
If you tremble, you shake a little because you are frightened, cold, or excited.

trend trends noun
the way things seem to be changing. *The trend is for people to save their money.*

trespass trespasses trespassing trespassed verb
If you trespass, you go on other people's land without asking them for permission.

trial trials noun
1 a period of time in a law court when lawyers, judge, and jury try to find out whether somebody is guilty or innocent of a crime.
2 a test to find out how good a thing is.

triangle triangles noun
1 a shape with three straight sides.
2 a small musical instrument with three metal sides that you play by hitting it with a short metal rod. ▲ Say **try**-ang-gul.
triangular adjective
a triangular shape.

triathlon triathlons noun
a race including swimming, bicycling, and running.

tribe tribes noun
a group of people from shared ancestry that speak the same language and live in the same area.

trick tricks noun
1 something that is done to cheat others or to try to make them believe that something that is not true.
2 something that looks as if it could not be done. *a magic trick.*

trick tricks tricking tricked verb
To trick others is to cheat them or try to make them believe something that is not true.

trickle trickles trickling trickled verb
When liquid trickles, a small amount of it flows slowly. *When Ben heard that his dog had died, tears slowly trickled down his cheeks.*

tricycle tricycle noun
a vehicle like a bicycle with three wheels. ▲ Say **try**-sik-ul.

trim trims trimming trimmed verb
If you trim something, you cut small pieces off it so that it has a better shape and looks neat. *Connie is trimming Joe's hair.*

trip trips noun
a journey to a place and back again. *We went on a school trip to New York City just before Christmas.*

trip trips tripping tripped verb
If you trip, you knock your foot on something and fall over. *She tripped over the cat.*

triple adjective
having three parts or done three times. *He's a triple winner.* or *the Triple Crown in horse racing.*

triplet triplets noun
one of three people or animals who have the same mother and were born at the same time.

triumph triumphs noun
a great success in something that you have had to try hard to do. *The acrobat's performance was a triumph.* ▲ Say **try**-umf.

trod trodden past of **tread**.

trolley trolleys noun
a streetcar.

Trees

Cedar of Lebanon

hornbeam

Douglas-fir

hybrid black-poplar

common juniper

golden weeping willow

sea black thorn

red oak

spindle

box

pendulculate oak

common jujube

guelder rose

dragon tree

petticoat palm

VOCABULARY

broad-leaved
trees with broad, flat leaves are deciduous. The leaves drop in the fall.

deciduous
trees that shed their leaves in the fall.

evergreen
conifers that keep their needlelike leaves in the winter.

hardwood
the wood of slow-growing, broad-leaved or deciduous trees. The wood is strong and used for making furniture.

heartwood
the oldest, hardest wood at the center of the trunk.

softwood
the wood of evergreen trees. The word is misleading as some "softwoods" are "hard."

trombone trombones noun
a large brass musical instrument that
you play by blowing into it and
moving one tube in and out of
another tube to change the notes.
trombonist noun.

trophy trophies noun
a prize such as a silver cup that is
given to a person who has won a
competition or tournament. *Sarah
won a big trophy at the horse show.*
▲ Say **troh**-*fee.*

tropical adjective
to do with the tropics, the very hot
parts of the world near the equator.
a tropical rainforest.

trot trots trotting trotted verb
When a horse trots, it moves quickly.
trot noun.

trouble troubles noun
a problem or a difficult or worrying
situation. ▲ Say **trub**-*el.*
in trouble.
If you are in trouble, you have done
something wrong and made
somebody angry who might punish
you. *If you break the window with that
ball, you'll be in big trouble.*

trough troughs noun
a long, narrow container
that has food
or water in it
for animals.
▲ Say **troff**.

trousers noun
pants.

truant truants noun
a student who stays away from school
without permission.
truancy noun.

truck trucks noun
a large motor vehicle that moves
things by road.

trudge trudges trudging
trudged verb
If you trudge somewhere, you
walk slowly because you are tired
or angry. *We trudged home through
the mud.*
▲ Say **trudj**.

true truer truest adjective
If something is true, it is based on
known facts and is accurate, not made
up or guessed at. *a true story.* ■ The
opposite is **false**.
truly adverb
very. *It was a truly funny story, and we
all laughed loudly.*

trumpet trumpets noun
a brass musical instrument that you
play by blowing into it.
trumpeter noun.

trunk trunks noun
1 the round, hard stem of a tree that
  the branches grow from.
2 the long nose of an elephant.
3 the main part of your body from
  the top of your legs to your
  shoulders—not your head, arms,
  or legs.
4 a large, strong box for carrying
  things in on a long trip or for
  storing things. *a steamer trunk.*

trust trusts trusting trusted verb
If you trust others, you believe that
they are good and honest and will not
do anything to hurt you.
trust noun.

truth noun
what is true, accurate, and correct.
I'm sure that she's telling the truth.

try tries trying tried verb
1 If you try to do something, you do
  your best to do it.
2 If you try something, you test it to
  see what it is like. *Try this soup and
  tell me if it needs more salt.*

T-shirt T-shirts noun
a shirt made of cotton with short
sleeves and no collar or buttons that
you pull over your head.

tub tubs noun
a big container that you take a bath in.

tube tubes noun
1 a long, round, hollow thing, like
  a pipe.
2 a long, thin container that you
  squeeze to get the contents out.

tuck tucks tucking tucked verb
If you tuck something, you push the
end of it under something or into
something else. *He tucked his shirt into
his pants.*

tuft tufts noun
a clump of hair or grass.

tug tugs tugging tugged verb
If you tug something, you pull hard at
it. *The baby kept tugging at my hair.*

tulip tulips noun
a plant that grows from a bulb and
has a long stem and a bright flower
in the shape of a cup.

tumble tumbles tumbling
tumbled verb
If you tumble, you fall suddenly,
rolling over and over. *The child tumbled
down the hill.*

tuna tunas noun
a huge ocean fish. *We eat tuna
in sandwiches.*

tune tunes noun
a series of musical notes that are nice
to listen to.

tunnel tunnels noun
a long hole under the ground or
through a hill. *the Lincoln Tunnel.*
tunnel verb

The moles have tunneled large burrows in the backyard.

turban turbans noun
a long strip of material wound around the head.

turf noun
short, thick grass. *After the football game, the turf was torn up.*

turkey turkeys noun
a large bird that does not fly and that is usually raised on a farm for its meat.

ocellated turkey

common turkey

turn turns turning turned verb
1 When something turns, it moves around so that it faces in a different direction or goes in a different direction. *The car turned right at the traffic lights.* or *He turned around and looked behind him.*
2 When something turns, it goes around. *The wheel turned.*
3 When you turn something, you turn it around. *She turned the handle.*
4 When something turns into something else, it changes to become that thing. *A caterpillar turns into a butterfly.*

turn turns noun
a time when you do something that other people have done before you and that other people will do after you. *It's my turn to use the computer.*

turtle turtles noun
a reptile with a hard shell that lives on land or in the water.

tusk tusks noun
a long, pointed tooth that comes right outside the mouth of an animal such as an elephant.

TV TVs noun
short for television. *She's upstairs watching TV.*

twice adverb
two times. *I've been to see the movie twice now. How many times have you seen it?*

twig twigs noun
a small branch of a tree.

twilight noun
a time after sunset before it gets completely dark. ▲ Say **twy**-*lite.*

twin twins noun
one of two people or animals who have the same mother and were born at the same time.

twinkle twinkles twinkling twinkled verb
When something twinkles, it shines with little flashes of light. *The stars were twinkling.*

twirl twirls twirling twirled verb
to turn or spin around and around. *She twirled her hair around her fingers.*
twirl noun.

twist twists twisting twisted verb

1 If you twist something, you turn it around and around. *She twisted the screwdriver to tighten the screw.*
2 When you twist something, you bend it or turn it around. *He twisted the wires together.*
twist noun.

twitch twitches twitching twitched verb
To twitch is to make a small, quick movement. *The big rabbit's nose suddenly twitched.*
twitchy adjective.

tycoon tycoons verb
A tycoon is a rich and powerful businessman or businesswoman.

type types typing typed verb
When you type, you press the keys on a keyboard to write something.
▲ Rhymes with **pipe.**

type types noun
1 a kind of thing. *An apple is a type of fruit.*
2 the size and style of printed letters and numbers. *big black type.*
▲ Rhymes with **pipe.**

typewriter typewriters noun
a machine with keys that you press to print letters and numbers on paper.

typhoon typhoon noun
a violent tropical storm of wind and rain. Typhoons usually happen in the western part of the Pacific Ocean.
▲ Say ti-**foon.**

typical adjective
A typical thing is the most usual of that type of thing. *a typical Midwestern town.* or *a typical summer storm.*
▲ Say **tip**-*i-cal.*

tyrannosaur tyrannosaurs noun
a huge dinosaur with small front legs, a large head, and sharp teeth. It walked on its hind legs and ate meat.

tyrant tyrants noun
a cruel and unfair ruler.
tyrannical adjective.

udder udders noun
the part of a cow, goat, or sheep that hangs under the its body, near the back legs, and that produces milk.

ugly uglier ugliest adjective
not pretty.
■ The opposite is **beautiful**.

ukulele ukuleles noun
a small, four-stringed Hawaiian guitar.

umbrella umbrellas noun
a thing that you hold over your head to stay dry when it rains. The frame of an umbrella is covered with a round piece of material and connected to a handle.

uncle uncles noun
Your uncle is the brother of your mother or your father, or the husband of your aunt.

unconscious adjective
1 If you are unconscious, you are in a type of deep sleep and you do not know what is happening. *When she fell downstairs and hit her head, she was unconscious for an hour.*
■ The opposite is **conscious**.

uncover uncovers uncovering uncovered verb
1 When you uncover something, you take off the thing or things that cover it. *He uncovered the box and looked inside.*

2 to find something that was hidden or not known about. *A treasure was uncovered by a farmer digging in a field.* or *The plot to blow up the building was uncovered.*

underground adjective, adverb
below the surface of Earth. *Rabbits build their burrows underground.*

undergrowth noun
all the bushes and other plants that grow under trees. *thick undergrowth.*

underline underlines underlining underlined verb
If you underline something, you draw a line under it to make people notice it. *Please write the date and underline it with a ruler.*

underneath preposition
below or under something. *I found my shoes underneath the bed.*

underpass underpasses noun
a road that goes underneath a railroad or another road.

understand understands understanding understood verb
to know what something means, how it works, or why it happens.

underwear noun
clothing, such as an undershirt and underpants, that you wear beneath your other clothes.

undo undoes undoing undid undone verb
If you undo a package, you open it.

undress undresses undressing undressed verb
to take off clothes.
■ The opposite is **dress**.

unemployed adjective
A person who is unemployed does not have a job and is not working.
unemployment noun.

uneven adjective
not straight or level.
■ The opposite is **even**.

unfair unfairer unfairest adjective
not just or fair. ■ The opposite is **fair**.

unfold unfolds unfolding unfolded verb
to open something out so that it lies flat.

unicorn unicorns noun
A unicorn is an imaginary animal similar to a horse but with one horn sticking out of the front of its head.

uniform uniforms noun
a set of clothes, usually for work, sports, or school, that people wear to show that they belong to the same group.

union unions noun
a group of workers that come together to talk to their managers about any problems at work.

unit units noun
1 one part of something.
2 an amount used in measuring or counting. *A foot is a unit of length, a pound is a unit of weight, and a minute is a unit of time.* ▲ Say **you**-nit.

unite unites uniting united verb
If things or people unite, they join together or do something together. *The colonists united to fight for independence.* ▲ Say *you*-**nite**.

universe noun
Earth, the Sun, the Moon, and all the other planets and stars in space.

university universities noun
a place where people can go to study things when they finish high school; college. *Nancy wanted to go to the same university that her mother had gone to.*

unkind unkinder unkindest adjective
not nice to others.
■ The opposite is **kind**.

unlike preposition
not the same as. ■ The opposite is **like**.

unlikely unlikelier unlikeliest
adjective
if something is unlikely, it is probably not going to happen.
■ The opposite is **likely**.

unload unloads unloading unloaded
verb
To unload is to take things off a ship or vehicle. *The cargo was unloaded at the dock last Friday.* ■ The opposite is **load**.

unlock unlocks unlocking unlocked
verb
When you unlock something, you turn a key to open it.
■ The opposite is **lock**.

untie unties untying untied
to undo knots. *Michael had to untie a lot of ribbon to open his presents.*

until preposition
up to a certain time or day. *Dad is in his office until 6 o'clock every evening.* or *I can't come out to play on Saturday until I've cleaned my room.*

unusual adjective
not ordinary. ■ The opposite is **normal** or **usual**.

upload verb
to transfer data, such as photos, from your computer to the Internet.

upper adjective
above or higher than another thing. *He has a cut on his upper lip.*

upright adjective, adverb
If something like a bottle is upright,

it is standing up, with the top facing upward.
Connie is standing upright.

upset upsets upsetting upset verb
1 If you upset people, you make them unhappy. *She upset me when she said that my idea was stupid.*
2 If you upset something like a drink, you knock it over and spill it.

upside-down adjective, adverb
If something is upside-down, the bottom is at the top and the top is at the bottom. *This sloth is hanging upside-down.*

upstairs adjective, adverb
on or to an upper floor. *My bedroom is upstairs.*

up-to-date adjective
new and current. *News is information that is up-to-date.*

upward, upwards adverb
going to a higher place. *The balloon moved upward.*

urgent adjective
so very important that it must be done immediately. *She made an urgent phone call to the doctor.*
urgency noun.

use uses using used verb
1 If you use something, you do a job with it. *You use scissors to cut things.* or *Do you know how to use your new computer?*
2 To use also means to take something. *Don't use all the glue.* ▲ Say **youzz**.

used to
1 If you used to do something, you did it before, but you do not do it now. *I used to go swimming every Tuesday, but now I play tennis.*
2 Used to can also mean knowing somebody or something well. *We are all used to her jokes.* ▲ Say **yoosd**-*to*.

use uses noun
what you can do with something. *This bag has many uses.* ▲ Say **youss**.

useful adjective
If people or things are useful, they help you in some way. *Simon was very useful and he helped with the baby.*
usefulness noun.

useless adjective
If something is useless, it is not good for anything and you cannot use it. *This plate is useless because it is broken.* ■ The opposite is **useful**.

usual adjective
If something is usual, it happens often or most of the time.
■ The opposite is **unusual**.
usually adverb
I usually go to school by bike.

utensil utensils noun
a tool or container, especially one used for cooking.

utter utters uttering uttered verb
To make a sound or to say something. *He uttered a cry of pain.*

vacant adjective
empty and not being used.
vacancy noun

vacation vacations noun
a time when you do not go to school
or work and when you might travel
to a nice place like a different country
or a beach.

vaccination vaccinations noun
an injection that stops you from
getting an illness.
▲ Say *vak-si-**nay**-shun.*
vaccinate verb.

vacuum cleaner vacuum cleaners
noun
a machine that sucks up dirt from
rugs.

vague vaguer vaguest adjective
not clear or definite.
▲ Say **vayg.**

vain vainer vainest adjective
Vain people are too proud of
themselves, especially of how they look.

valentine valentines noun
a special greeting card that you send
to someone you like or love on
February 14.

valley valleys noun
low land between hills or mountains.

valuable adjective
1 worth a lot of money. *a valuable
necklace.*
2 useful and helpful. *He gave me some
valuable advice.*

value noun
1 the amount of money that
something is worth. *What is the value
of your house?*
2 how useful and helpful something is.
*The instructions you gave me were of
great value in helping me make the
machine work.*

vampire vampires noun
in stories, a dead person who drinks
people's blood.

van vans noun
a medium-size, covered motor vehicle
with doors at the back and on the
sides.

vandal vandals noun
a person who breaks or
damages property on purpose.
*Vandals have smashed the
telephone booth.*

vanilla noun
a flavor that comes from the pod of
a tropical plant and is used in sweet
foods. *vanilla ice cream.*

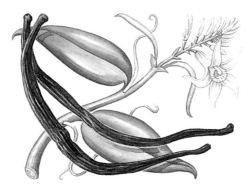

vanish vanishes vanishing vanished
verb
If something vanishes, it suddenly
disappears.

vanity noun
being vain and very proud of what
you look like.

variety varieties noun
1 a number of different types of
something. *They had a variety
of skirts and dresses in the sale.*
2 a type or sort of thing. *There
are lots of different varieties of
breakfast cereal.*
3 a lot of different things happening.
I like a lot of variety in my life.
▲ Say *ver-**eye**-i-tee.*

different varieties of breakfast cereal

various adjective
several different things. *You can buy
these towels in various colors.*
▲ Say **vair**-ee-us.

varsity adjective
A varsity team is the first, or best,
team of players in a sport.

vary varies varying varied verb
If something varies, it keeps changing.
*I take sandwiches to school every day, but
what goes in them varies.*
▲ Say **vair**-ee.

vase vases noun
a jar or container for putting flowers in.
▲ Say **vase.**

vast vaster vastest adjective
very, very large. *The Sahara is a vast
desert.*

vegan vegans noun
a vegetarian who only eats plant
products.

vegetable vegetables noun
a plant that people eat. Cabbages,
carrots, and potatoes are vegetables.
▲ Say **vej**-te-bul. ◆ Look at page 176.

vegetarian vegetarians noun
a person who does not eat meat or fish.
▲ Say *veg-e-**tair**-ee-un.*

174

vehicle vehicles noun
a thing that takes people or goods from one place to another. Buses, cars, trucks, and trains are all vehicles.
▲ Say **vee**-*i-cul*.

veil veils noun
a piece of material that some women wear over their faces or heads.

vein veins noun
one of the tubes in your body that carries blood back to your heart.

velvet noun
cloth that is thick and soft on one side.

verb verbs noun
a word that tells you what somebody or something does or what is happening. Think, run, and cut are all verbs. *What are you thinking?*

verdict verdicts noun
the result that the jury, and sometimes the judge, decide at the end of a trial in a court.

verse verses noun
a part of a poem or song made of several lines.

version versions noun
1 a changed form of something. *We bought the newest version of the computer game.*
2 one person's way of telling a story or what happened that is a little different from other people's. *In Harry's version of the story, the bull didn't chase her to the gate, she just ran.*

vertical adjective
standing straight up. *a vertical post.*
■ The opposite is **horizontal**.

vessel vessels noun
1 a ship or large boat.
2 a container for liquid.

vest vests noun
an article of clothing with no sleeves that is worn over over a shirt.

vet vets noun
a person whose job is to treat animals and help them get well when they are sick or hurt.

viaduct viaducts noun
a long bridge that carries a road or railroad over a valley.
▲ Say **veye**-*a-duct*.

vibrate vibrates vibrating vibrated verb
When something vibrates, it shakes very quickly. *The floor vibrated every time a train went past.*
▲ Say **veye**-**brate**.
vibration noun.

vice president vice presidents noun
the second highest official in the U.S. government.
vice presidency noun.

vicious adjective
cruel and violent. *a vicious attack.*
▲ Say **vish**-*us*.

victim victims noun
a person who has been attacked, hurt, robbed, or killed.

victory victories noun
a success in winning a battle or game.

view views noun
1 what you can see from one place. *We had a good view of the mountains.*
2 a person's opinion or what he or she thinks about something. *In my view, he fell over because he wasn't looking where he was going.*
▲ Say **vyou**.

vile viler vilest adjective
horrible. *That color is vile.*

village villages noun
a group of houses and other buildings in the country. *Villages are smaller than towns.*

villain villains noun
a very bad person, especially in a movie, story, or play. *The villain was jailed at the end of the movie.* ▲ Say **vil**-*un*.

vine vines noun
a climbing plant that grapes grow on.

vinegar noun
a sour liquid used to add flavor to food.

vineyard vineyards noun
a place where grape vines are grown for making wine. ▲ Say **vin**-*yard*.

violent adjective
1 a violent person uses force or weapons to hurt somebody else.
2 very strong or rough. *a violent storm.*

violet violets noun
a small plant with small white or purple flowers.

violin violins noun
a musical instrument with strings stretched across a wooden frame. *You play a violin by holding it under your chin and moving a stick called a bow across the strings.*
violinist noun.

virtual reality noun
an image made by a computer that surrounds you and that looks real and acts in real time.

Vegetables

1 savoy cabbage	9 broccoli	17 parsnips	25 celery
2 white cabbage	10 artichoke	18 zucchini	26 butternut
3 cauliflower	11 yam	19 carrot	squash
4 pumpkin	12 lettuce	20 red onion	27 green onions
5 lollo rosso	13 snow peas	21 string bean	28 cucumber
6 leek	14 peas	22 Brussels sprouts	29 sweet potato
7 corn	15 flat beans	23 potato	30 rutabaga
8 asparagus	16 French beans	24 radish	

virtue noun
a kind of goodness. *Honesty is a virtue.*

virus viruses noun
1 a tiny germ that causes a disease. *Colds and flu are caused by viruses.*
2 a computer program that damages the data in a computer system or network.

visible adjective
If something is visible, you can see it. ▲ Say **viz**-*i-bul*. ■ The opposite is **invisible**.

vision noun
a person's ability to see. *He has excellent vision.* ▲ Say **vish**-*un*.

visit visits visiting visited verb
If you visit people somewhere, you go to see them. *Matt visited his friend Sabrina in the hospital.*
visitor noun.

vitamin vitamins noun
one of the substances that are naturally in food that you need to stay healthy.

vocabulary vocabularies noun
1 all the words that somebody knows.
2 a list of words and what they mean.

voice voices noun
the sound that you make when you speak or sing.

volcano volcanoes noun
a mountain with an opening called a crater in the top, from which very hot melted rock and gases sometimes pour out when it erupts.

volume volumes noun
1 the amount of space inside something or the amount of space that something takes up. *What's the volume of that gas tank?*
2 a book in a set of books. *The first volume of a 20-volume encyclopedia.*
3 how loud a sound is. *Will you please turn down the volume of your iPod?*

volunteer volunteers noun
a person who does something without being paid and without being made to do it. *hospital volunteers.*

vote votes voting voted verb
If you vote for people, you choose them by putting your hand up, by making a mark on a piece of paper, or by using a special machine. *Have you voted yet?*
voter noun.

vowel vowels noun
the letters a, e, i, o, u, and sometimes y are vowels.

voyage voyages noun
a long journey by sea or in space. ▲ Say **voy**-*ij*.
voyager noun.

VOTE FOR
JOHN OLIVER

vulture vultures noun
a very large bird that eats dead animals. *The California condor is a type of vulture.*

ash and smoke

lava

magma chamber

Earth's layers

177

Ww

wade wades wading waded verb
To wade is to walk through deep water. *He waded across the stream.*

wag wags wagging wagged verb
When a dog wags its tail, it moves it quickly from side to side and up and down.

wages noun
the money that people are paid for the work that they do.

wagon wagons noun
a cart that is used to carry people and things from one place to another. It has four wheels and is usually pulled along by horses.

wail wails wailing wailed verb
If somebody wails, that person shouts or makes a sad cry because he or she is hurt or sad.

waist waists noun
Your waist is the narrow, middle part of your body. *Jack is wearing a belt around his waist.*

waistline noun
what your body measures around your waist.

wait waits waiting waited verb
If you wait, you stay where you are because you are expecting something. *We waited half an hour for the bus.*

waiter waiters noun
a person who brings you food in a restaurant or café.

wake wakes waking woke or waked verb
1 When you wake, you stop sleeping. *I woke up at 7 o'clock.*
2 When you wake someone, you make them stop sleeping. *I woke him at 5 o'clock.*

walk walks walking walked verb
When you walk, you move along on your feet. *I walk to the park every day.*
walk noun
We took the dog for a walk.

wall walls noun
1 one of the sides of a building or a room. *I helped paint my bedroom walls.*
2 something made of bricks or stones that you can see around some gardens. *We climbed over the wall and into the secret garden.*

wallet wallets noun
a small, flat case for keeping paper money and credit cards in.

wand wands noun
a stick that fairies and magicians wave when they do magic. *The fairy princess waved her magic wand.*

wander wanders wandering wandered verb
When you wander, you walk around slowly without going in any particular direction. *We wandered around in the woods looking for mushrooms to study in our science class.*

want wants wanting wanted verb
When you want something, you need it or you would like to have it. *Do you want an apple or an orange?*

war wars noun
a time when armies of different countries are fighting. ■ The opposite is **peace**.

ward wards noun
a big part of a hospital. *a surgical ward.*

wardrobe wardrobes noun
a person's clothes. *She has a big wardrobe of winter clothes.*

warehouse warehouses noun
a building where goods are kept before they are taken to stores or other places. *It took a few weeks to get our new sofa from the furniture warehouse.*

warm warmer warmest adjective
quite hot but not too hot. *The cat sat by the fire to stay warm.* ■ The opposite is **cool**.
warmth noun
I felt the warmth of the Sun on my skin.

warn warns warning warned verb
If you warn people, you tell them about something dangerous or bad that may happen. *He warned us not to swim in the river because it was very deep.* or *Dad warned us not to be late or he'd get upset.*

warning warnings noun
something that tells you about a danger that may happen. *The sign on the gate said, "Warning! Keep out—dangerous bull in field."*

wart warts noun
a hard lump on your skin. ▲ Rhymes with **sort**.

wash washes washing washed verb
When you wash something, you use soap and water to clean it. *He washed his face with a sponge before going to bed.*

wash noun
laundry; clothes that you need to wash or that you have washed. *I put the wash in the washing machine.*

washing machine washing machines noun
a machine that washes, rinses, and spins laundry; a washer.

wasp wasps noun
a flying insect with a narrow middle part of its body and a sting.

waste noun
1 What is left after you have digested your food, which is sent out of your body.
2 garbage and trash.
3 Something is a waste when you use too much of it or do not use it carefully. *It's a waste to throw away food.*

waste wastes wasting wasted verb
1 If you waste something, you use more than you need. *Don't waste water by letting the hose run.*
2 To waste also means not to make good use of something. *Don't waste time watching too much TV.*

watch watches watching watched verb
If you watch something, you look at it for a long time. *We watched the football game.* or *Watch how I do this trick.*

watch watches noun
a small clock that you wear around your wrist.

water noun
the clear liquid that is in seas, lakes, and rivers. *All living things need water.*

water waters watering watered verb
When you water plants, you pour water over them to help them grow.

waterfall waterfalls noun
a place on a river where a lot of water falls over high rocks or down a mountain.

waterproof adjective
If something is waterproof, it does not let water go through it. *a waterproof jacket.*

wave waves noun
1 a curved line of water moving across a sea. *The waves crashed up onto the shore.*
2 a vibrating movement like a wave on the sea that carries sound or light. *sound waves.*
3 a curving shape in your hair.
4 a movement with your hand that you make when you say "hello" or "goodbye" to somebody.

wave waves waving waved verb
When you wave, you move your hand up and down to say hello or goodbye to somebody. *My sister waved goodbye as she got on the bus.*

wax noun
material that candles are made out of. Wax is hard when it is cold, but it gets soft and melts when you heat it.

weak weaker weakest adjective
1 a weak person or thing has little power or strength. *She felt weak after her illness.* or *weak knees.*
2 likely to break very easily. *That branch is too weak to support your weight.*

3 A weak drink has a lot of water or milk in it. *weak tea.*
■ The opposite is **powerful** or **strong**.
● A word that sounds like **weak** is **week**.

wealthy wealthier wealthiest adjective
rich. *wealthy businessmen.*

weapon weapons noun
something such as a gun, spear, sword, or bow and arrow that people use to fight with.

wear wears wearing wore worn verb
1 When you wear clothes, you have them on your body. *Lindsay is wearing a blue dress.* or *Steve wore jeans.*
2 When something wears out, you cannot use it anymore because it is broken or too old. *These socks are worn out—they have holes in them.*
3 When something wears you out, it makes you very tired. *After running all the way to school, I was worn out.*

weather noun
The weather is how hot, cold, windy, rainy, or dry it is outside. *The weather forecast tells you what the weather will be like for the next few days.*

weave weaves weaving wove woven noun
1 When you weave, you make a piece of cloth using a tool called a loom. The loom has rows of thread fixed at each end, and you move another thread in and out of these.

2 to make something like a basket or a mat by twisting thin strips of wood or straw in and out of each other.

web webs noun
a net that a spider makes to catch flies.

web-footed adjective
having feet with a piece of skin between the toes, such as geese and ducks have.

wedding weddings noun
When two people get married, they have a ceremony called a wedding.

weed weeds noun
a wild plant that grows in yards and parks and that you do not want. *Thistles are weeds.*

thistle

mayweed

week weeks noun
a measure of time. There are seven days in a week—Monday, Tuesday, Wednesday, Thursday, Friday, Saturday, and Sunday. There are 52 weeks in a year. ● A word that sounds like **week** is **weak**.

weekend weekends noun
Saturday and Sunday.

weep weeps weeping wept verb
If people weep, they cry. *She wept because her cat had died.*

weigh weighs weighing weighed verb
1 You weigh something on a scale to find out how heavy it is.
2 Weigh also means how heavy you are. *How much do you weigh?*

weight weights
noun
1 how heavy somebody or something is. *What's the weight of this boy?*
2 a piece of metal weighing a certain amount that you use on a scale to find out how heavy something is.
weighty adjective
a weighty problem.

weird weirder weirdest
adjective
Something that is very strange or unusual. *I heard a weird noise in the house last night.*

welcome welcomes welcoming welcomed verb
If you welcome people, you show that you are happy to see them. *She came to the door to welcome us.*

well better best adjective, adverb
1 When you do something well, you do it in a good way. *Gerry plays the guitar very well.*
2 If you are well, you feel healthy.

well wells noun
a well is a deep hole in the ground with water or oil at the bottom.

wept past of **weep**.

west noun
1 the direction in which the Sun sets in the evening. ■ The opposite is **east**, **eastern**.
2 The West is the part of the United States that used to be the frontier. *The West has lots of open spaces like prairies and deserts.*
west adjective, **western** adjective
west adverb
The boat was sailing west.

western westerns noun
a movie or book about cowboys and the Wild West.

wet wetter wettest adjective
Something that is wet is covered with or full of water or another liquid. *You will get wet if you go out in the rain.* ■ The opposite is **dry**.

whale whales noun
a very large mammal that lives in the sea. Whales need air to breathe. A young whale is called a calf.

blue whales

wheat noun
a plant that farmers grow. We use its seeds, called grain, to make flour.

wheel wheels noun
A wheel is a round thing on something like a car, truck, or bicycle. Wheels turn around and around to move things along the ground.

wheelchair wheelchairs noun
a special chair with wheels for somebody who cannot walk very well.

whether conjunction
if. *I don't know whether I can come tonight.*

whine whines whining whined verb
To whine is to make a long, miserable sound because you want something.

whip whips whipping whipped verb
1 If you whip others, you hit them with a long piece of rope or leather.
2 to stir cream or eggs very fast until they become stiff.

whisk whisks whisking whisked verb
When you whisk things such as eggs or cream, you beat them very quickly. **whisk** noun.

whisker whiskers noun
one of the long hairs that cats, mice, and some other animals have on their faces.

whisper whispers whispering whispered verb
When you whisper, you speak very quietly so that other people cannot hear you. *She whispered in his ear.*

whistle whistles noun
1 an instrument that you blow into to make very high sounds. *He blew a whistle to end the football game.*
2 a high sound that you make when you blow through your lips.
whistle verb.

whole adjective
all of something. *He ate the whole cake.*
● A word that sounds like **whole** is **hole**. ■ The opposite is **part**.
whole noun
Two halves make a whole.

wick wicks noun
a piece of string that goes through the middle of a candle. When you light the wick, the candle burns.

wicked wickeder wickedest adjective
very bad or cruel. *In the fairy tale, Snow White's stepmother was a wicked witch.*

wide wider widest adjective
1 Something that is wide measures a lot from one side to the other. *Freeways are very wide roads.*
■ The opposite is **narrow**.
2 Wide also means how much something measures. *The window is three feet wide.*

widow widows noun
a woman whose husband is dead.

widower widowers noun
a man whose wife is dead.

width noun
how wide something is. *He measured from side to side to find the width of the box.*

wife wives noun
A man's wife is the woman that he is married to.

wig wigs noun
a thing made of real or fake hair that covers your head. Actors and bald people sometimes wear wigs.

wild wilder wildest adjective
1 Wild animals are animals that are not kept by people for food or as pets. Foxes and badgers are wild animals.
■ The opposite is **tame**.
2 Wildflowers and wild plants are not planted by people.

will wills noun
the part of your mind that makes you want to do things or decide what you want to do. *She has the will to win the race.* or *He cleaned his bedroom against his will.*

willing adjective
If you are willing, you are ready and happy to do what is wanted. *Are you willing to go to the store for me?*

willow willows noun
a tree with long, narrow leaves that grows close to water. Weeping willows have thin branches that hang downward.

wilt wilts wilting wilted verb
If a plant wilts, it droops because it needs water.

win wins winning won verb
When you win a race or game you come first and do better than everybody else. *Karen won the marathon.*

wind winds noun
air that is moving very fast. *The wind blew the sailboat along.* ▲ Rhymes with **tinned**.
windy adjective.
windy weather.

wind winds winding wound verb
1 When you wind a clock or a watch, you turn a key or a knob so that it starts working.
2 When you wind something like string around another thing, you twist it around and around. *They wound the yarn into a ball.*
3 When a road or a river winds, it has lots of bends in it.
▲ Rhymes with **find**.

windmill windmills noun
a tall building with large pieces of wood, called sails, on top that turn around in the wind. As the sails turn, they make machines inside work to grind corn into flour or to make electricity.

window windows noun
a hole covered by glass in the wall of
a building that lets in light and air.

windshield windshields noun
the window at the front of a car.

windsurf windsurfs windsurfing
windsurfed verb
To windsurf is to ride over water on
a special board with a sail.
windsurfer noun.

wine wines noun
Wine is an alcoholic drink usually
made from grapes.

wing wings noun
1 Birds, bats, and insects like bees
have wings that they flap when they
fly around.
2 The wings of an airplane are the
two flat parts on each side that help
it move through the air.

wink winks winking winked verb
If you wink at somebody, you
close and open one eye very quickly.
*She winked at me to show that it was
a joke.*

winter noun
the season of the year between fall
and spring. Winter is the coldest time
of the year.

wipe wipes wiping wiped verb
When you wipe something, you move
a cloth over it to clean or dry it.
I wiped the table clean after dinner.

wire wires noun
a long, thin piece of metal that
bends easily. Copper wire is used to
carry electricity. Many fences are
made of wire.

wise wiser wisest adjective
A person who is wise knows and
understands a lot about many things.
*Mom says that you get wiser as you
get older.*
wisdom noun.

wish wishes wishing wished verb
If you wish for something, you want
to have it or you want it to happen
very much. *I wish I was good at sports.*
wish noun.

witch witches noun
a woman in fairy tales who has magic
powers. *The prince rescued the princess
from the wicked witch.*

wither withers withering
withered verb
When a plant withers, it becomes dry
and dies. *The flowers withered and died
in the hot Sun.*

witness witnesses noun
a person who sees something
important happen and can tell other
people about it later. The *police are
looking for a witness to the accident.*

wives plural of **wife**.

wizard wizards noun
a man in fairy tales who has magic
powers.

wobble wobbles wobbling
wobbled verb
When something wobbles, it shakes
a little from side to side. *The Jell-o
wobbled on the plate.*
wobbly adjective.

woke past of **wake**.

wolf wolves noun
a wild animal that looks like a big
dog, with a pointed nose and pointed
ears. Wolves hunt in groups called
packs. A young wolf is called a cub.

woman women noun
a grown-up female person.

won past of **win**.

wonder wonders wondering
wondered verb
To wonder is to think about something
that you do not know the answer to.
I wonder why snakes have no feet.
wonder noun
They gazed with wonder at the fireworks.

wonderful adjective
very beautiful or very good. *We had
a wonderful vacation.*

wood woods noun
the material that trees are made of.
Tables and chairs are usually made
of wood. You can also use wood to
make paper.
wooden adjective
a wooden table.

woodpecker woodpeckers noun
a bird with a sharp beak that makes holes in wood and trees to find food.

woods noun
a place where a lot of trees grow close to each other.

wool wools noun
the soft, thick hair that grows on sheep and some other animals. Wool is used for making cloth and for knitting.
woolen adjective
woolen gloves.
woolly adjective.

word words noun
We use words when we speak or write. Words are made up of the letters of the alphabet, and each word means something. *Angela looked up the meaning of a word in the dictionary.*

wore past of **wear**.

work works working worked verb
1 When you work, you do or make something as a job. *Wendy works in a fast-food restaurant.*
2 To work also means to do something that takes a lot of time and effort. *I worked hard to finish the essay.*
3 When a machine works, it does what it should do. *The radio isn't working.*
work noun.

world noun
1 the planet that we live on and all its countries and people.
2 the universe.

worm worms noun
a small creature with a long, thin body and no legs. Many worms live in the dirt in gardens.

worn past of **wear**.
worn adjective
My socks are so worn that they have holes.

worry worries worrying
worried verb
If you worry, you keep thinking about bad things that might happen. *Dad worries when I'm home late from school.*

worship worships worshiping
worshiped verb
To worship is to pray to God or Allah.

worth adjective
having a certain value. If something is worth $80, you could sell it for $80. *This bike is worth $80.*

wound wounds wounding
wounded verb
To wound is to hurt or injure somebody. *He was tackled and wounded in the leg.* ▲ Say **wooned**.
wound noun.

wound past of **wind**.
▲ Say **wownd**.

wove, woven past of **weave**.

wrap wraps wrapping wrapped verb
If you wrap something, you cover it with paper or cloth. *He wrapped up the birthday present.* or *She wrapped the baby in a light blanket.*

wreck wrecks wrecking
wrecked verb
To wreck is to break or destroy something completely so that you cannot use it. *The fire wrecked the house.*

wreck wrecks noun
a car, boat, or an aircraft that has been badly damaged in an accident.

wreckage wreckages noun
the broken parts of something that has been badly damaged.

wrench wrenches noun
a tool for tightening and undoing pieces of metal.

wrestle wrestles wrestling
wrestled verb
To wrestle is to fight with somebody and try to push that person onto the ground. **wrestler** noun.

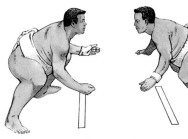
Sumo wrestlers

wring wrings wringing wrung verb
If you wring something that is wet, you twist and squeeze it to get water out of it. *He wrung out the wet towel.*

wrinkle wrinkles noun
a crease or line in your skin. *The old man's face was full of wrinkles.*
wrinkle verb
He wrinkled his forehead.
wrinkled adjective
wrinkled skin.

wrist wrists noun
Your wrist is the thin part of your arm just above your hand.

write writes writing wrote
written verb
When you write, you make words with a pen or pencil. *Felix wrote his name at the top of the paper.* ● A word that sounds like **write** is **right**.
writer noun.

writing noun
the words that you make on paper with a pen or pencil. *Rosemary has very neat writing.*

wrong adjective
1 If something is wrong, it is incorrect. *The answer to that problem is wrong.* ■ The opposite is **right**.
2 bad. *Being unkind to animals is wrong.*

wrung past of **wring**.

Xx

x-ray X-rays noun
a picture that shows the bones and other parts inside your body so that doctors can see if anything is broken or damaged.
x-ray adjective, **x-ray** verb.

xylophone xylophones noun
a musical instrument with a row of wooden or metal bars of different lengths that you hit to make musical notes. ▲ Say **zy-lo-fone**.

Yy

yacht yachts noun
a large boat with sails or an engine.

yard yards noun
There are three feet in a yard.

yawn yawns yawning yawned verb
When you yawn, you open your mouth wide and breathe in, as you do when you are very tired.

year years noun
a measure of time. There are 12 months in a year.
yearly adjective, adverb
a yearly visit.

yeast noun
a substance that is used to make bread rise.

yell yells yelling yelled verb
If you yell, you shout very loudly.

yogurt noun
a thick, slightly sour liquid food made from milk and often flavored.
▲ Say **yoh-gert**.

yoke yokes noun
a wooden frame that goes across the back of two oxen pulling a plow or cart to make them stay together.
● A word that sounds like **yoke** is **yolk**.

yolk yolks noun
the yellow part inside an egg.
▲ Say **yoke**.

young younger youngest adjective
not having lived for many years or for as many years as somebody else. *I'm younger than my grandpa.*
▲ Say **yung**.
■ The opposite is **old**.

youth youths noun
1 the time when a person is young. *He spent his youth in Oregon.*
2 a young man.
3 all young people. *the youth of today.* or *a youth program.*
▲ Say **yooth**.

Zz

zap zapping zapped verb
To zap is to shoot somebody or destroy something in a comic or computer game.

zebra zebras noun
an animal like a horse with black and white stripes. Zebras live in Africa.

zero zeros noun
the number 0. You write ten with a one and a zero–10.

zinc noun
a hard, bluish-white metal. *A coating of zinc protects iron and steel from rust.*

Zip Code Zip Codes noun
a set of numbers at the end of your address on an envelope or a package that comes after the name of your state. It tells the postal service where you live.

zipper zippers noun
two long strips of fabric with metal or plastic teeth that fit together to fasten two edges of material.
zip verb.

zombie zombies noun
in stories, a dead body brought back to life by witchcraft.

zone zones noun
an area in a town or country used for a special purpose. *a work zone.* or *a no-parking zone.*

zoo zoos noun
a place where wild animals are kept so that people can look at them.

zoology noun
the scientific study of animals.
▲ Say **zoh-ol-uh-jee**.
zoological adjective, **zoologist** noun
zoological gardens or *Lou wanted to be a zoologist and to study animals from the rainforest.*

The Kingfisher Children's Illustrated
Thesaurus

Aa

abandon verb forsake, give up, leave in the lurch, surrender, sacrifice ▷ *leave, quit*

abate verb lessen, slacken, dwindle, fade

abbey noun monastery, priory, cloister, church

abbreviate verb shorten, cut, contract, reduce ▷ *abridge* ☆ **expand**

abdicate verb resign, retire, renounce ▷ *quit*

ability noun aptitude, knack, flair, talent, gift, skill ☆ **inability**

able adjective skillful, competent, talented, strong ▷ *clever* ☆ **incapable**

abnormal adjective unusual, exceptional, erratic ☆ **normal**

abode noun home, residence, haunt, dwelling, lodging

abolish verb destroy, cancel, do away with, exterminate ☆ **restore**

abominable adjective detestable, foul, hateful, horrible, loathsome, atrocious ▷ *awful* ☆ **desirable**

about preposition & adverb near, nearly, touching, concerning, around

above preposition & adverb over, beyond, exceeding, on high, aloft ☆ **below**

abridge verb condense, compact ▷ *abbreviate*

abroad adverb overseas, far, away, apart, adrift ☆ **home**

abrupt adjective 1 sudden, curt, blunt, brusque 2 steep, hilly ☆ **smooth**

absent adjective not present, away, elsewhere, missing ☆ **present**

absent-minded adjective distracted, heedless, forgetful ☆ **attentive**

absolute adjective perfect, complete, certain, positive ▷ *utter* ☆ **imperfect**

absorb verb take in, soak up, assimilate, devour, pull in, swallow, consume ☆ **emit**

absorbed adjective intent, rapt, engrossed, preoccupied

abstain adjective refuse, refrain, give up, keep from, avoid, forbear ☆ **indulge**

abstract 1 adjective theoretical, intangible 2 verb withdraw, steal, remove, take away

absurd adjective preposterous, nonsensical, foolish ▷ *silly* ☆ **sensible**

abundant adjective ample, profuse, rich, plentiful, overflowing ☆ **scarce**

abuse 1 verb damage, injure, spoil, maltreat, hurt, misuse ☆ **protect** 2 noun mistreatment, attack

accelerate verb speed up, hasten, quicken, urge ▷ *hurry* ☆ **delay**

accent noun 1 stress, beat, rhythm, emphasis 2 dialect, brogue *Eileen speaks with an Irish brogue*, drawl, pronunciation

accept verb receive, take, admit, adopt, take on ☆ **refuse**

accident noun chance, casualty, disaster, calamity, mishap ☆ **purpose**

acclaim verb applaud, praise, approve ☆ **denounce**

accommodate verb oblige, lodge, receive, admit, adapt ☆ **deprive**

accompany verb be with, go with, escort, attend, convoy ☆ **abandon**

accomplice noun ally, confederate, helper, partner, conspirator

accomplish verb perform, fulfill, finish, complete ▷ *achieve* ☆ **fail**

accord 1 verb agree, consent, harmonize, allow ☆ **differ** 2 noun agreement, harmony

account noun 1 bill, invoice, record, score 2 tale, story *Mary told us the story of her trip to Washington*, narrative, history

accumulate verb collect, grow, gather, hoard, increase, amass ☆ **scatter**

accurate adjective careful, exact, faithful, precise ▷ *correct* ☆ **defective**

accuse verb charge, incriminate, taunt, denounce ☆ **defend**

accustom verb acclimatize, get used to, familiarize ☆ **estrange**

ache 1 noun pain, twinge 2 verb hurt, pain, sting, smart

achieve verb fulfill, accomplish, reach ▶ *attain* ★ fail

achievement noun accomplishment, attainment, exploit, deed, completion ▶ *feat*

acid adjective sharp, vinegarish, acrid, sour, tart ★ sweet, mellow

acknowledge verb admit, avow, recognize, own, accept, yield ★ disclaim

acquaint verb inform, tell, teach, notify, advise ★ deceive

acquaintance noun **1** friend, pal, associate **2** knowledge *You will need some knowledge of Spanish if you visit Mexico*, familiarity, experience

acquainted adjective aware, familiar, informed

acquire verb gain, earn, obtain, get, capture ★ forfeit, lose

acquit verb discharge, release, exonerate, dismiss, liberate ★ accuse

acrid adjective bitter, harsh, sour ▶ *acid* ★ mellow

across adjective & preposition crosswise, athwart, slantingly, over, against ★ along

act **1** noun deed, performance, action, step, presentation **2** verb operate, work, function, perform *Our class will perform a play by Shakespeare*

action noun operation, movement, feat, deed, exercise ★ rest

actual adjective correct, true, positive, certain ★ possible

acute adjective sharp, pointed, keen, penetrating, severe, distressing ★ blunt

adapt verb fit, adjust, accommodate, suit, conform

adaptable adjective flexible, usable, adjustable

add verb **1** total, combine, tote up ★ subtract **2** affix, annex, connect ★ detach

address **1** noun residence, place, home, domicile **2** verb talk to, speak to, accost, call

adept adjective expert, adroit, handy, skillful ▶ *clever* ★ clumsy

adequate adjective **1** sufficient, ample *The boat was small, but there was ample room for two people*, plenty **2** equal, able, qualified

adjacent adjective near, neighboring, next to, bordering, touching ★ separate

adjoin verb border, touch, verge, annex

adjust verb **1** regulate, rectify, correct, amend, revise **2** get used to *Our puppy quickly got used to her new home*

administer verb **1** execute, perform, carry out, conduct, direct, manage **2** give, dole out

admirable adjective praiseworthy, commendable, excellent ★ despicable

admiration noun adoration, affection, approval, delight, respect ★ contempt

admire verb approve, esteem, appreciate ▶ *respect* ★ despise

admit verb **1** pass, permit, grant, concede, allow, let in, acknowledge **2** confess, own up ★ deny

ado noun hubbub, commotion, fuss *Let's start the meeting without any more fuss*, excitement

adopt verb assume, select, choose, employ, apply, take over

adore verb worship, idolize, admire, revere, venerate ★ despise

adorn verb beautify, decorate, embellish, deck, garnish ★ deface

adrift adverb loose, afloat, floating, distracted

adroit adjective handy, skillful, dexterous, expert ▶ *adept* ★ awkward

adult adjective grown-up, mature, full-grown ★ immature

advance verb **1** progress, increase, further, go, go on, proceed ★ retreat **2** lend *Helen said she will lend me the money*, load

advanced adjective beforehand, ahead, modern

advantage noun benefit, upper hand, opportunity, assistance, boon ★ hindrance

adventure noun experience, escapade, venture, undertaking

adversary noun foe, opponent, antagonist, rival ▶ *enemy* ★ ally

adverse adjective unfavorable, hard, hostile, unfortunate ▶ *unlucky* ★ fortunate

advice noun counsel, suggestion, guidance

advise verb counsel, urge, suggest, prompt, inform, persuade ★ deter

afar adverb far, far off, away, abroad ★ near

affable adjective courteous, gracious, easy, frank, open ★ haughty

A
B
C
D
E
F
G
H
I
J
K
L
M
N
O
P
Q
R
S
T
U
V
W
X
Y
Z

A B C D E F G H I J K L M N O P Q R S T U V W X Y Z

affair noun **1** matter, business, concern **2** romance, liaison

affect verb **1** assume, adopt, feign, sham, put on airs **2** influence, change, sway *Your argument did not sway my opinion*

affection noun desire, fondness, feeling, kindness, liking ▶ *love* ☆ **indifference**

affectionate adjective warm-hearted, fond, loving ▶ *tender* ☆ **indifferent**

affirm verb assert, state, declare, endorse, maintain ☆ **deny**

affix verb attach, fasten, unite, append ☆ **detach**

afflict verb trouble, ail, distress, upset

afford verb **1** be wealthy, be rich **2** produce, provide *The stream provided good, clean water*, yield, bear ☆ **deny**

afraid adjective timid, cautious, frightened, alarmed ▶ *fearful* ☆ **fearless**

after *preposition* behind, later, following, succeeding ☆ **before**

again adverb **1** frequently, repeatedly, anew, afresh **2** furthermore, moreover

against *preposition* opposite, over, opposing, resisting ☆ **for**

age 1 noun period, date, time **2** noun old age, senility ☆ **youth 3** verb grow old, mature

aged adjective ancient, antiquated ▶ *old* ☆ **youthful**

agent noun doer, actor, performer, operator, worker, representative

aggravate verb **1** increase, make worse, worsen ☆ **mitigate 2** irritate, annoy

aggressive adjective offensive, warlike, military, pushy ☆ **peaceful**

aghast adjective astonished, dumbfounded, bewildered ☆ **calm**

agile adjective nimble, active, fleet, brisk, alert ▶ *lithe* ☆ **clumsy**

agitate verb disturb, trouble, excite, stir, fluster ☆ **smooth**

ago adverb past, gone, since ☆ **hence**

agony noun torture, torment, distress, pangs ▶ *pain* ☆ **comfort**

agree verb accord, fit, harmonize, combine, tally, suit ☆ **differ**

Aircraft

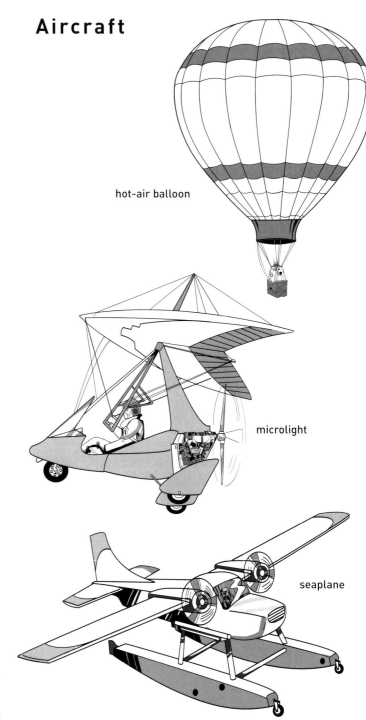

hot-air balloon

microlight

seaplane

agreeable adjective obliging, welcome, acceptable, grateful ▶ *pleasant* ☆ **disagreeable**

agreement noun understanding, harmony, concord ☆ **dispute**

ahead adverb **1** forward, onward **2** before, in advance ☆ **behind**

aid verb assist, support, encourage, serve ▶ *help* ☆ **hinder**

aim noun object, goal, purpose, end, intention

aisle noun path, corridor, passage, way ISLE

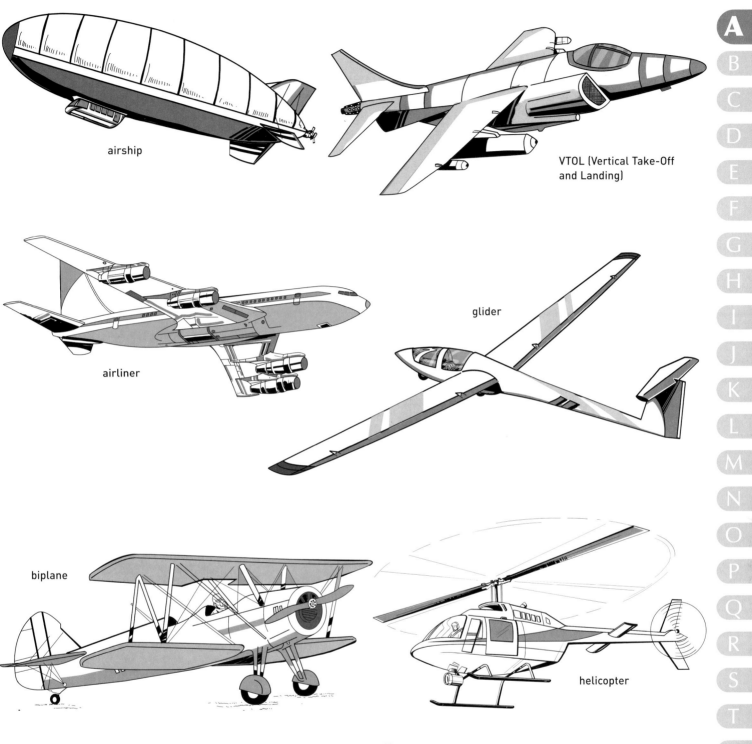

airship

VTOL (Vertical Take-Off and Landing)

airliner

glider

biplane

helicopter

akin adjective related, similar, allied, like ★ **dissimilar**

alarm verb frighten, terrify, startle ▶ *scare* ★ **comfort**

alert adjective active, ready, wakeful, watchful ▶ *agile* ★ **drowsy**

alien 1 adjective foreign, strange, remote ★ **akin**
2 noun foreigner, stranger

alike adjective similar, resembling, allied, like ★ **unlike**

alive adjective living, breathing, warm, alert, brisk ★ **dead**

all adjective whole, entire, complete, total ★ **none**

allot verb apportion, give, allocate, dispense, grant ★ **retain**

allow verb grant, permit, concede, owe, tolerate, entitle ★ **forbid**

ally noun friend, companion, supporter, accomplice, colleague ★ **foe**

almost adjective nearly, about, around, approximately, well-nigh

A

alone adjective lone, lonely, lonesome, forlorn ★ **together**

aloud adverb loudly, noisily, clamorously, audibly ★ **silently** ALLOWED

already adverb at this time, now, just now, previously

alter verb modify, vary, convert, transform ▷ *change* ★ **retain** ALTAR

altogether adverb completely, wholly, outright, entirely, totally ★ **partially**

always adverb ever, forever, eternally ★ **never**

amass verb collect, accumulate, heap, pile ★ **scatter**

amaze verb astound, surprise, stun, dumbfound ▷ *astonish*

ambition noun aspiration, desire, longing, zeal, aim ▷ *goal*

amend verb revise, mend, correct, repair, improve ▷ *alter*

amiable adjective affable, kindly, pleasant, amicable ▷ *agreeable* ★ **unfriendly**

amount noun figure, volume, sum, number, total

ample adjective bountiful, liberal, sufficient, plentiful ▷ *abundant* ★ **insufficient**

amplify verb increase, raise, enlarge, elaborate *Our teacher explained the problem and went on to elaborate on the details*, make louder ★ **abbreviate**

amuse verb entertain, charm, beguile, please ★ **bore**

ancestor noun forebear, parent, forefather, antecedent, predecessor

ancient adjective aged, antique, primeval, time-honored ▷ *old* ★ **modern**

anger noun wrath, ire, resentment, indignation, fury ▷ *rage*

angry adjective wrathful, irate, resentful, furious, infuriated, indignant ★ **good-tempered**

angle noun 1 corner, bend, fork, branch 2 aspect, phase, point of view *We argued at first, but then I saw Tom's point of view*

anguish noun torment, torture, pain ▷ *agony* ★ **ease**

announce verb broadcast, declare, propound, reveal, herald ▷ *proclaim* ★ **conceal**

annoy verb tease, vex, irritate, disturb, harass ▷ *upset* ★ **soothe**

answer noun reply, response, solution *It was a difficult puzzle, but Emma came up with the solution* ★ **question**

anticipate verb expect, prepare, hope for, foresee, predict

anxious adjective fearful, afraid, apprehensive, worried ★ **carefree**

apart adverb away, separately, asunder, loosely ★ **together**

aperture noun slit, hole, orifice, opening, cleft

apologize verb express regret, excuse, explain, plead, atone ★ **insult**

apparel noun clothes, robes, vestments, raiment, trappings, attire

apparent adjective plain, conspicuous, unmistakable, clear ▷ *obvious* ★ **obscure**

appeal verb address, request, urge, entreat, invite, ask ▷ *attract*

appear verb emerge, become visible, seem, look, come into view ★ **disappear**

appearance noun aspect, look, shape, form, impression, likeness

appease verb pacify, moderate, satisfy, stay, soften ★ **provoke**

appetite noun hunger, palate, relish, liking

applaud verb clap, cheer, praise, approve, encourage ★ **denounce**

apply verb 1 use, appropriate, employ 2 devote, direct, dedicate *Sue was dedicated to her job and worked very hard*

appoint verb name, assign, nominate, engage

appreciate verb esteem, recognize, respect, value, enjoy

appropriate 1 verb use, employ, adopt 2 adjective fitting, proper *To do a job well, you should use the proper tools*, timely, correct

approve verb acclaim, admire, appreciate, favor, agree ★ **disapprove**

approximate adjective near, close, rough

apt adjective 1 fit, clever, liable, likely ★ **unfitted** 2 liable, prone, inclined *Jack and Meg are both inclined to be late, so we'll wait a while*

ardent adjective passionate, warm, eager, fervent, intense, dedicated ★ **indifferent**

arduous adjective hard, laborious, tough, strenuous ▷ *difficult* ★ **easy**

Apes

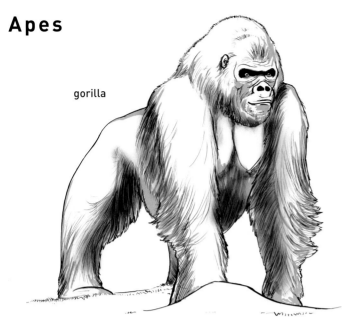

gorilla

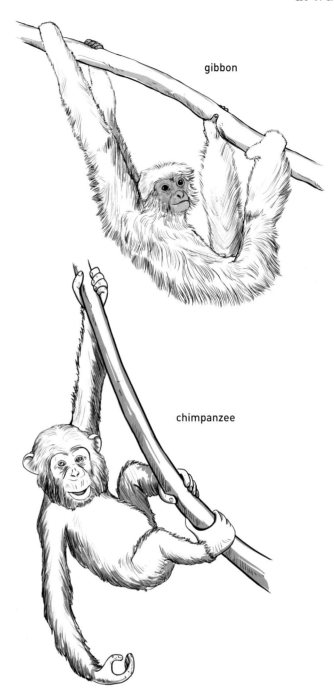

gibbon

orangutan

chimpanzee

area noun district, region, place, expanse, tract

argue verb **1** discuss, debate, talk over **2** quibble, quarrel, disagree

arid adjective parched, sterile ▶ *dry* ★ moist

arise verb **1** awaken, get up **2** begin, come into existence, originate, crop up, take place

army noun troops, legion, force, soldiery

around adverb about, encircling, on every side ★ within

arouse verb awaken, excite, disturb, alarm ★ pacify

arrange verb sort, order, dispose, deal, classify ★ confuse

arrest verb seize, take prisoner, hold, detain, stop ★ release

arrive verb reach, attain, land, get to, appear ★ depart

arrogant adjective supercilious, proud, haughty, conceited, disdainful ★ modest

art noun skill, artistry, cleverness, talent

artful adjective cunning, knowing, crafty, wily, sly ★ innocent

A B C D E F G H I J K L M N O P Q R S T U V W X Y Z

191

article noun 1 thing, object, substance 2 essay, treatise, typescript

artificial adjective invented, fictitious, fabricated, synthetic ★ real

ascend verb climb, rise, go up, get up, move up, scale, mount ★ descend

ashamed adjective shamefaced, abashed, confused ★ proud

ask verb demand, query, inquire, appeal ▶ request ★ answer

aspect noun front, face, side appearance, presentation, look, expression

aspire verb wish, long, desire, aim, hope, crave

ass noun 1 donkey, mule 2 fool, dunce, idiot, jerk, dolt

assault verb attack, assail, set upon, charge, invade ★ defend

assemble verb meet, gather, convene, come together, muster, collect ★ disperse

assent verb agree, comply, accept, consent ★ dissent

assert verb pronounce, maintain, state, aver ▶ declare ★ deny

assess verb estimate, evaluate, appraise

assign verb appoint, name, apportion, entrust

assist verb aid, support, protect, maintain, sustain ▶ help ★ obstruct

association noun union, connection, companionship, society, company, club

assortment noun variety, kind, sort, batch, parcel, collection

assume verb 1 believe, accept, suppose, admit 2 confiscate, take, possess oneself of

assure verb promise, guarantee, warrant, encourage ★ deter

astonish verb startle, surprise, confound, alarm, scare ▶ amaze

astound verb stagger, stupefy ▶ astonish

astray adjective lost, gone, vanished, missing, loose ★ safe

astute adjective shrewd, brainy, knowing, sharp, acute, crafty ★ simple

atrocious adjective monstrous, enormous, shameful, cruel, abominable, vile

attach verb fasten, append, unite, tie ▶ connect ★ unfasten

attack verb assault, invade, set upon, pounce, descend upon ★ defend

attain verb extend, master, obtain, acquire, grasp ▶ reach ★ fail

attempt verb endeavor, strive, seek, tackle ▶ try ★ abandon

attend verb 1 listen, heed, notice, observe, follow ★ disregard 2 be present

attentive adjective mindful, particular, heedful, observant ★ careless

attire noun costume, robes, clothes, garments ▶ apparel

attitude noun disposition, bearing, outlook, posture, position, aspect

attract verb 1 draw, influence, tempt, prompt, pull, drag 2 fascinate, enchant, captivate ★ repel

attractive adjective agreeable, beautiful, handsome, pretty, tempting ★ repellent

avail noun benefit, advantage, use, help, profit

available adjective convenient, handy, ready, attainable, accessible

avenge verb retaliate, revenge, pay back ★ pardon

average adjective usual, ordinary, mediocre, so-so, normal, standard ★ extreme

avid adjective eager, greedy, grasping

avoid verb shun, elude, quit, keep clear of, evade ▶ dodge ★ seek

awake verb wake, rouse, arouse, awaken, stir

award verb reward, give, bestow, grant, donate ★ withdraw

aware adjective conscious, sensible, informed, assured ★ unaware

away adverb absent, not present, afar, elsewhere ★ near

awe noun fear, dread, shock, consternation, wonder

awful adjective fearful, terrible, alarming, dreadful ★ commonplace OFFAL

awkward adjective ungainly, unwieldy, uncouth, clownish, gawky ▶ clumsy ★ dexterous

awry adjective crooked, askew, amiss, twisted, wrong ★ straight

Bb

babble verb prattle, blab, cackle, chatter, gossip

baby noun babe, infant, child, toddler, tot

back 1 adjective after, rear, hind, posterior ★ front
2 verb uphold, support *The party will support Tina Johnson at the next election*, endorse, be loyal to

backer noun supporter, ally, champion

backward adjective slow, shy, reluctant, unwilling, retarded ▸ *dull* ★ forward

bad adjective 1 imperfect, dreadful, unsound, awful, atrocious 2 naughty, wrong, wicked, badly behaved
3 rotten *This barrel is full of rotten apples*, spoiled ★ good

badge noun emblem, hallmark, symbol, crest

badger verb bother, annoy, nag ▸ *pester*

bad-mannered adjective impolite, boorish, uncivil ▸ *rude* ★ polite

baffle verb puzzle, perplex, frustrate, bewilder, mystify ▸ *puzzle*

bag noun net, sack, pouch, purse, backpack

bail verb scoop, ladle, dip

bait 1 verb tease, bother, goad, rib, needle ▸ *pester*
2 noun decoy, lure, snare BATE

bake verb cook, roast, harden, fire

balance verb weigh, adjust, equalize, compare

bald adjective hairless, severe, stark, bare, unadorned

balk verb hinder, baffle, thwart, obstruct, foil ★ aid

ball noun 1 dance, masquerade 2 globe, orb, sphere

ballad noun song, serenade, ditty

ballot noun vote, election, franchise, poll

ban verb prohibit, forbid, deny, stop

band noun 1 stripe, strip, zone, belt 2 orchestra, ensemble, group BANNED

bandit noun outlaw, robber, highwayman, thief, crook

bang verb crash, slam, smash, collide

banish verb expel, eject, exclude, exile, deport, cast out ▸ *dismiss* ★ welcome

bank noun 1 shore, ledge, terrace, coast, embankment
2 safe, vault, treasury

banner noun ensign, standard, streamer ▸ *flag*

banquet noun meal, feast, repast

banter verb chaff, tease, ridicule, joke

bar verb 1 obstruct, block, blockade, forbid, shut out
2 fasten, bolt, lock, latch

bare adjective 1 barren, empty, void 2 naked, unclothed, severe, blunt *We expected a polite reply, but got a blunt refusal*, bald BEAR

barely adverb hardly, scarcely *The well had run dry, and there was scarcely enough water for all of us*, just, simply

bargain 1 noun pact, deal 2 adjective low-priced, cheap

bark noun 1 rind, husk, peel 2 yelp, growl, cry

barrel noun cask, keg, drum, tub, cylinder

barren adjective bare, unfertile, empty ▸ *arid* ★ fertile BARON

barrier noun obstruction, obstacle, block, fence

barter verb swap, exchange, trade

base 1 adjective low, sordid, cheap, corrupt
2 adjective dishonorable, vile 3 adjective humble, menial 4 noun bottom, foundation 5 verb found *The book* Robinson Crusoe *was founded on a true story* BASS

bashful adjective shy, timid, modest, coy ★ bold

basin noun bowl, pot, sink, tub

batch noun lot, amount, assortment, collection

batter verb beat, strike, shatter, break, smash

battle verb clash, combat, fight, struggle, wrestle

bawl verb shout, yell, roar, bellow ★ whisper

bay 1 noun inlet, gulf, basin, bight 2 verb bark, yelp BEY

be verb exist, live, breathe

beach noun shore, sands, seaside, strand BEECH

beacon noun signal, lamp, light, guide

beak noun snout, bill, nose

beam noun 1 ray, light, streak 2 plank, joist, girder

bear verb 1 tolerate, put up with, endure, suffer ★ protest 2 bring, fetch, carry BARE

bearing noun manner, behavior, appearance, attitude, posture *He was a tall man with a military manner* BARING

bearings noun direction, whereabouts, location *In the storm, we totally lost our location*

beat verb 1 strike, pound, thrash ▸ *batter* 2 throb, flutter, thump *My heart thumped when I heard the sound of shouting in the street* BEET

beautiful adjective handsome, lovely, graceful, delicate, gorgeous ▶ *pretty* ★ ugly

beauty noun elegance, charm, loveliness, grace ★ ugliness

because 1 conjunction for, owing to, by reason of, since *Since Paul and Jane are here, I will stay, too*, as 2 adverb consequently

beckon verb signal, call, nod, summon

becoming adjective graceful, suitable, comely, fitting, attractive

before 1 preposition ahead, in front of, forward, preceding 2 adverb earlier *Here is a pie that I baked earlier*, previously ★ after

beg verb ask, request, entreat, beseech, plead, pray

begin verb commence, initiate, found, launch ▶ *start* ★ end

beginner noun novice, recruit, learner, student, pupil

beginning noun start, opening, origin, outset, foundation ★ end

behavior noun conduct, demeanor, manners ▶ *bearing* ★ misbehavior

behind 1 preposition after, following *Bill arrived to meet us, with his dog following* 2 adverb in the rear of, later, afterward ★ before

being noun creature, animal

belief noun faith, confidence, opinion, trust ★ disbelief

believe verb trust, assent, have faith in, think, suspect ★ disbelieve

bellow verb roar, shout, cry ▶ *bawl*

belong verb relate to, pertain, be owned by

below adverb under, beneath, underneath ★ above

belt noun strap, sash, girdle, strip

bend verb curve, incline, turn, yield, relax ★ straighten

benefit noun advantage, profit, good, favor, aid, blessing ★ disadvantage

beside adverb alongside, side by side, next to, abreast, together ★ apart

besides adverb in addition, furthermore, also, moreover

best adjective choice, prime, unequalled, finest ★ worst

bestow verb award, donate, confer, present ★ deprive

betray verb deceive, dupe, expose, unmask, inform on ★ protect

better adjective superior, finer, preferable *I think it would be preferable to visit the museum this afternoon instead of this morning* ★ worse

between preposition amid, among, betwixt

beware verb be careful, refrain from, heed, avoid, mind

bewilder verb confound, dazzle, mystify, confuse ▶ astonish ★ enlighten

beyond adverb over, farther, past, more, after ★ near

bicker verb quarrel, dispute, wrangle, argue ★ converse

bid verb proffer, present, tender, request, propose

big adjective 1 large, great, wide, huge, bulky, fat 2 important ★ small

bill noun 1 statement *This is a statement of your investments with us*, account, invoice, check, chit, reckoning 2 beak, mouth 3 poster, advertisement

bin noun box, can, case, chest, crate, tub

bind verb tie, fasten, secure, lace, swathe ★ untie

birth noun origin, beginning, source, creation ★ death BERTH

bit noun morsel, piece, fragment, part, crumb ★ whole

bite verb gnaw, chew, rend, chomp BIGHT, BYTE

bitter adjective 1 harsh, sour, tart ▶ *acid* 2 severe, stern ▶ *sarcastic* ★ mellow

blame verb chide, rebuke, reproach, criticize, accuse, condemn ★ praise

bland adjective soft, mild, gentle, soothing, tasteless

blank adjective empty, bare, void, bleak ★ full

blare verb blast, boom, clang, roar, sound

blast verb explode, split, discharge, burst

blaze verb burn, flare, glare, flicker

bleak adjective bare, open, exposed, dismal, stormy, chilly, raw, desolate *The farm was a cold and desolate place in the winter* ★ sheltered

blemish noun spot, stain, mark, speck, flaw, blotch

blend verb mix, unite, harmonize, merge, fuse, combine ★ **separate**

bless verb hallow, praise, exalt, endow, enrich, consecrate ★ **curse**

blessing noun advantage, boon, approval, godsend ★ **curse**

blight noun pest, plague, disease

blind adjective **1** eyeless, sightless *These salamanders live in underground caves and are sightless*, unsighted, unseeing **2** ignorant, unnformed

blink verb wink, twinkle, glitter, gleam

bliss noun joy, ecstasy, rapture, blessedness, happiness ★ **misery**

block **1** noun lump, mass, chunk **2** verb obstruct, bar, arrest BLOC

bloom **1** noun flower, blossom, bud **2** verb blossom, flourish, flower, thrive ★ **decay**

blot noun stain, blotch ▶ *blemish*

blow **1** verb puff, gust, blast **2** noun shock, stroke, impact, bang

blue adjective azure, turquoise, indigo, navy, ultramarine, cobalt BLEW

bluff **1** adjective frank, brusque, abrupt, outspoken *Freda Jones will never be elected mayor; she's too outspoken* **2** verb deceive, pretend *The lion closed its eyes, pretending that it had not seen the antelope*, conceal

blunder **1** noun mistake, error, slip, fault *It was my fault that the plates were broken*, oversight **2** verb slip, err, bungle ★ **correct**

blunt adjective **1** plain, abrupt, curt ▶ *bluff* **2** dull, not sharp

blush verb redden, color, crimson, flush

board **1** noun plank, table **2** noun committee, council **3** verb live *The new teacher is going to live next door*, lodge, accommodate BORED

boast verb swagger, swell, bluster ▶ *brag*

boat noun ship, vessel, craft, bark, barge

body noun **1** corpse, trunk, carcass **2** corporation, company, society

bog noun swamp, morass, marsh, quagmire

The body

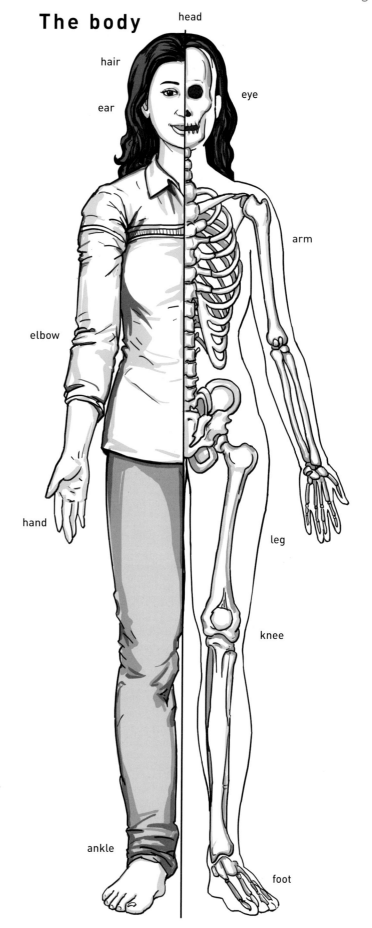

head
hair
ear
eye
arm
elbow
hand
leg
knee
ankle
foot

bogus adjective fake, false, spurious, sham, counterfeit
★ genuine

boil verb cook, steam, poach, seethe, foam

boisterous adjective tempestuous, stormy, uncontrolled, loud, noisy ★ serene

bold adjective fearless, courageous, adventurous, valiant, daring ▸ *brave* ★ fearful BOWLED

bolt 1 verb run away, take flight, flee *After the revolution, the queen had to flee the country* 2 verb devour, gorge, eat ▸ *gulp* 3 noun lock, latch, fastening

bond noun tie, link, joint, band, fastening

bonny adjective fair, handsome, healthy, shapely, buxom ▸ *pretty* ★ plain

bonus noun premium, benefit, award, prize

booby noun blockhead, sap, oaf, chump, nincompoop, dunce, fool, numbskull ★ oracle

boom noun 1 thunder, roar, rumble, blast 2 prosperity *After the recession came years of prosperity*

boon noun blessing, windfall, advantage ▸ *benefit* ★ drawback

boorish adjective unrefined, loutish, bad-mannered, rude, clumsy ★ refined

boost verb strengthen, raise up, heighten

border noun fringe, edge, margin, frontier

bore verb 1 tire, weary, fatigue *We were fatigued by the long bus ride home* 2 drill, punch, perforate BOAR

bored adjective uninterested, tired, jaded, fed-up BOARD

borrow verb take, imitate, adopt, assume, raise money ★ lend

boss noun 1 stud, knob 2 chief, manager *Helen is the manager of the new beauty salon*, employer

bossy adjective domineering, tyrannical, overbearing ▸ *arrogant* ★ modest

bother verb alarm, annoy, concern, distress ▸ *disturb*

bottom noun underside, deepest part, floor ▸ *base* ★ top

bough noun branch, limb, shoot BOW

boulder noun rock, slab, stone

bounce verb leap, spring, bound, bump, jump

bound verb rebound, prance ▸ *bounce*

boundary noun bounds, limits, border, frontier ▸ *barrier*

Bridges

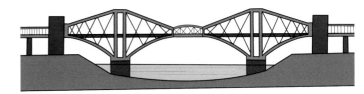

cantilever

girder

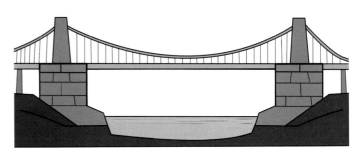

suspension

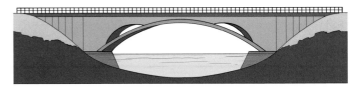

arch

bascule bridge	rope bridge
drawbridge	swing-span bridge
footbridge	viaduct

bounty noun donation, gift, grant ▸ *bonus*

bow verb bend, nod, stoop, kneel, yield, submit BOUGH

bowl noun plate, basin, dish, vessel, casserole BOLL

box 1 noun carton, case, chest, coffer *The town's coffers were empty, so they had to raise taxes*, pack 2 verb fight, spar, punch

196

boy noun lad, youth, child, youngster

brag verb crow, swagger, gloat ▶ *boast*

braid verb entwine, weave, plait BRAYED

branch noun **1** shoot, limb, twig ▶ *bough*
2 department, office, division

brand noun **1** trademark, emblem, label
This label shows that the cloth is of high quality
2 blot, stigma, stain

brandish verb flourish, parade, shake, swing, wave

brash adjective brazen, foolhardy, hasty, impetuous, impudent ▶ *rash*

brave **1** adjective audacious, fearless, daring, dauntless, gallant, heroic ▶ *bold* ★ **cowardly**
2 verb dare, defy, endure

break verb batter, brust, crack, snap, fracture, shatter BRAKE

breathe verb draw in, gasp, inhale, sniff, gulp, wheeze, emit

breed verb reproduce, produce, cause, bear, rear, multiply, propagate

bribe verb corrupt, buy, grease the palm, fix

brief adjective short, little, concise, terse, crisp, curt ★ **lengthy**

bright adjective **1** clear, cloudless, fair, airy **2** cheerful, genial *We were pleased to find so many genial members in the club* **3** clever, ingenious, acute ★ **dull**

brilliant adjective **1** lustrous, shining, radiant, dazzling, luminous **2** clever, intelligent ★ **dull**

brim noun edge, brink, rim, fringe

bring verb bear, fetch, deliver, carry, convey

bring about verb bring off, accomplish, achieve, cause, make happen

bring up verb breed, develop, raise, educate, foster

brink noun margin, border, boundary, limit

brisk adjective agile, alert, busy, energetic, active, nimble, invigorating ★ **sluggish**

brittle adjective breakable, fragile, delicate ▶ *frail*

broad adjective wide, expansive, roomy, open, vast, large ★ **narrow**

brood verb sigh, agonize, dwell on *You must try to forget your disappointment and not dwell on it*, languish BREWED

brook noun stream, creek, rivulet, watercourse

brow noun forehead, face, front, brink, edge, summit

bruise verb damage, discolor, blemish, injure, wound BREWS

brusque adjective abrupt, discourteous, gruff ▶ *blunt* ★ **polite**

brutal adjective cruel, inhumane, savage, barbarous, bloodthirsty ★ **humane**

bubble noun drop, droplet, blob, bead

buckle noun catch, clasp, clip, fastening

bud noun sprout, germ, shoot

budge verb propel, push, roll, shift, slide

build verb make, form, assemble, construct, erect, put up ★ **demolish** BILLED

bulge noun bump, swelling, lump, billow

bulky adjective big, huge, unwieldy, massive, cumbersome *I never liked that chair; it's too big and cumbersome to move*

bully **1** noun ruffian, tease, bruiser, tyrant, tough **2** verb tease, harass, oppress, terrorize

bump verb collide, hit, knock, strike, jab, jolt

bunch noun batch, bundle, cluster, collection, lot

bundle noun group, mass, heap, pack, parcel

bungle verb botch, blunder, mess up, ruin, fumble ★ **succeed**

burden noun **1** load, weight **2** strain, hardship *We suffered great hardship during the war*

burly adjective beefy, big, hefty, brawny, muscular ★ **frail**

burn verb blaze, flare, glow, singe, scorch, char, incinerate

burst verb break open, crack, explode, shatter, erupt

bury verb inter, conceal, cover up, hide, entomb, lay to rest BERRY

business noun **1** occupation, career, profession **2** company, enterprise, firm **3** problem, duty, affair

busy adjective active, brisk, industrious, lively, bustling ★ **lazy**

buy verb acquire, get, purchase, procure *If I can procure the right software, I'll do the job for you* ★ **sell** BY, BYE

Cc

cab noun taxi, taxicab

cabin noun 1 hut, chalet, cottage, shack 2 berth, compartment

cabinet noun 1 cupboard, closet 2 council, committee

cackle verb chuckle, giggle, snicker

café noun restaurant, coffee shop, snack bar

cage verb shut up, confine, imprison ★ free

calamity noun catastrophe, disaster, misadventure ▶ *mishap* ★ blessing

calculate verb reckon, figure, estimate ▶ *count*

call verb 1 cry out, shout, hail 2 name, designate 3 summon, telephone 4 visit, drop in

calling noun occupation, job, profession

callous adjective unfeeling, harsh, hard-bitten ★ sensitive

calm 1 verb soothe, ease, pacify, comfort 2 adjective easy, composed, mild ▶ *peaceful* ★ excited

can noun tin can, tin, jar, container, canister

cancel verb abolish, erase, put off, obliterate ★ confirm

candid adjective fair, honest, open, sincere, truthful ▶ *frank* ★ devious

capable adjective talented, able, competent, ▶ *clever* ★ incompetent

capacity noun 1 space, volume, extent 2 ability, aptitude *Jenny has an aptitude for learning languages*, intelligence

caper 1 verb dance, gambol, frolic 2 noun prank, joke, jest, lark

capital 1 noun cash, assets, funds, finance 2 adjective chief, excellent, important

captain noun chief, head, commander, master, skipper

capture verb seize, arrest, trap ▶ *catch* ★ release

car noun automobile, vehicle, conveyance, carriage, coach

carcass noun body, corpse, skeleton

care 1 verb take care, beware, heed, mind 2 noun attention, protection ★ carelessness

careful adjective heedful, prudent, watchful ▶ *cautious* ★ careless

careless adjective neglectful, slack, casual, thoughtless ★ careful

carelessness noun inaccuracy, negligence, slackness ★ care

caress verb hug, stroke, cuddle, embrace, pet, pat

carriage noun car, coach, buggy, baby buggy

carry verb bring, convey, lift, support ▶ *bear*

carry on verb continue, maintain, persist

carry out verb perform, achieve, fulfill, do

cart noun wagon, pushcart, buggy, wheelbarrow

carton noun bin, case, package, crate ▶ *box*

carve verb sculpt, cut, chisel, fashion, whittle ▶ *shape*

case noun chest, bin, carton ▶ *box*

cash noun money, coins, bills, coinage CACHE

cask noun barrel, keg, drum

cast verb 1 mold, form, shape 2 fling, heave, sprinkle ▶ *throw* CASTE

casual adjective accidental, chance, random ▶ *occasional* ★ regular

catch verb grasp, seize, arrest ▶ *capture* ★ miss

catching adjective infectious, contagious

cause 1 verb bring about, create, provoke 2 noun reason, source, origin CAWS

caution noun watchfulness, heed, vigilance, prudence ▶ *care* ★ recklessness

cautious adjective careful, discreet, prudent ▶ *watchful* ★ heedless

cavity noun dent, hole, gap, hollow

cease verb stop, conclude, end, refrain, terminate ★ begin

celebrate verb commemorate, observe, honor, glorify, rejoice, praise

cell noun chamber, cavity, cubicle, compartment SELL

cellar noun basement, vault, crypt, cave SELLER

cement 1 verb glue, stick, bind, gum, unite 2 noun plaster, mortar, adhesive

censor verb cut, examine, take out CENSER

censure verb blame, rebuke, reprimand, chide ▶ *scold* ★ praise

center noun middle, core, heart, nucleus

ceremony noun ritual, custom, performance

certain adjective **1** decided, definite, undoubted ▶ *sure* ★ **dubious** **2** particular *I had a particular reason for inviting you*, special

certainty noun confidence, assurance, trust, sureness ★ **doubt**

certificate noun document, permit, deed, diploma, testimonial

chafe verb rub, rasp, grate, irritate

chain verb bind, fetter, shackle, tether, bond

challenge verb dare, demand, dispute, defy, object to

chamber noun room, apartment, bedroom, compartment, hollow

champion noun defender, victor, master, winner ★ **loser**

chance noun **1** fortune, hazard, luck, gamble, lottery, wager **2** opportunity, occasion, risk ★ **certainty**

change verb alter, vary, turn, shift, reform, transform ★ **preserve**

chant verb intone, drone, croon, recite ▶ *sing*

chaos noun turmoil, confusion, disorder, pandemonium ★ **order**

chapter noun clause, division, part, period *It was a period in my life that I will never forget*, phase

character noun **1** letter, mark, emblem, device **2** reputation *She had a reputation for being very generous*, temperament, qualities

charge noun **1** attack, stampede, advance **2** cost, amount, price **3** accusation, blame *The men were all guilty, but it was Harry Smith who took the blame*, indictment

charm verb please, delight, enchant, bewitch ▶ *attract* ★ **irritate**

charming adjective delightful, appealing, lovely, pleasant ▶ *attractive* ★ **disgusting**

chart noun map, sketch, diagram, plan

chase verb hunt, pursue, follow, run after, hurry

chaste adjective virgin, pure, virtuous, innocent ★ **immodest** CHASED

chastise verb punish, whip, flog, beat, scold, tell off

chat verb converse, gossip ▶ *talk*

chatter verb babble, gossip ▶ *talk*

cheap adjective inexpensive, low-priced, bargain, reasonable, inferior ★ **expensive**

cheat verb swindle, bilk, defraud, fleece ▶ *trick*

check **1** verb inspect, compare, examine *The customs officer examined our luggage*, make sure **2** noun bill, invoice, reckoning

cheek noun audacity, boldness, impertinence, insolence

cheer verb **1** comfort, console, elate, buck up **2** applaud *The audience applauded the leading soprano*, clap, hail

cheerful adjective lively, bright, happy, merry, joyful ▶ *happy* ★ **sad**

cheery adjective blithe, breezy, bright, merry ★ **downcast**

cherish verb caress, hold close, care for, shelter, treasure

chest noun **1** case, coffer ▶ *box* **2** bosom, torso

chew verb bite, gnaw, grind, munch ▶ *eat*

chide verb scold, criticize, blame, tell off

chief adjective main, principal, leading, foremost ★ **minor**

child noun baby, infant, youth, juvenile

chilly adjective cool, crisp, brisk, cold, unfriendly ★ **warm**

chip verb & noun crack, splinter, dent, flake

chirp verb & noun warble, trill, cheep, twitter

choice **1** noun option *I had no option but to take the job*, preference, alternative **2** adjective select, dainty, precious, cherished, special

choke verb throttle, suffocate, gag, strangle ▶ *stifle*

choose verb pick, elect, decide, prefer ▶ *select* CHEWS

Churches and places of worship

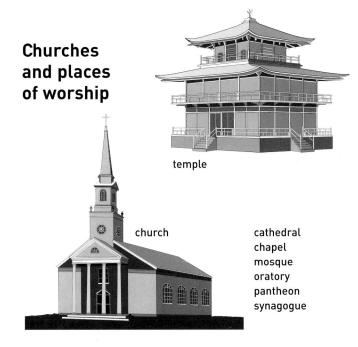

temple

church

cathedral
chapel
mosque
oratory
pantheon
synagogue

chop   verb cut, hack, clip, cleave, sever, lop

chubby   adjective plump, buxom, portly, round, stout
★ slim

chum   noun comrade, pal, friend, buddy, companion

chuck   verb throw, toss, fling, heave, sling

chuckle   verb cackle, chortle, snicker, giggle
★ laugh

chunk   noun piece, lump, mass, portion, slab

churlish   adjective brusque, harsh, impolite, morose
Dad had a headache and was in a morose mood ▶ surly
★ polite

circle   noun **1** ring, band   **2** company, group, class

circular   **1** adjective round, disklike   **2** noun handbill,
notice, poster

circulate   verb broadcast, distribute, publicize

cistern   noun tank, sink, basin, reservoir

cite   verb mention, specify, name, quote SIGHT, SITE

civil   adjective polite, courteous, polished ▶ *affable*
★ churlish

claim   verb demand, ask, require, insist, call for

clamor   noun babel, blare, din, row, hubbub, racket
▶ *noise* ★ silence

clamp   verb fasten, fix, hold, grasp

clap   verb applaud, acclaim, cheer

clarify   verb **1** make clear, explain, simplify   **2** cleanse,
purify

clash   verb **1** battle, conflict, quarrel   **2** bang, crash,
clang, clatter

clasp   **1** verb grasp, grip, seize, hold, fasten   **2** noun
buckle, catch, pin

class   noun category, type, sort, grade, group, species

classical   adjective pure, refined, scholarly, elegant,
polished, well-proportioned

classify   verb grade, sort, arrange, catalog

clean   **1** adjective pure, fresh, spotless, unsoiled   **2** verb
cleanse, scrub ▶ *wash* ★ dirty

cleanse   verb purify, scour ▶ *clean* ★ defile

clear   adjective **1** bright, fair, fine, light ★ dim
2 distinct, audible, lucid ★ vague   **3** free, open, empty

cleft   noun crack, cranny, slit, split, aperture

clever   adjective able, astute, apt, brainy, skillful,
talented ▶ *expert* ★ foolish

cliff   noun precipice, height, bluff, crag, overhang

climax   noun crisis, head, summit, turning point

climb   verb mount, scale, ascend, soar, go up

cling   verb adhere, attach, embrace, grasp, hold

clip   **1** noun fastener, clasp   **2** verb trim, prune,
snip, cut

clog   verb block, dam up, hinder, jam, impede

close   **1** verb (kloz) shut, bolt, bar, obstruct *The drapes
were thick and obstructed a lot of light*, end   **2** adjective
(klos) near, neighboring, adjacent ★ far   **3** adjective
heavy, stuffy, uncomfortable

closet   noun cupboard, cabinet

clothing   noun garments, dress, attire, raiment

cloud   noun vapor, fog, billow, haze

clown   noun buffoon, comedian, jester, joker

club   noun **1** cudgel, stick, truncheon   **2** company,
group, society

clue   noun evidence, inkling, lead, sign CLEW

clump   noun cluster, group, bunch

clumsy   adjective awkward, gawky, ungainly,
blundering ★ graceful

clutch   verb snatch, clasp, grasp, seize, grip

clutter   noun litter, muddle, mess

coach   noun **1** bus, car, carriage, vehicle   **2** trainer,
tutor, instructor

coarse   adjective **1** rough, unrefined, unpolished
2 brutish, rude, uncivil ★ refined COURSE

coat   noun **1** jacket, blazer, windbreaker   **2** fleece, fur,
skin, hide

coax   verb cajole, wheedle, urge, persuade, beguile
We sat for hours as Aunt Anna beguiled us with stories
★ dissuade COKES

coddle   verb pamper, spoil, indulge, baby, mollycoddle

coffer   noun casket, case, chest, treasury

cog   noun tooth, prong

coil   verb twist, wind, loop

coincide   verb match, agree, accord, synchronize, tally

cold   adjective cool, chilly, frigid, freezing, frosty, frozen
★ hot

collapse   verb founder, topple, break down, crumple,
fall down

collect   verb accumulate, amass, assemble, save
▶ *gather* ★ scatter

collide   verb crash, smash, hit, strike, meet

colossal adjective enormous, gigantic, immense, massive ▶ *huge* ★ **tiny**

column noun **1** pillar, post, shaft **2** file *The file of soldiers marched on parade*, line, procession

combat verb battle, contend, contest, oppose, defy ★ **submit**

combine verb unite, join, link, fuse, merge, mix ★ **separate**

come verb arrive, appear, enter, reach, advance ★ **go**

come by verb get, procure, acquire *I acquired a new TV in the sale*

comfort verb cheer, hearten, calm, soothe, console ★ **torment**

comfortable adjective restful, convenient, cozy, agreeable ★ **uncomfortable**

comforting adjective cheering, encouraging, consoling

command verb **1** order, dictate, direct **2** rule, dominate

commence verb start, begin, initiate, originate ★ **finish**

comment verb mention, remark, observe, point out

commiserate verb sympathize, show pity, be sorry for

commit verb carry out, do, enact, perform, promise, entrust

common adjective **1** ordinary, vulgar, habitual, customary **2** public, social, communal

commonplace adjective everyday, humdrum, ordinary, obvious ★ **rare**

commotion noun excitement, flurry, stir, uproar ▶ *fuss*

communicate verb tell, disclose, impart, reveal

community noun society, partnership, association ▶ *group*

compact adjective dense, close, tight, firm, condensed, concise

companion noun comrade, friend, chum, colleague, comrade, escort ★ **rival**

company noun association, league, alliance, business, firm

compare verb match, liken, equal, parallel

compartment noun cubicle, alcove, bay, cell, carriage

compassion noun kindness, mercy, sympathy, charity, understanding ▶ *pity* ★ **indifference**

compel verb make, coerce, drive, force *We could not understand the signs, so we were forced to guess where to check in*, urge ★ **coax**

compensate verb make good, refund, reimburse, repay, reward, ★ **injure**

compete verb contest, contend, rival, strive, oppose, challenge

competent adjective able, adapted, capable ▶ *clever* ★ **incompetent**

competition noun game, match, contest, tournament, rivalry, race

compile verb amass, put together, unite ▶ *collect*

complacent adjective self-satisfied, contented ▶ *smug* ★ **different**

complain verb protest, gripe, grumble, grouse ▶ *nag* ★ **rejoice**

complement verb complete, round off, add to, supplement, match COMPLIMENT

complete **1** verb finish, accomplish, achieve **2** adjective finished, fill, entire

complex adjective complicated, intricate, mixed, tangled ★ **simple**

complicated adjective entangled, involved ▶ *complex*

compliment verb flatter, admire, congratulate ▶ *praise* ★ **insult** COMPLEMENT

comply verb agree to, assent to, abide by, perform, yield ★ **refuse**

compose **1** verb make up, put together, form, construct, write **2** calm, quell

composure noun assurance, calm, confidence ★ **exuberance**

compound noun mixture, alloy, blend, combination

comprehend verb grasp, discern, take in ▶ *understand* ★ **misunderstand**

compress verb condense, contract, abbreviate ▶ *squeeze* ★ **expand**

comprise verb contain, consist of, include, embody, encompass

compromise verb **1** meet halfway, strike a balance, adjust, agree **2** imperil, weaken, jeopardize

compulsory adjective forced, necessary, obligatory *Everyone in the school has to go to the meeting; it's obligatory*, required ★ **voluntary**

A B C D E F G H I J K L M N O P Q R S T U V W X Y Z

201

compute verb calculate, figure, reckon, estimate

computer noun calculator, laptop, PC

comrade noun companion, pal, chum, buddy ▶ *friend* ✶ **enemy**

conceal verb bury, camouflage, cover ▶ *hide* ✶ **reveal**

concede verb allow, admit, yield, acknowledge, surrender ✶ **dispute**

conceit noun vanity, self-importance, arrogance ▶ *pride* ✶ **modesty**

conceited adjective proud, vain, arrogant ✶ **modest**

conceive verb create, design, devise *We devised a way to get the work done*, form, think up, develop

concentrate verb focus on, centralize, heed, pay attention

concept noun idea, thought, theory, view

concern 1 verb affect, touch 2 noun affair, matter, interest, business

concerning preposition as regards, respecting, about

concise adjective brief, condensed, short ▶ *compact* ✶ **expansive**

conclude verb 1 finish, terminate ▶ *end* 2 deduce, judge, reckon, presume

conclusion noun result, termination, end

concoct verb contrive, hatch, plan, devise, invent

concord noun agreement, understanding, goodwill, harmony ✶ **discord**

concrete 1 adjective actual, definite, real 2 noun cement, mortar

concur verb approve, agree, coincide, consent ✶ **disagree**

condemn verb blame, denounce, reprove, sentence, disapprove ✶ **approve**

condense verb compress, concentrate, abridge, thicken ✶ **expand**

condition noun shape, way, state, position, plight, situation ▶ *predicament*

condone verb overlook, disregard, forgive, excuse ✶ **censure**

conduct 1 noun attitude, bearing, behavior 2 verb guide, direct, lead, steer, pilot

confederate noun accomplice, ally, associate, partner

confer verb bestow, grant, award, give, present

conference noun discussion, meeting, forum

confess verb admit, acknowledge, own up, divulge ✶ **deny**

confide verb tell, divulge, reveal, whisper, entrust

confidence noun assurance, belief, boldness, firmness ✶ **doubt**

confident adjective certain, assured, poised, fearless ✶ **diffident**

confine verb restrict, limit, detain, imprison, constrain ✶ **free**

confirm verb verify, assure, approve, endorse, attest ✶ **deny**

confiscate verb seize, impound, commandeer *The house was commandeered by the army*

conform verb agree with, comply with, yield, adjust

confound verb perplex, mystify, puzzle, baffle, fluster ▶ *bewilder* ✶ **enlighten**

confront verb challenge, defy, face, oppose, menace

confuse verb baffle, bemuse, mystify ▶ *bewilder* ✶ **clarify**

congenial adjective companionable, natural, sympathetic, agreeable ▶ *friendly* ✶ **disagreeable**

congested adjective jammed, crowded, clogged, packed, teeming ✶ **clear**

congratulate verb rejoice, compliment, praise, wish one joy ✶ **commiserate**

congregate verb assemble, meet, come together, converge ✶ **disperse**

congress noun meeting, assembly, council, convention

conjecture verb guess, surmise, suspect, imagine, assume

connect verb unite, join, combine, fasten, link ✶ **disconnect**

conquer verb beat, crush, overcome, overpower, triumph ▶ *defeat* ✶ **surrender**

conscientious adjective moral, scrupulous, careful, diligent ▶ *honest* ✶ **careless**

conscious adjective alert, alive, aware, sensible, responsible ✶ **unconscious**

consecutive adjective chronological, in sequence, successive, continuous

consent verb assent, permit, concur, approve, comply ▶ *agree* ✶ **oppose**

conserve verb keep, preserve, protect, save, store up, safeguard ★ waste

consider verb discuss, examine, ponder, reflect *Alone on the island, I reflected on all that had happened,* take account of ★ ignore

considerable adjective abundant, ample, great, large, noteworthy, important ★ insignificant

consist of verb comprise, be composed of, contain, include

consistent adjective uniform, constant, regular, steady ★ inconsistent

console verb comfort, cheer, sympathize, soothe, solace ★ upset

conspicuous adjective noticeable, marked, apparent, obvious, prominent ★ inconspicuous

conspire verb intrigue, scheme, plot *He was jailed for plotting against the government*

constant adjective 1 regular, stable, uniform ▶ *consistent* 2 loyal, faithful, staunch, true ★ fickle

consternation noun dismay, horror, fear, awe, stupefaction ▶ *alarm* ★ composure

constitute verb compose, comprise, set up, fix, form, establish ★ destroy

constrict verb tighten, strain, tauten, draw together, choke, pinch ★ expand

construct verb erect, compose, compound, assemble ▶ *build* ★ demolish

consult verb ask, seek advice, discuss, confer, debate

consume verb use up, absorb, eat up, devour

contact noun touch, connection, communication

contagious adjective catching, infectious

contain verb comprise, consist of, hold, accommodate, enclose

contaminate verb pollute, soil, stain, sully, taint, infect

contemplate verb think, reflect, deliberate, consider, ponder

contempt verb disdain, scorn, disregard, derision ★ admiration

contend verb compete, contest, conflict, strive, struggle ★ concede

content 1 adjective (con-*tent*) satisfied, smug 2 verb satisfy, delight, gratify 3 noun (*con*-tent) matter, text, subject

contest 1 noun (*con*-test) competition, game, match, tournament 2 verb (con-*test*) dispute, argue

continue verb go on, keep up, endure, last, persist ★ stop

contract 1 verb (con-*tract*) condense, lessen, shrink 2 noun (*con*-tract) agreement, pact, understanding

contradict verb deny, dispute, challenge, oppose

contrary adjective opposed, adverse, counter, opposite ★ agreeable

contrast 1 noun (*con*-trast) difference, disparity, comparison 2 verb (con-*trast*) compare, differ, oppose, distinguish

contribute verb donate, present, bestow, provide ★ withhold

contrive verb form, fashion, construct, create, design, invent

control verb command, direct, dominate, lead, supervise

convene verb call together, rally, meet, muster *We mustered on the dock before boarding the ship,* assemble ★ dismiss

convenient adjective hardly, fit, helpful, suitable, accessible ★ awkward

conversation noun talk, chat, communication, discussion

convert verb alter, change, transform, adapt

convey verb carry, transport, conduct, bear, transmit

convict 1 noun (*con*-vict) prisoner, captive, criminal 2 verb (con-*vict*) find guilty, condemn

convince verb assure, persuade, prove to, win over

cook verb boil, broil, heat, warm, steam, fry, stew, bake

cool adjective 1 chilly, frigid ▶ *cold* 2 self-composed, calm, relaxed

cooperate verb collaborate, combine, aid, assist, join forces

cope with verb deal, handle, struggle, grapple, manage

copy verb duplicate, reproduce, imitate, mimic, simulate

cord noun string, rope, twine, line CHORD

cordial adjective hearty, sincere, congenial, jovial, affable ★ hostile

core noun heart, kernel, pith, crux *Now we're getting to the crux of the problem,* center CORPS

corner noun angle, bend, crook, cavity, cranny, niche, compartment

corpse noun body, carcass, remains

correct adjective true, actual, accurate, exact, precise ★ wrong

correspond verb 1 fit, harmonize, agree, coincide 2 write letters

corridor noun hallway, passage, aisle

corroborate verb confirm, certify, endorse, establish ★ contradict

corrode verb erode, waste, eat away, rust

corrupt 1 adjective dishonest, fraudulent, rotten 2 verb bribe, deprave, entice

cost noun 1 charge, amount, price, outlay 2 penalty, forfeit, sacrifice

costly adjective expensive, valuable, precious

costume noun suit, outfit, ensemble, attire, dress

cot noun bed, bunk, berth

cottage noun bungalow, cabin, chalet, shack, lodge

couch noun sofa, davenport, chaise longue

council noun assembly, committee, congress, convention COUNSEL

counsel 1 noun lawyer, attorney, advocate 2 verb advise, instruct, recommend COUNCIL

count verb add up, calculate, check, compute, reckon, tally

counter 1 noun token, coin, disk 2 noun bar, bench 3 adjective against, opposed

counterfeit adjective forged, fraudulent, fake, bogus *She entered the country on a bogus passport*, false

country 1 noun nation, people, realm, state 2 adjective rural, boondocks, boonies, sticks

couple 1 noun pair, brace, two 2 verb link, yoke, unite, join, connect

courage noun bravery, valor, boldness, gallantry, daring, pluck ★ cowardice

courageous adjective brave, bold, fearless, valiant ▶ *plucky* ★ cowardly

course noun 1 route, channel, path, road, track, trail 2 policy, plan, manner COARSE

court 1 noun alley, courtyard, atrium 2 noun bar, law court, tribunal 3 noun palace, retinue 4 verb woo, flatter

courteous adjective considerate, polite, refined, elegant ★ discourteous

courtesy noun politeness, civility, manners, gentility, respect

cove noun inlet, bay, creek, firth

cover 1 verb conceal, hide, secrete 2 verb include, embody, incorporate 3 noun cap, case, lid, canopy

covet verb want, envy, fancy, hanker after, long for, crave

cow verb frighten, bully, terrorize, scare, subdue

coward noun weakling, craven, funk, sneak ★ hero COWERED

cowardice noun fear, funk, faint-heartedness ★ courage

cowardly adjective fearful, weak, scared, spineless, timid ★ courageous

cower verb cringe, grovel, flinch, crouch

coy adjective demure, skittish, blushing, bashful, shy ★ forward

crack 1 noun slit, split, cleft, cranny, crevice, breach 2 verb snap, split, splinter

craft noun 1 cunning, deceit 2 ability, cleverness, expertise 3 occupation, business 4 boat, ship, plane

crafty adjective cunning, artful, wily, shrewd

cram verb ram, stuff, squeeze, press

cramp verb restrict, obstruct, hinder, confine

crash verb bang, clash, clatter, break, fall, topple, collapse

crass adjective stupid, oafish, boorish, obtuse, gross, vulgar, coarse ★ sensitive

crave verb long for, hanker after, need, yearn for, beg, plead

crawl verb creep, drag, slither, grovel

crazy adjective insane, mad, berserk, deranged, idiotic ★ sane

creak verb grate, grind, rasp, groan CREEK

crease noun fold, pucker, ridge, tuck

create verb bring into being, compose, concoct, make, invent, devise

creation invention, handiwork, foundation, production ★ destruction

creature noun animal, beast, being, brute *It was a huge brute—the biggest crocodile I'd ever seen*, person

credible adjective believable, likely, plausible ★ incredible

credit noun **1** acclaim, kudos, merit **2** belief, faith, confidence

creek noun stream, brook, rivulet CREAK

creep verb crawl, slither, squirm, wriggle

crest noun top, crown, pinnacle

crestfallen adjective downcast, dejected, discouraged ★ elated

crevice noun cleft, chink, crack, cranny, gap

crew noun team, company, party, gang

crime noun misdemeanor, offense, fault, felony

criminal **1** noun culprit, convict, felon, crook **2** adjective unlawful, wicked

cringe verb cower, flinch, duck, shrink, grovel

cripple verb disable, mutilate, paralyze, weaken, damage

crisis noun climax, turning point, catastrophe, disaster

crisp adjective brittle, crumbly, crunchy, firm, crusty

critical adjective crucial, all-important, acute, grave

criticize verb find fault with, disapprove of, condemn ★ praise

crony noun accomplice, ally, confederate, comrade, chum ▶ *friend*

crooked adjective **1** bent, bowed, distorted, twisted **2** dishonest, criminal

crop **1** noun harvest, gathering, yield **2** verb graze, shorten, browse

cross **1** adjective angry, annoyed, crusty **2** verb bridge, pass over **3** noun crucifix

crouch verb stood, squat, bow, cringe

crow **1** verb gloat, shout, brag, bluster **2** noun blackbird, raven

crowd noun mob, multitude, flock, assembly, swarm, throng

crowded adjective jammed, packed, congested, cramped

crucial adjective decisive, critical, acute

crude adjective raw, unrefined, rustic, unpolished ▶ *coarse* ★ refined

cruel adjective unkind, brutal, inhuman, ruthless ▶ *savage* ★ kind

cruise noun voyage, trip, sail, crossing CREWS

crumb noun bit, morsel, seed, grain, scrap, shred

crumble verb decay, grind, powder, crunch

crumple verb crinkle, crush, wrinkle, pucker

crunch verb chew, grind, masticate, munch ▶ *crush*

crush verb squash, mash, pound, compress

cry verb **1** exclaim, call, shout, shriek **2** weep, bawl, blubber, sob

cuddle verb hug, embrace, fondle, cosset, pet, snuggle

cue noun hint, key, nod, sign, signal

cull verb choose, pick, thin out, amass, collect

culprit noun criminal, convict, felon, offender, malefactor

cultivated adjective refined, civilized, cultured, educated, trained ★ neglected

cumbersome adjective bulky, awkward, clumsy, hefty ★ convenient

cunning adjective artful, astute, crafty

curb verb check, tame, restrain

cure **1** noun remedy, medicine, drug **2** verb heal, remedy, treat, attend

curious adjective **1** odd, peculiar, singular **2** inquisitive, prying, nosy

curl verb coil, twist, curve, crimp

current **1** adjective present, contemporary, topical, fashionable **2** noun stream, course, flow, electrical flow CURRANT

curse **1** verb swear, condemn, damn **2** noun oath, denunciation

curt adjective brusque, blunt, churlish, crusty, gruff ▶ *terse* ★ polite

curtail verb trim, shorten, clip, truncate ▶ *abbreviate* ★ lengthen

curve noun loop, hook, curl, twist, wind, coil ▶ *bend*

cushion noun pillow, bolster, pad, support

custom noun habit, usage, convention, rite ▶ *fashion*

customer noun purchaser, buyer, client, patron

cut verb carve, whittle, chisel, cleave, sever, gash, slice

cut off verb disconnect, interrupt, stop

cute adjective charming, attractive, pretty, dainty

cutting adjective sharp, biting, bitter, sarcastic

A B C D E F G H I J K L M N O P Q R S T U V W X Y Z

Dd

dab verb blot, swab, touch, pat

dabble verb toy, meddle, tinker, trifle, putter

daft adjective crazy, silly, innocent, idiotic, cracked, dopey ★ **bright**

dagger noun knife, dirk, bayonet, stiletto

daily 1 adjective everyday, normal, common *It is quite to see squirrels in the woods* 2 noun newspaper

dainty adjective delicate, charming, exquisite, choice, tasty

daily verb play, trifle, dawdle, linger, loiter

damage noun harm, sabotage, vandalism, injury, hurt

damn verb curse, swear, condemn, criticize ★ **bless**

damp adjective humid, clammy, dank ▶ *moist* ★ **dry**

damsel noun girl, maiden, lady, woman

dance verb hop, skip, jump, prance, frolic, gambol

danger noun peril, hazard, risk, jeopardy, menace ★ **safety**

dangerous adjective perilous, precarious, unsafe, risky, hazardous ★ **safe**

dangle verb hang, swing, sway

dank adjective sticky, muggy, moist, soggy ▶ *damp*

dapper adjective spruce, natty, neat, stylish, trim ▶ *smart* ★ **scruffy**

dare verb brave, face, risk, defy, challenge, venture

daring adjective adventurous, dashing, bold, fearless ▶ *brave* ★ **timid**

dark adjective dusky, swarthy, shady, dim, dingy, shadowy ★ **light**

darling noun pet, love, dear, favorite, beloved, precious

darn verb mend, sew, patch, repair

dart 1 noun arrow, missile 2 verb dash, hurtle *The express train hurtled through the tunnel*, charge, gallop

dash verb rush, gallop, run, career, fly, hasten

date 1 noun time, point 2 noun appointment *I have an appointment to see the doctor*, engagement, 3 verb become old, become dated

daub verb plaster, spread, smear, dab, paint

daunt verb intimidate, terrify, scare, confront

dauntless adjective fearless, gallant, courageous ▶ *brave* ★ **discouraged**

dawdle verb linger, loiter, lag, waste time ▶ *dally* ★ **hurry**

dawn noun beginning, daybreak, daylight, morning, sunrise ★ **dusk**

Dances

ballet	minuet
bolero	morris dance
bop	polka
cha-cha	polonaise
Charleston	quadrille
conga	quickstep
disco	rumba
fandango	samba
foxtrot	square dance
gavotte	tango
Highland fling	tap dance
hip-hop	tarantella
jitterbug	two-step
jive	twist
line dance	waltz
mazurka	

flamenco

daze verb deaden, muddle, blind, dazzle ▶ *bewilder* DAYS

dazzle verb blind, glare, confuse ▶ *daze*

dead adjective deceased, departed, gone, lifeless, dull ☆ alive

deaden verb paralyze, blunt, muffle, drown

deadly adjective fatal, lethal, mortal, baleful, venomous

deaf adjective hard of hearing, unhearing, heedless

deal verb bargain, trade, market, communicate, traffic, give out

dealer noun merchant, trader, tradesman

dear 1 adjective darling, beloved, loved, cherished *These old books are some of my most cherished possessions* 2 expensive, high-priced, costly DEER

death noun decease, end of life, mortality ☆ life

debate verb argue, discuss, dispute, question, contend

debris noun trash, junk ▶ *garbage*

debt noun obligation, debit, dues, liability ☆ credit

decay verb 1 decompose, rot *The potatoes had been left too long and had rotted*, spoil 2 decline, sink, dwindle, waste

deceive verb dupe, hoax, trick, cheat, mislead ▶ *betray* ☆ enlighten

decent adjective respectable, chaste, proper, fair, modest ☆ indecent

decide verb determine, rule, judge, resolve

declare verb avow, state, profess, proclaim, announce

decline 1 verb descend, dwindle *The profits of the business had dwindled*, drop, fall 2 verb refuse, say no ☆ assent 3 noun descent, slope, slant, dip, pitch

decorate verb embellish, adorn, ornament

decoy 1 verb entice *We were enticed into the café by the smell of roasting coffee*, ensnare, mislead, tempt 2 noun lure, bait

decrease verb diminish, lessen, wane, decline, reduce, downsize ☆ increase

decree noun law, edict, manifesto, rule, decision

decrepit adjective senile, infirm, crippled, feeble, frail ☆ robust

dedicate verb devote, apportion, assign, surrender, pledge

deduce verb draw, infer, conclude, glean, surmise, reason

deduct verb subtract, take from, remove, withdraw ☆ add

deed noun 1 act, feat, stunt 2 document, paper, contract *Michael was under contract to play ball for the team for three years*

deep adjective 1 profound *The accident taught us a profound lesson about friendship*, bottomless, low 2 learned, wise, sagacious

deface verb disfigure, deform, injure, mar, blemish ☆ adorn

defeat verb beat, conquer, overcome, vanquish ☆ triumph

defect noun flaw, fault, weak point, blemish, error

defective adjective imperfect, faulty, deficient, insufficient ☆ perfect

defend verb protect, guard, fortify, support, sustain, uphold ☆ attack

defer verb postpone, put off, adjourn, waive, yield ☆ hasten

defiant adjective mutinous, rebellious, resistant, aggressive ☆ submissive

deficient adjective wanting, imperfect, defective, faulty ☆ superfluous

defile verb taint, infect, pollute, sully, disgrace ☆ cleanse

define verb explain, interpret, designate, mark out, specify ☆ obscure

definite adjective clear, certain, clear-cut, distinct ▶ *sure* ☆ vague

deform adjective misshape, distort, contort, twist, warp

defraud verb fleece, swindle, embezzle, diddle ▶ *cheat*

defy verb resist, withstand, disregard, challenge, disobey ☆ obey

degrade verb humble, debase, corrupt, downgrade, cheapen ☆ improve

degree noun grade, step, measure, rate, scale *Our answers were scored on a scale from one to ten*, class

dejected adjective depressed, downcast, crestfallen, disheartened ▶ *gloomy* ☆ elated

delay verb postpone, put off, detain, halt, hinder, impede ☆ hurry

deliberate 1 adjective willful, calculated, intentional, planned ☆ **unintentional** 2 verb reflect, contemplate, discuss

delicate adjective dainty, refined, soft, luxurious, modest, fragile, tender ☆ **harsh**

delicious adjective palatable, luscious, mellow, savory, choice ▶ *scrumptious* ☆ **unpleasant**

delight noun enjoyment, pleasure, rapture, bliss ▶ *happiness* ☆ **displease**

delightful adjective enjoyable, cheery, enchanting, lovely ▶ *agreeable* ☆ **horrible**

deliver 1 verb transfer, hand over, bear *She came bearing gifts for the whole family*, carry, convey 2 free, liberate, release

delude verb cheat, hoax, hoodwink, mislead ▶ *deceive* ☆ **guide**

deluge noun inundation, swamp, spate ▶ *flood*

demand verb 1 request, ask, appeal, entreat 2 badger, pester, nag *My sister has been nagging me to take her to the park*

demeanor noun bearing, manner, conduct, air

demented adjective distracted, foolish, insane ▶ *mad* ☆ **sane**

demolish verb destroy, wreck, ruin, smash, overthrow, knock down ☆ **build**

demon noun fiend, imp, devil, evil spirit

demonstrate verb prove, exhibit, illustrate ▶ show

demote verb degrade, downgrade, relegate ☆ **promote**

demur verb hesitate, object, protest, doubt, waver ☆ **consent**

demure adjective coy, sedate, staid, sober, prudish, discreet ☆ **indiscreet**

den noun 1 nest, cave, haunt, lair 2 hideaway, retreat *This little room is my retreat, where I can sit and think*, study

denote verb designate, indicate, mean, show, point out

denounce verb decry, defame, attack, brand ▶ *accuse* ☆ **praise**

dense adjective 1 thick, solid, stout, compact ☆ **sparse** 2 stupid, thick, stolid, obtuse ☆ **smart** DENTS

dent noun notch, cavity, chip, dimple, hollow

deny verb 1 refuse, reject, repudiate 2 disagree with *I am afraid that I disagree with what you say*, oppose, contradict ☆ **admit**

depart verb quit, go, retire, withdraw, vanish ▶ *leave* ☆ **arrive**

department noun section, division, office, branch, province

depend on verb lean on, rely upon, trust in

depict verb describe, sketch, portray, outline, draw

deplorable adjective distressing, disastrous, shameful, scandalous ☆ **excellent**

deplore verb regret, lament, mourn ☆ **celebrate**

deport verb banish, exile, expel, oust

deposit verb drop, lay, place, put, bank, entrust, save ☆ **withdraw**

depot noun 1 warehouse, storehouse 2 terminus, station

depraved adjective corrupted, immoral, evil, sinful, vile *After calling me vile names, he left* ☆ **upright**

depreciate verb 1 devalue, lesson, lose value *From the moment it was bought, the car began losing value*, reduce 2 belittle, disparage, deride ☆ **appreciate**

depress 1 verb dishearten, dispirit, cast down ☆ **cheer** 2 flatten, push down

depressed adjective dispirited, disheartened, despondent, fed up

deprive verb take away, rob, starve, divest *The traitor had been divested of all her honors* ☆ **bestow**

depth noun pit, shaft, well, chasm, gulf, abyss

deputy noun agent, delegate, lieutenant, assistant, councillor

derelict adjective abandoned, deserted *The* Mary Celeste *sailing ship was found deserted in the Atlantic Ocean*, forlorn

deride verb laugh at, jeer at, ridicule ▶ *mock* ☆ **praise**

derive verb develop *Many English words developed from Norman-French*, obtain, arise from, originate

descend verb fall, drop, lower, decline, collapse ▶ *sink* ☆ **ascend**

describe verb depict, portray, detail, define, tell

desert 1 noun (*dez*-ert) wasteland, wilderness 2 adjective desolate, arid, barren 3 verb (dez-*ert*) forshake, leave ▶ *abandon* DESSERT

deserve verb be worthy of, merit, warrant, be entitled to ☆ **forfeit**

design noun drawing, painting, plan, pattern, scheme

desirable adjective 1 agreeable, pleasing, good 2 attractive, alluring, adorable

desire verb 1 wish, require, need, want, crave 2 long for, yearn after, pine for *My sister lived abroad but always pined for home* ☆ detest

desist verb abstain, avoid, break off, cease, end

desolate adjective lonely, forlorn, miserable, wretched, alone ☆ cheerful

despair noun depression, misery, hopelessness, sorrow ▷ *gloom* ☆ hope

desperate adjective drastic, reckless, frantic, rash, wild ☆ hopeful

despicable adjective contemptible, low, detestable, degrading ☆ noble

despise verb abhor, detest, loathe, look down on ▷ *hate* ☆ prize

despite preposition in spite of, notwithstanding

despondent adjective depressed, dispirited, brokenhearted ▷ *miserable* ☆ cheerful

destination noun goal, terminus, end, objective, journey's end

destiny noun fate, lot, fortune, future, prospect, doom

destitute adjective poor, needy, bankrupt, penniless, poverty-stricken, ☆ wealthy

destroy verb ruin, demolish, spoil, smash, exterminate ▷ *wreck* ☆ create

destruction noun desolation, downfall, ruin, defeat, havoc ☆ creation

detach verb separate, part, divide, loosen, undo ☆ attach

detail noun item, fact, circumstances, point

detain verb delay, retard, restrain, arrest, hold up, hinder, impede ☆ release

detect verb notice, discover, observe, scent, track down ☆ miss

deter verb prevent, hold back, check, stop ▷ *detain* ☆ encourage

deteriorate verb become worse, worsen, corrode, decline, decompose ☆ improve

determine verb find out, decide, identify, choose, regulate

detest verb abhor *Lucy was a peaceful person who abhorred violence*, loathe, despise ▷ *hate* ☆ adore

devastate verb lay waste, ravage, overwhelm ▷ *destroy*

develop verb mature, ripen, grow up, evolve, extend ☆ restrict

deviate verb diverge, differ, vary, contrast, wander ☆ conform

device noun apparatus, contrivance, instrument, appliance

devil noun imp, evil spirit, demon, fiend, Satan

devious adjective tricky, sly, subtle, cunning, roundabout ☆ forthright

devise verb contrive, fashion, form, plan, conceive

devoid adjective barren, empty, free, without, lacking ☆ endowed

devote verb allocate, allot, give, assign, dedicate

devoted adjective dedicated, devout, loyal, caring, ardent ☆ indifferent

devour verb swallow, gulp, gorge, consume ▷ *eat*

devout adjective pious, devoted, religious, faithful, passionate ☆ insincere

dexterous adjective able, active, deft, nimble ▷ *skillful* ☆ clumsy

diagram noun outline, plan, sketch, draft, chart, drawing

dictate verb speak, utter, say, instruct, ordain, command

die verb expire, finish, end, pass away, perish, cease ☆ live DYE

differ verb 1 vary, contrast, diverge *In this case, my views diverge strongly from yours* 2 argue, conflict, clash

difference noun variance, distinctness, divergence, subtlety ☆ agreement

different adjective contrary, variant, distinct, original, unusual ☆ same

difficult adjective hard, puzzling, baffling, complex, laborious ☆ easy

difficulty noun trouble, bother, predicament ☆ ease

diffidently adjective bashful, reserved, retiring, timid, unsure ▷ *shy* ☆ confident

dig verb burrow, excavate, grub, delve, scoop

digest 1 verb (di-*gest*) absorb, assimilate, dissolve 2 noun (*di*-gest) abridgment, condensation, précis

209

digit noun **1** number, figure, cipher, **2** finger, toe, thumb

dignified adjective grave, majestic, noble, lofty, grand ★ **undignified**

dignity noun grandeur, merit, fame, gravity, nobility

dilapidated adjective neglected, unkempt, crumbling, decayed

dilemma noun quandary, plight, difficulty, predicament

dilute verb water down, weaken, reduce, thin

dim adjective dark, faint, pale, gloomy ▶ *obscure* ★ **bright**

diminish verb reduce, lessen, decrease, become smaller ★ **enhance**

din noun uproar, racket, babble, commotion, pandemonium ▶ *noise* ★ **quiet**

dingy adjective murky, dark, dreary, somber, gloomy ▶ dismal ★ **bright**

dip verb sink, subside, immerse, plunge

dire adjective alarming, appalling, awful, horrible ▶ *terrible* DYER

direct **1** adjective straight, even, blunt, candid **2** verb aim, level, train, point

direction noun course, trend, way, track, route

dirt noun impurity, filth, grime, muck, soil

dirty adjective unclean, impure, filthy, sordid, squalid, nasty ★ **clean**

disable verb cripple, lame, maim, disarm

disadvantage noun inconvenience, burden, damage, loss, obstacle ★ **advantage**

disagree verb differ, revolt, decline, refuse, dissent, argue ★ **agree**

disagreeable adjective unpleasant, obnoxious, unwelcome, offensive ★ **agreeable**

disappear verb vanish, dissolve, fade, melt, depart, expire ★ **appear**

disappoint verb frustrate, disillusion, let down, dismay, dissatisfy ★ **please**

disapprove verb condemn, denounce, criticize, reproach ★ **approve**

disaster noun calamity, catastrophe, accident, misfortune ★ **triumph**

disbelief noun incredulity, distrust, doubt, suspicion ★ **belief**

discard verb eliminate, get rid of, reject, scrap *Once we got a new car, I scrapped the old one*, throw away ★ **adopt**

discern verb note, discover, distinguish

discharge verb **1** dismiss, give notice to, expel **2** detonate, emit, fire

disciple noun follower, learner, student, attendant

discipline noun correction, training, self-control, obedience

disclaim verb repudiate, disown, renounce, deny, reject ★ **acknowledge**

disclose verb discover, show, reveal, expose, betray ▶ *divulge* ★ **conceal**

disconcert verb abash, confuse, confound, upset, baffle ★ **encourage**

disconnect verb separate, detach, cut off, sever, uncouple ★ **connect**

disconsolate adjective distressed, sad, forlorn, melancholy, desolate ▶ *unhappy* ★ **cheerful**

discontented adjective displeased, disgruntled, unsatisfied, reluctant ★ **content**

discord noun disagreement, strife ★ **concord**

discourage verb depress, dismay, dispirit, dishearten *I don't want to dishearten you, but our vacation is canceled*, put off ★ **encourage**

discouraged adjective crestfallen, daunted, depressed, downcast, ★ **encouraged**

discourteous adjective blunt, crude, churlish, outspoken, abrupt ★ **courteous**

discover verb locate, surprise, unearth, uncover ▶ *find* ★ **conceal**

discreet adjective prudent, cautions, careful, tactful, sensible ★ **indiscreet** DISCRETE

discriminate verb distinguish, penetrate, favor, judge, assess ★ **confound**

discuss verb confer, consider, talk over, debate, argue

disdain noun ridicule, scorn, contempt, derision ★ **admiration**

disease noun infection, contagion, illness, plague, ailment, sickness

disfigure verb blemish, deface, deform, mar, scar, spoil ★ **adorn**

disgrace noun scandal, dishonor, shame, infamy, stigma ★ **honor**

Dogs

Afghan hound	Irish setter
Airedale	Labrador
beagle	Old English sheepdog
bloodhound	Pekingese
borzoi	pointer
boxer	pug
Chihuahua	Saint Bernard
chow	saluki
Doberman pinscher	spaniel
golden retriever	terrier
Great Dane	whippet
greyhound	

dalmatian

poodle

bassett hound

bulldog

German shepherd

collie

dachshund

disguise verb conceal, mask, falsify, cloak, deceive, fake

disgust 1 noun revulsion, loathing, distaste *The house was dirty, and I entered it with distaste* 2 verb repel, revolt, nauseate ☆ **admire**

dish noun plate, platter, bowl

dishearten verb depress, cast down, deter, deject ▶ *discourage* ☆ **encourage**

dishonest adjective deceitful, unscrupulous, shady, crooked ☆ **honest**

disintegrate verb crumble, molder, decompose, rot, fall apart ☆ **unite**

dislike verb hate, loathe, detest, abhor, abominate ▶ *despise* ☆ **like**

dismal adjective dreary, ominous, cheerless, depressing ▶ *hopeless* ☆ **cheerful**

dismiss verb banish, discard, abandon, dispel, repudiate, release ☆ **appoint**

disobey verb rebel, transgress, resist, defy, ignore ☆ **obey**

disorder noun confusion, disarray, commotion, chaos ☆ **order**

dispel verb disperse, drive away, dismiss, allay, scatter ☆ **collect**

dispense verb distribute, arrange, allocate, supply, measure out ☆ **accept**

disperse verb scatter, separate, break up, spread abroad, distribute ☆ **gather**

display verb show, exhibit, unfold, expose, flaunt *He flaunts his expensive clothes to his friends*, flourish ▶ *reveal* ☆ **hide**

displease verb annoy, anger, irritate, upset, vex, offend, infuriate ☆ **please**

dispose verb arrange, place, position, regulate, order

dispose of verb discard, dump, destroy, eliminate, throw away ☆ **keep**

dispute 1 noun conflict, quarrel, argument 2 verb argue, refute, contend

disregard verb overlook, misjudge, despise, ignore, snub ☆ **heed**

disreputable adjective discreditable, dishonorable, disgraceful ▶ *shameful* ☆ **honorable**

dissect verb examine, scrutinize, analyze, dismember

dissent noun disagreement, difference, repudiation, opposition ☆ **assent**

dissimilar adjective different, diverse, unlike, various ☆ **similar**

dissolve verb melt, thaw, break up, fade

dissuade verb deter, discourage, warn, put off ☆ **persuade**

distance noun extent, remoteness, range, reach, span, stretch

distinct adjective 1 separate, independent, detached 2 clear, conspicuous, lucid ☆ **hazy**

distinguish verb discern, discover, differentiate

distinguished adjective important, notable, great, famed, celebrated ☆ **ordinary**

distort verb deform, misshape, twist, bend, buckle

distract verb 1 beguile, bewilder, disturb, confuse 2 entertain

distress verb harass, embarrass, trouble, grieve ▶ *worry* ☆ **soothe**

distribute verb give out, deliver, disperse, circulate ▶ *dispense* ☆ **collect**

district noun area, community, locality, *Pat and Mike have moved to a new locality*, neighborhood, region

distrust verb suspect, discredit, doubt, disbelieve ☆ **trust**

disturb verb annoy, bother, disquiet, unsettle, upset, confuse ☆ **calm**

dither verb waver, hesitate, falter, oscillate

dive verb plunge, pitch, swoop, descend, drop

diverse adjective different, various, dissimilar, numerous, separate ☆ **identical**

divert verb 1 alter, change, deflect 2 entertain, gratify

divest verb disrobe, undress, strip

divide verb separate, dissect, part, divorce, distribute, apportion, split, ☆ **join**

division noun portion, fragment, section, compartment, department

divorce verb annual, cancel, separate, divide, part, split up

divulge verb betray, disclose, tell, announce, broadcast, uncover

dizzy adjective giddy, confused, shaky, wobbling, muddled, staggering

do verb 1 carry out, perform, act 2 be adequate, suffice

do away with verb destroy, abolish, eliminate, kill

do up verb fasten, tie, fix

docile adjective amenable, tame, meek, orderly, manageable ☆ **uncooperative**

doctrine noun article, belief, creed, dogma, teaching

document noun paper, deed, certificate, form

dodge verb avoid, parry, duck, elude, fend off

dogged adjective obstinate, morose, sullen, persistent, steadfast ☆ **docile**

doleful adjective dismal, woebegone, depressing, rueful, sad ▶ *gloomy* ☆ **merry**

domestic 1 adjective homey, household *The children always help with the household chores*, family, internal 2 domesticated, tame

dominant adjective masterful, superior, supreme, prevalent ☆ **subordinate**

dominate verb rule, control, direct, tyrannize, overbear ☆ **yield**

donation noun gift, present, contribution

doom noun judgment, fate, verdict, destiny, destruction

door noun entrance, doorway, gate, gateway, portal

dose noun draft, potion, quantity, amount

doubt verb hesitate, waver, demur, suspect, mistrust, be dubious ☆ **trust**

doubtful adjective suspicious, dubious, indefinite, uncertain, unclear ☆ **certain**

dour adjective austere, dreary, grim, hard, severe ☆ **cheery**

dowdy adjective dull, plain, dingy, frumpish ▶ *shabby* ☆ **elegant**

downcast adjective crestfallen, downhearted, dejected ▶ *miserable* ☆ **happy**

downfall noun ruin, overthrow, misfortune, disgrace, failure

downright adjective blunt, candid, absolute, forthright, straightforward

doze verb snooze, slumber, sleep, nod off, drowse

drab adjective colorless, cheerless, dull, gloomy, gray
▶ *dreary* ★ bright

draft verb sketch, outline, draw, design, plan

drag verb draw, pull, haul, tug, tow, lug

drain 1 verb draw, strain, drip, percolate, empty, dry, drink up 2 noun conduit, sewer, pipe

dramatic adjective theatrical, exciting, surprising, sensational ★ ordinary

drape verb hang, suspend, droop, cover

drastic adjective extreme, dire, desperate, harsh, radical ★ mild

draw verb 1 pull, tug, drag, haul 2 sketch, design, depict, portray

drawback noun weakness, shortcoming, failing, defect, handicap ★ advantage

dread noun fear, terror, horror, alarm, awe, dismay
▶ *fright* ★ confidence

dreadful adjective fearful, terrible, horrible, alarming
▶ *awful* ★ comforting

dream noun trance, vision, fancy, reverie, fantasy, illusion

dreary adjective dingy, gloomy, somber, cheerless
▶ *dismal* ★ bright

drench verb saturate, soak, steep, flood

dress 1 noun clothing, vestments, costume, grab, apparel, attire 2 verb wear, put on, don

dress up verb playact, don costumes

drift verb float, flow, wander, stray, meander
The little stream meandered through lush countryside

drill 1 verb teach, exercise, train, discipline
2 bore, penetrate, pierce

drink verb imbibe, swallow, absorb, quaff, sip

drip verb drop, ooze, percolate, drizzle, trickle

drive verb 1 make, compel, force, oblige, prod, goad
2 propel, direct, operate, actuate

drivel noun nonsense, babble, twaddle, bunkum, gibberish

drizzle verb dribble, mizzle, shower, spit ▶ *rain*

droll adjective whimsical, comical, comic
▶ *funny*

droop verb flag, sink, decline, languish, drop, bend, wilt

drop 1 verb fall, sink, dip, plunge, plummet
2 noun droplet, globule, drip

drown verb sink, immerse, swamp, submerge, extinguish

drowsy adjective sleepy, somnolent, dazed, tired

drudge verb toil, labor, struggle, plod, slave

drug verb dope, deaden, sedate, stupefy, poison

dry adjective 1 arid, parched, moistureless, dried up
★ wet 2 uninteresting, boring, tedious, prosaic, dull

dubious adjective suspicious, fishy, suspect, untrustworthy ▶ *doubtful* ★ trustworthy

duck 1 noun waterfowl 2 verb plunge, submerge, dip, dodge, lurch

due adjective 1 owing, unpaid, payable 2 just, fair, proper 3 scheduled, expected DEW, DO

duel noun combat, contest, battle, swordplay

duffer noun blunderer, bungler, booby, dolt

dull adjective 1 stupid, stolid, obtuse, dim-witted
2 blunt, not sharp 3 boring, uninteresting, tedious

dumb 1 adjective silent, speechless, mute 2 foolish, stupid ▶ *dull* ★ intelligent

dummy 1 noun mannequin, puppet, doll 2 noun blockhead, dimwit 3 adjective artificial, fake, false

dump verb deposit, ditch, empty, throw away

dunce noun dimwit, dolt, blockhead, duffer, ignoramus
★ genius

dungeon noun cell, prison, jail, vault

dupe verb cheat, defraud, deceive, outwit

duplicate noun copy, facsimile, replica, reproduction

durable adjective lasting, enduring, permanent, stable, reliable ★ fragile

dusk noun twilight, nightfall, evening, gloaming
★ dawn

dusty adjective grimy, dirty, filthy, grubby ★ polished

duty noun 1 obligation, responsibility, allegiance, trust, task 2 impost, tax, excise

dwell verb stop, stay, rest, linger, tarry, live, reside

dwell on verb emphasize, linger over, harp on

dwindle verb diminish, decrease, decline, waste, shrink, become smaller ★ increase

dye noun pigment, coloring matter, color, stain, tint DIE

Ee

eager adjective avid, keen, ambitious, ardent, zealous
▶ *enthusiastic* ✶ **indifferent**

early adjective advanced, forward, soon ✶ **late**

earn verb make money, deserve, merit, rate, win, acquire ✶ **spend** URN

earnest adjective serious, sincere, determined, eager, zealous ✶ **flippant**

earth noun **1** soil, dust, dry land **2** world, globe, sphere, our planet

ease noun **1** calm, repose, rest, quiet, peace **2** dexterity, deftness ✶ **difficulty**

easy adjective effortless, smooth, simple, practicable ✶ **difficult**

eat verb consume, dine, chew, swallow, gorge

ebb verb flow back, fall back, recede, decline, wane ✶ **flow**

eccentric adjective queer, strange, odd, erratic, whimsical ▶ *peculiar* ✶ **normal**

echo verb vibrate, reverberate, imitate

economical adjective moderate, reasonable, frugal ▶ *thrifty* ✶ **expensive**

ecstasy noun joy, happiness, delight, elation ▶ *bliss* ✶ **torment**

edge noun border, rim, brink, fringe, margin, tip ▶ *end*

edible adjective eatable, comestible, safe, wholesome ✶ **inedible**

edit verb revise, correct, adapt, censor, publish

educate verb instruct, teach, tutor, coach, train

educated adjective learned, cultured, erudite, literate, well-bred ✶ **ignorant**

eerie adjective weird, unearthly, uncanny, awesome

effect **1** noun outcome *What was the outcome of your interview?* end, result **2** verb cause, make, bring about, accomplish

effective adjective operative, serviceable, competent ✶ **useless**

efficient adjective competent, proficient, able ▶ *effective* ✶ **inefficient**

Eating verbs

breakfast
chew chomp consume
devour dig in dine drink
eat eat up
feast feed finish off
gobble gorge gulp guzzle
imbibe
lap up lunch
masticate munch
nibble nosh
partake peck at pick at
quaff
relish
sample savor set to sip slurp
snack swallow sup swig swill
taste tuck in
wash down wine and dine
wolf down

effort noun exertion, toil, labor, accomplishment ▶ *feat*

eject verb drive out, force out, expel, evict, oust, discharge

elaborate adjective complex, elegant, ornate, intricate ★ simple

elated adjective excited, gleeful, joyous, overjoyed ▶ *pleased* ★ downcast

elderly adjective old, aged, ancient ★ youthful

elect verb choose, determine, vote, select, pick

elegant adjective redefined, luxurious, polished, classical ▶ *graceful* ★ inelegant

elementary adjective easy, effortless, basic, clear ▶ *simple* ★ complex

elevate verb raise, erect, hoist, upraise ▶ *lift* ★ lower

eligible adjective qualified, suitable, acceptable, proper ▶ *fit* ★ unfit

eliminate verb do away with, abolish *The government has abolished many old laws*, exterminate, erase, delete ★ keep

elude verb evade, avoid, depart, dodge, escape

embarrass verb abash, confuse, disconcert, fluster, shame

emblem noun badge, mark, brand, sign, crest, device

embrace verb 1 hug, squeeze, cuddle, caress, hold 2 include *The census figures include all households*, encompass, enclose

emerge verb come out, exit, appear, arise, turn up ★ disappear

emergency noun crises, danger, extremity, predicament ▶ *plight*

eminent adjective famous, noted, renowned, well-known, esteemed ▶ *important* ★ unknown

emit verb give off, belch, radiate, discharge, eject, vent ★ absorb

emotion noun sentiment, feeling, fervor, passion

emotional adjective affected, sensitive, responsive, temperamental ★ cold

emphasize verb accentuate, accent, intensify ▶ *stress* ★ understate

employ verb engage, hire, retain, apply, adopt ▶ *use*

employee noun worker, staff member, jobholder

empty 1 adjective bare, barren, vacant *That house has been vacant for months*, hollow, unoccupied ★ full 2 verb discharge, drain, unload, pour out ★ fill

enchant verb enthrall, bewitch, delight, gratify ▶ *charm* ★ bore

enclose verb surround, encircle, encompass, contain, include ★ open

encounter verb come upon, meet, experience, face

encourage verb cheer, hearten, console, comfort, support ▶ *urge* ★ dissuade

encroach verb intrude, transgress, overstep, trespass, infringe

end 1 noun conclusion, finish, limit, boundary *This river marks the boundary of the county* 2 verb complete, close, terminate ▶ *finish* ★ start

endanger verb hazard, imperil, jeopardize ▶ *risk* ★ protect

endeavor verb aspire, aim, strive, struggle, try ▶ *aim*

endless adjective ceaseless, continuous, everlasting, limitless

endorse verb undersign, uphold, support, guarantee, vouch for ★ disapprove

endow verb settle upon, invest, award, bequeath, provide ▶ *bestow* ★ divest

endowed adjective talented, gifted, enhanced

endure verb bear, tolerate, suffer, go through, experience, cope with

enemy noun foe, adversary, rival, antagonist, opponent ★ friend

energetic adjective dynamic, lively, vigorous, brisk ▶ *active* ★ sluggish

energy noun vigor, endurance, stamina, vitality, force, power

enforce verb apply, administer, carry out

engage verb 1 employ, hire, charter, rent 2 occupy *That new book has occupied my mind for weeks*, oblige, operate 3 pledge, betroth

engine noun machine, device, motor, turbine, appliance

engrave verb etch, stipple, incise, sculpture, carve, chisel

engrossed adjective absorbed, fascinated, enthralled ★ bored

A
B
C
D
E
F
G
H
I
J
K
L
M
N
O
P
Q
R
S
T
U
V
W
X
Y
Z

enhance verb intensify, strengthen, amplify, improve
☆ decrease

enigma noun riddle, puzzle, cryptogram, mystery, problem

enjoy verb like, be fond of, delight in, appreciate, savor
▶ *relish* ☆ detest

enjoyable adjective likable, amusing, delicious
▶ *agreeable* ☆ disagreeable

enlarge verb amplify, make bigger, expand, extend, magnify, increase, broaden ▶ *swell* ☆ shrink

enlighten verb inform, teach, explain to, educate, instruct ☆ confuse

enlist verb conscript, employ, engage, muster, sign up, volunteer

enmity noun animosity, acrimony, bitterness, hostility, antagonism, antipathy ▶ *hatred* ☆ friendship

enormous adjective immense, vast, tremendous, massive ▶ *huge* ☆ tiny

enough adjective sufficient, adequate, ample, plenty
☆ insufficient

enrage verb aggravate, incite, incense, infuriate
▶ *anger* ☆ soothe

enrich verb decorate, embellish, adorn, improve
☆ impoverish

enroll verb sign up, enlist, register, accept, admit
☆ reject

enslave verb bind, conquer, dominate, overpower, yoke ☆ free

ensue verb develop, follow, result, arise ▶ *happen*
☆ precede

ensure verb confirm, guarantee, insure, protect, secure

entangle verb tangle, snarl, ensnare, complicate
▶ *bewilder* ☆ extricate

enter verb go in, arrive, enroll, invade, commence, penetrate ☆ leave

enterprise noun endeavor, adventure, undertaking, concern, establishment

entertain verb amuse, charm, cheer, please, divert, beguile ☆ bore

enthrall verb captivate, charm, entrance, fascinate
☆ bore

enthusiasm noun fervor, ardor, interest, hobby, passion, eagerness

entice verb attract, beguile, coax, lead on, wheedle

entire adjective complete, intact, total, whole, full
☆ partial

entirely adjective absolutely, wholly, utterly *Our old dog came here, utterly tired and exhausted*, altogether
☆ partially

entitle verb 1 allow, authorize, empower *As president, I am empowered to sign this document*, enable 2 call, christen, term, name

entrance 1 noun (*en*-trance) way in, access *There is an access to the garden on the far side*, doorway, gate, opening 2 verb (en-*trance*) bewitch, captivate, charm ☆ repel

entreat verb beg, beseech, implore, ask

entry noun access, admission, admittance ▶ *entrance*
☆ exit

envelop verb wrap, wind, roll, cloak, conceal, enfold

envious adjective jealous, grudging, covetous *Arlene cast a covetous eye at my new jacket*, resentful
☆ content

environment noun surroundings, neighborhood, vicinity, background

envy verb covet, grudge, desire, crave, resent

episode noun occasion, affair, circumstance, happening, installment

equal adjective 1 matching, like, alike, same ☆ different 2 fit *I'm not sure if Joe is really fit for this job*

equip verb furnish, provide, supply, fit out, rig

equipment noun stores, supplies, outfit, tackle *When we arrived at the lake, Sam realized that he'd left his fishing tackle behind*, gear

equivalent adjective equal, comparable, alike, similar, interchangeable ☆ unlike

era noun epoch, age, generation, period, time

eradicate verb uproot, weed out, remove, stamp out
▶ *abolish*

erase verb cancel, rub out, obliterate, eliminate
▶ *delete* ☆ mark

erect 1 adjective upright, upstanding, rigid *The tent had a rigid metal frame* ☆ relaxed 2 verb build, construct, put up ☆ demolish

err verb be mistaken, blunder, go astray, mistake, misjudge, sin

errand noun mission, assignment, duty, job ▶ *task*

erratic adjective eccentric, irregular, unstable, unreliable ★ stable

erroneous adjective untrue, false, faulty, inaccurate ▶ *wrong* ★ correct

error noun mistake, fault, flaw, fallacy, untruth ▶ *blunder* ★ truth

erupt verb blow up, explode, burst, vent ▶ *discharge*

escape verb break free, get away, dodge, elude, evade ▶ *flee* ★ capture

escort 1 noun (*es*-cort) guard, conductor, aide, attendant, procession 2 verb (es-*cort*) accompany, conduct

especially adverb chiefly, principally, notably

essay noun 1 effort, trial 2 theme, manuscript, composition *Whoever writes the best composition gets a prize*

essence noun 1 extract, juice, perfume 2 substance *He spoke well, but there was no substance to his speech*, core, pith, character

essential adjective necessary, needed, vital, requisite ★ superfluous

establish verb situate, place, station, found, organize, set up ★ upset

estate noun property, land, fortune, inheritance

esteem verb honor, respect, admire ▶ *like* ★ dislike

estimate verb consider, calculate, figure, assess, reckon

estrange verb alienate, antagonize, separate ★ unite

eternal adjective endless, ceaseless, forever, immortal, undying ★ temporary

evacuate verb leave, desert, quit ▶ *abandon* ★ occupy

evade verb elude, avoid, get away from, escape from ★ face

evaporate verb vanish, dissolve, disappear, condense, dry up

even adjective 1 smooth, plane, flat, flush 2 balanced, equal ★ uneven 3 yet, still

evening noun eve, eventide, sunset ▶ *dusk* ★ morning

event noun occurrence, incident, happening

ever adverb always, evermore, perpetually, forever ★ never

everlasting adjective continual, endless, permanent, lasting ★ temporary

everyday adjective common, frequent, daily, familiar ★ occasional

everything noun all, the whole, the lot

evict verb expel, eject, cast out, remove, kick out

evidence noun appearance, proof, sign, token, testimony

evident adjective obvious, apparent, plain, visible, conspicuous ★ obscure

evil verb wicked, sinister, wrong, bad, hurtful, sinful ★ good

exact adjective accurate, precise, definite, correct ▶ *right* ★ inexact

exaggerate verb magnify, overstate, overestimate, amplify ★ minimize

examine verb check, inspect, scrutinize, test, quiz, question

example noun case, sample, specimen, pattern, model, illustration

exasperate verb provoke, anger, annoy, aggravate ★ soothe

excavate verb mine, quarry, shovel, dig up, discover, unearth ★ bury

exceed verb excel, surpass, better, beat, outstrip

excel verb outdo ▶ *exceed*

excellent adjective admirable, good, superb, exquisite ▶ *splendid* ★ inferior

except preposition with the exception of, barring, save, saving, omitting

exceptional adjective unique, unusual, rare *Margaret has a rare gift for the piano*, uncommon ★ common

excess noun too much, extreme, glut, extravagance, extreme ▶ *surplus* ★ scarcity

exchange verb trade, barter, swap, convert, change

excite verb inflame, inspire, provoke, rouse, thrill ★ quell

excited adjective ablaze, wild, ecstatic, frantic, thrilled ★ bored

exclaim verb state, say, utter, ejaculate, declare, cry out

exclude verb bar, shut out, prevent, boycott, forbid, leave out ☆ **include**

exclusive adjective only, personal, choice, particular, special ☆ **inclusive**

excuse verb forgive, pardon, absolve, exempt, release ☆ **accuse**

execute verb 1 accomplish, do, carry out *The work was carried out just as I had expected*, achieve 2 put to death, hang

exempt verb excuse, release, discharge, relieve, exonerate

exercise 1 noun performance, lesson, lecture, training 2 verb apply, train, practice *We have been practicing tennis for months*

exert verb apply, exercise, strain, struggle, toil

exhale verb breathe out, expel, expire ☆ **inhale**

exhaust 1 verb use up *We have used up all the butter*, consume, deplete, empty 2 overtire, fatigue, weaken

exhibition noun spectacle, show, fair, pageant, display

exhilarate verb invigorate, animate, stimulate, thrill ☆ **discourage**

exile verb deport, banish, relegate, transport, dismiss

exist verb be, live, breathe, subsist, stand

exit noun way out, outlet, egress, door

expand verb inflate, spread, dilate, extend, amplify ▷ *swell* ☆ **contract**

expansive adjective affable, genial, friendly, open, comprehensive

expect verb look out for, anticipate, assume, foresee, contemplate

expedition noun 1 outing, excursion, exploration, quest *As a child, I spent long hours in the library in the quest for knowledge* 2 speed, dispatch, alacrity

expel verb evict, eject, discharge, throw out ☆ **admit**

expend verb spend, lay out, waste, consume, use up ▷ *exhaust* ☆ **save**

expensive adjective costly, high-priced, valuable, rich ☆ **cheap**

experience 1 noun training, practice, wisdom, knowledge 2 verb encounter, try, undergo, endure

experiment noun trial, test, check, venture

expert noun specialist, master, authority, professional ☆ **novice**

expire verb 1 breathe out, exhale 2 die, lapse *The lease on this house will lapse at the end of the year*, run out ☆ **begin**

explain verb elucidate, spell out, define, expound, teach ☆ **mystify**

explanation noun definition, outline, answer, meaning

explode verb detonate, blow up, go off, burst, discharge

exploit 1 noun deed, feat, act, stunt 2 verb take advantage of, profit by

export verb ship, send out, send abroad

expose verb show, reveal, exhibit, present, lay bare, betray ☆ **cover**

express 1 verb phrase, voice, put into words, utter 2 verb squeeze out 3 adjective speedy, fast

expression noun 1 phrase, idiom, sentence, statement 2 look, countenance, appearance

exquisite adjective dainty, subtle, fine, refined ▷ *beautiful* ☆ **coarse**

extend verb stretch, reach, lengthen ▷ *expand* ☆ **shorten**

extent noun breadth, expanse, width, bulk, mass, reach, duration

exterior 1 noun outside, surface 2 adjective external, outer, outdoor ☆ **interior**

extinct adjective defunct, dead, exterminated ☆ **living**

extinguish verb put out, blow out, abolish, destroy, quench ☆ **establish**

extract verb take out, select, remove, withdraw ☆ **insert**

extraordinary adjective unusual, incredible, strange, uncommon, marvelous ☆ **common**

extravagant adjective wasteful, reckless, prodigal, lavish ☆ **stingy**

extreme adjective 1 excessive, outrageous, intense ☆ **moderate** 2 farthest, final, remote, furthest

extricate verb loose, loosen, remove, retrieve, pull out

exultant adjective rejoicing, jubilant, joyous, triumphant ▷ *elated* ☆ **depressed**

Ff

fable noun myth, legend, story, fantasy ⭐ fact

fabric noun cloth, textile, material

fabulous adjective imaginary, legendary *Many tales have been told about the legendary deeds of Robin Hood*, mythical, marvelous ▷ *wonderful*

face 1 noun countenance, visage 2 noun front, frontage, facade *The original facade was kept when the building was renovated* 3 verb confront, be opposite

facetious adjective frivolous, jocular, humorous, witty, comical ▷ *funny* ⭐ serious

facility noun ease, readiness, quickness, adroitness, knack

facsimile noun replica, copy, repro, photocopy

fact noun truth, deed, occurrence, event, reality, actuality ⭐ fiction

factory noun plant, mill, works, shop

factual adjective true, actual, accurate, correct ▷ *real* ⭐ false

fad noun craze, fashion, passion, desire, mania *My sister has a mania for teddy bears*, vogue

fade verb discolor, bleach, dwindle, dim

fail verb collapse, fall, miss, trip, lose, flop ⭐ succeed

failing noun frailty, weakness, fault, flaw ▷ *defect*

failure noun collapse, crash, fiasco, downfall ⭐ success

faint 1 adjective indistinct *The writing was so indistinct that we could hardly read it*, soft low, dim, feeble 2 verb swoon, pass out, collapse FEINT

fair adjective 1 just, equal, reasonable ⭐ unfair 2 mediocre *He was not a good piano player, just mediocre*, average, moderate 3 blond, light-skinned, beautiful

faith noun trust, confidence, belief, fidelity, creed

faithful adjective 1 loyal, constant, staunch, true ⭐ faithless 2 accurate, dependable *My watch is very dependable; it keeps accurate time* ⭐ inaccurate

faithless adjective false, unfaithful, untrue ⭐ faithful

fake adjective false, fictitious, pretended ▷ *bogus* ⭐ genuine

fall verb 1 fall down, stumble, drop 2 decline, dwindle *My mother's investment had dwindled and was worthless*, lower ⭐ rise

fall down verb stumble, lose one's balance

fall through verb collapse, fail, founder *The family business had foundered during the recession*

fallacy noun flaw, fault, mistake, illusion, deception

false adjective 1 untrue, counterfeit, fake, inaccurate 2 dishonest, disloyal ⭐ reliable

falsehood noun lie, fiction, fable, fabrication, untruth, fib ⭐ truth

falter verb reel, totter, stumble, waver, tremble

fame noun glory, distinction, honor, eminence, renown

familiar 1 adjective common, frequent, well-known 2 intimate *Dan and Mary are intimate friends of mine*, close, dear

famine noun scarcity, hunger, shortage, starvation

famished adjective hungry, starving, ravenous

famous adjective famed, well-known, celebrated, legendary *My grandmother was very attractive; her beauty was legendary*, notorious ⭐ unknown

fan verb ventilate, cool, blow, stimulate

fanatic noun enthusiast, zealot, follower, fan

fanciful adjective romantic, fantastic, imaginary, unreal ⭐ ordinary

fancy 1 adjective decorative, beautiful, ornamental 2 verb desire, hanker after *I had been hankering after a sea cruise all year*, yearn

fantastic adjective strange, bizarre, unfamiliar, romantic ▷ *fanciful* ⭐ ordinary

far adjective distant, faraway, remote ⭐ near

fare 1 verb manage *I managed fairly well while my parents were away*, get along, happen 2 noun charge, cost, fee 3 noun food, meals, menu

farewell *interjection* goodbye, so long, adieu *We bade our hosts adieu as we drove off*

farm 1 verb cultivate, raise, grow 2 noun farmstead, homestead, ranch, holding *We owned a small holding of land in the west*

fascinate verb bewitch, beguile, enthrall, engross ⭐ bore

fashion 1 noun style, fad, mode, manner 2 verb form, carve, sculpt, devise

A B C C D E F G H I J K L M N O P Q R S T U V W X Y Z

fast 1 adjective rapid, quick, speedy, brisk   2 verb starve, famish, go hungry

fasten verb fix, tie, attach, bind, hitch, truss
☆ **unfasten**

fat 1 adjective stout, corpulent *Uncle Harry was a corpulent old man* ▸ *plump* ☆ **thin**   2 noun grease, oil, tallow, shortening

fatal adjective deadly, lethal, destructive, mortal
☆ **harmless**

fate noun fortune, destiny, future, lot, portion

fathom verb unravel, understand, follow, comprehend

fatigue 1 noun tiredness, weariness   2 verb tire, exhaust, languish *The survivors of the shipwreck languished in the boat*

fault noun 1 defect, flaw, imperfection   2 blame, responsibility, error

faulty adjective imperfect, defective, unreliable, unsound, broken   ☆ **perfect**

favor 1 noun kindness, courtesy, benefit   2 verb indulge, prefer, approve   ☆ **disapprove**

favorite 1 noun choice, darling, preference
2 adjective best-liked, chosen, preferred

fawn verb crouch, crawl, grovel FAUN

fear 1 noun fright, alarm, terror, panic, shock
☆ **courage**   2 verb dread, be afraid, doubt

fearful adjective timid, anxious, alarmed, worried
▸ *afraid*   ☆ **courageous**

fearless adjective gallant, courageous, daring, valiant
My sick mother made a valiant effort to keep working
▸ *brave*   ☆ **timid**

feast noun banquet, repast, dinner

feat noun deed, exploit, achievement, performance, stunt FEET

feature noun mark, peculiarity, distinction, characteristic

fee noun charge, commission, cost

feeble adjective frail, faint, flimsy, puny   ▸ *weak*
☆ **strong**

feed verb nourish, sustain, foster, nurture *These plants must be nurtured if they are going to survive*

feel verb touch, handle, perceive, comprehend, know, suffer

feign verb fake, pretend, act, sham FAIN

feint noun bluff, pretense, dodge, deception FAINT

fellow noun companion, comrade, associate, colleague

female adjective feminine, womanly, girlish, maidenly
☆ **male**

fence 1 noun barrier, paling, barricade   2 verb dodge, evade, parry *The sudden attack was parried by the defenders*, duel

ferocious adjective fierce, savage, brutal, grim, vicious
☆ **gentle**

fertile adjective fruitful, productive, rich, abundant
☆ **barren**

fervent adjective warm, passionate, enthusiastic, zealous ▸ *ardent*

festival noun celebration, carnival, fete, jubilee

festive adjective convivial, jovial, sociable, gleeful, cordial ☆ **somber**

fetch verb bear, bring, carry, deliver, convey

fete noun bazaar, carnival, fair, festival

fetter verb manacle, handcuff, shackle, restrain

feud noun dispute, grudge, conflict, discord
☆ **harmony**

fever noun illness, infection, passion, excitement, heat, ecstasy

few adjective scant, scanty, meager, paltry, not many

fiasco noun washout, calamity, disaster, failure

fib noun lie, falsehood, untruth

fickle adjective unstable, changeable, faithless, disloyal
☆ **constant**

fiction noun stories, fable, myth, legend, invention
☆ **fact**

fidelity noun faithfulness, loyalty, allegiance *I owe allegiance to my family and my country* ☆ **treachery**

fidget verb be nervous, fret, fuss, jiggle, squirm

field noun farmland, grassland, green, verdure, meadow, prairie

fiend noun devil, demon, imp, beast, brute

fiendish adjective atrocious, cruel, devilish, diabolical

fierce adjective barbarous, cruel, brutal, merciless
▸ *savage* ☆ **gentle**

fiery adjective passionate, inflamed, excitable, flaming
☆ **impassive**

fight noun & verb conflict, argument, encounter, combat, contest, battle

figure 1 noun symbol, character, numeral 2 noun form, shape, model 3 verb calculate, reckon *Bella has reckoned the amount correctly*

filch verb steal, thieve, sneak, purloin *Someone has purloined the letters from our mailbox*

file 1 verb scrape, grind, grate, rasp 2 noun binder, case, folder

fill verb load, pack, cram, replenish, occupy ★ empty

filter verb sieve, sift, refine, clarify, screen, percolate PHILTER

filth noun impurity, dirt, soil, slime, smut, grime, squalor, muck ★ purity

filthy adjective unclean, impure, nasty, foul ▶ *dirty* ★ pure

final adjective terminal, closing, ultimate, conclusive ▶ *last*

find verb discover, achieve, locate, obtain, perceive, meet with *Our plans met with the committee's approval* ★ lose FINED

fine 1 adjective thin, minute, smooth, slender 2 adjective excellent, sharp, keen, acute 3 noun forfeit, penalty

finesse noun skill, competence, deftness

finger 1 verb feel, grope, handle, touch 2 noun digit, thumb, pinkie

finish verb accomplish, complete, close, conclude ▶ *end* ★ begin

fire 1 noun blaze, conflagration, heat 2 verb ignite, light, discharge, shoot

firm 1 adjective stable, steady, solid, substantial 2 noun company, business

first adjective beginning, earliest, initial, chief, principal

fishy adjective suspicious, dubious, doubtful ★ honest

fissure noun breach, cleft, crack, cranny FISHER

fit adjective 1 apt, suitable, fitting, able 2 trim, hale, healthy, sturdy

fitting adjective proper, suitable, appropriate, correct ★ unsuitable

fix 1 verb repair, mend, attach, fasten 2 noun predicament, jam, pickle, plight *After the earthquake, the town was in a desperate plight*

flabby adjective baggy, drooping, feeble, sagging, slack

flag 1 verb droop, languish, dwindle, fail 2 noun banner, ensign, colors *The regimental colors were flying at half-mast*

Flags

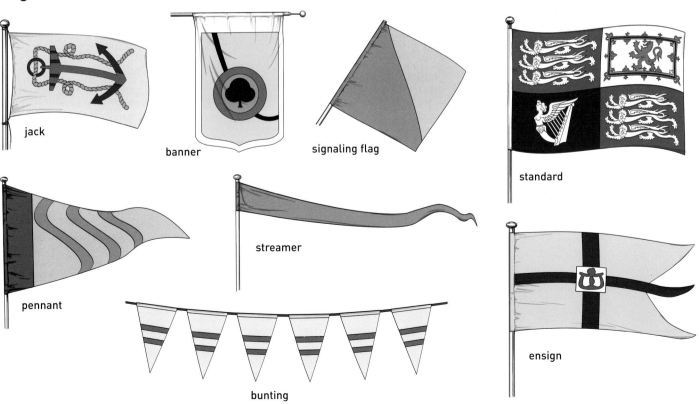

jack

banner

signaling flag

standard

pennant

streamer

ensign

bunting

221

flagrant adjective blatant, bold, brazen, arrant
⭐ secret

flair noun knack, talent, faculty, ability, gift FLARE

flame noun fire, blaze, radiance

flap verb agitate, flutter, wave, swing, dangle

flare 1 verb blaze, burn, glare, flash, glow 2 noun signal, beacon FLAIR

flash verb gleam, glimmer, sparkle, twinkle, scintillate

flat 1 adjective level, smooth, even, horizontal 2 noun apartment, chambers

flatter verb blandish, toady, soft-soap, butter up, curry favor *He gives me presents but only to curry favor with me*
⭐ criticize

flavor noun taste, savor, tang, aroma, quality

flaw noun fault, defect, blemish, mark, weakness

flawless adjective perfect, immaculate, faultless, sound ⭐ imperfect

flee verb escape, abscond, run away, bolt, vanish
⭐ stay FLEA

fleet 1 adjective rapid, speedy, quick, nimble ▸ *swift*
⭐ slow 2 noun navy, armada, flotilla *A flotilla of yachts sailed up the river*

fleeting adjective passing, brief, momentary, temporary ⭐ lasting

flexible adjective pliant, pliable, supple, elastic

flicker verb blaze, glitter, flare, burn, sparkle

flimsy adjective slight, meager, fragile, trivial, rickety, weak, feeble ⭐ sturdy

flinch verb cower, cringe, shrink, wince *I had twisted my ankle and winced with pain as I climbed the hill*

fling verb throw, pitch, cast, heave ▸ *hurl*

flippant adjective saucy, pert, brash, impudent, glib
⭐ earnest

float verb drift, glide, hover, sail, swim

flock noun herd, drove, crush, group

flog verb beat, chastise, flay, lash, spank

flood verb deluge, engulf, inundate *The town was inundated when the river overflowed*, drown, swamp

floor noun deck, base, bottom, platform, level, story

flop verb flap, fall, drop, droop, fall flat

florid adjective ruddy, flushed, red, ornate ⭐ pale

flounce verb bounce, fling, jerk, spring, bob

flounder 1 verb bungle, fail, falter, fumble 2 noun flatfish

flour noun meal, bran, farina FLOWER

flourish verb 1 shake, brandish, flaunt 2 blossom, bloom, prosper ▸ *thrive*

flow verb run, stream, glide, sweep, swirl ▸ *gush* FLOE

flower noun & verb blossom, bloom, bud FLOUR

fluent adjective vocal, facile, articulate *Sally is very articulate and has a great command of language*, flowing, fluid

fluid adjective watery, flowing, liquid, runny
⭐ solid

flummox verb baffle, confuse, fluster, confound ▸ *bewilder* ⭐ enlighten

flush 1 verb glow, bloom, blush 2 verb douse, drench, rinse 3 adjective level, even

fluster verb bother, confuse, perturb ▸ *fuss* ⭐ calm

flutter verb wave, flap, flop, flitter, hover, flit

fly 1 verb take flight, glide, soar, float 2 verb escape, hasten 3 noun winged insect

foam noun froth, scum, lather, suds, surf

foe noun enemy, opponent, rival, adversary ⭐ friend

fog noun mist, vapor, haze, cloud

foil 1 verb defeat, overcome, elude 2 noun sheet metal, tin foil, film, flake

fold noun & verb crease, hem, seam, crimp, pleat FOALED

follow verb 1 pursue, succeed, come after 2 understand, catch on to

folly noun silliness, foolishness, absurdity, craziness ▸ *nonsense* ⭐ wisdom

fond adjective tender, loving, caring ▸ *affectionate* ⭐ hostile

fondle verb pet, stroke, cuddle, caress, coddle

food noun nourishment, nutriment, provender, provisions, fare

fool 1 noun idiot, dunce, clown, blockhead, simpleton 2 verb deceive, trick, swindle

foolhardy adjective reckless, impetuous, madcap ▸ *rush* ⭐ cautious

foolish adjective absurd, ridiculous, daft ▸ *silly* ⭐ wise

for *preposition* on behalf of, toward, because of ★ **against** fore, four

forbid *verb* bar, ban, prohibit, deter, hinder, prevent ★ **allow**

force 1 *noun* energy, strength, might, power 2 *verb* make, compel, coerce *You can't coerce me into doing what I don't want to do*, push

fore *adjective* first, front, leading FOR, FOUR

forecast *verb* foresee, predict, foretell, prophesy

foreign *adjective* alien, strange, remote, exotic, outlandish ★ **domestic**

foremost *adjective* chief, leading, principal, uppermost

forfeit *verb* abandon, give up, lose, relinquish, sacrifice ★ **reward**

forge *verb* 1 counterfeit, falsify, copy, imitate 2 construct, form, make, fashion

forgery *noun* fake, dud, counterfeit, imitation, phony

forget *verb* overlook, neglect, lose sight of ★ **remember**

forgive *verb* pardon, absolve, reprieve, let off, overlook ★ **blame**

forlorn *adjective* lonely, desolate, miserable, wretched ★ **hopeful**

form 1 *verb* make, fabricate, fashion, contrive, create 2 *noun* manner, fashion, style 3 *noun* shape, figure *I made a clay figure of a pirate*

formal *adjective* stiff, solemn, ceremonial, ritualistic, aloof ★ **informal**

former *adjective* earlier, previous, prior ★ **later**

formidable *adjective* awful, terrible, alarming, terrifying, serious ★ **trivial**

forsake *verb* abandon, give up, desert, discard, leave ▷ *quit* ★ **resume**

forth *adverb* ahead, forward, onward, outward

forthright *adjective* frank, candid, direct, bald, blunt ★ **devious**

forthwith *adverb* immediately, directly, at once, instantly ★ **soon**

fortify *verb* 1 strengthen, confirm, corroborate, hearten 2 garrison, protect, buttress *The old house was crumbling and the walls needed to be buttressed* ★ **weaken**

fortitude *noun* courage, endurance, bravery, composure ▷ *strength* ★ **cowardice**

fortunate *adjective* happy, felicitous, auspicious, rosy ▷ *lucky* ★ **unfortunate**

fortune *noun* 1 affluence, wealth, treasure 2 chance, destiny, fate

forward 1 *adverb* onward, forth, ahead, before 2 *adjective* progressive, bold, audacious ★ **modest** 3 *verb* advance, send, transmit

foster *verb* 1 help, promote, aid 2 care for, cherish, nurse

foul *adjective* mucky, nasty, filthy, dirty, murky ★ **fair** FOWL

found *verb* create, build, erect, establish

foundation *noun* establishment, base, basis, groundwork *You will pick up Spanish easily, since you already have the groundwork from your classes*

fountain *noun* spring, well, reservoir, source

fowl *noun* bird, chicken, poultry FOUL

foxy *adjective* crafty, slick, cunning, tricky ▷ *artful* ★ **naive**

fraction *noun* portion, part, division ▷ *fragment*

fracture *noun* break, cleft, crack, fissure, opening ▷ *split*

fragile *adjective* brittle, frail, delicate, dainty ▷ *flimsy* ★ **robust**

fragment *noun* portion, bit, chip, morsel, piece ▷ *fracture*

fragrance *noun* aroma, smell, odor ▷ *scent*

frail *adjective* weak, feeble, infirm ▷ *fragile*

frame *noun* framework, casing, shape, mount, chassis

frank *adjective* sincere, candid, open, honest, blunt ▷ *truthful* ★ **insincere**

frantic *adjective* excited, furious, distracted, wild, mad ▷ *frenzied* ★ **calm**

fraud *noun* deceit, fake, extortion, swindle ▷ *forgery*

fraudulent *adjective* sham, fake, counterfeit ▷ *bogus* ★ **genuine**

fray *noun* combat, contest, battle, brawl ▷ *rumpus*

freak *adjective* abnormal, bizarre *A snowstorm in the tropics would be bizarre*, odd, unusual ★ **common**

free 1 *adjective* unhindered, at liberty, liberated, unrestricted 2 *adjective* gratuitous, gratis, without cost 3 *verb* let loose, unleash, release

freeze *noun* ice, frost, refrigerate FREES, FRIEZE

frenzied adjective agitated, excited, furious, hysterical *Lisa became hysterical when she saw the house on fire* ▸ *frantic* ⋆ **placid**

frequent adjective repeated, numerous, recurrent, common ▸ *regular* ⋆ **rare**

frequently adverb often, many times, commonly ⋆ **rarely**

fresh adjective new, young, vigorous, blooming, recent, wholesome ⋆ **stale**

fret verb worry, harass, irritate, torment ▸ *vex* ⋆ **calm**

friction noun **1** rubbing, grating, contact, abrasion **2** ill-feeling, discord, dispute

friend noun companion, associate, ally, crony *On Saturdays, my father plays golf with some of his cronies*, pal ▸ *chum*

friendly adjective affable, amicable, kindly, cordial ▸ *genial* ⋆ **hostile**

friendship noun affection, fellowship, fondness, harmony ▸ *concord* ⋆ **enmity**

fright noun alarm, dread, dismay, terror ▸ *fear* ⋆ **calm**

frighten verb daunt, dismay, scare, alarm ▸ *terrify* ⋆ **reassure**

frightful adjective alarming, shocking, ghastly ▸ *horrible* ⋆ **pleasant**

frigid adjective cool, chilly, icy, frozen, wintry ⋆ **warm**

fringe noun edge, border, limits, outskirts

frisky adjective lively, spirited, playful, active ⋆ **quiet**

frivolous adjective frothy, facetious, flippant, foolish ▸ *trivial* ⋆ **serious**

frock noun robe, dress, gown, smock

frolic verb gambol, caper, frisk, sport

front noun fore, brow, forehead, face, facade, beginning ⋆ **back**

frontier noun border, boundary, edge, limit

frosty adjective chilly, frigid, frozen, freezing ▸ *cold* ⋆ **warm**

froth noun scum, bubbles ▸ *foam*

frown verb glower, grimace, glare ▸ *scowl* ⋆ **smile**

frugal adjective thrifty, economical, careful, sparing *We were poor in the old days and needed to be sparing with our money* ▸ *meager* ⋆ **wasteful**

fruitful adjective fertile, productive, flourishing ⋆ **barren**

fruitless adjective unprofitable, sterile, barren, pointless ⋆ **fruitful**

frustrate verb thwart, balk, foil, hinder, defeat ⋆ **fulfill**

fugitive noun escapee, runaway, deserter

fulfill verb perform, render, please, accomplish, achieve ⋆ **frustrate**

full adjective loaded, packed, laden, charged, abundant, complete ⋆ **empty**

fumble verb grope, spoil, mismanage, flail ▸ *bungle*

fun noun sport, frolic, gaiety, jollity, entertainment, amusement

function **1** noun service, purpose, activity **2** noun affair, party, gathering **3** verb act, operate, work

fund noun stock, supply, pool, store, treasury *The city treasury has cash surplus this year*, reserve

fundamental adjective basic, essential, primary, rudimentary ⋆ **unimportant**

funny adjective comical, droll, amusing, ridiculous ▸ *humorous* ⋆ **solemn**

furious adjective agitated, angry, fierce, intense ▸ *frantic* ⋆ **calm**

furnish verb **1** supply, provide, offer **2** equip

furrow noun groove, channel, hollow, seam, rib

further **1** adjective extra, more, other, supplementary **2** verb advanced, aid, hasten

furtive adjective secretive, sly, hidden ▸ *stealthy* ⋆ **open**

fury noun anger, frenzy, ferocity, passion ▸ *rage* ⋆ **calm**

fuse verb melt, smelt, combine, merge, solder, weld, integrate ▸ *join*

fuss noun stir, excitement, tumult, bustle, bother, commotion ▸ *ado* ⋆ **calm**

fussy adjective busy, faddish, fastidious, finicky, exacting ⋆ **plain**

futile adjective useless, in vain, hopeless *It was hopeless; the bag was too big for Leo to carry*, barren, forlorn, ineffective ⋆ **effective**

future adjective forthcoming, coming, impending, eventual

fuzzy adjective murky, foggy, misty, unclear

Gg

gain verb get, win, acquire, attain, profit

gale noun storm, wind, hurricane, tornado, cyclone

gallant adjective courageous, noble, chivalrous ▶ *brave*

gallop verb dash, run, career, rush

gamble verb bet, risk, wager, chance GAMBOL

gambol verb prance, romp, frisk, frolic ▶ *jump* GAMBLE

game noun 1 sport, pastime, contest, competition ★ **work** 2 quarry, prey

gang noun crew, team, troop, crowd, cluster, party

gap noun space, blank, hole, break, cranny, chink, opening, crack, interval

gape verb yawn, stare, gaze, gawk ▶ *look*

garbage noun trash, rubbish, refuse, waste, slop, litter

garden noun flower bed, vegetable patch, patio, park, yard

garment noun clothes, dress, attire, robe, costume ▶ *clothing*

garret noun attic, loft, cupola

gas noun vapor, fume, mist, smoke

gasp verb gulp, pant, choke ▶ *breathe*

gate noun door, portal, gateway GAIT

gather verb 1 collect, pick up, pick, draw, amass, assemble, flock, hoard, acquire ★ **disperse** 2 understand *I understand that you were picked as team captain*, assume, judge

gathering noun meeting, assembly, function, affair, company, collection

gaudy adjective flashy, cheap, tawdry, loud, showy

gaunt adjective thin, lean, skinny, spare ▶ *haggard* ★ **robust**

gauge 1 noun measure, meter, rule 2 verb judge, measure, estimate *We must estimate the number of beans in the jar*, probe GAGE

gaze verb stare, look, regard, contemplate

gear noun tackle, array, accessories, machinery, harness, equipment

gem noun jewel, stone, treasure

general adjective normal, usual, habitual, customary, total, whole ★ **local**

generous adjective free, liberal, kind ★ **selfish**

genial adjective cheerful, cheery, sunny, hearty, cordial, pleasant ▶ *jolly* ★ **cold**

genius noun brilliance, prowess, talent, power, skill, cleverness, brains ★ **stupidity**

genteel adjective refined, polished, civil, courteous, well-bred, polite, elegant ★ **boorish**

gentle adjective 1 easy, mild, soft, kind, moderate, tender, humane 2 gradual, faint, feeble, slight *The field had a slight slope that was perfect for sledding*

genuine adjective 1 real, authentic, true, sound 2 sincere, honest, candid, frank ★ **false**

germ noun microbe, seed, embryo, nucleus

gesture noun sign, signal, motion, nod, shrug, movement

get verb 1 acquire, obtain, gain, win, receive, secure, achieve, inherit ★ **forfeit** 2 understand, catch on *It took Johnny quite a while to catch on to what I meant*, fathom, figure out, learn

get up verb arise, awake, awaken

get rid of verb discard, reject, throw away, scrap

ghastly adjective shocking, hideous, horrible, fearful, terrible, frightful

ghost noun spook, spirit, specter, banshee, phantom, apparition

ghostly verb uncanny, haunted, eerie, weird

giant adjective mammoth, huge, colossal, enormous, tremendous, immense ▶ *big, gigantic* ★ **tiny**

gibber verb gabble, prattle, jabber

gibberish noun nonsense, drivel, garbage

gibe verb jeer, sneer, scoff, deride ▶ *taunt*

giddy adjective dizzy, whirling, reeling, unsteady, wild, reckless

gift noun 1 present, donation, bounty, boon 2 talent, skill *Her skill in painting was unbelievable*, ability, power

gigantic adjective stupendous, titanic, colossal ▶ *giant* ★ **minute**

giggle verb chuckle, chortle, cackle, snicker ▶ *laugh*

gingerly adverb carefully, daintily, warily, cautiously

girder noun rafter, joist, beam

girl noun maid, maiden, miss, damsel, young woman, lass, wench

girlish adjective maidenly, dainty, feminine

girth noun circumference, perimeter, fatness, breadth

gist noun essence, substance, kernel, nub, pith, significance

give verb **1** donate, grant, distribute, bestow **2** bend, yield *The wooden footbridge suddenly yielded under his weight and crashed into the stream*, relax, recede **3** produce, yield **4** pronounce, utter, emit ⭐ take

give back verb return, restore

give forth verb emit, send out, radiate

give in verb surrender, quit, yield

give off verb belch, emit, exude

give up verb surrender, give in, relinquish, hand over

giver noun donor, bestower, presenter

glad adjective joyful, joyous, delighted, pleased ▷ *happy* ⭐ sorry

gladden verb make happy, gratify, delight, elate ▷ *please* ⭐ grieve

gladly adverb freely, readily, cheerfully, willingly

glamour noun romance, interest, fascination, attraction, enchantment

glance **1** noun look, glimpse, peep **2** verb peer, notice **3** brush, shave, graze *Fortunately, she only grazed her knee*

glare **1** verb blaze, glow, flare, sparkle, dazzle **2** frown, glower, stare

glaring adjective **1** sparkling, dazzling **2** blatant, notorious, conspicuous

glass noun tumbler, goblet, cup, beaker, mirror, looking glass

glaze verb polish, gloss, burnish, varnish

gleam verb sparkle, glitter, flash, glisten, twinkle

glee noun jollity, gaiety, elation, triumph ▷ *happiness*

glib adjective fluent, slick, smooth, slippery, facile, talkative

glide verb slide, slither, slip, soar, sail, skate, skim, fly

glimmer verb sparkle, scintillate, flicker, glow, gleam

glimpse verb spy, spot, glance, view

glisten verb shine, glitter, glow, gleam

glitter verb gleam, sparkle, flash, glint, glisten, scintillate

gloat verb whoop, exult, crow, revel, triumph

globe noun ball, sphere, planet, earth, world

gloom noun darkness, gloaming, dusk, shadow, dimness, bleakness ⭐ light

gloomy adjective cheerless, black, dark, bleak, cloudy, overcast, dismal, dour, glum, melancholy ▷ *dreary* ⭐ happy

glorious adjective brilliant, lustrous, noble, exalted, renowned ▷ *splendid*

glory noun brilliance, radiance, pride ▷ *splendor*

gloss noun luster, sheen, shimmer, polish ▷ *glaze*

glossy adjective shiny, burnished, sleek, slick, polished

glow noun & verb glare, glitter, bloom, blush, flush, shine, gleam, twinkle

glower verb frown, stare, scowl, glare

glue **1** noun paste, gum, cement, mucilage, adhesive, rubber cement **2** verb stick, fasten

glum adjective sullen, sulky, morose, miserable, dejected, downcast ▷ *gloomy*

glut noun abundance, plenty, too much, surplus

glutton noun gorger, stuffer, crammer, pig, gormandizer, gourmand

gnash verb grind, chomp, bite, crunch

gnaw verb chew, nibble, bite, champ, consume

go verb **1** walk, pass, move, travel, depart, proceed **2** stretch, reach, extend *The prairie extended as far as the mountains*

go after verb pursue, chase, follow

go ahead verb progress, proceed, continue

go away verb leave, depart, vanish, disappear

go back verb return, resume, withdraw

go by verb pass, elapse, vanish

go in verb enter, advance, invade, penetrate

go in for verb enter, take part, participate, compete

go off verb explode, blow up, depart

go on verb continue, advance, proceed, move ahead, keep up

go up verb climb, mount, rise ▷ *ascend*

goad verb prod, incite, impel, drive, urge, sting, worry

goal noun target, ambition, aim, object, destination

gobble verb devour, gorge, swallow, gulp, bolt

goblin noun sprite, demon, gnome, elf

God noun the Creator, the Father, the Almighty, Allah, Jehovah, the Divinity, the Holy Spirit, King of Kings, the Supreme Being

godless adjective unholy, unclean, wicked, savage, profane ★ **righteous**

golden adjective excellent, precious, brilliant, bright

good adjective 1 excellent, admirable, fine 2 favorable *The calm weather provides favorable conditions for waterskiing*, advantageous, profitable 3 righteous, moral, true *He has always been a kind and true friend* 4 clever, skillful, expert 5 fit, proper, suited ★ **bad**

goodness noun excellence, merit, worth, honesty, kindness ▶ *virtue* ★ **evil**

goods noun wares, commodities, cargo, load, material, belongings

gorge 1 verb swallow, gulp, devour ▶ *eat* 2 noun canyon, glen, valley

gorgeous adjective beautiful, ravishing, stunning, superb, magnificent

gossip verb chat, chatter, prattle, tittle-tattle

gouge verb excavate, groove, dig out

govern verb rule, reign, manage, direct, guide, control, conduct, command

government noun rule, administration, supervision, parliament

governor noun director, manager, leader, chief, overseer, head of state

gown noun robe, dress, frock

grace noun elegance, refinement, polish, symmetry ▶ *beauty*

graceful adjective beautiful, lovely, shapely, refined ▶ *elegant*

gracious adjective amiable, kind, suave, urbane, affable, elegant ★ **churlish**

grade noun 1 class, rank, degree 2 slope, gradient, incline, slant

gradual adjective by degrees, step-by-step, continuous, little by little ★ **sudden**

graft 1 verb splice, insert, bud, plant 2 noun bribery, corruption

grain noun fiber, crumb, seed, particle, atom, bit, drop

grand adjective splendid, impressive, stately, magnificent, wonderful, superb

grandeur noun magnificence, splendor, majesty, lordliness

grant 1 noun bounty, award, subsidy 2 verb bestow, donate *We all donated money to the charity*, confer, give

grapple verb struggle, tussle, wrestle, seize, grasp, clutch

grasp verb 1 grip, seize, take, grab, hold 2 understand, comprehend

grasping adjective greedy, avaricious, covetous, miserly ★ **generous**

grate 1 verb rasp, file, jar, clash, rub, grind 2 annoy, irritate, vex 3 noun fireplace GREAT

grateful adjective thankful, appreciative, obliged, indebted

gratify verb delight, satisfy, please, content, enchant, indulge, favor ★ **displease**

gratitude noun thankfulness, appreciation, obligation

grave 1 adjective solemn, sober, momentous, dignified, majestic 2 essential, important *I have important news to tell you* 3 noun tomb, vault, shrine

gravity noun 1 seriousness, solemnity, importance, significance 2 force, gravitation, weight

graze verb 1 scrape, brush, shave, glance 2 browse, crop, bite GRAYS

grease noun fat, suet, tallow, oil

great adjective 1 large, considerable, bulky, huge, ample 2 important, elevated, noted *Here is a list of noted politicians* 3 main, chief, principal GRATE

greedy adjective gluttonish, voracious, grasping, selfish, acquisitive ★ **unselfish**

green adjective 1 emerald, jade, turquoise 2 ungrown, immature, raw *During baseball training, the raw recruits learn the ropes*, untrained ★ **expert**

greet verb welcome, accost, hail, salute, salaam, address

grief noun woe, sadness, regret, distress, anguish ▶ *sorrow* ★ **joy**

grievance noun injury, hardship, complaint, wrong, trial ★ **boon**

grieve verb lament, deplore, mourn, sorrow, be sad, afflict, hurt ★ **rejoice**

grievous adjective lamentable, deplorable, grave, critical, severe, mortal

grill 1 verb fry, broil 2 noun grating, grid

grim adjective 1 serious, stern, harsh, solemn, dour, forbidding 2 horrid, dreadful, terrible ▶ *somber* ★ **mild**

grime noun filth, soil, dust, soot ▶ *dirt*

Groups of animals

a drove of cattle
a flock of birds
a herd of elephants
a mob of kangaroos
a pack of wolves
a pride of lions
a school of porpoise
a sloth of bears
a swarm of bees
a troop of monkeys
a colony of seals
a cete of badgers
a skulk of foxes

a gaggle of geese

grin   noun & verb smile, beam, smirk, simper

grind   verb **1** scrape, file, crush, powder   **2** sharpen, whet, grate

grip   verb grasp, grab, snatch, clasp, seize ▶ *hold*
★ **loosen**

grisly   adjective horrid, horrible, dreadful, ghastly
▶ *grim*

grit   noun **1** powder, dust, sand, gravel   **2** nerve, mettle, pluck ▶ *courage*

groan   verb moan, complain, grumble, creak

GROWN

groom   **1** noun husband, bridegroom   **2** noun stable boy, servant, hostler   **3** verb spruce, tidy, preen

groove   noun furrow, ridge, corrugation, channel, rut, score

grope   verb feel, handle, finger, manipulate, touch, pick

gross   adjective **1** large, bulky, unwieldy, massive
2 coarse, vulgar, crude   **3** outrageous, glaring, flagrant
The driver was arrested for a flagrant disregard of the speed limit

grotesque   adjective deformed, malformed, misshapen, freakish, abnormal, bizarre

ground   noun **1** dry land, soil, earth, dust   **2** bottom, base, foundation

grounds   noun **1** foundation, cause, basis, excuse
2 dregs, sediment, silt   **3** gardens, parkland, estate

group   noun **1** division, section, branch   **2** gang, throng, cluster, bunch, class, set

grovel   verb fawn, crouch, crawl, toady, cringe, wallow, cower

grow   verb **1** increase, advance, expand, extend, develop, raise   **2** sprout, germinate, shoot

growl   verb snarl, snap, threaten, thunder

growth   noun expansion, development, advance
▶ *increase*

grow up   verb mature, develop, ripen

grubby   adjective messy, dirty, mucky

grudge   noun & verb hate, envy, dislike, spite

gruesome   adjective frightful, hideous, ghastly ▶ *grisly*

gruff adjective husky, throaty, croaky, blunt, churlish, crusty, curt ★ **affable**

grumble verb complain, snivel, murmur, growl, protest

grumpy adjective disgruntled, dissatisfied, surly, sour, irritable, sullen ★ **affable**

grunt noun & verb snort, groan ★ **growl**

guarantee noun warranty, assurance, security, pledge

guard 1 noun protector, sentry, guardian, watchman 2 verb protect, defend, watch over, shelter, shield

guess verb surmise, conjecture, judge, think, suspect, suppose

guest noun visitor, caller GUESSED

guide 1 noun pilot, director, leader, controller 2 verb steer, navigate, lead, direct, manage, conduct *Our teacher conducted us to the bus, and we all climbed aboard*

guild noun club, trade union, association, federation, fellowship, band, society

guile noun knavery, foul play, trickery, deceit, cunning, fraud ★ **honesty**

guilty adjective blameworthy, sinful, wicked, wrong ★ **innocent**

guise noun garb, pose, posture, role, aspect *The salesman's aspect was a little too friendly; we did not trust him*, appearance GUYS

gulch noun valley, gully, ravine

gulf noun 1 bay, basin, inlet 2 chasm, opening, abyss, depths

gullible adjective credulous, innocent, naive, trusting

gully noun trench, ditch, channel, ravine

gulp verb swallow, consume, guzzle, devour

gun noun rifle, cannon, revolver, pistol, automatic, shotgun

gurgle verb ripple, murmur, purl, babble

gush verb stream, spurt, spout, flow, run, pour out

gust noun blast, blow, squall, wind

gusto noun relish, zest, eagerness, zeal, pleasure

gutter noun moat, ditch, dike, drain, gully, channel, groove

guzzle verb gulp, imbibe, drink, swill, quaff

habit noun 1 custom, practice, routine, way, rule 2 mannerism *He has an odd mannerism of drumming his fingers on the table*, addiction, trait

hack verb chop, mangle, gash, slash

hackneyed adjective stale, trite, commonplace, tired ★ **new**

hag noun crone, harridan, witch, virago *I know I have a temper, but Julia is a real virago*

haggard adjective drawn, wan, pinched, thin ▶ *gaunt* ★ **hale**

haggle verb bargain, barter, bicker, dispute ★ **yield**

hail 1 verb salute, call to, accost, welcome, greet 2 noun sleet, frozen rain, ice storm HALE

hair noun locks, mane, tresses, strand

hale adjective hearty, robust, sound, fit ▶ *healthy* ★ **ill** HAIL

half noun division, fraction, segment

hall noun entrance, foyer, corridor, lobby, vestibule *There is a coat rack and an umbrella stand in the vestibule of her house* HAUL

hallow verb sanctify, consecrate, bless, dedicate, make holy

hallucination noun illusion, fantasy, delusion, mirage, dream ★ **reality**

halt verb end, pause, rest, cease ▶ *stop* ★ **start**

halting adjective faltering, hestitating, wavering, awkward ★ **fluent**

hammer 1 verb beat, pound, bang 2 noun mallet, gavel *The judge banged his gavel and called for order*

hamper 1 verb hinder, interfere, impede, curb ★ **aid** 2 noun basket, creel *The fisherman carried a creel to put his catch in*, crate

hand 1 verb give, pass, present, yield 2 noun fist, palm

handicap noun defect, disability, drawback, restriction ★ **advantage**

handicraft noun skill, hobby, art, workmanship, craft, occupation

handle 1 noun shaft, holder, grip 2 verb feel, touch, finger, work, wield

handsome adjective 1 good-looking, graceful, attractive 2 generous, lavish *Aunt Betsy is always lavish with presents for the children* HANSOM

handy adjective ready, convenient, deft, skilled ✶ clumsy

hang verb dangle, suspend, sag, droop, swing

hanker for verb long for, yearn for, crave, desire ✶ dislike

haphazard adjective accidental, random, aimless, casual ▶ *chance* ✶ deliberate

hapless adjective ill-fated, luckless, unlucky ▶ *miserable* ✶ lucky

happen verb occur, take place, come about, result

happening noun event, incident, occurrence, occasion

happiness noun delight, ecstasy, gaiety, joy, enjoyment ▶ *bliss* ✶ unhappiness

happy adjective cheerful, blithe, content, joyous, jubilant ▶ *merry* ✶ unhappy

harass verb beset, annoy, upset, bother ▶ *distress* ✶ assist

harbor 1 noun port, anchorage, mooring 2 noun refuge, shelter, safety *At last we were back in the safety of our home* 3 verb give shelter to

hard adjective 1 firm, stony, rocky, solid ✶ soft 2 difficult, tough *I had a very tough problem to solve, perplexing* ✶ easy 3 stern, severe, callous, ruthless

hardly adverb seldom, rarely, scarcely, slightly

hardship noun trouble, suffering, want ▶ *difficulty* ✶ ease

hardy adjective rugged, sturdy, tough, healthy, stout, sound ▶ *robust* ✶ weak

hark verb listen, hear ▶ *listen*

harm 1 noun damage, mischief, ruin, wrong, abuse, sin 2 verb abuse, blemish, hurt *I'm sorry, I didn't mean to hurt you*, injure ✶ benefit

harmful adjective injurious, evil, wicked, damaging ✶ harmless

harmless adjective safe, gentle, innocuous, innocent ✶ harmful

harmony noun agreement, conformity, accord, unity, goodwill ✶ discord

harp 1 noun lyre, stringed instrument 2 verb harp on, dwell on *I tried to forget the cold, but Carol continued to dwell on it*, allude to

harrow verb agonize, taunt, distress, torture, harry ▶ *harass* ✶ hearten

harsh adjective 1 jarring, coarse, rough 2 severe, strict, ruthless ✶ mild

harvest verb plow, harrow, reap, pluck

hash noun 1 mess, confusion, muddle 2 stew, goulash, meat loaf

hassle noun argument, bother, difficulty, squabble, struggle

haste noun rush, bustle, dispatch, urgency, swiftness ▶ *hurry* ✶ delay

hasten verb hurry, hustle, quicken, accelerate, speed up ✶ dawdle

hasty adjective hurried, rushed, abrupt, indiscreet ✶ deliberate

hate verb abhor, detest, loathe ▶ *despise* ✶ love

hateful adjective abominable, loathsome, odious, despicable ✶ pleasing

haughty adjective arrogant, disdainful, scornful, snobbish ✶ humble

haul verb pull, draw, tug, drag, heave HALL

have verb possess, occupy, own, receive, take in

haven noun harbor, port, refuge, retreat, sanctum, shelter

havoc noun wreckage, ruin, destruction, disorder, mayhem

hay noun pasture, silage, grass, straw HEY

haze noun cloud, vapor, fog, mist HAYS

hazy adjective foggy, misty, murky, vague, uncertain ✶ clear

head 1 noun visage, skull, cranium, pate 2 adjective chief, main, principal, boss

heading noun caption, headline, title, inscription

headlong adjective rough, dangerous, reckless ▶ *rash*

heal verb soothe, treat, cure, mend, restore HEEL, HE'LL

healthy adjective fine, fit, hearty, sound, vigorous ▶ *hale* ✶ sick

heap noun pile, mass, mound, collection

hear verb listen to, hearken, overhear HERE

hearten verb assure, encourage, embolden, inspire
★ dishearten

heartless adjective brutal, callous, cold ▷ *unkind* ★ **kind**

hearty adjective cordial, sincere, earnest, honest, jovial
★ **cold**

heat noun **1** warmth, temperature **2** passion, ardor,
fervor *She spoke with great fervor about what she believed*

heave verb fling, cast, hurl, hoist, pull, tug

heavenly adjective beautiful, blessed, divine, lovely
★ **hellish**

heavy adjective weighty, hefty, ponderous, loaded ★ **light**

hectic adjective excited, fast, frenzied, wild ▷ *frantic*
★ **leisurely**

heed verb listen, pay attention, follow, respect, obey
★ **ignore**

heedless adjective thoughtless, reckless, unwary, rash
▷ *careless*

height noun **1** altitude, stature **2** top, apex, peak,
zenith ★ **depth**

hellish adjective abominable, awful, inhuman, fiendish
★ **heavenly**

help **1** noun aid, support, assistance **2** verb lend
a hand *We all lent a hand in building the hut*, aid, assist
★ **hinder**

helpful adjective caring, considerate ▷ *useful*
★ **useless**

helping noun ration, portion, piece, serving
Mike would like a second serving. He's still hungry, share

helpless adjective incapable, powerless, unfit, forlorn
▷ *weak* ★ **strong**

hem noun edge, border, fringe, margin

hence adverb accordingly, thus, therefore, henceforth

herd noun crowd, crush, flock, group, mass, mob,
horde HEARD

here adverb present, attending, hereabouts, in this
place HEAR

heritage noun inheritance, legacy, birthright, tradition

hermit noun recluse, solitary, monk

hero noun champion, daredevil, star, idol, conqueror
★ **villain**

Headgear

beret

Stetson

yarmulke

cycling helmet

fez

heroic adjective bold, fearless, lionhearted, gallant
▷ *brave* ★ **cowardly**

heroine noun celebrity, goddess *Marilyn Monroe was
a goddess of the silver screen*, idol, star, lead

hesitate verb falter, dither, doubt, wait

hew verb chop, cut, fashion, carve, sculpt HUE

hidden adjective concealed, covered, veiled, unseen
★ **open**

hide verb conceal, cover, obscure, bury, cloak
★ reveal HIED

hideous adjective repulsive, unsightly, gruesome, horrible ▶ *ugly* ★ **beautiful**

hiding noun beating, thrashing, caning

high **1** adjective tall, towering, lofty, elevated **2** shrill *The referee blew a shrill blast on his whistle*, treble, strident **3** expensive, costly ★ **low**

highbrow adjective brainy, educated, intellectual

hijack verb raid, kidnap, seize, snatch, steal

hike verb walk, ramble, tramp

hilarious adjective amusing, gleeful, jocular, entertaining ▶ *funny* ★ **serious**

hill noun hummock, rise, climb, height, elevation, slope

hinder verb hamper, impede, obstruct, slow down, frustrate ▶ *handicap* ★ **help**

hindrance noun impediment, obstruction, check, barrier ★ **aid**

hint noun clue, inkling *We had an inkling of what was inside the box*, whisper, tip, suggestion

hire verb charter, rent, lease, retain, engage ★ **dismiss** HIGHER

hiss verb boo, hoot, jeer, deride, whistle ▶ *ridicule* ★ **applaud**

history noun narration, account, saga, story, chronicle *The new book is a chronicle of the progress of equal rights*

hit **1** verb strike, slap, beat, batter, whack **2** verb collide, strike, clash ★ **miss** **3** noun stroke, collision, blow, success, triumph

hitch **1** verb attach, connect, fasten **2** noun delay, holdup, problem, snag *The work went smoothly for hours, until we hit a snag*

hoard verb accumulate, save, collect, treasure ★ **squander** HORDE

hoarse adjective raucous, croaky, husky, throaty ★ **mellow** HORSE

hoax noun trick, deception, fraud, joke, spoof, lie

hobble verb dodder, falter, shuffle, stagger

hobby noun pastime, amusement, recreation, interest

hoist verb lift, raise, erect, heave

hold **1** verb have, possess, own, retain, keep, grasp **2** verb contain, accommodate *This cabin can accommodate four people* **3** verb stop, arrest **4** noun fortress, keep, storeplace HOLED

hole noun aperture, slot, perforation, opening, cavity WHOLE

hollow **1** adjective concave, empty, vacant **2** adjective insincere, artificial **3** noun basin, depression *Water had accumulated in a small depression*, crater, channel

holy adjective sacred, pure, consecrated, blessed, hallowed ★ **wicked** WHOLLY

home noun house, dwelling, homestead

homely adjective **1** humble, unpretentious, comfortable, modest **2** ordinary, plain, simple **3** unattractive, plain

honest adjective upright, fair, sincere, honorable ★ **devious**

honesty noun integrity, honor, sincerity, morality ★ **dishonesty**

honor noun morality, honesty, reputation, integrity, uprightness ★ **disgrace**

honorable adjective honest, respectable, high-minded, virtuous ★ **dishonest**

hook noun clasp, link, catch, fastener, barb *The fishhook ended in a number of small barbs*

hoop noun loop, ring, band, circle

hoot verb call, cry, howl, shout, shriek, yell

hop verb jump, leap, skip, spring, vault, caper

hope verb anticipate, envision, envisage, desire, expect, foresee ★ **despair**

hopeful adjective expectant, confident, optimistic ★ **pessimistic**

hopeless adjective despairing, desperate, downhearted, unattainable ★ **hopeful**

horde noun crowd, gang, band, throng, swarm *The ice-cream truck attracted a swarm of children* HOARD

horrible adjective awful, atrocious, frightful, ghastly ▶ *horrid* ★ **agreeable**

horrid adjective beastly, bloodcurdling, dreadful, frightening ▶ *horrible* ★ **pleasant**

horror noun dread, fear, fright, outrage, panic, loathing ★ attraction

horse noun mount, charger, hack, stallion, mare, filly, colt, foal HOARSE

hose noun 1 tubing, pipe 2 socks, stockings HOES

hospitable adjective sociable, neighborly, charitable, welcoming ★ hostile

host noun 1 entertainer, master of ceremonies, MC, sponsor 2 army, band, legion, horde

hostile adjective unfriendly, antagonistic, alien, malevolent ★ friendly

hot 1 adjective warm, fiery, scalding, roasting, heated ★ cold 2 pungent, peppery, sharp

hotel noun inn, hostelry *The stagecoach pulled in to a local hostelry for refreshment*, tavern, motel, resort

house noun home, residence, dwelling, abode

hovel noun cabin, shed, den, shack, shanty

hover verb fly, float, hang, dally, linger

howl verb hoot, cry, bellow, shriek ▶ *scream*

hub noun center, axis, focal point, pivot

hubbub noun babel, bedlam, chaos, clamor, uproar ▶ *row* ★ calm

huddle verb cluster, flock, gather, herd, nestle ★ separate

hue noun color, dye, shade, tinge, tint HEW

huff noun anger, passion, mood, pique *Amy stormed off in a fit of pique* ▶ *sulk*

hug verb clasp, embrace, enfold ▶ *cuddle*

huge adjective enormous, monstrous, colossal, immense ▶ *vast* ★ tiny

hum verb drone, croon, buzz, pulsate, throb

human adjective reasonable, understandable, mortal ▶ *humane* ★ inhuman

humane adjective benign, forgiving, gentle, lenient, kind ★ inhumane

humble adjective low, lowly, meek, unassuming ▶ *modest* ★ arrogant

humbug noun bluff, bunkum, claptrap *The salesman's goods were cheap, and he talked a lot of claptrap about them*, quackery, trickery

humdrum adjective monotonous, commonplace, everyday, boring ▶ *dreary* ★ exceptional

humid adjective clammy, damp, moist, wet, vaporous ★ dry

humiliate verb embarrass, humble, abash, degrade, deflate ★ boost

humor 1 noun comedy, fun, banter, whimsy 2 verb flatter, coax, pamper, spoil

humorous adjective amusing, droll, comical, whimsical ▶ *funny* ★ serious HUMERUS

hunch 1 noun feeling, guess, idea, inkling 2 verb crouch, curl up, squat *We squatted in the long grass, where we were out of sight*

hunger 1 noun craving, desire, starvation 2 verb crave, desire, hanker

hungry adjective famished, starving, voracious

hunt verb chase, seek, scour, search, stalk, trail

hurdle noun barrier, fence, hedge, obstruction

hurl verb cast, fling, heave, pitch, throw, propel, toss

hurry verb dash, hustle, quicken, accelerate ▶ *hasten* ★ dally

hurt 1 verb harm, wound, pain, sting, suffer 2 verb upset, annoy, distress 3 adjective rueful, sad, offended

hurtful adjective cutting, cruel, distressing, wounding ★ kind

hurtle verb chase, charge, dash, rush, speed, tear

hush verb calm, quiet down, soothe ★ disturb

husky adjective croaking, gruff, harsh ▶ *hoarse*

hustle verb bustle, speed, hasten ▶ *hurry*

hut noun cabin, shelter, shanty, shack

hymn noun anthem, chant, carol, psalm HIM

hypnotize verb mesmerize, fascinate, spellbind *We stood spellbound as we watched the trapeze artist*, bewitch

hypocrite noun fraud, deceiver, impostor, mountebank

hysterical adjective 1 distraught, mad, delirious, beside oneself 2 comical, hilarious, farcical ★ calm

Ii

icy adjective freezing, frozen, cold, frigid, frosty

idea noun notion, thought, belief, fancy, impression, image

ideal adjective perfect, absolute, supreme, best, model, complete

identical adjective same, alike, twin, duplicate, equal *different*

identify verb detect, recognize, know, distinguish, spot

identity noun existence, self, singularity, individuality

idiot noun imbecile, moron, fool, dimwit, dolt

idiotic adjective crazy, stupid, simple, fatuous *foolish* *sane*

idle adjective 1 unoccupied, unemployed, unused 2 lazy, frivolous, sluggish *active* IDOL

idol noun 1 image, icon, god, fetish 2 hero, favorite, star *Buster Keaton was a star of silent movies* IDLE

ignite verb kindle, set light to, spark off, catch fire

ignorant adjective unknowing, ill-informed, unread, stupid, dumb *wise*

ignore verb disregard, neglect, omit, overlook, pass over *note*

ill adjective 1 ailing, diseased, frail, infirm, sick, unwell *well* 2 hostile, malicious *Cinderella's sisters were cruel and malicious*, evil, harmful

ill-mannered adjective coarse, crude, boorish, uncivil *rude* *polite*

ill-tempered adjective bad-tempered, curt, irritable *good-tempered*

ill-treat verb abuse, harm, injure, neglect, oppress *care for*

ill will noun animosity, hard feelings, dislike, hatred, hostility *malice* *goodwill*

illegal adjective unlawful, wrong, villainous, illicit, contraband *legal*

illegible adjective unreadable, indecipherable, obscure, indistinct *legible*

illegitimate adjective illegal, unlawful, improper, wrong *legitimate*

illiterate adjective uneducated, unlearned, unlettered, unread, untaught *literate*

illness noun ailment, attack, complaint, disease, disorder

illuminate verb brighten, clarify, enlighten, light up *darken*

illusion noun apparition, fancy, fantasy, mirage, deception *reality*

illustration noun picture, drawing, explanation, sketch

image noun likeness, effigy, portrait, replica, reflection, double

imaginary adjective unreal, fanciful, fictitious, visionary *real*

imagination noun idea, notion, thought, illusion, conception, fancy, vision, impression *reality*

imagine verb assume, believe, invent, pretend, think up *visualize*

imbecile noun blockhead, fool, idiot, bungler, dolt

imitate verb emulate, follow, reproduce, simulate, mock *copy*

immaculate adjective clean, spotless, faultless, stainless *pure* *soiled*

immature adjective callow, raw, crude, childish, unripe *mature*

immediate adjective 1 instant, instantaneous, prompt 2 nearest, next, neighboring *As children, my mother and father lived in neighboring houses* *distant*

immediately adverb at once, directly, without delay, forthwith

immense adjective tremendous, enormous, vast *huge* *tiny*

immerse verb plunge, dip, douse, submerge *sink*

imminent adjective impending, approaching, looming, close

immobile adjective at rest, at a standstill, motionless *moving*

immodest adjective shameless, barefaced, indelicate, improper *modest*

immoral adjective evil, unscrupulous, vicious, vile, depraved *wicked* *moral*

immortal adjective undying, eternal, everlasting, constant ☆ mortal

immune adjective exempt, resistant, safe, protected ☆ susceptible

imp noun rascal, urchin, elf

impact noun blow, shock, stroke, collision, crash, knock

impair verb damage, spoil, devalue, cheapen, harm ▶ *hinder* ☆ enhance

impart verb communicate, render, bestow, disclose *I am unable to disclose where I heard that story* ▶ *tell*

impartial adjective unbiased, candid, fair-minded, impersonal ☆ biased

impatient adjective intolerant, irritable, hasty, curt ☆ patient

impede verb hamper, interfere with, obstruct ▶ *hinder* ☆ aid

impel verb goad, incite, urge, actuate, push ▶ *drive* ☆ dissuade

impending adjective approaching, coming, forthcoming, looming ☆ remote

imperfect adjective defective, unsound, blemished, flawed ▶ *faulty* ☆ perfect

imperial adjective august, majestic, lofty, regal, royal, grand

imperious adjective arrogant, domineering, overbearing ☆ humble

impersonal adjective aloof, detached, remote, neutral, cold ☆ friendly

impersonate verb imitate, mimic, masquerade as, pose as, portray

impertinent adjective insolent, impudent, discourteous ▶ *saucy* ☆ polite

impetuous adjective sudden, unexpected, impulsive, spontaneous ▶ *hasty* ☆ careful

implement 1 verb accomplish, bring about, fulfill *I was able to fulfill my dream of going to Japan* 2 noun instrument, tool, gadget

implicate verb connect, entangle, involve, throw suspicion on ☆ absolve

implicit adjective implied, indicated, understood, tacit

implore verb beseech, entreat, beg, crave, plead

imply verb hint at, intimate, insinuate ▶ *suggest* ☆ declare

impolite adjective discourteous, ill-mannered ▶ *rude* ☆ polite

import 1 verb bring in, carry in 2 noun meaning, purport *When I grew old enough, I realized the purport of my mother's advice*, sense

important adjective significant, essential, serious, substantial ▶ *great* ☆ trivial

imposing adjective impressive, massive, magnificent ▶ *stately* ☆ modest

impossible adjective hopeless, not possible, unworkable, unacceptable ☆ possible

impostor noun impersonator, masquerader, deceiver, fraud, pretender, quack

impoverish verb bankrupt, diminish, weaken, ruin, beggar ☆ enrich

impractical adjective impossible, unworkable, idealistic, unusable ☆ practical

impress verb 1 influence, affect, sway, inspire 2 emboss *She wore a crown of gold embossed with diamonds*, engrave, indent

impression noun 1 belief, concept, fancy, effect 2 dent, imprint, stamp, printing *The book had sold 5,000 copies, and a new printing was planned*

imprison verb jail, lock up, confine ☆ free

improbable adjective doubtful, unlikely, implausible ▶ *dubious* ☆ probable

impromptu adjective improvised, spontaneous, ad lib, unrehearsed ☆ planned

improper adjective 1 erroneous, false, unsuitable 2 immoral *My parents always taught me that lying and cheating were immoral*, indecent ▶ *wrong* ☆ proper

improve verb make better, repair, restore, improve on, refine ☆ diminish

impudent adjective impertinent, audacious, brazen, disrespectful ▶ *rude* ☆ polite

impulse noun motive, drive, force, inclination, urge, wish

impulsive adjective sudden, unexpected, reckless ▶ *impetuous* ☆ cautious

impure adjective contaminated, corrupted, foul, corrupt ☆ pure

inaccessible adjective remote, isolated, unattainable ☆ accessible

inaccurate adjective erroneous, incorrect, imprecise ▶ *faulty* ☆ accurate

inactive adjective inert, static, dormant, quiet, unoccupied ☆ active

inadequate adjective deficient, unequal, incapable ▶ *unfit* ☆ adequate

inane adjective absurd, ridiculous, stupid, senseless ▶ *silly* ☆ sensible

inappropriate adjective improper, wrong, incorrect, unsuitable, unfitting ☆ appropriate

inattentive adjective unheeding, indifferent, careless, neglectful ☆ attentive

incapable adjective helpless, inadequate, unable, unfit, weak ☆ capable

incense 1 verb (in-*cense*) enrage, infuriate, annoy 2 noun (*in*-cense) fragrance *We walked through fields where the fragrance of wildflowers was wonderful*, aroma, perfume

incentive noun motive, impulse, drive, spur, lure

incident noun event, happening, episode, circumstance, occurrence

incidental adjective casual, chance, accidental, random, minor

incite verb encourage, urge, drive, goad, impel, provoke ▶ *prompt* ☆ restrain

incline 1 noun (*in*-cline) slant, slope, grade, gradient 2 verb (in-*cline*) tend, verge, lean to, bias, favor

inclined adjective liable, prone, disposed, favorable

include verb contain, cover, incorporate, embody, comprise ☆ exclude

inclusive adjective comprehensive, all-embracing ☆ exclusive

income noun earnings, royalty, revenue, receipts, profits ☆ expenses

incomparable adjective incredible, first-rate, superb ▶ *unrivaled* ☆ ordinary

incompetent adjective incapable, inadequate, inept, helpless ▶ *clumsy* ☆ competent

incomplete adjective unfinished, partial, imperfect, wanting ☆ complete

incomprehensible adjective unintelligible, perplexing, puzzling ☆ comprehensible

inconceivable adjective incredible, unlikely, strange ▶ *extraordinary* ☆ comprehensible

inconsiderate adjective tactless, careless, insensitive ▶ *thoughtless* ☆ considerate

inconsistent adjective incongruous, unstable, unpredictable ☆ consistent

inconspicuous adjective indistinct, faint, hidden, ordinary ☆ conspicuous

inconvenient adjective annoying, awkward, difficult, troublesome ☆ convenient

incorrect adjective erroneous, imprecise, mistaken ▶ *wrong* ☆ correct

increase 1 verb add to, boost, magnify, heighten 2 noun addition *We heard the news today that Emily has had an addition to her family*, rise, enhancement ☆ decrease

incredible adjective unbelievable, amazing, farfetched, wonderful ☆ ordinary

incriminate verb implicate, accuse, indict ▶ *blame* ☆ acquit

indecent adjective immodest, improper, impure, coarse ☆ decent

indeed adverb actually, truly, really, very much, positively

indefinite adjective uncertain, unsure, unreliable, dubious ▶ *vague* ☆ certain

indelicate adjective coarse, immodest, indecent ▶ *unseemly* ☆ delicate

independent adjective free, self-reliant, separate, self-governing ☆ dependent

indicate verb show, point out, denote, suggest, symbolize, flag, signal

indifference noun disinterest, unconcern, apathy, coldness ☆ interest

indifferent adjective uninterested, cold, casual, apathetic, listless ☆ interested

indignant adjective annoyed, resentful, wrathful ▶ *angry* ☆ pleased

indirect adjective devious, roundabout, incidental ☆ direct

indiscreet adjective incautious, thoughtless, ill-advised ▶ *hasty* ☆ discreet

indiscriminate adjective confused, bewildered, careless ▶ *random* ☆ deliberate

indispensable adjective necessary, crucial, vital ▶ *essential* ☆ unnecessary

indistinct adjective faint, dim, unclear, obscure, murky ▶ *vague* ★ **distinct**

individual 1 adjective single, odd, special, exclusive 2 noun person, being *Sharon enjoys the company of other human beings*, creature

indulge verb gratify, humor, pamper, satisfy, spoil

industrious adjective busy, hard-working, diligent, conscientious ★ **lazy**

inedible adjective deadly, poisonous, harmful, uneatable ★ **edible**

inefficient adjective negligent, incapable ▶ *incompetent* ★ **efficient**

inelegant adjective awkward, ungainly, crude, coarse ▶ *clumsy* ★ **elegant**

inept adjective awkward, absurd, unskilled ▶ *clumsy* ★ **skillful**

inert adjective inactive, passive, static, sluggish, listless, dead ★ **alive**

inevitable adjective unavoidable, certain, sure, necessary ★ **uncertain**

inexact adjective imprecise, inaccurate ▶ *erroneous* ★ **exact**

inexpensive adjective low-priced, reasonable, economical ▶ *cheap* ★ **expensive**

inexperienced adjective inexpert, unskilled, untrained ▶ *inept* ★ **experienced**

infallible adjective perfect, unerring, faultless ▶ *reliable* ★ **faulty**

infamous adjective notorious, shady, scandalous, shameful, disgraceful ★ **glorious**

infant noun baby, child, little one, toddler

infatuated adjective in love, beguiled, charmed, fascinated, smitten

infect verb contaminate, blight, defile, pollute

infectious adjective catching, contagious

infer verb reason, conclude, judge, understand

inferior adjective second-rate, lesser, lower, poor, mediocre, imperfect ★ **superior**

infinite adjective eternal, unending, endless, immense, unbounded

infirm adjective weak, feeble, frail, senile, decrepit ★ **healthy**

inflame verb inspire, provoke, excite, stimulate, arouse ★ **cool**

inflate verb expand, dilate, swell, pump up, blow up ★ **deflate**

inflict verb apply, burden, deal, deliver, force

influence 1 noun authority, control, guidance, force 2 verb affect, impress, inspire *After Annie visited her old neighborhood, she was inspired to write a poem*, prejudice

inform verb tell, let know, acquaint, warn, enlighten

informal adjective casual, easy, familiar, relaxed, simple ★ **formal**

information noun knowledge, news, intelligence, advice

infrequent adjective unusual, uncommon, occasional ▶ *rare* ★ **frequent**

infringe verb disobey, violate, encroach, trespass, flout

infuriate verb anger, enrage, madden, incense, vex ▶ *annoy* ★ **calm**

ingenious adjective clever, resourceful, shrewd, adroit, inventive ★ **clumsy**

ingenuous adjective honest, open, simple, trusting, sincere ★ **artful**

ingratiate verb curry favor, flatter, grovel, toady *We distrusted Tim; he was always trying to toady himself with the teacher*

ingredient noun component, element, part, factor

inhabit verb live in, dwell in, reside in, dwell, occupy

inhale verb breathe in, inspire, sniff, suck in ★ **exhale**

inherit verb succeed to, acquire, take over, receive

inhospitable adjective unfriendly, desolate, unkind, unsociable ★ **hospitable**

inhuman adjective barbaric, brutal, beastly, heartless, savage

inhumane adjective callous, cruel, pitiless, ruthless ▶ *inhuman* ★ **humane**

initiate verb start, launch, teach, instruct, train ▶ *begin*

initiative noun ambition, drive, enterprise, resourcefulness

inject verb inoculate, infuse, vaccinate

injure verb hurt, mar, spoil, wound, blemish, deform, disfigure

inkling noun suspicion, impression, notion, clue

inlet noun bay, gulf, basin, bight, estuary, harbor

inn noun hotel, motel, lodge, tavern IN

innocent adjective guiltless, faultless, stainless, virtuous, blameless ★ **guilty**

inoffensive adjective harmless, safe, gentle, quiet ► *innocent* ✶ **malicious**

inquire verb ask, examine, inspect, check, question

inquisitive adjective nosy, snooping, eager, inquiring, ► *curious*

insane adjective demented, mad, frenzied, crazy, wild, lunatic ✶ **sane**

inscribe verb write, stamp, cut, carve, etch

inscription noun heading, caption, legend, epitaph, label

insecure adjective perilous, unsafe, hazardous, dangerous, unconfident, uncertain ✶ **secure**

insensible adjective **1** unconscious, stunned, knocked out *The reigning champion was knocked out in the third round* **2** insensitive, numb, stupefied

insensitive adjective impassive, indifferent, thick-skinned, unruffled, insensible ✶ **sensitive**

inseparable adjective indivisible, devoted, intimate, close

insert verb put in, inset, introduce, place, interleave ✶ **remove**

inside adverb indoors, inner, inward, within ✶ **outside**

insight noun awareness, intelligence, judgment, knowledge ► *wisdom*

insignificant adjective unimportant, nonessential, meager, irrelevant ► *humble* ✶ **important**

insincere adjective pretended, deceptive, dishonest, two-faced, false ✶ **sincere**

insinuate verb suggest, imply, signify, get at, intimate

insipid adjective tasteless, flat, flavorless, bland, banal ✶ **tasty**

insist verb assert, maintain, request, require, demand, persist ✶ **waive**

insolent adjective impudent, impertinent, discourteous, insulting, fresh, rude ✶ **respectful**

inspect verb examine, check, oversee, supervise, superintend

inspiration noun motive, stimulus, brain wave, ► *encouragement*

inspire verb hearten, prompt, provoke, excite ► *encourage* ✶ **deter**

install verb establish, plant, set, position, fix, introduce

instance noun example, case, occasion, occurrence INSTANTS

instant **1** adjective immediate, instantaneous *I pressed the button, and there was an instantaneous explosion*, rapid **2** noun moment, minute, flash, jiffy

instantly adverb at once, right away, immediately, now ► *forthwith* ✶ **later**

instead adverb alternatively, preferably, rather

instead of adverb in place of, in one's place, on behalf of

instinct noun ability, knack, intuition, feeling, sixth sense

institute **1** noun association, college, establishment, organization **2** verb begin, start *The people raised enough money to start a new program to help the poor*, found, open

instruct verb teach, direct, order, educate, coach, drill, train

instrument noun device, gadget, implement, contraption, tool

insufferable adjective unbearable, intolerable, impossible ✶ **tolerable**

insufficient adjective inadequate, lacking, scanty, wanting ► *sparse* ✶ **sufficient**

insulate verb protect, shield, isolate, set apart

insult noun & verb slander, slight, snub, abuse, outrage ✶ **compliment**

insure verb guarantee, protect, warrant, assure

intact adjective whole, unharmed, uncut, complete, in one piece, sound ✶ **damaged**

integrity noun honor, uprightness, honesty, goodness, purity ✶ **dishonesty**

intellectual adjective scholarly, studious, thoughtful ► *intelligent* ✶ **foolish**

intelligent adjective acute, astute, brainy, brilliant, intellectual ► *clever* ✶ **stupid**

intend verb mean, aim, determine, ordain, plan, project

intense adjective extreme, ardent, earnest, forcible, passionate ► *keen* ✶ **mild** INTENTS

intention noun aim, intent, project, design, notion, end, goal

intercept verb stop, arrest, confiscate, delay, obstruct ► *thwart*

interest noun appeal, fascination, zest, activity, concern ✶ **boredom**

Musical instruments

saxophone

accordion

drum

guitar

interesting adjective appealing, fascinating, absorbing, entertaining ★ **boring**

interfere verb meddle, intrude, interrupt, butt in, tamper ★ **assist**

interior adjective internal, inner, inside, inward ★ **exterior**

interlude noun pause, interval, intermission, spell, recess

internal adjective inner, inward ▶ *interior* ★ **external**

interpret adjective explain, define, construe

interrogate verb question, examine, ask, inquire, quiz ▶ *investigate*

A B C D E F G H I J K L M N O P Q R S T U V W X Y Z

239

interrupt adjective break in, butt in, interject, disturb, hold up, suspend

interval noun space, period, term, intermission ▷ *interlude*

intervene verb break in, interrupt, intrude, mediate, arbitrate ▷ *interfere*

interview noun conference, inquiry, enquiry, meeting, consultation, talk

intimate 1 adjective near, close, familiar, private, secret ⋆ **distant** 2 verb hint at, suggest *The evidence suggests that the defendant has not been telling the truth* ▷ *insinuate*

intimidate verb daunt, overawe, cow, bully, frighten, browbeat ⋆ **persuade**

intolerant adjective bigoted, unfair, small-minded, dogmatic ⋆ **tolerant**

intoxicated adjective drunk, inebriated, tipsy

intrepid adjective daring, heroic, unafraid, bold, gallant ▷ *fearless*

intricate adjective complex, complicated, elaborate, tricky ⋆ **simple**

intrigue 1 noun plot, scheme, affair, liaison 2 verb attract, enchant *The old man enchanted us with his stories*, captivate, scheme

introduce verb 1 put in, insert, inject 2 acquaint, present

intrude verb interrupt, interfere, invade, trespass ⋆ **withdraw**

inundate verb flood, deluge, engulf, immerse, submerge, swamp *We advertised for a new assistant and were swamped with replies*

invade verb break in, penetrate, assault, assail ▷ *enter* ⋆ **withdraw** INVEIGHED

invalid 1 adjective (in-*val*-id) null, void *These tickets are void—they are more than a year old*, useless 2 noun (*in*-val-id) patient, sufferer, sick person, disabled person

invaluable adjective precious, costly, priceless, valuable ⋆ **worthless**

invent verb fabricate, conceive, devise, make up, originate, concoct

invention noun creation, gadget, contrivance, discovery

investigate verb explore, examine, research, inquire, search, study

invisible adjective hidden, concealed, out of sight, unseen, masked ⋆ **visible**

invite verb ask, beckon, attract, summon, urge, encourage ⋆ **force**

involve verb comprise, complicate, entangle, include, take in

inward adjective hidden, inner, internal, secret, inside ⋆ **outward**

irate adjective incensed, cross, annoyed, furious, infuriated ▷ *angry* ⋆ **calm**

irksome adjective annoying, irritating, disagreeable ⋆ **pleasing**

ironic adjective satirical, derisive, mocking, scornful

irregular adjective uncertain, unsettled, disordered, singular ▷ *odd* ⋆ **regular**

irrelevant adjective immaterial, unnecessary, unrelated ⋆ **relevant**

irresistible adjective charming, compelling, overpowering, fascinating ⋆ **resistible**

irresponsible adjective undependable, unreliable, feckless, flighty ⋆ **responsible**

irritable adjective bad-tempered, edgy, fretful, peevish ▷ *cross* ⋆ **cheerful**

irritate verb annoy, vex, irk, offend, provoke ▷ *bother* ⋆ **please**

island noun isle, islet, key, atoll, cay

issue 1 verb flow, ooze, bring out, circulate, publish 2 noun edition, printing, publication *My book of poems was ready for publication*, impression 3 problem, question, concern

itch 1 verb prickle, tingle, irritate 2 noun impulse, motive, desire *I have always had a strong desire to work in a hospital*

item noun point, particular, thing, object, article

Jj

jab verb poke, prod, push, stab, dig

jabber verb chatter, gabble, mumble, babble

jacket noun coat, jerkin, cover, case, sheath

jagged adjective rough, broken, uneven ★ smooth

jail noun prison, penitentiary, lockup, brig

jam 1 noun jelly, preserves, marmalade 2 verb crowd, pack *We were packed in the bus like sardines*, crush, squeeze JAMB

jar 1 noun jug, beaker, ewer, vase, pitcher, pot 2 verb jog, rattle, grate *That singer's voice really grates on me*, grind

jaunt noun & verb trip, journey, cruise, travel, tour

jaunty adjective lighthearted, showy, dapper, debonair

jealous adjective envious, covetous, grudging

jealousy noun envy, covetousness, distrust, spite

jeer verb laugh at, deride, mock, ridicule, insult ▶ *taunt*

jeopardy noun peril, risk, hazard ▶ *danger* ★ safety

jerk noun & verb yank, pull, drag, jog, jolt, tug

jersey noun pullover, sweater

jest noun joke, jape, spoof, banter, chaff

jester noun clown, buffoon, prankster, comedian

jet noun & verb spurt, squirt, flow, gush

jetty noun wharf, dock, quay, pier

jewel noun gem, stone, trinket, charm, locket

jibe verb mock, scoff, scorn, sneer, taunt ▶ *jeer*

jiffy noun instant, flash, minute, moment

jilt verb abandon, brush off, desert, drop, forsake

jingle verb tinkle, clink, chink, ring, jangle

job noun task, work, chore, place, office, post, position

jocular adjective gleeful, witty, jolly ▶ *funny* ★ serious

jog verb 1 prod, nudge, shove, shake 2 run, sprint, trot

join verb 1 unite, link, combine, connect, attach ★ separate 2 enlist, sign up *Bill has signed up for tennis*

joint 1 noun junction, knot, union, connection 2 adjective shared, united, mutual *It's in our mutual interest to work this out*

joke noun gag, trick, frolic, lark, jape, game, prank ▶ *jest*

jolly adjective jovial, cheerful, blithe, frisky ▶ *merry* ★ sad

jolt noun & verb jar, shock, shove, rock, jerk, bump

jostle verb push, shove, shoulder, thrust, elbow

jot 1 noun atom, bit, grain, particle 2 verb note, scribble, take down

journal noun 1 ledger, account book 2 diary, newspaper, magazine *I'm the editor of the school magazine*

journey noun excursion, trip, tour, jaunt, ramble

jovial adjective jolly, festive, cordial, affable, cheerful ▶ *merry* ★ sad

joy noun rapture, enchantment, delight, pleasure, charm ▶ *bliss* ★ sorrow

joyful adjective joyous, enjoyable, pleasurable, happy, jovial, delighted ★ sorrowful

jubilant adjective exultant, gleeful, happy, overjoyed, excited ★ depressed

judge 1 noun justice, magistrate, referee, umpire 2 verb assess *We can ask the jeweler to assess the value of these pearls*, decide, find, appraise, estimate

judgment noun 1 decision, opinion, verdict *The jury gave a verdict of "not guilty,"* decree, finding 2 intelligence, understanding, valuation

judicious adjective prudent, discreet, expedient, wise ★ indiscreet

jug noun beaker, ewer, urn, vase ▶ *jar*

juggle verb conjure, manipulate

juice noun essence, extract, sap, fluid, nectar

jumble noun medley, mixture, muddle, tangle, clutter

jump verb spring, bound, hop, skip, vault ▶ *leap*

junction noun 1 union, combination, joint, connection 2 crossroads, intersection, juncture, crossing

jungle noun forest, bush, wilderness

junior adjective lesser, younger, subordinate ★ senior

junk noun trash, debris, rubbish, waste, clutter, litter, scrap, garbage, refuse

just 1 adjective sound, regular, orderly, exact, fair, honest, impartial 2 adverb exactly, precisely 3 adverb only, merely

justice noun equity, impartiality, fairness, right ★ injustice

justify verb vindicate, acquit, condone, uphold, legalize

jut verb bulge, extend, stick out, overhang, project *We took shelter where the cliff projects over the path* ★ recede

juvenile 1 adjective adolescent, youthful, childish ★ mature 2 noun boy, girl, child, youngster, youth

A B C D E F G H I J K L M N O P Q R S T U V W X Y Z

Kk

keen 1 adjective eager, ardent, earnest, diligent
2 sharp *Her wit is as sharp as a razor*, acute, fine ☆ **dull**

keep 1 verb hold, retain, collect, possess ☆ **abandon**
2 verb care for, maintain, shelter *We have arranged to shelter the refugees* 3 noun tower, dungeon, castle, fort, stronghold

keeper noun jailer, warden, attendant, caretaker, janitor, custodian

keeping noun compliance, obedience, accord

keep on verb continue, go on, endure, persist ☆ give up

keepsake noun souvenir, token, memento, reminder, relic

keg noun barrel, cask, tub, drum, container

ken noun grasp, grip, understanding, mastery, knowledge

kerchief noun scarf, headscarf, shawl, neckerchief

kernel noun core, heart, hub, center, gist, nub COLONEL

kettle noun boiler, cauldron, cooking pot, teakettle

key 1 noun opener 2 noun solution, clue, answer
3 noun cay, isle, island, atoll 4 adjective essential, fundamental, vital, critical QUAY

kick verb 1 boot, strike with the foot, punt, hit
2 complain, grumble, rebel *The people rebelled against the harsh rule of the new king*, resist

kidnap verb abduct, capture, seize, snatch, steal, hijack

kill verb slay, assassinate, destroy, massacre, slaughter
▷ *murder*

killjoy noun spoilsport, wet blanket *I don't want to be a wet blanket, but I'm tired and want to go home*, grouch, complainer ☆ **optimist**

kin noun race, kindred, offspring, kind, family, relative

kind 1 adjective gentle, kindly, genial, good-natured, amiable ☆ **unkind** 2 noun style, character, sort, variety

kindle verb 1 light, ignite, set fire to 2 inflame
The mayor's words only inflamed the people even more, excite, provoke, rouse

kindness noun good nature, charity, amiability, affection, tenderness ☆ **cruelty**

king noun monarch, sovereign, majesty, ruler, emperor

kink noun 1 knot, loop, bend, coil 2 freak, eccentricity, whim *This strange tower was built as the result of a whim by the eccentric designer*

kiss verb salute, embrace, smooch, buss

kit noun set, outfit, baggage, effects, gear, rig

knack noun flair, talent, ability, genius, gift ▷ *skill*

knave noun cheat, rascal, villain, scamp, scoundrel
▷ *rogue* NAVE

knead verb form, squeeze, mold, shape, press NEED

kneel verb bend the knee, genuflect *The nun genuflected before the altar and then said her rosary*, bow down, worship

knife noun scalpel, blade, dagger, cutter

knight noun cavalier, champion, soldier, warrior, baronet NIGHT

knit verb weave, crochet, spin, twill, link, loop

knob noun boss, bump, handle, opener, button

knock verb hit, slap, punch, bang, smite, strike

knock out 1 verb stun, make insensible, render unconscious 2 noun success, hit, triumph

knoll noun barrow, hill, mound, hillock

knot noun 1 tie, bond, join, loop, kink, snarl, tangle
2 cluster, group NOT

know verb perceive, discern, notice, identify
▷ *understand* NO

know-how noun skill, knowledge, talent

knowing adjective astute, knowledgeable, intelligent, perceptive ☆ **ignorant**

knowledge noun understanding, acquaintance, learning, wisdom, scholarship, information, sapience
☆ **ignorance**

kudos noun prestige, distinction, fame, glory, recognition

Ll

label noun badge, tag, ticket, sticker, docket, slip

labor noun & verb toil, work, drudge, strain, struggle

laborious adjective 1 hard-working, diligent 2 strenuous, arduous *Digging potatoes is arduous work*, hard ☆ **easy**

lack 1 noun need, want, absence, deficiency, scarcity *During the hot weather, there was a scarcity of water* 2 verb need, require, want, miss

laconic adjective terse, curt, brief, concise ☆ **wordy**

lad noun boy, fellow, kid, youth, chap

laden adjective loaded, burdened, hampered, weighed down ☆ **empty**

ladle verb dip, scoop, dish, shovel

lady noun woman, female, dame, damsel, matron, mistress

lag verb dawdle, loiter, tarry, saunter ▷ *linger* ☆ **lead**

lagoon noun pool, pond, lake, basin

lair noun den, nest, retreat, hideout, hole

lake noun lagoon, loch, pond, spring, reservoir

lam verb beat, hit, clout, knock ▷ *strike*

lame adjective 1 crippled, hobbled, disabled 2 weak, feeble *That's a feeble excuse for missing school*, inadequate, unconvincing

lament verb deplore, mourn, grieve, sorrow ▷ *regret* ☆ **rejoice**

lamp noun lantern, light, flare, torch, flashlight

lance 1 noun spear, pike, javelin, shaft 2 verb puncture, pierce, cut

land 1 noun country, district, tract, area, nation, region 2 verb alight, arrive, carry, touch down *We had engine trouble, so the aircraft touched down in the desert*

landlord noun host, hotelier, innkeeper, owner

landmark noun milestone, milepost, beacon, monument, signpost

landscape noun scenery, view, prospect, countryside, panorama

lane noun alley, drive, passage, way LAIN

language noun tongue, speech, utterance, dialect, jargon

languid adjective leisurely, unhurried, sluggish, slow, easy ☆ **lively**

languish verb decline, droop, flag, pine, suffer, yearn ☆ **flourish**

lanky adjective tall, rangy, gangling, scrawny ☆ **squat**

lantern noun lamp, flashlight, torch

lap 1 verb lick, drink, sip, sup 2 noun circuit, course, distance 3 noun thighs, knees

lapse verb expire, die, pass, elapse, go by, deteriorate LAPS

larder noun pantry, storeroom, cellar

large adjective big, ample, substantial, great, broad ▷ *huge* ☆ **small**

lark noun adventure, escapade, spree, joke, frolic, gambol

lash 1 verb beat, cane, whip, flay, flog 2 noun prod, goad, drive, whip

lass noun girl, maiden, maid, young woman

last 1 adjective final, concluding, latest, utmost, aftermost ☆ **first** 2 verb remain, linger *The foggy weather lingered for most of the morning*, endure, stay

latch noun bolt, bar, padlock, fastener

late adjective tardy, behindhand, departed, slow ☆ **early**

lately adverb recently, latterly, formerly

lather noun suds, foam, bubbles, froth

latter adjective final, last, latest, recent, closing ☆ **former**

laud verb compliment, praise, applaud, glorify ☆ **blame**

laugh verb chuckle, giggle, guffaw, snicker ☆ **cry**

launch 1 verb start, begin, commence, establish, initiate 2 noun motorboat

lavish 1 adjective abundant, generous, liberal, extravagant 2 verb waste, squander *My parents left me a small fortune, but I squandered it all*, give

law noun rule, ordinance, regulation, edict, decree

lawful adjective legal, legitimate, rightful ☆ **illegal**

lawyer noun attorney, counsel, jurist, barrister, solicitor, advocate

lax adjective careless, casual, slack, relaxed, vague
★ strict LACKS

lay 1 verb put, set *It's time for dinner; let's set the table*, deposit, place, spread 2 verb impute, charge 3 adjective nonprofessional, amateur

layer noun seam, sheet, thickness, tier

lazy adjective idle, inactive, slothful, slow, sluggish
★ active

lead verb conduct, guide, escort, direct, command
★ follow

leader noun guide, pilot, conductor, chief, head, master

leaf noun frond, blade, sheet LIEF

league noun band, association, society, guild, group

leak verb trickle, ooze, seep, exude, flow out LEEK

lean 1 adjective spare, slim, thin, skinny *Lina has no flesh on her; she is very skinny*, 2 verb bend, curve, tilt, incline LIEN

leap verb spring, bound, jump, hop, skip

learn verb find out, ascertain, determine, acquire knowledge, understand

learned adjective cultured, educated, scholarly, literate
★ ignorant

learning noun scholarship, education, knowledge
▷ *wisdom* ★ ignorance

least adjective fewest, smallest, slightest, lowest, tiniest
★ most LEASED

leave 1 verb abandon, desert, forsake, quit, go 2 bequeath, bestow 3 noun vacation, furlough *Jack is on a furlough from the army*, permission

lecture noun talk, speech, address, sermon

ledge noun shelf, ridge, step

legacy noun bequest, inheritance, gift

legal adjective legitimate, lawful, valid, sound ★ illegal

legend noun 1 fable, myth, tale, fiction 2 inscription *The box bore a brass plate with an inscription*, heading, caption

Lights

arc lamp
candle
chandelier
electric light
fluorescent lamp
footlights
gaslight
headlight
lantern
night-light
reading light
spotlight
sunlamp
table lamp
torch

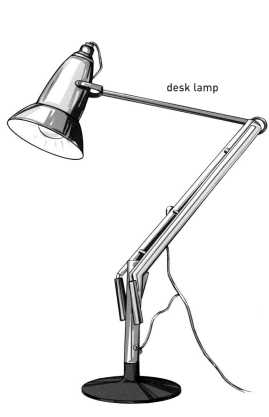

desk lamp

flashlight

bulb

legible adjective clear, readable, understandable, distinct ⋆ **illegible**

legitimate adjective legal, lawful, proper, rightful ▷ *genuine* ⋆ **illegal**

leisurely adjective unhurried, slow, easy, carefree, tranquil ⋆ **hectic**

lend verb loan, advance, provide, supply, grant, lease ⋆ **borrow**

lengthen verb extend, elongate, stretch, draw out, prolong ⋆ **shorten**

lengthy adjective long, drawn out, long-winded ▷ *tedious* ⋆ **short**

lenient adjective tolerant, merciful, sparing, forbearing, indulgent ⋆ **severe**

less adjective lesser, smaller, inferior, lower

lessen verb reduce, cut, become smaller, diminish, decrease ⋆ **increase** LESSON

lesson noun instruction, lecture, information, teaching, exercise LESSEN

let 1 verb allow, permit, suffer, authorize *The mayor authorized our school to hold the celebrations in the park*, grant 2 lease

let down verb 1 lower, take down 2 betray, abandon, disappoint ⋆ **satisfy**

letter noun 1 dispatch, communication, epistle, message 2 character *The book was printed in Hebrew characters*, sign, symbol

level 1 noun plane, grade 2 adjective even, flat, smooth ⋆ **uneven** 3 verb aim, direct, point 4 verb demolish *Many houses were demolished during the earthquake*, destroy

liable 1 adjective answerable, accountable, responsible 2 apt *My parents are apt to be annoyed if I play loud music*, prone, inclined

liar noun deceiver, fibber, teller of tales LYRE

libel verb slander, malign, blacken, defame, slur ⋆ **praise**

liberal adjective openhanded, generous, openhearted, free, lavish

liberate verb set free, save, release, ⋆ **restrict**

liberty noun freedom, independence ⋆ **slavery**

license verb allow, permit, entitle ⋆ **ban**

lie 1 noun untruth, falsehood 2 verb recline *I plan to recline on the sofa for the afternoon*, lounge, repose ▷ *loll* 3 verb tell a lie, fib, invent LYE

life noun being, existence, activity, energy ⋆ **death**

lift verb raise, erect, hoist, elevate, hold up ⋆ **lower**

light 1 noun radiance, glow, shine, glare, brightness 2 noun lamp, beacon, flame 2 verb ignite, illuminate, kindle *The scouts kindled a fire to cook their food* 3 adjective fair, light-colored, sunny ⋆ **dark** 4 lightweight, buoyant, airy ⋆ **heavy**

like 1 adjective similar, resembling, akin ⋆ **unlike** 2 verb admire, love, adore, cherish, prize ⋆ **dislike**

likely adjective probable, expected, possible

likeness noun 1 resemblance, appearance 2 photograph *That's a wonderful photograph of my grandmother*, portrait

likewise adverb also, too, furthermore, further

limb noun leg, arm, extension, branch, shoot, bough

limit 1 noun barrier, boundary, border, edge, end, restraint 2 verb reduce, restrict *The heavy rain was restricted to the hilly countryside*, confine ⋆ **free**

limited adjective restricted, reduced, narrow, confined ⋆ **unrestricted**

limp 1 adjective flabby, flimsy, flexible 2 verb hobble, falter, shuffle

line noun 1 stripe, streak, dash, bar 2 cord, thread 3 row, queue, file 4 calling *Being an opera singer is a noble calling but a difficult one*, occupation

linger verb loiter, lag, dally, tarry, delay ▷ *dawdle* ⋆ **speed**

link 1 noun bond, tie, connection, joint 2 verb unite, join, couple, bracket ⋆ **separate**

liquefy verb liquidize, melt

liquid noun fluid, liquor, solution, juice

list 1 noun schedule, table, catalog, register 2 verb tilt, lean, heel *The yacht heeled over as it turned into the wind*, careen, slope

listen verb hear, hearken, hark, heed

listless adjective languid, dull, lethargic, lifeless ▷ *sluggish* ⋆ **lively**

literally adverb actually, faithfully, precisely, really ⋆ **loosely**

literate adjective educated, well-educated, learned, lettered ☆ **illiterate**

lithe adjective agile, nimble, flexible, supple ☆ **stiff**

litter noun clutter, jumble, rubbish, mess, refuse

little **1** adjective small, tiny, short, slight, trivial, petty ▷ *small* ☆ **large** **2** adverb hardly, rarely, seldom

live **1** adjective alive, living, existing, active, alert ☆ **dead** **2** verb be, subsist, breathe, exist

lively adjective active, brisk, vivacious, animated, agile ☆ **listless**

livid adjective **1** angry, enraged, furious, mad **2** ashen *We were really scared, and Bob's face was ashen*, grayish, pale, leaden

living **1** adjective alive, existing **2** noun job, occupation, work, livelihood

load **1** noun freight, cargo, goods, burden **2** verb fill, pack, burden, pile up, stack LODE, LOWED

loaf **1** verb waste time, idle, dally, dawdle **2** noun block, cube, lump, cake

loan **1** noun credit, advance, allowance **2** verb allow, lend, advance *The bank advanced me the money to pay the mortgage* LONE

loath or **loth** adjective reluctant, disinclined, opposed

loathe verb abhor, detest, despise, dislike ▷ *hate* ☆ **like**

lobby noun hallway, entrance, vestibule, foyer

local adjective regional, district, provincial

locate verb find, discover, detect, unearth

lock **1** noun bolt, fastener, latch, clasp **2** verb bolt, fasten, secure **3** noun floodgate, weir **4** noun curl, braid, tress *I kept a tress of her hair in a locket*

lodge **1** verb stay at, put up, shelter, get stuck *A fishbone got stuck in his throat*, remain **2** noun inn, hotel

lofty adjective **1** tall, high, noble, great **2** proud, exalted, arrogant ☆ **modest**

logical adjective fair, justifiable, reasonable, sound ☆ **illogical**

loiter verb lag, trail, linger, dally, dawdle, hang around

loll verb recline, sprawl, lounge, lie, rest, flop

lone adjective single, sole, lonely, separate, unaccompanied LOAN

lonely adjective alone, forsaken, friendless, remote, forlorn, lonesome

long **1** adjective lengthy, extended, expanded ☆ **short** **2** verb crave, hanker, yearn, desire

look **1** verb appear, seem **2** verb peer, glance, watch, behold **3** noun appearance, glance, gaze *Her gaze fell upon me, and I had to answer the next question*

loom verb menace, portend, rise, emerge, appear

loop noun bend, circle, coil, noose, twist

loophole noun escape, way out, excuse, get-out

loose adjective **1** slack, separate, apart, flimsy, flabby, baggy **2** free, relaxed, **3** vague, indefinite

loosely adverb freely, separately, vaguely

loosen verb slacken, relax, undo, detach, release, unfasten ☆ **tighten**

loot noun booty, haul, swag, spoils, plunder LUTE

lord noun noble, ruler, duke, marquess, earl, viscount, baron

lose verb **1** mislay, misplace, miss ☆ **find** **2** be defeated, suffer defeat *The rebels suffered defeat at the hands of the army*, fail ☆ **win**

loser noun failure, dud, flop ☆ **winner**

loss noun damage, harm, forfeit, ruin, misfortune ☆ **gain**

lost adjective mislaid, missing, gone, vanished, strayed, ruined ☆ **found**

lot noun **1** group, batch, assortment **2** fate, portion, fortune **3** plot, patch, land

lotion noun balm, salve, ointment, cream, liniment

loud adjective **1** noisy, blatant, shrill, blaring, deafening **2** gaudy, vulgar, tasteless ☆ **quiet**

lounge **1** verb recline, lie, loll, sprawl, laze **2** noun lobby *Tea was served in the hotel's lobby*, reception room, waiting room

lout noun oaf, clod, boor, lummox

lovable adjective winsome, charming, attractive, fascinating ☆ **hateful**

love **1** verb adore, idolize, worship, dote on, cherish, treasure **2** noun affection, passion, devotion, ardor ☆ **hate**

---

lovely adjective charming, delightful, beautiful, adorable ☆ hideous

low adjective 1 base, vulgar, crude, improper 2 not high, flat, level 3 soft, faint, muffled, deep 4 humble, modest, lowly 5 cheap, inexpensive ☆ high LO

lower 1 verb let down, fall, descend 2 verb debase, disgrace, degrade 3 adjective inferior, lesser, smaller, minor

loyal adjective constant, staunch *Bill was Kathy's staunch friend for years*, true ▶ *faithful* ☆ disloyal

lucid adjective clear, obvious, intelligible, bright ▶ *transparent* ☆ murky

luck noun chance, fortune, success, windfall ☆ misfortune

lucky adjective fortunate, successful, blessed, charmed, favored ☆ unlucky

ludicrous adjective absurd, foolish, silly, outlandish, ▶ *ridiculous*

lug verb pull, draw, drag, haul, tow, heave

luggage noun baggage, suitcases, trunks, boxes

lull 1 verb calm, dwindle, cease, slacken, subside 2 noun calm, hush, respite

lumber 1 noun timber, wood, boards, logs 2 verb plod, shuffle, stomp

luminous adjective shining, radiant, bright

lump noun bit, piece, chunk, block, knob, swelling *I noticed a rather painful swelling on my arm*

lunatic noun insane person, maniac, psychopath

lunge verb push, thrust, plunge, charge, pounce

lurch verb lean, list, reel, rock, stagger, stumble

lure verb attract, draw, decoy, ensnare, invite ▶ *tempt* ☆ repulse

lurid adjective ghastly, disgusting, grim, grisly, melodramatic, sensational

lurk verb slink, skulk, crouch, hide, prowl, snoop

luscious adjective juicy, succulent, mellow, delicious, scrumptious ☆ nauseous

lush adjective wild, luxuriant, green, rich, abundant

lust noun desire, passion, craving, greed

luster noun brightness, brilliance, gleam, sheen

lusty adjective hale, hearty, vigorous, energetic, rugged, tough ☆ weak

luxury noun affluence, wealth, richness, comfort, bliss

lyre noun harp, zither LIAR

Mm

macabre adjective ghastly, grisly, hideous, horrible ▶ *ghostly*

machine noun engine, contrivance, device

mad adjective 1 angry, furious 2 lunatic, crazy ▶ *insane* ☆ sane

madcap adjective flighty, reckless, thoughtless, impulsive

magazine noun 1 periodical, publication 2 storehouse, depot, arsenal

magic 1 noun wizardry, witchcraft, sorcery, conjuring 2 adjective bewitching *She greeted me with a bewitching smile*, fascinating, miraculous

magician noun conjuror, wizard, witch, sorcerer, juggler

magistrate noun judge, justice, bailiff

magnanimous adjective forgiving, generous, charitable, liberal ☆ paltry

magnate noun industrialist, merchant, tycoon, VIP, leader MAGNET

magnet noun lodestone, attraction, bait, draw MAGNATE

magnetic adjective attracting, attractive, absorbing, entrancing, alluring, mesmerizing ▶ *charming* ☆ repulsive

magnificent adjective majestic, noble, grand, brilliant, superb ▶ *splendid* ☆ modest

magnify verb enlarge, increase, exaggerate ▶ *enhance* ☆ diminish

maid noun 1 maiden, virgin, miss, damsel 2 maidservant, domestic help, waitress MADE

mail noun 1 letters, post, correspondence, epistles 2 armor *The knight's armor was made of breastplates and chain mail*, shield MALE

maim verb mutilate, injure, mangle, crush ▶ *disable* ☆ heal

main 1 adjective leading, principal, head, chief, central *Such important matters are dealt with at our central office*, 2 noun channel, duct, line, pipe

mainly adverb chiefly, generally, mostly, on the whole, usually

247

maintain verb **1** sustain, keep, support, provide for **2** affirm, advocate *The chairman advocated an increase in charges*, assert

majestic adjective dignified, grand, noble, august, elevated ▷ *magnificent* ☆ **unimportant**

major **1** adjective senior, chief, leading, more important, greater ☆ **minor** **2** noun officer, soldier

majority noun greater number, most part, bulk, mass ☆ **minority**

make verb **1** build, construct, fabricate, fashion **2** compel, drive, coerce **3** designate *Two days after her boss retired, Liz was designated as the new head of the department*, appoint

make up verb **1** invent, fabricate, create **2** forgive and forget, bury the hatchet *At last, my brother and sister stopped arguing and decided to bury the hatchet*

makeshift adjective improvised, temporary, stopgap *I fixed the car engine, but it was only a stopgap repair* ☆ **permanent**

malady noun illness, sickness, ailment, affliction, disease

malevolent adjective malign, baleful, venomous, malicious ▷ *hostile* ☆ **benevolent**

malice noun bitterness, rancor, spite, enmity ▷ *hatred* ☆ **kindness**

malicious adjective malignant, spiteful, resentful, bitter ▷ *hateful* ☆ **kind**

maltreat verb bully, harm, abuse, injure ▷ *hurt* ☆ **assist**

mammoth adjective giant, colossal, enormous, massive ▷ *huge* ☆ **small**

man **1** noun male, sir, mankind, humankind, gentleman **2** noun valet, manservant **3** verb equip, fit out, arm, crew

manage verb **1** direct, control, administer **2** get along *I get along just fine on my own*, fare, cope with ☆ **fail**

manager noun director, superintendent, overseer, supervisor, boss

mandate noun authority, command, instruction, warrant

maneuver verb direct, drive, guide, handle ▷ *manipulate*

mangle verb crush, deform, destroy, maul ▷ *maim*

mania noun madness, delirium, craze, fad, enthusiasm, passion

manifest verb signify, suggest, demonstrate, display ▷ *show* ☆ **hide**

manipulate verb work, handle, wield, use, conduct, control ▷ *operate*

manly adjective male, masculine, brave, bold, strong ▷ *fearless*

manner noun fashion, style, form, mode, demeanor, bearing, way MANOR

manor noun estate, country house, chateau, hall MANNER

mansion noun house, castle, residence ▷ *manor*

mantle noun canopy, cape, covering, hood, shroud, cloak MANTEL

mantel noun fireplace shelf, mantelpiece MANTLE

manual **1** adjective hand-operated, physical *Working in a car factory, his job required a lot of physical labor* **2** noun guide, guidebook, handbook

manufacture verb make, build, fabricate, create, produce ▷ *construct*

manuscript noun **1** script, article, essay, theme **2** handwriting, autograph

many adjective numerous, varied, various, frequent, countless ☆ **few**

map noun chart, plan, diagram, outline

mar verb deface, disfigure, injure, blemish, damage ▷ *spoil* ☆ **enhance**

march verb stride, walk, pace, step, file, trek

margin noun edge, border, rim, side, boundary, brim, brink ☆ **center**

mariner noun seaman, sailor, seafarer, deckhand, tar, seadog

mark **1** noun feature, emblem, impression *The letter had a hand-stamped impression on it*, blemish **2** verb scratch, blemish, stain **3** verb take notice of, observe

marked adjective noticeable, conspicuous, apparent, clear, striking ☆ **slight**

market noun grocery store, supermarket, bazaar

maroon verb desert, beach, strand, abandon, cast away ☆ **rescue**

marry verb wed, get married, espouse, mate, unite ☆ **separate**

marsh noun swamp, mire, moor, morass, bog

marshal verb gather, group, deploy, assemble MARTIAL

martial adjective military, militant, hostile, warlike
⭐ peaceful MARSHAL

marvel noun miracle, wonder, spectacle, sensation

marvelous adjective wonderful, wondrous, fabulous, spectacular ▷ *remarkable* ⭐ ordinary

masculine adjective manlike, manly, strong, robust, strapping ▷ *male* ⭐ feminine

mash verb crush, squash, pulverize, grind

mask 1 noun camouflage, veil, domino
2 verb conceal, disguise *Aladdin went to the marketplace disguised as a beggar*, shield ⭐ uncover

mass noun batch, combination, hunk, load, quantity, lump

massacre verb exterminate, butcher, murder, slaughter, kill

massive adjective big, large, bulky, enormous
▷ *huge* ⭐ small

master 1 noun controller, director, leader, captain, champion 2 verb tame *Our job on the ranch was to tame the wild horses*, control, defeat, subdue

match 1 noun light, fuse, taper, Lucifer 2 verb copy, pair, equal, tone with

mate 1 noun spouse, husband, wife, companion, chum, comrade 2 verb breed, join, wed, yoke

material 1 noun fabric, textile, cloth, stuff, matter
2 adjective actual, real, concrete *There was concrete evidence of the prisoner's innocence*

maternal adjective motherly, parental, kind, affectionate, protective

matter 1 noun affair, concern, subject, topic
2 noun stuff, material, substance *This rock contains some sort of mineral substance* 3 noun trouble, distress
4 verb signify, count, affect

mature adjective ripe, mellowed, seasoned, developed, grown-up, adult ⭐ immature

maul verb batter, beat, molest, paw ▷ *mangle*

maxim noun saying, motto, axiom, proverb

maximum adjective supreme, highest, most, greatest, top, largest ⭐ minimum

maybe adverb possibly, perhaps, perchance

maze noun labyrinth, puzzle, tangle, confusion
▷ *muddle* MAIZE

meadow noun grassland, field, mead, pasture

meager adjective thin, spare, slight, flimsy, sparse
▷ *scanty* ⭐ substantial

meal noun repast, dinner, lunch, breakfast, supper
▷ *feast*

mean 1 verb signify, denote, express, suggest
2 adjective cruel, base, low, paltry, miserly ⭐ generous
3 average, medium MIEN

meaning noun significance, explanation, sense

means noun 1 resources, money, wealth 2 technique, ability *She has the ability to become a professional soccer player*, method

measure 1 noun meter, gauge, rule 2 noun limit, extent, amount 3 verb estimate, value, quantify *It is hard to quantify how much damage has been done*

meat noun flesh, viands, victuals, food, muscle, brawn MEET, METE

mechanical adjective 1 automatic, machine-driven
2 routine, unthinking

medal noun award, decoration, ribbon, prize, trophy MEDDLE

meddle verb interfere, intervene, intrude, tamper MEDAL

medicine noun remedy, cure, physic, medicament, nostrum, drug

mediocre adjective average, common, inferior, middling ▷ *ordinary* ⭐ excellent

meditate verb ponder, puzzle over, think, reflect, contemplate

medium 1 noun means, agency, center 2 noun conditions, setting, atmosphere *I like school because it has such a wonderful atmosphere of learning* 3 adjective average, fair ▷ *mediocre*

medley noun assortment, jumble, collection, hodgepodge

meek adjective docile, humble, quiet, patient, uncomplaining ▷ *mild* ⭐ arrogant

meet verb come together, converge, join, flock, assemble, encounter MEAT, METE

meeting noun gathering, assembly, convention

melancholy adjective glum, gloomy, unhappy, sad
▷ *miserable* ⭐ cheerful

mellow adjective 1 ripe, rich, full-flavored ⭐ unripe
2 jovial, cheerful 3 smooth, soothing, delicate *The dessert had a smooth, delicate flavor*

Measurements

inch
foot
yard
mile
cup
pint
quart
gallon
ounce
pound
ton
millimeter
centimeter
meter
kilometer
milliliter
liter
milligram
gram
kilogram
tonne

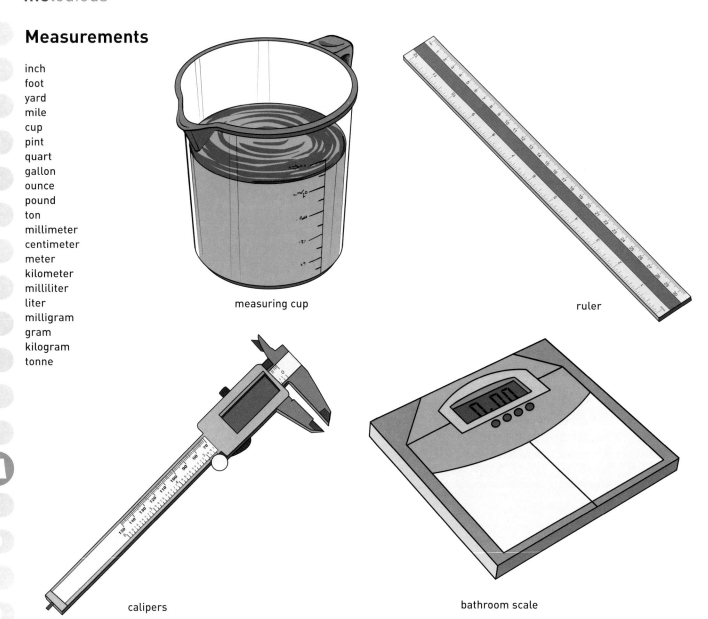

measuring cup

ruler

calipers

bathroom scale

melodious adjective sweet, mellow, silver-toned, rich, resonant ▸ harsh

melody noun tune, air, lay, song, chant, theme

melt verb dissolve, liquefy, soften, thaw ▸ solidify

member noun 1 fellow, associate, representative, comrade 2 limb, part, portion, leg, arm

memorable adjective unforgettable, fresh, indelible, noticeable, striking ▸ *conspicuous*

memorial noun monument, memento, relic, mausoleum *The emperor was buried in the ancient mausoleum*

memorize verb learn, commit to memory, remember

memory noun recall, recapture, recollection, renown ▸ *fame*

menace verb threaten, intimidate, frighten, alarm ▸ *bully*

mend verb restore, correct, promote, improve rectify, heal ▸ *repair* ▸ damage

menial 1 adjective servile, ignoble, base 2 noun flunky, underling, lackey

mental adjective intellectual, theoretical *Edward's knowledge of music is purely theoretical; he can't play or sing*, abstract ▸ physical

mention verb declare, announce, observe, disclose, speak of, say

mercenary 1 adjective acquisitive, grasping, greedy ▸ *selfish* 2 noun soldier of fortune *The men who were killed were not patriots but soldiers of fortune*, freelance, hireling

250

merchandise noun wares, goods, commodities, cargo, freight, stock

merchant noun dealer, trader, marketeer, vender, retailer, tradesman

merciful adjective humane, clement, lenient, compassionate, sparing, forgiving ★ **merciless**

merciless adjective callous, cruel, pitiless, unrelenting, inhuman ★ **merciful**

mercy noun compassion, clemency, forgiveness, forbearance, grace ▶ *pity* ★ **cruelty**

mere adjective pure, unmixed, absolute, unaffected, simple, paltry

merge verb mix, mingle, combine, fuse, blend, weld ▶ *unite*

merit 1 noun excellence, quality, virtue, worth, caliber ▶ *talent* ★ **failing** 2 verb deserve, be worthy of

merry adjective jolly, gleeful, cheerful, mirthful, sunny ▶ *happy* ★ **melancholy**

mesh noun net, lattice, snare, netting, tangle, trap, web

mess 1 noun muddle, confusion, clutter, jumble, chaos ▶ *plight* ★ **order** 2 dining hall, mess hall, dining room

message noun communication, letter, missive, notice, note, dispatch *The reporter sent a dispatch to her newspaper editor*

messenger noun courier, runner, agent, bearer, carrier, herald

mete verb measure, apportion, distribute, divide, deal MEAT, MEET

meter noun 1 measure, gauge, rule 2 cadence *He recited some of his poems, which had a peculiar cadence to them*, rhythm, lilt, swing

method noun routine, usage, way, means, system, rule, manner ▶ *mode*

mettle noun spirit, life, fire, animation, ardor, boldness ▶ *courage*

middle 1 noun center, heart, midst 2 adjective medium, average, normal

midget 1 noun dwarf, gnome, pygmy 2 adjective little, miniature, small ▶ *tiny* ★ **giant**

mien noun appearance, air, look, manner, expression MEAN

miffed adjective annoyed, nettled, offended, hurt ▶ *upset* ★ **delighted**

might 1 noun strength, ability, power, force, energy 2 verb past tense of **may** *She might not have gone had she known it would snow* MITE

mighty adjective strong, powerful, potent, stupendous ▶ *hefty* ★ **weak**

mild adjective moderate, calm, gentle, genial, docile ▶ *meek* ★ **harsh**

military adjective martial, soldierly, warlike

mill 1 noun grinder, works, factory, plant 2 verb crush, grind, pulverize *The rock was pulverized and used for making roads*, grate, pound

mimic verb impersonate, copy, simulate, imitate

mince verb shred, chop, crumble, grind, hash MINTS

mind 1 noun brain, intellect, soul, spirit 2 verb listen to, obey, follow orders 3 verb take care of, look after 4 verb be careful, watch out for

mine 1 noun quarry, colliery, shaft, deposit, tunnel 2 noun bomb, explosive 3 verb excavate, dig out 4 pronoun belonging to me *This store is mine*

mingle verb mix, blend, combine ▶ *merge*

miniature 1 adjective tiny, small, dwarf, midget, minute 2 noun small portrait

minimum adjective least, smallest, lowest, slightest ★ **maximum**

minister noun 1 clergyman, vicar, priest 2 ambassador, diplomat *My aunt was a diplomat working in the Brazilian embassy* 3 secretary, cabinet member

minor adjective lesser, smaller, lower, junior, trivial, trifling ★ **major** MINER

mint 1 verb stamp, forge, cast 2 adjective new, perfect, untarnished 3 noun peppermint, plant

minute 1 noun (*min*-it) flash, instant, moment 2 adjective (my-*nyute*) slight, tiny, small ▶ *miniature* ★ **huge**

miracle noun marvel, wonder, phenomenon

miraculous adjective supernatural, amazing, wondrous, prodigious ★ **ordinary**

mire noun slime, muck, ooze, mud

mirror 1 noun looking glass, reflector 2 verb imitate, simulate, reflect *The essay reflected my feelings about my old home*, copy

mirth noun hilarity, laughter, jocularity, fun, frolic, jollity ★ melancholy

misbehave verb do wrong, disobey, offend, be naughty ★ behave

miscellaneous adjective various, varied, divers, sundry, mixed, jumbled

mischief noun roguery, pranks, damage, hurt, annoyance, harm

mischievous adjective rascally, villainous, naughty, destructive, spiteful ★ good

misconduct noun misbehavior, wrongdoing, naughtiness, rudeness

miser noun niggard, skinflint, scrooge, penny pincher, tightwad ★ spendthrift

miserable adjective forlorn, wretched, pitiable, desolate, suffering ★ cheerful

misery noun sorrow, woe, grief, anguish, distress ▶ *unhappiness* ★ happiness

misfit noun eccentric *Professor Jones is something of an eccentric and comes to lectures in her slippers*, dropout, oddball, nonconformist

misfortune noun adversity, bad luck, hardship, evil, calamity ▶ *disaster* ★ luck

misgiving noun distrust, mistrust, doubt, apprehension, anxiety ▶ *qualm* ★ confidence

mishap noun misadventure, blow, accident ▶ *misfortune*

misjudge verb underestimate, overestimate, overrate, underrate ▶ *mistake*

mislay verb lose, misplace, miss

mislead verb deceive, lead astray, hoodwink, take in, outwit ▶ *bluff*

miss 1 verb fail, fall short of, skip, pass over, mistake 2 verb grieve over, yearn for, lament 3 noun girl, young woman, damsel

missile noun projectile, arrow, dart, pellet, shot, rocket

mission noun errand, task, assignment, object, objective, end, aim ▶ *quest*

mist noun moisture, dew, vapor, fog, cloud MISSED

mistake 1 noun error, fault, lapse, blunder, oversight 2 verb slip up, misunderstand, confuse

mistaken adjective erroneous, untrue, false, fallacious ▶ *wrong* ★ correct

mistrust verb disbelieve, distrust, doubt, fear ▶ *suspect* ★ trust

misunderstand verb mistake, misinterpret, take wrongly ★ grasp

misuse verb exploit, abuse, corrupt

mite noun 1 grain, atom, morsel, particle 2 bug, parasite *The plants were infested with parasites* MIGHT

mitigate verb allay, ease, abate, moderate, justify ★ aggravate

mix verb blend, whip, mingle, combine ▶ *stir*

mix up verb confuse, confound, muddle, jumble ▶ *bewilder*

mixture noun miscellany, medley, jumble, blend

moan verb wail, groan, grouse, grumble, grieve

mob noun crowd, mass, gang, flock, rabble, company, throng

mobile adjective active, portable, wandering, movable ★ immobile

mock 1 verb mimic, imitate, jeer at, laugh at, ridicule ▶ *flatter* 2 adjective pretended, artificial

mode noun fashion, style, vogue, manner, way, form ▶ *method* MOWED

model noun 1 pattern, original, prototype *This car is a prototype, but we will produce many like it in the future* 2 mannequin 3 replica, representation

moderate adjective reasonable, medium, gentle, mild, quiet, modest ▶ *fair*

modern adjective new, up-to-date, modish, stylish, recent

modest adjective bashful, demure, diffident, unassuming, humble ★ vain

modesty noun humility, diffidence, reserve, shyness, decency ★ vanity

modify verb transform, convert, change, alter, revise, redesign

moist adjective damp, humid, watery, clammy, dank ▶ *wet* ★ dry

moisture noun damp, dampness, liquid, wetness

mold 1 verb form, shape, fashion, cast, create 2 noun pattern, matrix 3 noun earth, loam

moldy adjective mildewed, putrid, bad

molest verb annoy, bother, pursue, attack, torment ▶ *harry*

moment noun **1** second, instant, twinkling
2 importance, worth, weight *I think your argument has
some weight, and I agree with you*

momentous adjective notable, outstanding, decisive,
important ★ insignificant

monarch noun king, sovereign, ruler, emperor, prince
The head of state in Monaco is a prince

money noun wealth, cash, coin, legal tender

mongrel noun hybrid, mixed, crossbreed, dog

monitor **1** noun listener, auditor, watchdog, prefect
2 verb check, supervise, oversee

monologue noun lecture, oration, speech,
recitation, sermon

monopolize verb control, take over, appropriate
▶ *dominate* ★ share

monotonous adjective tedious, uninteresting, dull,
prosaic *His speech was so prosaic that I almost dropped off
to sleep*, repetitive ▶ *tiresome*

monster noun beast, fiend, villain, brute

monstrous adjective hideous, frightful, dreadful,
terrible, criminal ▶ *wicked*

mood noun state of mind, humor, temper,
disposition *My grandmother's gentle disposition won
her many friends*

moody adjective morose, sulky, sullen, peevish,
cantankerous *I didn't like Uncle Harry; he was a
cantankerous old man* ★ cheerful

moor **1** verb tether, picket, tie, chain, anchor, secure
2 noun heath, moorland MORE

mop noun **1** sponge, swab, towel **2** hair, tresses,
locks, mane

mope verb be dejected, grieve, moon, pine, sulk

moral adjective virtuous, good, honest, honorable
▶ *upright* ★ immoral

morbid adjective gruesome, macabre, melancholy

more **1** adjective in addition, also, beyond, extra,
further **2** adverb better, again, longer MOOR

morning noun dawn, daybreak, daylight, cockcrow
*I rose at cockcrow, saddled my horse, and was off to
Richmond*, sunrise ★ evening MOURNING

morose adjective glum, sullen, sulky, broody, taciturn
▶ *moody* ★ cheerful

morsel noun bit, bite, piece, scrap, nibble

mortal adjective **1** human, feeble, ephemeral **2** fatal,
final, deadly, severe

most **1** adjective greatest nearly all **2** adverb mostly,
chiefly, mainly, utmost

mostly adverb as a rule, principally, usually, normally

mother **1** noun female parent, mom, mommy, mama
2 verb nurse, protect, rear, care for

motherly adjective caring, comforting, loving,
maternal, gentle

motion noun **1** movement, locomotion, action, passage
2 proposal *I vote that we accept the proposal*, suggestion

motionless adjective stationary, still, transfixed,
stable, inert ★ moving

motive noun reason, purpose, occasion, impulse, cause
▶ *spur*

mottled adjective speckled, spotted, pied, piebald

motto noun saying, slogan, watchword, maxim *My
mother's maxim was "Always look on the bright side,"* proverb

mound noun hillock, pile, knoll, rise, mount

mount verb ascend, climb, rise, vault

mourn verb lament, deplore, sorrow, regret, weep
▶ *grieve* ★ rejoice

mournful adjective doleful, somber, cheerless,
sorrowful ▶ *melancholy* ★ joyful

mouth noun aperture, opening, entrance, orifice,
inlet, jaws

mouthful noun bite, morsel, sample, taste, tidbit

move verb **1** march, proceed, walk, go **2** propose,
suggest, recommend **3** propel, drive, impel

moving adjective touching, affecting, stirring *The
band played a stirring rendition of "Amazing Grace,"*
emotional

much **1** adjective abundant, considerable, ample
2 adverb considerably, greatly, often **3** noun lots, loads,
heaps, plenty

muck noun dirt, filth, mire, ooze, mud, scum

muddle **1** noun confusion, clutter, jumble, mix-up
2 verb bungle, tangle, confound ▶ *bewilder*

muff verb botch, mismanage, miss, spoil ▶ *muddle*

muffle verb **1** deaden, mute, muzzle, silence **2** wrap,
envelop, wind, swaddle

mug **1** noun face, looks **2** noun cup, beaker, tankard
3 verb attack, beat up, rob

muggy adjective clammy, dank, damp, humid, close ☆ dry

mull verb meditate *I meditated over the weekend before deciding what to do*, consider, study, think about

multiply verb increase, spread, grow, extend, intensify ☆ decrease

multitude noun crowd, legion, throng, swarm, horde ☆ handful

mum adjective dumb, silent, quiet, mute

munch verb crunch, chew, bit, nibble ▶ eat

murder verb slay, assassinate, butcher, destroy, slaughter ▶ *kill*

murky adjective foggy, cloudy, dark, gloomy, dull, misty ☆ bright

murmur noun & verb whisper, mutter, mumble, drone

muscular adjective brawny, athletic, burly, beefy, powerful ▶ *robust* ☆ puny

muse verb meditate, ponder, puzzle over, brood, deliberate

must 1 verb ought to, should, be obliged to 2 noun duty, necessity, requirement

muster verb marshal, collect, assemble, rally *The troops rallied and prepared to attack again*, enroll

musty adjective moldy, rank, mildewy, decayed

mute adjective silent, speechless, voiceless, soundless ☆ loud

mutilate verb injure, hurt, cut, damage, hack ▶ *maim*

mutiny noun & verb protest, revolt, strike, riot

mutter verb mumble, grouse, grumble ▶ *murmur* ☆ exclaim

mutual adjective common, reciprocal, interchangeable ▶ *joint* ☆ one-sided

mysterious adjective obscure, unrevealed, unexplained, secret ▶ *hidden* ☆ clear

mystery noun puzzle, enigma, secrecy, riddle, problem

mystify verb confuse, bamboozle, hoodwink, puzzle, mislead ▶ *baffle* ☆ enlighten

myth noun fable, legend, supposition, fabrication, tradition, fantasy ☆ fact

mythical adjective fabulous, fabled, legendary, traditional, imaginary ☆ true

nab verb arrest, apprehend, seize, catch, capture, grab

nag 1 verb pester, hector, heckle, badger, annoy, henpeck, scold *My parents scolded me for coming home late* 2 noun horse, pony

nail 1 noun brad, peg, pin, spike, tack 2 verb hammer, fix, tack, peg 3 verb capture, catch, seize

naive adjective innocent, unworldly, unsophisticated, simple, trusting ☆ cunning, sophisticated

naked adjective nude, bare, unclothed, undressed ☆ clothed

name 1 noun title, description, designation 2 noun character, reputation *A good reputation is very important to me*, distinction 3 verb christen, style, term, entitle

nap 1 verb sleep, doze, drowse, rest 2 noun down, fiber, fuzz *Velvet is a cloth with a kind of fuzz on the surface*

narrate verb describe, tell, recite, yarn

narrow adjective slender, fine, small ▶ *thin* ☆ wide

nasty adjective dirty, mucky, foul, offensive, unpleasant ▶ *squalid* ☆ nice

national adjective civil, governmental, public, general

native adjective natural, inborn, aboriginal, domestic, local

natural adjective frank, genuine, innate, instinctive, ordinary, usual

naturally adjective absolutely, certainly, frankly, normally

nature noun 1 temper, personality, disposition 2 the world, the outdoors, landscape

naughty adjective mischievous, rascally, wicked, disobedient ▶ *bad* ☆ well-behaved

nauseous adjective disgusting, sickening, repulsive, revolting ☆ pleasant

nautical adjective maritime *Ancient Greece was a great maritime nation*, seamanlike, naval, sailing

navigate verb voyage, cruise, sail, guide, pilot

navy noun ships, fleet, armada, flotilla

near adjective close, nearby, adjacent, bordering, beside ▶ *nigh* ★ remote

nearly adverb about, almost, all but, thereabouts, roughly

neat adjective 1 tidy, spruce, smart, stylish ★ untidy 2 skillful, clever, adroit *I admire your adroit handling of that tricky situation*, ingenious

necessary adjective needed, essential, basic, required, compulsory ★ optional

need 1 verb require, want, crave ▶ *demand* ★ have 2 noun distress, want, necessity, deprivation *During the long war, the people suffered many deprivations* KNEAD

needed adjective wanted, desired, lacking ▶ *necessary* ★ unnecessary

needless adjective pointless, unnecessary, superfluous, useless ★ necessary

needy adjective destitute, down-and-out, deprived ▶ *poor* ★ well-off

neglect verb overlook, ignore, scorn, slight, disregard ▶ *spurn* ★ cherish

neglected adjective unkempt, abandoned, dilapidated, uncared for ★ cherished

negligent adjective neglectful, forgetful, slack, indifferent ▶ *careless* ★ careful

negotiate verb bargain, deal, treat, haggle, mediate

neighborhood noun vicinity, surroundings, district, area, locality *There are many fine houses in this locality*

neighborly adjective hospitable, friendly, kind, obliging ▶ *helpful*

nerve noun 1 mettle, guts, pluck, courage 2 audacity, impudence *Mr. Thompson already owes us money, and yet he has the impudence to ask for more*

nervous adjective tense, taut, jumpy, flustered, anxious, timid ★ confident

nest noun den, burrow, haunt, refuge, resort

nestle adjective cuddle, snuggle, huddle, nuzzle

net 1 verb catch, trap, lasso, capture 2 noun lattice, mesh, trap, web, lace *I have some new lace curtains* 3 adjective clear *I made a clear $15,000 after taxes*, final, lowest

nettle verb exasperate, annoy, ruffle, pique ▶ *vex*

neutral adjective impartial, unbiased, fair-minded, unprejudiced ★ biased

never adverb at no time, not at all, under no circumstances ★ always

new adjective recent, just out, current, latest, fresh, unused ▶ *novel* ★ old GNU, KNEW

news noun information, intelligence, tidings, account, bulletin

next adjective 1 following, succeeding, after, later 2 adjacent, adjoining *I live on Park Street, and my friend lives on the adjoining street*, beside

nibble verb bite, peck, gnaw, munch ▶ *eat*

nice adjective 1 pleasant, agreeable, amiable, charming, delightful ★ nasty 2 precise, accurate, fine, subtle

niche noun compartment, hole, corner, recess, place

nick verb dent, score, mill, cut, scratch

nigh adjective next, close, adjacent, adjoining ▶ *near* ★ distant

night noun dark, darkness, dusk, evening ★ day KNIGHT

nimble adjective active, agile, spry, lithe, skillful ▶ *deft* ★ clumsy

nip verb cut, snip, pinch, twinge, bite

no 1 adjective not any, not one, none 2 adverb nay, not at all KNOW

noble adjective dignified, lofty *My aunt is very important and has a lofty position on the council*, generous, grand, stately, elevated ★ base

nod verb 1 beckon, signal, indicate, salute 2 sleep, doze, nap

noise noun din, discord, clamor, clatter, hubbub, tumult, uproar ★ silence

noisy adjective loud, boisterous, turbulent, rowdy, clamorous ★ quiet

nominate verb appoint, assign, elect, choose, propose, suggest

nonchalant adjective casual, unperturbed, calm, blasé *We enjoyed the new musical, but Sue has been to so many shows that she was very blasé about it*, cool, detached ★ anxious

nondescript adjective commonplace, colorless, dull, ordinary ▸ *plain* ★ **unusual**

none pronoun not one, not any, not a part, nil, nobody NUN

nonsense noun absurdity, balderdash, drivel, rot, garbage, twaddle ★ **sense**

nook noun compartment, hole, corner, alcove, crevice, cubbyhole, cranny ▸ *niche*

noose noun loop, bight, snare, rope, lasso

normal adjective usual, general, average, sane, lucid, rational, standard ★ **abnormal**

nose noun 1 beak, bill, neb, snout 2 prow, stem, bow, front

nosy adjective inquisitive, curious, prying, snooping, intrusive

nostalgia noun homesickness, longing, pining, regret, remembrance

notable adjective eventful, momentous, outstanding, great, celebrated ▸ *famous* ★ **commonplace**

notch noun dent, nick, score, cut, cleft, indentation

note noun 1 letter, message, communication 2 remark, record, report 3 fame, renown, distinction 4 bank note, bill

noted adjective eminent, renowned, celebrated, great ▸ *famous* ★ **obscure**

nothing noun zero, naught, null, nil, zip ★ **something**

notice 1 noun announcement, advice, sign, poster 2 verb note, remark, observe *After observing that his bike had a flat tire, Joel knew that he would have to walk to school*, perceive, make out, see ★ **ignore**

notify verb inform, tell, intimate, announce, declare ★ **withhold**

notion noun idea, conception, opinion, belief, judgment

notorious adjective infamous, questionable, scandalous, blatant

notwithstanding adverb nevertheless, nonetheless, however, despite

nourish verb feed, sustain, nurture, comfort, support ★ **starve**

nourishing adjective beneficial, healthful, nutritious, wholesome

novel 1 adjective fresh, unusual, original, unique, rare, uncommon 2 noun fiction, story, book, romance, tale

novice noun beginner, learner, apprentice, tyro, pupil ★ **expert**

now adverb at this moment, at present, at once, instantly, right away

now and then adverb from time to time, sometimes, occasionally

nude adjective bare, naked, unclothed, stripped, undressed

nudge verb poke, push, prod, jog, shove, dig

nuisance noun offense, annoyance, plague, trouble, bore, pest, irritation

nullify verb annul, invalidate, cancel, quash ▸ *abolish* ★ **establish**

numb adjective deadened, insensible, dazed, stunned, unfeeling ★ **sensitive**

number 1 noun figure, amount, volume, quantity, sum 2 noun crowd, throng, multitude *The new president's visit to the town was watched by a multitude of people* 3 noun figure, symbol ▸ *numeral* 4 verb count, reckon, tally

numeral noun symbol, figure, character, cipher

numerous adjective many, divers, several, plentiful ▸ *abundant* ★ **few**

nun noun sister, religious, abbess, prioress NONE

nurse 1 verb attend, care for, foster, support, sustain 2 noun hospital attendant, caretaker

nursery noun 1 children's room, baby's room 2 greenhouse, hothouse, garden

nurture verb feed, nourish, cherish, foster, tend ▸ *nurse*

nutritious adjective healthful, substantial, health-giving ▸ *nourishing* ★ **bad**

oaf noun brute, lout, blockhead, dolt, ruffian, lummox

obedient adjective respectful, obliging, lawabiding, servile, dutiful ★ rebellious

obey verb comply, conform, submit, heed, mind, behave ★ disobey

object 1 verb (ob-*ject*) protest, complain, argue, oppose, refuse ★ agree 2 noun (*ob*-ject) thing, article, commodity, item 3 noun mission, purpose *The purpose of my visit is to end this conflict*, end

objectionable adjective displeasing, distasteful, disagreeable, repugnant ★ pleasant

obligation noun responsibility, liability, commitment ★ choice

oblige verb 1 require, compel, force, make 2 gratify, please, help ▶ *assist* ★ displease

obliging adjective helpful, polite, agreeable, courteous ▶ *willing* ★ unkind

obliterate verb blot out, efface, erase, wipe out, destroy

oblivious adjective unmindful, absentminded, heedless, unaware ★ aware

obnoxious adjective repulsive, revolting, offensive ▶ *unpleasant* ★ pleasant

obscene adjective dirty, unclean, vile, filthy, nasty, immoral, indecent ★ decent

obscure 1 adjective indistinct, dim, vague, hidden, confusing *The language of a legal document can be very confusing* ▶ *doubtful* ★ clear 2 verb conceal, hide, cloud, darken, cover ▶ *hide* ★ clarify

observant adjective attentive, watchful, heedful ▶ *alert* ★ inattentive

observation noun 1 attention, study, supervision 2 utterance, comment, remark, statement *The police issued a statement*

observe verb 1 abide by *I intend to abide by the my parents' rules*, adhere to, carry out, keep up 2 note, notice, perceive, watch ▶ *see* 3 utter, remark, mention

obsolete adjective dated, outmoded, unfashionable, out-of-date ★ current

obstacle noun obstruction, barrier, bar, hindrance ▶ *drawback* ★ advantage

obstinate adjective determined, dogged, unyielding, perverse *As a child, I upset my parents by my perverse behavior* ▶ *stubborn* ★ docile

obstruct verb hinder, impede, block, bar, choke ▶ *restrain* ★ help

obstruction noun hindrance, restraint, impediment, snag

obtain verb acquire, achieve, gain, procure, attain ▶ *get* ★ lose

obtuse adjective dull, stupid, unintelligent, stolid, thick, blunt ★ bright

obvious adjective plain, evident, self-evident, explicit, apparent ▶ *clear* ★ obscure

occasion noun 1 affair, episode, occurrence, circumstance 2 reason, purpose, motive

occasional adjective casual, rare, infrequent, periodic ★ frequent

occult adjective hidden, unrevealed, secret, mysterious, supernatural *Edgar Allan Poe wrote tales of the supernatural* ★ open

occupant noun owner, resident, proprietor, tenant

occupation noun 1 activity, employment, calling, job 2 possession, tenancy, residence

occupied adjective 1 busy, employed, active 2 settled, populated, peopled ★ unoccupied

occupy verb inhabit, live in, reside, dwell in, own, possess, hold

occur verb take place, befall, turn out, come to pass, result ▶ *happen*

occurrence noun happening, affair, circumstance, incident, occasion ▶ *event*

ocean noun sea, main *The pirates of the Spanish Main were the curse of shipping*, deep, tide

Oceans and bodies of water

Arctic	bay	sound
Atlantic	fjord	straits
Indian	gulf	
Pacific	lagoon	
Southern	loch	

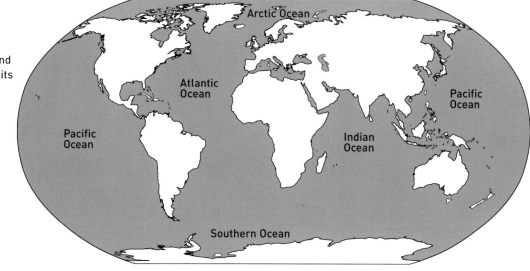

odd adjective **1** single, unmatched **2** singular, peculiar, quaint, queer ★ **ordinary** **3** surplus, leftover, remaining

odds and ends noun leavings, debris *The bag had split, and there was debris everywhere*, leftovers, oddments, remains

odious adjective hateful, offensive, detestable ▷ *abominable* ★ **pleasant**

odor noun **1** scent, aroma ▷ *fragrance* **2** stink, stench, reek ▷ *smell*

odorous adjective fragrant, perfumed, aromatic, sweet-smelling

off **1** adverb away from, over, done **2** preposition along, against, opposite, distant ★ **on** **3** adjective bad, moldy, rotten

offend verb **1** insult, hurt, wound, outrage, displease **2** transgress, sin ★ **please**

offense noun insult, outrage, attack, crime, hurt

offensive adjective insulting, offending, rude, repugnant, hurtful, distasteful

offer **1** verb propose, proffer, present, tender, attempt **2** noun bid, endeavor, proposal

offering noun sacrifice, donation, gift, present

offhand adjective **1** brusque, casual, curt, informal, abrupt **2** informal, improvised, impromptu *The singer gave an impromptu performance* ★ **planned**

office **1** noun bureau, department, room **2** position, appointment, post

officer noun **1** official, administrator, functionary, executive **2** military rank, policeman, minister *A minister from the French Embassy made a speech*

official **1** adjective authorized, authentic, proper, formal ★ **unofficial** **2** noun executive, officeholder, bureaucrat *The city bureaucrats take months to get a job done*

officious adjective interfering, meddlesome, self-important

offspring noun child, children, descendant, heir, family

often adverb frequently, regularly, recurrently, time after time, repeatedly ★ **seldom**

ointment noun lotion, salve, cream, balm, embrocation, liniment

old adjective **1** ancient, antique, aged, antiquated **2** crumbling, decayed *Beneath the ivy were the decayed remains of the castle wall*, decrepit ★ **new** **3** out-of-date, old-fashioned, passé **4** aged, mature, elderly ★ **young**

ominous adjective menacing, threatening, foreboding, sinister

omit verb leave out, neglect, let go, overlook, skip ★ **include**

once adverb formerly, at one time, previously

one **1** adjective sole, alone, lone, whole **2** noun unit, single thing

one-sided adjective unequal, unfair, unjust, biased

only **1** adjective exclusive, single, sole, lone, solitary **2** adverb solely, barely, exclusively

onset noun start, outbreak, assault, attack, onslaught

onslaught noun charge, attack, bombardment

ooze **1** noun mire, muck, slime **2** verb bleed, discharge, emit, exude, leak

open **1** verb uncover, unlock, unfasten **2** verb start, commence, begin **3** adjective uncovered, clear, evident, apparent ★ **closed** **4** adjective frank, honest, candid, fair

opening noun **1** aperture, mouth, crevice, recess, hole **2** commencement, beginning

openly adverb candidly, frankly, plainly, sincerely ★ **secretly**

operate verb function *Despite its age, the old car continued to function*, work, manipulate, drive ▶ *perform*

operation noun performance, movement, action, motion, proceeding

opinion noun view, concept, judgment, belief, point of view

opponent noun antagonist, rival, competitor, contestant, foe ▶ *enemy* ★ **ally**

opportune adjective timely *It had started to rain, so the timely arrival of the bus was welcome*, convenient, fortunate, suitable ★ **untimely**

opportunity noun occasion, chance, opening, scope, moment

oppose verb withstand, resist, obstruct, confront, hinder ▶ *defy* ★ **support**

opposite adjective **1** facing, fronting **2** conflicting, opposing, contrary, adverse ★ **same**

opposition noun antagonism, defiance, hostility, difference ▶ *resistance* ★ **cooperation**

oppress verb crush, depress, harass, overpower, overwhelm

optimist noun hopeful person, perfectionist ★ **pessimist**

optimistic adjective hopeful, cheerful, confident, positive ★ **pessimistic**

option noun preference, choice, alternative

optional adjective possible, voluntary, unforced, open ★ **compulsory**

opulent adjective rich, affluent, prosperous, well-to-do ▶ *wealthy* ★ **poor**

oration noun sermon, lecture, speech, discourse

orb noun globe, ball, sphere

orbit noun **1** path, passage, trajectory **2** province, realm, domain *The river, the forest, and the castle were all within her domain*

ordeal noun trial, nightmare, torment, agony

order **1** noun arrangement, pattern, grouping,

organization **2** noun command, law, rule, decree *A decree was issued forbidding the hunting of deer* **3** noun shipment, consignment **4** verb direct, instruct, command **5** verb arrange, control, conduct

orderly adjective regular, methodical, trim, neat, well-mannered ★ **messy**

ordinary adjective common, usual, commonplace, general, customary ★ **extraordinary**

organization noun **1** association, group, institute, establishment **2** structure, arrangement, system

organize verb arrange, form, structure, establish, classify ★ **disorganize**

origin noun beginning, start, basis, foundation, root, source ★ **end**

original adjective **1** first, aboriginal, ancient, former, primary **2** fresh, new, novel *Traveling by camel was a novel experience*

originate **1** verb create, conceive, compose **2** arise, begin ▶ *start* ★ **end**

ornament **1** noun decoration, adornment, tracery, pattern **2** trinket, curio, knickknack

ornate adjective decorated, adorned, flowery, embellished, showy, garish ★ **plain**

oust verb expel, eject, evict, dismiss, propel ▶ *overthrow*

out **1** adjective away, outside, absent ★ **in** **2** adjective open, revealed, uncovered **3** adverb loudly, aloud, audibly

out of order adjective broken, not working

out of sorts adjective sick, ill, poorly, gloomy, fed up

outbreak noun epidemic *An epidemic of cholera had hit the village*, rebellion, eruption, explosion, flare-up

outburst noun eruption, explosion ▶ *outbreak*

outcast noun exile, castaway *Robinson Crusoe was a castaway on a desert island*, derelict, refugee

outcome noun effect, consequence, conclusion, result

outcry noun commotion, row, uproar, tumult, shouting, hue and cry ▶ *clamor*

outdated adjective old, antique, old-fashioned, unfashionable, obsolete ★ **modern**

outdo verb surpass, excel, beat, outclass, eclipse

outfit noun ensemble, set *My mother bought a new set of dishes for half price in the sale*, rig, equipment, gear

outing noun excursion, picnic, expedition, trip, ramble

outlandish adjective strange, erratic, odd, queer, quaint, bizarre ★ **ordinary**

outlaw noun bandit, highwayman, hoodlum, desperado *Billy the Kid was a desperado in the Wild West*, robber

outlet noun exit, egress, way out, vent, spout, nozzle, opening ★ **inlet**

outline 1 noun diagram, plan, blueprint, sketch, framework, summary 2 verb draw, sketch, describe

outlook noun view, prospect, forecast, attitude, aspect, prognosis

output noun yield, product, produce, achievement, manufacture

outrage 1 noun disgrace, injury, offense, affront 2 verb offend, insult, shock, violate

outrageous adjective insulting, offensive, exorbitant, monstrous ★ **acceptable**

outright 1 adjective complete, thorough, absolute, wholesale 2 adverb at once, completely, entirely, altogether

outset noun first, opening, beginning ▸ *start* ★ **finish**

outside 1 noun exterior, surface, front 2 adjective exterior, external, outward, surface

outsider noun stranger, foreigner, alien, misfit *Gulliver was something of a misfit in the land of the tiny Lilliputians*

outskirts noun limits, bounds, boundary, outpost, suburb

outspoken adjective frank, open, straightforward, blunt, direct ▸ *candid* ★ **tactful**

outstanding adjective striking, pronounced, conspicuous, notable ▸ *exceptional* ★ **ordinary**

outward adjective exterior, outside, outer, superficial *From a distance, my father and Bill Jones look alike, but it's really just superficial*

outwit verb get the better of, swindle, defraud, dupe ▸ *cheat*

over 1 adjective concluded, ended, done with, settled 2 prep. above, more than, exceeding 3 adverb aloft, above, beyond, extra

overall 1 adjective complete, inclusive, total, broad 2 adverb by and large, on the whole

overbearing adjective domineering, dictatorial, haughty, pompous ▸ *arrogant* ★ **modest**

overcast adjective cloudy, heavy, dark, murky, dull ★ **bright**

overcome adjective overwhelm, conquer, crush, defeat, vanquish ▸ *subdue*

overdo verb overwork, exaggerate, go too far *I didn't mind your eating one of my apples, but taking all four was going too far*

overdue adjective delayed, belated, late, behindhand ★ **early**

overflow verb swamp, deluge, inundate, submerge, soak, spill

overhaul verb 1 repair, mend, fix, inspect, examine 2 overtake, pass, gain on

overhead adverb above, upward, aloft, on high ★ **below**

overhear verb listen, eavesdrop, snoop, spy

overjoyed adjective elated, jubilant, rapturous ▸ *delighted* ★ **disappointed**

overlap verb overrun, go beyond, coincide, overlay

overlook verb 1 disregard, pardon, condone, ignore 2 neglect, miss, pass over 3 inspect, check, examine

overpower verb conquer, crush, master, subdue, vanquish ▸ *defeat*

overseas adjective abroad, foreign ★ **domestic**

overseer noun inspector, supervisor, boss, manager, master, mistress

oversight noun omission, blunder, error, fault, lapse ▸ *mistake*

overtake verb catch up, pass, outdo, outstrip, pass ▸ *overhaul*

overthrow verb defeat, beat, topple ▸ *overpower*

overture noun 1 (in music) prelude, opening, introduction 2 offer, proposal, invitation

overwhelm verb overcome, stun, shock, overpower, deluge, inundate *The reply to our advertisement was huge; we were inundated with letters*

overwhelming adjective all-powerful, formidable, breathtaking, shattering ★ **insignificant**

owe verb be in debt, incur, be due

own 1 verb possess, occupy, hold 2 verb admit, confess, grant 3 adjective individual, personal, private

owner noun proprietor, possessor, landlord

Pp

pace 1 noun & verb step, tread, stride 2 noun speed, rate, velocity, tempo

pacify verb appease, calm, moderate, tranquilize ▶ *soothe* ★ **aggravate**

pack 1 noun bundle, bunch, swarm, crowd, group 2 verb cram, load, fill, throng

package noun parcel, packet, bundle, box, carton

packet noun bag, pack, container, parcel ▶ *package*

pact noun contract, treaty, agreement, arrangement PACKED

pad 1 noun tablet, notepad, jotter 2 noun foot, paw 3 verb fill, pack, shape, stuff, cushion

paddle 1 noun oar, sweep, scull 2 verb row, steer, propel 3 verb wade, splash, swim

pagan noun heathen, idol worshiper, infidel

page noun 1 sheet, leaf, paper 2 boy, attendant, bellhop, messenger

pageant noun fair, parade, procession, exhibition, masque ▶ *show*

pail noun bucket, churn, tub, container PALE

pain 1 noun ache, pang, throb, twinge, spasm, cramp 2 verb hurt, sting, ache ▶ *ail* PANE

painful adjective aching, throbbing, sore, agonizing ★ **painless**

painstaking adjective scrupulous *Carly kept a scrupulous record of everything that she spent*, careful, diligent, particular ★ **negligent**

paint verb color, draw, daub, varnish, stain

painting noun drawing, illustration, picture, mural, design

pair noun couple, brace, two, twins, twosome PARE, PEAR

pal noun chum, friend, buddy, crony ▶ *comrade* ★ **enemy**

palace noun castle, chateau, stately home *In England you can visit stately homes belonging to the aristocracy*, mansion

pale adjective pallid, ashen, pasty, colorless, faint, feeble, white ★ **ruddy** PAIL

pallid adjective ashen, colorless, livid *The man had a livid scar across his forehead*, waxen ▶ *pale*

paltry adjective petty, mean, shabby, trifling, pitiable, trashy ★ **significant**

pamper verb humor, indulge, coddle, fondle ▶ *spoil* ★ **neglect**

pan noun container ▶ *pot*

pandemonium noun uproar, clatter, row, rumpus, din, chaos *The ice storm reduced the airline schedule to total chaos* ▶ *noise* ★ **calm**

pander verb indulge, pamper, please, give in to

pane noun panel, glass, window PAIN

panel noun 1 pane, rectangle, insert 2 jury, group, committee, forum *There will be a forum of all the candidates before the election*

pang noun ache, throe, twinge, throb ▶ *pain*

panic 1 noun fright, alarm, fear, terror 2 verb scare, frighten, startle, stampede ★ **relax**

pant verb puff, snort, blow, gasp, heave

pantry noun larder, buttery, storeroom, cupboard

paper noun stationery, document, deed, article, dossier *The police have a dossier on all known criminals in this town*

Paper

blotting paper	parchment
carbon paper	rice paper
cardboard	stationery
crepe paper	tissue paper
manila paper	toilet paper
newsprint	vellum
notepaper	wallpaper
papyrus	writing paper

parade 1 noun procession, march, display ▶ *pageant*
2 verb display, exhibit, flaunt, show off

paralyze verb cripple, disable, incapacitate, deaden, stun

paramount adjective leading, chief, supreme, outstanding ▶ *foremost* ★ **minor**

paraphernalia noun baggage, equipment, gear

parasite noun sponger, hanger-on, leech, scrounger

parcel noun batch, bundle, lot ▶ *package*

parched adjective arid, scorched, withered, dry, thirsty

pardon verb excuse, forgive, acquit, condone, absolve ★ condemn

pare verb skin, peel, uncover, strip, scrape, shave PAIR, PEAR

parent noun father, mother, guardian, originator

park 1 noun garden, green, grounds, playground, woodland 2 verb leave *You can leave your car outside our house*, position, station

parlor noun drawing room, living room, sitting room

parody noun caricature, burlesque, satire, imitation

parry verb avoid, avert, fend off, rebuff, repel

parsimonious adjective niggardly *The factory workers received a niggardly sum for their work*, sparing, miserly, stingy ▶ *frugal* ★ **generous**

part 1 noun piece, fragment, portion, scrap 2 noun character, role *My sister has a leading role in the play*, duty 3 verb separate, divide, detach 4 verb depart, quit, leave

partial adjective 1 imperfect, limited, part, unfinished 2 biased, favorable to, inclined

partially adverb incompletely, somewhat, in part

participate verb take part, share, cooperate

particle noun morsel, atom, bit, seed, crumb, grain, scrap

particular adjective 1 choosy, fastidious, scrupulous 2 strange, odd, peculiar 3 special, distinct, notable *Old John Cotton was one of the notable citizens of our city*

partly adverb in part, incompletely, to some degree, up to a point ★ **totally**

partner noun colleague, associate, ally, helper

party noun 1 function, celebration, festivity, social 2 group, faction *A small faction on the committee wanted the park to be closed*, body

pass 1 verb exceed, overstep, outstrip 2 verb experience *He experienced little pain after the operation*, suffer, undergo 3 verb neglect, ignore 4 noun permit, ticket, passport 5 noun defile, gap, notch, passage

passage noun 1 corridor, pathway, alley 2 journey, cruise, voyage 3 sentence, paragraph, clause

passenger noun traveler, commuter, wayfarer

passing adjective casual, fleeting, hasty, temporary, brief ★ **permanent**

passion noun desire, ardor, warmth, excitement, zeal ▶ *emotion* ★ **calm**

passionate adjective ardent, impetuous, fiery, earnest, enthusiastic ★ **indifferent**

past 1 adjective finished, ended, former, gone ★ **present** 2 preposition after, exceeding, beyond 3 noun history, yesterday ★ **future** PASSED

paste noun glue, cement, gum, adhesive

pastime noun recreation, sport, fun, hobby, amusement

pasture noun grass, field, meadow, mead

pat 1 verb tap, caress, fondle, stroke, touch 2 adverb timely, exactly *Celia arrived at exactly the right moment*, precisely

patch verb mend, patch up, sew, darn, cobble

path noun way, track, road, route, course, footway

pathetic adjective pitiable, sad, wretched, miserable, poor, puny *We picked out the puniest pup in the litter for a pet*

patience noun endurance, perseverance, composure, calmness, restraint ★ **impatience** PATIENTS

patient adjective forbearing, long-suffering, persevering, understanding ★ **impatient**

patriotic adjective loyal, nationalistic, public-spirited jingoistic

patrol verb police, watch, guard, protect, tour

patronize verb 1 assist, encourage, foster, buy from 2 talk down to, condescend

pattern noun 1 model, standard, prototype 2 arrangement, decoration, ornament

pause 1 verb halt, cease, suspend, stop, delay 2 noun lull, intermission, break, interruption, breather, rest PAWS

pay 1 verb reward, award, support, compensate, discharge 2 noun payment, salary, wages, compensation

peace noun harmony, calm, concord, serenity, quiet, tranquility ★ **tumult** PIECE

peaceful adjective serene, quiet, restful, harmonious ▶ *tranquil* ★ **disturbed**

peak noun summit, apex, top, crown, pinnacle

peal verb ring, strike, clamor, chime, resound, toll, clang PEEL

peasant noun farmer, rustic, sharecropper, countryman, yokel

peculiar adjective **1** singular, odd, curious, unusual, uncommon, strange **2** unique, private, special, distinctive

peddle verb sell, hawk, canvas, trade, vend, retail

peddler noun hawker, street trader, trader

pedestal noun base, stand, plinth, support

peek noun & verb glimpse, blink, look ▶ *peer*

peel **1** verb skin, strip, pare, scale **2** noun skin, covering, rind, coat PEAL

peer **1** verb peep, stare, look, gaze **2** noun aristocrat, lord, noble **3** noun equal, fellow, counterpart PIER

peerless adjective unequaled, unique, beyond compare, unbeatable

peevish adjective cross, childish, grumpy, crusty, irritable ▶ *testy* ★ **good-tempered**

peg noun hook, knob, pin, post, hanger, fastener

pelt **1** verb beat, bombard, thrash, throw **2** verb rain cats and dogs, teem, pour **3** noun skin, hide, fleece, fur

pen **1** noun quill, ballpoint **2** noun cage, coop, hutch, stall **3** verb write, autograph, scribble

penalty noun fine, forfeit, punishment, price ★ **reward**

pending adjective awaiting, unfinished, doubtful, uncertain, undecided

penetrate verb **1** pierce, perforate, stab, permeate *The aroma of lilacs and roses permeated the house* **2** discern, see through, comprehend

penetrating adjective **1** sharp, perceptive, understanding **2** shrill, stinging

pennant noun flag, streamer, bunting, banner

penniless adjective destitute, needy, poverty-striken ▶ *poor* ★ **wealthy**

pensive adjective thoughtful, reflective, wistful, preoccupied

people **1** noun folk, society, the public, populace, inhabitants **2** verb populate, inhabit, settle

pep noun punch, energy, high spirits, vigor ▶ *vitality*

peppery adjective **1** biting, caustic *I'm afraid that your essay wasn't very good; the teacher made some very caustic comments*, hot-tempered, angry **2** hot, pungent, sharp

perceive verb feel, sense, observe, notice, make out, understand ▶ *see*

perch **1** verb alight, light, sit, squat, roost **2** noun rod, pole, staff, roost **3** noun fish

perfect **1** adjective (*per*-fect) absolute, ideal, sublime, excellent, splendid, faultless ★ **imperfect** **2** verb (per-*fect*) complete, finish, fulfill, refine

perforate verb puncture, drill, punch, penetrate

perform verb **1** carry out, do, fulfill, accomplish **2** play, act, stage, present *The local drama group will present a new play next week*

performer noun actor, player, singer, entertainer, artist

perfume noun scent, essence, aroma, odor

perhaps adverb possibly, perchance, maybe, conceivably

peril noun hazard, jeopardy, menace, risk, insecurity ▶ *danger* ★ **safety**

period noun spell, time, duration, term, interval, course, span, age

periodical **1** noun magazine, publication, journal, gazette, review **2** adjective regular, routine, recurring, repeated

perish verb die, pass away, wither, disintegrate, expire, shrivel

perky adjective bouncy, bright, cheerful, lively ▶ *sprightly* ★ **dull**

permanent adjective endless, ageless, timeless, constant ▶ *durable* ★ **fleeting**

permission noun authorization, sanction, privilege, warrant *The police have a warrant for your arrest* ★ **prohibition**

permit **1** verb (per-*mit*) allow, grant, agree, empower **2** noun (*per*-mit) warrant, license, pass

perpendicular adjective upright, erect, sheer, steep, vertical ★ **horizontal**

perpetrate verb commit, do, inflict, perform, practice, execute

perpetual adjective everlasting, ceaseless, eternal, never ending ▶ *endless* ★ **fleeting**

A B C D E F G H I J K L M N O P Q R S T U V W X Y Z

perplex verb mystify, baffle, bewilder, confound
▷ *puzzle* ★ **enlighten**

persecute verb harass, molest, plague, badger
▷ *bother* ★ **pamper**

persevere verb persist, hold out, hang on, endure,
continue ★ **give up**

persist verb remain, stand fast, abide, carry on
▷ *persevere* ★ **stop**

persistent adjective tenacious, relentless, stubborn,
obstinate ★ **weak**

person noun individual, human, being, somebody,
personage, character

personal adjective individual, intimate, private,
special, peculiar

personality noun individuality, character, disposition,
nature

perspective noun outlook, aspect, proportion

perspire verb sweat, exude, ooze

persuade verb convince, wheedle, blandish, entice,
cajole *I cajoled my mother into buying me a new swimsuit*,
induce ▷ *coax* ★ **discourage**

pert adjective saucy, flippant, jaunty, cheeky, brash
★ **shy**

perturb verb upset, disturb, trouble, distress, fluster
▷ *bother* ★ **reassure**

peruse verb read, study, pore over, browse, inspect,
scrutinize, examine

pervade verb penetrate, permeate, spread, saturate, soak

perverse adjective contrary, wayward, opposite,
disobedient ▷ *stubborn* ★ **reasonable**

pessimist noun defeatist, killjoy, wet blanket, cynic
*Uncle Bert is a real cynic; he even thinks that the lottery
is fixed* ★ **optimist**

pessimistic adjective cynical, dismal, fatalistic,
defeatist, downhearted ★ **optimistic**

pest noun nuisance, plague, blight, curse, vexation, bug

pester verb nag, hector, badger, annoy, disturb, harass
▷ *bother*

pet 1 verb fondle, caress, baby, cosset, cuddle
2 noun favorite, beloved, dear 3 adjective endearing,
cherished, dearest

petition noun plea, appeal, entreaty, round robin,
request

petrified adjective spellbound, frightened, scared,
terrified

petty adjective 1 paltry, cheap, inferior, trifling ▷ *trivial*
★ **important** 2 mean, measly, stingy

petulant adjective fretful, displeased, querulous,
irritable ▷ *peevish*

phantom 1 noun apparition, specter, spook, ghost
2 adjective spooky, ghostly, imaginary

phase noun aspect, appearance, angle, view, period,
point FAZE

phenomenal adjective remarkable, outstanding,
marvelous, miraculous, incredible

phenomenon noun marvel, rarity, curiosity, sensation,
spectacle

philanthropic adjective charitable, kind, generous,
humane, benevolent, bountiful, public-spirited
★ **selfish**

philosophical adjective calm, cool, logical,
thoughtful, impassive, unruffled

phobia noun dread, fear, awe, neurosis, hang-up
*My father has a hang-up about bats; he can't stand
them*, horror

phrase noun expression, idiom, saying, utterance,
sentence FRAYS

physical adjective 1 material, substantial, solid,
concrete 2 bodily, personal, sensible

pick 1 verb select, choose, single out, gather 2 noun
pike, pickax

picket 1 noun patrol, scout, sentinel, lookout, guard
2 noun post, rail, panel, fence 3 verb strike, demonstrate

pickle 1 noun preserve 2 noun difficulty, predicament
3 verb cure, salt, preserve, souse

picture 1 noun painting, tableau, portrait, illustration,
drawing 2 noun movie, film 3 verb illustrate, imagine,
fancy

picturesque adjective attractive, artistic, pictorial,
scenic

piece noun portion, fragment, lump, morsel, bit
▷ *scrap* PEACE

pier noun wharf, dock, quay, jetty PEER

pierce verb perforate, drill, bore ▷ *penetrate*

piercing adjective 1 loud, deafening, shrill, penetrating
2 keen, sharp, cutting

pigment noun color, dye, hue, paint, stain

pile noun & verb heap, mass, stack, load, store

pilfer verb purloin, rifle, rob, filch ▶ *steal*

pilgrim noun traveler, wanderer, wayfarer

pilgrimage noun excursion, journey, mission, tour, trip, crusade

pillage verb plunder, ravage, loot, ransack *Thieves broke into the museum and ransacked all the cases*, rifle

pillar noun column, shaft, tower, obelisk, monument

pillow noun cushion, bolster, support

pilot noun 1 guide, steersman, coxswain, helmsman, helmswoman 2 aviator, flyer

pimple noun zit, blemish, swelling, boil

pin 1 noun fastener, clip, spike, peg 2 verb fix, fasten, attach, join, tack

pinch 1 verb nip, squeeze, crush, tweak 2 verb pilfer, steal 3 noun dash, drop, splash 4 noun crisis, difficulty, jam

pine verb hanker, yearn, long for, languish *The flowers in the pot are languishing from lack of water*, sicken

pinnacle noun summit, top, crest, peak, apex

pioneer noun founder, leader, trailblazer, explorer, innovator

pious adjective devout, godly, holy, moral, religious, virtuous

pipe 1 noun tube, duct, passage, hose, conduit 2 whistle, flute

piquant adjective appetizing, spicy, tangy, savory, pungent

pique verb annoy, displease, irritate, affront, vex PEAK

pirate 1 noun corsair *In days of old the ships in the Mediterranean were often raided by corsairs*, buccaneer, privateer, sea rover 2 verb copy, plagiarize, steal

pistol noun gun, revolver, automatic PISTIL

pit noun 1 hole, hollow, crater, trench, mine 2 dent, dimple, depression

pitch 1 verb fling, throw, cast, sling, toss 2 verb fall, drop, descend 3 verb raise, set up, erect 4 noun angle, slope, degree 5 noun sales message

pitcher noun jar, beaker, crock, jug, ewer, vessel

piteous adjective pitiful, heartbreaking, mournful ▶ *pathetic*

pitiless adjective merciless, unmerciful, cruel, unrelenting ★ **merciful**

pity 1 noun mercy, compassion, charity, tenderness 2 verb spare, forgive, grieve for, sympathize with

pivot 1 noun axle, axis, hinge, turning point, spindle, swivel 2 verb revolve, rotate, turn, spin

placate verb appease, pacify, soothe, satisfy ▶ *humor* ★ **infuriate**

place 1 noun spot, locality, site, situation, position 2 noun house, apartment, residence 3 verb put, deposit, establish, allocate, arrange

placid adjective peaceful, quiet, serene, mild ▶ *restful* ★ **ruffled**

plague 1 noun epidemic, disease, contagion, pest, blight 2 verb persecute, pester *We were pestered by flies*, infest, annoy ▶ *badger*

plain 1 adjective unadorned, simple 2 adjective obvious, clear, apparent 3 adjective blunt, direct, candid 4 adjective smooth, level, flat 5 noun prairie, plateau, tableland PLANE

Planets

The eight planets (and one dwarf planet) of our solar system travel around a star we call the Sun.

Earth
Jupiter
Mars
Mercury
Neptune
Pluto (dwarf planet)
Saturn
Uranus
Venus

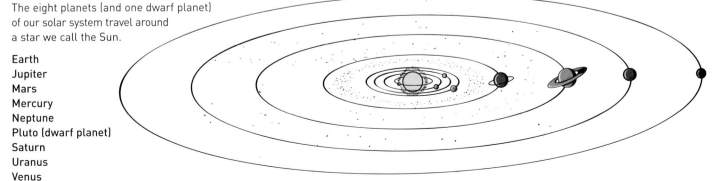

plan 1 noun design, chart, diagram, drawing
2 noun project, proposal, arrangement, scheme
3 verb design, prepare, arrange, invent

plane 1 adjective level, even, flat, smooth
2 noun aircraft 3 noun smoothing tool PLAIN

planned adjective prepared, ready, arranged

plant 1 verb sow, scatter, implant 2 verb place,
set, establish 3 noun herb, shrub, vegetable
4 noun equipment, machinery, factory

plaster 1 noun cement, mortar, paste 2 noun
bandage, dressing 3 verb spread, smear, daub

plastic 1 adjective moldable, pliable, malleable, soft,
supple 2 noun thermoplastic

plate 1 noun dish, platter, palette 2 noun sheet, panel
3 verb laminate, cover, gild, anodize

platform noun rostrum *I was called up to the rostrum to
receive my prize*, stage, stand, dais

plausible adjective believable, credible, convincing,
glib, persuasive ★ unlikely

play 1 verb sport, gambol, frisk, romp, frolic 2 verb
perform, act, represent 3 noun drama, performance
4 noun sport, amusement, recreation

player noun actor, sportsman, artist, musician,
performer, contestant

playful adjective frisky, frolicsome, larky, lively, sportive
★ serious

plead verb appeal, argue, ask, implore, request, beseech

pleasant adjective affable, agreeable, cheerful, nice
▶ *charming* ★ unpleasant

please verb 1 gratify, enchant, amuse, entertain
▶ *delight* 2 like, choose, wish, prefer

pleased adjective delighted, gratified, satisfied
▶ *contented* ★ annoyed

pleasing adjective agreeable, enchanting, entertaining
▶ *satisfying* ★ unpleasant

pleasure noun delight, joy, amusement, entertainment,
enjoyment ▶ *fun* ★ trouble

pledge 1 noun promise, vow, undertaking, warrant,
oath 2 verb bind, contract, promise, undertake

plentiful adjective lavish, ample, profuse, bountiful
▶ *abundant* ★ scanty

plenty noun enough, profusion, affluence ▶ *abundance*
★ scarcity

pliable adjective supple, flexible, pliant, malleable,
moldable, bendy ★ rigid

plight noun predicament, difficulty, condition,
dilemma *We made it to the train station on time, but when
we realized that we had forgotten our tickets, we were in a real
dilemma*, jam

plod verb toil, labor, drudge, slog, grind

plot 1 noun scheme, plan, intrigue 2 noun story,
narrative 3 verb hatch, intrigue, scheme

pluck 1 verb gather, pick, pull, yank, catch 2 noun
courage, determination, bravery

plucky adjective courageous, daring, heroic, hardy
▶ *brave* ★ feeble

plug 1 noun stopper, cork, bung 2 verb stop, block,
choke, cork 3 verb publicize, boost, promote, push

plum 1 noun prize, bonus, treasure 2 adjective best,
choice, first-class

plump adjective buxom, stout, chubby, rotund, pudgy
★ skinny

plunder 1 noun booty, loot, swag, spoils 2 verb fleece,
rob, ransack, pillage, loot

plunge verb dive, pitch, submerge, duck, immerse,
swoop, hurtle

poach verb 1 pilfer, steal, filch, purloin 2 steam, cook

pocket 1 noun compartment, pouch, sack, bag 2 verb
filch, pinch, steal

poem noun ode, verse, rhyme, ballad, lyric

poetic adjective artistic, elegant, graceful, flowing, lyrical

poignant adjective moving, touching, pathetic, biting,
penetrating

point 1 noun spike, barb, pike, prong, end, tip 2 noun
locality, place, spot 3 noun aspect, object, aim, purpose
4 noun headland, cape 5 verb aim, direct, level, train

pointless adjective meaningless, senseless, silly, vague,
feeble ▶ *absurd* ★ significant

poise 1 noun confidence, assurance, dignity,
self-possession, balance 2 verb stand, hover, brood over

poison 1 noun venom, virus, toxin 2 verb taint, fester,
corrupt, infect

poisonous adjective deadly, evil, lethal *Don't touch
those red berries; they're lethal*, noxious, toxic, venomous

poke verb jab, push, nudge, jostle, ram, thrust, stab,
prod ▶ *shove*

pole noun stick, stave, stake, rod, post, bar, mast, shaft, spar

policy noun course, action, practice, rule, procedure, guidelines

polish 1 verb burnish, buff, smooth, brighten, clean 2 noun gloss, glaze, shine 3 noun refinement, grace, culture

polished adjective 1 glossy, burnished, shiny 2 refined, cultivated, cultured

polite adjective courteous, attentive, civil, well-bred, elegant, discreet ★ impolite

poll 1 noun election, vote, count, census, ballot 2 verb survey, canvas, vote

pollute verb adulterate, debase, befoul, taint, poison, corrupt ★ purify

pomp noun ceremony, show, splendor, pageantry, magnificence ★ simplicity

pompous adjective showy, self-important, bombastic ▶ *pretentious* ★ modest

ponder verb meditate, consider, reflect, deliberate, think about

pool 1 noun lagoon, pond, lake 2 noun accumulation, funds, reserve, kitty 3 verb combine, contribute, share

poor adjective 1 destitute, penniless, miserable ★ rich 2 low quality, faulty, feeble, shoddy *That shirt may be cheap, but it's shoddy and won't last* ★ superior
PORE, POUR

poorly 1 adjective ailing, ill, sick, seedy 2 adverb badly, inexpertly, crudely ★ well

pop verb 1 bang, burst, crack, explode 2 slide, slip, insert

popular adjective 1 well-liked, favorite, in favor, fashionable 2 current, common, vulgar, prevailing

pore verb scan, examine, peruse, scrutinize POOR, POUR

portable adjective lightweight, convenient, transportable ▶ *handy* ★ awkward

portion noun piece, fragment, share, fraction ▶ *part*

portly adjective plump, stout, fat, burly, bulky

portrait noun likeness, painting, picture, profile

portray verb describe, depict, represent, picture, illustrate, impersonate

pose 1 verb stand, poise, posture, position 2 noun position, stand, guise, stance *If you want to learn to play golf well, you need a good stance*

position noun 1 spot, situation, location, place, site 2 job, post 3 posture, attitude 4 rank, standing, status

positive adjective 1 certain, sure, confident ★ doubtful 2 real, true, absolute ★ negative 3 precise, definite, unmistakable

possess verb have, own, hold, occupy ★ lose

possessions noun wealth, assets, property, goods

possible adjective conceivable, imaginable, likely, feasible, attainable ★ impossible

possibly adverb perhaps, maybe, perchance conceivably

post noun 1 rail, pole, beam, banister, stake 2 position, employment, job 3 mail

poster noun placard, bill, advertisement, sign

posterior adjective hind, behind, after, rear ★ front

postpone verb put off, defer, shelve, adjourn ▶ *delay* ★ advance

posture noun bearing, stance, attitude, carriage

pot noun basin, bowl, pan, vessel, container, jar

potential 1 adjective possible, probable, latent, dormant, budding 2 noun ability, talent, capacity ▶ *flair*

potion noun beverage, medicine, mixture, tonic, brew

pouch noun bag, poke, sack, purse, pocket, wallet

pounce verb strike, lunge, spring, swoop, fall upon ▶ *attack*

pound 1 verb beat, batter, crush, hammer 2 noun enclosure, compound, pen 3 noun weight

pour verb spout, jet, gush, spill, cascade, rain
PORE, POUR

pout verb grimace, glower, sulk, scowl, mope ★ smile

poverty noun 1 distress, need, bankruptcy, privation ▶ *want* 2 scarcity, shortage ★ plenty

powder 1 noun dust, sand, ash, grit, bran 2 verb pulverize, crunch, grind

power noun 1 authority, command, control, ability 2 energy, force, strength

powerful adjective mighty, vigorous, forceful ▶ *strong* ★ weak

practical adjective 1 useful, effective, workable 2 experienced, qualified, trained ▶ *skilled* ★ impractical

practice noun **1** custom, habit, usage **2** work, conduct, performance, action ★ theory **3** verb carry out, apply, do, execute ▶ *perform*

praise **1** verb acclaim, applaud, glorify, exalt ★ criticize **2** noun applause, flattery, compliment, approval ★ criticism PRAYS, PREYS

prance verb gambol, frolic, romp, caper, swagger

prank noun trick, joke, antic, lark, jape, stunt

prattle noun & verb chatter, jabber, gossip, drivel, babble

pray verb beg, beseech, entreat, implore, request PREY

prayer noun petition, entreaty, worship, devotion, supplication

preach verb lecture, moralize, advocate *The president advocated a program to feed the poor*, urge, proclaim

precarious adjective perilous, hazardous, insecure, dangerous ▶ *risky* ★ safe

precaution noun forethought, provision, anticipation, care, providence ▶ *prudence*

precede verb lead, head, usher, go before, preface ★ follow

precious adjective valuable, cherished, treasured, dear, beloved ▶ *costly* ★ worthless

precise adjective **1** definite, exact, pointed, accurate **2** formal, particular, strict ★ vague

precisely adverb absolutely, just so, exactly, correctly

precision noun exactitude, accuracy, care, detail

precocious adjective fast, smart, clever ★ backward

predicament noun situation, state, condition, embarrassment, fix ▶ *plight*

predict verb foresee, foretell, prophesy, presage, divine

predominant adjective leading, main, powerful, superior, ruling, controlling ★ minor

preen verb prance, swagger, strut, spruce up, doll up, groom

preface noun introduction, prelude, prologue, preamble, foreword

prefer verb choose, select, desire, like better, fancy ▶ *favor* ★ reject

prejudice **1** noun bigotry, intolerance, bias, discrimination **2** verb influence, warp, twist, distort, undermine ★ benefit

prejudiced adjective biased *My opinion of Jessica is biased; she's my little sister*, bigoted, one-sided, unfair, intolerant ★ fair

preliminary adjective introductory, preparatory, opening, initial ★ final

premature adjective untimely, previous, early, immature ★ late

premeditated adjective calculated, planned, prearranged, intentional ★ spontaneous

premier **1** noun prime minister, first minister, head of government **2** adjective chief, first, head, leading, principal

premises noun grounds, house, building, lands

prepare verb arrange, adapt, provide, get ready, concoct, plan ★ demolish

preposterous adjective absurd, ridiculous, laughable ▶ *unreasonable* ★ reasonable

prescribe verb indicate, order, propose, recommend, specify

presence noun **1** existence, appearance, aspect **2** nearness, neighborhood, proximity PRESENTS

present **1** noun (*pres*-ent) gift, donation, bounty, favor **2** (*pres*-ent) adjective here, on the spot, ready, current **3** verb (pre-*sent*) offer, tender, bestow, award, exhibit

presently adverb soon, shortly, before long, immediately

preserve **1** verb protect safeguard, conserve, shield ▶ *keep* **2** noun jam, jelly, relish

press **1** verb bear down, depress, clamp, jam, compress, flatten **2** noun printing machine **3** noun newspapers, reporters, journalism

pressure noun **1** strain, tension, stress, urgency **2** weight, compression, force

prestige noun repute, authority, weight, power

presume verb infer *I infer from your smile that you have passed your exam*, suppose, grant, take for granted, assume

presumptuous adjective arrogant, bold, audacious, insolent ▶ *forward* ★ modest

pretend verb **1** make believe, simulate, sham, feign, masquerade **2** aspire, claim, strive for

pretext noun excuse, pretense, guise, device

pretty adjective attractive, beautiful, comely, dainty, bonny ▷ *lovely* ⋆ **ugly**

prevail verb obtain, overcome, predominate ▷ *triumph* ⋆ **lose**

prevalent adjective current, common, popular, in use, accepted ⋆ **uncommon**

prevent verb avert, forestall, ward off, discourage, stop ▷ *hinder* ⋆ **help**

previous adjective former, prior, earlier, premature, untimely ⋆ **later**

prey noun quarry, chase, booty, victim PRAY

prey on verb plunder, fleece, oppress, terrorize

price noun cost, amount, expense, payment, value, worth

priceless adjective 1 invaluable, precious, cherished, costly 2 amusing, comic, humorous, hilarious *The clown's antics were hilarious*

prick verb jab, jag, puncture, stab, pierce

pride noun conceit, arrogance, vanity, egotism, self-importance, honor, exaltation, pleasure PRIED

prim adjective puritanical, demure, starchy, priggish ⋆ **informal**

primary adjective first, original, chief, essential, fundamental

prime adjective 1 principal, chief, basic, original 2 best, finest, choice

primitive adjective 1 simple, austere, crude 2 uncivilized, savage, barbarous

principal 1 adjective main, chief, head, leading, foremost 2 noun head, leader, boss, director PRINCIPLE

principle noun 1 law, regulation, rule, doctrine 2 virtue, worth, integrity, rectitude *The president of the club was honored by the mayor as a "person of high moral rectitude"* ⋆ **wickedness** PRINCIPAL

print 1 verb impress, stamp, brand, publish 2 noun impression, printing, imprint

prior 1 adjective previous, former, earlier, preceding 2 noun abbot, monk

prison noun jail, penitentiary, dungeon, lock up

private adjective 1 particular, personal, special, own 2 solitary, remote *He spent his vacations in a remote cabin,* quiet ⋆ **public**

privilege noun 1 advantage, benefit, exemption 2 right, authority, entitlement, prerogative *It was the emperor's prerogative to pardon offenders*

prize 1 noun reward, premium, trophy, honor 2 noun booty, spoils, plunder 3 adjective best, champion, winning 4 verb value, appreciate, cherish 5 verb force, lever, pry, lift, raise PRIES

probable adjective likely, presumable, reasonable, possible ⋆ **improbable**

probe verb 1 poke, prod 2 examine, investigate, scrutinize

problem 1 noun puzzle, question, riddle, poser, quandary 2 difficulty, dilemma, snag, predicament, complication

proceed verb 1 advance, continue, go on, progress ⋆ **recede** 2 arise, flow, spring, emanate *A strong sulfurous odor emanated from the crater of the volcano*

process 1 noun procedure, operation, movement, system, method 2 verb convert, alter, handle, refine

procession noun parade, pageant, march, cavalcade

proclaim verb declare, announce, advertise, publish, expound

procure verb secure, acquire, win, gain, attain, get ⋆ **lose**

prod verb goad, poke, nudge, incite, urge, shove

prodigal adjective extravagant, reckless, lavish ▷ *spendthrift* ⋆ **thrifty**

prodigious adjective 1 miraculous, abnormal, amazing, remarkable ▷ *extraordinary* ⋆ **ordinary** 2 huge, mighty ▷ *enormous* ⋆ **tiny**

produce 1 noun (*pro*-duce) product, output, yield, crop, harvest 2 verb (pro-*duce*) provide, yield, create, deliver, put forward

product noun output, crop, harvest, return, merchandise, commodity

profane adjective impious, blasphemous, unholy, worldly, sinful ⋆ **sacred**

profess verb declare, avow, acknowledge, own

profession noun 1 occupation, career, job, calling, employment 2 avowal, admission

professional adjective skilled, efficient, experienced ▷ *expert* ⋆ **amateur**

A B C D E F G H I J K L M N O **P** Q R S T U V W X Y Z

proffer verb present, offer, tender, submit

proficient adjective competent, able, skilled, trained ▷ *expert* ☆ **clumsy**

profit 1 noun benefit, gain, advantage, acquisition ☆ **loss** 2 verb improve, gain, reap, acquire ☆ **lose** PROPHET

profound 1 adjective deep, penetrating, fathomless 2 wise, shrewd, learned, sagacious *The leader of the tribe was old, wise, and sagacious* ☆ **shallow**

profuse adjective bountiful, extravagant, exuberant, prolific, sumptuous ▷ *lavish* ☆ **sparse**

progress 1 noun (*prog*-ress) advancement, growth, development ☆ **decline** 2 verb (pro-*gress*) advance, proceed, go, forge ahead, travel, grow

prohibit verb forbid, bar, deny, ban, obstruct, hinder ▷ *prevent* ☆ **permit**

project 1 noun (*pro*-ject) work, affair, plan, scheme, undertaking 2 verb (pro-*ject*) propel, hurl, jut, protrude 3 verb contrive, scheme, plan 4 verb protrude, bulge, stick out

prolific adjective fruitful, creative, productive, fertile ☆ **scarce**

prolong verb lengthen, stretch, draw out, spin out ▷ *extend* ☆ **shorten**

prominent adjective 1 famous, notable, distinguished ☆ **minor** 2 projecting, standing out, bulging, jutting

promise 1 noun commitment, undertaking, warrant, pledge 2 verb agree, guarantee, vow

promote adjective 1 cultivate, advance, assist ▷ *encourage* 2 dignify, elevate, upgrade, honor ☆ **degrade**

prompt 1 adjective punctual, timely, quick, smart, ready ☆ **tardy** 2 verb hint, remind, urge ▷ *encourage* ☆ **deter**

prone adjective 1 inclined, apt, liable, disposed ☆ **unlikely** 2 prostrate *The sea-sick sailor lay prostrate on the ship's deck*, face down, precumbent ☆ **upright**

pronounce verb 1 speak, utter, say, articulate 2 declare, decree, proclaim

pronounced adjective outstanding, striking, noticeable ▷ *distinct* ☆ **vague**

proof noun evidence, testimony, confirmation, criterion, scrutiny ☆ **failure**

prop noun & verb stay, brace, truss, support

propel verb start, push, force, impel, send ▷ *drive* ☆ **stop**

proper adjective 1 correct, without error, right, accurate, exact 2 respectable, decent, becoming, seemly ☆ **improper** 3 personal, own, special ☆ **common**

property 1 noun possessions, wealth, chattels, buildings, belongings 2 quality, virtue, characteristic, peculiarity

prophecy noun forecast, divination, prediction, prognostication

prophesy verb predict, foretell, foresee, declare

proportion 1 noun ratio, percentage, part, fraction 2 adjustment, arrangement

proposal noun proposition, offer, outline

propose verb 1 put forward, offer, suggest 2 ask for the hand of, ask to marry, pop the question

proprietor noun owner, possessor, landlady, landlord

prosaic adjective factual, tedious, uninteresting, boring, unimaginative, everyday, dull, mundane, ordinary ☆ **interesting**

prosecute verb 1 indict, put on trial, summon, sue 2 continue, pursue, carry on, conduct ☆ **abandon**

prospect noun 1 outlook, forecast, promise, expectation 2 view, landscape, vista, aspect

prosper verb succeed, flourish, grow ☆ **fail**

prosperous adjective affluent, wealthy, rich, successful, thriving ☆ **unsuccessful**

protect verb defend, preserve, guard, secure, shelter, support ☆ **endanger**

protest 1 verb (pro-*test*) complain, object, dispute, challenge ☆ **accept** 2 noun (*pro*-test) objection, complaint, dissent, outcry

protracted adjective extended, drawn out, lengthy, prolonged ☆ **shortened**

protrude verb project, bulge, jut ☆ **recede**

proud 1 adjective arrogant, haughty, supercilious, boastful ☆ **humble** 2 lofty, majestic, noble, splendid ☆ **mean**

prove verb show, demonstrate, authenticate, confirm, verify ★ **disprove**

provide verb supply, furnish, equip, contribute, afford ★ **withhold**

province noun **1** realm, sphere, orbit, place, department **2** region, state, county

provoke verb prompt, incite, excite, enrage, inflame ▶ *aggravate* ★ **appease**

prowess noun ability, strength, might, bravery ▶ *valor* ★ **clumsiness**

prowl verb stalk *Somewhere in the darkness, a large gray cat stalked its prey*, roam, slink

prudent adjective careful, cautious, discreet, shrewd ▶ *thrifty* ★ **rash**

prudish adjective straitlaced, narrow-minded, demure, priggish ▶ *prim*

prune **1** verb cut, shorten, trim, crop **2** noun dried plum

pry verb snoop, peep, meddle, intrude

public **1** adjective communal, civil, popular, social, national **2** noun the people, the populace, society

publish verb broadcast, distribute, circulate, communicate, bring out

pucker verb fold, crease, cockle, furrow, wrinkle ★ **straighten**

puerile adjective callow, immature, juvenile

puff verb inflate, swell, blow, pant, distend

pull verb **1** haul, drag, tow, heave ★ **push** **2** gather, pluck, detach, pick

pump verb **1** inflate, expand, swell, inject, siphon **2** interrogate, question, grill

punch verb **1** strike, beat, hit, cuff **2** puncture, pierce, perforate, bore

punctual adjective prompt, on time, precise, exact, timely ★ **tardy**

puncture noun perforation, hole, leak, wound

pungent adjective sharp, bitter, poignant, biting ▶ *acrid* ★ **mild**

punish verb chastise, correct, discipline, chasten, reprove, scold

puny adjective feeble, weak, frail, small, petty, stunted, insignificant ★ **large**

pupil noun student, scholar, schoolchild, learner

puppet noun **1** doll, marionette **2** cat's-paw *The prisoner was not the true culprit, but only the ringleader's cat's-paw*, figurehead, pawn

purchase **1** verb buy, procure, secure, obtain, get ▶ *buy* ★ **sell** **2** noun bargain, investment

pure adjective **1** immaculate, spotless, stainless, clear ▶ *clean* ★ **impure** **2** virtuous, chaste, honest, blameless

purely adverb simply, barely, merely, only

purge verb **1** purify, clean, cleanse, scour **2** liquidate, exterminate, kill

purify verb clean, clarify, wash, purge

purloin verb rob, thieve, take, filch, pilfer ▶ *steal*

purpose noun intent, design, will, goal, target

purse **1** noun handbag, wallet, pouch, reticule **2** verb pucker, crease, compress, wrinkle

pursue verb **1** follow, track, trace ▶ *chase* **2** practice, maintain, work for

pursuit noun **1** hunt, chase, follow, hue and cry **2** occupation, hobby, interest *Stamp collecting has always been one of my main interests*

push **1** verb shove, thrust, press, drive, propel **2** noun advance, assault, drive

put verb **1** set, place, deposit, repose, lay **2** express, propose, state

put down verb **1** write, jot down, record, note **2** crush, humiliate, subdue, insult

put off verb **1** postpone, defer, delay, adjourn **2** dishearten, unsettle, perturb

putrid adjective decomposed, rotten, rancid, rank, stinking ★ **wholesome**

putter verb dabble, fiddle, tinker, mess around

puzzle **1** verb baffle, confuse, mystify, perplex ▶ *bewilder* **2** noun conundrum, brainteaser, problem, dilemma

puzzling adjective baffling, curious, strange, bewildering ▶ *peculiar*

quack noun impostor, charlatan *She pretended to tell fortunes by cards, but she was nothing but a charlatan*, humbug, fake

quaff verb imbibe, swallow ► *drink*

quagmire noun bog, mire, marsh ► *swamp*

quail verb tremble, flinch, shrink, cower, succumb ★ **withstand**

quaint adjective curious, whimsical, fanciful, singular, old-fashioned, droll

quake 1 verb tremble, quaver, shiver, quiver, shudder 2 noun shock, convulsion, tremor *The tremors from the earthquake were felt hundreds of miles away*

qualification noun 1 fitness, capacity, ability, accomplishment 2 restriction, limitation, modification *The engineer's design was accepted with certain modifications*

qualify verb 1 empower, enable, fit, suit 2 moderate, limit, restrict

quality noun 1 characteristic, condition, power 2 excellence, worth, goodness

qualm noun doubt, misgiving, hesitation

quandary noun difficulty, doubt ► *dilemma*

quantity noun amount, number, volume, sum

quarrel 1 noun dispute, squabble, wrangle, disagreement ★ **harmony** 2 verb argue, bicker, brawl, squabble ★ **agree**

quarry noun 1 game, prey, object, victim, target 2 mine, excavation, pit

quarter noun 1 area, territory, place, district 2 one fourth 3 mercy *The commander of the invading army showed mercy to the local defenders*, grace, lenience

quarters noun lodgings, dwelling, billet, rooms

quash verb abolish, nullify, suppress, overthrow, subdue

quaver verb shake, tremble, shiver, shudder, vibrate, oscillate, quake

quay noun pier, dock, wharf, landing, jetty KEY

queasy adjective bilious, squeamish, sick, faint

queer adjective trange, odd, whimsical, peculiar

quell verb crush, stifle, extinguish, defeat

quench verb 1 douse *We carefully doused our campfire before leaving the site*, put out, cool, check 2 slake *The cattle rushed to the river and slaked their thirst*, cool, allay

query 1 noun question, doubt, objection 2 verb ask, inquire, question, doubt ★ **accept**

quest noun chase, hunt, search, pursuit, venture

question 1 noun query, inquiry, interrogation, 2 noun topic, problem, issue 3 verb ask, inquire, interrogate ★ **answer**

questionable adjective doubtful, uncertain, undecided, unbelievable ★ **certain**

queue noun 1 row, line, procession, lineup 2 pigtail, coil, braid, ponytail CUE

quibble verb argue, trifle, split hairs, carp *If you like our plan, don't carp about the details*

quick adjective 1 speedy, rapid, express, swift ► *fast* 2 alert, active, agile, lively ★ **slow** 3 clever, intelligent, acute ★ **dull** 4 hasty, sharp, touchy ★ **mild**

quicken verb accelerate ► *hasten* ★ **delay**

quiet 1 adjective silent, soundless, noiseless, hushed ★ **noisy** 2 adjective placid, smooth, undisturbed ★ **busy** 3 noun peace, rest, tranquility, silence ★ **tumult**

quilt noun blanket, cover, comforter, eiderdown

quip noun joke, gag, gipe, jest, wisecrack, retort

quirk noun pecularity, curiosity, foible *Despite his age and one or two foibles, old Uncle Fred was very agile*, mannerism ► *habit*

quit verb 1 cease, desist, stop 2 leave, depart, relinquish 3 give up, surrender

quite adverb absolutely, altogether, wholly

quits adjective even *If I pay what I owe, it makes us even*, all square, level, equal

quiver 1 verb tremble, quake, shiver, shudder 2 noun holster, scabbard, sheath

quiz 1 verb question, ask, examine, grill 2 noun test, examination, contest *Barbara was the winner of the spelling bee*

quizzical adjective 1 incredulous, skeptical, suspicious 2 whimsical, teasing, amused

quota noun allowance, allocation, ration

quotation noun 1 extract, selection, passage 2 cost, estimate, price

quote verb recite, cite, recount, recollect, tell, mention

Rr

rabble noun crowd, mob, riffraff

race 1 noun competition, contest, chase, dash
2 noun people, nation, folk, stock, breed, tribe
3 verb run, speed, hurry, scamper, gallop, sprint

rack 1 noun shelf, stand, frame, framework
2 verb distress, strain, torment, pain WRACK

racket noun 1 uproar, noise, hubbub, tumult
▶ *din* 2 fraud, deception, swindle

racy adjective 1 pungent, piquant, zestful
2 spirited, smart, lively

radiant adjective 1 brilliant, bright, luminous,
shining 2 splendid, glorious, happy ★ dull

radiate verb 1 gleam, sparkle, beam, shine
2 emit, spread, diffuse

radical adjective 1 extreme, fanatical, deep-seated
2 original, fundamental *The new teacher made some
fundamental changes to our lessons*, natural ★ superficial

raffle noun draw, sweepstakes, lottery

rafter noun joist, girder, beam, support

ragamuffin noun scarecrow, urchin ▶ *waif*

rage 1 noun wrath, fury, ferocity, passion, madness
▶ *anger* 2 verb rave, fret, fume *The mad bull was fuming
with rage as we leaped over the fence*, storm, flare up

ragged adjective shabby, seedy, shaggy, rough, torn
★ smart

raid 1 noun invasion, attack, strike, sortie
2 verb attack, invade, ransack, plunder, maraud
The ship was attacked and plundered by pirates RAYED

rail 1 noun post, picket, fence, railing 2 verb scold,
rant, blast, reproach

rain noun & verb deluge, drizzle, flood, shower,
torrent REIGN, REIN

raise verb 1 elevate, lift, erect, hoist *The flag was
hoisted as the ship came into port* ★ lower 2 excite,
awaken, rouse 3 promote, increase, advance
4 cultivate, grow, breed RAZE

rake verb grope, scrape, collect, gather, assemble

rally verb 1 meet, assemble, convene *The members
of the club will convene next month* ★ disperse
2 encourage, restore, reunite

ram verb 1 cram, crowd, push, pack, stuff, poke,
wedge 2 charge, beat, crash, drive

ramble verb 1 stroll, meander, saunter, roam, rove
2 chatter, digress *Joe's speech was very long, as he kept
digressing from the point*, dodder

ramp noun gradient, slope, incline, grade

rampage 1 noun storm, rage, riot, uproar, tumult
2 verb rave, rush, run wild *Someone left the gate open,
and the pigs ran wild in the cabbage patch*

ramshackle adjective unstable, shaky, unsteady,
flimsy, rickety ▶ *decrepit* ★ stable

rancid adjective sour, curdled, rank, putrid, musty

rancor noun spite, grudge, animosity, hatred
▶ *malice* RANKER

random adjective haphazard, vague, casual,
accidental ▶ *chance* ★ deliberate

range 1 noun extent, length, span, magnitude, area
2 noun kind, sort, class, order 3 verb wander, rove,
roam, stray

rank 1 noun grade, class, position, level 2 adjective
foul, musty, offensive, coarse 3 adjective luxuriant,
fertile, dense *The whole county was covered with dense
forest*

rankle verb burn, smolder, fester, be embittered

ransack verb plunder, pillage, search, scour

ransom 1 noun release, deliverance, payoff,
price 2 verb rescue, redeem *Jill was lazy at school
to begin with, but she later redeemed herself with hard work*,
liberate

rant verb rave, declaim, bluster, roar, shout

rap verb tap, pat, strike, knock

rapid adjective speedy, quick, swift ▶ *fast* ★ slow

rapt adjective engrossed, intent, captivated,
fascinated, delighted RAPPED, WRAPPED

rapture noun bliss, ecstasy, delight ▶ *joy* ★ sorrow

rare adjective 1 unusual, uncommon, scarce,
occasional 2 valuable, fine, precious ★ common
3 underdone, lightly cooked

rascal noun rogue, knave, villain, scamp, scoundrel,
blackguard ★ gentleman

rash 1 adjective headstrong, audacious, hasty, foolhardy ▶ *reckless* ⭐ **cautious** 2 noun eruption, outbreak, epidemic *There has been an epidemic of chickenpox in our neighborhood*

rashness noun audacity, carelessness, hastiness, recklessness ⭐ **carefulness**

rasp 1 verb file, grate, grind 2 verb irk, irritate, vex 3 noun file, tool

rate 1 noun pace, tempo *It took us a while to get used to the tempo of life in the city*, velocity, speed 2 noun tax, charge, cost 3 verb appraise, assess, estimate, merit, value

rather adverb 1 somewhat, to some extent, sort of 2 first, preferably, sooner

ration 1 noun portion, share, allotment, helping 2 verb allocate, allot, restrict, control

rational adjective 1 sensible, sound, wise, intelligent, sane ⭐ **irrational** 2 reasonable, fair, proper ⭐ **absurd**

rattle verb 1 jangle, jingle, vibrate 2 muddle, confuse, daze ▶ *bewilder*

raucous adjective harsh, hoarse, rough, strident, gutteral

ravage verb devastate, destroy, pillage, ransack, desolate, wreck

rave verb 1 rant, ramble *The old man rambled on for hours about his youth*, roar, rage, storm 2 favor, be ecstatic about

ravenous adjective hungry, starving, famished, voracious ▶ *greedy*

ravishing adjective beautiful, bewitching, delightful, charming ▶ *enchanting*

raw adjective 1 uncooked 2 unripe, green *I was pretty green during the first six months in the job*, inexperienced 3 sensitive, painful, tender 4 cold, exposed, chilly

ray noun beam, gleam, glimmer, shaft, stream, spark

raze verb demolish, destroy, flatten, obliterate, ruin RAISE, RAYS

reach 1 verb arrive at, gain, get to, attain, grasp 2 verb stretch, extend 3 noun extent, length, grasp, distance, scope

react verb respond, reverberate *The sound of the church bell reverberated through the village*, behave, respond

read verb 1 peruse, pore over, study, browse, understand 2 recite, orate REED

readily adverb easily, eagerly, freely, gladly, promptly ⭐ **reluctantly**

ready adjective 1 prepared, alert, prompt, willing ⭐ **reluctant** 2 convenient, handy ⭐ **remote** 3 skillful, facile, expert ⭐ **clumsy**

real adjective 1 genuine, authentic, factual ⭐ **false** 2 substantial, existent, actual ⭐ **imaginary** REEL

realistic adjective 1 authentic, lifelike 2 practical, down-to-earth *Sue is a real romantic type, but her boyfriend is much more down-to-earth*, unromantic, businesslike, pragmatic ⭐ **fanciful**

realize verb 1 understand, comprehend, feel 2 earn, gain, obtain, acquire

really adverb truly, indeed, actually, absolutely

realm noun domain, province, sphere *My mother has taken up writing and is very involved in the sphere of books*, region, territory, field

reap verb harvest, gather, obtain, realize, derive, gain ⭐ **squander**

rear 1 noun back, end, tail, behind, posterior 2 adjective hind, after, following 3 verb foster, breed, educate 4 verb lift, raise, elevate

reason 1 noun purpose, motive, basis, cause, explanation 2 noun wisdom, sense, intellect 3 verb consider, think, argue

reasonable adjective 1 sensible, valid, rational ⭐ **absurd** 2 moderate, fair, just, modest 3 inexpensive, low priced *Everything in the new supermarket is low priced* ⭐ **excessive**

reassure verb inspire, hearten, convince ▶ *encourage* ⭐ **discourage**

rebate noun refund, repayment, discount, allowance

rebel 1 verb (re-*bel*) revolt, mutiny, disobey, resist 2 noun (*reb*-el) revolutionary, mutineer *Fletcher Christian was the leader of the mutineers on the ship*, traitor

rebellious adjective defiant, disobedient, mutinous, resistant ⭐ **obedient**

rebuke verb reprimand, reproach, scold, tell off ⭐ **praise**

recall verb 1 recollect, remember 2 cancel, overrule, countermand *We were just about to pull down the building when our orders were countermanded*, call back

recede verb ebb, retreat, flow back, decline, shrink, withdraw, return ⭐ **proceed**

receipt noun acknowledgment, voucher

Receptacles

bowl

plastic container

recent adjective late, new, fresh, novel, modern, current ★ **out-of-date**

recently adverb lately, currently, latterly

receptacle noun container, holder, vessel, bowl

reception noun 1 entertainment, function, party 2 acceptance, acknowledgment

recess noun 1 alcove, corner, socket, niche, slot, nook 2 intermission, interlude, pause

recession noun slump, stagnation, depression ★ **boom**

recipe noun formula, method *I'll show you my secret method of making angel food cake; it never fails*, prescription

recite verb recount, chant, speak, declaim, relate, describe

reckless adjective unwary, incautious, daring, brash, heedless ▶ *rash* ★ **cautious**

reckon 1 verb calculate, figure, count, tally *I have checked the accounts, and my figures tally with yours*, account 2 judge, expect, believe, guess, surmise

reclaim verb recover, redeem, reform, retrieve, restore, salvage

recline verb lounge, sprawl, lie, rest, loll, repose

recognize verb 1 recall, recollect, remember, identify, know 2 see *I will explain my idea slowly, and you will see what I mean*, comprehend, understand

recoil verb 1 rebound, backfire, boomerang 2 falter, flinch, shrink, quail *My little brother quailed at the sound of the thunder*

recollect verb recall, recognize, place ▶ *remember* ★ **forget**

recommend verb suggest, advise, propose, commend, approve ★ **veto**

recompense 1 noun payment, compensation, remuneration 2 verb reimburse, repay ▶ *reward*

reconcile verb 1 accept, harmonize, pacify, placate ★ **estrange** 2 adjust, settle, square

record 1 verb (re-*cord*) note, register, enter, inscribe, list 2 noun (*rec*-ord) album, disk, platter, CD, LP, MP3 3 chronicle, archive, almanac *We'll get hold of the almanac and check the time of high tide*, register 4 performance, championship

recount verb 1 (re-*count*) relate, tell, recite, describe 2 (*re*-count) count again

recover verb 1 reclaim, retrieve, redeem, regain 2 get better, recuperate, revive ★ **worsen**

recreation noun pastime, sports, amusement, fun

recruit 1 noun trainee, beginner, apprentice 2 verb enlist, enroll, draft, mobilize

rectify verb correct, put right, repair, remedy, restore, adjust, reset

recuperate verb get better, rally, improve, mend ▶ *recover* ★ **worsen**

recur verb return, reappear, come back, repeat, revert

redden verb crimson, color, flush ▶ *blush*

redeem verb 1 buy back, compensate for, exchange 2 save, liberate, free

reduce verb 1 lessen, diminish, curtail, contract 2 overcome, defeat, humiliate

reek verb smell, stink, fume, exhale, smoke

reel 1 verb roll, rock, shake, stagger, falter, totter 2 noun spool, bobbin, spindle REAL

refer verb relate, connect, associate, assign, belong

referee noun umpire, arbitrator, judge

reference noun **1** allusion, insinuation, innuendo
From your innuendo, it seems that you think I'm joking! ▶ hint
2 testimonial, recommendation, credentials

refine verb clarify, purify, filter, process, cultivate

refined adjective **1** civilized, cultivated, cultured
▶ *polite* **2** purified, pure, clarified ★ **coarse**

reflect verb **1** think, contemplate, deliberate, consider
2 mirror, copy, imitate, image

reform verb **1** improve, correct ▶ *rectify* **2** remodel,
reorganize, revamp

refrain **1** verb avoid, abstain, forbear, resist, keep from
2 noun chorus, melody, tune

refresh verb rejuvenate, renew, restore, cheer, enliven
★ **exhaust**

refrigerate verb chill, cool, freeze

refuge noun haven, harbor, asylum, sanctuary
▶ *shelter*

refugee noun exile, fugitive, emigrant

refund verb repay, rebate, reimburse *I must reimburse you
for everything that you spent on my behalf*, pay back, return

refuse **1** verb (re-*fuze*) decline, say no, demur, repudiate
2 noun (*ref*-use) trash, garbage, rubbish, waste

refute verb deny, dispute, disprove, discredit
★ **prove**

regain verb recover, get back, retrieve, redeem

regal adjective royal, princely, majestic, noble, stately

regard **1** verb esteem, revere, honor, respect ★ **dislike**
2 verb notice, observe, see, gaze **3** noun affection,
esteem, fondness, repute ★ **contempt**

regardless **1** adjective heedless, neglectful, indifferent
★ **careful** **2** adverb anyhow, anyway, in any case

region noun area, zone, territory, locality, province,
country

register **1** noun roll, roster, record, archives *We can
trace the town's history from the ancient archives* **2** verb
enter, record, inscribe, enroll, sign on

regret **1** verb repent, rue, deplore, lament, mourn,
apologize ★ **welcome** **2** noun remorse, sorrow, apology,
grief

regular adjective **1** normal, customary, periodical,
formal ★ **unusual** **2** orderly, steady, unchanging
★ **variable**

regulate verb **1** control, manage, govern, determine
2 adjust, measure, time, correct

regulation noun **1** rule, law, command, bylaw
The club bylaws require us to elect a new secretary
2 order, control, government

rehearse verb repeat, practice, drill, prepare, run
through

reign **1** noun rule, sway, power, control **2** verb govern,
rule, dominate, command RAIN, REIN

rein verb & noun bridle, hold, check, harness RAIN,
REIGN

reinforce verb support, strengthen, toughen, harden,
stiffen ★ **weaken**

reject **1** verb (re-*ject*) discard, get rid of, throw out,
refuse, repel, deny **2** noun (*re*-ject) castoff, scrap

rejoice verb glory, exult, cheer, please, triumph
▶ *delight* ★ **lament**

relapse **1** verb revert, backslide, turn back, recede
2 noun repetition, recurrence, setback

relate verb describe, recount, tell, mention, detail

related adjective associated, allied, connected, linked,
akin ★ **different**

relative **1** noun kinsman, kinswoman, cousin,
relation, sibling *I have four siblings—three sisters and
one brother* **2** adjective comparative, approximate,
relevant

relax verb diminish, loosen, ease, reduce, relieve,
unwind ★ **tighten**

relaxed adjective composed, cool, easygoing, mellow
▶ *casual* ★ **tense**

release verb let go, loose, liberate, acquit, discharge
▶ *free* ★ **detain**

relent verb relax, soften, yield, ease, give in, unbend
★ **harden**

relentless adjective unmerciful, remorseless, grim,
pitiless ▶ *cruel* ★ **humane**

relevant adjective applicable, pertinent, appropriate,
apt ▶ *suitable* ★ **irrelevant**

reliable adjective dependable, trustworthy,
responsible, honest ▶ *sound* ★ **unreliable**

relic noun fragment, vestige, antique, keepsake,
memento *This brooch is a memento of my great-grandmother;
she wore it often*

relief noun aid, assistance, respite, support, succor ▶ *help* ★ **aggravation**

relieve verb release, support, comfort, lighten, relax, console ★ **aggravate**

religious adjective pious, devout, orthodox, devoted, God-fearing, faithful

relinquish verb renounce, let go, waive, disclaim, give up ▶ *abandon* ★ **retain**

relish 1 verb enjoy, like, approve ▶ *appreciate* ★ **loathe** 2 noun savor, flavor, tang, gusto *The fried chicken was a great success; everyone ate with enormous gusto*, zest, sauce

reluctant adjective hesitant, averse, loth, disinclined, squeamish ★ **willing**

rely on verb depend on, count on, believe in

remain verb 1 stay, tarry, dwell, wait, rest ★ **depart** 2 persist, last, endure

remainder noun remnant, residue, leavings

remark verb 1 utter, observe, state, mention ▶ *say* 2 notice, perceive, note ▶ *see*

remarkable adjective unusual, surprising, curious, prominent ▶ *outstanding* ★ **ordinary**

remedy 1 noun cure, restorative, medicine 2 noun relief, solution, treatment, corrective 3 verb relieve, heal, cure, put right

remember verb recollect, recognize, think back ▶ *recall* ★ **forget**

remind verb suggest, hint, cue, prompt

remit verb 1 relax, desist, slacken, modify, excuse, forgive 2 pay, square, settle up

remnant noun residue, remains, rest ▶ *remainder*

remorse noun regrets, contrition, pity

remote adjective 1 distant, far, isolated ★ **near** 2 unrelated, alien, foreign ★ **significant**

remove verb dislocate, take away, transfer, withdraw, carry off

rend verb split, fracture, tear apart, sever, break

render verb 1 give, present, surrender, deliver 2 play, execute, perform

renew verb 1 modernize, mend, prolong, renovate 2 reissue *Next week we start to reissue some of the old silent movies*, revive

renounce verb disown, disclaim, give up, repudiate, forsake ★ **retain**

renowned adjective eminent, noted, famed, notable ▶ *celebrated* ★ **obscure**

rent 1 verb hire, lease, let, charter 2 noun tear, rip, break, crack, fissure 3 noun fee, payment

repair 2 verb fix, mend, correct, remedy, rectify *We are sorry that there was an error in your account; we will rectify it right away* 1 noun restoration, adjustment

repast noun meal, food, snack, spread

repay verb 1 refund, reimburse, pay 2 avenge, retaliate, revenge, punish

repeal verb revoke, annul, abolish, quash *The man's innocence was proved, and his sentence was quashed* ▶ *cancel* ★ **establish**

repeat verb duplicate, renew, reiterate, do again

repel verb 1 repulse, deter, reject, push back 2 revolt, disgust, nauseate ★ **attract**

repellent adjective distasteful, hateful, discouraging ▶ *repulsive* ★ **attractive**

repent verb sorrow, deplore, grieve ▶ *regret*

replace verb 1 supersede, succeed, follow, substitute 2 put back, reinstate, restore

replenish verb fill, refill, restock, furnish, provide, top up ★ **empty**

replica noun facsimile, copy, likeness, duplicate

reply 1 verb answer, respond, rejoin, retort, acknowledge 2 noun answer, response, acknowledgment, riposte

report 1 noun statement, account, message, communication, tidings 2 noun noise, explosion, bang 3 verb tell, disclose, reveal, expose

repose 1 verb rest, settle, lie down, sleep, recline 2 noun ease, peace, quiet, tranquility ★ **tumult**

represent verb 1 depict, picture, portray, illustrate 2 stand for, mean, denote

representative 1 noun agent, delegate, envoy, deputy 2 adjective typical, figurative

repress verb restrain, suppress, bottle up, smother, stifle

reprimand 1 verb admonish, blame, rebuke ▶ *chide* 2 noun reproach, talking-to, scolding ★ **praise**

reproach verb scold, reprove, reprimand, blame ▶ *rebuke* ★ **approve**

reproduce verb 1 copy, duplicate, imitate, simulate 2 breed, multiply, generate

reprove verb reproach, reprimand ▶ *rebuke* ★ **approve**

repudiate verb renounce, disown, disavow, disclaim
★ acknowledge

repugnant adjective unattractive, disagreeable,
offensive ▶ *repulsive*, ★ pleasant

repulse verb repel, rebuff, drive back, reject ▶ *spurn*
★ attract

repulsive adjective obnoxious, disgusting, loathsome
▶ *repugnant* ★ attractive

reputation noun standing, position, esteem, honor,
good name

request 1 verb demand, beg, entreat, beseech ▶ *ask*
2 noun petition, entreaty, invitation

require verb 1 need, want, demand, crave 2 expect,
cause, instruct

rescue 1 verb save, set free, liberate, recover, release
2 noun liberation, deliverance, salvation *Salvation for the
shipwrecked crew came when the coast guard lifted them to safety*
★ capture

research verb examine, explore, investigate, inquire
▶ *study*

resemble verb look like, mirror, take after, be like ★ differ

resent verb resist, begrudge, dislike, take exception to
★ like

resentful adjective offended, bitter, piqued, huffy
▶ *indignant* ★ contented

reserve 1 verb hoard, retain, withhold ▶ *keep* 2 noun
modesty, shyness, restraint 3 noun supply, backlog, stock

reservoir noun lake, spring, pool, container

reside verb live, occupy, inhabit, lodge ▶ *dwell*

residence noun house, home, habitation, dwelling,
mansion RESIDENTS

resign verb retire, abdicate, step down, give notice,
abandon ▶ *quit* ★ join

resign oneself to verb accept, comply, reconcile
Robinson Crusoe became reconciled to loneliness on his island,
yield, give in ▶ *submit* ★ resist

resist verb withstand, oppose, defy, refrain, hinder
▶ *thwart* ★ submit

resistance noun defiance, obstruction, opposition,
hindrance ★ acceptance

resolute adjective determined, resolved, obstinate,
stubborn, dogged *Despite the bad weather, the climbers were
dogged in their will to reach the peak* ★ weak

resolve 1 verb determine, intend, decide 2 verb decipher,
unravel, disentangle 3 noun resolution, purpose, will

resort 1 verb frequent, haunt, visit 2 noun alternative,
chance, course 3 noun spa, watering place, hotel,
vacation spot

resourceful adjective clever, ingenious, bright

respect 1 noun esteem, honor, regard, repute, dignity
2 verb esteem, honor, revere, venerate *The names of the
pioneers and explorers will always be venerated*

respectable adjective decent, admirable, honest,
honorable, proper ★ disreputable

respectful adjective deferential, courteous, polite,
dutiful ★ disrespectful

respite noun break, halt, interval, lull, recess, letup

respond verb answer, reply, retort, tally, accord, agree
★ differ

responsible adjective 1 accountable, dependable,
sensible ▶ *reliable* ★ unreliable 2 liable, guilty

rest 1 noun repose, relaxation, peace, tranquility
2 noun break, pause, respite, spell 3 noun remainder,
residue, balance 4 verb repose, settle, sleep, relax WREST

restful adjective peaceful, quiet, calm, placid
★ disturbing

restless adjective uneasy, fitful, agitated, nervous, fretful
★ calm

restore verb 1 replace, reinstate, return 2 refurbish,
recondition, renovate *We renovated this old sofa, which we
found in a junk shop*

restrain verb stop, prevent, hold back, subdue ▶ *check*
★ encourage

restrict verb confine, limit, cramp, handicap ▶ *regulate*
★ free

result 1 noun effect, consequence, outcome, end
★ cause 2 verb ensue, happen, turn out, follow, emerge,
occur

resume verb renew, recommence, start again, go back to
▶ *continue* ★ interrupt

retain verb hold, restrain, withhold, detain ▶ *keep*
★ relinquish

retaliate verb avenge, reciprocate, fight back, repay,
retort ★ submit

retire verb 1 retreat, go back ▶ *withdraw* ★ advance
2 abdicate, resign, relinquish

retort 1 noun riposte, reply, rejoinder 2 verb return, answer, reply

retract verb recant, deny, disavow, take back, revoke ★ maintain

retreat 1 verb retire, depart, shrink ▶ *withdraw* ★ advance 2 noun sanctuary *This section of the park is being made into a bird sanctuary*, shelter, den, haven

retrieve verb redeem, recover, regain, rescue ▶ *salvage* ★ lose

return 1 verb rejoin, come back, reappear 2 verb restore, give back, repay, refund 3 noun form, tax form, document, list

reveal verb disclose, expose, show, display, uncover, divulge ★ hide

revel 1 verb make merry, celebrate, have fun 2 noun celebration, gala, party, spree

revenge 1 noun vengeance, reprisal, retaliation 2 verb avenge, get one's own back

revenue noun income, receipts, earnings

revere verb honor, esteem, regard, adore, venerate, respect ★ despise

reverse 1 verb cancel, change, overrule, repeal, revoke 2 noun adversity, disaster, bad luck, misfortune 3 adjective backward, contrary, opposite *We turned the car around and drove back in the opposite direction*

review 1 verb reconsider, examine, survey 2 noun inspection, examination 3 noun synopsis, journal, magazine REVUE

revise verb edit, amend, improve, rewrite, alter

revive verb awaken, rally, recover, refresh, restore, invigorate ▶ *rouse*

revoke verb repeal, abolish *The principal refuses to abolish the school dress code*, cancel, quash, reverse, withdraw

revolt 1 verb rebel, mutiny, riot 2 verb nauseate, sicken, disgust 3 noun rebellion, uprising, revolution

revolting adjective obnoxious *The chemical factory's chimney was giving off obnoxious fumes*, repulsive, offensive ▶ *repugnant* ★ pleasant

revolve verb rotate, spin, gyrate, turn

reward 1 noun award, payment, benefit, bonus, profit ★ punishment 2 verb compensate, repay, remunerate ★ punish

rhyme noun verse, poem, ditty, ode RIME

Rivers and waterways

arroyo	pool
brook	pond
canal	river
channel	spring
creek	strait
lake	stream
loch	surf

waterfall

rhythm noun beat, pulse, throb, stroke, timing

ribald adjective smutty, vulgar, coarse, gross

rich adjective 1 wealthy, prosperous, affluent, opulent ★ poor 2 fertile, loamy, fruitful, abundant ★ barren 3 delicious, sweet, luscious, delicate

rid verb get rid of, unburden, expel, free

riddle 1 noun puzzle, cryptogram, enigma 2 verb puncture, bore, perforate, pierce

ride 1 verb sit, travel, drive, journey 2 noun journey, jaunt, lift, trip

ridge noun 1 groove, furrow, fold 2 highland, chain, range *A range of hills could be seen in the distance*

ridicule 1 noun scorn, derision, travesty, sarcasm, mockery 2 verb deride, mock, jeer, banter *His banter can be amusing, but he doesn't know when to stop and sometimes offends people*

ridiculous adjective laughable, absurd, foolish, preposterous ▶ *silly* ★ sensible

rife adjective common, current, frequent, prevalent ▶ *widespread* ★ scarce

rifle 1 verb loot, rob, plunder ▶ *ransack* 2 noun gun, musket, firearm

rift noun 1 fissure, breach, crack 2 disagreement, clash, break

A B C D E F G H I J K L M N O P Q **R** S T U V W X Y Z

right **1** adjective correct, proper, true ☆ **incorrect** **2** adjective honest, upright, fair **3** adjective seemly, fit, suitable, becoming ☆ **improper** **4** noun truth, justice, honesty ☆ **wrong** RITE, WRITE

righteous adjective honorable, upright, moral

rigid adjective **1** stiff, firm, inflexible **2** stern, austere, harsh ☆ **flexible**

rigorous adjective stern, severe, strict, rigid

rim noun border, margin, edge, verge *We knew that we were on the verge of disaster*, brink

ring **1** noun circle, band, collar **2** noun bell, chime, tinkle **3** verb chime, strike, jingle, sound WRING

riot **1** noun uproar, tumult, brawl, broil ☆ **calm** **2** verb revolt, rampage, rebel

ripe adjective **1** mellow, mature, seasoned **2** developed, adult, full-grown

rise **1** verb ascend, mount, soar, arise, grow ☆ **fall** **2** verb appear, occur, happen ☆ **vanish** **3** noun ascent, advance, increase ☆ **fall**

risk **1** verb chance, dare, hazard, gamble **2** noun adventure, peril, danger, jeopardy ☆ **safety**

risky adjective perilous, chancy, dangerous, tricky, uncertain ☆ **safe**

rite noun custom, ritual, practice RIGHT

rival **1** adjective opposing, competing, conflicting **2** noun opponent, adversary ☆ **associate**

river noun stream, waterway, brook, torrent *Before the rains came, this torrent was only a trickle*

road noun street, avenue, drive, lane, highway, freeway, route, way RODE, ROWED

roam verb rove, ramble, range, stroll, wander

roar verb bellow, bawl, yell, blare, cry

rob verb cheat, defraud, loot, plunder ▷ *steal*

robber noun bandit, brigand, thief, crook

robe noun costume, dress, gown, habit

robust adjective strong, healthy, lusty, sturdy ▷ *vigorous* ☆ **delicate**

rock **1** noun stone, boulder, cobble, pebble, crag, reef **2** verb totter, reel, sway, falter **3** verb quiet, still, tranquilize, soothe

rod noun baton, stick, stave, pole, perch, cane

rogue noun rascal, blackguard, scamp, knave ▷ *scoundrel* ☆ **gentleman**

role noun character, post, duty, function *At the end of the party, my function will be to clear up*

roll **1** noun record, register, list **2** noun spool, scroll, reel **3** verb revolve, rotate, turn **4** verb smooth, level, press **5** verb lurch, reel, pitch, ROLE

romance noun **1** love story, novel, love affair **2** adventure, excitement, fantasy, glamour

romantic adjective **1** amorous, passionate, loving **2** visionary, fanciful *Many people have a fanciful idea of how things were in the old days*, fantastic, extravagant ☆ **ordinary**

romp verb gambol, caper, frolic, prance, play

roof noun ceiling, covering, cover, canopy

room noun **1** apartment, chamber, area, compartment, salon **2** space, capacity

root noun **1** seed, source, radicle **2** basis, element, stem, origin

rope noun cable, cord, hawser, line, lasso

rosy adjective **1** cheerful, encouraging, hopeful, optimistic **2** pink, flesh-colored

rot **1** verb corrupt, crumble, decay, perish **2** noun bunkum *The last speaker at the meeting was talking a lot of bunkum*, balderdash, nonsense

rotate verb revolve, turn, spin, pivot, gyrate

rotten adjective **1** decayed, putrid, decomposed, fetid **2** deplorable, despicable, nasty, vicious **3** sick, ill, poorly

rough adjective **1** wrinkled, craggy, coarse, shaggy, broken **2** rude, crude, imperfect **3** blunt, gruff, brusque, discourteous RUFF

round **1** adjective circular, rotund, spherical **2** noun ring, circle, loop

rouse verb **1** waken, arouse, excite, disturb **2** anger, inflame, incite ☆ **calm**

rout verb crush, defeat, conquer, overthrow

route noun road, track, way, journey, direction

routine noun usage, practice, formula, technique, method, habit *After being alone for so long, I have gotten into the habit of talking to myself*

rove verb tramp, roam, wander, stroll, drift

row **1** noun (*ro*) string, line, queue, rank, column **2** verb paddle, scull ROE **3** noun (rhymes with *now*) fight, squabble, noise, quarrel, argument, dispute ☆ **calm**

rowdy adjective rough, unruly, boisterous, noisy, wild ☆ **quiet**

Rulers, monarchs, and leaders

caesar
czar
czarina
emperor
empress
king
mikado
mogul
president
prime minister
prince
princess
queen
rajah
sultan

pharaoh

royal adjective sovereign, princely, stately, majestic
▶ *regal*

rub verb stroke, brush, scrub, wipe, polish

rubbish noun debris, trash, junk, garbage

rude adjective **1** coarse, primitive, ill-bred, impolite, boorish, bad-mannered **2** crude, formless, shapeless
★ polished ROOD, RUED

rue verb be sorry for, deplore, grieve ▶ *regret*

ruffian noun hoodlum, hooligan, lout, scoundrel, rogue,
▶ *rascal*

ruffle verb **1** fluster, worry, excite, agitate **2** crumple, rumple, crease

ruffled adjective upset, worried, flustered, harassed, bothered, irritated

rugged adjective **1** rough, craggy, shaggy, ragged
2 rigorous, robust, strong, strenuous

ruin verb **1** demolish, wreck, damage, smash
2 bankrupt, impoverish, overwhelm

rule **1** verb control, govern, command, manage, direct
2 verb decide, determine, judge **3** noun law, regulation
4 noun straightedge

ruler **1** noun leader, director, king, queen, monarch, governor **2** rule, straightedge

rumble verb roar, thunder, boom, roll

rumor noun hearsay, report, gossip, scandal

rumpus noun uproar, racket, riot, commotion, hurly-burly ★ calm

run **1** verb hurry, hasten, speed, sprint ★ saunter
2 verb leak, flow, ooze **3** verb operate, propel, drive
4 noun race, course

run away verb escape, flee, bolt, abscond ★ stay

rupture verb & noun break, burst, puncture, split

rural adjective rustic, countrified, pastoral ★ urban

ruse noun dodge, hoax, scheme, trick, ploy RUES

rush verb & noun dash, speed, hurry, scramble, stampede, rampage ★ saunter

rust noun corrosion, mold, blight, mildew, stain, deterioration

rustic adjective rural, pastoral, country, homely, simple

rustle noun & verb crackle, swish, murmur, whisper

rut noun furrow, channel, groove, score, track

ruthless adjective cruel, savage, harsh, ferocious, pitiless ★ merciful

A B C D E F G H I J K L M N O P Q **R** S T U V W X Y Z

S s

sack 1 noun bag, pouch, pack 2 verb rob, plunder, pillage 3 discharge, dismiss, lay off SAC

sacred adjective holy, blessed, hallowed, spiritual, consecrated, revered ★ profane

sacrifice 1 noun offering 2 verb forfeit, give up, relinquish ▶ *abandon*

sad adjective sorrowful, melancholy, unhappy, mournful, woeful ▶ *sorry* ★ happy

sadden verb mourn, grieve, distress, lament, dishearten, disappoint ★ please

safe 1 adjective secure, protected, sure ★ unsafe 2 noun vault, coffer, cashbox, strongbox

safety noun shelter, security, sanctuary, protection, refuge ★ danger

sag verb bend, slump, curve, bow, decline, flag ▶ *droop* ★ bulge

sage 1 adjective wise, sensible, shrewd, sagacious ★ foolish 2 noun wise person, savant *We were taught by an old savant of the university, Professor Hankins, philosopher* ★ fool

said adjective expressed, stated

sail verb cruise, voyage, navigate, float, skim SALE

sailor noun seafarer, mariner, pilot, shipmate, captain, jack-tar, seadog SAILER

sake noun motive, reason, purpose, object, principle

salary noun pay, earnings, reward, wages, income

sale noun auction, transaction, selling, trade, disposal SAIL

sally noun jest, joke, crack, riposte ▶ *quip*

salute 1 verb greet, accost, welcome, hail, honor 2 noun greetings, welcome, acknowledgment

salvage verb save, conserve, rescue, restore, reclaim ▶ *preserve* ★ abandon

same adjective 1 identical, duplicate, alike, similar 2 aforesaid, aforementioned *I leave all my possessions to my wife, the aforementioned Angela Gomez*

sample 1 noun specimen, example, model, pattern, illustration 2 verb inspect, try, taste

sanction verb permit, allow, authorize, approve

sanctuary noun retreat, shelter, shrine, asylum, haven ▶ *refuge*

sane adjective normal, rational, reasonable, lucid ▶ *sensible* ★ insane

sap verb bleed, drain, exhaust, reduce, weaken ★ strengthen

sarcastic adjective biting, cutting, sardonic, cynical, ironic, caustic *My cousins made some caustic remarks after I played the violin*

satire noun invective, sarcasm, burlesque, ridicule, parody

satisfaction noun contentment, delight, gratification, compensation ★ grievance

satisfy verb gratify, fulfill, appease, suit, please ▶ *delight* ★ disappoint

saturate verb soak, steep, drench, souse, waterlog *I am afraid that old canoe is too waterlogged to ever be used again*

saucy adjective forward, pert, impudent, cheeky, disrespectful ★ civil

saunter verb roam, loiter, wander, linger, dawdle, amble ▶ *stroll* ★ hasten

savage 1 adjective barbaric, wild, uncivilized, ferocious, brutal ★ civilized 2 noun brute, oaf, barbarian

save verb 1 liberate, set free, rescue, protect, guard 2 keep, preserve, salvage, hoard, put aside ★ squander

savory adjective appetizing, flavorful, luscious, agreeable ★ tasteless

say verb speak, utter, state, pronounce, talk, tell, assert

saying noun proverb, statement, adage, idiom, maxim, aphorism

scale 1 noun measure, balance, calibration 2 noun crust, plate, flake 3 noun clef, key *I will play this next piece in the key of C*, mode 4 verb climb, ascend, clamber up

scamp noun knave, rogue, rascal, scoundrel, scalawag *Someone rang our doorbell, but when I opened the door, the scalawag had gone*

scamper verb hurry, run, scurry, hasten, sprint, scoot ▶ *rush*

scan verb examine, glance at, scrutinize, pore over ▶ *check*

scandal noun disgrace, libel, slander, offense, infamy, rumor, discredit ★ honor

scanty adjective meager, insufficient, sparse, inadequate, poor, scant ★ **plenty**

scar 1 noun blemish, mark, stigma, wound 2 verb brand, damage, disfigure

scarce adjective rare, infrequent, sparse, scanty, uncommon ★ **common**

scarcity noun lack, deficiency, dearth, rarity, infrequency ★ **abundance**

scare verb frighten, startle, shock, alarm, dismay ★ **reassure**

scatter verb spread, disperse, strew, broadcast, disseminate ▶ *sprinkle* ★ **collect**

scene noun sight, spectacle, vision, view, exhibition, landscape SEEN

scent 1 noun aroma, tang, fragrance, smell, odor 2 verb detect, sniff, smell CENT, SENT

schedule noun timetable *We checked the timetable before buying our train tickets*, program, catalog, diary

scheme noun plot, plan, project, design, proposal, idea

scholar noun 1 pupil, student, schoolchild, learner 2 intellectual *That café is a favorite gathering place for intellectuals*, savant, academic

scholarly adjective learned, educated, literate, cultured ★ **illiterate**

scoff verb sneer, mock, deride, jeer, ridicule ★ **respect**

scold verb rebuke, admonish, reprove, find fault with ▶ *chide* ★ **praise**

scoop 1 verb bail, ladle, spoon, excavate, gouge, hollow 2 noun exclusive, inside story, coup

scope noun extent, margin, compass, range, latitude, field

scorch verb sear, burn, singe, blister, shrivel

score verb 1 cut, mark, scratch 2 register, record, win

scorn 1 noun mockery, disdain, ridicule, disregard 2 verb despise, mock, spurn, slight ★ **respect**

scoundrel noun rascal, knave, thief, rogue, villain ▶ *vagabond* ★ **gentleman**

scour verb 1 cleanse, rinse, scrub, purge 2 search, seek, ransack, rake

scourge 1 verb beat, whip, thrash, cane 2 noun curse, evil, misfortune, plague ★ **blessing**

scowl verb & noun frown, glower, grimace, glare ★ **smile**

scramble 1 verb clamber, climb 2 verb jostle, struggle, swarm, push 3 noun turmoil, bustle, confusion ★ **order**

scrap 1 noun piece, morsel, bit, portion, fragment, grain 2 verb abandon, discard, junk

scrape 1 verb scratch, groove, abrade, file, grate, scour 2 noun predicament, fix, difficulty

scratch verb & noun wound, cut, mark, score

scream verb & noun screech, cry, shriek, howl, yell

screen 1 noun awning *Before the ceremony, an awning was erected over the entrance to the hotel*, canopy, shade, protection 2 verb protect, hide, conceal, veil

screw verb twist, turn, wrench, tighten, compress

scribble verb write, scrawl, scratch

scribe noun writer, penman, clerk, historian

script noun handwriting, manuscript, text, words, libretto *Sir Arthur Sullivan wrote the music for* The Mikado, *and W. S. Gilbert wrote the lyrics and libretto*

scrub 1 verb scour, brush, mop, cleanse 2 noun brushwood, undergrowth

scruffy adjective messy, dirty, frowzy, seedy, shabby, sloppy ▶ *slovenly* ★ **neat**

scrumptious adjective delightful, delicious, appetizing, exquisite

scrupulous adjective painstaking, particular, rigorous, strict, conscientious ★ **careless**

scrutinize verb examine, inspect, peruse, study

scuffle verb & noun tussle, skirmish, fight, struggle, squabble

scum noun dross, foam, froth, dregs, crust

scuttle verb 1 scramble, scamper, scoot, hurry 2 destroy, smash, wreck

seal 1 noun signet, stamp 2 noun cork, bung, closure 3 noun sea mammal 4 verb fasten, close, shut

seam 1 noun ridge, scar, lode, furrow 2 hem, pleat, tuck SEEM

search 1 verb seek, quest, hunt, trail, track, scour, explore 2 noun exploration, investigation, quest, pursuit

season 1 noun period, time, occasion, term 2 verb accustom, acclimatize, mature 3 verb flavor, spice, salt

seat 1 noun bench, chair, stool, sofa, couch, throne 2 noun headquarters, place, site 3 verb accommodate, locate, place

secret adjective mysterious, hidden, concealed, obscure, private ★ **public**

section noun division, group, department, segment, portion

secure 1 adjective safe, protected 2 adjective confident, certain, sure, stable ⋆ **uncertain** 3 verb fasten, protect, close, lock ⋆ **unfasten** 4 verb acquire, procure, obtain ⋆ **lost**

sedate adjective staid, sober, demure, earnest ▶ *steady* ⋆ **flippant**

see verb 1 behold, witness, sight, observe 2 heed, watch, examine, note 3 understand, comprehend, know SEA

seedy adjective shabby, squalid, poor, grubby, unkempt ▶ *slovenly* ⋆ **spruce**

seek verb look for, search, inquire, endeavor, hunt

seem verb appear, look like, sound like, look as if SEAM

seemly adjective fit, suitable, proper, decent, decorous ⋆ **unseemly**

seethe verb simmer, fizz, bubble, boil, foam

seize verb grasp, snatch, take, clutch, arrest ▶ *grab* ⋆ **abandon** SEAS, SEES

seldom adverb rarely, infrequently, hardly, scarcely ⋆ **often**

select 1 adjective choice, preferred, fine, prime *All the fruit on the trees in the orchard is in its prime,* first-class ⋆ **common** 2 verb choose, pick out, single out, prefer

selfish adjective greedy, self-centered, narrow, illiberal ▶ *stingy* ⋆ **generous**

sell verb vend, market, retail, trade, peddle ⋆ **buy**

send verb transmit, dispatch, forward, mail, direct ⋆ **detain**

send for verb command, order, summon, request ⋆ **dismiss**

sensation noun 1 feeling, perception, impression, awareness 2 excitement, commotion, scandal

sensational adjective exceptional, scandalous, lurid ▶ *exciting* ⋆ **ordinary**

sense noun 1 sensation, impression, feeling 2 understanding, mind, tact, intellect 3 wisdom, significance, meaning CENTS, SCENTS

senseless adjective silly, stupid, absurd ▶ *foolish* ⋆ **sensible**

sensible adjective 1 wise, intelligent, astute, shrewd 2 reasonable, rational 3 conscious, aware, mindful ⋆ **senseless**

sensitive adjective 1 susceptible, responsive, acute, impressionable *Because Rachel is at such an impressionable age, her mother does not want her to see the movie* 2 touchy, thin-skinned

sentence noun 1 phrase, clause 2 judgment, decision, condemnation, doom

sentimental adjective romantic, tender, emotional

separate 1 adjective disconnected, apart, detached ⋆ **united** 2 verb detach, part, divide, break, disconnect ⋆ **unite**

sequel noun continuation, consequence, result, outcome

serene adjective tranquil, calm, peaceful, undisturbed, clear ⋆ **tempestuous**

series noun sequence, progression, succession, run, string

serious adjective grave, earnest, solemn, thoughtful, severe, grim ⋆ **trivial**

serve verb attend, assist, aid, oblige, help, officiate, act

service noun 1 aid, help, assistance, attendance, employment 2 ceremony, rite *Stuart is studying the marriage rites of the Inca*

set 1 noun group, pack, outfit, series 2 verb settle, put, place, seat, locate 3 verb stiffen, congeal, harden 4 adjective decided, resolved, determined, fixed

setback noun defeat, delay, problem, snag, holdup ⋆ **advantage**

settle verb 1 establish, regulate, fix 2 pay, liquidate, finish 3 populate, colonize 4 live, dwell, reside

several adjective various, numerous, sundry, separate

severe adjective strict, rigid, unkind, hard, austere ▶ *stern* ⋆ **lenient**

sew verb stitch, tack, baste, fasten, seam SO, SOW

shabby adjective torn, ragged, mean, shoddy, tacky ▶ *squalid* ⋆ **neat**

shack noun hut, cabin, shanty, shed, hovel

shackle verb & noun manacle, handcuff, chain, rope, fetter

shade noun 1 shadow, gloom, darkness, dusk 2 blind, awning, screen 3 color, tint, hue, tone 4 ghost, spirit, wraith *Out of the darkness, a wraithlike figure loomed up before us*

shadow 1 noun shade 2 verb follow, stalk, tail

shady adjective 1 shadowy, shaded ⋆ **sunny** 2 crooked, infamous, disreputable ⋆ **honest**

Ships and boats

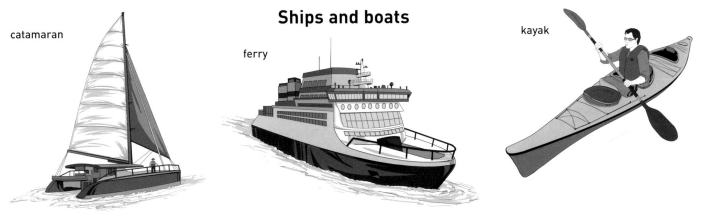

catamaran

ferry

kayak

motorboat (speedboat)

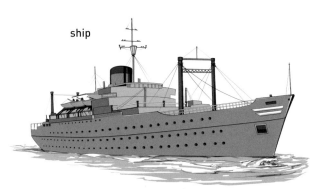

ship

shaft noun **1** pillar, column, support **2** hilt, handle, rod **3** mine, pit, well, tunnel

shaggy adjective hairy, tousled, unkempt, rough ★ smooth

shake verb flutter, tremble, throb, shudder ▶ *quiver*

shallow adjective **1** not deep **2** trivial, empty, silly, empty-headed ★ profound

sham adjective false, imitation, counterfeit, forged ▶ *bogus* ★ genuine

shame noun & verb dishonor, discredit ▶ *disgrace*

shameful adjective disgraceful, scandalous, outrageous ▶ *disreputable* ★ honorable

shape **1** noun form, structure, outline, pattern **2** verb form, fashion, make, create

share **1** verb allot, divide, participate, cooperate **2** noun portion, allotment, allowance

sharp adjective **1** acute, keen, pointed **2** clear, distinct, clean-cut **3** painful, severe, intense **4** pungent, acrid, acid **5** alert, shrewd, acute ▶ *clever* ★ dull

shatter verb smash, wreck, break, fracture, ruin ▶ *destroy*

shave verb shear, crop, slice, shred, graze, trim

shear verb fleece, strip, cut ▶ *shave* SHEER

sheath noun scabbard, quiver, holster, holder, case, casing

shed **1** noun hut, barn, lean-to, shanty **2** verb cast off, molt *Our parrot is molting and leaving feathers all over the carpet*, spill **3** verb beam, radiate

sheepish adjective timid, diffident, foolish, embarrassed, shamefaced ★ unabashed

sheer adjective **1** absolute, simple, pure, unmixed **2** transparent, filmy, thin **3** steep, abrupt, perpendicular *The trail ended at the foot of a huge, perpendicular cliff* SHEAR

shell noun pod, case, husk, hull, shuck, crust

shelter **1** noun roof, sanctuary, safety, home, retreat, cover **2** verb shield, cover, protect, screen ★ expose

shield noun & verb guard, screen, safeguard ▶ *shelter*

shift **1** verb alter, move, change, displace, remove **2** noun turn, spell, stint

shifty adjective untrustworthy, devious, treacherous ▶ *wily* ★ honest

shine verb & noun glow, gleam, glitter, sparkle, flash

ship **1** noun boat, barge, craft, vessel **2** verb export, send, transport

shirk verb dodge, avoid, shun, evade, slack

shiver verb quaver, quiver, shake, shudder ▶ *tremble*

shock **1** noun blow, jolt, clash, collision **2** noun scare, start, turn **3** verb stupefy, daze, stun

285

shocking adjective scandalous, awful, frightful ▶ *horrible* ★ **agreeable**

shoot verb **1** fire, discharge, bombard, propel **2** verb germinate *We grew some beans in a glass jar and watched them germinate*, grow, bud, sprout **3** noun bud, twig, sprout CHUTE

shop **1** noun store, market, emporium **2** verb buy, market, purchase

shore **1** noun beach, coast, strand, seashore, seaside **2** verb prop, support, bolster up, brace

short adjective **1** brief, concise, condensed ★ **long** **2** deficient, incomplete, scanty ★ **full** **3** sharp, severe, bad-tempered **4** small, puny, squat, diminutive, tiny ★ **tall**

shortcoming noun defect, fault, flaw, inadequacy, ▶ *weakness*

shorten verb cut, crop, abbreviate, lessen ▶ *diminish* ★ **lengthen**

shortened adjective abbreviated, abridged, condensed ★ **enlarged**

shortly adjective presently, soon, before long, directly

shout noun & verb cry, scream, roar, shriek, cheer, whoop, bellow

shove verb push, jostle, prod, nudge, move, propel ★ **pull**

show **1** verb display, parade, exhibit, flaunt, reveal ★ **hide** **2** verb prove, testify to, demonstrate **3** verb explain, teach, instruct **4** noun exhibition, display, ceremony, play

shower **1** verb scatter, spray, sprinkle, rain **2** noun downpour, cloudburst **3** noun barrage, volley, discharge

shred **1** noun particle, piece, scrap, tatter, fragment **2** verb tear, rip, strip

shrewd adjective profound, deep, discerning ▶ *wise* ★ **obtuse**

shriek noun & verb screech ▶ *shout*

shrill adjective treble, high-pitched, screeching, ear-piercing

shrink verb **1** contract, dwindle, shrivel, become smaller **2** flinch, cringe, recoil, withdraw

shrivel verb wither, contract, wrinkle, decrease, pucker, parch ▶ *wilt*

shudder verb shake, quake, tremble ▶ *quiver*

shuffle verb **1** mix, jumble, rearrange **2** hobble, limp

shun verb avoid, elude, ignore, spurn, steer clear of ★ **accept**

shut verb fasten, close, secure, slam, bar, latch, lock ★ **open**

shut up verb **1** imprison, cage, intern **2** be silent, hold one's tongue, be quiet

shy **1** adjective bashful, diffident, timid, wary, shrinking ★ **bold** **2** verb flinch, quail, recoil

sick adjective **1** ill, poorly, ailing, unwell, feeble **2** weary, fed up, displeased **3** nauseated

side noun **1** border, edge, flank, margin, half **2** party, sect, group, team SIGHED

sift verb strain, drain, separate, screen, sieve, riddle

sigh verb **1** grieve, lament, moan, complain **2** wheeze, breathe

sight **1** noun appearance, spectacle, scene, mirage **2** noun seeing, perception, visibility **3** verb behold, glimpse, observe CITE, SITE

sign **1** noun symbol, emblem, mark **2** noun omen, token **3** noun signboard, signpost, placard **4** verb endorse, autograph, inscribe

signal **1** noun beacon *As soon as the ships were sighted, beacons were lit all along the coast*, sign, flag, indicator **2** adjective distinguished, impressive, outstanding

significant adjective symbolical, meaningful, weighty ▶ *important* ★ **unimportant**

signify verb denote, indicate, suggest, imply ▶ *mean*

silence noun quiet, hush, peace, tranquility ★ **noise**

silent adjective hushed, noiseless, soundless, still, mute ▶ *quiet* ★ **noisy**

silly adjective absurd, senseless, stupid, fatuous ▶ *foolish* ★ **wise**

similar adjective resembling, alike, harmonious, common ▶ *like* ★ **different**

simple adjective **1** elementary, plain, uncomplicated ▶ *easy* **2** trusting, open, naive ★ **intricate**

simply adverb merely, purely, barely, solely, only

sin **1** noun misdeed, wrong, vice, evil, wickedness **2** verb err, offend, trespass, stray, do wrong

since **1** conjunction because, as, for, considering **2** preposition subsequently, after

sincere adjective true, unaffected, frank, open, truthful ▶ *genuine* ★ **insincere**

Singers

alto
baritone
bass
basso profundo
cantor
chorister
contrabass
contralto
countertenor
mezzo-soprano
prima donna
soprano
tenor
treble
vocalist

sing verb vocalize, warble, yodel, trill, croon, chant, carol, hum, chirp

singe verb scorch, burn, scald, sear, char

singer noun vocalist, minstrel, songster, chorister, crooner

single adjective **1** one, only, sole **2** solitary, alone, separate **3** unmarried, celibate *The priests of the Roman Catholic Church are celibate*

singular adjective odd, peculiar, curious, surprising ▷ *unusual* ★ ordinary

sinister adjective menacing, threatening, unlucky, disastrous ▷ *evil* ★ harmless

sink **1** verb drop, dip, descend, decline ▷ *fall* ★ rise **2** noun basin, drain

sit verb perch, seat, squat, roost, rest, settle

site noun spot, plot, locality, place, station, post ▷ *situation* CITE, SIGHT

situation noun **1** position, location, place, site, whereabouts, standpoint **2** predicament, plight, state

size noun **1** dimensions, proportions, measurement **2** magnitude, bulk, volume, weight SIGHS

skeptical adjective doubtful, unbelieving, incredulous ▷ *dubious* ★ convinced

sketch **1** noun drawing, picture, cartoon **2** noun draft, blueprint, outline **3** verb draw, portray, depict, outline

skillful adjective adroit, able, adept, dexterous, expert, competent ▷ *clever* ★ clumsy

skill noun ability, expertness, knack, facility ▷ *talent*

skim verb brush, touch, graze, float, glide

skimp verb stint, scrimp, economize, scrape

skin noun peel, rind, hide, husk, pelt

skinny adjective thin, lean, scraggy, weedy ★ fat

skip verb **1** jump, hop, dance, caper **2** pass over, miss, disregard, omit

skirmish noun & verb scuffle, fight, affray, scrap, combat, clash

skirt **1** noun petticoat, kilt **2** noun border, hem, edge, margin **3** verb border, flank, evade, avoid

skulk verb lurk, hide, cower, slink, sneak

slab noun board, stone, boulder, piece, chunk

slack adjective **1** limp, flabby, loose, relaxed ★ tight **2** lazy, sluggish ▷ *idle* ★ busy

slander verb libel, malign, accuse, abuse ▷ *defame* ★ praise

slant **1** verb & noun incline, angle, cant ▷ *slope*

slap verb smack, whack, strike, hit, spank

slash verb & noun cut, slit, gash, hack, rip

slaughter verb slay, butcher, massacre ▷ *kill*

slave **1** noun bondsman, bondswoman, serf, vassal, drudge, captive **2** verb drudge, toil, labor, grind

slavery noun bondage, enslavement, serfdom, servility, drudgery, captivity ★ freedom

slay verb murder, massacre ▷ *kill* SLEIGH

sleek adjective shiny, smooth, glossy, slick

sleep verb & noun snooze, nap, doze, drowse, repose, slumber

slender adjective **1** narrow, thin, fine, slight ▷ *slim* ★ thick **2** trivial, inadequate, meager

slice **1** verb shred, shave, cut, strip, segment **2** noun segment, piece, cut, slab

slick adjective **1** shiny, smooth ▷ *sleek* **2** glib, suave, plausible

slide verb slip, slither, glide, skim, skate

slight **1** adjective delicate, tender ▷ *slender* **2** adjective small, little, meager, trifling, trivial ★ significant **3** noun & verb snub, insult, disdain

slim adjective fine, slight ▷ *slender* ★ fat

slime noun mire, ooze, mud, filth

sling **1** verb hurl, toss, throw **2** noun loop, bandage, strap, support

287

slink verb prowl, creep, sidle, sneak ▶ *skulk*

slip **1** verb slide, slither, glide **2** verb fall, lurch, drop, slip over **3** verb & noun blunder, slip up

slippery adjective **1** smooth, glassy **2** tricky, untrustworthy, cunning ▶ *shifty* ★ trustworthy

slit verb gash, cut, rip ▶ *slash*

slogan noun motto, catchword, war cry, saying

slope **1** noun slant, grade, gradient, incline, ascent, descent, rise **2** verb lean, incline, descend, ascend

sloppy adjective **1** careless, slipshod, inattentive ▶ *slovenly* **2** dowdy, messy, tacky **3** dingy, dirty

slot noun recess, opening, hole, groove

slovenly adjective slipshod, careless, negligent, disorderly, sloppy, untidy, dowdy

slow **1** adjective inactive, tardy, late, slack, leisurely ▶ *sluggish* ★ fast **2** verb slow down, slacken, lose speed, relax ★ accelerate SLOE

sluggish adjective slothful, lazy, inactive, languid, indolent, lifeless ▶ *idle* ★ brisk

slumber verb snooze, doze ▶ *sleep* ★ awaken

sly adjective cunning, tricky, furtive, sneaky, artful ▶ *wily* ★ frank

smack verb slap, strike, spank ▶ *hit*

small adjective **1** minute, tiny, slight, diminutive ▶ *little* ★ large **2** trivial, petty, feeble, paltry, inferior

smart **1** adjective alert, bright ▶ *intelligent* **2** adjective elegant, neat, spruce, dressy ★ dull **3** verb sting, burn, throb ▶ *ache*

smash verb break, hit, destroy, wreck, demolish

smear verb plaster, daub, coat, varnish, cover, spread, smudge

smell noun aroma, fragrance, scent, perfume, stink, stench, odor, tang

smile verb grin, simper, smirk, beam ▶ *laugh*

smoke **1** noun vapor, mist, gas **2** verb fume, reek, whiff, smolder, vent

smooth **1** adjective level, even, flat, plain, sleek ★ rough **2** verb flatten, level, press

smother verb choke, throttle, stifle, restrain

smudge noun & verb mark, smear, blur, stain, blight

smug adjective self-satisfied, content, complacent, conceited

smut noun dirt, smudge, blot, spot, smear

snack noun lunch, repast, morsel, bite

snag noun catch, complication, drawback, hitch

snap verb **1** break, crack, snip **2** snarl, growl

snare **1** verb trap, catch, seize, net **2** noun trap, noose, pitfall

snatch verb seize, grab, clutch, grip, take, pluck, grasp

sneak **1** verb slink, prowl, crouch ▶ *skulk* **2** noun wretch, coward, informer

sneer verb jeer, scoff, gibe, scorn, ridicule, taunt

sniff verb smell, breathe in, inhale, scent

snivel verb weep, cry, blub, sniffle

snobbish adjective condescending, snooty, lofty, patronizing, stuck-up

snoop verb pry, eavesdrop, peep, peek, sneak

snooze verb doze, nap, slumber ▶ *sleep*

snub verb slight, slur, spurn, cut ▶ *humiliate*

snug adjective cozy, sheltered, secure, safe, restful ▶ *comfortable*

so adverb accordingly, thus, therefore, likewise SEW, SOW

soak verb moisten, wet, douse, saturate, steep

soar verb glide, fly, rise, hover, tower SORE

sob verb lament, cry, sigh ▶ *weep*

sober adjective temperate, abstemious *Uncle Arthur was very abstemious and never drank anything alcoholic*, calm, composed, serious, somber ★ excited

sociable adjective companionable, affable, friendly, genial ★ withdrawn

social adjective neighborly, civic, public **2** convivial ▶ *sociable*

soft adjective **1** pliable, plastic, flexible, supple ★ hard **2** kind, gentle, mild ▶ *tender* ★ harsh **3** low, faint, quiet ★ loud

soften verb **1** melt, dissolve, mellow ★ solidify **2** moderate, diminish, quell

soil **1** noun earth, dirt, mold **2** verb foul, dirty, sully, taint

sole adjective only, single, lone, one SOUL

solemn adjective **1** grim, serious ▶ *somber* **2** impressive, stately, sedate ★ frivolous

solid adjective **1** steady, firm, stable, sturdy **2** dense, compact, hard ★ soft

solidify verb congeal, harden, clot, cake, set ★ soften

solitary adjective alone, lonely, remote, separate, only

solution noun **1** blend, mixture, brew, fluid **2** answer, explanation

solve verb unravel, untangle, elucidate ▶ *explain* ★ **complicate**

somber adjective dark, serious, solemn, grim, gloomy, funereal ★ **bright**

some adjective any, more or less, about, several SUM

sometimes adverb at times, from time to time, occasionally

somewhat adverb in part, a little, not much

song noun air, tune, carol, ballad, ode, ditty *The new pop song was based on an old sailors' ditty*

soon adverb presently, shortly, before long

soothe verb pacify, appease, mollify, ease, lull, comfort ★ **irritate**

sordid adjective shabby, miserable, dirty, base ▶ *squalid*

sore **1** adjective tender, aching, painful, inflamed **2** adjective annoyed, upset, grieved **3** noun ulcer, boil, carbuncle SOAR

sorrow **1** noun grief, woe, remorse, anguish ★ **joy** **2** verb mourn, grieve, lament ★ **rejoice**

sorrowful adjective sad, disconsolate, mournful, dejected ★ **joyful**

sorry adjective **1** pained, grieved, hurt, dejected, doleful ★ **glad** **2** wretched, mean, poor, shabby ★ **delighted**

sort **1** noun kind, type, variety, group, class **2** verb sift, arrange, catalog, classify

soul noun spirit, substance, mind, vitality, fire, essence SOLE

sound **1** noun noise, din, tone ★ **silence** **2** verb blare, blast *We were startled by a blast from the trumpets*, blow **3** adjective hearty, virile, whole, perfect ▶ *healthy* ★ **unfit**

sour adjective **1** tart, rancid, bitter, acid ★ **sweet** **2** morose, peevish ▶ *harsh* ★ **genial**

source noun origin, spring, fount, cause, beginning

souvenir noun token, memento, keepsake, reminder, relic

sow **1** noun (rhymes with *how*) female pig **2** verb (rhymes with *mow*) plant, scatter, strew SEW, SO

space noun **1** extent, expanse, capacity, room, accommodation **2** the universe, the heavens, firmament

spacious adjective roomy, extensive, commodious, broad, wide ★ **restricted**

span **1** noun stretch, reach, extent, length **2** verb cross, bridge, link, connect

spare **1** adjective extra, reserve, surplus **2** adjective bare, meager, poor, scanty ▶ *sparse* **3** verb afford, preserve, give, allow

sparkle verb glitter, glow, gleam, glint, twinkle

sparse adjective scanty, thin ▶ *meager* ★ **dense**

spate noun flood, flow, deluge, rush, torrent

speak verb say, utter, talk, pronounce, lecture, express

spear noun pike, javelin, lance

special adjective distinct, different, unique, individual ▶ *particular* ★ **common**

species noun breed, kind, sort, class, family

specific adjective definite, exact, precise ▶ *special*

specimen noun sample, example, type, model, pattern

speck noun dot, speckle, spot, particle

spectacle noun sight, scene, exhibition, presentation ▶ *display*

spectacles noun glasses, eyeglasses

spectacular adjective wonderful, fabulous, surprising ▶ *marvelous*

spectator noun onlooker, witness, observer

speech noun **1** talk, tongue *The people spoke a strange tongue that we had never heard*, language **2** address, lecture

speed noun velocity, rapidity, dispatch, pace, tempo *The tempo of life in the quiet seaside town was much too slow for us*

speedy adjective swift, rapid, fleet, quick, lively ▶ *fast* ★ **slow**

spell **1** noun charm, magic, witchcraft **2** noun period, term, space, time **3** verb form words, write out

spend verb **1** expend, lay out, lavish, pay, disburse **2** exhaust, use up

spendthrift noun wastrel, squanderer, prodigal ★ **miser**

sphere noun **1** globe, ball, orb, planet **2** realm, orbit, domain, field

spice noun seasoning, flavoring, zest, relish, savor

spill verb pour, stream, run, overflow, spurt, upset

spin verb revolve, rotate, turn, whirl, make thread

spine noun backbone, needle, quill *The porcupine is covered in sharp quills*, ridge

289

Spices

pepper

nutmeg

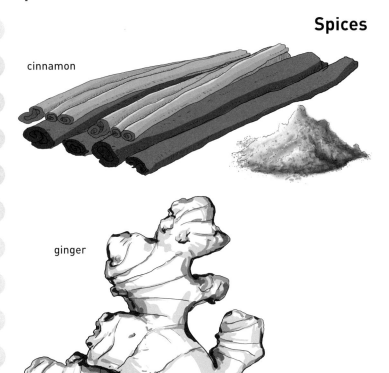

cinnamon

ginger

spirit noun **1** essence, substance, nature, character **2** soul, air, breath **3** vigor, energy, courage **4** phantom, specter, ghost

spiritual adjective **1** religious, divine, unworldly, holy **2** pure, immaterial

spite **1** noun malice, rancor, hostility, hatred **2** verb grudge, annoy, offend, injure

spiteful adjective vicious, malicious, vindictive ▷ *hateful* ☆ **kind**

splash verb wet, spatter, shower, sprinkle

splendid adjective grand, brilliant, magnificent, showy, glorious ▷ *sumptuous* ☆ **ordinary**

splendor noun glory, pageantry, brilliance ▷ *pomp*

split verb cleave, sever *Our family quarreled with our cousins and severed relationships for years*, crack, snap, splinter

spoil verb **1** hurt, injure, harm **2** deface, disfigure, destroy **3** rot, decompose, putrefy, decay

spoiled adjective decayed, rotten, broken up, corroded

spontaneous adjective natural, impulsive, self-generated, voluntary

spoof noun **1** hoax, joke, bluff, prank, satire **2** quip, jest, wisecrack

sport **1** noun game, amusement, fun, athletics, recreation **2** verb play, frolic, gambol, romp

spot **1** noun dot, speck, mark, stain, blemish **2** verb espy, notice, recognize, distinguish

spotless adjective pure, clean, unstained, faultless, perfect

sprawl verb recline, stretch, extend, lie ▷ *lounge*

spray verb sprinkle, squirt, splash, shower

spread verb **1** scatter, strew, sow, circulate **2** extend, stretch, expand, open

sprightly adjective lively, vivacious, cheerful, agile ▷ *brisk* ☆ **sluggish**

spur verb arouse, drive, urge, incite

spurious adjective fake, counterfeit, false ▷ *bogus* ☆ **genuine**

spurn verb reject, scorn, disdain, disregard ▷ *snub* ☆ **respect**

spurt verb **1** stream, squirt, emerge, gush **2** hurry, hasten, rush

spy **1** noun agent, detective, observer, snooper, scout **2** verb see, glimpse, pry, peek, spot

squabble noun & verb quarrel, clash, fight, row ▷ *dispute*

squad noun group, company, troop, force, band, team

squalid adjective foul, dirty, untended, poverty-stricken ▶ *sordid* ⋆ **clean**

squall 1 noun blast, gust, blow, tempest 2 verb blubber, cry, bawl, howl

squander verb misspend, waste, fritter, lavish

squash verb 1 mash, crush, squelch, pound 2 quell, suppress, humiliate

squat 1 adjective dumpy, stocky, tubby, plump 2 verb crouch, sit, roost, perch

squeal verb squawk, squeak, cheep, grunt, cry

squeamish adjective fastidious, delicate, finicky, nauseous

squeeze verb compress, press, constrict, force, pinch

squirm verb wriggle, fidget, flounder, twist ▶ *writhe*

squirt verb spray, splash ▶ *spurt*

stab verb & noun cut, jab, puncture, wound, thrust

stable 1 adjective firm, steady, solid, constant, durable, lasting ⋆ **unstable** 2 noun barn, cowshed, shed, stall

stack 1 noun pile, pack, bundle, sheaf, heap 2 verb assemble, pile up, amass

staff noun 1 stick, cane, pole, rod 2 team, workers, force, personnel

stage 1 noun platform, dais, scaffold, podium *The famous conductor stood on the podium and raised his baton*, arena 2 noun step, degree, position 3 verb perform, produce, present, put on

stagger verb reel, totter, waver, lurch

stagnant adjective motionless, inactive, still, quiet, sluggish

staid adjective serious, steady, earnest, sober, demure ▶ *sedate* ⋆ **frivolous** STAYED

stain 1 noun blemish, blur, spot, blot 2 noun disgrace, shame 3 verb tarnish, sully, blemish, defile

stair noun step, rung, spoke, footrest STARE

stake 1 noun stick, stave, paling, spike, pole ▶ *staff* 2 noun bet, claim, wager, involvement 3 verb prop, secure, support STEAK

stale adjective 1 musty, old, tasteless, faded 2 common, trite, banal, flat ⋆ **fresh**

stalk verb 1 hunt, chase, follow, pursue, shadow 2 swagger, strut, stride, parade

stall 1 verb tarry, delay, hedge, obstruct, hamper ⋆ **advance** 2 noun compartment, booth, stand, bay

stalwart adjective rugged, sturdy, stout, lusty ▶ *valiant* ⋆ **timid**

stamina noun endurance, vitality, strength, power, energy ⋆ **weakness**

stammer verb stutter, falter, hesitate, stumble

stamp 1 verb print, imprint, mark, impress 2 noun impression, mark, print, brand 3 noun kind, make, genus, cast 4 noun seal, sticker

stand 1 noun board, counter, table, platform ▶ *stall* 2 verb rest, put, locate, place 3 verb tolerate, put up with, abide, endure ⋆ **oppose** 4 verb arise, get up, be erect ⋆ **sit**

standard 1 adjective normal, regular, uniform 2 noun pattern, criterion, norm 3 noun flag, banner, ensign

staple adjective main, principal, important, leading

stare verb gaze, gape, look, peer STAIR

stark adjective severe, plain, downright, bare, absolute

start 1 verb commence, begin, found, initiate 2 verb depart, set out, leave 3 verb startle, jump, wince 4 noun beginning, commencement 5 noun shock, scare, fit

startle verb frighten, alarm, scare, surprise ▶ *start*

starve verb be hungry, famish, want

state 1 noun condition, situation, position 2 noun country, nation, commonwealth 3 verb declare, say, express, utter ▶ *speak*

stately adjective imposing, grand, dignified ▶ *magnificent* ⋆ **commonplace**

statement noun 1 declaration, utterance, remark, motto 2 bill, account, invoice

station 1 noun post, spot, site, position, terminal 2 verb park, place, put, establish *We got there early to establish our place in the line*

stationary adjective still, unmoving, standing, fixed ⋆ **mobile** STATIONERY

stationery noun paper, envelopes, ink, pens, pencils STATIONARY

statue noun carving, bust, figure

staunch adjective constant, faithful, true, firm ▶ *loyal* ⋆ **unfaithful**

stay 1 verb endure, last, remain, stand, linger 2 verb check, curb, prevent 3 noun halt, wait ▶ *stop*

steady 1 adjective firm, fixed, established, constant ▷ *staunch* ☆ **uncertain** 2 verb brace, stabilize, stiffen

steal verb 1 thieve, pilfer, filch, swipe ▷ *rob* 2 slink, flit, creep ▷ *prowl* STEEL

stealthy adjective furtive, sneaky, sly, secret ▷ *underhanded* ☆ **open**

steep 1 adjective sheer, sharp, hilly, precipitous 2 verb bathe, soak, souse, submerge

steer verb guide, direct, pilot, control

stem 1 noun stalk, shoot, stock, trunk 2 verb arise from, flow from 3 verb check, resist, restrain

step 1 noun pace, tread, stride, gait 2 noun action, method, deed 3 verb walk, skip, trip, pace STEPPE

sterile adjective 1 barren, unfertile, arid 2 sanitary, disinfected

stern 1 adjective strict, severe, harsh, grim ▷ *austere* ☆ **mild** 2 noun aft end, rear, poop *The name of the ship was displayed in large letters on the poop*

stew verb 1 cook, simmer, boil 2 worry, fuss

stick 1 noun stave, pole, rod, cane, staff 2 verb adhere, cling, cleave, glue, paste, seal

sticky adjective gluey, gummy, adhesive

stick out verb project, bulge, extrude ▷ *jut* ☆ **recede**

stiff adjective 1 inflexible, firm, stable, unyielding ▷ *rigid* ☆ **flexible** 2 formal, stilted, prim, precise ☆ **yielding**

stifle verb suffocate, throttle, gag, muzzle ▷ *smother*

stigma noun 1 blot, blur, scar ▷ *blemish* 2 disgrace, dishonor ▷ *shame* ☆ **credit**

still 1 adjective fixed, stable, static 2 adjective calm, quiet, serene, tranquil, noiseless, hushed ▷ *peaceful* ☆ **agitated** 3 verb quiet, hush, muffle ▷ *calm* ☆ **agitate**

stimulate verb inspire, provoke, arouse, motivate ▷ *excite* ☆ **discourage**

sting verb prick, wound, pain, hurt, injure

stingy adjective miserly, tightfisted, selfish, niggardly ▷ *tight* ☆ **generous**

stink verb smell, whiff, reek

stint 1 noun job, task, chore 2 noun turn, spell, share, quota 3 verb limit, stop, scrimp, restrict ☆ **squander**

stir 1 verb move, excite, spur, agitate ▷ *stimulate* 2 verb whisk, mix, blend 3 verb waken, arouse ☆ **calm** 4 noun flurry, fuss, uproar

stock 1 adjective standard, regular, established, normal 2 noun reserve, hoard, supply 3 verb provide, supply, equip, hoard

stocky adjective thickset, chunky, sturdy, pudgy ▷ *squat* ☆ **willowy**

stodgy adjective dull, heavy, tedious, boring

stolid adjective stupid, dull, mindless, unintelligent ▷ *stodgy* ☆ **quick**

stoop verb bend, crouch, kneel, bow

stop 1 verb cease, desist, end, terminate, halt ☆ **start** 2 verb prevent, forestall, avoid 3 verb arrest, hold, fix 4 noun pause, end, cessation *A cessation of hostilities came into force after the peace agreement*

store 1 verb put by, reserve, hoard, save ☆ **use** 2 noun stock, supply, reserve 3 noun market, shop, emporium

story noun 1 yarn, tale, narrative, account, anecdote 2 untruth, lie, fib 3 floor, landing, level, flight, deck

storm 1 noun tempest, gale, cyclone, hurricane, tornado ☆ **calm** 2 noun turmoil, upheaval, attack 3 verb rage, rant, fume, attack

stout adjective 1 sturdy, tough, robust ▷ *strong* ☆ **weak** 2 fat, corpulent ▷ *plump* ☆ **thin**

stow verb deposit, store ▷ *pack*

straight adjective 1 right, undeviating, unswerving ▷ *direct* 2 frank, candid, truthful ▷ *honest* ☆ **crooked** STRAIT

straightforward adjective open, outspoken, reliable, trustworthy ☆ **devious**

strain 1 noun tension, fatigue, exertion ▷ *stress* ☆ **relaxation** 2 noun melody, tune, air 3 verb struggle, labor ▷ *toil* ☆ **relax** 4 verb wrench, injure 5 verb filter, sift, separate

strait noun channel, sound, narrows STRAIGHT

straitlaced adjective prim, prudish, strict, puritanical *My family was rather puritanical, and we were not allowed to play any games on Sundays*

strand 1 noun coast, beach, shore 2 noun hair, fiber, tress, lock 3 verb desert, maroon, abandon

strange adjective 1 unusual, incredible, extraordinary, curious ▷ *odd* ☆ **commonplace** 2 foreign, alien, remote

stranger noun outsider, foreigner, visitor, newcomer ▷ *alien* ☆ **acquaintance**

strangle verb constrict, choke, garrote, throttle

strap noun belt, harness, thong, leash

stray verb **1** wander, deviate, depart, rove **2** sin, err, do wrong

streak noun stroke, stripe, band, line, bar, strip

stream **1** noun current, course, drift, brook, creek, run **2** verb flow, gush, spurt, pour

strength noun **1** power, force, might ▶ *energy* **2** boldness, nerve, intensity ★ **weakness**

strenuous adjective laborious, resolute, determined ▶ *earnest* ★ **weak**

stress **1** noun tension, force, effort ▶ *strain* **2** noun accent, emphasis **3** verb emphasize, accentuate

stretch verb expand, reach ▶ *extend* ★ **shorten**

strict adjective **1** severe, rigorous, rigid, austere ▶ *stern* ★ **lenient** **2** scrupulous, punctilious, accurate ▶ *precise* ★ **inaccurate**

stride noun & verb walk, step, tread, parade, march

strife noun struggle, contest, quarrel, friction ▶ *conflict* ★ **peace**

strike **1** verb beat, smite, collide, knock ▶ *thump* **2** verb discover, unearth **3** noun assault, thrust, attack **4** noun walkout, boycott

striking adjective eye-catching, wonderful ▶ *extraordinary* ★ **commonplace**

strip **1** verb take off, peel, skin, shave, remove **2** noun ribbon, stroke, streak, line

stripe noun streak, band, bar, chevron *Soldiers in the army have chevrons on their sleeves to indicate their rank*, rule ▶ *strip*

strive verb endeavor, attempt, aim, compete ▶ *try* ★ **yield**

stroke **1** noun shock, blow, knock, thump **2** noun seizure, fit, convulsion **3** verb pat, rub, caress, smooth, comfort

stroll verb & noun walk, promenade, saunter, tramp, ramble

strong adjective **1** powerful, vigorous, hardy, muscular ▶ *robust* **2** solid, secure, fortified ★ **weak** **3** potent, hot, spicy ▶ *pungent*

structure noun **1** building, edifice, erection **2** construction, organization, composition

struggle **1** verb endeavor, labor, battle, wrestle ★ **yield** **2** noun conflict, battle ▶ *fight* **3** noun distress, trouble ▶ *effort*

strut **1** noun support, mainstay, prop **2** verb parade, prance, swagger

stubborn adjective **1** dogged, persistent, tenacious **2** pigheaded, perverse, willful ▶ *obstinate* ★ **docile**

stuck-up adjective vain, conceited ▶ *snobbish* ★ **modest**

studious adjective scholarly, learned, thoughtful ▶ *diligent* ★ **thoughtless**

study **1** verb read, peruse, research, scrutinize, examine, train ▶ *learn* **2** noun learning, meditation, thought, contemplation ▶ *research*

stuff **1** verb fill, congest, pack, crowd **2** noun textile, fabric, material, goods

stumble verb **1** stagger, lurch, fall ▶ *trip* **2** stammer, falter ▶ *stutter*

stump **1** verb perplex, mystify, confuse ▶ *bewilder* **2** noun stub, tip, log, root

stun verb knock out, overpower, stupefy, dumbfound ▶ *confound*

stunt noun deed, feat, achievement, performance ▶ *exploit*

stupefy verb daze, muddle, bewilder, astonish, flabbergast ▶ *shock* ★ **revive**

stupendous adjective astounding, amazing, overwhelming ▶ *wonderful* ★ **ordinary**

stupid adjective simple, stolid, dull, senseless ▶ *foolish* ★ **clever**

stupidity noun inanity, silliness, feebleness, foolishness ★ **brilliance**

sturdy adjective rugged, stalwart, tough, strapping ▶ *hardy* ★ **weak**

stutter verb stumble, falter ▶ *stammer*

style **1** noun mode, vogue, fashion, way, manner, form **2** verb name, call, christen STILE

suave adjective agreeable, elegant, polite, pleasant, sophisticated *After living in the city for many years, my sister had developed very sophisticated tastes*

subdue verb suppress, soften, tame, tone down, moderate, mellow ▶ *repress*

subject **1** noun (*sub*-ject) matter, topic, theme **2** noun subordinate, dependant **3** adjective dependent, subordinate, liable **4** verb (sub-*ject*) rule over, subdue, subjugate

submerge verb plunge, immerse, sink ▪ **raise**

submissive adjective yielding, servile, meek ▸ *obedient* ▪ **obstinate**

submit verb **1** yield, give in, accede, surrender, hand over **2** offer, tender, present

subordinate adjective junior, minor, subject, dependent, secondary ▪ **superior**

subscribe verb sign, enroll, register, agree, assent

subsequent adjective later, following, succeeding, after ▪ **former**

subside verb decline, peter out, decrease, diminish, wane *I used to go mountaineering, but my interest waned after a while* ▸ *abate* ▪ **rise**

substance noun **1** matter, object, stuff, material **2** essence, kernel, meaning ▸ *gist*

substantial adjective **1** steady, sturdy, firm ▸ *stable* **2** ample, large, real, solid ▪ **imaginary**

substitute **1** noun alternative, makeshift, stopgap **2** verb swap, change, replace, duplicate

subtle adjective **1** shrewd, fine, delicate **2** clever, crafty, perceptive

subtract verb take away, withdraw, deduct, remove ▪ **add**

succeed verb **1** flourish, prosper, thrive, triumph ▪ **fail** **2** follow, inherit, replace ▪ **precede**

success noun prosperity, triumph, victory, achievement ▪ **failure**

successful adjective victorious, prosperous, fortunate, thriving ▪ **unlucky**

suck verb inhale, take in, draw in, imbibe

sudden adjective unexpected, abrupt, impulsive, swift, prompt ▪ **gradual**

suffer verb **1** bear, endure, put up with **2** encounter, undergo ▸ *sustain*

sufficient adjective adequate, ample, plenty ▸ *enough* ▪ **deficient**

suffocate verb smother, choke ▸ *stifle*

suggest verb recommend, advise, submit, hint, intimate

suit **1** verb fulfill, gratify, please, suffice, accommodate, befit **2** noun ensemble, outfit, costume

suitable adjective fitting, appropriate, correct, proper, becoming ▪ **unsuitable**

suite noun **1** set, series, succession **2** apartment, rooms

sulk verb pout, grouch, brood, mope

sulky adjective glum, morose, churlish, moody ▸ *sullen* ▪ **genial**

sullen adjective gloomy, heavy, dismal, cheerless ▸ *sulky* ▪ **cheerful**

sum noun amount, total, whole, entirety SOME

summary noun synopsis, précis, abstract, summing-up, outline, analysis

summit noun peak, pinnacle, top, apex, zenith ▪ **base**

summon verb call, beckon, command, invite, muster ▪ **dismiss**

sumptuous adjective profuse, costly, gorgeous, splendid ▸ *lavish* ▪ **frugal**

sundry adjective different, separate, several ▸ *various*

sunny adjective bright, cheerful, light, clear ▸ *radiant* ▪ **gloomy**

superb adjective magnificent, stately, gorgeous ▸ *grand* ▪ **commonplace**

supercilious adjective contemptuous, haughty, arrogant ▸ *snobbish* ▪ **modest**

superficial adjective slight, imperfect, shallow, skin-deep ▸ *trivial* ▪ **profound**

superfluous adjective in excess, inessential, spare ▸ *surplus* ▪ **essential**

superior adjective **1** better, greater, higher, loftier ▸ *excellent* **2** eminent, conspicuous, principal ▪ **inferior**

supersede verb succeed, replace, displace, suspend, usurp *The president's authority was usurped by the military* ▪ **continue**

supervise verb superintend, control, manage ▸ *direct*

supple adjective lithe, pliable, flexible, bending

supplement **1** noun addition, complement, sequel, postscript **2** verb supply, add, fill

supply **1** verb provide, furnish, yield, contribute, purvey ▪ **retain** **2** noun hoard, reserve ▸ *stock*

support **1** verb uphold, bear, sustain, maintain, help ▸ *favor* ▪ **oppose** **2** verb hold up, prop, strut, brace **3** verb endure, tolerate, suffer **4** noun maintenance, upkeep

suppose verb assume, presume, believe, imagine, imply ▸ *consider*

suppress verb restrain, extinguish, destroy, stop ▸ *quell* ▪ **incite**

supreme adjective dominant, highest, greatest, maximum ▪ **lowly**

sure adjective 1 certain, positive, definite   2 secure, steady, safe   3 permanent, abiding, enduring
★ uncertain

surface noun 1 area, expanse, stretch   2 outside, exterior, covering ★ interior

surge 1 verb swell, rise, heave, rush   2 noun ripple, billow, wave SERGE

surly adjective morose, cross, testy, touchy, crusty
▶ *sullen* ★ affable

surmise verb guess, speculate, conjecture, suspect
▶ *presume* ★ know

surpass verb eclipse, outdo, outstrip, excel, exceed
▶ *beat*

surplus noun excess, remainder, balance, residue
★ shortcoming

surprise 1 verb startle, astonish, amaze ▶ *astound*
2 noun amazement, astonishment ▶ *wonder*

surrender verb quit, give up, yield, submit
▶ *relinquish*

surround verb enclose, encircle, encompass

survey 1 verb (sur-*vey*) look at, examine, scrutinize
▶ *study* 2 verb estimate, measure   3 noun (*sur*-vey)
assessment, appraisal

survive verb live, exist, continue, outlast, abide
★ surrender

susceptible adjective sensitive, impressionable, inclined, capable ★ insensitive

suspect 1 verb (sus-*pect*) disbelieve, doubt, distrust
2 adjective (*sus*-pect) unbelievable, questionable, dubious

suspend verb 1 interrupt, delay, arrest, adjourn, postpone ▶ *stop* ★ continue   2 expel, throw out
3 swing, dangle ▶ *hang* ★ drop

suspense noun anticipation, waiting, abeyance
The club couldn't decide on a new leader, so the matter was left in abeyance, stoppage, uncertainty ▶ *tension* ★ decision

suspicious adjective incredulous, skeptical, doubtful, suspecting ★ trustful

sustain verb 1 uphold, keep, maintain, provide for
2 suffer, undergo, experience   3 nourish, nurture, feed

swagger verb 1 parade, prance ▶ *strut* 2 brag, bluster
▶ *boast*

swallow 1 verb absorb, consume, eat, digest, devour, drink ▶ *gulp* 2 noun mouthful, gulp   3 noun bird

swamp 1 noun fen, bog, marsh, morass, quagmire
2 verb submerge, submerse, overflow, deluge ▶ *drench*

swap verb exchange, switch, trade, barter

swarm 1 noun throng, horde, shoal, flock, crowd
2 verb teem, abound, jam, mass, crowd, cluster

swarthy adjective dusky, dark, brown, tawny

sway 1 verb swing, rock, totter, lean, incline ▶ *waver*
2 noun rule, authority, control ▶ *influence*

swear verb 1 promise, warrant, affirm, attest   2 curse, damn, blaspheme

sweat verb perspire, ooze, leak, exude, swelter
During that time of the year, it was very hot and we sweltered all day

sweep verb brush, scrub, clean, scour

sweet adjective 1 sugary, syrupy, luscious ★ sour
2 melodic, tuneful, musical, mellow ★ discordant
3 gentle, tender, mild, lovable ★ unpleasant   4 fragrant, pure, clean, fresh, wholesome, aromatic ★ putrid

swell verb expand, distend, inflate, bulge ▶ *enlarge*
★ contract

swerve verb veer, deviate, skid, skew, lurch ▶ *waver*

swift adjective speedy, rapid, quick ▶ *fast* ★ slow

swill 1 verb swig, consume, imbibe, tipple ▶ *gulp*
2 noun refuse, garbage, waste

swim verb bathe, wade, paddle, float, glide

swindle 1 noun trick, fraud, blackmail, racket
2 verb hoodwink, deceive, hoax, dupe, rip off ▶ *cheat*

swine noun pig, boar, sow, porker, hog

swing 1 verb hang, suspend, dangle, lurch, reel
2 noun tempo, time

switch 1 verb change, exchange, alter, trade, substitute, swap   2 noun lever, pedal, control, button

swivel verb pivot, spin, rotate, revolve, turn

swoop verb pounce, descend, stoop, plummet, plunge

sword noun rapier, blade, foil, épée, cutlass, saber, steel
SOARED

symbol noun character, figure, numeral, letter, sign, token, emblem CYMBAL

sympathetic adjective thoughtful, understanding, kind, affectionate ★ indifferent

system noun 1 method, plan, order, scheme, arrangement, routine   2 network, organization
a hierarchical organization

Tt

table noun 1 board, stand, slab, tablet, counter, stall 2 list, catalog, schedule, index, statement

tablet noun 1 pill, capsule, lozenge 2 board, table, pad

tack 1 noun thumbtack, nail, pin, brad 2 noun aim, direction, set 3 verb affix, fasten, join, stitch

tackle 1 noun outfit, gear, rig, harness 2 verb grasp, halt, intercept, seize 3 verb deal with *I dealt with the problem of the missing map*, undertake, set about

tact noun diplomacy, judgment, skill, discretion *If you want your secret to be kept, you had better not rely on his discretion* TACKED

tactful adjective diplomatic, wise, subtle, prudent *discreet* ☆ **tactless**

tactics noun strategy, campaign, method, procedure

tactless adjective inconsiderate, gauche, clumsy, boorish ▷ *inept* ☆ **tactful**

tag noun label, ticket, docket, slip, sticker

taint verb sully, tarnish, infect, stain, soil, contaminate ▷ *defile* ☆ **purify**

take verb 1 grasp, grab, seize, procure 2 receive, accept, obtain 3 carry, convey, lead, conduct 4 interpret, understand

take place verb occur, happen, befall *Our parents were concerned about what might befall us when we left school*

tale noun story, fable, anecdote, yarn, narrative TAIL

talent noun knack, genius, gift, ability, aptitude ☆ **stupidity**

talk 1 verb speak, say, utter, gossip 2 verb describe, comment on, talk about 3 noun speech, chatter, conversation 4 noun lecture, speech, discourse

tall adjective lanky, lofty, big, high, towering, giant ☆ **short**

tally verb 1 count, enumerate, compute 2 agree, conform, coincide ☆ **disagree**

tame 1 adjective domesticated, gentle, mild, docile *Although we found it in the woods, the kitten was docile* ☆ **savage** 2 adjective flat, dull, boring, tedious 3 verb train, discipline, domesticate

tamper with verb meddle, interfere, damage, tinker

tang noun smell, scent, aroma, flavor, savor, taste

tangible adjective concrete, solid, substantial, real, material ☆ **spiritual**

tangle noun & verb twist, muddle, jumble, knot

tantalize verb tease, taunt, thwart, disappoint ▷ *frustrate* ☆ **satisfy**

tantrum noun rage, fit, hysterics, storm

tap 1 verb pat, hit, knock, rap, strike 2 noun faucet, spout, cock, nozzle, bung

tape noun ribbon, filament, braid, strip, riband

taper verb dwindle, narrow, contract, decline, wane, narrow ☆ **widen** TAPIR

tardy adjective slow, sluggish, reluctant, slack ▷ *late* ☆ **prompt**

target noun goal, aim, ambition, purpose, butt, end, victim

tariff noun tax, rate, toll, duty, payment, schedule of fees

tarnish verb stain, sully *Mark's reputation at school was sullied after he was accused of stealing*, spot, darken, blemish, rust ☆ **brighten**

tarry verb delay, stall, wait, loiter ▷ *linger* ☆ **hurry**

tart 1 adjective acid, sour, sharp, pungent 2 noun pie, quiche, pastry, flan

task noun job, stint, chore, assignment, undertaking

taste 1 noun bite, mouthful, flavor, savor, tang 2 verb try, sip, sample, relish

tasteful adjective artistic, graceful, elegant, smart ▷ *refined* ☆ **tasteless**

tasteless adjective 1 flavorless, insipid 2 gaudy, inelegant ▷ *vulgar* ☆ **tasteful**

tasty adjective appetizing, piquant, savory ▷ *delicious* ☆ **disgusting**

tattle verb gossip, tittle-tattle, blab, prattle

taunt verb jibe, reproach, rebuke, ridicule, scoff at ▷ *sneer* ☆ **compliment**

taut adjective tense, tight, stretched ▷ *rigid* ☆ **relaxed** TAUGHT

tawdry adjective flashy, loud, gaudy, showy ▷ *vulgar* ☆ **superior**

tax 1 noun levy, duty, impost, tithe, toll 2 verb load, oppress, overburden TACKS

teach verb instruct, educate, tutor, coach, guide, train

teacher noun educator, professor, lecturer, schoolmaster, schoolmistress, coach, tutor

team noun party, group, gang, crew, company TEEM

tear verb **1** rip, rend, tatter, shred **2** dash, bolt, rush, sprint TARE

tearful adjective weepy, moist, wet, sobbing, sad

tease verb annoy, harass, vex, irritate, torment ▶ *tantalize* ★ soothe TEAS, TEES

tedious adjective wearisome, tiresome, irksome, exhausting ▶ *boring* ★ fascinating

teem verb abound, swarm, overflow, increase, be full ★ lack TEAM

tell verb **1** disclose, speak, state, talk, utter **2** discern, discover, distinguish

temper **1** noun temperament, disposition, nature, humor **2** noun anger, annoyance, passion **3** verb moderate, soften, weaken, restrain

temporary adjective short, limited, impermanent, brief ★ permanent

tempt verb entice, invite, attract, persuade ▶ *lure* ★ deter

tenacious adjective **1** stubborn, firm, obstinate, unwavering ★ weak **2** adhesive, glutinous

tenant noun occupant, householder, occupier

tend verb **1** take care of, manage, serve, guard ★ neglect **2** affect, lean, incline, verge ★ diverge

tendency noun disposition, leaning, inclination, bent ★ aversion

tender **1** adjective delicate, soft ▶ *fragile* **2** adjective mild, kind, sympathetic ▶ *gentle* **3** adjective raw, painful, sore **4** verb proffer *Charlotte proffered her services as a babysitter*, present, volunteer, bid

tense adjective tight, strained, taut, nervous, edgy ★ relaxed TENTS

tension noun strain, stress, rigidity, suspense, worry ★ relaxation

term **1** noun expression, denomination, title, phrase **2** noun time, season, spell *We stayed in Hong Kong for a spell during our trip to the Far East*, duration **3** verb entitle, call, dub

terminate verb cease, stop, end, conclude ▶ *finish* ★ begin

terrible adjective frightful, terrifying, fearful, dreadful ▶ *horrible* ★ superb

terrify verb petrify, shock, appall, alarm ▶ *frighten*

territory noun region, area, expanse, dominion, land ▶ *country*

terror noun alarm, panic, horror, dismay ▶ *fright* ★ confidence

terse adjective brief, concise, short, pithy, abrupt ▶ *curt* ★ long-winded

test **1** noun examination, trial, check, proof, experiment **2** verb examine, try out, check, quiz, analyze

testy adjective irritable, bad-tempered, touchy, peevish ▶ *cross* ★ genial

tether noun rope, cord, lead, leash, chain

text noun contents, reading, passage, clause

thanks noun gratitude, credit, appreciation

thaw verb **1** melt, fuse, liquefy, soften ★ freeze **2** unbend, relax

theft noun robbery, fraud, larceny, plundering

theme noun subject, text matter, topic

theory noun idea, supposition, concept, hypothesis

therefore adjective consequently, hence, accordingly

thick adjective **1** dense, solid, bulky, compact **2** stiff, set, congealed **3** viscous, gummy, stodgy ★ thin

thief noun crook, robber, burglar, bandit, pirate

thin adjective **1** slender, slim, slight, lean, skinny ★ fat **2** waferlike, delicate, flimsy **3** watery, dilute, unsubstantial ★ thick

thing noun article, object, something, being, substance

think verb **1** ponder, consider ▶ *reflect* **2** conceive, imagine ▶ *fancy* **3** surmise, conclude ▶ *reckon*

thirsty adjective parched, dry, craving, burning

thorn noun barb, prickle, bramble, thistle

thorough adjective outright, absolute, complete, utter ★ haphazard

though conjunction although, even though, notwithstanding, however, yet

thought noun reflection, consideration, study, concept, deduction

thoughtful adjective **1** pensive, studious, contemplative **2** considerate, kind, heedful, careful ★ thoughtless

thoughtless adjective heedless, careless, rash, neglectful ▶ *indiscreet* ★ thoughtful

thrash verb **1** whip, flog, hit **2** stir, pitch *The sea was rough—each wave pitched the small boat closer to the rocks*, toss

thread noun filament, twist, yarn, fiber

A B C D E F G H I J K L M N O P Q R S T U V W X Y Z

threadbare adjective 1 shabby, ragged, worn 2 commonplace, hackneyed, stale ★ fresh

threaten verb intimidate, bully, blackmail ▶ *menace* ★ reassure

thrifty adjective frugal, careful, economical, saving, sparing ★ wasteful

thrilling adjective exciting, gripping, stimulating

thrive verb prosper, flourish, succeed, grow, increase ★ decline

throb 1 noun tick, beat, palpitation 2 verb beat, palpitate, vibrate

throng 1 noun crowd, horde, mob 2 verb pack, crowd, swarm, fill

throttle verb choke, smother ▶ *strangle*

through preposition by way of, by means of, as a result of

throw verb fling, cast, hurl, project, propel, thrust ★ keep THROE

thrust verb & noun push, project, drive, force, prod

thug noun hoodlum, bandit, assassin, mugger, ruffian

thump verb & noun beat, hit, knock, bang, wallop

thunderstruck adjective openmouthed, amazed, astounded, staggered

thus adverb accordingly, so, therefore, consequently

thwart verb frustrate, balk, baffle, hinder, obstruct ★ assist

ticket noun pass, label, card, coupon, token

tickle verb 1 caress, stroke, pat, brush 2 titillate, convulse, amuse 3 delight, gratify

tidbit noun delicacy, morsel, dainty, snack, treat

tide noun stream, current, drift, ebb, flow TIED

tidings noun information, intelligence, report, advice ▶ *news*

tidy adjective 1 neat, well-kept, spruce, orderly 2 ample, large, substantial

tie 1 verb join, attach, secure *Be sure to secure the gate so that the dogs can't get out,* unite ▶ *fasten* 2 noun cravat, necktie, bow tie 3 noun bond, connection

tight adjective 1 fast, close, compact, tense ▶ *taut* ★ loose 2 miserly, tightfisted ▶ *stingy* ★ generous

tighten verb strain, tauten, constrict, cramp, crush ▶ *squeeze* ★ loosen

till 1 preposition until, up to, as far as 2 verb plow, cultivate, tend 3 noun cash drawer, cash register

tilt verb & noun slant, slope, incline, lean, list, tip

time noun 1 period, duration, season, age, era, term, span 2 meter, measure, tempo, rhythm THYME

timid adjective fearful, afraid, timorous, diffident, modest ▶ *shy* ★ bold

tinge verb & noun color, tincture, tint, stain, shade

tingle verb thrill, throb, tickle, vibrate

tinker verb meddle, fiddle *Bill fiddled with the old clock for ages, trying to make it work,* patch up, putter, trifle

tinkle verb jingle, jangle, ring, clink

tint noun dye, hue, tinge, shade ▶ *color*

tiny adjective small, diminutive, puny, wee ▶ *little* ★ huge

tip 1 noun apex, peak, point, extremity ▶ *top* 2 noun gratuity, gift, donation, reward 3 noun information, hint, tip-off 4 verb list, lean, tilt ▶ *slope*

tipsy adjective inebriated, drunk, drunken

tire verb exhaust, bore, fatigue, harass, weaken

tiresome adjective wearisome, tedious, boring ▶ *humdrum* ★ interesting

title noun 1 name, denomination, term, style, designation 2 claim, interest *My brother and I share an interest in the family business,* ownership

toady verb fawn, crawl, grovel, crouch, cringe

toast 1 noun pledge, compliment, salutation 2 verb brown, roast, heat

together adverb collectively, jointly, simultaneously, at the same time ★ separately

toil verb & noun struggle, labor, travail ▶ *work* ★ relaxation

token noun memento, keepsake, symbol, omen ▶ *souvenir*

tolerable adjective endurable, supportable, bearable, passable ★ unbearable

tolerant adjective forbearing, indulgent *Sally's parents are very indulgent with her and buy her whatever she wants,* liberal, easygoing ▶ *lenient* ★ intolerant

tolerate verb accept, bear with, put up with, endure, suffer ▶ *allow* ★ resist

toll 1 verb ring, strike, chime, clang 2 noun charge, duty, tax, levy

tone noun 1 pitch, loudness, noise, note 2 emphasis, accent, inflection 3 temper, manner, attitude 4 color, cast, hue, shade

Titles

pope

professor

admiral
ambassador
archbishop
baron baroness
brigadier
cardinal
chancellor
colonel
commodore
count countess
czar czarina
dame
dean
duke duchess
earl
emir
emperor empress
general
governor
infanta
kaiser
khan
king
knight
lama
lieutenant
lord lady
madame
maharajah maharani
major
marshal
mayor
mogul
monsieur
pope
priest
prince princess
professor
queen
rabbi
senator
señor señora
sergeant
shogun
signor signora
shah
sheik
sheriff
sultan sultana

shogun

sultan

too adverb **1** also, as well, besides **2** extremely, very, unduly

tool noun **1** implement, utensil, machine, agent **2** pawn, puppet, cat's-paw, stooge TULLE

top noun **1** summit, pinnacle, peak **2** lid, cover, stopper, cap **3** upper surface ⭑ **bottom** **4** noun spinning toy **5** adjective highest, best, uppermost *After climbing for four days, we reached the uppermost part of mountain*

topic noun subject, motif, question ▶ *theme*

topical adjective contemporary, popular, up-to-date

topple verb collapse, founder, overturn, totter ▶ *fall*

topsy-turvy adjective upside-down, overturned, confused, chaotic

torment verb & noun pain, distress ▶ *torture* ⭑ **ease**

torrent noun flood, stream, cascade, cataract, waterfall ⭑ **trickle**

torture verb agonize, rack, anguish ▶ *torment*

toss verb fling, hurl, pitch, cast, project, heave ▶ *throw*

total **1** noun aggregate, whole, sum, completion **2** verb add, tot up, reckon **3** adjective complete, entire

totally adverb completely, absolutely, entirely, utterly ⭑ **partially**

touch **1** verb feel, finger, fondle, handle, stroke **2** verb move, affect, concern **3** verb beat, hit, collide with **4** verb adjoin *Our house is situated at a spot where three streets adjoin*, meet, border **5** noun tinge, hint, suspicion

touchy adjective peevish, petulant, snappish ▶ *moody*

tough **1** adjective hard, strong, vigorous, rugged, sturdy **2** adjective arduous, difficult **3** noun hoodlum, hooligan, bruiser, bully

tour noun trip, journey, jaunt, excursion, voyage, ride, visit

tournament noun contest, championship, competition ▶ *match*

tow verb haul, drag, tug, haul, heave ▶ *pull* TOE

tower **1** verb soar, dominate, surmount **2** noun turret, spire, belfry

toy **1** noun plaything, doll, game **2** verb play, tinker, fiddle, twiddle

trace **1** verb trail, track, follow, pursue, discover **2** verb sketch, draw, copy **3** noun trail, track, spoor **4** noun drop, speck, vestige

track verb search out, follow ▶ *trace*

tract noun **1** area, space, extent, plot **2** booklet, leaflet, pamphlet TRACKED

trade **1** verb barter, exchange, buy, sell, patronize **2** noun occupation, work, livelihood, business

tradition noun custom, convention, practice

traffic **1** noun business, barter ▶ *trade* **2** transportation, vehicles, movement

tragedy noun catastrophe, disaster, adversity ▶ *calamity* ⭑ **comedy**

tragic adjective disastrous, catastrophic, miserable, wretched ▶ *deplorable* ⭑ **comic**

trail noun spoor, track ▶ *trace*

train **1** verb teach, educate, instruct, drill, school **2** noun chain, procession, series

traitor noun rebel, mutineer, renegade, quisling, betrayer

tramp **1** noun vagabond, wanderer, vagrant, bum, hobo ▶ *beggar* **2** noun jaunt, stroll, ramble **3** verb roam, rove, range, walk, travel

trample verb tread on, walk on, flatten ▶ *crush*

tranquil adjective peaceful, placid, serene, restful ▶ *calm* ⭑ **restless**

transaction noun business, performance, dealing, negotiation, proceeding

transfer verb move *My sister is being moved to the head office after her promotion*, displace, change ▶ *exchange*

transmit verb dispatch, forward, relay ▶ *send* ⭑ **receive**

transparent adjective clear, lucid, crystal, diaphanous

transport **1** verb carry, convey, conduct, transfer ▶ *move* **2** noun transportation

trap **1** verb ensnare, catch, net **2** noun snare, pitfall, noose, decoy ▶ *ambush*

trash noun garbage, junk, debris, rubble ▶ *rubbish*

travel **1** verb & noun trek, voyage, cruise ▶ *journey*

treacherous adjective **1** traitorous, unfaithful, false, deceptive ▶ *disloyal* ⭑ **faithful**

tread verb **1** dangerous, risky, precarious, tricky ⭑ **reliable** **2** step, walk, tramp, march, go **3** stride, gait, walk, step

treason noun treachery, betrayal, sedition

treasure **1** noun hoard, fortune, riches, wealth **2** verb appreciate, esteem ▶ *value*

treat **1** verb deal with, handle, manage, serve **2** verb regale, entertain **3** verb doctor, attend **4** noun banquet, entertainment, fun

treaty noun agreement, covenant, alliance

tremble verb quake, quaver, shudder, flutter ▶ *shake*

tremendous adjective 1 immense, enormous ▶ *huge* 2 terrible, dreadful, awful

tremor noun quiver, shake, flutter, ripple ▶ *vibration*

trench noun ditch, moat, trough, gully, gutter

trend noun tendency, inclination, direction

trespass 1 verb infringe, overstep, intrude 2 noun offense, sin, transgression

trial noun 1 endeavor, testing, experiment 2 ordeal, grief, suffering 3 essay, proof 4 hearing, lawsuit

tribe noun clan, family, race, group, set

tribute noun 1 ovation, compliment, praise 2 dues, toll, tithe, tax

trick 1 noun fraud, artifice, wile, cheat, deception 2 noun jape, prank, frolic 3 noun juggling, stage magic, conjuring 4 verb deceive, defraud

trickle verb leak, ooze, seep, drip, drop, dribble

trifle 1 noun bauble, plaything, foolishness, nonsense 2 verb dabble, idle, play with

trifling adjective paltry, petty, worthless, slight ▶ *trivial* ★ important

trim 1 verb prune, clip, shorten, crop 2 verb ornament, smarten, decorate 3 adjective tidy, neat, orderly ★ scruffy

trinket noun bauble, bead, jewel, ornament, toy

trip noun 1 journey, excursion, jaunt ▶ *tour* 2 verb stumble, fall, slip

tripe noun garbage, trash, nonsense, twaddle *This is a silly story; I've never read such twaddle*

trite adjective hackneyed, ordinary, corny ▶ *stale*

triumph noun victory, success, achievement ▶ *conquest* ★ defeat

trivial adjective trifling, common, unimportant, ordinary, useless ▶ *trite* ★ important

troop 1 noun band, gang, group, pack, team, unit 2 verb flock, crowd, swarm TROUPE

trophy noun prize, award, cup, souvenir

trot verb canter, jog, scamper, scurry

trouble 1 noun disturbance, annoyance, calamity, misfortune ▶ *misery* 2 verb disturb, annoy, harass ▶ *distress* ★ delight

true adjective 1 accurate, precise, factual, correct ★ inaccurate 2 faithful, loyal, constant 3 pure, real ▶ *genuine* ★ false

trunk noun 1 body, torso, stem, stalk 2 chest, case, box 3 proboscis *The tapir's proboscis is not as large as the elephant's trunk*, nose, snout

truss verb fasten, secure, strap, tie ▶ *bind* ★ untie

trust 1 noun faith, confidence, belief 2 verb believe in, credit, depend on ★ doubt TRUSSED

trustful adjective trusting, innocent, naive ▶ *gullible* ★ cautious

trustworthy adjective dependable, credible, honorable ▶ *reliable* ★ unreliable

truth noun 1 reality, fact, precision ▶ *accuracy* ★ falsehood 2 integrity, faith, honor ▶ *fidelity* ★ deceit

truthful adjective reliable, frank, open ▶ *honest* ★ false

try 1 verb endeavor, attempt ▶ *strive* 2 verb examine, try out ▶ *test* ★ abandon 3 noun trial, attempt, effort

trying adjective bothersome, annoying, troublesome

tub noun basin, bowl, pot, barrel, keg, tun

tube noun pipe, spout, duct, hose, shaft

tuck verb stow, fold, pack, pleat, hem

tug verb drag, tow, haul, heave ▶ *pull* ★ push

tumble verb drop, descend, trip, topple, stumble ▶ *fall*

tumult noun noise, rumpus, racket, uproar, disturbance, disorder ★ peace

tune noun melody, harmony, air, strain ▶ *song*

tunnel noun subway, shaft, passage, gallery

turn 1 verb spin, revolve, whirl ▶ *rotate* 2 verb bend, curve ▶ *twist* 3 verb change, alter ▶ *convert* 4 verb spoil ▶ *sour* 5 noun stint, spell, chance 6 noun rotation ▶ *revolution* TERN

twaddle noun balderdash, nonsense, drivel, rigmarole, piffle ▶ *bunkum* ★ sense

twinge noun pain, pang, spasm, gripe ▶ *ache*

twinkle verb glitter, gleam, glisten, glimmer ▶ *sparkle*

twist verb 1 bend, curve, turn 2 warp, contort, writhe 3 wind, intertwine *The octopus intertwined its tentacles around the large clam*, encircle

twitch verb jerk, jump, jiggle, blink, flutter

type 1 noun kind, sort, character, description 2 noun prototype, model, pattern 3 noun letter, symbol 4 verb typewrite, keyboard, key in

typical adjective characteristic, symbolic, regular, stock, representative ★ abnormal

tyrant noun despot, autocrat, dictator, martin

A B C D E F G H I J K L M N O P Q R S T U V W X Y Z

Uu

ugly adjective unsightly, ungainly, frightful, ghastly, hideous, horrid, nasty ⋆ **beautiful**

ultimate adjective furthest, farthest, most distant, extreme, eventual ▷ *final*

umpire noun referee, judge, mediator

unabashed adjective brazen, unconcerned, undaunted ▷ *composed* ⋆ **sheepish**

unable adjective helpless, incapable, powerless ⋆ **able**

unaccustomed adjective inexperienced, unfamiliar ▷ *strange* ⋆ **familiar**

unaffected adjective natural, sincere, true, artless ▷ *naive* ⋆ **impressed**

unafraid adjective courageous, dauntless, intrepid ▷ *fearless* ⋆ **afraid**

unanimous adjective harmonious, consenting, agreeing ▷ *united*

unassuming adjective diffident, reserved, quiet, simple ▷ *modest* ⋆ **forward**

unattached adjective single, free, loose ▷ *separate* ⋆ **committed**

unattended adjective alone, unwatched, ignored ▷ *abandoned* ⋆ **escorted**

unavoidable adjective inevitable, irresistable, certain ▷ *necessary* ⋆ **uncertain**

unaware adjective ignorant, unheeding, unknowing, forgetful ▷ *oblivious* ⋆ **aware**

unbalanced adjective 1 top-heavy, lopsided, uneven 2 insane, unhinged *He seems to have become unhinged ever since he lost his job*, crazy, eccentric

unbearable adjective unacceptable, intolerable ▷ *outrageous* ⋆ **acceptable**

unbiased adjective impartial, fair, just ▷ *neutral* ⋆ **prejudiced**

uncanny adjective weird, ghostly, unearthly, creepy ▷ *eerie*

uncertain adjective doubtful, vague, chancy, indefinite ▷ *dubious* ⋆ **certain**

uncivilized adjective primitive, barbaric, coarse, gross ▷ *vulgar* ⋆ **civilized**

uncomfortable adjective awkward, embarrassed, cramped, self-conscious ⋆ **comfortable**

uncommon adjective rare, scarce, infrequent, extraordinary ▷ *unusual* ⋆ **common**

unconscious adjective 1 ignorant, unheeding ▷ *unaware* 2 insensible, senseless, stunned ⋆ **conscious**

unconventional adjective unorthodox, peculiar *I have my own peculiar way of looking at things*, individualistic ▷ *eccentric* ⋆ **conventional**

uncouth adjective crude, coarse, clumsy, vulgar ▷ *boorish* ⋆ **polite**

uncover verb expose, discover, show, divulge ▷ *reveal* ⋆ **conceal**

under 1 adverb underneath, below, beneath 2 preposition less than, lower than, subject to

undergo verb endure, tolerate, bear, suffer ▷ *sustain*

underground adjective secret, concealed, private, hidden, subversive

underhand adjective stealthy, undercover, deceitful ▷ *sneaky* ⋆ **honest**

underneath adjective beneath, under ▷ *below* ⋆ **above**

underrate verb undervalue, understate, disparage, belittle ⋆ **exaggerate**

understand verb comprehend, appreciate, grasp, sympathize ▷ *realize* ⋆ **misunderstand**

understudy noun stand-in, deputy, substitute, reserve, replacement

undertake verb attempt, commence, contract, embark on ▷ *tackle*

undesirable adjective objectionable, distasteful ▷ *unpleasant* ⋆ **desirable**

undignified adjective improper, inelegant, clumsy ▷ *unseemly* ⋆ **graceful**

undo verb unfasten, disentangle, unravel, free ▷ *release* ⋆ **fasten**

undress verb disrobe, strip, remove, take off ▷ *divest* ⋆ **dress**

unearthly adjective eerie, uncanny, supernatural ▸ *ghostly*

uneasy adjective uncomfortable, restive, self-conscious, edgy ✶ calm

unemployed adjective unoccupied, redundant, out of work

uneven adjective irregular, rough, bumpy, lopsided, unequal ✶ even

unexpected adjective abrupt, impulsive, chance, surprising ▸ *sudden* ✶ normal

unfair adjective prejudiced, one-sided, partial, unjust ✶ fair

unfaithful adjective faithless, untrue, dishonest ▸ *false* ✶ faithful

unfamiliar adjective alien, obscure, fantastic, bizarre ▸ *strange* ✶ familiar

unfasten verb release, open, unlatch, untie ▸ *undo* ✶ fasten

unfinished adjective incomplete, imperfect, lacking, crude ✶ finished

unfit adjective unqualified, unsuitable, incapable, unsuited ✶ suitable

unfold adjective open, expand, develop, reveal, disclose, unwrap ✶ withhold

unforeseen adjective surprising, sudden, accidental ▸ *unexpected* ✶ predictable

unforgettable adjective memorable, impressive, noteworthy, exceptional

unfortunate adjective deplorable, lamentable, adverse, hapless ▸ *unlucky* ✶ fortunate

unfriendly adjective antagonistic, surly, cold ▸ *hostile* ✶ friendly

ungainly adjective gawky, awkward, graceless, unwieldly ▸ *clumsy* ✶ graceful

ungrateful adjective thankless, selfish, ungracious, ill-mannered ✶ grateful

unhappiness noun depression, misery, sadness

unhappy adjective miserable, dismal, luckless *As hard as he tried, the luckless Tom was always last in the race*, melancholy ▸ *sad* ✶ happy

unhealthy adjective 1 unwholesome, harmful 2 sick, ill, diseased ✶ healthy

uniform 1 noun regalia, livery *It was a very grand affair, with the footmen in full livery*, costume, dress 2 adjective stable, steady, unchanging, level ✶ varied

unimportant adjective puny, trivial, insignificant ▸ *petty* ✶ important

unintentional adjective inadvertent, involuntary, unwitting ▸ *accidental* ✶ deliberate

union noun 1 alliance, association, league 2 accord, agreement, harmony 3 fusion, blend, compound

unique adjective original, exceptional, exclusive, single, sole ✶ commonplace

unit noun entity, single, one, individual

unite verb join, combine, connect, merge, blend, fuse ✶ separate

united adjective joined, combined, undivided ▸ *unanimous* ✶ separated

unity noun union, harmony, uniformity, agreement ✶ disagreement

universal adjective general, all-embracing, entire, worldwide *Our company has products that are sold worldwide*

unjust adjective partial, prejudiced, unfair, wrong ▸ *biased* ✶ just

unkempt adjective disheveled, shabby, sloppy, slovenly, ungroomed ▸ *scruffy* ✶ neat

unkind adjective inhuman, heartless, brutal, callous ▸ *cruel* ✶ kind

unknown adjective hidden, mysterious, undiscovered, dark ✶ familiar

unless conjunction if not, except when

unlike adjective unrelated, dissimilar, distinct ▸ *different* ✶ similar

unlikely adjective rare, improbable, doubtful, incredible, unheard of ▸ *dubious* ✶ likely

unlucky adjective unfortunate, luckless, ill-fated, unhappy ✶ lucky

unnatural adjective 1 artificial, stilted, strained 2 inhuman, cruel ▸ *heartless* ✶ natural

unnecessary adjective nonessential, excess, superfluous ▸ *needless* ✶ necessary

unoccupied adjective 1 uninhabited, empty, deserted ▸ *vacant* 2 idle, spare ▸ *unemployed* ✶ occupied

303

unpleasant adjective disagreeable, displeasing, objectionable ▶ *offensive* ✶ **pleasant**

unpopular adjective obnoxious *I was glad to leave the party; I had been forced to talk to some obnoxious people,* detested, shunned, rejected ▶ *disliked* ✶ **popular**

unqualified adjective **1** unable, incompetent, inadequate ▶ *unfit* **2** complete, thorough, absolute

unreal adjective imaginary, fictional, artificial, false, fanciful ✶ **real** UNREEL

unreasonable adjective **1** extravagant, excessive, extreme ✶ **moderate** **2** far-fetched, absurd, foolish ✶ **rational**

unreliable adjective untrustworthy, undependable, irresponsible ▶ *fickle* ✶ **reliable**

unrest noun **1** defiance, disquiet, protest, rebellion **2** anxiety, distress, worry ✶ **calm**

unrestricted adjective unrestrained, unlimited, open, free, unhindered ✶ **limited**

unripe adjective green, immature, callow *I was just a callow youth in those days, but I hope I have learned something since then,* unseasoned, unready ✶ **ripe**

unrivaled adjective inimitable, unequaled, matchless, peerless ✶ **inferior**

unruly adjective disorderly, troublesome, restive ▶ *rowdy* ✶ **orderly**

unseemly adjective incorrect, indecent, improper, unbecoming, shocking ✶ **seemly**

unselfish adjective generous, liberal, charitable, hospitable ▶ *kind* ✶ **selfish**

unstable adjective unsteady, shaky, inconstant, fickle, volatile ✶ **stable**

unsuitable adjective improper, unacceptable, unfitting, inconsistent ✶ **suitable**

untidy adjective bedraggled, disorderly, muddled, messy ▶ *slovenly* ✶ **tidy**

untie verb unfasten, unravel, free, release ▶ *undo* ✶ **tie**

until preposition till, as far as, up to

untimely adjective inopportune, ill-timed, premature ✶ **opportune**

unusual adjective strange, queer, exceptional, quaint, curious ▶ *odd* ✶ **normal**

unwilling adjective averse, disinclined, grudging, opposed ▶ *reluctant* ✶ **willing**

upheaval noun disturbance, disruption, overthrow, turmoil

uphold verb sustain, keep up, endorse ▶ *support*

upkeep noun maintenance, care, conservation, support, expenses ✶ **neglect**

upper adjective higher, superior, elevated, uppermost ✶ **lower**

upright adjective **1** sheer, steep, perpendicular ✶ **horizontal** **2** honorable *Josephine was one of the most honorable people I had ever met,* ethical, virtuous ✶ **dishonest**

uproar noun hubbub, noise, disorder, tumult, turmoil ▶ *clamor*

upset **1** verb bother, perturb, unsettle, annoy **2** verb overthrow, overturn, topple **3** adjective disturbed, confused, worried

upside-down adjective **1** overturned, upturned **2** chaotic, muddled, jumbled

urge **1** verb goad, plead, spur, beseech ✶ **deter** **2** noun encouragement, compulsion ▶ *impulse*

urgent adjective important, earnest, intense, vital ✶ **trivial**

use **1** verb employ, practice, apply **2** verb consume, exhaust, deplete, expend **3** noun usage, wear

useful adjective valuable, favorable, practical, beneficial ✶ **useless**

useless adjective trashy, paltry, futile *Trying to train a cat to fetch is a futile activity,* inefficient ▶ *worthless* ✶ **useful**

usual adjective common, general, habitual, familiar ▶ *normal* ✶ **exceptional**

utensil noun tool, implement, instrument, apparatus, device

utilize verb employ, apply, exploit ▶ *use*

utmost adjective extreme, supreme, greatest, ultimate, last, distant

utter **1** adjective thorough, absolute, complete **2** verb declare, pronounce, speak ▶ *say*

utterly adverb extremely, completely, entirely, fully, wholly

Vv

vacant adjective **1** empty, unoccupied, exhausted ★ **occupied 2** stupid, blank, expressionless, mindless

vacation noun holiday, rest, recess, break

vagabond noun vagrant, tramp, loafer, beggar, rover, bum, hobo

vague adjective indefinite, imprecise, inexact, uncertain ▶ *obscure* ★ **certain**

vain adjective **1** conceited, arrogant ▶ *proud* ★ **modest 2** fruitless, useless, worthless ▶ *futile* VANE, VEIN

valiant adjective stout, valorous, worthy, gallant ▶ *brave* ★ **cowardly**

valid adjective genuine, authentic, official *No one is allowed into the meeting without an official pass*, proper

valley noun gorge, dale, dell, glen, vale

valor noun courage, fortitude, heroism, gallantry ▶ *bravery* ★ **cowardice**

valuable adjective **1** costly, precious, priceless, expensive ★ **worthless 2** meritorious *She was awarded the medal for meritorious service during the war*, righteous, worthy

value 1 noun worth, benefit, merit, price **2** verb appreciate, esteem, prize, treasure **3** verb appraise, assess, rate, estimate

van noun truck, vehicle, wagon, cart

vandalize verb damage, sabotage, harm, ruin

vanish verb **1** disappear, fade, dissolve ★ **appear 2** exit, depart, go

vanity noun pride, conceit, pretension ★ **modesty**

vanquish verb conquer, defeat, overpower, subdue ▶ *beat*

vapor noun steam, fog, mist, moisture, smoke

variable adjective changeable, fickle, unsteady, fitful, wavering ★ **invariable**

Vehicles

ambulance	hearse	taxi
automobile	jeep	tractor
bulldozer	limousine	tram
bus	motorcycle	trap
cab	rickshaw	trolley
car	roller skates	truck
cart	scooter	skateboard
chariot	sedan	streetcar
fire engine	stagecoach	wagon
go-kart	tank	wheelchair

bicycle

varied adjective various, diverse *She was a woman of diverse interests*, miscellaneous, mixed, assorted ★ uniform

variety noun 1 assortment, array, mixture, medley *The singers entertained us with a medley of their hits* 2 sort, type, kind, class, category, breed, brand

various adjective mixed, different, many ▶ *varied*

vary verb differ, alter, change, diversify, diverge

vase noun jug, jar, beaker ▶ *pitcher*

vast adjective great, enormous, extensive, huge, wide ▶ *immense* ★ narrow

vault 1 noun grave, mausoleum, cellar, crypt, dungeon 2 verb jump, clear, bound, leap, hurdle

veer verb swerve, skid, turn, tack, deviate, change

vehement adjective impassioned, fiery, passionate, ardent, eager, zealous ▶ *strong* ★ indifferent

vehicle noun 1 automobile, car, conveyance, carriage, cart 2 agency, means, expedient

veil 1 noun cloak, cover, wimple, curtain 2 verb hide, conceal, shade, screen ★ expose VALE

vein noun 1 seam, strain, streak, stripe, thread, course 2 disposition, mood, style, phrasing VAIN

velocity noun rate, pace, tempo, rapidity, impetus *After I won the school prize, I had greater impetus to work hard* ▶ *speed*

venerable adjective respectable, revered, august, dignified, honored ▶ *sage*

vengeance noun reprisal, retaliation ▶ *revenge* ★ pardon

venomous adjective 1 poisonous, toxic, vitriolic 2 spiteful, malicious, hostile ▶ *vindictive*

vent 1 verb discharge, emit, express, let fly, release 2 noun aperture, duct, opening, outlet

ventilate verb 1 aerate, cool, fan, blow 2 express, debate, discuss, examine

venture 1 noun enterprise, undertaking, endeavor 2 verb risk, bet, hazard ▶ *chance*

verbal adjective stated, said, expressed, spoken, unwritten ★ written

verdict noun decision, judgment, finding, conclusion, opinion

verge 1 noun border, brink, edge, boundary 2 verb incline, tend, border, come close to

verify verb confirm, declare, authenticate, corroborate *The witness corroborated the story told by the defendant* ★ discredit

versatile adjective adaptable, variable, adjustable, handy ★ inflexible

verse noun poem, rhyme, stave, canto, jingle, doggerel *Call this stuff poetry? It's just doggerel!*

version noun account, form, interpretation, adaptation, type

vertical adjective upright, erect, sheer, perpendicular, steep ★ horizontal

very 1 adverb extremely, exceedingly, greatly, intensely, 2 adjective exact, real, true, actual, genuine

vessel noun 1 bowl, pot, canister, container, basin, jar 2 craft, ship, boat

vestige noun remains, remnant, hint, glimmer, residue, trace

veteran 1 noun old timer, master, old hand, expert ★ novice 2 adjective experienced, practiced, adept ★ inexperienced

veto 1 verb ban, reject, prohibit, stop, forbid ★ approve 2 noun embargo *The United Nations placed an embargo on the selling of arms to the two countries*, prohibition, disapproval ★ assent

vex verb annoy, provoke, trouble, irritate, harass ▶ *displease* ★ soothe

vibrate verb shake, quiver, oscillate, fluctuate ▶ *tremble*

vice noun evil, failing, fault ▶ *sin* ★ virtue

vicinity noun area, environs, neighborhood ▶ *surroundings*

vicious adjective evil, sinful, malignant, immoral, vile ▶ *wicked* ★ virtuous

victim noun sufferer, scapegoat, martyr, prey, pawn, dupe

victor noun winner, conqueror, champion, prizewinner ★ loser

victory noun success, triumph, achievement ▶ *conquest* ★ **defeat**

view 1 noun landscape, sight, panorama, spectacle 2 noun estimation, belief, theory, opinion 3 verb watch, see, behold, witness

vigilant adjective attentive, wary, alert, guarded ▶ *watchful* ★ **lax**

vigor noun energy, vim, stamina, might, power ▶ *strength* ★ **weakness**

vigorous adjective forceful, energetic, powerful, dynamic ▶ *active* ★ **weak**

vile adjective low, wretched, contemptible, miserable, nasty, evil ▶ *despicable* ★ **noble**

villain noun blackguard, knave *You are nothing but a knave who is out to steal my money*, sinner, rascal ▶ *rogue* ★ **hero**

vim noun stamina, zip, strength ▶ *vigor*

vindicate verb warrant, sustain, support, defend, establish ▶ *justify* ★ **accuse**

vindictive adjective vengeful, unforgiving, grudging, spiteful ▶ *malicious* ★ **merciful**

violate verb 1 disobey, oppose, defy, resist, infringe ★ **obey** 2 abuse, defile, outrage, desecrate

violent adjective furious, rabid, rampant, forcible, tempestuous ★ **calm**

virile adjective manly, masculine, vigorous, vibrant ▶ *strong* ★ **weak**

virtually adverb almost, nearly, practically, substantially

virtue noun goodness, honesty, chastity, purity ▶ *quality* ★ **vice**

virtuous adjective chaste, innocent, honorable, moral ▶ *righteous* ★ **wicked**

visible adjective perceptible, discernible, apparent, exposed, obvious ★ **invisible**

vision noun 1 apparition, specter, ghost, mirage 2 concept, revelation, foresight

visit 1 noun call, sojourn, stay, excursion 2 verb call on, drop in, tarry, stay

visitor noun guest, company, tourist, caller

visual adjective seeable, observable, visible

vital adjective 1 essential, indispensible, critical, crucial ▶ *necessary* 2 alive, vibrant, virile, dynamic *Our team won a number of games after we had been trained by the new dynamic coach*, energetic

vitality noun stamina, virility, vigor ▶ *strength*

vivacious adjective lively, spirited, vital, animated, merry ▶ *sprightly* ★ **languid**

vivid adjective 1 clear, bright ▶ *brilliant* 2 vigorous, strong, lucid ★ **dull**

vocal adjective articulate, eloquent, spoken, strident, vociferous ★ **quiet**

vocation noun occupation, calling, job, mission, career, pursuit

vogue noun style, fashion, mode, popularity

voice 1 noun speech, articulation, utterance 2 noun choice, preference, opinion 3 verb utter, express, proclaim, pronounce

void 1 adjective bare, barren, empty 2 adjective invalid, canceled, useless 3 noun cavity, chasm, space, opening, nothingness

volatile adjective 1 lively, changeable, fickle, giddy 2 elusive, fleeting, evaporable

volley noun discharge, fusillade, barrage, shower

volume noun 1 bulk, capacity, mass, quantity ▶ *amount* 2 loudness, amplitude 3 book, edition, tome

voluntary adjective free-willed, optional, intended, gratuitous ★ **compulsory**

vomit verb spew, disgorge, puke, throw up

vote 1 noun ballot, election, poll, referendum 2 verb ballot, poll, choose, elect

vow 1 verb promise, swear, assure, vouch, testify 2 noun oath, pledge, promise

voyage noun journey, cruise, passage, trip

vulgar adjective 1 common, coarse, crude, indelicate, rude ★ **elegant** 2 native, ordinary, common

vulnerable adjective unprotected, unguarded, exposed, defenseless, tender ★ **strong**

wad noun bundle, chunk, block, plug

waddle verb wobble, totter, shuffle, toddle

wag 1 verb waggle, shake ▶ *vibrate* 2 noun wit, humorist, joker

wage 1 noun fee, pay, salary, remuneration 2 verb carry out, fulfill, undertake

wager 1 verb gamble, bet, speculate, chance, hazard 2 noun pledge, stake, bet

wagon noun cart, truck, van ▶ *vehicle*

waif noun orphan, stray, foundling

wail 1 verb deplore, weep, grieve, lament ▶ *cry* ☆ rejoice 2 noun lamentation, weeping, grief, moan, howl

wait verb 1 expect, await, bide, stay, stop ▶ *linger* 2 attend, serve WEIGHT

waive verb relinquish, disclaim, disown, forego, defer ▶ *renounce* WAVE

wake verb awaken, stimulate, excite ▶ *arouse*

wakeful adjective 1 restless, awake 2 alert, wary, watchful

walk 1 verb advance, march, step, progress, move 2 noun stroll, hike ▶ *ramble* ☆ run 3 noun lane, alley, way 4 noun sphere, field, career *I started my career in journalism, but I later went into politics*, interest

wallow verb 1 flounder, stagger, tumble 2 delight, enjoy, revel

wan adjective pale, ashen, feeble, sickly, pallid ▶ *weak* ☆ robust

wand noun mace, baton, stick, scepter, rod

wander verb stray, meander, roam, stroll, deviate

wane verb droop, decline, decrease, lessen, ebb *As the little boat neared the rocks, Fred's courage ebbed away*, sink ☆ wax WAIN

wangle verb fiddle, contrive, fix, arrange

want 1 verb desire, covet, crave, need, require 2 noun need, necessity, demand 3 noun dearth, deficiency ▶ *scarcity* ☆ plenty

wanton adjective 1 unscrupulous, irresponsible 2 playful, frolicsome, wild 3 dissolute, immoral

war noun hostilities, fighting, bloodshed, enmity, strife ☆ peace WORE

ward noun 1 pupil, minor, charge 2 district, quarter WARRED

ward off verb prevent, forestall, avoid, stop ▶ *avert*

wardrobe noun 1 locker, cupboard, closet 2 outfit, clothes, apparel

warm 1 adjective tepid, hot, lukewarm 2 adjective sympathetic ▶ *warmhearted* 3 adjective eager, hot, zealous 4 verb heat, bake, cook, prepare

warn verb caution, admonish, advise, alert, apprise WORN

warning noun caution, admonition, forewarning, alarm, tip

warp verb contort, bend, twist, kink, deform ☆ straighten

warrant 1 verb guarantee, certify, justify, permit, allow 2 noun assurance, permit, license, authority *She produced documents that showed her authority on the board of directors*

wary adjective cautious, alert, careful, heedful ▶ *prudent* ☆ rash

wash 1 verb bathe, scrub, rinse, cleanse, wet 2 noun washing, cleaning

waste 1 noun garbage, debris, trash, rubbish 2 verb squander, spend, lavish, fritter 3 verb wither, decay, shrivel, perish WAIST

wasteful adjective lavish, prodigal, spendthrift ▶ *extravagant* ☆ economical

watch 1 verb note, observe, guard ☆ ignore 2 verb inspect, look at, oversee 3 noun timepiece 4 noun guard, sentry, watchman

watchful adjective attentive, observant, vigilant ▶ *wary* ☆ inattentive

water verb wet, bathe, wash, douse, drench, sprinkle, spray

wave 1 verb brandish, flourish, waft, swing 2 noun breaker, billow, undulation WAIVE

waver verb falter, hesitate, vacillate *There's no time to vacillate; make up your mind* ☆ decide

wax verb increase, rise, grow, expand, enlarge ☆ wane

way noun **1** route, road, path, passage, track
2 technique *The company introduced a new technique for making glass*, procedure, method, style WEIGH

wayward adjective contrary, perverse, obstinate ▶ *stubborn* ★ **docile**

weak adjective **1** feeble, frail, puny, helpless, delicate **2** foolish, soft, senseless, stupid **3** thin, watery, insipid **4** fragile, flimsy, tumbledown ★ **strong** WEEK

weaken verb enfeeble, relax, sag, flag ▶ *languish* ★ **strengthen**

weakness noun defect, fault, frailty, flaw ★ **strength**

wealth noun riches, luxury, prosperity, money, opulence ★ **poverty**

wealthy adjective rich, affluent, prosperous, opulent ★ **poor**

wear verb **1** dress in, don **2** rub, scrape, waste, consume **3** last, endure, remain WARE

weary **1** adjective exhausted, tired, fatigued ★ **fresh** **2** verb exhaust, tire, bore ★ **refresh**

weather noun climate, clime, conditions

weave verb braid, plait, unite, blend

web noun net, tissue, webbing, textile, netting

wed verb marry, join, link, splice, tie the knot

wedge **1** noun block, chock, lump, chunk **2** verb crowd, force, jam, push, thrust, squeeze

wee adjective little, small, minute ▶ *tiny* ★ **large**

weep verb blubber, snivel, sob, whimper ▶ *cry* ★ **rejoice**

weigh verb balance, estimate, ponder, examine, consider WAY

weight noun **1** load, pressure, burden, heaviness **2** importance, onus, significance, gravity WAIT

weighty adjective heavy, hefty, ponderous, onerous ★ **trivial**

weird adjective eerie, supernatural, unearthly, mysterious ▶ *uncanny*

welcome **1** adjective pleasing, desirable ▶ *agreeable* **2** verb greet, accost, hail, salute **3** noun greeting, salutation, acceptance

Weather conditions

Hot weather
close drought heat wave hot humid muggy sultry sweltering torrid tropical

Cold weather
arctic bitter blizzard brisk chilly cold cold snap cool freeze freezing frost glacial hail icy nippy subzero

Wet weather
deluge
downpour
drizzle
mizzle
precipitation
rainy
showers
sleet
slush
snowing
soaking

Overcast weather
cloudy dark foggy foul hazy misty murky overcast smoggy

Windy weather
blowy blustery
breeze draft
dust devil
flurry gale
gusty hurricane tornado
turbulent windy

309

welfare noun well-being, comfort, happiness, benefit, advantage ☆ **harm**

well **1** adjective robust, healthy, hearty, sound ☆ **ill**
2 adverb properly, suitable, adequately, accurately
☆ **badly** **3** noun fountain, spring

well-off adjective comfortable, prosperous ▷ *wealthy*
☆ **poor**

wet adjective **1** moist, damp, watery, drenched
2 adjective drizzling, showery, raining **3** verb soak, moisten, dampen

wheedle verb coax, cajole, inveigle *We were inveigled into buying some of the local lace*, persuade ☆ **coerce**

whet verb **1** sharpen, hone, strop ☆ **blunt** **2** excite, stimulate, rouse ☆ **dampen**

whim noun fancy, humor, desire, urge, notion, impulse

whine verb **1** howl, wail, whimper, moan **2** complain, grouse, grumble WINE

whip verb **1** flog, lash, thrash, chastise, spank **2** whisk, mix, blend

whirl verb twirl, spin, rotate, revolve, whir ▷ *twist*

whisk verb beat, brush, hasten, hurry, sweep ▷ *whip*

whisper **1** noun murmur, hint, suggestion, breath
2 verb breathe, murmur, divulge, buzz, intimate
☆ **shout**

whistle noun & verb cheep, chirp, warble, call

whole adjective **1** all, entire, total, intact **2** sound, complete, unbroken ☆ **part** HOLE

wholesome adjective healthful, nutritious, beneficial, sound, good ☆ **noxious**

wicked adjective infamous, corrupt, depraved, unrighteous, sinister, sinful ▷ *evil* ☆ **virtuous**

wickedness noun corruption, depravity, iniquity, sinfulness, villainy ▷ *evil*

wide adjective broad, ample, extended, spacious, roomy, extensive, vast ☆ **narrow**

widespread adjective prevalent, far-flung, extensive, sweeping, universal *The use of a universal language would be of great help in the United Nations* ☆ **limited**

wield verb **1** brandish, flourish, manipulate **2** control, command, exert, maintain

wild adjective **1** savage, ferocious, fierce, untamed
☆ **tame** **2** violent, unrestrained, boisterous ☆ **civilized**
3 careless, insane, reckless ☆ **sane**

wilderness noun desert, jungle, wasteland, wilds, outback

will **1** noun resolution, decision, zeal, accord **2** noun order, wish, command, request, demand **3** noun legacy, testament **4** verb choose, desire, elect

willful adjective temperamental, headstrong, deliberate ▷ *obstinate* ☆ **docile**

willing adjective disposed, zealous, ready, earnest
▷ *agreeable* ☆ **unwilling**

wilt verb wither, waste, sag, dwindle ▷ *ebb*

wily adjective cunning, sly, tricky, deceitful ▷ *crafty*
☆ **sincere**

win verb succeed, gain, get, acquire, procure ▷ *triumph*
☆ **lose**

wince verb shrink, quail, flinch *My little sister didn't flinch once when she had her vaccination*, start ▷ *cringe*

wind (rhymes with *pinned*) noun breeze, blast, gust, gale

wind (rhymes with *mind*) verb coil, turn, twist, bend
WINED, WHINED

wink noun & verb blink, flutter, flicker, glint

winner noun champion, master ▷ *victor*

wipe verb clean, brush, mop, remove, swab

wire noun **1** cable, telegraph, telegram **2** cable, cord

wisdom noun judgment, discretion, tact, thought, reason ☆ **folly**

wise adjective sensible, profound, astute, subtle, discreet ▷ *sage* ☆ **foolish**

wish **1** verb desire, crave, want, hanker for, long for
2 noun command, will, desire, liking

wistful adjective **1** pensive, musing, wishful **2** forlorn, melancholy, soulful

wit noun **1** fun, humor, levity, pleasantry **2** brains, sense, judgment, intelligence ☆ **stupidity**

witch noun enchantress, sorceress, crone, hag

withdraw verb **1** retire, retreat, depart, leave ▷ *flee*
2 extract, take out

withdrawn adjective unsociable, retiring, reclusive, aloof, solitary ☆ **sociable**

wither verb waste, fade, pine, languish ▷ *shrivel*

withhold verb retain, reserve, restrain, hold back
▷ *keep* ☆ **grant**

Borrowed words

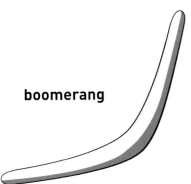

boomerang

Modern French
police
rendezvous
liaison
menu

Dutch
boss
brandy
decoy
landscape

Scandinavia
fjord
geyser

lemming
ombudsman
ski

Italian
balcony
cameo
fiasco
influenza

German
blitz
delicatessen
dollar
kindergarten

Chinese
kowtow
sampan
typhoon
wok

Japanese
bonsai
judo
karate
origami

Turkish
coffee
kiosk

Spanish
armada
fiesta
macho
patio
siesta
sombrero

Afrikaans
aardvark
apartheid

Boer
trek
veldt

Inuit
anorak
igloo
kayak
parka

Gaelic
blarney
bog
brat
brogue
smithereens

Aztec
avocado
cocoa
tomato

Arabic
admiral
alcohol
algebra
alkali
sherbet
sofa
zero

Aboriginal languages
boomerang
dingo
budgerigar
kangaroo

Persian
bazaar
caravan
divan
paradise

tulip
turban

Hindi
bungalow
chintz
cot
pajamas
thug
veranda

Native American
chipmunk
moccasin
moose
papoose
wigwam

---

within adjective inside, interior, inner

withstand verb resist, oppose, confront ▷ *defy* ☆ support

witness 1 noun spectator, onlooker, bystander *One of the bystanders at the accident came forward togive evidence*, signatory 2 verb behold, observe, see, attest

witty adjective funny, jocular, waggish, amusing ▷ *comical* ☆ dull

wizard noun sorcerer, magician, conjurer

woe noun sorrow, sadness, grief, misery, trouble ☆ joy WHOA

woman noun lady, girl, female, wife

wonder 1 noun marvel, miracle, rarity, curiosity 2 noun bewilderment, surprise, amazement ▷ *awe* 3 verb speculate, question, marvel, muse

wonderful adjective marvelous, fabulous, spectacular, superb ▷ *splendid* ☆ commonplace

woo verb make love, court, pursue

wood noun 1 lumber, timber, planks 2 forest, woods, copse, woodland, grove, thicket WOULD

word noun 1 expression, term, utterance 2 pledge, promise 3 tidings, news, information

work 1 noun toil, drudgery, labor, grind 2 noun task, job, stint, chore 3 verb operate, function, manipulate, run, drive

world noun globe, earth, sphere, planet

worry 1 verb bother, annoy, disturb ▷ *trouble* ☆ soothe 2 noun vexation, anxiety, concern, fear ☆ delight

worsen verb aggravate, decline, deteriorate, degenerate ☆ improve

worship 1 verb revere, adore, esteem, honor, praise ☆ despise 2 noun adoration, devotion, reverence

worth noun value, benefit, merit, caliber *This year's students were of a high caliber*, dignity

worthless adjective valueless, paltry, trifling, useless ▷ *cheap* ☆ valuable

worthwhile adjective valuable, helpful, useful, beneficial ☆ useless

worthy adjective upright, admirable, excellent, honest, fine ☆ vile

wound 1 verb hurt, injure, gash, pain, distress ▷ *harm* ☆ heal 2 noun injury, bruise, harm

wrangle verb & noun squabble, fight, row, scrap ▷ *quarrel* ☆ accord

wrap verb fold, envelop, enclose, cover, clothe, conceal ☆ unfold RAP

wrath noun fury, ire, rage, passion ▷ *anger* ☆ pleasure

wreck 1 verb demolish, smash, ruin, destroy, spoil, ravage ☆ repair 2 noun derelict, hulk, shipwreck, ruin

wrench verb twist, wring, strain, sprain, pull

wrestle verb struggle, battle, combat, grapple, tussle ▷ *fight*

wretch noun vagabond, blackguard, villain, rogue
▸ *scoundrel*

wretched adjective **1** dejected, abject, miserable
▸ *despicable* **2** saddening, pathetic ▸ *pitiful* ★ **joyful**

wriggle verb twist, writhe, squirm, worm *My hamster wormed his way under the couch, and it took some time before we could get him back out*, dodge

wring verb choke, squeeze, throttle, strangle, twist RING

wrinkle noun & verb crease, pucker, ruffle, rumple, crinkle, furrow

write verb inscribe, pen, sign, scrawl, scribble RIGHT, RITE, WRIGHT

writer noun **1** scribe, penman, clerk **2** author, essayist, narrator, playwright, poet, dramatist

writhe verb wind, twine, weave, twist ▸ *wriggle*

written adjective recorded, set down, documentary, transcribed

wrong **1** adjective unjust, unfair, immoral, wicked **2** adjective false, mistaken, erroneous **3** verb injure, hurt, abuse **4** noun offense, atrocity, iniquity, sin, injustice ★ **right**

wry adjective crooked, askew, awry, aslant, twisted, distorted ★ **straight** RYE

Yy

yank verb draw, pull, snatch ▸ *jerk*

yap verb **1** bark, yelp **2** prattle, blather, gossip, jaw

yard **1** noun lawn, garden, courtyard, court, quadrangle **2** three feet

yarn noun **1** story, account, tale, narrative **2** thread, wool, linen, twist

yawn verb gape, open

yearly adjective **1** annual, perennial, per annum *We shall pay a salary of $50,000 per annum* **2** adverb every year, annually

yearn verb ache, crave, desire, pine, hunger for ★ **dislike**

yell verb shriek, squawk, whoop, screech, shout
▸ *bellow* ★ **whisper**

yield **1** verb produce, provide, furnish, supply **2** verb surrender, give in, submit ★ **withstand** **3** verb abdicate, resign, renounce **4** noun crop, harvest, product, output

yielding **1** adjective obedient, submissive, unresisting ★ **stubborn** **2** plastic, malleable, flexible ★ **solid**

yoke **1** verb join, couple, link, harness **2** noun chain, bondage *The children of Israel moved out of bondage in the land of Egypt*, enslavement YOLK

yokel noun bumpkin, rustic, boor, peasant

young adjective youthful, tender, juvenile, junior, little ★ **old**

youngster noun child, youth, boy, girl, kid, lad, adolescent

youth noun **1** adolescence, prime, salad days ★ **age** **2** lad, boy ▸ *youngster*

youthful adjective boyish, girlish, young, spry, juvenile, lively ★ **aged**

Yule noun Christmas

Zz

zany adjective crazy, nutty, droll, goofy, eccentric, wacky, loony, loopy ▸ *funny* ★ **serious**

zeal noun devotion, eagerness, enthusiasm, keenness, ardor ★ **apathy**

zealous adjective devoted, fervent *Dave was a fervent supporter of the school's football team*, fanatical, earnest ▸ *eager* ★ **apathetic**

zenith noun climax, height, apex, peak

zero noun nothing, nada, zip, naught, nil, nullity, aught

zest noun **1** relish, gusto, appetite, keenness **2** flavor, piquancy, taste **3** rind, peel

zone noun area, district, region, tract, sector

zoom verb flash, fly, shoot, streak, hurtle, whiz

Parts of speech

noun: cheetah, antelope
*The **cheetah** is chasing the **antelope**.*

adjective: foreign
*I collect **foreign** stamps.*

noun
the name of a person, place, thing, or idea.
*Tom's **video** on **justice** and **freedom**
was in his **house** in **San Jose**.*

pronoun
stands in place of a noun.
***He** gave **her** a bar of soap. **It** was scented.*

adjective
a word that describes a noun.
*It was a **cold**, **frosty** day, so she wore a **large**, **woolen** hat.*

verb
a word expressing action or being.
*When she **broke** the window, she **felt** unhappy.*

adverb
gives more information about an adjective or another adverb.
*The **very** large horse galloped **quickly** around the course.*

conjunction
a word that joins words or phrases.
*Jane **and** Dan went to work, **but** we stayed at home.*

preposition
shows the relationship between one noun and another.
*The cat is sitting **on** the mat. The mouse is **under** the table.*

interjection
a word that expresses a strong feeling.
***Ouch!** That hurts. **Oh!** How nice.*

verb: to dry
*Hal **is drying** his face.*

adverb: upside-down
*The sloth is hanging **upside-down**.*

Pronunciation notes

Whenever you see this symbol in the dictionary ▲ a note will follow to help you pronounce a word properly. Sometimes the word will be spelled out for you using these symbols. Other times it will be rhymed with a less difficult word. Pronouncing some words can seem hard but you will find it easier if you say the word out loud. Remember: Practice makes perfect!

Get used to these sounds and soon you'll have no problems, even with the longest, most complicated words!

Consonant sounds

Symbol used	As in:
p	**p**an
b	**b**ed
t	**t**ip
d	**d**ip
k	**c**ar, **k**ey
g	**g**et
f	**f**at
v	**v**an
th	**th**in and **th**ough
s/ss	**s**oup
z	**z**ero, bar**s**
sh	**sh**ip and plea**s**ure
h	**h**ot
ch	**ch**ips
j	**j**ump
m	**m**an
n	**n**o
ng	si**ng**
w	**w**et
l	**l**et
r	**r**ed
y	**y**et

Vowel sounds

Symbol used	As in:
i	b**i**t
e	b**e**d
a	m**a**t
o	d**o**g
u	c**u**t and p**u**ll
ee	s**ee**n, happ**y**
oo	f**oo**l, l**u**minous, n**ew**
ar/ah	c**ar**, f**a**ther
or	f**ou**r, t**o**re, p**oo**r
ay/a+e	s**ay**, m**a**ke
y/ye	fl**y**, b**i**cycle
oy	b**oy**, p**oi**nt
oh/o+e	m**o**ment, b**oa**t
ow	c**ow**
ai	h**ai**r

Word games

Dictionaries are not just for looking up words. You can have a lot of fun with them too. These word games will help you improve your wordpower. You can play them on your own, or you can team up with your friends and have a wordpower competition.

Rhyming phrases
Think of a noun and then find an adjective that rhymes with it. We've started you off with a couple. How many pairs can you make?

fat/cat
green/bean

Guess what I am defining
1 living things so tiny that you cannot see them without a microscope.
2 a kind of dancing that tells a story.
3 a long hole dug in the ground along the side of a road so that water can drain away.

Do you know the word—the plural—for more than one ...
sheep, deer, child, goose, calf, mouse, man, foot, city, loaf?

Snakewords
This snake is made up of words that go together to make new words. What is the longest snakeword you can make?

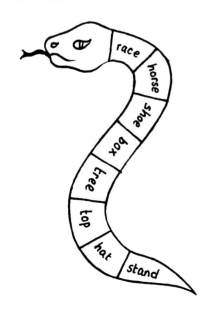

Clockwise games
How many words can you find reading clockwise around this circle?

What's the word?
Look at these pictures and guess what each pair has in common.

Tongue twisters
Try to say these tongue twisters ten times very quickly:

Freddy thrush flies through a thick fog.
She sells seashells by the seashore.
The six Sheiks' sixth sheep's sick.
The Leith police dismisseth us.
Still the stinking steamer sank.

Which is the most difficult to say? Try to make up some tongue twisters of your own.

Spot the odd one
hat bat mat dot fat
cleaner kinder fastest bigger

grunt squeak quack ring hiss
bicycle train bus toboggan

Can you match the opposites in this list?
deep	end
late	remember
hot	sad
careful	early
above	shallow
forget	narrow
happy	below
tall	careless
wide	cold
begin	short

Can you complete the following words?
butter........*(clue:* an insect)
king ....*(clue:* a bird)
key............*(clue:* as on a piano)
port...........*(clue:* be carried)
sea ....*(clue:* ocean plant)
sea ....*(clue:* summer or fall)
tight..........*(clue:* a circus act)
toad ....*(clue:* don't eat it)

Secret messages
An easy way to write a secret message is to write the words backwards. So instead of writing ELEPHANT, you would write TNAHPELE.
Can you figure out what this message says?

TEEM EM NI EHT
TNARUATSER
TA EMITHCNUL.

Similar meaning
Can you match all the words with similar meanings?
harmful	chat
piece	find
discover	leave
even	damaging
begin	frightened
feel	touch
talk	start
angry	smooth
afraid	cross
go	bit

Answers on page 316

Spellchecker

Words we use all the time and how to spell them. The words in **heavy black type** are some words which are difficult to spell.

a

about
ache
address
advertisement
after
ago
all
already
also
always
am
an
and
any
anybody
anyone
anything
anyway
anywhere
are
aren't = are not
as
at
away

b

be
became
because
become
been
being
best
better
business
but
by
bye

c

calendar
came
can
cannot = can not
can't = can not
career
ceiling
come
could
couldn't = could not

d

did
didn't = did not
do
does
doesn't = does not
doing
done
don't = do not
down
Dr. = Doctor
during

e

each
either
else
ever
every
everybody
everyone
everywhere

f

few
first
for
friend
from

g

gave
get
getting
give
go
goes
going
gone
gorilla
got

h

had
hadn't = had not
handkerchief
has
have
haven't = have not
he
he'll
her
here
hers
herself
he's = he is
him
himself
his
how
hurrah

i

I
I'd = I had
if
I'll = I shall, I will
I'm = I am
in
into
is
isn't = is not
it
its
it's = it is
itself
I've = I have

j

jewelry
just

k

kilogram
kilometer

l

last
least
less
let's = let us
lot

m

made
make
many
may
me
might
mile
mine
Miss
mom
more
most
Mr.
Mrs.
Ms.
much
must
mustn't = must not
my
myself

n

needn't = need not
neither
nephew
next
niece
nobody
none
nonsense
no one
nothing
now
nowhere

o

o'clock
of
off
OK
on
once
only
or
other
our
ours
ourselves
out
over

p

perhaps
probably
put
putting

s

same
shall
shan't
she
she'll = she will
she's = she is
should
shouldn't = should not
since
sir
so
some
somebody
someone
something
sometime
somewhere
soon
sorry
success
such

t

than
that
the
their
theirs
them
themselves
then
there
these
they
they'd = they had
they'll = they will
they're = they are
they've = they have
this
those
to
today
tomorrow
tongue
tonight
too

u

up
upon
us

v

very

w

was
wasn't = was not
way
we
we'd = we had
we'll = we shall, we will
went
were
we're = we are
weren't = were not
while
who
who'll = who will
whom
who's = who is
whose
why
will
with
won't = will not
worst
would
wouldn't = would not

y

yet
you
you'd = you had
you'll = you will
your
you're = you are
yours
yourself
you've = you have

315

Useful information

Days of the week
Monday
Tuesday
Wednesday
Thursday
Friday
Saturday
Sunday

Monday's child is fair of face
Tuesday's child is full of grace
Wednesday's child is full of woe
Thursday's child has far to go
Friday's child is loving and giving
Saturday's child works hard for a
    living
But the child that is born on the
    Sabbath day,
Is bonny and blithe, good and gay.

Months of the year
January
February
March
April
May
June
July
August
September
October
November
December

Mnemonics
A mnemonic (▲ say *nem-on-ik*) is a little rhyme or catch phrase that helps us remember something. For instance, there is an old spelling rule "I before e except after c," as in *field*, *ceiling*. And this rhyme:

Thirty days hath September,
April, June, and November.
All the rest have thirty-one
Excepting February alone
    which has 28 days and 29 days
    each leap year.

Symbols
Here are some everyday symbols:
¢   cent
$ dollar
@   at. *Flowers @ $1 a bunch.*
%   percent

Seasons
spring, summer, fall, winter

Numbers
1	one	first
2	two	second
3	three	third
4	four	fourth
5	five	fifth
6	six	sixth
7	seven	seventh
8	eight	eighth
9	nine	ninth
10	ten	tenth
11	eleven	eleventh
12	twelve	twelfth
13	thirteen	thirteenth
14	fourteen	fourteenth
15	fifteen	fifteenth
16	sixteen	sixteenth
17	seventeen	seventeenth
18	eighteen	eighteenth
19	nineteen	nineteenth
20	twenty	twentieth
21	twenty-one	twenty-first
30	thirty	thirtieth
40	forty	fortieth
50	fifty	fiftieth
60	sixty	sixtieth
70	seventy	seventieth
80	eighty	eightieth
90	ninety	ninetieth
100	one hundred	hundredth
1,000	thousand	thousandth
1,000,000	million	millionth
1,000,000,000	billion	billionth

Time
60	seconds in one minute
60	minutes in one hour
24	hours in one day
7	days in one week
4	weeks in one month
12	months in one year
10	years in one decade
100	years in a century
1,000	years in a millennium

Measurement
U.S. customary:
12 inches = 1 foot
3 feet = 1 yard
5,280 feet = 1 mile
16 ounces = 1 pound

Metric:
10 millimeters = 1 centimeter
100 centimeters = 1 meter
1,000 meters = 1 kilometer
1,000 grams = 1 kilogram

Answers to word games on page 314

Guess what I am defining
1 bacteria. **2** ballet. **3** ditch.

Do you know the plural?
sheep, deer, children, geese, calves, mice, men, feet, cities, loaves.

What's the word?
bulb, cone, horn

Match the opposites
deep/shallow   late/early
hot/cold   careful/careless
above/below   forget/remember
happy/sad   tall/short
wide/narrow   begin/end

Complete the words
butterfly, kingfisher, keyboard, portable, seaweed, season, tightrope, toadstool.

Spot the odd one
dot (the other words are spelled with an a)
fastest (the other adjectives are comparatives)
ring (the other words are noises animals make)
toboggan (all the other vehicles have wheels)

Secret message
Meet me in the restaurant at lunchtime.

Similar meaning
harmful/damaging
bit/piece
even/smooth
talk/chat
go/leave
discover/find
feel/touch
start/begin
cross/angry
afraid/frightened

Did you know what the symbols were on page 158?

wheelchair access

e-mail

restroom

parking

restaurant

telephone

first aid

bicycle route

Countries and people

Some countries and the adjectives that go with them.

Austria

Belarus

Brazil

China

Fiji

Greece

Guatemala

Nepal

Country	Adjective	Country	Adjective
Afghanistan	Afghan	Lebanon	Lebanese
Albania	Albanian	Liberia	Liberian
Algeria	Algerian	Libya	Libyan
Angola	Angolan	Luxembourg	Luxembourger
Argentina	Argentinean	Malawi	Malawian
Austria	Austrian	Malaysia	Malaysian
Australia	Australian	Mali	Malian
Bangladesh	Bangladeshi	Mauritania	Mauritanian
Belgium	Belgian	Mexico	Mexican
Belarus	Belarussian	Mongolia	Mongolian
Benin	Beninese	Morocco	Moroccan
Bhutan	Bhutanese	Myanmar (Burma)	Burmese
Bolivia	Bolivian	Namibia	Namibian
Brazil	Brazilian	Nepal	Nepalese
Cambodia	Cambodian	Netherlands	Dutch
Cameroon	Cameroonian	New Zealand	New Zealander
Canada	Canadian	Nicaragua	Nicaraguan
Chad	Chadian	Niger	Nigerien
Chile	Chilean	Nigeria	Nigerian
China	Chinese	Norway	Norwegian
Colombia	Colombian	Pakistan	Pakistani
Congo	Congolese	Panama	Panamanian
Costa Rica	Costa Rican	Paraguay	Paraguayan
Cuba	Cuban	Peru	Peruvian
Cyprus	Cypriot	Philippines	Filipino
Czech Republic	Czech	Poland	Polish
Denmark	Danish	Portugal	Portuguese
Ecuador	Ecuadorean	Romania	Romanian
Egypt	Egyptian	Russia	Russian
England	English	Saudi Arabia	Saudi Arabian
Ethiopia	Ethiopian	Scotland	Scottish
Fiji	Fijian	Senegal	Senegalese
Finland	Finnish	Slovakia	Slovakian
Gambia	Gambian	South Africa	South African
Greece	Greek	Spain	Spanish
Guatemala	Guatemalan	Sri Lanka	Sri Lankan
Guinea	Guinean	Sudan	Sudanese
Guyana	Guyanese	Sweden	Swedish
Haiti	Haitian	Switzerland	Swiss
Honduras	Honduran	Syria	Syrian
Hungary	Hungarian	Tanzania	Tanzanian
Iceland	Icelandic	Thailand	Thai
India	Indian	Tunisia	Tunisian
Indonesia	Indonesian	Turkey	Turkish
Iran	Iranian	Uganda	Ugandan
Iraq	Iraqi	United Kingdom	British
Ireland	Irish	United States	
Israel	Israeli	of America	American
Italy	Italian	Uruguay	Uruguayan
Jamaica	Jamaican	Venezuela	Venezuelan
Japan	Japanese	Vietnam	Vietnamese
Jordan	Jordanian	Wales	Welsh
Kenya	Kenyan	Yemen	Yemeni
Korea	Korean	Zambia	Zambian
Kuwait	Kuwaiti	Zimbabwe	Zimbabwean

New Zealand

Slovakia

Syria

Tunisia

Turkey

Uganda

Venezuela

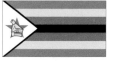
Zimbabwe

Our fifty states and their capitals

State	Capital	State	Capital	State	Capital
Alabama:	Montgomery	Louisiana:	Baton Rouge	Ohio:	Columbus
Alaska:	Juneau	Maine:	Augusta	Oklahoma:	Oklahoma City
Arizona:	Phoenix	Maryland:	Annapolis	Oregon:	Salem
Arkansas:	Little Rock	Massachusetts:	Boston	Pennsylvania:	Harrisburg
California:	Sacramento	Michigan:	Lansing	Rhode Island:	Providence
Colorado:	Denver	Minnesota:	St. Paul	South Carolina:	Columbia
Connecticut:	Hartford	Mississippi:	Jackson	South Dakota:	Pierre
Delaware:	Dover	Missouri:	Jefferson City	Tennessee:	Nashville
Florida:	Tallahassee	Montana:	Helena	Texas:	Austin
Georgia:	Atlanta	Nebraska:	Lincoln	Utah:	Salt Lake City
Hawaii:	Honolulu	Nevada:	Carson City	Vermont:	Montpelier
Idaho:	Boise	New Hampshire:	Concord	Virginia:	Richmond
Illinois:	Springfield	New Jersey:	Trenton	Washington:	Olympia
Indiana:	Indianapolis	New Mexico:	Santa Fe	West Virginia:	Charleston
Iowa:	Des Moines	New York:	Albany	Wisconsin:	Madison
Kansas:	Topeka	North Carolina:	Raleigh	Wyoming:	Cheyenne
Kentucky:	Frankfort	North Dakota:	Bismarck		

Our presidents and their native states

President	Native State	President	Native State
George Washington:	Virginia	Benjamin Harrison:	Ohio
John Adams:	Massachusetts	William McKinley:	Ohio
Thomas Jefferson:	Virginia	Theodore Roosevelt:	New York
James Madison:	Virginia	William Howard Taft:	Ohio
James Monroe:	Virginia	Woodrow Wilson:	Virginia
John Quincy Adams:	Massachusetts	Warren G. Harding:	Ohio
Andrew Jackson:	South Carolina	Calvin Coolidge:	Vermont
Martin Van Buren:	New York	Herbert Hoover:	Iowa
William Henry Harrison:	Virginia	Franklin D. Roosevelt:	New York
John Tyler:	Virginia	Harry S. Truman:	Missouri
James K. Polk:	North Carolina	Dwight D. Eisenhower:	Texas
Zachary Taylor:	Virginia	John F. Kennedy:	Massachusetts
Millard Fillmore:	New York	Lyndon B. Johnson:	Texas
Franklin Pierce:	New Hampshire	Richard M. Nixon:	California
James Buchanan:	Pennsylvania	Gerald R. Ford:	Nebraska
Abraham Lincoln:	Kentucky	Jimmy (James Earl) Carter:	Georgia
Andrew Johnson:	North Carolina	Ronald Reagan:	Illinois
Ulysses S. Grant:	Ohio	George H.W. Bush:	Massachusetts
Rutherford B. Hayes:	Ohio	Bill (William Jefferson) Clinton:	Arkansas
James A. Garfield:	Ohio	George W. Bush:	Connecticut
Chester A. Arthur:	Vermont	Barack Obama:	Hawaii
Grover Cleveland:	New Jersey		

How our states got their names

Alabama—Native American for tribal town.

Alaska—Originally an Inuit word, *alakshak*, meaning "peninsula," "great lands," or "land that is not an island."

Arizona—Spanish version of Pima Native American word for "little spring place," or Aztec *arizuma*, meaning "silver-bearing."

Arkansas—French name for Quapaw— "downstream people"—a Siouan people.

California—Name given by the Spanish conquistadors. It was the name of an imaginary island in a Spanish romance written in the 1500s.

Colorado—From Spanish for "red."

Connecticut—From Mohican and other Algonquin words meaning "long river place."

Delaware—Named after Lord De La Warr, an early governor of Virginia.

Florida—Named by Ponce de Leon on "Flowery Easter," or Pasqua Florida, Easter Sunday 1513.

Georgia—Named for King George II of England.

Hawaii—Possibly from the native word for homeland: *Hawaiki* or *Owhyhee*.

Idaho—Said to be an invented name meaning "gem of the mountains." May also be a Kiowa Apache term for the Comanche.

Illinois—French for *Illini* or "land of *Illini*," an Algonquin word meaning "men" or "warriors."

Indiana—Means "land of the Indians."

Iowa—Native American word translated as "here I rest" or "beautiful land."

Kansas—Sioux word for "south wind people."

Kentucky—Indian word translated as "dark and bloody ground," "land of tomorrow," or "meadowland."

Louisiana—Named after the French King Louis XIV, who first claimed the territory.

Maine—Named after an ancient French province. It is also a descriptive term that refers to the mainland rather than to the coastal islands.

Maryland—After Queen Henrietta Maria, wife of King Charles I of England.

Massachusetts—From a Native American tribe named after "large hill place."

Michigan—From Chippewa words, *mici gama*, meaning "great water."

Minnesota—From Dakota Sioux word meaning the "cloudy water" or "sky-tinted water" of the Minnesota River.

Mississippi—Probably Chippewa; *mici zibi*, "great river" or "gathering in of all the waters." Also an Algonquin word: *messipi*.

Missouri—An Algonquin Native American term meaning "river of the big canoes."

Montana—Latin or Spanish for "mountainous."

Nebraska—From an Omaha or Otos Native American word meaning "broad water" or "flat river."

Nevada—A Spanish word meaning "snow-clad."

New Hampshire—Named in 1629 by Captain John Mason, after his home county in England.

New Jersey—Named after England's Isle of Jersey.

New Mexico—Spaniards in Mexico applied this term to land north and west of the Rio Grande in the 1500s.

New York—Named in 1644 after the Duke of York and Albany.

North/South Carolina—Named after King Charles I of England.

North/South Dakota—Dakota is a Sioux word for "friend or "ally."

Ohio—Iroquois word for "fine or good river."

Oklahoma—Choctaw word meaning "red man."

Oregon—Possibly named after the words on a French map: "*Ouaricon-sint.*"

Pennsylvania—Named after William Penn, who had first suggested calling the region "Sylvania," which means "woodland."

Rhode Island—Possibly named *Roode Eylandt*, meaning "red clay," by a Dutch explorer.

Tennessee—*Tanasi* was the name of Cherokee villages on the Little Tennessee River.

Texas—Variant of word used by Caddo and other Native Americans to mean "friends" or "allies."

Utah—From a Navajo word meaning "upper," or "higher up." The Spanish form is Yutta.

Vermont—From French words *vert* (green) and *mont* (mountain).

Virginia—Named by Sir Walter Raleigh in honor of Queen Elizabeth, who was known as the Virgin Queen of England.

Washington—Named after George Washington.

West Virginia—Took this name when the western counties of Virginia refused to secede from the U.S. in 1863.

Wisconsin—A Native American name believed to mean "grassy place" in Chippewa.

Wyoming—From the Algonquin words for "large prairie place," "at the big plains," or "on the great plain."

The publishers would like to thank the following for contributing to this book:

Illustrators:
Rachel Fuller, Ron Hayward, Karen Hiscock, Ruth Lindsay, Jerry Malone, Patrick Mulrey, Rob Perry, Jim Robins, David Russell, Sue Sharples, Rob Shone, Guy Smith (Mainline), Harry Titcombe.

Artists:
Fred Anderson, Arcana, Liz Butler, Joanne Cowne, Angelika Elsebach, Michael Fisher (Garden Studio), Lee Gibbons, Peter Goodfellow, Ray Grinaway, Geoff Hamilton, David Holmes (Garden Studio), Richard Hook, John James, Terry Lambert, Alan Male, Andrew Macdonald, Janos Marffy, Josephine Martin, William Olliver, Bruce Pearson, Eric Rowe (Linden Artists), Roger Stewart, Ian Thompson, Guy Troughton, Phil Weare (Linden Artists).

Models:
Muriel Adamson, Aju Ahilan, Rachel Beaumont, Sarah Beaumont, Rose Bernez, Ben Clewley, Harriet Coombes, Charlotte Coombes, Belinda Cotton, Samantha Cotton, Veronique Dulout, Toby Flaux, Hugo Flaux, Jazz-Ann Fletcher, Ella Fraser-Thoms, Phoebe Fraser-Thoms, Marianne Gingell, Nick Goodall, Freddie Godfey-Smythe, Jessie Grisewood, John Grisewood, Natasha Howell, Peter Jewell, Flora Kent, Sajni Lakhani, Rudy Logue, Jazz Logue, Joe Mangione, Ned Miles, April McGhee, Alice McGhee, Riya Pabari, Rishi Pabari, Ricky Sachdev, Neil Sachdev, Daksha Sachdev, Angelina Sidonio, Domenic Sidonio, Sam Tyler.

Truly Scrumptious Ltd.: for Tara Saddiq.
Tiny Tots to Teen: for Lucy Russell.
Scallywags: for Connie Kirby, David Watts, Jordan White, Joe Wood, James Workman.

Hannah Landis, St. Bartholomew's Hospital for the physical therapy equipment.
Nice Irma's, London.
Footes Musical Instruments, London.
G.K. Locksmiths, London.
Advisory Services, London ("Roger" Clutton, Ray Coventry, William Greaves, Kil Hamilton, Jon Meakin, John Pearson, Roger and Linda Stong, and Peter Footman).